THE REFORMS OF
THE COUNCIL OF CONSTANCE
(1414-1418)

STUDIES IN THE HISTORY
OF
CHRISTIAN THOUGHT

EDITED BY

HEIKO A. OBERMAN, Tucson, Arizona

IN COOPERATION WITH

HENRY CHADWICK, Cambridge
JAROSLAV PELIKAN, New Haven, Connecticut
BRIAN TIERNEY, Ithaka, New York
ARJO VANDERJAGT, Groningen

VOLUME LIII

PHILLIP H. STUMP

THE REFORMS OF
THE COUNCIL OF CONSTANCE
(1414-1418)

THE REFORMS OF
THE COUNCIL OF CONSTANCE
(1414-1418)

BY

PHILLIP H. STUMP

E.J. BRILL
LEIDEN · NEW YORK · KÖLN
1994

The paper in this book meets the guidelines for permanence and durability of the Committee on Production Guidelines for Book Longevity of the Council on Library Resources.

Library of Congress Cataloging-in-Publication Data

BX
830
1414
.S78
1993

Stump, Phillip H.
  The Reforms of the Council of Constance (1414-1418) / by Phillip
H. Stump.
    p.   cm. — (Studies in the history of Christian thought, ISSN
0081-8607 ; v. 53)
  Includes bibliographical references and index.
  ISBN 9004099301
  1. Council of Constance (1414-1418) 2. Schism, The Great Western,
1378-1417. 3. Church renewal—Catholic Church—History. I. Title.
II. Series.
  BX830 1414.S78   1993
  262'.52—dc20   93-31994
                                                            CIP

Die Deutsche Bibliothek - CIP-Einheitsaufnahme

Stump, Phillip H.:
The Reforms of the council of Constance : (1414-1418) / by
Phillip H. Stump. – Leiden ; New York ; Köln : Brill, 1993
  (Studies in the history of Christian thought ; Vol. 53)
  ISBN 90–04–09930–1
NE: GT

ISSN   0081-8607
ISBN   90 04 09930 1

PRINTED IN THE NETHERLANDS

CONTENTS

PREFACE

This book began as a doctoral dissertation, guided by the scholar who founded the modern study of reform ideas, Gerhart Ladner. There is no way I can adequately express my appreciation to him for his example and inspiration.

Most of the initial research was done at Tübingen University in Germany between 1974 and 1976 with the support of a DAAD Fellowship and the hospitable reception of the Institut für Spätmittelalter und Reformation and its director, Heiko Oberman. I am deeply grateful for the support and encouragement of Professor Oberman and the scholars and staff at the Institute, particularly Christoph Burger, Manfred Schulze, Egon Gindele, and Suse Rau, as well as of the visiting scholars at the Institut, especially Theo Bell, Marilyn Harran, and Thomas Brady. I owe a special debt of thanks to Werner Krämer for his advice, encouragement, and hospitality when I visited him in Mainz.

The canonistic background of the Constance reform ideas became much clearer to me during my work as a research fellow at the Institute of Medieval Canon Law in Berkeley from 1977–80. I owe special thanks to the director, Stephan Kuttner, and to my colleagues John Sawicki, Tom Izbicki, Stephanie Jefferis Tibbets, and Steven Horwitz.

Constantin Fasolt and Thomas Izbicki read the entire draft of the book and gave me invaluable advice and correction from the perspectives of their studies of earlier and later reform eras.

I have been fortunate to receive advice and training from leading scholars of diverse confessional backgrounds who are striving to understand that period of history in which the confessions underwent their fateful separation. Since I believe that the judgments of historians, as much as they strive for objectivity, are nevertheless influenced by their confessional backgrounds, let me state here that I am a Protestant of the Reformed (Presbyterian) tradition; at the same time I am committed to ecumenical dialogue, and I hope for the reunion of the churches. To what degree these convictions have influenced my view of the Council of Constance, the reader must judge.

In the process of revision, my original dissertation, published in 1978, has become a new and different study. For the dissertation, I had relied almost entirely on printed editions of Constance sources. Subsequent examination of the manuscripts, made possible by financial assistance from the American Philosophical Society and the Lynchburg College Committee for Faculty Research and Development, revealed that the existing editions are often incomplete or unreliable. The *Acta concilii Constanciensis* of Heinrich Finke did invaluable service in making accessible to scholars much of the unusually rich documentation for the council's reform deliberations. However, Finke edited the reform speeches and tracts in a partial manner, excising large sections which he regarded as repetitive or unimportant. His edition of the most important document, the record of the reform committee deliberations, though in many ways a major advance over the earlier edition of Hardt, seriously obscured the nature of the manuscript record. Thus I have produced a new edition as an appendix to this volume. Much of the revised study below consists of a detailed analysis of these concrete reform deliberations. In the second half of the book I have presented an analysis of the ideas and images of reform which provides a summary of some of the dissertation's findings, and an expansion of others; it also includes additional examples.

The Lynchburg College Library staff has been exceedingly generous with their time in helping me to locate and secure sources whose obscurity often fascinated and sometimes exasperated them; I owe special thanks to Virginia Dunn, Carol Pollock, Elizabeth Henderson, and Rayetta Knight. My former student, Dee Blackstock, gave me valuable assistance with computer data entry. Copies from the Vienna and Kues manuscripts cited in the bibliography below were kindly provided by the Hill Monastic Microfilm Library, St. John's Abbey and University, Collegeville, Minnesota.

Finally, my greatest debt of gratitude is to my wife Marion, and our children David, Katie, and Jennifer for their patience and support for a project that took me away from them far too often.

PROLOGUE

In 1378, upon the death of Pope Gregory XI the college of cardinals unanimously elected as his successor Bartolomeo Prignano, the Archbishop of Bari, who took the name Urban VI.[1] Afterwards, the cardinals affirmed that their election had taken place in complete freedom. But some six months later the same cardinals had become so convinced of the error of their choice that they declared that their election had not been made freely and was therefore invalid. They thus unanimously declared that Urban VI was not pope and they proceeded to elect a new pope, Cardinal Robert of Geneva, who took the name Clement VII. But Urban VI did not cease to believe he was pope; he remained in Rome and appointed new cardinals to replace those who had deserted him. Half the lands of Europe continued to give obedience to him; the rest of western Christendom gave its allegiance to Clement VII, who established his rival papacy at Avignon. Urban's predecessor had in fact only recently brought the papacy back to Rome after it had sojourned some seventy years in that Provençal town (1309–1377). The woes of this Babylonian captivity, as Petrarch named it, were now succeeded by the even greater woes of nearly forty years of schism. There had been frequent schisms in the western Church in the preceding centuries, but none had lasted so long nor had been so serious as this, the Great Western Schism.

In this schism it was not possible to determine who was the legitimate pope.[2] The roughly equal portions of Europe which supported each of the rival papacies hardened into *de facto* separate churches, which were called "obediences" and whose tenacity was responsible for prolonging and intensifying the schism. Many

---

[1] The best overall study of the events of the Schism and the fifteenth century councils is still Volume 14 of the *Histoire de l'Eglise* of Fliche and Martin: Étienne Delaruelle, E.-R. Labande, and Paul Ourliac, *L'Église au temps du Grand Schisme et de la crise conciliaire, 1378–1449* (Paris, 1962–64). It is now supplemented by the excellent survey of Giuseppe Alberigo, *Chiesa conciliare: Identità e significato del conciliarismo* (Brescia, 1981). For the events of the schism leading up to Constance, see Aldo Landi, *Il papa deposto (Pisa 1409): L'idea conciliare nel Grande Schisma* (Turin, 1985). The first volume of Walter Brandmüller's long-awaited history of the Council of Constance is now in print: *Das Konzil von Konstanz (1414–1418)*. Vol. 1: Bis zur Abreise Sigismunds nach Narbonne (Paderborn, 1991).

[2] Karl August Fink, "Zur Beurteilung des grossen abendländischen Schisma," *ZKG*, 73 (1962), 335–43.

hoped that the schism would end with the death of one or other of the popes. But upon the death of each of the original contenders (Urban VI in 1389 and Clement VII in 1394) successors were elected by the respective colleges of cardinals and each received the continued allegiance of his obedience. Western Christendom faced the realization that the two-headed monster of the schism would not die a natural death. So Christians proposed more active solutions for ending the schism, such as military force, mutual resignation of both contending popes, or arbitration by a third, neutral party. The King of France and most of the French clergy sought on two separate occasions (1398 and 1407) to compel the Avignon pope Benedict XIII to reach a compromise for ending the schism by withdrawing their obedience from him. When all these solutions proved unworkable, Europe ultimately turned to a solution which had been proposed by many persons almost from the beginning of the schism: the convocation of a general council attended by representatives of both obediences which would deal with the rival popes and reunite the Church.

One major reason for the delay in adopting this solution was the fact that the positive law of the Church required that general councils could only be summoned into being by popes, and neither of the rivals was willing to issue such a summons. Some suggested that the council could be summoned by the cardinals or the emperor in such an emergency situation. However, the validity of a council which had been convoked in such a manner would have been subject to question; thus any solution of the schism which it might enact would run the danger of having its validity questioned on technical grounds. Finally, the cardinals of the two rival obediences jointly convoked the general council of Pisa in the year 1409 without the sanction of either pope. This council succeeded in securing the acceptance of its actions by neither obedience in its entirety. Neither of the rival popes recognized his deposition at the hands of the Pisa fathers, and the election of a new pope, Alexander V, by the cardinals at the council only compounded the crisis by adding a third rival line of popes to the schism. Alexander V, upon his death in 1410 was succeeded by John XXIII, who took his place as representative of the new "Pisa line" of popes alongside the older Avignon and Roman lines which were represented at this time by Benedict XIII and Gregory XII respectively. The monster had sprouted a new head.

It was in this context that King Sigismund, the emperor-elect of the Holy Roman Empire, was able to convince Pope John XXIII to summon a new general council to meet at Constance in 1414. In fall of that year, representatives from almost every region of Europe began to assemble in the little Swabian town on Lake Constance. Thousands of persons made their appearance there during the three and one-half years the council was in session.[3] To this council belongs the honor of finally ending the schism. It deposed the pope who had convoked it and thereby secured the promised resignation of the Roman pope Gregory XII. After winning to itself the support of virtually the entire obedience of Benedict XIII, which consisted chiefly of the Iberian kingdoms, it proceeded to depose him as well, secure in the knowledge that its deposition would be effective.[4] The council went on to elect a new pope, Martin V, who became the undisputed head of a reunited western Christendom.

The council's victory had not been easily won. Scarcely four months after it had begun to meet the council faced a serious threat. In late March, 1415, Pope John XXIII, sensing that the council planned to take action against him, fled from Constance, and numerous supporters followed him, including a number of cardinals. In the face of these developments, which called into question its very right to continued existence, the council acted decisively. First, they decreed formally that they had been duly convoked and had full authority to continue meeting and acting even without the presence of the pope. Then on April 6, 1415,[5] the

---

[3] Delaruelle, 139ff. In his study of the lists of participants, Johannes Riegel identified 2,290 persons who attended the council in some sort of official capacity. See Johannes Riegel, *Die Teilnehmerlisten des Konstanzer Konzils: Ein Beitrag zur mittelalterlichen Statistik* (Freiburg, 1916) and Jürgen Miethke, "Die Konzilien als Forum der öffentlichen Meinung im 15. Jahrhundert," *DA* 37 (1981) 736–773 at 747.

The following is drawn from Miethke's summary of Riegel's data:

Highest prelates (popes, cardinals, patriarchs, and their legates)	32
Archbishops and their procurators	27
Bishops and their procurators	142
Generals of orders and abbots	119
Heads of ecclesiastical corporations	75
Envoys of such corporations	72
Curial officials	335
Envoys of universities	27
Secular lords or their envoys	92
Representatives of towns	195
Other lay nobles and freemen	1176

Among all these groups 409 individuals can be identified as university graduates.

[4] Although Benedict did not admit his deposition, the area of his obedience had been reduced to the small expanse of his family patrimony in Peñiscola, Spain: see Delaruelle, 219–221.

[5] The decree was originally read in the fourth general session, March 30, the day before Easter Sunday; however, in reading the decree, Zabarella suppressed the words "reform in head and members," necessitating the re-enactment of the

council enacted its now most famous decree. "Haec sancta synodus," began the decree; "this holy council" receives its power
directly from God; and all persons of whatever rank or status, even
if it be papal, are bound to obey the council in matters of faith,
union, and reform of the Church in head and members.[6]

Nineteenth century liberals were fond of pointing to the revolutionary quality of this decree, seeing in it the precursor of the
principles of modern constitutional monarchy.[7] Many modern
ecumenists are seeking to prove that the decree still holds the
binding force of law for the Church.[8] My study will ask how the
Constance fathers themselves understood the decree's words "reformation in head and members." Since this reform was the third of
the three great tasks of the council in which the council's authority
was established as supreme within the Church, this study will
indirectly help to shed light on the ecclesiological views of the
Constance fathers. The first two tasks were rather specific: the
combatting of heresies and the ending of schisms. The specific
alleged heresies with which the council dealt were those of the
Hussites and Wycliffites. It condemned certain of their doctrines,
and, to its shame, it burned John Hus himself and another Hussite
leader, Jerome of Prague, despite safe conducts granted to them. In
addition to solving the Great Western Schism, the Council also

---

decree in its full form during the following session. On this, see Hasso Hofmann,
*Repräsentation: Studien zur Wort- und Begriffsgeschichte von der Antike bis ins 19. Jahrhun-
dert* (Berlin, 1974), 259; also Thomas Morrissey, "The Decree 'Haec Sancta' and
Cardinal Zabarella: His Role in its Formulation and Interpretation," *AHC* 10
(1978) 145–176.
    [6] *Conciliorum oecumenicorum decreta*, ed. J. Alberigo, et al. 3d ed. (Bologna, 1973),
409–410: "In nomine sanctae et individuae Trinitatis, Patris et Filii et Spiritus
sancti. Amen. Haec sancta synodus Constantiensis generale concilium faciens, pro
exstirpatione praesentis schismatis, et unione ac reformatione ecclesiae Dei in
capite et in membris fienda. . . . Et primo declarat, quod ipsa in Spiritu sancto
legitime congregata, generale concilium faciens, et ecclesiam catholicam militan-
tem repraesentans, potestatem a Christo immediate habet, cui quilibet cuiuscumque status vel dignitatis, etiam si papalis exsistat, obedire tenetur in his quae
pertinent ad fidem et exstirpationem dicti schismatis, ac generalem reformationem
dictae ecclesiae Dei in capite et in membris." Brandmüller's suggested new
translation of the phrase "etiam si papalis exsistat" as "even if someone should
exist who held the papal power" (implying the council's judgment that all three of
the papal claimants were illegitimate) is intriguing, but the use of the word
"papalis" as a substantive to mean "someone who holds the papal power" seems
unlikely. See *Konzil von Konstanz* (above, n. 1) 254–256.
    [7] John Figgis referred to it as "probably the most revolutionary official docu-
ment in the history of the world"; see *Studies of Political Thought from Gerson to Grotius*
(Cambridge, 1916), 41; on Figgis, see also Francis Oakley, "Figgis, Constance,
and the Divines of Paris," *AHR* 75 (1969) 368–86.
    [8] See below, p. 14.

entertained hopes of bringing about a re-union with the Greek Christians; two decades later the Council of Basel-Ferrara-Florence went on to do so, although its success was an illusory one. Alongside these specific, limited, and well-defined tasks the third task, reform, sounds surprisingly vague and all-inclusive. It will be the purpose of this study to investigate the nature of the Constance reform ideas and the degree to which the council was able to translate these ideas into effective practical reform measures.

PART I

THE CONTEXT

CHAPTER ONE

HÜBLER, HALLER, *HAEC SANCTA* AND REFORM

Past interpretations of the Council of Constance have usually proceeded either from the perspective of political history or that of
ecclesiology. Each perspective provides a corrective on the other.
Political history enables us to look at the evolution of thought at
Constance in its historical context rather than as a reflection of
timeless questions about the nature of the church. The ecclesiological perspective provides a corrective to the efforts of political
historians to view the conciliar movement as a precursor of later
secular political movements. The two principal past studies of the
Constance reforms were written primarily from the perspective of
political history. Ironically, they viewed the reforms from almost
diametrically opposed political perspectives. In 1867, Bernhard
Hübler saw the reforms as an effort to provide a parliamentary
government for the universal church.[9] A generation later, in 1901,
Johannes Haller saw them as a reflection of nascent national churches in Europe.[10] Both authors, from their different perspectives,
generally regarded the Constance reforms as failures. More recently, especially in the years around the Second Vatican Council,
studies of conciliarism as a movement shifted the emphasis back to
ecclesiology. These newer studies, while not addressing the Constance reforms directly, did shed light on the ideological content of
the reforms. Still more recent studies have examined conciliarism
from the combined perspectives of ecclesiology and political history, above all those of G.H.M Posthumus Meyjes, Antony Black,
Werner Krämer, Giuseppe Alberigo, and Karl August Fink. Of
these, only Fink has examined the Constance reforms themselves
from both perspectives. On the basis of his intimate knowledge of
the functioning of the papal curia before and after Constance, Fink

---

[9] Bernhard Hübler, *Die Constanzer Reformation und die Concordate von 1418*. Leipzig,
1867.
[10] Johannes Haller, *Papsttum und Kirchenreform, vier Kapitel zur Geschichte des
ausgehenden Mittelalters* (Berlin, 1903, repr. Berlin 1966). On Haller's accomplish-
ments, influence, and biases, see most recently Heribert Müller, "Der bewunderte
Erbfeind: Johannes Haller, Frankreich und das Französische Mittelalter," *HZ* 252
(1991) 265–317. Müller also weighs the role of Haller's strong Protestant commitment.

reached a very different conclusion about the success of the reforms than had Hübler and Haller.[11] His remarks, suggestive as they were, only sketched the outlines of a new approach to the Constance reforms.

I believe the most promising approach is one which combines the perspectives of ecclesiology and political history with a third perspective—that of reform ideology itself. Gerhart Ladner developed the study of the history of reform ideas.[12] One of Ladner's students, Louis Pascoe, used his methodology to analyze the reform thought of Jean Gerson and Pierre d'Ailly.[13] The present study will apply the same method to examine the conciliar reform deliberations themselves. The individual reforms will be analyzed in all their concrete diversity, a diversity which reflects above all the divergent concrete interests of the various estates in the church which were represented at Constance. However, I will argue that unifying conceptions of reform, which in most cases had long histories, were present at the council and facilitated the development of a coherent common program which must be regarded as a remarkably successful product of collegial deliberation.

1. Hübler: Reform as "ecclesiastical parliamentarism"

Hübler viewed the Constance reforms as efforts to place constitutional controls on papal absolutism, which he believed had developed during the course of the Middle Ages. For him the central reforms were efforts to establish the council as the supreme authority in the Church, analogous to a nineteenth century parliament in secular government. So, for example, certain reforms provided for the regular meeting of general councils and gave them legislative authority and even power to remove the pope from office and regulate his administration through legislation; other reforms established the college of cardinals as a sort of privy council[14] and

---

[11] Karl August Fink, "Papsttum und Kirchenreform nach dem Grossen Schisma," *Theologische Quartalschrift* 126 (1946) 110–122 at 114–115.

[12] Gerhart Ladner, *The Idea of Reform* (Cambridge, Mass., 1959). Professor Ladner's articles on reform have been been re-edited in *Images and Ideas in the Middle Ages: Selected Studies in History and Art*, 2 vols. (Rome, 1983).

[13] Louis Pascoe, *Jean Gerson: Principles of Church Reform* (Leiden, 1973) and "Theological Dimensions of Pierre d'Ailly's Teaching on Papal Plenitude of Power," *AHC* 11 (1979) 357–366.

[14] Hübler, 75: "Staatsrath." On p. 74 Hübler describes the role to be given the cardinals as "die Machtstellung eines kirchlich-constitutionellen Regierungsfactors."

still others gave the general council parliamentary power over the papal pursestrings.[15]

Excursus II of Hübler's book is subtitled "A Contribution to the History of Ecclesiastical Parliamentarism."[16] In it he depicted the slow emergence of the central principle of conciliar superiority. He felt that its full unfolding was only possible when the conciliar theorists departed from the foundation of the canon law of their time. He did acknowledge that one group of conciliar thinkers remained within the basic framework of the canon law. They grounded the council's right to judge the pope upon the canon *Si papa* (D.40 c.6) which, although it stated clearly the rule that the pope was to be judged by no one, provided an exception to this rule in the case that the pope should fall into heresy. By extending the concept of heresy to include all notorious crimes such conciliar theorists sought to establish the authority of the council to judge and depose a schismatic or criminal pope, even a pope who merely scandalized the Church through his maladministration.

Hübler felt that this basis for the conciliar theory was very limited and unsatisfactory. He argued that the principle of conciliar superiority could only be fully developed when the theorists found their basis in the natural rather than the positive man-made law. Strongly influenced by Aristotle and using arguments based on natural law, the conciliarists established that the foundation of all ecclesiastical power lay in the universal Church. The practical execution of that power lay only partly with the pope. Ultimately, it rested with the general council, which represented the universal Church and had the right to convene itself even without the pope, if he failed in his duty to convoke it. The council had power to decide disputes in which the pope was involved, to correct an erring pope, and even to depose a pope for the common good or utility of the whole Church. Thus the council as representative of the universal Church could make laws which it could force the pope to obey and could punish him for disobedience. These rights of the council were firmly established in the decree *Haec sancta*.

Such was Hübler's characterization of the version of conciliar theory which had such great advantages over the version developed on the meager basis of positive law. He contrasted both versions to another tactic which had been adopted to deal with the Schism and

---

[15] *Ibid.*, 109: "constitutionelles Budgetrecht."
[16] *Ibid.*, 360ff.: "Die Restauration der Generalsynoden durch die Doctrin des 14. u. 15. Jahrhunderts. Ein Beitrag zur Geschichte des kirchlichen Parlamentarismus."

with overweening papal power: the withdrawal of obedience from the pope. The French king and clergy had employed this tactic unsuccessfully on two separate occasions, 1397 and 1406. They had withdrawn their obedience from the Avignon pope Benedict XIII in an effort to force him to come to terms with the Roman pope and end the Schism. At the same time they had proclaimed a series of "liberties" or rights of the clergy in France which had been infringed upon by the papacy and which the French clergy reclaimed for themselves during the time of withdrawal of obedience. Chiefly they refused to pay papal taxes and to accept persons named by the pope to fill French ecclesiastical offices. For Hübler the "doctrine" of withdrawal of obedience was destructive; it was a sign of the decay of discipline of the times. Rather than seeking a solution that would apply to the whole Church, this doctrine was divisive. It was, in the final analysis, only a reaction to an even more dangerous doctrine of the times which approved the development of separate national churches and would have made the Schism permanent. The conciliar theory which the Council of Constance sought to realize provided a much more constructive approach by allowing the continued existence of the papal monarchy while transforming it into a parliamentary, constitutional one.

Hübler assumed that this theory of ecclesiastical parliamentarism departed completely from the past and that the positive law of the late Middle Ages would have regarded it as "the sheerest heresy". Ironically, Hübler's views here were based largely on earlier papalist ecclesiological polemic against the conciliar movement, which had sought to show that heretical theses of William of Ockham and Marsiglio of Padua lay at the heart of conciliarism.[17] Ockham's nominalism allegedly provided the basis for conciliar doctrines because it regarded all human institutions including the Church as contingent and not firmly grounded in any necessary metaphysical order.[18]

During the last half-century much progress has been made to-

---

[17] Karl Wenck, "Konrad von Gelnhausen und die Quellen der konziliaren Theorie," *HZ* 76 (1896) 6 ff; K. Hirsch, *Die Ausbildung der konziliaren Theorie im 14. Jahrhundert* (Vienna, 1903); A. Kneer, *Die Entstehung der konziliaren Theorie* (Rome, 1893); *The Council of Constance*, trans. Louise Loomis, ed. John Mundy and Kennerly Woody (New York, 1961), 8–9.

[18] H. Arquillière, "L'origine des théories conciliaires," *Séances et travaux de l'Académie des Sciences Morales et Politiques*, 175 (1911) 573–586. Recently, Antony Black has, on the contrary, shown what a strong role realist thought about the church played in the conceptions of Basel conciliarists like Heimerich van de Velde; see Antony Black, *Council and Commune: The Conciliar Movement and the Fifteenth-century Heritage* (London/Shepherdstown, 1979), 82–84.

ward the correction of such misconceptions. The basis of this progress has been a much more careful analysis of the primary source material of the period made possible above all by Heinrich Finke's extensive investigation and publication of hitherto unedited sources. One of Finke's students, Hermann Heimpel, finally settled the question of authorship of one of the key conciliar tracts, *De modis uniendi et reformandi ecclesiam*.[19] The authorship of this tract, which clearly borrowed and approved ideas of Marsiglio of Padua, had long been attributed to Gerson, whose thought thus had been assumed to be tainted (or distinguished) by radical, heretical, democratic doctrines of popular sovereignty. In a detailed biographical study Heimpel went further to suggest that the true author of the tract, Dietrich of Niem, was also not as radical a thinker as his approval of Marsiglio might suggest, since he drew ideas quite eclectically and inconsistently from many sources. In fact, Heimpel showed that Dietrich's invectives were not so much theoretical treatises as they were personal expressions of animosity towards specific popes in whose service he worked as a curial official.[20]

Michael Seidlmayer, another student of Finke, on the basis of an investigation of important Spanish documents from the early years of the Great Schism, found that the first call for a general council originated with three Italian cardinals, who wished to submit the disputed election of Urban VI to the authority of the universal Church as a supreme judge.[21] Building on the earlier research of Bliemetzrieder,[22] he observed that the Italian cardinals, as well as succeeding advocates of the "conciliar idea", were able to draw on a wealth of accumulated ideas for support, all of which had a continuous history which antedated the thought of Marsiglio and Ockham and lay quite within the borders of orthodoxy.[23]

Many of the fundamental results of the research of the last decades in this area were presaged by Seidlmayer's summary of the four-fold sources of the conciliar ideas: 1) canon law; 2) Aristotelian social and political teaching; 3) theological arguments; and 4) historical rights and practices in the Church which had fallen into disuse. The most interesting research has been in the field of canon

---

[19] Hermann Heimpel, *Dietrich von Niem* (Münster, 1932), 77–121.
[20] *Ibid.*, 47.
[21] Michael Seidlmayer, *Die Anfänge des grossen abendländischen Schismas: Studien zur Kirchenpolitik insbesondere der spanischen Staaten und zu den geistigen Kämpfen der Zeit* (Münster, 1940), 179.
[22] Franz Bliemetzrieder, *Das Generalkonzil im grossen abendländischen Schisma* (Paderborn, 1904), 75f.
[23] *Ibid.*, 173ff.

law, starting with the seminal study of Brian Tierney. Tierney demonstrated the firm canonistic basis for the conciliar doctrines,[24] the central core of which had been recognized but underestimated by Hübler: the canonists' interpretation of the crucial canon *Si papa*, which allowed for judgment of a heretical pope. The teaching of a number of key canonists supported the opinion that the general council was the agency which was authorized to judge and depose such a heretical pope and that the concept of heresy could be extended in this case to include any notorious papal crime such as simony and perhaps even maladministration. Tierney further showed that even the legislation of the popes themselves during the crucial period of the development of the papal monarchy had provided important material for conciliar thought. It did so directly in its consideration of the relationship between pope and universal Church and indirectly in statements concerning the diffusion of power among head and members within ecclesiastical corporations such as monasteries and cathedral churches. Canonists in their commentaries came to apply the latter statements to the relationship between the pope and council as head and members of the universal Church considered as a corporation. In his concluding chapter Tierney suggested that one of the leading conciliar thinkers, the canonist Cardinal Zabarella, drew all these materials together into a coherent and workable conciliar theory based entirely on canon law.

As for the Aristotelian social and political teachings, leading conciliar thinkers used them in orthodox ways, as Georges de Lagarde has shown. They did not borrow ideas so much from Ockham and Marsiglio as from the writings of Thomas Aquinas and his students.[25] Louis Pascoe has analyzed the influence of Aristotelian conceptions on the reform thought of Gerson and d'Ailly, two of the leading conciliarists at Constance.[26] He shows that they combined their Aristotle quite comfortably with their Pseudo-Dionysius. Yves Congar[27] has traced the background of this hierarchical thought, especially in the use of Pseudo-Dionysian

---

[24] Brian Tierney, *The Foundations of the Conciliar Theory: The Contribution of the Canonists from Gratian to the Great Schism* (Cambridge, 1955).

[25] Georges de Lagarde, *La naissance de l' esprit laïque au déclin du moyen âge*, (Louvain/Paris, 1956–63), 2:50–85 and 331ff., and 3:364ff. But see Miethke, 737–740, who argues that influence of Ockham and Marsiglio on conciliarists is easily underestimated.

[26] Pascoe, "Theological dimensions" (See above, n. 13), 360–65.

[27] Yves Congar, "Aspects ecclésiologiques de la quérelle entre mendiants et séculiers dans la séconde moitié du XIIIe siècle et le début du XIVe," *Archives d'histoire doctrinale et littéraire du moyen âge* 36 (1961) 35–151.

principles in the context of the struggles between the secular priests and the friars in the thirteenth and fourteenth centuries. These studies have shown clearly how hierarchical and clerical was the thought of conciliar theologians and have provided a valuable corrective to the somewhat fanciful, but widespread earlier characterization of theologians like Gerson as democratic, laicist revolutionaries.

Though Hübler's theory is thus highly problematic, his analysis of the concrete reforms is often accurate. A number of reforms deliberated at Constance could be classed as "constitutional" reforms, in that they would have subjected the pope and curia to the regular oversight of either the council or the college of cardinals. Other "constitutional" reforms would have reorganized the central administrative organs of the church—pope, cardinals, and curia. Though they did not amount to "ecclesiastical parliamentarism," they did envisage the council as a supreme authority in the church. We shall return to them later.

2. Haller: Reform as decentralization

Other reforms fit Hübler's model less well. The reforms which had seemed most urgent to many reformers were those regarding papal provisions, annates, and services. Hübler tended to treat these as conciliar efforts to regulate papal powers of taxation and appointment to office. Great disagreement at the council occurred in the deliberation of these matters, causing reform activity to slow down and even stop.[28] Hübler felt that it was narrow particularism, especially in the form of nationalism, which divided the reformers and enabled the curialists, or "conservatives" to prevent them from enacting these reforms.[29] When the reforms could not be enacted by universal legislation, the reformers had to turn to particularized, national concordats.

There is considerable irony in the fact that Hübler blamed particularism for the failure of the reforms of papal powers of taxation and appointments to ecclesiastical offices. For these same reforms, regarded from another vantage point, were themselves very strong expressions of particularism. They were in fact, often the efforts of local prelates to reassert their powers; and they were

---

[28] Hübler, 17, 41.
[29] *Ibid.*, 42, 44–45, 62, especially 38: "An die Stelle der ecclesia Dei reformanda in capite et in membris traten die kleinlichen Local- und Privatinteressen der Landes Kirchen."

thus attempts to decentralize the Church rather than to provide
controls over the papal exercise of power through another central
organ, the council. Several decades after Hübler, Johannes Haller
chose to look at the reforms as decentralization. But he mistook the
localism of the prelates for emerging nationalism. The Gallican
withdrawal of obedience from the pope, which Hübler had regarded as a dangerously particularistic counter-current to the
movement for ecclesiastical parliamentarism became for Haller
the epitome of late medieval reform. Haller went on to identify the
assertion of autonomy of national churches as the core of the reform
movement, and he suggested that it found its ultimate expression in
the reform work of the Councils of Constance and Basel.[30]

For Haller the reform movement which culminated in the Councils of Constance and Basel began in the years just before 1400, not
with the writings of Conrad of Gelnhausen and Henry of Langenstein, as Hübler had posited.[31] The papal centralization which the
reformers attacked had its roots in a much earlier period, even
before it reached its full blossom under the popes at Avignon.
Criticisms of the effects of papal centralization were as old as the
centralization itself, but the new reformers attacked the very foundations of the papal centralization in a systematic and thorough
way. The movement found classic expression in two pivotal works,
the *De squaloribus* (or *De praxi*) *Romane curie* (1403) and the *Speculum
aureum de beneficiis ecclesiasticis* (1404/5); in the complete development
it received in the most important writing of this period, the *De modis
uniendi et reformandi ecclesiam* (1410), it was nothing short of a call for
revolution.

Haller argued that the ideas expressed in these three crucial
treatises were derived from the program of reform first announced
several years earlier in the French synod of 1398 as part of the
French clergy's withdrawal of obedience from Benedict XIII. This

---

[30] Haller, 465–479. Haller's views were taken up and expressed even more
sharply by succeeding scholars; see, e.g., Richard Zwölfer, "Die Reform der
Kirchenverfassung auf dem Konzil zu Basel," *Basler Zeitschrift für Geschichte und
Altertumskunde*, 28 (1929), 141–247 and 29 (1930) 1–58.

[31] Building on Haller's model, Howard Kaminsky has pointed to the fundamental difference between the earlier view of the council in the *via concilii* or *via
iustitie*—that the council was to act as judge to determine which pope was
legitimate—and the later view of the council in the *via cessionis*, ultimately the *via
eiectionis*, in which the council would compel both rival popes to abdicate or would
depose them both. Kaminsky argues that the councils of Pisa and Constance were
implementations of this later view, which originated—for uniquely French political reasons—in the withdrawal of obedience enacted in the French synod of 1398.
See "The Politics of France's Subtraction of Obedience from Pope Benedict XIII,
27 July, 1398," *Proceedings of the American Philosophical Society* 115 (1971) 366–97.

program, eloquently summarized in a speech of the canonist Pierre
Leroy at that synod, became known as the "Gallican liberties". It
was a call for the restoration of the ancient rights and immunities of
the church, which, according to the reformers, had been usurped
by the popes. For Haller, the reform movement which found expression at the Council of Constance was the program of the
Gallican liberties extended to the whole church. The French, having won their freedom from the pope, preached this gospel of liberty
to the rest of Europe in the fifteenth century just as they would their
gospel of political liberty in the eighteenth.

How did the French arrive at this gospel? Haller wisely argued
against attributing any major role to the ideas of Marsiglio of
Padua. Less wisely, he also ruled out a delayed influence of William
Durant the Younger (Haller: his ideas find no literal echoes in the
Gallican ideas) and the use of canonistic sources (Haller: the
relevant ones were too sparse and scattered to be useful).[32] Instead,
the French developed their program by imitating a ready
example—the freedom which the English church had won from the
papacy over the preceding two centuries. Like the English, the
French were in the process of creating a "national church"; the
Germans and other nations in turn followed the French example.

Such is Haller's argument. Its analysis of the political situation
in France during the years before the council was keenly percep-
tive. Howard Kaminsky has followed Haller's lead in investigating
the politics of the subtraction of obedience in 1398 and the important role played by Simon de Cramaud in this action and its
aftermath.[33] Haller also rightly stressed the central role of the ideas
of Pierre Leroy and of the three seminal reform tracts mentioned
above and correctly called attention to the manner in which their
fundamental reform ideas overlap with one another and form much
of the basis for later reform ideas. We shall have to deal with them
extensively in our discussion of reform at Constance. The problems
with Haller's interpretation lie chiefly in his views concerning the
sources and the implications of these ideas. I believe that he fundamentally misinterpreted their implications because he viewed
them backward from the perspective of the Council of Basel (his

---

[32] Haller, 371–373. Haller is aware of the impact of Durant's work on D'Ailly
and Gerson, but he underestimates it. On Durant, see Constantin Fasolt, *Council
and Hierarchy: The Political Thought of William Durant the Younger* (Cambridge, Engl.,
1990), and below p. 229 n. 91.

[33] Howard Kaminsky, "Politics"; and *Simon de Cramaud and the Great Schism*
(New Brunswick, N.J., 1983).

area of greatest scholarly expertise), and from the context of his own times (an age of intense nationalism).

It is revealing to contrast Haller's views with those of Victor Martin in his monumental study of the origins of Gallicanism.[34] Martin warned strongly against interpreting Gallicanism as a sort of ecclesiastical nationalism. While agreeing with Haller that the schism played midwife to Gallicanism he placed the birth in the synod of 1406/07 rather than that of 1398[35] (thus after the appearance of the three crucial tracts in which Haller had detected such strong "Gallican" influence), and while Martin accepted Haller's argument that France closely followed England's fourteenth century example, he argued that the allegedly "English" ideas were in fact originally French ideas of the early fourteenth century repatriated in France during the Schism.[36] Furthermore, the English example itself was not fully applicable to France, which had accepted the canon law of the church to a much greater degree than England. Because France accepted the canon law, the Gallicans' remedy was to oppose one part of the canon law to another. They exalted the canons of the councils and the decrees of ancient popes over the decretals of the recent popes, in order to attack the papal rights of taxation and appointments to office which were sanctioned by the recent decretals.

Haller and Martin rightly identified in the program of "Gallican liberties" important constituent elements of the ideas of reform set forth at the Council of Constance, but they did not give sufficient attention to the canonistic and theological sources which underlay both the Gallican liberties and other reform thought at Constance. They noted that Leroy was a canonist—the leading one of his day according to Guillaume Fillastre;[37] and Martin showed how Gallicans used earlier canon law texts to challenge papal decretals. But the canonists were also able to use the decretal law itself to restrain papal power by requiring the popes to follow the laws which their predecessors had made for lesser prelates. Tierney's classic study cited above[38] demonstrated the manner in which the canonist Francesco Zabarella applied the decretal law concerning the relationship between bishop and chapter in a cathedral church to the

---

[34] Victor Martin, *Les origines du Gallicanisme* (Paris, 1939, repr. Geneva, 1978).
[35] Martin, *Gallicanisme*, 29 n.2.
[36] Martin, *Gallicanisme*, 348–357; see especially p. 352, n.3.
[37] Louis Bourgeois du Chastenet, *Nouvelle histoire du concile de Constance: Preuves* (Paris, 1718) 199 and 209, cited by Martin, *Gallicanisme*, 1:357 n.2.
[38] Tierney, *Foundations*; see n. 24 above.

relationship between pope and cardinals in the Roman church. Numerous reforms proposed at Constance required the pope to receive the counsel, and/or consent and/or subscription of the cardinals before taking certain weighty actions which affected the welfare of the universal church; these were almost certainly patterned on similar measures in papal decretals concerning the relationship between bishop and chapter.

Although LeRoy was a canonist, he drew many of his ideas about the restraint of papal power from arguments developed by theologians over the preceding century and one-half, especially in the dispute between seculars and mendicants. That dispute and the ideas surrounding it were still quite current at the time of the Council of Constance. A convenient summary of these ideas may be seen in a request submitted by the envoys of the University of Paris to the Constance reform committee calling for the revocation of Alexander V's bull which granted privileges to the mendicants.[39] What Leroy above all took from the theologians was a hierarchical conception of the church which he and they used as a basis from which to attack the encroachments of the papacy on the powers of the intermediate levels (the prelates) in the hierarchy.[40] Haller had signalled this strong hierarchical strain of thought in the Gallicans and noted that it had little in common with Marsiglio of Padua's democratic ideas.[41] However, he did not stress sufficiently the degree to which the canonistic and theological ideas of reform cross-fertilized each other.

Hermann Heimpel has demonstrated that this cross-fertilization occurred in a very direct way through the collaboration of theologians and canonists in the writing of important tracts, including the seminal *De squalores* (or *De praxi*).[42] Haller had identified its author

---

[39] ACC.2.690–698. For analysis, see below, pp. 245–249.

[40] See above, n. 27 for Congar's fundamental study of the earlier development of these ideas. The strong hierarchical element in Gerson's ecclesiology is explored by Pascoe, *Gerson*, 17–48 and by G.H.M. Posthumus Meyjes, *Jean Gerson: Zijn kerkpolitiek en ecclesiologie* ('s-Gravenhage, 1963), 210–251. On the other hand, mendicants frequently expressed pro-papal ideas. At Constance there were few who did so; Leonardo Dati was the most notable. See Thomas Izbicki, "The Council of Ferrara-Florence and Dominican Papalism," in *Christian Unity*, ed. Giuseppe Alberigo (Louvain, 1991), 429–443; and Brian Tierney, " 'Divided Sovereignty' at Constance: A Problem of Medieval and Early Modern Political Theory," *AHC* 7 (1975) 238–256.

[41] See Haller, 362–63 and 73–77.

[42] Hermann Heimpel, "Studien zur Kirchen- and Reichsreform des 15. Jahrhunderts: II. Zu zwei Kirchenreform-Traktaten des beginnenden 15. Jahrhunderts: Die Reformschrift 'De praxi curiae Romanae' ('Squalores Romanae curiae,' 1403) des Matthäus von Krakau und ihr Bearbeiter; Das 'Speculum aureum de

as the theologian Matthew of Cracow, but he did not know who
added the canonistic citations; Heimpel identified him as Job Vener, who also worked later with another theologian, Konrad Soest,
to produce the Heidelberg Postillen. In turn, the canonist Paulus
Vladimiri was strongly influenced by the theological arguments in
Matthew's treatise when he produced his own work, the *Speculum
aureum*, another of Haller's three seminal treatises. Matthew died in
1410, but both Vener and Vladimiri were in Constance and played
important roles there in the reform activity. Heimpel has shown
that Vener and Vladimiri were part of a larger network of reformers that spread across Europe in a "reform rectangle" linking
the cities of Prague, Krakow, Heidelberg, and Padua. The main
links were the universities in these cities, but also the court of
Ruprecht, the Count Palatine of the Rhine, where both Matthew
and Job were employed—Matthew as royal councillor, Job as
protonotary. Vladimiri studied under Zabarella at Padua and
taught there under Zabarella's leadership from 1404–1410.[43]

3. The ecclesiological context

It is above all ecclesiologically oriented studies which in the past
three decades have thoroughly demonstrated the role of orthodox
canonistic and theological theory in the shaping of conciliar
thought. At almost the same time Tierney published his seminal
Foundations of the Conciliar Theory, Ludwig Buisson examined many
of the same sources in his *Potestas und caritas*.[44] Then, in the years
surrounding Vatican II a spate of studies analyzed the significance
of the decrees *Haec sancta* and *Frequens*.[45] Hans Schneider offers an

---

titulis beneficiorum' (1404/5) und sein Verfasser," *Sitzungsberichte der Universität
Heidelberg, phil.-hist. Klasse*, 1974, no. 1; *Die Vener von Gmünd und Strassburg, 1162–
1447* (Göttingen, 1982).

[43] Heimpel, *Die Vener*, 2:700–701. Heimpel also believes that there may have
been a tie between Zabarella and the Count Palatine Ruprecht, who was also
emperor-elect between 1400 and 1410; Zabarella had written a consilium justifying the deposition of Wenceslas which had paved the way for Ruprecht's election.
However, the calling of the Council of Pisa by the cardinals caused Zabarella and
the Palatinate to take very different stances. See Klaus Wriedt, "Der Heidelberger
Hof und die Pisaner Kardinäle: Zwei Formen des Konzilsgedankens," in *Aus
Reichsgeschichte und nordischer Geschichte (Festgabe für K. Jordan)*, ed. Horst Fuhrmann,
et al. (Kiel, 1972), who stresses the Palatinate's rejection of a council convoked
and ruled by cardinals.

[44] Ludwig Buisson, *Potestas und caritas: Die päpstliche Gewalt im Spätmittelalter*
(Cologne, 1958).

[45] See esp. Hans Küng, *Strukturen der Kirche* (Freiburg, 1962) and Paul De-
Vooght, *Les pouvoirs du concile et l'autorité du pape au concile de Constance* (Paris, 1965)

outstanding overview of this scholarship and its divergent interpretations; he also shows how interpretations of the Council of
Constance have been shaped since the fifteenth century by
papalist-conciliarist polemic.[46] Building on Schneider's study,
Giuseppe Alberigo, in a study of great importance published in
1981, argues that the papalist interpretation of conciliarism as an
extreme democratic position based on the heretical views of Marsiglio of Padua and William of Ockham began with Eugenius IV
and his supporters after the breach with the Council of Basel.[47]
Most of the main strands of all the future "papalist" polemic about
"conciliarism" were established in Juan de Torquemada's *Summa
de ecclesia*.[48] Alberigo seeks to go back before the beginning of the
polemic to ask how the contemporaries themselves viewed the
decree *Haec sancta*. In other words, he seeks to place the decree in its
historical context, in a narrower sense within the events of the
council itself, and in a broader sense within the entire conciliar
epoch from 1378 to 1462.

Alberigo concludes that the decree was a valid decree, accepted
with little controversy at the time of the council. He finds that on
the whole few statements were made about the decree at the council
itself after its passage—and virtually none that either questioned
the decree's validity on the one hand or attempted to use it in order
to support a radical conciliarism on the other. In the understanding
of the council fathers the decree asserted the council's power over

---

and "Le conciliarisme aux conciles de Constance et de Bâle. Compléments et
précisions," *Irenikon* 36 (1968) 61–75, for the positive arguments. Doubts are
raised by August Franzen, "Zur Vorgeschichte des Konstanzer Konzils vom
Ausbruch des Schismas bis zum Pisanum," and "Das Konzil der Einheit," in *Das
Konzil von Konstanz (Festschrift H. Schäufele)*, ed. August Franzen et al. (Freiburg,
1964), 3–35 and 69–112; and by Helmut Riedlinger, "Hermeneutische Überlegungen zu den Konstanzer Dekreten," *ibid.*, 214–238. Erwin Hänggi offers quite
cogent criticism of Franzen and Riedlinger's arguments in a review in *Zeitschrift für
Schweizerische Kirchengeschichte* 60 (1966) 187–194. The studies of Hubert Jedin
remain fundamental: *Bischöfliches Konzil oder Kirchenparlament? Ein Beitrag zur Ekklesiologie der Konzilien von Konstanz und Basel*, 2d ed. (Basel, 1965), and the first
chapter of *Geschichte des Konzils von Trient*, v. 1 (Freiburg, 1951).

[46] *Der Konziliarismus als Problem der neueren katholischen Theologie: Die Geschichte der
Auslegung der Konstanzer Dekrete von Febronius bis zur Gegenwart* (Berlin, 1976).

[47] Alberigo, *Chiesa conciliare* (see above, n. 1), 9–10.

[48] On Torquemada, see Thomas Izbicki, *Protector of the Faith: Cardinal Johannes
de Turrecremata and the Defense of the Institutional Church* (Washington, D.C., 1981). In
his article "Papalist Reaction to the Council of Constance: Juan de Torquemada
to the Present," *Church History* 55 (1986) 7–20, Izbicki shows how Torquemada
originated the papalist argument that the crucial superiority decree *Haec sancta*
was not valid since at the time of its enactment the Council of Constance was a
council of only one obedience.

the pope in the abnormal situation in which there was a schismatic
or heretic pope, and under normal conditions it accorded the council
a regular role in the government of the church alongside the pope.[49]
Alberigo notes the various efforts at Constance to define the respective roles of the pope and council as supreme authorities within the
church.[50]

Alberigo does not look more closely at the specific reform ideas of
the council. However, he regards the demand for reform as the
unifying theme in the thought of the whole generation of Europeans
which flourished during the Councils of Pisa and Constance. He
divides the conciliar era into three generations which came of age in
the era of the early Schism, the decade 1410–20, and the period
after 1435 respectively.[51] The second generation includes all the
great reformers at Constance; Alberigo finds their thought to be
characterized by the tension between reform in the sense of renewal
on the one hand and restoration in the sense of reinstating the
conditions before the schism on the other. The third generation
inherited this tension; but by their time the restoration had proved
superficial, since the underlying reality had changed so profoundly
during the Schism; and the renewal had become a delusion. By the
time of the third generation "diverse and contrasting modes of
understanding reform" had emerged, especially since the Council
of Constance had adjourned leaving the demand for reform unsatisfied.

Alberigo's historical approach admirably removes the study of
Haec sancta from the rigid matrix of the polarized ecclesiological
discussion. It also offers promising perspectives for understanding
the Constance reforms. I would argue that the Council of Constance did not leave the reform demands unsatisfied, that it in fact
nourished hope for continued reform, but that diverse and con-
strasting modes of understanding reform were already present at
Constance. It is these modes that my study proposes to analyze.

4. The Constance reforms

The indispensable general survey of late medieval conciliar reform
is now the fundamental recent study of Johannes Helmrath.[52] The

---

[49] Pp. 349–352.
[50] See, for example, pp. 200–201, 211–212.
[51] Pp. 19–21.
[52] Johannes Helmrath, "Reform als Thema der Konzilien des Spätmittelalters," in *Christian Unity*, ed. Giuseppe Alberigo. (Louvain, 1991), 75–152. See also

best recent introduction to the reform work of the Council of Constance is found in an article by Walter Brandmüller published in the same year as Alberigo's study.[53] In it Brandmüller expressed agreement with the criticism of Hübler's and Haller's anachronistic models which I had set forth in my 1978 doctoral dissertation. I had suggested there that anachronistic views of the goals of the reformers had led to a too hasty verdict that the reforms were failures, and I had outlined a more accurate understanding of the reformers' goals based on their diverse but overlapping concrete interests. Brandmüller agreed, noting the tantalizing suggestion of Karl August Fink that the Constance reforms were not such failures as earlier scholarship has made them out.[54] However, as a "historian and theologian" Brandmüller remained deeply dissatisfied with the Constance reforms, calling it a "historical scandal" that the whole reform work of the council exhausted itself in the struggle to resolve conflicting economic interests among the clergy.[55] According to Brandmüller, even such an important reform decree as "Frequens," which established the regular meeting of general councils, was ultimately an attempt at "institutionalization of reform" and thus unable to bring about real spiritual renewal.[56] Brandmüller was disappointed that the Constance reformers did not aim higher. I will argue that they did aim higher. What appears to us as an institutional reform was for the Constance fathers the reform of the living body of Christ in head and members, animated by the Holy Spirit. Modern scholars have often echoed the observation of some of the council fathers themselves that the most significant *reformatio* to be enacted at Constance was that which ended the *de-formatio* of a three-headed church. It is easy to miss the full

---

his earlier study of the Council of Basel: *Das Basler Konzil, 1431–1449: Forschungsstand und Probleme* (Cologne, 1987). In both studies, Helmrath brings together a rich harvest of primary and secondary sources and concisely and accurately summarizes the state of the question on all important topics. His hypotheses concerning disputed matters and his identification of areas for further research establish an agenda for all further study of conciliar reform. Of particular value is his focus on the implementation of the reforms at both the central and regional levels.

[53] "Causa reformationis: Ergebnisse und Probleme der Reformen des Konstanzer Konzils," *AHC* 13 (1981), 49–66.

[54] Brandmüller, "Causa reformationis," 62 n. 55. See above, n. 11. To Fink's statements could be added similar remarks by E.F. Jacob and Hubert Jedin.

[55] Brandmüller, "Causa reformationis," 63: "Dass sich aber das gesamte Reformwerk der nach Teilnehmerzahl, Dauer und Problemstellung bedeutendsten Kirchenversammlung des Mittelalters in dem Versuch, ökonomische Verteilungskämpfe innerhalb des Klerus zu beenden, erschöpfte, ist ein historischer Skandal."

[56] Brandmüller, "Causa reformationis," 57.

impact of this statement. For the Constance reformers, ending the schism meant ending the abuses of the schism. The studies of Favier, Baix, Esch, and others have shown how enormous those abuses were.[57]

Even the reforms that appear most crassly as squabbles over conflicting economic interests were often pictured by the reformers in much more exalted terms. What is needed is to combine a close analysis of the concrete reform measures with an analysis of the ways in which the reformers imagined the results of these measures. We are fortunately in an excellent position to make such an analysis because the tracts and speeches written and delivered at the council as well as the records of the reform committee deliberations and the official acta of the council itself offer an extraordinarily complete record of the council's reform ideology. In a fascinating article, Jürgen Miethke has called attention to this rich common stock of ideas circulating at Constance, to which the individual speakers and writers added their own endlessly diverse nuances.[58] He observes that the audience for the tracts written at the council was quite literally an audience—tracts were often read in public session, slowly and over several sessions so that hearers could make their own copies.[59] (Finke and Arendt have argued conversely that the very numerous speeches delivered at the council were often circulated in manuscript form for reading and copying.)[60] The writers and speakers also had at their disposal an unusually rich collection of important earlier writings. The councils, as international fora, offered an unprecedented opportunity for the participants to share with each other these writings, which had earlier circulated primarily within various "closed publics" (circles of friends, universities, religious orders, etc.).[61]

---

[57] Jean Favier, *Les finances pontificales à l'époque du Grand Schisme d'Occident* (Paris, 1966); François Baix, *La Chambre apostolique et les "Libri Annatarum" de Martin V (1417–1431)* (Brussels and Rome, 1947; and Arnold Esch, "Simonie-Geschäft in Rom 1400: 'Kein Papst wird das tun, was dieser tut,'" *Vierteljahrschrift für Sozial- und Wirtschaftsgeschichte* 61 (1974), 433–457.

[58] Miethke (see above, n. 3), 741–742. See also Johannes Helmrath, "Kommunikation auf den spätmittelalterlichen Konzilien," in *Die Bedeutung der Kommunikation für Wirtschaft und Gesellschaft*, ed. Hans Pohl (Stuttgart, 1989), 116–172.

[59] Miethke, 754–755 notes 61 and 61a, cites very interesting evidence from colophons of manuscripts.

[60] ACC.2.369–370; Paul Arendt, *Die Predigten des Konstanzer Konzils* (Freiburg, 1933), 5–6.

[61] Miethke, 760–767; see esp. p. 767: "Auf den Konzilien konnten die geschlossenen Öffentlichkeiten und Verbreitungskreise, die sonst nur so schwer zu überschreiten oder miteinander zu verbinden waren, wenigstens für eine Zeitlang miteinander verschmelzen . . ."

Miethke's main thesis is that there was not a common idea of "conciliarism" at the councils of Pisa, Constance, and Basel, but rather a common stock of ideas from which "conciliarists" drew different "conciliar ideas."[62] What he says about conciliar ideas is even more true of reform ideas. Ideas of reform and renewal can and must be treated as a distinct genre of ideas, not as subsets or reflections of different ecclesiological or political stances. After looking at the concrete reform proposals themselves in Chapters 3 through 6, I will turn to the wider ideology of reform. In Chapter 7 I will examine the common stock of arguments from which reformers drew. In the study of reform ideology, Gerhart Ladner has shown the importance of dealing not only with arguments, but also with the very words and images which are used to describe reform. To borrow a suggestive concept of Jacques LeGoff, we need to consider the "imaginary" of reform.[63] "Imaginary" as an adjective is virtually synonomous today with "unreal," but LeGoff uses it as a collective noun to refer to that which is in the imagination. What is imagined is not necessarily unreal; in fact, one of the ways we perceive reality is through our imagination. In this study, I would like to use the concept of the "imaginary" primarily in a more prosaic way—to mean a working collection of images analogous to a vocabulary (a working collection of words). Used in this sense it precisely parallels Miethke's concept of the common stock of arguments. In Chapter 8 I will look at the way words and images convey conceptions of change. Like the god Janus, renewal ideas look forward and backward at once and thus involve a more complex view of the past and future than a simple idea of progress. Finally, in Chapter 9, I will consider the ways in which the words and images are used to describe the subjects and objects of reform.

Here we will return to the ecclesiological questions and to the relationship between reform and the decree *Haec sancta*. However, we will be placing these questions in the framework of reform thought rather than vice versa. Louis Pascoe, who was, like myself, trained by Gerhart Ladner in the study of reform ideas, demonstrated in his study of Gerson mentioned above how an understand-

---

[62] It is also possible to talk about different languages of discourse used by different reformers in different contexts; this challenging idea is suggested in a recent article by Antony Black, "Political Languages in Later Medieval Europe," in *The Church and Sovereignty, c. 590–1915: Essays in honour of Michael Wilks*, ed. Diana Wood (Oxford, 1991), 313–28.

[63] Jacques LeGoff, *L'Imaginaire médiéval: Essais* (Paris, 1985). In his preface, pp. i–xxi, LeGoff explains his concept of the "imaginary."

ing of ideas of reform can shed light on ecclesiology.[64] Gerson's synthesis of conciliarism with a strong hierarchical view of the church belies all attempts to identify "conciliarism" with an "ascending theory of government." Gerson's view was held by a large group of reformers for whom the council was supreme because it represented the universal, hierarchical church, which had alone been promised infallibility by Christ. This universality is underlined not only in the phrase *uniuersalem ecclesiam representans* in *Haec sancta*, which explains why the council receives power directly from Christ, but also in the phrase *generalem reformationem dictae ecclesiae Dei in capite et in membris*, which explains the council's authority to regulate the exercise of papal power.

The crucial phrase *in capite et in membris* evokes strongly the concept of the church as the body of Christ and signals the close connections of conciliar reform with corporatist thought. Antony Black's studies of later conciliar thought at Basel have quite rightly stressed these connections, even though corporatism was not as strong at Constance as at Basel.[65] Black notes clearly the differences between "Constantian" and "Basilean" conciliar thought.[66] However, a number of his observations about reform at Basel apply also to Constance. For example, he views the Basel reform program as one of decentralization, but he rightly criticizes Haller's view that the reformers wanted to build national or territorial churches. Even though the reforms had the *effect* of strengthening the territorial rulers' control over their churches, this was not the *intent* of the reformers. He argues that at Basel the reformers rejected such an alliance and that conversely the lay princes in fact impeded reform by their neutrality stance.[67] Black also rightly rejects Haller's characterization of the reformers' aims as "revolutionary."[68] The actions taken by the council were revolutionary, but the reforms they envisaged were not. Black would argue that they saw themselves as

---

[64] Pascoe, *Gerson*, 17–48.

[65] Antony Black, *Monarchy and Community: Political Ideas in the Later Conciliar Controversy, 1430–1450* (Cambridge, 1970); and especially *Council and Commune* (see above, n. 18).

[66] *Council and Commune*, 21–22, 31–32, 55–56. His most incisive formulation of the difference is found in his recent survey article "The Conciliar Movement," in *The Cambridge History of Medieval Political Thought*, ed. J.H. Burns (Cambridge, 1988) 573–587, at 579–580, where he says that Gerson's ideas of "mixed government" at Constance were "inverted" at Basel "to make the *council* the primary recipient and the pope the derivative recipient, of Christ's authority. The theory of mixed government was now replaced almost wholly by one of community sovereignty."

[67] Pp. 45–48.

[68] P. 37.

conserving a conciliar polity of the church. Thus, in many ways Black also revives Hübler's idea of the council as a parliament.[69] I believe this approach points toward a third way of viewing the Constance reforms, which invokes the insights of Hübler and Haller while avoiding their anachronisms.

This study pursues that third way by viewing the Constance reforms as a chapter in the history of reform ideology, by observing the tension between the concrete reforms and the images with which reformers envisioned them, and above all by analyzing the diverse attitudes of reformers toward change. All reform thought reflects a fundamental ambivalence between moving back and moving forward. Alberigo stresses the tension between restoration and reform in the longings of the generation that came of age in the years of Pisa and Constance. He implies that both hopes were doomed to disappointment—reform insofar as it aimed too far, and restoration insofar as it sought only a return to the pre-schism status quo. Alberigo's phrase—"verso la normalizzazione della chiesa,"[70] strangely but not unaptly evokes Warren Harding's "return to normalcy" in the 1920s. After the Schism, just as after World War I, normalcy was an illusion, because the underlying reality had changed so drastically. I will argue, however, that the Constance reformers cherished few illusions. They looked backward in order to correct the enormous abuses of the Schism, and they did so with remarkable success. They looked forward in order to prevent such abuses in the future in a way that would keep pace with changing realities—through the frequent celebration of general councils.

---

[69] Pp. 191–193.
[70] Pp. 205–227.

CHAPTER TWO

THE STRUGGLE FOR REFORM

The only complete survey of the Constance reform deliberations remains that of Hübler.[1] He presented the deliberations as a tug-of-war, a series of bursts of activity followed by slowdowns and then impasses which could only be resolved by compromises. For him the parties at the opposing ends of the rope were the reformers, led by the the emperor-elect, versus those who opposed reform, led by the cardinals and curia; he labelled these parties the "liberals" and "conservatives", respectively. For him, the overall results of these compromises were disappointing since the liberals were outmaneuvered by the conservatives.

1. Hübler's view of the reform negotiations

Serious consideration of reform at the council began in the summer of 1415, after the deposition of John XXIII and the resignation of Gregory XII and after the trial and condemnation of John Hus. The conservatives stalled consideration of any reform proposal until after the reform party's leader, Sigismund, had left for negotiations with the adherents of Benedict XIII. The cardinals seized this opportunity to propose the formation of a reform committee, whose deliberations they thus expected to control. During the last half of 1415 this committee produced a comprehensive program of reform, but reform activity stagnated in 1416 pending Sigismund's return. When he returned in January, 1417, attention again focused on union, especially after the arrival of the Spanish delegations. The reform party and the conservatives now clashed over whether reform should take place before the election of the new pope, resulting in what Hübler called the two "priority struggles."

The "first priority struggle" lasted from April 3 to July 22 and was precipitated by the refusal of the Castilian delegates to join the council until the plans for the election were fixed. Hübler suggested that the cardinals were co-opting the Castilians so that they could delay reform by pushing the issue of the election to the fore. After

---

[1] Hübler, 3–64.

the Castilians were finally seated, the cardinals caused further delay by demanding new security decrees from Sigismund. Finally a compromise was reached on July 13; Sigismund granted a new security pledge, and the cardinals agreed that reform at least *in capite et curia Romana* would be enacted before the election. Soon after the deposition of Benedict XIII on July 26, a new reform committee, which included Spanish delegates but no cardinals, was formed and quickly prepared the reform in head and Roman curia for enactment. At this point the "second priority struggle" ensued. Agreement could not be reached on all the reforms. The cardinals demanded that the mode of election be discussed concomitantly with the reforms; Sigismund refused. Each side blamed the other for stalling. The cardinals organized the three Latin nations against the emperor-elect and the liberals. This struggle was finally resolved by a second compromise. The reforms upon which agreement could be reached would be enacted and the council would proceed to the election, provided that the future pope be bound to work with the council to enact reform in the remaining areas. Accordingly, the five reform decrees on which the nations had agreed were enacted in the thirty-ninth general session (October 8), and in the fortieth session (October 30) a decree was passed which bound the future pope to a reform pledge or guarantee (*cautio de reformatione fienda*), by which he would enact reform under eighteen headings. The first three of the decrees of the thirty-ninth session did make an effort to put into practice the "constitutional principles" of the council, which had called for transferring the center of gravity from the papal *plenitudo potestatis* to the council.

However, a break with these constitutional principles had begun with the fateful coalition of the three Latin nations against the German and English nations. Ecclesiastical liberalism had grown tired. Moreover, the division of the reform, and the reduction of further reforms to those *in capite et curia Romana* showed that particularist interests were gaining the upper hand. And, as the liberals had feared, bringing about reform after the election was very difficult. A third reform committee, composed of six cardinals and six representatives from each of the five nations, was established soon after the election. It worked zealously, but the divisions among the nations were so great that the pope and cardinals were able to sit back and watch as the reforms once again reached a stalemate. Here the German nation took the initiative and presented its own proposal (*Avisamenta*) for a separate agreement with the pope. In reply, the pope made his own proposal for reform (Hübler called it the *Reformacte*), and a third and final compromise ensued. In the forty-third session, March 21, 1418, the council enacted the seven further reform decrees upon which agreement had been reached. Reform under the remaining headings was to be enacted as far as possible in separate agreements or concordats between the pope and the individual nations. The texts of these concordats were included in the acta for the forty-third session, but further changes were still made before the final promulgation of the concordats over the next several months. The reforms enacted in these concordats were of little importance, and in any event all the concordats, except the English one, were temporary, enacted for a five-year period only.

Such is the gist of Hübler's analysis. Hübler defined the terms for all future analyses. He identified and named the phases of the negotiations and the principal documents; underlined the central role played by the three successive reform committees; and sorted out the main terms of the compromises which emerged from what he called the two "priority struggles" of 1417. What might seem to be a weakness, his down-playing of the influence of secular political struggles, I believe to be fundamentally correct. Even though we know much more about these struggles as a result of documents discovered by Finke and analyses of Valois, Crowder,[2] and others, there is still little evidence that they had any major effect on the reform negotiations.

And yet Hübler's view is in serious need of revision in several respects. Finke's newly published sources alter Hübler's view of the process of the negotiations both before and after the election. The most serious problem, however, is Hübler's reduction of the struggle for reform at Constance to a conflict between a liberal reform party led by the emperor and a conservative curialist party led by the cardinals. This view is anachronistic and over-simplified; it seriously distorts the historical reality. After re-examining the chronological framework of the reform negotiations in this chapter, I will argue that we can only understand the outcome by examining separately the development of each major group of reforms.

2. Reform during the early months of the council

Most of the council's efforts during its early months were devoted to ending the Schism and condemning the alleged heresies of Wyclif and Hus. The council did not begin formal deliberation of reforms

---

[2] See below, nn. 29, 32, and 39.

until after decisive actions had occurred in both areas: the deposition of John XXIII (May 29), the resignation of Gregory XII (July 4), the departure of Sigismund for negotiations with the adherents of Benedict XIII (July 18); the condemnation of the heretical theses attributed to Wyclif (May 4) and the trial and death by burning of Hus (July 6).

Even during this time, however, there had been much informal discussion of reform. Many delegations brought with them treatises on reform and lists of reform proposals which had been drawn up over the preceding decade, and new reform proposals were circulated during the council's early months. The trial of John XXIII had also caused the council fathers to think directly about reform issues. Most of the charges brought against John XXIII had to do with his maladministration of the church; they represent a virtual catalogue of the abuses which the reformers sought to attack.[3] After the trial a reformer could respond to curialist claims that popes cannot commit simony by pointing to the council's conviction of John XXIII for this crime.[4] Some of the most ardent reformers had remained loyal to Gregory XII and Benedict XIII. In the condemnation of John XXIII, their reforming zeal could jibe nicely with their affection for these popes. Conversely, the disillusioned reformers of John's own obedience included cardinals and other curial officials who were deeply disturbed by his mismanagement of the curia and the papal states, especially his alienation of lands and rights of the Roman church. The condemnation of this mismanagement provided a strong model for later reforms. If the council could condemn abuses of papal power in a reigning pope, it could presumably also take action to prevent those abuses by limiting the exercise of papal power in the future.

This concept was of fundamental importance for reform at the council. It was based in turn on the idea that the council represented the universal church and thus had the ultimate authority for the governance of the church. As much as this idea appears to foreshadow later secular ideas of representative, parliamentary

---

[3] ACC.3.157–209; see Finke's introduction, pp. 11–29; Finke also makes reference to the complaints against John's mismanagement which appeared at the same time in the pamphlet literature which is also edited in this section of the ACC.

[4] See anonymous tract against annates (partially edited by Finke, ACC.2.592–600), Paris, BN, MS lat. 14644, fol. 361r: Oportet supponere quod papa potest comittere symoniam et cum ipso committi potest iuxta nota in c. Si papa xl. di [D.40 c.6]. . . . et in hoc non insisto quia iste dominus Jo. XXIII ex isto crimine symonie per generale concilium nuperime et merito dampnatus est multis ad hoc racionibus et auctoritatibus sacrum mouentibus concilium.

government, we must also note its unfortunate close connection with the idea of combatting heresy. The canonists who had argued that the council has power to judge and depose a pope for maladministration based this power on an extension of the council's power to judge a pope for heresy. This connection was made very visible at Constance, when during the spring of 1415 the condemnation of John XXIII proceeded in tandem with the condemnation of the Wycliffite and Hussite teachings.[5]

3. The process of reform deliberations

Hübler was correct in stating that the cardinals took the initiative in establishing the first reform committee just after Sigismund's departure for Spain, and surely one major reason for this timing was, as Hübler suggested, their desire to deliberate the reforms at a time when he couldn't influence them. We should not make too much of this, however. The time after his departure was the logical time to begin reform deliberations since further conciliar action on union had to await the results of his successful negotiations with the Spanish. Sigismund's primary concern at the council was ending the schism rather than reform. Even when he returned from Spain, the reform deliberations remained insulated from his influence.

It is true that lay princes and kings did make their influence strongly felt at Constance, especially in the negotiations concerning union. It was urgent that they should be involved, since only their active cooperation could unite the separate obediences of the rival popes. In this sense the Council of Constance was indeed the first great world congress of nations.

Lay princes did also have interests in the reforms, very concrete interests. The weakening of papal patronage rights and taxation of the clergy offered them the possibility of increasing their own patronage and taxation. Obviously, these reforming interests could clash with those of the clergy itself, except to the extent that individual clerics hoped to avail themselves of lay patronage. The emperor and other lay princes did share with the clerical reformers

---

[5] For example, May 2, 1415 (the same day that the books and memory of Wyclif were condemned), both John XXIII and the Hussite Jerome of Prague were formally cited by the council as part of their condemnation proceedings. See also Edith Tatnall "The Condemnation of John Wyclif at the Council of Constance," in *Councils and Assemblies*, ed. C.J. Cuming and Derek Baker (Cambridge, Engl., 1971), 209–218, at 211–213.

a general reforming desire to insure appointment of the most qualified candidates. They did exert influence on reforms. I will try to point out the evidence for this influence, but will argue that it in fact worked most often to *impede* the enactment of reforms, i.e. those reforms which threatened the princes.

The reform committee was the arena where the reforms were hammered out, and secular princes had no direct influence over its deliberations. To understand why, we must examine briefly a document discovered by Finke which outlines the council's procedures for deliberation and voting.[6] Once the reform committee had agreed on the draft of a reform measure, they submitted it to the individual nations. Then the measure passed to a conference committee composed of two deputies elected from each nation, which tried to iron out the differences between the nations and produce a final version acceptable to all. This revised version was then resubmitted to the nations for vote.[7] If approved by all of them it could be enacted in general session; if disapproved it was presumably returned to the reform committee.

---

[6] The older study of the council's order of procedure by Friedrich Stuhr, *Die Organisation und Geschäftsordnung des Pisaner und Konstanzer Konzils* (Schwerin, 1891) is thus now superseded on these matters. The significance of the new documents discovered by Finke (ACC.2.742–758) is discussed by Johannes Hollnsteiner, "Studien zur Geschäftsordnung am Konstanzer Konzil: Ein Beitrag zur Geschichte des Parlamentarismus und der Demokratie," in *Abhandlungen aus dem Gebiete der mittleren und neueren Geschichte: Eine Festgabe zum siebzigsten Geburtstag Heinrich Finke gewidmet* (Münster, 1925), 240–56; repr. in *Das Konstanzer Konzil*, ed. Remigius Bäumer (Darmstadt, 1977), 121–142 (Hollnsteiner had also been delegated by Finke to write the introductory material for the edition of these documents, ACC.2.576–578.) The text of the documents consists of a set of proposals, and there is no evidence that they were ever formally enacted. However, Hollnsteiner argues convincingly that they probably present a close approximation of the procedure actually followed.

[7] To enact a reform by conciliar decree required the unanimous consent of all four, later five nations. Fillastre reports an unsuccessful attempt in the summer of 1416 to change this rule so that only the approval of three of the four nations would be required. Within each nation decision was made by majority vote, but it is not completely clear who was entitled to vote. Intense debates on this question occurred in early 1415, but no uniform practice was established. Instead each nation established its own procedure. A proposal aired in the German nation May 14, 1415 urged that the nation follow the example of the French nation, which had clearly defined who had the right to vote and organized the seats and voting order according to rank. We have the record of one roll call vote taken in the French nation in October–November 1415. Those who voted included patriarchs, bishops, abbots, envoys of lay princes, curial officials, priors, university professors, archdeacons, and miscellaneous lower clergy and monastic personnel, even two persons identified as *sine titulo*. The proposed order of business discussed above called for extending the right to vote to anyone who held an office, including parish priests, and to all university graduates; however, there was resistance to part of the plan and we do not know whether it was followed.

It is significant that reform bills went directly to the nations for deliberation and voting. Other measures had to pass first through the council's steering committee, known as the "general deputies." For reform measures, the reform committee thus acted in place of the general deputies, and reforms were relatively insulated from the other political matters of the council. Whatever influence Sigismund exercised over the steering committee—and it may have at times been great[8]—it did not affect reform matters. When the influence of secular princes was felt, it was either expressed by individual members of the reform committee[9] or it was exerted in the negotiations between the nations concerning the reforms after they had been drafted by the committee.[10]

We have a wonderful window into the deliberations of the reform committee itself in the form of manuscripts containing collections of proposed reform decrees drafted by the committee. Hübler knew only the records which had been edited by Hardt from two Viennese manuscripts. Finke discovered six new records in four manuscripts unknown to Hardt and argued that the records in all the manuscripts, including Hardt's two, were unofficial copies of reform drafts at various stages in the committee's deliberations.[11] In his new edition of these materials, Finke showed how a study of the

---

[8] Hartmut Boockmann cautions against over-estimating the ability of secular princes, including Sigismund, to affect the proceedings at the council; see "Zur politischen Geschichte des Konstanzer Konzils," *ZKG* 85 (1974) 45–63 at 52–53.

[9] Fillastre tells us that the cardinals requested the removal from the reform committee of Robert Hallum, Andreas Lascari, and Bernard de la Planche, referring to them as "illi, qui notorie erant inimici Romane ecclesie et curie atque cardinalium"; these men were known to be cronies of Sigismund. Fillastre's earlier remarks strongly suggest that the cardinals' demand was in retaliation for a demand of the German and English nations that no Italian member of the reform committee be a member of the curia. (ACC.2.134)

[10] Unfortunately, we have no official record of the deliberations of the reforms within the nations. One manuscript does contain a record of proposals sent from the reform committee for consideration in the French nation, but it contains no record of the nation's deliberation of them; on the other hand one manuscript of the second reform committee's drafts contains notes concerning the German and Spanish nations' deliberation of some of the drafts. (See below, p. 55) We also have a detailed official record of the French nation's deliberations concerning annates in autumn 1415, but this occurred before the reform committee had produced drafts on this matter. The letters of Peter Pulka and of the envoys of the University of Vienna often contain detailed unofficial reports of the deliberations of reforms in the German nation and of the negotiations among the nations in early 1418. They are edited by F. Firnhaber, "Petrus de Pulka, Abgesandter der Wiener Universität am Concilium zu Constanz," *Archiv für die Kunde österreichischer Geschichts-Quellen* 15 (1856) 1–70, repr. Graz, 1970. The best official record of the reform stance of the French and German nations is found in their Avisamenta.

[11] See below, the introduction to my new edition of these materials, where I also identify three new manuscript records of the committee's deliberations.

successive drafts of a reform measure could be used by the historian to reconstruct the probable course of the deliberations concerning that reform. Several of the manuscripts contain corrections and marginal notations which reflect revisions of previous drafts and which also give other valuable information concerning the deliberations, including names of authors of drafts and of committee members[12] and also dates, votes, sub-committees, points of disagreement, and further disposition of measures.

The manuscript records suggest that the committee worked feverishly during the summer and fall of 1415. By December, its program had reached a relatively finished form—a core collection of proposals which appears in most of the manuscripts in almost the same order. In my edition below, I have called this the "Common Collection." Then, in 1416, activity seems to have slowed. The document concerning conciliar procedure mentioned above informs us that a large backlog of such reforms awaited consideration by the nations in 1416, resulting from the council's preoccupation with other business, or perhaps from "a certain negligence."[13] Possibly members of the German and English nations were delaying consideration of reforms until Sigismund's return since he had asked that no important business should be concluded in his absence.[14] The procedural document, probably reflecting the concern

---

[12] These records cite the names of fourteen members of the reform committee; see ACC.2.561–562. The names are as follows (references are to page numbers from the edition below unless otherwise noted): Pierre d'Ailly, cardinal of Cambrai (V, c.14); Francesco Zabarella, cardinal of Florence (Common, c.20); Alemanno Ademari, cardinal of Pisa (Common, c.20); Jean Mauroux, patriarch of Antioch (Common, c.38); Nicholas Bubbewyth, bishop of Bath (V, c.14); Francesco da Montepulciano, bishop of Arezzo (Common, c.14); Nikolaus Lubich, bishop of Merseburg (Common, c.6, para.17; see below p. 122, n.51); Enrico Scarampi, bishop of Belluno-Feltre (see Sawicki and Stump, "Evidence," 53); Job Vener (D², c.7); Robert Appleton (Common, c.6, para.17); Angelo Bagliani (the *auditor camere* mentioned in Common, c.6, para.17; see below, p. 199); and three persons who cannot be identified more precisely: prior Celestinarum (V, c.14), Michael Bolosonis (?) (Common, c.6, para.17), abbas Vandrigii (or Vandingii) (Common, c.6, para.17). In addition, Fillastre mentions the names of four members of the second reform committee (ACC.2.133–34): Robert Hallum, bishop of Salisbury; Andreas Lascari, bishop-elect of Posen; Élie Lestrange, bishop of LePuy; and Bernard de la Planche, vicar of Bordeaux. It is also possible that Pier Paolo Vergerio was a member of the committee; see below, p. 276.

[13] ACC.2.751: "quia hucusque aliis impedientibus negociis vel forte quedam in curia pauca de illis adhuc inter naciones sunt deliberata . . ." I am suggesting an emendation of the phrase "quedam in curia" in Finke's edition to "quadam incuria," which appears in one of the two versions of the text (Finke doesn't cite this variant; the version he cites reads "qdam in Curia".)

[14] See his instructions to the council recorded in Cerretano's journal, ACC.2.286: "Primo supplicat predictus d. rex, quatinus in eius absencia sacrum

of other council members lest such reforms be pushed through hastily after Sigismund's return, required that a certain portion of the finished reform bills be sent to the nations each week and that only one further week be allowed for deliberation and voting on these in the nations. It required that all those "whose interests are affected by the reforms," including the cardinals, were to have a hearing in these deliberations. However, the main reason for inaction was probably that the nations wished to wait until the remaining obedience of Benedict XIII joined the council.

In spite of the lull, numerous signs of reforming activity appear in 1416. The extensive additions to the Common Collection which appear in two of the manuscripts probably reflect deliberations of the committee in that year. Moreover, the other four manuscripts of the Common Collection contain, alongside it an impressive set of reforms that may have been deliberated in 1416. Hardt dubbed this text the *Decretales*, because its reforms are phrased as proposed conciliar decrees organized according to the titles of the *Decretales Gregorii IX*.[15] A number of important tracts against annates may have been written in this period;[16] the ongoing debate concerning the system of papal provisions and taxation is also revealed by a heated exchange between Maurice Rvačka and Cardinal Zabarella July 26, 1416.[17] Gerson's tract "Ad reformationem contra simoniam," probably appeared in this year,[18] and finally, on November 1, 1416, Pierre d'Ailly published his treatise on reform.[19]

After Sigismund's return in January of 1417 and the arrival of the delegations from the former obedience of Benedict XIII, the *causa unionis* seized center stage. Hübler assumed that Sigismund and the liberals at this time insisted that reform take place before the election, thus precipitating the priority struggles. However, in the spring of 1417, Sigismund was very anxious to complete the work of union, first by the deposition of Benedict XIII, and then

---

concilium non procedat ad aliquam conclusionem arduorum negotiorum, set solum fiant avisamenta in omnibus et teneantur parata, ut cum sua serenitas revertetur ad concilium, cito possit eligi summus pontifex." The instructions appear to date from April 5, 1416. They go on to say "Tertio supplicat, quod procedatur in reformacione universalis ecclesie et totius cleri, ymmo et cuiuslibet status christianitatis et maxime in reformacione capitis."

[15] See below, pp. 159–162.

[16] These include the three tracts edited by Finke ACC.2.592–605; also the second annate tract of Paulus Vladimiri. See Chapter 7 below for analysis of these tracts.

[17] See Chapter 7, p. 174 n.6 and 175 n.10 below.

[18] *G*.6.179–181. Glorieux dates it "after June 1416."

[19] Ed. H.1.407f.; see Oakley, pp. 246–47, 250–252.

perhaps by a vote of acclamation for a new pope who would be Sigismund's own protégé. The formalities of Benedict's trial and deposition were protracted and painstaking, and in the midst of these, the newly arrived Castilian delegates greatly complicated the issue of election when they called into question the council's right to determine the election procedure. Peter Pulka suspected the machinations of the cardinals behind the Castilian's actions. Building on Pulka's suspicions, Hübler believed that the cardinals and the "conservative party" were trying to stall reform. But the matter was not so simple.

4. The summer of 1417

The chief primary source concerning the "priority struggles", Cardinal Fillastre's journal, invites consideration of the events in a polarized fashion, as a struggle between the cardinals and Sigismund. Hübler's view was strongly influenced by the excerpts from Fillastre to which he had access, excerpts drawn from the complete manuscripts by the Vatican librarian, Emmanuel Schelstrate, who had also viewed the struggle in polarized fashion.[20] A closer reading of the complete text of Fillastre's journal suggests that for the cardinals the overriding issue was not delay of reform, but protection of their interests in the papal election. Documents published by Finke concerning the role of the Spanish nation at the council strongly suggest that the Castilians needed little encouragement from the cardinals in their refusal to join the council until the mode of election was firmly settled. They were very disturbed about the decree which the council had passed giving the Aragonese a disproportionate number of votes in the Spanish nation at the council. Indeed, the instructions which the Castilian envoys carried with them to the council commanded them not to unite with the council until the question of voting was favorably settled.[21] The cardinals

---

[20] Hübler cited them directly from Schelstrate's edition. Many of the excerpts were taken from Schelstrate into von der Hardt's edition of the Constance acta and in this way influenced scholars who did not read Schelstrate's edition. On Schelstrate's use of Fillastre, see ACC.4.xiii. On the priority struggles see also Odilo Engels, "Der Reichsgedanke auf dem Konstanzer Konzil," *Historisches Jahrbuch*, 86 (1966) 80–106, and most recently Heimpel, *Vener*, 2:743–759.

[21] On these questions, see Bernhard Fromme, "Der erste Prioritätstreit auf dem Konstanzer Konzil," *RQ* 10 (1896) 509–18 at 509–10. See also Luis Suarez Fernandez, *Castilla, el cisma y la crisis conciliar (1378–1440)* (Madrid, 1960), 91 n.18, who agrees with Fromme on this point. Hübler (p. 18 n. 54) had based his suspicion on a hunch of Peter Pulka, p. 50: "Sed ipsi [castellani] forte ex dictis cardinalium moti se uniri nolebant."

seized upon this opportunity to shift the attention of the council to the issue of the election of the new pope and to impugn the decree of the fourteenth general session which had established the right of the council to determine how and when the election would occur. In answer to the Castilians' question about the security of the council, the cardinals stated that the passage of that decree had been the one occasion when the freedom of deliberation of the council had been impaired: they had agreed to the decree out of fear (caused not by Sigismund, but by Carlo Malatesta and the Patriarch of Antioch, Jean Mauroux.)[22]

Sigismund was deeply disturbed by this move of the cardinals. For him, too, the election was the overriding issue. His supreme goal throughout the council had been the termination of the Schism; to this he had devoted much expense and personal effort; the uniting of the rival obediences could hardly have been accomplished without his energetic diplomacy. In the summer of 1417, Sigismund must have been concerned above all to insure that the pope to be elected would retain the undivided allegiance of Christendom; given the experience of the past forty years, he believed that the cardinals would not be able to elect such a pope. At the same time, he expected to exercise strong influence himself over the choice of the new pope. When the cardinals called into doubt the decrees of the twelfth and fourteenth sessions concerning the election, Sigismund saw all his work endangered. He refused to even discuss the manner of election until after Benedict XIII had been deposed, saying he would rather be thrown into Lake Constance.[23]

The cardinals, far from worrying that Sigismund would delay the election in order to push reform, feared instead that he would try to have his own candidate for pope elected by conciliar acclamation immediately after the deposition of Benedict.[24] Thus, they took advantage wherever they could of developments which eroded the support of Sigismund and his principal allies.

Sigismund had a major prelate as trusted ally in each of the four nations; these prelates often served as presidents of their nations.

---

[22] See Pulka, 50. The cardinals' protest appears disingenuous when compared with Cardinal Zabarella's public statement three weeks after the fourteenth session. In his speech of July 24, 1415, recorded by Cerretanus, Zabarella praised Sigismund in highest terms for making Constance a free meeting place (ACC.2.254).

[23] ACC.2.103.

[24] ACC.2.101, 104. See also ACC.4.78–79; the Castilians said that Sigismund had told them he had the right to choose the new pope, since all the existing cardinals were illegitimate.

(Presidents were newly elected each month, but often were re-elected for several months; in addition to presiding over the meetings of their nations, the presidents meeting together with other elected deputies from each nation formed the steering committee which determined the agenda to be considered by the entire council.) Sigismund's allies were Bartolomeo de la Capra, archbishop of Milan (Italian nation), Jean Mauroux, Patriarch of Antioch (French nation), Johann Wallenrode, archbishop of Riga (German nation), and Robert Hallum, bishop of Salisbury (English nation). The cardinals recognized these prelates as their enemies; Fillastre, playing upon the acronym formed by the beginning letters of their four sees, complained that MARS ruled the council.[25]

The cardinals probably played a role in unseating de la Capra from the presidency of the Italian nation on June 1, 1417. However, they directed their most intensive efforts against Mauroux, possibly because they regarded him as Sigismund's most likely candidate for pope. In May, Olivier Guennet, the secretary of Cardinal Fieschi plotted to have him expelled from the French nation, and Mauroux had Guennet arrested.[26] The cardinals forced Mauroux to release him, and soon Mauroux was indeed expelled from the nation, a bitter blow to Sigismund. Later in the summer, during one of Sigismund's absences from Constance, the cardinals engineered Mauroux's removal from his important post as acting papal *camerarius* at Constance.[27]

By attacking Mauroux, the cardinals also helped to drive a further wedge between Sigismund and the French nation. Sigismund himself had already done much to antagonize the French, beginning with his open alliance with the English king, Henry V, in his war with France (Treaty of Canterbury, 1416). Bitter disputes between the French and English representatives occurred at Constance in 1417.[28] The French even challenged the right of the English to be a separate nation at the council. On the very eve of the crucial struggles of 1417 Sigismund had also aligned himself in the internal factional strife within France by forming an alliance with the duke of Burgundy, the bitter enemy of the Armagnac-Orleans faction which controlled the French government (Treaty of Constance,

---

[25] ACC.2.115.
[26] ACC.2.101–102.
[27] ACC.2.131.
[28] J.-P. Genet, "English Nationalism: Thomas Polton at the Council of Constance," *Nottingham Historical Studies* 28 (1984) 60–78.

April 29, 1417).[29] Three days later he had the electors of the Empire formally ratify the Treaty of Canterbury. The preceding March 22, Sigismund had sent a letter to Charles VI accusing him of prolonging the Schism. At about the same time Charles's ambassadors at the council sent a messenger to Charles to inform him of Sigismund's hostility; the messenger, Nicolas de la Capelle, was apprehended by Sigismund's agents and brought back to the council, where Sigismund caused his message to be read in public session before the embarrassed French ambassadors. The message, in cryptic language, seems to have expressed fear of a joint Anglo-Burgundian-Imperial military campaign against the Armagnac faction. It was not just the French at Constance who perceived such an alliance taking shape. The ambassador of the city of Lucca at the council sent back an explicit report in April of such an alliance against the count of Armagnac. Nicolas de la Capelle's message reported Sigismund's efforts in the council to brand the French king and his ambassadors as schismatics because of the count of Armagnac's continued adherence to Benedict XIII. On September 1, Sigismund went so far as to send a letter of defiance to the count of Armagnac saying he would support his faithful vassal, the duke of Burgundy, against the court.

Did Sigismund contemplate military action to overthrow the count of Armagnac and thus force French cooperation? Such a possibility is unlikely in the extreme. Political alliances with Henry V and the duke of Burgundy as well as any contemplated military action were probably for strictly political and military ends, mainly the atavistic reassertion of imperial rights in the old "Middle Kingdom."[30] On the other hand, Sigismund had ample reason to attack the count of Armagnac's ecclesiastical policy at the council, since the count was indeed the only major political figure who continued to support Benedict XIII after his deposition.[31]

The cardinals took the initiative and on Pentecost Saturday, May 29, 1417, presented their own proposal for the mode of the election. This proposal, drafted by D'Ailly and known by its incipit as *Ad laudem*, called for a conclave consisting of the Sacred College and a similar number of non-cardinals; a two thirds' majority of

---

[29] For the relations between Sigismund and the French, see Noël Valois, *La France et le Grand Schisme d'Occident* 4 (Paris, 1902), 377–379; the text of the Treaty of Constance was edited by Finke in ACC.4.479–484.

[30] Valois, *Schisme* 364–366.

[31] Valois, *Schisme* 4:349.

each group would be required for election.[32] Sigismund refused even to discuss *Ad laudem*; the German and English nations and at first the Aragonese followed him. However, on June 25, the entire Spanish nation, including the Aragonese, approved the schedule, a bitter blow for Sigismund.

Tensions grew. Fillastre claims that Sigismund wanted the cardinals to promise they would elect a pope friendly to him, whereas the cardinals demanded a new guarantee of security. The cardinals hoped to use such a new guarantee to impugn the election decree of Session 14, but Sigismund continued to retain the phrase "decretis concilii semper salvis," or similar words, in each new draft. Finally, however, on July 11, Sigismund offered a guarantee that the cardinals decided to accept, even though they still found it insufficient.

In this way the first priority struggle was resolved by a temporary truce which allowed the council to proceed to the deposition of Benedict XIII (July 26), as Sigismund wished, while leaving the cardinals the hope of retaining as much of their control over the election as possible. It was also agreed that reform of the Roman curia (*quoad curiam*) would precede the election, and both Sigismund and the cardinals agreed through proxies to a mutual promise that they would protect each others' rights and *status*. Between July 26 and August 1, a new reform committee was formed.[33] The cardinals even agreed that they would have no official representatives on the committee,[34] probably in an effort to facilitate negotiations and avoid delay of the election.

Indeed, when the new reform committee's work bogged down, the cardinals began to urge that the nations at least discuss the method of election while the reform negotiations were going on. Fillastre says that Sigismund would hear none of it.[35] Another deadlock and priority struggle ensued, which, according to Hübler,

---

[32] For Finke's edition of the schedule *Ad laudem* and other writings pertaining to it, together with introductory remarks on the events surrounding it, see ACC.3.613–671.

[33] On the dating, see Heimpel, *Vener*, 1:365–66 n.171.

[34] This concession was less significant than it might appear, since, according to Fillastre (ACC.2.145, 147) the decrees drafted by the committee were later subject to deliberations between the representatives of the cardinals and the nations: "Et semper agebatur per deputatos cardinalium et nationum omnium de concordando articulos reformacionis . . ."

[35] ACC.2.135. According to Fillastre, Sigismund, accompanied by legates of the German princes, approached the German nation saying that "multa dampna passi erant per Romanam curiam, quam petebant reformari. Et finaliter pro illa et aliis causis vel occasionibus non darentur deputati pro modo eleccionis, donec esset facta reformacio. . . ." Fillastre reads this as a ruse to delay the election.

this time finally prevented the enactment of a comprehensive reform program before the election. Since Hübler regarded Sigismund as the leader of the "reform party" at the council, he blamed
the failure of the comprehensive reform program on the progressive
isolation of the emperor-elect, caused by the defection of Sigismund's coalition partners (*Bundesgenossen*). The defection occurred
in two phases: first, the formation of a coalition of the three "Latin"
nations which joined the cardinals against Sigismund; and then the
final defection of the English nation, leaving Sigismund the support
of only his German nation.[36]

The crucial step in the formation of the Latin coalition, according to Hübler, was the adhesion of the French. Hübler wonders
why this nation, which had suffered more than any other from
papal abuses, abandoned the reform party; he finds two reasons.
First, they feared that the council might be stymied and the schism
perpetuated if the election was not held soon. Second, the highly
influential members of the French universities benefitted extensively from the papal system of patronage and feared that the council
would abolish or severely restrict papal provisions to offices if
reform took place before the election. Hübler does not mention here
the machinations of the cardinals to discredit Sigismund and win
support for themselves in the French nation, nor does he consider
Sigismund's partiality to the English and his tactless acts which
cost him French support (see above, pp. 33–34).[37] Nevertheless, I
believe he is right when he underlines the importance of the divided
interests within the French nation concerning reform. We shall
have much more to say about this.

The struggle reached a climax September 9, when the cardinals
and the three "Latin" nations tried to present to the council a
protest (Incipit: *Audite*) calling for the council to proceed to the
election or at least to consider the mode of election. The protest was
doubly unwelcome to Sigismund, not only because it implied that
those who deliberately delayed the election might be guilty of
abetting schism, but also because it caught him at a very weak
moment. The refusal of the Spanish nation to seat Sigismund's
preferred candidate as president September 1 had been followed

---

[36] The cardinals even tried to make inroads here, according to Hübler (p. 29
n.86), by bribing two of the leading reform prelates; however, Hübler cites no
source.

[37] He did not know about many of the cardinals' machinations because he did
not have the full text of Fillastre; and he was unaware of many of Sigismund's
moves or unwilling to cast aspersion on his leadership.

September 4 by a much greater calamity, the death of Sigismund's leading ally at the council, Robert Hallum, the bishop of Salisbury, leader of the English delegation, and one of the most outspoken advocates of reform at the council.[38] His death left an immense void. Three days later, while Sigismund was absent from Constance, the cardinals seem to have pressured the English nation finally to agree to send deputies to discuss the mode of election—at least, so Fillastre claims. At the September 9 meeting of the council Cardinal Adimari made reference to this agreement.

Fillastre recounts the ensuing exchange with high drama. Sigismund hotly denied Adimari's statement and summoned the leaders of the English nation. When questioned, they waffled, protesting that they had followed the German nation in the past and wanted to follow it in the future. Adimari then demanded that the Germans also send deputies since all the other nations had. When the German nation made no response, Adimari presented the protest of the cardinals and the three Latin nations to be read to the council by Philippe de Coëtquis, archbishop of Bourges. Sigismund fulminated: "By God, you won't read it." An Italian notary then countered, "Post it to the doors!" Sigismund exclaimed, "You'll be posted to the doors!" and delivered blows to the notary's chin and chest, shouting "These Italians and Frenchmen want to give us a pope. By God they shall not do it!" De Coëtquis asked for notarized copies of the protest and the meeting broke up. On September 11, Adimari finally read the protest at a public meeting. Sigismund strongly opposed this, and, when Adimari continued reading, he and his allies left the meeting; some voices jeered after them, "The heretics are leaving."

Sigismund was being outmaneuvered and he responded with somewhat desperate measures. This was not the first time Sigismund had used force at the council. Fillastre had missed no opportunity to point out examples—the stationing of armed men in an adjacent building during a tense meeting of the Spanish nation (to which the Spanish also went armed); the dispatch of two patrols to apprehend cardinals whom Sigismund believed to be fleeing by night from the council (next day it was found that the patrols had fired on one another and that the cardinals' flight had been only a rumor); the barring of the city gate to Italian, French, and Spanish representatives who wanted to leave the council on August 1 (Sigismund personally

---

[38] On Bishop Hallum see R.N. Quirk, "Bishop Robert Hallum and the Council of Constance," in *Friends of Salisbury Cathedral: Twenty-second Annual Report* (1952) 3–15.

stood in their way). The cardinals' red miters signified their impending martyrdom, writes Fillastre. One detects, however, a certain disingenuousness in this racy narrative. The cardinals' real fear was not the loss of their lives, but the loss of their interests as princes of the church and pope-makers.

In the week following the dramatic confrontation of September 9, Sigismund came to realize that the time had come for compromise. Hübler treats the compromise as though it was a package of measures agreed to at the same time. I believe there was in fact a series of compromises, an initial one on September 19 between Sigismund and the cardinals, and then at least three compromises of a more complex nature within the council itself.

The developments which shaped these compromises were much more complex than Hübler allowed. Reform was only one of the issues, and even at this time less important than the election. Sigismund still hoped to influence the election but must have realized that further delay was not likely to allow him to recoup any of his influence over the council. The specter of a new schism was also raised by the effort of many members to flee the council; at first Sigismund had them arrested and tried to force them to return, but this only caused more fear.

Many of the Spanish delegates had left because of the internal dispute within the Spanish nation which involved voting rights of the three main Spanish delegations (Portuguese, Aragonese, and Castilian), and one key factor in the final compromise was the resolution of this dispute. Before the arrival of the Castilians, the council had granted to the Aragonese the right to additional votes by proxy for all the prelates in the "overseas" possessions of the king of Aragon (chiefly Sardinia, Corsica, and Sicily). When the Castilians arrived they sharply protested this decree because it violated the Capitula Narbonensis which had been agreed upon by the Spanish and the council's envoys under Sigismund's leadership in early 1416. The council revoked the decree July 28, but the Aragonese lobbied throughout the summer to have their additional votes restored to them. Finally at the peak of tension in early September 1417, a dispute arose in the Spanish nation over the presidency, which normally rotated monthly among the three main groups. When the turn of the Portuguese candidate came, the Castilians protested on the pretext that he was a layman (as indeed were virtually all the members of Portugal's delegation to the council).

The moves of the English nation played an even greater role in the compromise. Their wavering support for Sigismund had been the crucial step in his isolation. C.M.D. Crowder argues that the English representatives wavered because they had received new instructions from Henry V commanding them not to support the delay of the election any further.[39] This new policy, says Crowder, resulted from Henry's concern to bring a speedy resolution to the council so that Sigismund would be free to undertake the military activities against France which he had promised in his alliance with Henry. Bishop Hallum's death, September 4, was "the chance that favored Henry's new intentions" (Crowder). Without Hallum's strong commitment to common action with the German nation, the English nation started to waver, especially under pressure from the cardinals. In a funeral sermon for Hallum preached September 9, Richard Fleming suggested that the council should not seek an "unlimited reform" which would delay the election unnecessarily.[40] Crowder suggests that the new stance was one of neutrality, designed to hasten the election without offending Sigismund. At the height of the tensions during the week of September 12, the legates of the English king offered their services as arbitrators between Sigismund and the cardinals.

The crucial element in the reconciliation on September 19 between the cardinals and Sigismund is revealed in a document which long remained hidden. In 1959, Professor E. Mályusz published the full text of this document, a charter signed September 19, 1417, by the twenty-three cardinals present at Constance at that time and addressed to Sigismund.[41] In the charter the cardinals promise that they will cause the new pope and his successors to provide to all the prelacies in the kingdom of Hungary those persons whom Sigismund and his successors nominate. These providees (except the archiepiscopal ones) will not be required to pay annates. Furthermore, the pope will not involve himself at all with

---

[39] C.M.D. Crowder, "Henry V, Sigismund and the Council of Constance, a Reexamination," *Historical Studies* 4 (1963), ed. G.A. Hayes-McCoy, 93–110. See Fillastre's account, ACC.2.147. On these matters, see also Thomas Morrissey, "The Emperor-elect Sigismund, Cardinal Zabarella, and the Council of Constance," *Catholic Historical Review* 69 (1983) 353–370.

[40] The relevant text in the sermon was transcribed by Vidal from a Klosterneuberg manuscript which had come into his possession. See J.M. Vidal, "Un recueil manuscrit de sermons prononcés aux conciles de Constance et de Bâle," *RHE* 10 (1909) 493–520 at 510–511. I have been unable to trace the current location of this manuscript. The passage Vidal quotes is not found in the text of the sermon as it is recorded in the two other manuscripts which are known to contain it.

[41] Elemér Mályusz, *Das Konstanzer Konzil und das königliche Patronatsrecht in Ungarn* (Studia historica academiae scientiarum Hungaricae, 18) (Budapest, 1959); the text of the agreement appears on pp. 8–9. The document is a 1447 copy of the

the collation of benefices in the kingdom of Hungary or lands annexed to it, and no legal cases will be taken out of the kingdom by the pope except those which devolve to him by legitimate appeal.[42] Through this charter Sigismund must have hoped to salvage for himself and his kingdom of Hungary rights which he had abandoned hope of gaining through general reforms to be enacted by the council. The document thus provides a good index of Sigismund's concrete interests in reform. It also suggests that the reformers at the council, even before the election, were not likely to bring about a reform which served these interests. Sigismund, in fact, had relatively little influence over the reform negotiations.

In the further compromises which ended the second priority struggle, the English again played an important role. Now the central figure was Henry Beaufort, bishop of Winchester and uncle to Henry V of England.[43] Bishop Beaufort appeared in the region of Constance in early October, dressed as a pilgrim. Henry had announced Beaufort's pilgrimage to the Holy Land on July 18, and Crowder argues that Henry sent him to secure a speedy conclusion to the Schism. Contemporaries suggested that he hoped himself to be elected pope.[44] Fillastre says that Beaufort came from neighbor-

---

original (which was destroyed in the Battle of Mohacs, 1526); it was discovered in 1931 in the town archives of Eperies. See also A. Czismadia, "Die Auswirkungen der 'Bulle' von Konstanz auf die Entwicklung des Oberpatronatsrechts," *Acta Iuridica Academiae Scientiarum Hungaricae* 2 (1960) 53–82 and Alexander Szentirmai, "De 'iure supremi patronatus' regum Hungariae," *Monitor ecclesiasticus* 86 (1961) 281–291. Szentirmai challenges the conclusions of Mályusz and Czismadia regarding the effects of the charter and the legitimacy of using it as a basis for the later claims concerning the patronage rights of the Hungarian state, but he in no way questions the authenticity of the document itself. See also Mályusz's study of Sigismund's reign in Hungary: *Kaiser Sigismund in Ungarn, 1387–1437* (Budapest, 1990); also Sabine Wefers, *Das politische System Kaiser Sigmunds* (Stuttgart, 1989).

[42] Mályusz, *Patronatsrecht*, 8: "... Promittimus bona fide eidem serenissimo regi, sicut eiusdem petitio subiungebat, nos facturos et efficaciter curaturos, quod sumpmus pontifex de proximo domino concedente assumendus et eiusdem in sede apostolica successores imperpetuum providebunt ecclesiis metropolitanis et kathedralibus et monasteriis prefati regni Hungarie de personis ydoneis, pro quibus supradictus rex et successores ipsius in regno Hungarie pro tempore supplicabunt, sine solutione annatarum uel alterius cuiuscunque exactionis. Ita tamen, quod hii, quos ad metropolitanas ecclesias promoveri postulaverit, moderatas solvant annatas ad instar ceterarum ecclesiarum nationis Germanice. Item quod sedes apostolica non intromittat se de collatione beneficiorum quorumcunque in regno Hungarie et aliis sibi annexis. Item quod nullus extrahatur extra sua regna predicta ad iudicia auctoritate litterarum apostolicarum, nisi cum cause predictorum regnorum per appellationem legitime fuerint ad sedem apostolicam devolute.

[43] On Beaufort, see G.L. Harriss, *Cardinal Beaufort: A Study of Lancastrian Ascendancy and Decline* (Oxford, 1989), especially pp. 91–95.

[44] See K.B. McFarlane, "Henry V, Bishop Beaufort, and the Red Hat, 1417–1421," *EHR* 60 (1945) 316–348.

ing Ulm to Constance at the request of the English representatives at the Council and that he played a key role there as mediator in the negotiations of Sigismund, the cardinals, and the national congregations which produced the major compromise. According to Fillastre the terms of the compromise were three fold: 1) A conciliar decree in the form of a guarantee (*cautio*) that reform would be enacted after the election; 2) the enactment before the election of those reform measures upon which agreement had already been reached by all the nations; and 3) the appointment of a commission to decide the method of election.

The *cautio* decree was enacted to satisfy the German nation, which still wanted reform to take place before the election. Further negotiations lasted for a month and produced further compromises on the exact text of the *cautio* decree and, at last, on the thorniest issue of all—the election procedure. It was a French cardinal, Simon de Cramaud, who finally drafted an acceptable compromise election procedure.[45] According to this compromise the conclave would be augmented on a one-time basis with thirty additional electors, six from each of the five nations; to be elected, a candidate would have to receive at least two-third of the votes of *each* nation's electors concomitantly with two-thirds of the votes of the cardinals. This plan was well suited to the election of a pope who would receive undisputed allegiance from all the former obediences; it was also likely to produce a very long conclave. Amazingly, however, the cries of *Habemus papam* greeted the election of Cardinal Odo Colonna as the new pope Martin V on November 11, only three days after the electors had entered the Constance Kaufhaus on November 8.[46]

In discussing the two priority struggles, Hübler's study and other earlier studies placed the emphasis on reform and assumed that the election was delayed because reformers feared that reform would not take place after the election. However, I would argue that in the second priority struggle, as in the first, what delayed the election was not primarily the fear of reformers, but the inability to arrive at an acceptable election procedure. To be sure, strong fears

---

[45] This plan and Cramaud's important role have been thoroughly investigated in the study of Howard Kaminsky, *Simon de Cramaud and the Great Schism* (New Brunswick, 1983). The plan was presented to the council on October 22 by Jacques Gelu.
[46] On the election see Karl August Fink, "Die Wahl Martins V.", in *Das Konzil von Konstanz*, 138–151 (repr. in *Das Konstanzer Konzil*, 306–322; and Dieter Girgensohn, "Berichte über Konklave und Papstwahl auf dem Konstanzer Konzil," *AHC* 19 (1987) 351–363.

were expressed by many reformers that to postpone reform until
after the election would be to table reform altogether. These fears
were summarized best by the cynicism of a group of anonymous
"theologians," writing in October. In two years the council had
scarcely reached agreement on a single specific measure. After the
election, the new pope would impede the reform, and the desire of
some to please the new pope, and the fear of others to displease him
would detract from the freedom of deliberations which the council
enjoyed *sede vacante*; everyone would be tired and want to go home,
as had occurred at the Council of Pisa.[47] Richental's report of
German and English fears echoes these thoughts: If reform were
delayed until after the election "everyone would ride home in
droves and thus reform would never take place, if it were all up to
the pope."[48] However, Richental's chronicle does not assume that
only the Germans and English passionately desired reform. The
other three nations desired that after the election the council would
choose "reformers (*reformatores*) who would meet together after the
election and would establish an order for how such times [as the
Schism] would never recur and how each cleric, secular or regular,
should conduct himself and how much benefit [nutz] he should
have in the office he now holds."[49]

The principal struggle in the summer of 1417 was not between a
reform party and an anti-reform party. The main bone of conten-
tion was the election. As for reform, the main struggle was among
different conceptions of reform. Many reformers actually preferred
to postpone some reforms until after the election. Even reformers

---

[47] See also the theses of Pier Paolo Vergerio, August 10, 1417 in ACC.3.667–69.
He spoke against even discussing the mode of election prior to enactment of
reform, because "desiderio electionis precipitaretur forsitan reformacio vel certe
dimitteretur imperfecta. Et eciam, si ullo modo prius constare possit, qui essent
futuri electores, reformacio circa eos et statum eorum redderetur minus libera. . . .
cum necessitas quedam habende reformacionis, ut constat sit permaxime necessaria, facultas vero eius perficiende vix unquam erit tanta, quanta nunc est,
quoniam raro vel nunquam solet existente generali concilio congregato vacare
papatus."

[48] Ulrich von Richental, *Chronik des Constanzer Conzils 1414 bis 1418*, ed. Michael
Buck (Stuttgart, 1882, repr. Hildesheim, 1962), 111: "so wurd menglich zerriten
[or haimriten] und beschäch die reformacion niemer, wann es dann alles an ainem
baupst stünde."

[49] Richental, 111: "Und do nun also nieman me baupst was, do hettend die
Ytalici, Hyspani und Gallici, die dry nationes gern gesehen, das man gewellet hett
und darnach reformaciones genomen hett, das sind das die nach der wal zesam-
men wärind gesessen und das die ain ordnung gemacht hettind, das sollich ziten
nit mer uff gestanden wurd und wie ieglicher pfaff, er wär gaistlich oder weltlich,
sich halten solt und wie vil nutz jeglicher haben solt in der dignität, so er dann
wär."

who wanted to enact all the reforms before the election came to realize that some compromise had to be reached to avoid the danger of postponing the election any further. The compromises concerning reform prepared the way for the more difficult compromise on the election procedure.

I am not arguing that there was no active opposition to reform. The cardinals surely opposed reforms that seemed too threatening to the prerogatives of the Roman church. Ironically, Cardinal Zabarella was one of the most astute guardians of those prerogatives. It was Zabarella who had omitted the words *reformatio in capite et in membris* from the decree *Haec sancta* when he formally read the decree in the fourth session, necessitating the re-enactment of the decree in the fifth session with the mutilated words restored.[50] Further, there is evidence that Zabarella acted as official censor of the sermons preached at the council, in which some of the strongest reform demands were expressed.[51] It was also Zabarella who urged the council to enact reforms in Sigismund's absence.[52] And, in the dispute with Maurice Rvačka mentioned above, Zabarella strongly defended the rights of the Roman church, justifying the annates as a sign of the subjection of other churches to Rome.[53] This was the same Zabarella who had played a leading role in the development of "conciliar theory" before he became a cardinal, and who, even as a cardinal at Constance, proposed several important reforms when he served on the first reform committee. However, in the late summer of 1417, the five main reforms on the table were ones which placed strong limits on the power of the Roman church. It may well be that Zabarella's death on September 26 played an important role in facilitating the compromise by which the five decrees of October 9 were enacted.

These five decrees were the first reforms passed by the council.[54] The reforms were of great significance, and they were effective—they were observed scrupulously by the new pope Martin V after his election. No further reforms were enacted at that time because the reformers could not yet agree on these reforms and because the

---

[50] For a more favorable view of Zabarella's role in the formulation of *Haec sancta*, see Thomas Morrissey, "The Decree 'Haec Sancta' and Cardinal Zabarella: His Role in its Formulation and Interpretation," *AHC* 10 (1978) 145–176.

[51] ACC.2.376.

[52] ACC.2.253–255.

[53] Texts of Maurice's reform demands and Zabarella's reply were preserved by Cerretanus, ACC.2.325–333.

[54] This was also observed in the acta themselves for this session (H.4.1434): "Istud est principium reformationis ecclesiae publicatum in publica sessione . . ."

cautio decree guaranteed that the reforms in head and curia would be enacted after the election. Thus, the compromises which ended the priority struggles were in no way a victory of conservatives over reformers. The council enacted significant reforms before the election and offered the promise of further reform after it. Whether that promise would be fulfilled depended on whether the conflicting conceptions of the reformers could be reconciled.

5. *Reform after the papal election*

Hübler argued that the urgency· of proceeding to reform immediately after the election was driven home by Martin V's issuance of his chancery rules the very day after his coronation, rules which included many practices the reformers had been seeking to curtail or eliminate. Though he thus echoed Hardt's interpretation of these chancery rules as an indication of Martin's anti-reform stance, Hübler wisely warned against the error of those historians who claimed that Martin deliberately and spitefully attempted to "divide and conquer" the nations by encouraging disunity among them.[55] He believed that Martin in fact needed only to sit back and watch that disunity play into his hands. Even this judgment is too harsh, however. Quite probably, Martin V took the lead in reform, first by encouraging the nations to agree on a common reform program,[56] and then by salvaging as much as possible of the remaining reforms in the national concordats. Of course, Martin at the same time did all he could to protect the interests of the papacy in the reform negotiations. But he knew that in the eyes of most Christians the legitimacy of his papal title depended on the authority of the council. The decrees of the fortieth session which had sanctioned the election were the same which contained the famous reform *cautio* which bound him to carry out reform under the eighteen articles. After Martin and his deputies had negotiated with the nations for four months and

---

[55] P. 45 n.135.

[56] Fillastre says that Martin called for the appointment of reform deputies soon after the election. Gobelinus Persona, however, says that it was the nations who took the initiative. See Gobelinus Persona, *Cosmodromius: Cosmidromius Gobelini Person und als Anhang desselben Verfassers Processus translacionis et reformacionis monasterii Budecensis*, ed. Max Jansen (Münster, 1900), 226. Pulka merely says that deputies were appointed by the pope and nations respectively (p. 62, letter of December 27: "statim coronato domino nostro papa deputabantur de singulis nationibus et collegio d. cardinalium certi reformatores. . . .") There seems to be no reason to doubt Fillastre's statement here.

achieved all the reforms the nations could agree on, he asked the council to decree that the *cautio* had been satisfied, and it did so.

Fillastre's diary has much to say about the reform deliberations in this period, especially about the disagreements. His reports are echoed by letters of Peter Pulka and the Cologne envoys to their respective universities. Unfortunately, we have no record of the third reform committee's deliberations. Formed soon after the election, the committee consisted of six deputies from each of the five nations meeting with six cardinals appointed by Martin. It also appears that the cardinals at times met separately with the deputies of each nation. Agreement on general reform was still very difficult, even though the French nation now strongly supported it. It is interesting that, when the French tried to enlist Sigismund's support, he replied that it was no longer "in his interest" to pursue a general reform.[57]

Pulka and Fillastre both cite the reforms of papal provisions as the thorniest issue. The divergence of opinions protracted negotiations for more than two weeks, after which deliberations were suspended altogether for more than a month.[58] During this period two important documents appeared, which are identified in the manuscripts as the *Avisamenta* of the German nation and the *Responsio* of the pope.[59] On the basis of these he concluded that Martin

---

[57] Hübler, 42 citing Gobelinus Persona's account excerpted in H.4.1503. See Gobelinus Persona, 226: "Unde nacio Gallicana regem adiit petens ab eo, ut papam ad reformandum ecclesiam dignaretur informare; qui respondit eis: 'Dum nos, ut reformacio fieret ecclesie, priusquam ad electionem summi pontificis procederetur, instabamus, vos nolentes acquiescere, papam, priusquam fieret reformacio ecclesie, habere voluistis. Et ecce papam habetis, quem et nos habemus; illum pro expeditione huiusmodi reformacionis adite, quoniam pro nunc nostri non interest, prout intererat sede Romana vacante.'" However, Fillastre (p. 160) says that in this period Sigismund and the legates of the kings of Aragon and Castile made many excessive demands; the king of Aragon, in particular, asked "multa iniqua et de rebus ecclesiarum sibi perpetuo concedendis." On these demands, see Karl August Fink, *Martin V. und Aragon* (*Historische Studien* 340; Berlin, 1938) 5-59 at 42. In ACC.4.168ff. appear a part of the official instructions of the king's ambassadors at the council. From these and other sources it appears that Alfonso asked to keep the revenues he had collected out of the former Avignon chamber while it was in Spain; he requested reduction of or exemption from the census for his overseas territories; and he desired the erection of eight new bishoprics and the right to nominate almost all the high church officials himself, including those who were to become cardinals. See also, most recently, Alan Ryder, *Alfonso the Magnanimous: King of Aragon, Naples, and Sicily, 1396–1458* (Oxford, 1990).

[58] Pulka, 62–65; ACC.2.162.

[59] Hübler called this *Responsio* the papal *Reformacte*; other scholars have referred to it more correctly in German as the papal "Reformentwurf" or in French as a "projet de réforme." In the manuscripts it is referred to as the *Responsio* or the

was pushed to issue a piece of legislation (Hübler called it the papal *Reformacte*; I prefer the term *Responsio*) because the German nation had taken the initiative after the election by airing their demands for reform in their Avisamenta. Most later historians assumed that this occurred because the Germans had given up on achieving a general reform. Finke, on the basis of his discovery of an analogous set of Avisamenta written by the French nation, offered a more convincing explanation. According to Finke, someone made the suggestion that the individual nations prepare position statements as a platform for further negotiation. These position statements were the Avisamenta. The papal Responsio, which followed on January 20, 1418, would then be the curia's own position statement drafted after considering those of the nations. Rather than efforts to achieve national solutions because the conciliar reforms had failed, the Avisamenta and Responsio were a final attempt to enact universal reforms by resolving the differences among the nations.[60] I would add that proceeding in this manner may well have been the new pope's idea. In the negotiations it appears that Martin, while carefully defending the papacy's interests, did not simply oppose the reforms, but rather was prepared to negotiate, perhaps even to take the lead in working out an acceptable compromise of conflicting interests. In the manuscript containing the French Avisamenta, Finke also discovered a very interesting document which I believe consists of excerpts from instructions sent to Constance with the royal embassy in late 1417 or early 1418 setting forth the stance of the French court on various reform issues.[61]

Reformatio of Martin V. Mansi's interpolation of the *Responsio* into the forty-third general session (27:1177) gives the false impression that it was enacted as legislation at that time; the manuscripts of the official acta of the council which Mansi reprinted in his edition show no trace of it where Mansi places it; see Phillip Stump, "The Official Acta of the Council of Constance in the Edition of Mansi," in *The Two Laws: Studies in Medieval Legal History Dedicated to Stephan Kuttner*, ed. Laurent Mayali and Stephanie Tibbetts (Washington, D.C., 1990), 232 and n.25.

[60] ACC.2.565–67.

[61] The text is edited in ACC.2.680–82. The rubric reads "Sequencia ab instruccionibus ecclesie Gallicane secundum materias occurrentes, que pro nunc tractantur, extracta sunt"; the marginal note, "Infrascripta exhibita fuerunt dominis ambaxiatoribus domini ducis Burgundie ex parte archiepiscopi Turonensis et ambaxiatorum ecclesie Gallicane die XXIII. Januarii anno domini MCCCCXVIII." See Finke's introductory remarks, *ibid.*, 568, and also his description of Paris BN lat. 14457, from which he edited this text, ACC.4.lii–lv. The portion of the manuscript containing this text was evidently a collection of documents assembled by Simon de Plumetot, a member of the Parlement of Paris. On Plumetot, see Gilbert Ouy, "Simon de Plumetot (1371–1443) et sa bibliothèque," in *Miscellanea codicologica F. Masai dicata* (Ghent, 1979), 353–81. Finke believed the *Instructiones* were drafted after the issuance of the papal *Responsio*, thus

Our best source on the final deliberations is a letter of Peter Pulka to the University of Vienna written March 23, two days after the forty-third general session on March 21.[62] At that session the seven reform decrees upon which agreement had been reached were promulgated. As for the other reforms, Pulka tells us that separate agreements were made on these between the deputies of the single nations and the cardinals appointed by the pope; these agreements were "not enacted in public session but were expedited privately by the chancery under the seal of the vicecancellarius."[63] He is referring to the concordats, which were thus not formally enacted in the forty-third session, though their text appears there in Mansi's edition of the acta.[64] Pulka indicates that the concordats were arrived at through negotiations between representatives of the pope and representatives of the nations concerning "articles in a certain decree"[65] (no doubt the papal *Responsio*). Pulka's description of the reforms relegated to the concordats is significant:

---

forming an intermediate step between the latter and the French Concordat. I would argue that their tentative wording, designed to cover many different outcomes, suggests an earlier date. They make no specific reference to the eighteen articles established in the fortieth session; it appears from the rubric that the extracts presented in this manuscript were taken from the original instructions and rearranged in the order of these articles.

[62] Pulka, 68–70. The Avisamenta of the German and French nations are found in Hardt 1:999–1012 (repr. Mansi 28:362–70) and ACC.2.673–79, respectively. The papal Responsio is available in either Hardt 1:1021–42 or Hübler, 128–57 (also in Mansi, 27:1177–84). The conciliar decrees are found in *Conciliorum oecumenicorum decreta*, ed. J. Alberigo et. al., 3d ed. (Bologna, 1973), 438–44 and 447–50.

[63] "Et omnia talia, quae non concernunt omnes nationes generaliter, sed unam specialiter non diffinientur in publica sessione, sed expedientur privatim per cancellarium sub sigillo vice-cancellarii." (p. 70)

[64] The best edition of the concordats is found in *Raccolta di concordati*, ed. Giovanni Mercati, 1 (Vatican, 1954), 144–68. While the concordats were officially proclaimed in the forty-third general session (see Mansi 27:1176D), they were not published in their final form until between one and four months later; see Hübler, 52–55. Hardt had known only a German, French, and English concordat. Hübler argued that Hardt's "French" concordat was really a "Romanic" concordat, meant to apply to all three Latin nations (though with some different provisions for France). See Anton Chroust, "Zu den Konstanzer Concordaten," *Deutsche Zeitschrift für Geschichtswissenschaft* 4.1 (1890) 1–13. In the meantime, copies of a separate Spanish concordat have been found; Mercati provides an edition of this concordat. To my knowledge, no separate Italian concordat has been discovered. On the different versions of the English concordat, see E.F. Jacob, *The Register of Henry Chichele, Archbishop of Canterbury, 1414–1443* (Oxford, 1937–47), clx–xlxi, and *id.*, "Wilkin's *Concilia* and the Fifteenth Century," *Transactions of the Royal Historical Society*. 4th ser., 15 (1932) 91–131 at 116–19.

[65] " ... tractatus super reformatione ecclesiae quoad certos articulos in quodam decreto contentos adhuc pendebat inter deputatos nationum ex una, et domini papae ex altera partibus ..." (p. 69)

"articles on which there could not be agreement among the nations, such as the collation of benefices and the qualifications of those who are to receive benefices and many other things concerning which there should perhaps not be a uniform regulation for all parts of the world."[66]

Hübler and others have regarded the results as disappointing, especially since the concordats (except the English one) were temporary, enacted for only a five-year period. I would argue on the contrary that the reforms were significant successes. Many reformers no doubt wished to go further; ironically, it was probably they above all who insisted that the concordats be only temporary, so that they would not bind the hands of the next council which was to meet in five years. Once again I will argue that the failure to enact the other reforms proposed at Constance resulted above all from the different interests of the reformers in "different parts of the world" and the diverse conceptions of reform among the reformers themselves. Let us now turn to an anaylsis of the interplay of these interests in the council's specific reform deliberations.

---

[66] " . . . super certos vero articulis super quibus non poterat fieri concordia nationum, ut super collatione beneficiorum et qualificatione beneficiandorum et aliis pluribus, super quibus etiam forte non expediret conformis ordinatio pro omnibus mundi partibus, concordaverunt nationes singillatim, quaelibet pro se cum dominis cardinalibus pro papae deputatis. . . ." (p. 69)

PART II

THE REFORMS

A BRIEF GUIDE TO THE RECORDS OF THE REFORM DELIBERATIONS

The four chapters which follow analyze the deliberations of specific measures by the council. Many readers will want to verify my analysis by consulting the sources on which it is based. Table 1 provides a schematic diagram of the stages of reform deliberations at the council. Each cell identifies the particular organ which conducted that stage of the negotiations and then lists in parentheses the sources which provide a record of that stage.

Reliable editions exist for the final decrees, the concordats, the national Avisamenta and the papal Responsio.[1] Unfortunately, no manuscript record remains from the third reform committee; however, reports in Cardinal Fillastre's journal and the letters of Peter Pulka to his university (he was ambassador of the University of Vienna to the Council) provide some insight into these negotiations. The most important sources for the negotiations by far are the records of the first and second reform committees. For these, the reader should refer to my new edition of their records provided as Appendix 1 to this volume. In the text of the next four chapters I have provided references to the relevant texts of the edition. The reader who wishes to understand the nature of the manuscript record should read the introduction to the edition. Here I would like to give some brief guidelines for the more general reader.

The first rule is that the records identified as "Common, c.1, etc., as well as those identified V, c.22, etc., are records of the first reform committee;[2] and those identified as S^2, W^2, and D^2 are records of the second committee. Most of the deliberations in the second committee represent continuations of deliberations begun in the first committee. The final column in Table 4, p.307, shows the

---

[1] See above, pp. 46, 47 nn. 62 and 64. Hübler provides a very helpful table (pp. 217–249) which enables the reader to compare the different provisions of the concordats with each other and with the papal *Responsio*. The edition of the French Avisamenta in the ACC contains numerous errors, some of them substantial. In my notes I have cited these texts from the manuscripts at relevant points.

[2] In addition there are several miscellaneous proposals which may be from the first committee or which may have been drafted between the times of activity of the two committees (see below, p. 297).

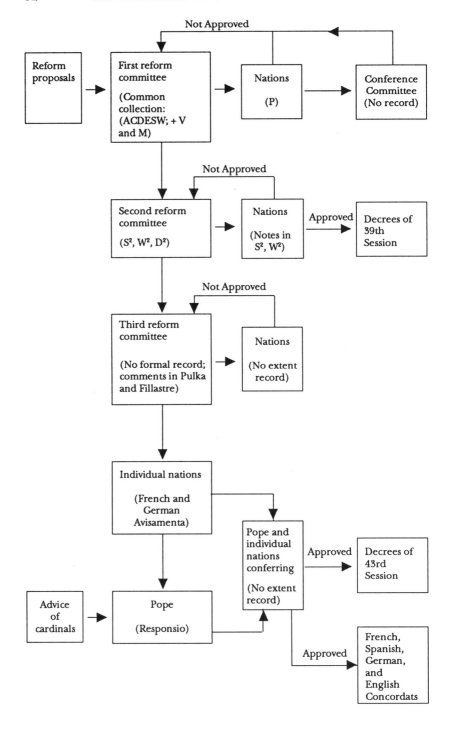

relationship between the deliberations of the two committees. Table 4 is also a concordance of the three manuscript records of the second committee; it shows that most of the records identified as being part of S^2 are also found in D^2 or W^2. I have edited S^2 in full, with variants from the proposals found also in D^2 and W^2. (The editions of D^2 and W^2 provide only the rubric, incipit and explicit of the texts which are found also in S^2.)

The manuscript records of the first reform committee, though more extensive and complicated than that of the second committee, show greater overall uniformity. Six of the records are sufficiently uniform in organization that we can refer to them as a "Common Collection," which I have edited as a single document. In lieu of providing separate incipit-explicit analyses of each manuscript, I have shown in Tables 1–3, pp. 299–306, the divergences among the manuscripts in contents and ordering of proposals. The six manuscripts fall into two distinct groups (ADS and CEW), which I have shown along the left and right sides of the table; in the two central columns I have placed the two Vatican manuscripts (M and V) which provide independent witnesses to the first committee's deliberations. Since the order of proposals in M and V diverges so greatly from that of the Common Collection, I have also provided incipit-explicit analyses of these two manuscripts. (These analyses follow the edition of the Common Collection; texts which appear only in V or M and not in the Common Collection are edited in full within the incipit-explicit analyses.) A ninth manuscript (P) provides an independent witness of the first five proposals in the Common Collection and is of considerable interest because it was used to communicate these to the French nation for deliberation.

I believe that the two groups ADS and CEW represent two distinct recensions, probably copied from two different official or semi-official records maintained in the committee. The record from which C, E, and W were copied may well have been a record maintained by the committee itself; the archetype of A, D, and S was more likely a record maintained by the representatives of the German nation on the committee. Both records, now lost, must have been continuously updated to reflect the results of ongoing deliberations of the measures. The divergent readings of the manuscripts reflect in part the different times at which groups of proposals in them were copied from the two evolving records.

Of the two Vatican manuscripts, V follows roughly the same overall chronological pattern of organization as the Common Collection, though V presents texts in order of their first introduction in the committee, whereas the main body of the Common Collection (cc.1–29) generally presents them in order of their first formal deliberation. The text of V (as opposed to V's marginal additions) thus almost always gives the earliest version of proposals. V often provides valuable information concerning the dates and results of deliberation, and in some cases it identifies the authors of the proposals and the presiding member of the committee at the time the measures were introduced. M, though it lacks these notes, often presents more complete and accurate texts than those in V. It includes many more proposals than V, including most of the additions to the Common Collection found otherwise only in D and S.

Manuscripts C, E, and W also present a set of marginal annotations recording dates and results of deliberations for many measures. The fact that the three manuscripts share these same notations in almost identical form suggests that the official record from which they were copied was also maintained in this format. In Table 5, p. , I have drawn together in chronological order all the references in the manuscripts to dates of deliberation of measures by the first reform committee. These enable us to reconstruct a rather full picture of the work of the committee, which was largely completed in the fall of 1415; in the introduction to the edition I have outlined the main phases of that work.

In addition to the annotations which it shares with C and E, W also presents a second set of annotations in a different hand and darker ink. These annotations consist of the words "Expeditus" or "Ponitur" placed next to measures; I believe that these notes record the approval or tabling of the measure by the committee. I would further argue that these annotations were made in the second reform committee, which used manuscript W as an official or semi-official record of the first committee's deliberations. The same hand marked some of these measures with the word "Membra", indicating that these measures were part of the reform of the members (and thus outside the immediate purview of the second reform committee, which was to devote its primary attention to the reform *in capite*.)

For convenience, I have identified the records of the second reform committee as W^2, S^2, and D^2, to distinguish them from the records of the first committee's Common Collection found in the same manuscripts. Thus, for example, W^2 refers to Vienna ÖNB lat. 5094, fols. 1–11, while W refers to the record of the Common Collection in the same manuscript, which immediately follows W^2, on fols. 13–26. (The superscripts are omitted in the critical apparatus except when needed for clarity. W^2 is also used to identify changes to texts in the Common collection made in a later hand in W. As explained below, p. 276, I believe these changes were made in the second reform committee.)

Two of the proposals in the Common Collection in W show extensive corrections and additions which must have been made in the second reform committee since they are in the same hand and darker ink mentioned above. These proposals reappear in S[2] with the additions and corrections already taken into the text of the proposals.

W[2]'s drafts of four of the five decrees enacted in the 39th Session contain notes which record the approval of the Spanish nation. This appears to have been the final stage in achieving general agreement on these measures (and it occurred in early October, just days before the 39th Session on October 9.) The one draft which lacks this notation (the later decree *Frequens*) is also the only one in which the wording of the amended version in W[2] is not already the wording of the final decree. Nine proposals in W[2] are marked with Arabic numbers in the margins (the numbers 1–10, omitting 7). I believe these represent proposals on which substantial agreement had been reached. (See p. 296 below for further details.)

In light of the above information, the reader can trace each reform through its various drafts in the two committees. Common, cc.1–29 are records of deliberations which had been concluded by the end of 1415. (Some of these records are in the form of drafts of proposals which the committee had approved, others are records of the committee's deliberations of the measures.) Common, cc.33–38 are records of measures on which deliberation continued beyond 1415 but was complete by the fall of 1416. Common, cc.30–32 and 39–51, as well as the proposals in V and M which do not appear in the Common Collection, must represent matters which the committee deliberated but on which it could achieve no conclusion. For almost all the measures the text of V presents the earliest version. For Common cc. 1–9, A, D and S seem generally to present earlier versions than C, E, and W, but for cc. 10–22, the text of E and W (and of C for cc.15–22) presents an earlier version than the text in A, D, and S. (These generalizations do not, however, apply to the long text of c.6, which is different in virtually every manuscript for reasons explained below, p. 280.) Common, cc. 24–29 appear in essentially the same version in all the manuscripts.

The reader who wishes to compare my edition with the earlier edition in the ACC can do so handily using the concordance in Table 6, p. 313. The table also shows which of the reform committee records relate to each of the final reform decrees and the articles in the concordats enacted at the council.

CHAPTER THREE

THE CONSTANCE FISCAL REFORMS

Hübler lamented that the reform deliberations continually reached impasses over the questions of reform of papal finances and provisions to offices. The council failed to reach significant agreement in these areas, and thus the momentum of reform bogged down. For Haller, Zwölfer, and others, these were *the* central reforms, the most essential steps in dismantling papal centralization and establishing the freedom of the national churches. The Council of Basel took up the work left unfinished at Constance and completed it by abolishing all major papal taxes and provisions.

The Constance reformers did focus very great attention on these two matters, and many of them did call in theory for the abolition of both papal taxes and papal provisions. I would argue, however, that their stances here were polemical, and that in practice their reform goals were focused differently. We can only understand those goals by looking closely at the actual course of reform deliberations, observing carefully the competing interests of the diverse groups involved. In an earlier study, I argued that the Constance reforms of papal taxation were far more successful than historians of the councils have acknowledged.[1] Here I would like to summarize the results of that study and then go on to make some comments about other fiscal reforms at the council.

1. Papal Taxation of the Clergy

Historians of papal finances have often pointed out the profound change that occurred beginning in Martin V's reign. Revenues from taxation of the clergy fell drastically—perhaps as low as one-third their former levels—and the popes partially compensated for this loss by expanding their seigneurial revenues in the

---

[1] See Phillip Stump, "The Reform of Papal Taxation at the Council of Constance (1414–1418)," *Speculum* 64 (1989) 69–105, and the supporting references there for all the material through p. 13 below. See also Andrea Gardi, "La Fiscalità pontificia tra medioevo ed età moderna," *Società e storia* 33 (1986) 509–557.

papal states. Historians of papal finance have not generally viewed these changes as the result of the Constance reforms, probably because historians of the councils have so persistently asserted that the reforms were failures. However, Jean Favier's magisterial study of papal finances during the Schism has enabled us to gauge much more accurately the effects of the Constance reforms.[2] It informs us about the amounts of revenues involved in the various types of tax and also the total revenues available to the popes of the Schism, the methods of collection, and the fiscal expedients used by the popes to deal with the frequent times of fiscal crisis.

Favier's findings are significant and often surprising. In the past historians of conciliar reform have focused on tenths (clerical income taxes) and on annates and services (taxes on the first year's revenues of the benefices of those who received them through papal provision or confirmation). They have tended to regard the council's effective abolition of three less well known papal taxes—the procurations, spoils, and fruits during vacancies—as essentially a cosmetic reform. Yet Favier's research shows that one of these three, the procurations, accounted for about twenty percent of the regular income of the popes at Avignon during the Schism, more than that derived from either the tenths or the annates. Its abolition was no mere cosmetic reform. Moreover, reformers eyed the papal collection of procurations as among the most egregious abuses since these moneys had originally been intended to support the visitation tours of bishops, archdeacons, and others who went out to maintain order and reform abuses in the churches under their authority. Expropriation of these moneys by the curia appeared to many as the very negation of reform.

Papal collection of spoils and fruits during vacancies also caused very great rancor. Spoils were the movable property of deceased prelates (prelates could not bestow these by testament without special permission), and fruits during vacancies were the revenues of vacant benefices from the time of their vacation until the successor took possession. While these taxes were not a major source of revenue (for the Avignon obedience, on the average less than four percent of the total), the popes continued to collect them in spite of the bitter complaint they engendered. Again, Favier's results are suggestive. Spoils yielded slim revenues because the popes had to take over the liabilities as well as the assets of the deceased prelates whose spoils they targeted. Financially strapped popes, ridden by

---

[2] Jean Favier, *Les finances pontificales à l'époque du Grand Schisme d'Occident* (Paris, 1966).

the frequent fiscal crises of the schism, continued to collect taxes which were both unpopular and unprofitable.

The Schism itself was the greatest crisis, splitting the revenues of the curia first two and later three ways. The ending of the Schism enabled the termination of marginal fiscal practices like the spoils.[3] However, the council's decision to abolish these taxes was not easily won. By tracing the successive drafts of these reform measures at Constance we can see that curial opposition was not the only, perhaps even not the most significant cause for delay. In considering the effects of any fiscal reform we must ask who would be the new owners of the revenues to be denied to the pope. The reformers themselves asked this, and their divergent answers slowed enactment of the reforms. For example, many reformers demanded that the spoils and fruits during vacancies be reserved for the successors in the benefices. However, others besides the pope competed for the collection of these revenues—prelates, collegiate bodies, and secular princes. Conflicting views and interests on these matters helped delay enactment, causing the reforms of the three taxes, initially all treated together in a single proposal, to be divided and continually revised. Ultimately, the abolition of spoils was recombined with that of procurations and enacted as a reform decree of the 39th session; rather than reserving spoils for the successors, the decree said they would belong to those to whom they would be due according to the *ius commune*. The abolition of papal collection of fruits during vacancies could not be enacted until the 43d session; and again, rather than reserving them for the successors, the decree left them to the "disposition of custom and privilege."

A number of princes had established the custom of collecting fruits during vacancies from some benefices. This is one of those areas in which the influence of the princes tended to work against reform at the council. Such is still more the case with the reform of tenths. The studies of Favier, Lunt, Hennig, and others have shown that the proceeds of papal tenths were very often assigned to the princes. Favier remarks that this was undoubtedly a major reason for the weakness of resistance to tenths. Conciliar reformers lamented that the Schism had been prolonged because popes had been able to use the granting of tenths to maintain the support of the princes in their rival obediences. The picture that increasingly emerges is one of conciliar reformers fighting on two fronts, against

---

[3] They had been revived by the end of the fifteenth century, however. See Stump, "Taxation," 102 n. 100.

predatory princes and egoistic papacy.

Combined curial and princely opposition helped to prevent enactment of the early proposals on tenths considered by the reform committee, which would have required that universal tenths be granted only in general council, indeed only with the consent of the council. That measure, if it had passed, would have made the tenths virtually useless to both pope and princes as a source of ready revenue, since the councils were to meet only once every ten years. In this light, Hübler's opinion that conciliar approval of tenths would have led to parliamentary power of the purse over the papal monarchy seems anachronistic.[4] Moreover, Favier shows that tenths accounted for a relatively small portion of the revenues of Avignon popes during the Schism—between eleven and seventeen percent, on the average.

The final decree on tenths, enacted in the 43d session, was by no means a failure, however. It declared that universal tenths could be imposed only in the case of great and heavy necessity which concerns the common good of the whole church, and then only with the consent and subscription of the cardinals and of the prelates whose opinion could be consulted. And for territorial tenths it required the consent (not the mere advice) of the territorial clergy.

The council also achieved significant successes in the reform of the taxes which had raised the most vocal and determined opposition of reformers—the annates and services. Favier shows that during the Schism the annates provided about the same proportion of the Avignon papal collectors' receipts as did the tenths. The services accounted for between ten and twenty percent of the total receipts of the Avignon camera during this period—roughly the same proportion of total receipts as the annates. However, the amounts of services received by the *papal* camera represented less than one-half the total amounts collected in services, since one-half of the common services went to the camera of the cardinals, and in addition to the common services (*servitia communa*), prelates owed petty services (*servitia minuta*) to the *familiares* of the pope and the cardinals. Common services were paid by prelates when the pope provided them to or confirmed their election to consistorial benefices (major abbacies and bishoprics and higher prelacies); the amount of services for each benefice was recorded in the papal camera and was in theory one-third of the first year's revenues.

---

[4] In this sense, also, William Durant the Younger's proposal for placing limits on papal power by conciliar control of papal revenues seems all the more proleptic. On Durant's proposal, see Fasolt, *Council*, 244–246, on his prolepsis, p. 319.

Annates were paid by those who received papal provision or confirmation to lesser benefices; the amount paid was in theory the net
annual revenue of the benefice (after expenses), as determined in
the tax registers for the the tenths. For untaxed benefices, the
amount was fixed at one-half the first year's income.

The reforms of annates and services were so controversial that
they were continually deferred by the reform committee, and ultimately no conciliar decree regarding them was enacted. Thus, all
the council's reforms of annates and services were relegated to the
national concordats, and historians of the councils have often treated these reforms as merely cosmetic. The nucleus of them was a
terse paragraph in a proposal presented by the cardinals (led by
Adimari) in the first reform committee which established the payment of the taxes in installments after peaceful possession of the
benefice and called for the reassessment of benefices which were too
heavily taxed. These were not trivial reforms. The first helped to
eliminate the most troublesome aspect of the taxes, their simoniacal
appearance. (During the Schism the popes had begun regularly to
demand full payment of the annates before granting the bulls which
gave to the beneficiary power to exercise his office.) The demand
for reassessment pointed the way to a truly significant reduction of
the taxes.

Historians who have deemed the Constance tax reforms failures
have generally pointed above all to the council's failure to abolish
the annates and services completely, something done only later by
the Council of Basel. Yet the council did achieve a major reduction
in these taxes in the land where they had weighed most heavily. As
a result of the French concordat, new prelates in the kingdom of
France henceforth paid only one-half the former amounts of services. They continued to pay them at this reduced rate even after
the total abolition of these taxes at the Council of Basel had failed
in practice.

Again, this victory was achieved in the face of strong opposition;
fortunately, an extensive notarial record of the debate concerning
annates in the French nation in the fall of 1415 gives us detailed
insight into the reasons for the opposition.[5] In this debate the
nation considered reinstating the famous provisions of the French
neutrality legislation of 1407, which had totally suspended the
payment of annates and services. The record of the deliberations

---

[5] See Stump, "Taxation," 84–96; the most accessible edition is found in found
in Edmond Martène, and Ursin Durand, *Thesaurus novus anecdotorum*, 2 (Paris,
1717), 1543–1609.

offers tantalizing insights into the opinions, posturings, and ma-
neuverings of different groups and individuals. Part of the maneuver-
ing involved the deliberately ambivalent use of the word *vacantia*,
which could mean either annates or services or both. The president, Jean Mauroux, must have also been involved in the ma-
neuverings; he may well have been double-dealing, since he also
held the post of acting papal camerarius at Constance (i.e., second
in command of the whole network of papal finance).[6]

The notaries made a record of the roll call vote in which 134
persons or their proxies expressed detailed opinions about the
actions to be taken. The results show widespread approval to
abolish the *vacantia*, but almost always coupled with expression of
willingess to "provide for the pope and cardinals." The most
ardent opponents of the taxes usually expressed this willingness,
but many prelates and clergy also feared that new modes of taxation might hurt them more than the annates and services had.
Curial opponents of the tax revolt were able to appeal to these
fears.

Just after the president, Jean Mauroux, summarized the vote of
the nation on November 2 by stating simply that the vast majority
agreed that the *vacantia* should be abolished, Jean d'Achéry rose
and clarified that this abolition should also explicitly include the
services; Mauroux immediately restated the conclusion to include
the services. Pandemonium broke out—protests, name-calling,
and recriminations, not just from the curial officials present, but
also from other members.[7] Part of the furor was triggered by
Mauroux's failure to state anything about replacement revenues.
In the end he did restate the conclusion to include them. However,
I would argue that a larger reason for the strong reaction was
D'Achéry's last-minute amendment. Most of the voters had understood *vacantia* to mean annates only. The much greater revenues
involved in services made the voters much more cautious about

---

[6] On Mauroux's role, see Stump, "Taxation," 90–91 n. 60.

[7] *Thesaurus*, 2:1560: "Ipse dominus patriarcha [Mauroux] nulla alia examina-
tione et concordia votorum facta, neque concordata dixit quod major pars et duplo
major fuit opinionis, quod dictae vacantiae non sunt nec fuerunt debitae, et quod
tamquam indebitae, tollantur. Et tunc dominus Johannes episcopus Silvanectensis
[D'Achéry] dixit quod non solum vacantiae, sed etiam communia et minuta
servitia, et omnia contingentia, et dependentia, tollantur. Et plures clamaverunt
quod placet. Et tunc idem dominus patriarcha dixit quod concludebat cum majori
parte, quod dictae vacantiae et servitia communia et alia inde sequuta tamquam
indebita tollantur, tam de praeteritis, quam praesenti et futuro temporibus. Et
tunc fuit magnum murmur in natione et tumultus maximus et magna turbatio
clamantium hinc et inde ad diversa . . ."

abolishing them. Yet, in the end it was the services rather than the annates that were reduced by one-half. The further negotiations suggest why.

The vote revealed the most ardent opponents of the annates and services to be the university graduates; they were the ones present who had some of the most realistic ambitions for obtaining a higher benefice, but would have had some of the greatest difficulty in paying the tax on the benefice, especially the services. In fact, Jean d'Achéry was a doctor of theology who had recently been promoted to the see of Senlis, and had requested a delay in the payment of his services because of his state of financial embarrassment.

These negotiations of the French nation were going on at the same time as the most intense work of the the reform committee was taking place. The German nation had not even begun to deliberate the annates and services, and it sent an appeal to the French nation not to act so independently in this matter. The French were much more concerned about annates and services because they suffered more under these taxes than clergy in other regions. Because of the presence of the papacy at Avignon for a century, a larger number of wealthy benefices in France had become subject to reservations than elsewhere. Evidence for this was presented as part of a position paper prepared for the French nation in November 1415 to support its action against the curial opponents (For further analysis of this paper, see Chapter 7 below.) That evidence is confirmed by a review of the tax records for services in all parts of Europe. In 1378, the proportion of services for secular prelacies drawn from the kingdom of France and the Dauphiné was 31% of the total for all of Europe. For this and other reasons the French crown, and especially the Parlement pushed strongly for abolition of these taxes, all the more so since it appeared increasingly likely that the papacy would never return to Avignon.

The French nation achieved more impressive results in their reform of annates and services than did the other nations. The concept for the most impressive result, the reduction of services, seems to have originated in the Instructions of the Gallican Church, as a temporary expedient, pending total abolition, and the French prelates introduced it in their Avisamenta. They asked for the same reduction in both annates and services; however, the pope finally granted only the reduction in services. Still, the lesser clergy were not entirely neglected. Before the Schism the tax rate for the tenth on all benefices in France had been reduced by one-half because of the devastation there from war, plague, and economic crisis. That reduction would have also resulted in a corresponding reduction of one-half in the amount of annates, if the collectors had not been instructed to collect the difference between the tax and the first year's revenues instead of the tax rate itself as the amount of the annates.[8] The French concordat at Constance made it clear that the collectors were to collect only the tax rate itself. For many, this meant a substantial reduction in annates.

The French lower clergy also shared in the results achieved by the other nations in their concordats, results which were by no means negligible. They helped eliminate the taint of simony by establishing installment payments of annates *after* peaceful possession of the benefice. They made benefices with less than 25 florins revenue truly exempt from the annates. They eliminated the obligations of beneficiaries to take over the debts of their predecessors for annates and services. And they halved the amount of existing personal debts for annates and services for any persons who paid the remainder within six months. All these changes regularized the collection of annates, eliminated abuses, and ultimately made them a much less important source of income for the curia, according to François Baix, who has studied the collection of annates in regions strong touched by papal provisions.[9] As for the reassessment of tax rates proposed by Adimari, this demand entered the concordats, and while there is not much evidence of tax rates being reduced, we know that some very wealthy, but notoriously underassessed sees had their taxes raised (it is easy to overlook this kind of real tax reform.) Finally, the concordats included several kinds of benefices that would be exempt from annates. The most notable exemption by far was benefices acquired through papal expectancies. We shall see in the next chapter that the numbers of these were vast.

The willingness of the papacy to concede so much is striking. Even more striking was the willingness of the cardinals to accede to the reduction of French services. The cardinals were not known for their self-effacement. Partly they were driven to accept the reduction in lieu of the still worse alternative of total abolition, which the French crown and Parlement threatened. However, their actions were also part of a wider compromise. This brings us to consider the cardinals' other revenues.

---

[8] See Stump, "Taxation," 100.

[9] François Baix, *La Chambre apostolique et les "Libri Annatarum" de Martin V (1417–1431)*. Brussels and Rome, 1947, ccxxxii, cclxvii, and especially cccviii.

2. Reforms of cardinals' revenues

Far more important to the cardinals than the services were the revenues they received from the numerous benefices they held in plurality and ruled in absentia. This pluralism and absenteeism were among the most egregious abuses which the reformers attacked. The cardinals were not usually violating the letter of the law, because they held the benefices in commendam—i.e., they had the right to collect the revenues even though they didn't hold title to the benefice.[10] Reformers had complained bitterly about the commendams and had suggested various measures for dealing with them. The *Capitula agendorum* suggested several means of providing an alternate revenue for the cardinals.[11] One was to increase the income of their cardinalitian titles in the suburbican churches by unions of sinecure benefices with these. This alone would not suffice; it might raise the revenues of the titles to at most 1,000 florins, but the *Capitula agendorum* indicated that realistic replacement revenues would be in the neighborhood of 4,000 florins.[12] Another possibility would be to suppress one benefice in each cathedral church and use the resulting revenues to support the cardinals. This would have been to shift the chief burden of support from the regular to the secular clergy and probably would have encountered fatal resistance.

The second reform committee, from which the cardinals were excluded, did address the reform directly and hammered out a far-sighted solution. They sought to eliminate the commendams in phases, gradually replacing them with alternate revenues to be provided by the pope. The initial record (W², c.20) called for the cardinals immediately to give up all charitable institutions which they held as benefices (hospitals, orphanages, etc.); and, within a year, all parish churches, "claustral offices,"[13] and other benefices with revenues less than 70 *livres tournois*. The long term plan was for the cardinals to give up all the benefices they held in plurality in exchange for compensation to replace the lost revenue from these benefices up to a total of 6,000 florins. (However, each cardinal

---

[10] On the commendams, see Guillaume Mollat, *La collation des bénéfices ecclésiastiques sous les papes d'Avignon, 1305–1378* (Paris, 1921), 34–38.

[11] ACC.4.560–561.

[12] Most of the manuscripts have 24,000 florins! This may have simply been the result of an early scribal error, or it may have been an effort to calculate a cardinal's total revenue from all sources, including services.

[13] This term does not appear to refer to offices of abbot or prior, but rather to more minor offices.

would be allowed to keep one prelacy in commendam, to which he could retire in old age; the income from this benefice to be calculated as part of the 6,000 florin maximum.) A cardinal would also give up any bishopric or abbacy held in commendam as soon as the pope assigned him an equivalent revenue from another source.

The record of the further negotiations concerning commendams in W^2 consists of two very interesting agreements which resulted from negotiations between representatives of the sacred college and representatives of the second reform committee (W^2, cc.16–17). In the first of these, the cardinals agreed to most of the measures in c.20.[14] In the second agreement (c.17), the cardinals identified the kinds of benefices which were not to be granted to cardinals created in the future. Parish churches and benefices with revenues of less than seventy florins were prohibited (but charitable institutions were not specifically mentioned—an oversight? or perhaps considered too obvious to mention?) What about the kinds of benefices which c.16 required cardinals to give up in exchange for compensation? Most of these were not to be granted to new cardinals (Bishoprics, however, could be granted, but not metropolitan sees. When a bishopric granted to a cardinal became vacant, the next holder had to be a non-cardinal.) No mention was made of any alternate source of revenue for these new cardinals.

The results were evidently the product of very tough negotiations. Individual cardinals demanded exceptions—Brogny and de Saluces to exceed the 6,000 florin limit; Cramaud to retain the archbishopric of Poitiers. The strangest, and saddest, exception was that for Cardinal Brancacci to hold "a certain preceptorship of a hospital of St. Anthony." It seems unbelievable that a cardinal with revenues up to 6,000 florins from commendams would have a personal exception made to allow him to maintain as an absentee landlord the small additional revenue from an institution designed to care for the poor. The fact that Brancacci lodged a formal petition in this matter with the nations suggests that he expected the results of these negotiations to be enacted. The cardinals' concern about even more far-reaching inroads on their revenues from commendams may have later played a role in their acquiescence to the reduction of the tax-rate for common services in France discussed above.

---

[14] They did not, however, include "claustral offices" among those to be given up immediately. They also limited the kinds of benefices to be given up in exchange for compensation; most significant among the benefices excluded were deaneries, which c.20 had desired to be surrendered above all others.

The cardinals were probably not sanguine about the pope's ability to find sufficient replacement revenues for the commendams. Nor were the reformers. In c.20 they had established a set of interim measures for the monastic benefices still retained by the cardinals pending compensation. In each monastery the cardinal should appoint a monk of the order to oversee discipline and observance of the rule; if he appointed a person to farm the revenues of the benefice, this person should likewise be of the same order, and in any case not a layman; and the cardinal must maintain the due number of religious in the monastery. As a result of the negotiations with representatives of the sacred college, these measures were even strengthened in c.16; the cardinal must provide for the monks decently and honestly from the revenues of the monastery and must visit the monastery personally and carry out needed repairs at his own expense (if he doesn't, the ordinary should compel him to do so or else deduct the repair expenses from the farmed revenues.)

After the papal election, the final negotiations on commendams followed closely the lines of the agreements in cc.16–17. However, the emphasis clearly shifted to future grants. Both the French and German Avisamenta did still contain statements about the cardinals giving up the commendams they presently held in exchange for compensation, but they were vague and general, simply referring to an article of the third reform committee which is no longer extant. In the final concordats, all that remained about existing commendams was the general statement that they should be given up in exchange for compensation, but no requirement to give them up within a certain time.

However, with regard to future commendams the concordats are quite clear. They specify classes of benefices which are not to be granted to the cardinals or to other prelates in commendam or titulum; these classes are the major ones listed in the agreements in W^2, c.16–17.[15] The Avisamenta had also wanted to go beyond those agreements and exclude cathedral churches and generally all benefices with cure of souls. The *Responsio*, however, did not accept this exclusion, and it did not appear in the concordats. Instead, the French and Spanish concordats did resurrect the exclusion of benefices with small revenues, though the limit was placed at fifty rather than seventy florins. Interestingly, the Spanish concordat omitted the exclusion of parish churches. The German Avisamenta

---

[15] In the German concordat the are divided between two articles, Articles 5 and 9.

had also included some of the guarantees from W^2, c.16 about the proper maintenance of religious houses still held by cardinals. The Responsio expanded these considerably, restoring virtually all the provisions included in the earlier agreements and even going beyond them. Almost none of these, however, except the German ones, entered the concordats.

The pope thus honored almost all the changes requested by the nations regarding future commendams, and he even went beyond the earlier agreements in some ways, especially by applying the restrictions on future commendams to those granted to other prelates as well as cardinals. The pope could and did bring about reforms of the members which the council might have had trouble enacting alone. We also have strong evidence that Martin V carried out some of the most important reforms of commendams agreed on in the concordats. Hermann Diener's study of grants of abbacies made in commendam between 1417 and 1523, based on a review of the records in the Vatican archives, shows that Martin V made very few such grants.[16] Of the approximately 700 abbacies filled in consistory during Martin's reign, only 2.5% were granted as commendams (in fact, less than 1% of abbacies outside Italy, which wasn't covered by the concordats.) By contrast, 21% and 63.2% of the grants were commendams in the later reigns of Pius II and Julius II, respectively. Diener expressed surprise at this result and remarked that it may have been "influenced by the reform movements of the Council of Constance." We can go much further and say that the low numbers were a direct result of the successful Constance reforms. Even though Diener's results concern only abbacies, these were among the most prevalent commendams and the ones which had produced the bitterest complaints from reformers. Thus, in the case of the commendams, even though cardinalitian rather than papal revenues were at issue, we again see striking evidence of the success of the Constance fiscal reforms.

3. Indulgences

The papal curia profited financially from indulgences in several ways. First, it received chancery fees for the preparation of letters of indulgence.[17] Such letters generally entitled the bearer to choose a

---

[16] Hermann Diener, "Die Vergabe von Klöstern als Kommende durch Papst und Konsistorium (1417–1523)," *QFIAB* 66 (1988) 270–283.
[17] William Lunt, *Papal Revenues in the Middle Ages* (New York, 1934), 459.

confessor, who was given power by the letter to hear the person's confession and to grant him or her the indulgence.[18] Some letters were granted directly to the individual by the papal curia; others were given to local institutions which the pope authorized to impart indulgences.[19] Sometimes the local churches had to compound with the papacy in order to receive this authorization; the curia stood to profit in this way as well. The indulgences administered by local churches were usually partial indulgences; they authorized the local church to grant from one to ten years to each recipient on certain feast days. Sometimes the popes granted this privilege to the local church for a fixed period of time; sometimes the grant was perpetual.[20] Alternatively, the local church might be empowered to send out people called quaestors, or indulgence preachers, who would distribute the indulgence to persons in exchange for alms. As Lunt points out, Chaucer's "Pardoner" was a quaestor. The pope alone had the power to grant a plenary indulgence, which removed all temporal penalties owed by the sinner and was generally given only in the hour of death. The indulgence for crusaders was also generally a plenary indulgence, and the papacy had started granting plenary indulgences also on other occasions, such as pilgrimage to certain churches (St. Mary Portiuncula, etc.) and, starting in 1300, for visit to the holy places of Rome during the year of Jubilee.[21] The interval between jubilee years was fixed at one hundred years by Boniface VIII, but Clement VI reduced it to fifty and Urban VI to 33 1/3 years.[22] Popes also granted indulgences on the model of the jubilee indulgence (*ad instar iubilei*), which authorized local churches to grant the jubilee indulgence to those who could not visit Rome.[23]

Indulgences administered by local churches do not appear to have yielded large revenues for the papacy. It was otherwise with the revenues derived from jubilee indulgences, *ad instar* indulgences, and indulgences collected *in partibus* by papal agents. To receive the jubilee indulgence, pilgrims had to visit and offer alms at three, later four Roman churches; these churches divided the alms with the papal chamber, which received from them all the bullion and three-quarters of the coined money collected. Huge

---

[18] Lunt, 447.
[19] Lunt, 493.
[20] Lunt, 476–79.
[21] Lunt, 459f.
[22] Nicolaus Paulus, *Geschichte des Ablasses im Mittelalter vom Ursprunge bis zur Mitte des 14. Jahrhunderts* (Paderborn, 1922–1923), 2:150–152.
[23] Lunt, 480–487.

sums of money were received from churches which compounded with the pope for the grant of an indulgence *ad instar iubilei* (one thousand florins for Milan in 1391, six hundred in 1396, one thousand for Cologne in 1394, etc.)[24] "*Ad instar*" indulgences were also granted in a similar manner for the Portiuncula indulgence and other famous indulgences.[25]

At the Council of Constance, reform of indulgences started with a proposal submitted to the reform committee September 25 by Nicholas Bubbewyth, the English Bishop of Bath and Wells, who was also president of the committee at that time.[26] Discussion followed, and when the votes were counted a majority was in favor of revoking all perpetual and *ad instar* indulgences and all indulgences granted *a pena et culpa* (often another name for plenary indulgences). They also declared that *questus non uendantur*, which seems to have forbidden the sale of proceeds from indulgences. A committee of three headed by D'Ailly was appointed to draft a formal constitution.

The reformers did thus not attack the concept of indulgences; they merely sought to remove particularly abusive forms of indulgence, especially the plenary and *ad instar* indulgences. Favier found that these were used by the Roman popes during the Schism with special frequency as a fund-raising effort in times of financial crisis. Boniface IX did revoke all the indulgences granted *a pena et culpa* and the *ad instar* indulgences, but things had come to such a pass that contemporaries suspected that he did so in order to grant new ones. (In fact, he did grant some new ones, but far fewer than before.)[27]

Immediately following the record of the deliberations on September 25 in the Vatican manuscripts we find what must be the constitution drafted by D'Ailly's sub-committee. Its preamble states the need to cut back human ambition (*ad succidendas ambitiones mortalium*) and expresses concern lest the treasury of merits be cheapened if poured out too profusely. It then revokes a whole list of indulgences granted by papal or other authority during the Schism—the jubilee and crusading indulgences,[28] as well as those for full or partial remission of sins over an unspecified time, and an

---

[24] Lunt, 493f.

[25] Lunt, 487.

[26] 26. V, c.14; M, c.38. The text in M is much less corrupt and more complete, although V has the correct name for the president and proposer.

[27] Paulus, 2:153–54.

[28] Note, however, that an addition in W[2] allows an exception for crusading indulgences for those fighting heretics and schismatics.

interesting assortment of *ad instar* indulgences. It threatens with excommunication prelates and laymen who allow the sale of these indulgences, and it requires the careful examination of all questors.

The fate of this decree remains a mystery. Most other reforms which appear in this manner in V and M are recorded also in the Common Collection, often with notes on further deliberations. No further trace of *Ad succidendas* appears in the manuscripts, although another, similar set of reforms is found among the second reform committee's deliberations (in W², c.22). It calls for revocation of all indulgences granted during the Schism, especially the *ad instar* ones, singling out for special opprobrium those emanating from cardinals for places at the Roman Curia; these granted one hundred days indulgence for each note that pilgrims sing for one hundred days as they circumambulate these places. "This tends more to the deception and derision of the Christian people than to the salvation of souls. . . . All such abuses and extortions of money are to be totally extirpated."

The council failed to enact a decree on indulgences. The Avisamenta of the French and German nations reveal a considerable difference of opinion. Whereas the German nation held to the strong demands of the two drafts discussed above, the French recommendations were remarkably mild; they counseled that caution be exercised in granting further indulgences, but they asked that all past indulgences remain in effect. In his Responsio Martin V offered to abolish all *ad instar* and perpetual indulgences *a pena et culpa* and *cum plena remissione* granted to localities; in his chancery rules he had already prohibited the cardinals from granting such perpetual indulgences.

The concordats reflect the logical outcome of the "national" differences. The French and Spanish concordats asked for no changes. The German concordat revoked all *ad instar* indulgences granted during the Schism; it was these that had brought such large sums to the curia in the form of compositions and which had led to such abuses. In the concordat Martin also promised to use restraint in granting future indulgences. On the whole, he followed this pledge, apparently even declining to proclaim the year of jubilee in 1423, even though flocks of pilgrims desired it.[29] The English concordat's article on indulgences is the most interesting. First, it was quite explicit about the real grievances of the prelates: The papal indulgence letters, sold far and wide by the quaestors,

---

[29] Paulus, 2:158–59, 185–86.

allow parishioners to choose confessors other than their ordinary bishops and priests. Some of the parishioners even assume the audacity of sinning because they think the indulgence protects them, and thus "they withdraw from their parish churches tithes and oblations and other debts, or they pay them less faithfully." The potency of the concordat's remedy was even more striking than the candor of its complaint. The English bishops were given the power to investigate and if need be to suspend, papal indulgences which they found to be scandalous, and of denouncing these to the pope for revocation. The power Martin thus conceded seems all the more remarkable since the English concordat was granted in perpetuity.

The German, and especially the English nations thus achieved notable victories in the reform of indulgences at Constance. Favier's findings again suggest that the differing zeal of the nations reflected their different experiences during the Schism at the hands of rival popes who used different fiscal expedients.[30] The Roman popes, to whose obedience the Germans and English belonged, made very frequent use of indulgences, especially during periods of crisis. They had at their disposal the city of Rome with its treasures of relics, the holy graves, and the other spiritualia which made possible the granting of indulgences in conjunction with the celebration of the holy year and of pilgrimages to Rome. The popes at Avignon during the Schism made much more restrained use of indulgences because they did not enjoy these "spiritual resources."

Even the Germans and English did not want to abolish indulgences, but rather to protect against their misuse and overuse. They wanted to protect them from being cheapened by overissue, like inflationary currency. The council, in fact, granted its own indulgences, though on a much more modest scale than the plenary indulgence granted by the Council of Basel in 1435.[31] The indulgences granted at Constance were not justified on the basis of the council's *plenitudo potestatis*, but rather on the basis of adding up the indulgences which each individual cardinal and prelate at the council could grant. The leading canonists, civilians and theologians at the council, including Zabarella, D'Ailly, and Caspar of

---

[30] Favier, 590–99.

[31] On this, see especially Pascal Ladner, "Der Ablass-Traktat des Heymericus de Campo: Ein Beitrag zur Geschichte des Basler Konzils," *Zeitschrift für Schweizerische Kirchengeschichte* 71 (1977) 93–140, at 97–103. Only some of the Basel fathers had reservations about the authority of the council to grant a plenary indulgence, whereas the *consilia* from Constance mentioned below never mention any thought of a plenary indulgence.

Perugia, wrote a set of consilia on the question of how great an indulgence could be granted in this manner.[32] The indulgences mentioned in the council's official acta as granted by the council *sede vacante* must have been indulgences of this variety.

4. Taxes and simony

We might expect that those who branded the annates and services outright as simony would have attacked them in the conciliar deliberations concerning simony. Such an attack was indeed made at the Council of Basel fifteen years later.[33] The Basel fathers' attempt to outlaw the annates and services in the context of a decree against simony occurred after a deadlock in the Basel negotiations concerning the simple abolition of the annates and services; the deadlock had resulted from disagreement about providing revenues to replace the income from these taxes. The proposed simony decree, in its turn, produced an even more intractable deadlock caused by the prelates' desire to maintain their own revenues collected for ordinations and other pontifical acts, revenues which would have been explicitly outlawed by the decree along with the annates and services. Ultimately the simony decree was abandoned and the Basel fathers returned to the direct consideration of annates and services. In their annates decree of June, 1435, they went ahead and abolished these taxes, postponing consideration of replacement revuenues; by failing to deal with replacement revenues, the council virtually assured Pope Eugenius IV's refusal to approve the annate decree. It is interesting that the final version of the annate decree also outlawed most of the revenues of the ordinaries which they had tried so hard to protect in their resistance to the simony decree.

At the Council of Constance the proposed decrees concerning simony did not mount as direct and explicit an attack on annates as did the Basel fathers, although some reformers at Constance pushed for such an attack. That they did so in one of the earliest

---

[32] Vienna, *Österreichische Nationalbibliothek* lat. 3896, fols. 230r–235v. Most of them agreed that the indulgences could be added together, but only up to a maximum of one year. They were basing their opinion above all on a classic opinion of Hostiensis in this matter. A few argued against this limit on the basis of the newer practice of the curia by which multiple hundred day indulgences of several cardinals added together could be granted for the same act; others counseled that more restraint be used in the granting.

[33] See Zwölfer, 198–247.

schedules in the Common Collection, *Contra labem simoniace* (c.3) shows how strongly some reformers felt about this matter. *Contra labem* attacked simony involved in the granting of benefices "whether within the curia or outside of it" and thus might have encompassed simony committed in papal provisions. A later draft specified that the decree pertained to acts of anyone of whatever status, even if it be that of a bishop, archbishop, patriarch or cardinal, adding the words "siue paciscendo" ("and by bargaining") to describe the way in which the simoniacal agreements were made. Could "siue paciscendo" be an oblique reference to the obligations which papal providees or confirmees made to the apostolic chamber to pay their services? Since these amounts were usually fixed and recorded in the *Libri taxarum*, it is likely that most reformers understood the phrase to mean only those amounts demanded by the chamber in excess of the services (often far in excess).

The last draft of *Contra labem* which we possess (S², c.8) reflects refinements which were probably made in the second reform committee. The earlier drafts had declared the penalty of deprivation of all offices *ipso facto* for all violaters of the decree, stating that the forfeited benefices could be freely conferred on new persons. They had also deprived of all benefices those who were negligent in enforcing the provisions of the decree. The wording of the final draft was more moderate and more workable. It provided for due process in the forfeiture of benefices before they could be granted out afresh (i.e., there had to have been legitimate declaration of the commission of the crime after all interested parties had been summoned), and it entirely replaced the penalty of deprivation for negligent enforcers by a statement requiring the ordinaries to enforce the decree under pain of punishment by their superiors. On the other hand, this final draft tightened the wording which defined the nature of the simony envisaged; it was explicitly stated to encompass simony incurred in the granting of benefices and "by pact or convention." This could refer to the obligations made to the chamber, but it could also refer to agreements made between people who exchanged benefices, or to someone who paid someone else to resign a benefice into their hands. Subsequent developments suggest that the language was left vague intentionally because of underlying disagreements in the reform committee and in the council at large.

The German Avisamenta approved the decree proposed in the reform committee; the French Avisamenta expressed dissatisfaction with it and offered a substitute decree. The proposed French decree explicitly condemned the assertion that the pope does not commit simony in the collation or confirmation of a benefice when he receives moneys or bargains to receive moneys (*de illis percipiendis paciscatur*). No new penalties are provided; the entire brunt of the draft is to make clear that the pope commits simony when he demands money for a collation or confirmation. It subjects to the canonical penalties anyone "who in the future, with corrupt intention, makes an agreement or promise, direct or indirect, concerning money or any other temporal commodity, to the pope or any other ordinary provisor, elector, presenter, patron, confirmer, or mediator, in the curia or outside it, before the collation, provision, confirmation, election, or presentation, and then afterwards receives, by the intervention of this money or agreement, a dignity, office, or benefice which he would not otherwise receive"; likewise, the person who confers the benefice in this manner, even if he holds the episcopal, archiepiscopal, patriarchal or cardinalitian dignity. For all its legal accuracy and all-inclusiveness, the proposed decree never mentioned the annates and services explicitly. Its list of office holders subject to the canonical penalties also stopped short of mentioning the papal dignity; in this crucial clause it agreed precisely with the earlier drafts. The words concerning bargaining and pacts could refer to the obligations made in curia. The ardent Gallicans surely understood it this way, but a strict constructionist could argue the contrary. The crucial qualifying clause, "with corrupt intent," hardly applies to the state of mind of a prelate obligating himself to pay the normal amount of services paid by his predecessors for over a century. The proposed simony decree in the French Avisamenta was the last effort of the Gallicans at Constance to brand the annates and services as simony. Even if it had been accepted by the council, its language was too vague and reserved to accomplish this goal.

In the end none of these proposals was enacted in the final decree. The final decree (the fourth of Session 43) is truncated in several ways. The arenga is shorted; the long, explicit listing of ranks of those who can be found guilty is removed and replaced by a short phrase; and the subject matter of the decree is reduced to future simony by the insertion of the word *deinceps* to qualify its measures. The difficulty of dealing with the simony-tainted ordinations and provisions of the Schism had proven insurmountable. With regard to future simony, the final decree contained two main sections: 1) Simoniacal ordinations: Those ordained simoniacally would be suspended immediately from all orders. Hübler notes that this provision tightened the existing law, which required suspension only from the order obtained simoniacally. 2) Simoniacal elections, provisions, etc.: These were declared null and void, *ipso facto*; revenues received by such simoniacal appointees were to be returned; those guilty of giving or receiving simoniacally were to be excommunicated *ipso facto* even if they were of "pontifical or cardinalitian" dignity. Hübler took "pontifical" here to refer to the pope, and said that this decree thus decided the question of whether the pope could commit simony.[34] However, the word pontifical here replaces the words "episcopal, archiepiscopal, patriarchal" in earlier drafts and thus almost certainly does not refer explicitly to the pope. Nor did it really need to; the council had already deposed a pope (John [XXIII]) for simony, among other crimes.

A decree against simony was not a workable way to attack the annates and services. The Basel fathers did not learn from the Constance reformers' experience. They were aware of the Constance deliberations, however. The portion of the Cusa manuscript which contains a copy of the reform committee deliberations was a collection of reform materials assembled for Cardinal Cesarini to aid him in developing his own program of reform at the Council of Basel. Some of the marginal glosses on *Contra labem* in this manuscript were almost certainly made at the Council of Basel (though not in the hand of either Cesarini or of Nicholas Cusanus, the later owner of the manuscript).[35] Among them is a note that stresses the need to declare that papal simony is subject to the decree; however, the glossator adds that this would better be accomplished by a separate decree such as the proposed decree on deposition of the pope (*Romanus pontifex*, Common, c.4). Constance reformers had tried to do that too, also without success, as we shall see in Chapter 5.

5. Conclusion

If we define success as the total abolition of annates, whether by branding them as simony or otherwise, then the reforms of the Council clearly failed. We have seen how narrow a definition that would be, how much it would exclude the really remarkable success of the reformers in significantly reducing the burden of papal taxation and in removing some of the worst abuses connected with curial revenues, even when this resulted in losses of major revenues for pope and cardinals. It is ironic that these very reforms have so

---

[34] Hübler, 147 n.73.
[35] See below, p. 290.

often been dismissed as merely cosmetic, or even singled out as epitomes of the failure of conciliar reform. The success of the reforms is all the more significant because the abuses in these areas were so great; virtually all the powers of the pope had been subjected to misuse for fiscal purposes during the Schism.

Several tiny clauses in fiscal reforms of the decrees and concordats were of momentous importance. *Rationi fore consentaneum et reipublice accommodum*: This phrase describes the abolition by the council of the spoils and procurations (S², c.10), some of the most serious and hated papal fiscal abuses, and shows the role of reason and the common good as unifying themes for the reformers. We shall return to the significance of these words in Chapters 5 and 9. *Debitum huiusmodi in successorem non transeat* (papal *Responsio*, Hübler, 138): By this phrase the pope freed recipients of papal provisions from the obligation to pay accumulated debts of their precedessors for annates. A remarkable reform, but also one which entailed a major conceptual shift on the important legal question of whether annates were an obligation attached to the benefice or the beneficiary. We shall see in Chapter 7 that the opposing opinion of French and German reformers on this question reflects the very great conceptual uncertainty about the whole system of benefices and taxes on benefices. Finally, *praeterquam uigore gratiarum exspectatiuarum* (Papal Responsio, Hübler, 138): This is the phrase that exempted from annates those who acquired their benefices through papal expectancies. An enormous number of benefices was affected, entailing a major loss of revenue to the pope, as we shall see in the next chapter. The significant point here is that Martin V had concluded that the power of patronage was more important than the revenues. A century later, Francis I made a similar decision in the Concordat of Bologna. The reformers at Constance were also well aware of the importance of patronage; one main reason they wanted reform before the election was that they feared the new pope's powers of patronage would make people less willing to pursue reform as zealously. However, their conceptual uncertainty and divided interests on the whole question of benefices and provisions made their reforms of papal patronage a less impressive success than the fiscal reforms. Even here, however, the reforms were far from failures, as I shall now attempt to demonstrate.

CHAPTER FOUR

REFORM OF PAPAL PROVISIONS

Alongside taxation, interference in the filling of church offices is the other principal phenomenon usually cited as an example of the the papal centralization of power in the Middle Ages. In this chapter I will argue that the Constance reforms in this area, like those of papal taxation, were more successful than generally acknowledged, especially when we view these reforms in the light of the complex competing interests of the various groups of reformers. The reformer's rhetoric tended to overstate the extent of papal interference, partially in response to misleading statements of papalist theorists concerning the right of the pope to fill all offices on the basis of the *plenitudo potestatis*. Not only was it difficult to put theory into practice, but even the theory itself seldom envisaged papal appointments as more than exceptions to the normal process. I will examine the rhetoric more closely in Chapter 7. In this chapter I will attempt to provide enough information about the theory and practice to place the reforms in their context.[1]

1. The development of papal provisions

Through papal provisions candidates received offices from the pope that would have under normal circumstances been granted by election or collation of the ordinaries. Our discussion would be easier if we could simply equate provisions with papal appointments; but this is not the case. A provision gave its recipient a right to a benefice (*ius ad rem*), but not secure possession of the benefice (*ius in re*).[2] This is because the pope's right to fill the benefice

---

[1] The major works on papal provisions are Guy Mollat, *La collation des bénéfices ecclésiastiques sous les papes d'Avignon, 1305–1378* (Paris, 1921) and Geoffrey Barraclough, *Papal Provisions: Aspects of Church History Constitutional, Legal and Administrative in the Later Middle Ages* (Oxford, 1935, repr. Westport, Conn., 1971). See also the important recent study concerning the operation of papal provisions in the collegiate churches of Zurich: Andreas Meyer, *Zürich und Rom: Ordentliche Kollatur und päpstliche Provisionen am Frau- und Grossmünster 1316–1523* (Tübingen, 1986).

[2] See Barraclough, *Papal Provisions*, 92–93. A provision was not "a direct administrative order, which admitted neither qualification nor refusal, but a statement of claim which could only be enforced with judicial cognizance."

competed with that of the ordinary collator. Provisions date from at
least the eleventh century; initially they were isolated appointments
to single offices, but soon the popes also reserved at times the right
to make provisions to all the offices in a certain diocese or realm. In
1265, a new phase began as Pope Clement IV in the decretal *Licet
ecclesiarum* (VI 3.4.2) made the first reservation which applied to the
universal church; he reserved the right to make provisions to all
offices vacated by persons who died in the papal curia.

At first, the popes did not justify their provisions on the basis of
the *plenitudo potestatis* to fill *every* office,[3] but rather on their right to
remove a cleric from *any* office; if they could remove from any office,
they could also appoint to any office. Even when canonistic theorists did invoke the *plenitudo potestatis*, their commentaries make it
clear that they did not expect it to be used widely in making
provisions. Indeed, the accepted canonical opinion at the time of
the Council of Constance held that if a papal provision competed
with the collation of an ordinary collator the collation of the ordinary would hold if it was made prior to the papal provision; i.e., the
person collated by the ordinary would not be ejected from his office
by a later papal provision. This was not true, however, in the case
of reserved benefices; here, said the canonists, the hands of the
ordinary were bound, and he was not allowed to collate to the office
before the pope made his provision. The canonists recognized this
as an exception to the *ius commune* of the church.[4] The general

---

Barraclough says that the only right, a *tenue ius*, conveyed by a papal rescript was
the *ius implorandi officium iudicis*. He says this was neither a *ius in re* nor a *ius ad rem*.
However, by the time of the Council of Constance a provision was considered to
convey a *ius ad rem*.

[3] Kenneth Pennington observes that Innocent IV was the first to use the
plenitudo potestatis to justify the exclusive right of the pope to bestow benefices while
a bishop was suspended; see *Pope and Bishops: The Papal Monarchy in the Twelfth and
Thirteenth Centuries* (Philadelphia 1984), 128. Earlier canonists, beginning with
Johannes Teutonicus, had connected papal provisions with the popes' right to
remove any cleric from his office (by calling him to Rome); *ibid.*, 124 and n.37.
Though Johannes remarked that the pope could remove even a bishop, he added
that he could not depose all the bishops, because this would disturb the universal
church (*uniuersalem ecclesiam turbaret*).

[4] Petrus de Ancharano, in his gloss on *Licet* says "In collationibus beneficiorum
uacantium in curia papa nititur ex speciali consuetudine que in hoc est fortior
quam ius commune competens pape in collationibus. quia ius commune facit quod
papa in beneficiis conferendis non irritet collationem ordinarii qui preuenit papam
in conferendo ut c. Dilectus supra eodem tit. sed specialis consuetudo super
uacantibus in curia hic facit plus. quia ligat manus ordinariorum ciuitatis quod
non prodest preuentio ergo potest consuetudo fortificare ius commune et eius
effectum augere: et effectus talis auctus recipit denominationem a consuetudine
non a iure communi ar. ff. de iusti. et iu. l. Ius ciuile [Dig. 1.1.6]. . . ." See Pietro
d'Ancarano, *Lectura super sexto decretalium* (1502). It is important to distinguish the
term *ius commune* here from the term *ius scriptum* (see below, n. 7).

reservation of *Licet ecclesiarum* was justified on the basis, not of the papal plenitude of power, but of a long-standing custom of papal provisions to benefices of clerics who died in the curia. One may surmise that the popes were able to establish this custom because they regularly knew about the vacancy of such benefices well before the ordinary collators did.[5] Despite this long-standing custom, *Licet* was not used in a thoroughgoing manner at first and had to be reinvigorated by the decretal *Presenti* (Boniface VIII, VI 3.4.34), which also expanded the definition of *in curia*.[6]

The decretals *Licet* and *Presenti* had been included in the *Liber sextus* of Boniface VIII and had thus become part of what the Constance reformers called the *ius scriptum*.[7] These reformers made a clear distinction between them and the subsequent general reservations, which were promulgated either in papal chancery rules or in decretals which were included in the Extravagantes collections. The chancery rules were by their nature temporary, valid only during the pontificate of the pope who issued them, but three pivotal *extravagantes* had a greater claim to permanency.

Exsecrabilis, issued by John XXII, November 19, 1317, and included in the *Extravagantes Joannis XXII*,[8] was ostensibly a measure directed against pluralism (the holding by a single individual of more than one benefice with cure of souls). Its practical effect, however, was to multiply considerably the numbers of papal provisions because it reserved to the pope the right to fill all the excess benefices which the pluralists were required to vacate.[9]

Ex debito, another decretal of John XXII,[10] formed the fundamental turning point in papal provisions, according to Guy Mollat.[11] Whereas the provisions made on the basis of reservations

---

[5] The ordinaries, however, had begun maintaining permanent procurators in the curia, so that they could make collations to offices vacant in curia before the pope did. It was partly to combat this that Clement enacted the general reservation of *Licet*; see Meyer, *Zürich*, 2.

[6] See Mollat, *Collation*, 10. Henceforth, *in curia* meant either at the papal residence or at the apostolic chancery or at a distance of two days' journey (40 Roman miles) from either.

[7] It is important to distinguish this term from that of the *ius commune* as used in the gloss of Petrus d'Ancharano cited in n. 3 above. Some reformers, such as Dietrich of Niem, used the term *ius commune* in place of the term *ius scriptum*, and others spoke of the *ius commune scriptum*; Hübler, following Bickell, used the two terms interchangeably.

[8] *Extrav. Io. XXII* 9, ed. Jacqueline Tarrant (Città del Vaticano 1983) 190–198.

[9] Mollat, *Collation*, 25–26.

[10] It was not included in his *Extravagantes* collection, however, but rather in the *Extravagantes communes* (Extrav. comm. 1.3.4)

[11] Mollat, *Collation*, 12. Meyer questions the importance attributed to this decretal by scholars, but he is talking about the situation in Germany. That in France was much different.

in *Licet* had affected relatively few benefices, *Ex debito* gravely hurt the rights of the ordinary collators. *Licet* had touched only benefices vacated by death; *Ex debito* reserved for the pope the right to provide to benefices vacated by resignation. Thus the benefices held by cardinals and curial officials became the pope's to grant out again, and from the time of John XXII a major increase in papal provisions is observable.

Ad regimen (Benedict XII, January 11, 1335, *Extrav. comm.* 3.3.13) was essentially a restatement of the reservations of *Praesenti* and *Ex debito* with a few additions and was thus the decretal which contained the most comprehensive collection of reservations; it was to *Ad regimen* that the Constance reformers thus directed their principal attention.

There was very good basis in canonistic legal theory for the demand that all the reservations not included in the *ius scriptum* be abolished. Such a demand was heard often at Constance. When Cardinal Adimari argued for retaining the reservations of the decretal *Ad regimen*, his justification was that it was so moderate *and established by custom that it can be taken for law*.[12] Thus, he tacitly acknowledged that it was not yet generally accepted as part of the *ius scriptum*, and, in arguing that it should be so accepted, he did not base his argument on the *plenitudo potestatis*, but rather on a long-standing custom (the same rationale that had been used earlier to justify the reservations of *Licet ecclesiarum*).

Another form of provision known as expectancies (*gratia expectativa*) may have been an even greater target for the reformers than the reservations. Here the provision was based not on a the pope's competition with the ordinary's collation to a vacant benefice (provision *iure concursus*) or on the pope's right to fill a reserved benefice (provision *iure reservationis*), but on the pope's granting of a grace to an individual to fill the next benefice which becomes vacant in the future in his diocese. Hence they may be called provisions *iure praeventionis*.[13]

The expectancy was thus a future interest, less certain than a provision to a specific reserved benefice.[14] It frequently happened that the bearer of an expectancy failed to receive the next available

---

[12] See below, p. 82.

[13] On expectancies, see Mollat, *Collation*, 31–34; Sabine Weiss, "Päpstliche Expectanzen in Theorie und Praxis," in *Ecclesia peregrinans: Josef Lenzenweger zum 70. Geburtstag*, ed. Karl Amon, et al. (Vienna, 1986), 143–152. See also the section in Meyer, *Zurich*, 29–32.

[14] The following explanation is based on Sabine Weiss's illuminating study cited in n. 13 above; see especially p. 151.

benefice; however, in this case the expectancy did not become invalid, but still authorized the holder to another vacant benefice. Thus it offered more security than a provision to a specific benefice *iure concursus*, where in the event of an alternate collation by the ordinary the providee faced a long, costly, and possibly unsuccessful legal battle. For a cleric who already had a good income, the expectancy offered a good possibility of increasing that income. Thus, in a curious manner the expectancies functioned somewhat like shares in the futures markets today. They were often acquired by persons who were already well endowed and who wished to seek security against the uncertainty of future investments. It is ironic that expectancies had been at least partly intended for poor clerics; one form of expectancy was specifically designated *in forma pauperum*. (However, studies have shown that this type of expectancy became increasingly rare.)[15] Expectancies were avidly sought by clerics. Whole groups of persons were regularly issued expectancies *en bloc*; the most notable of these mass grants were those given to the persons listed on the *rotuli* submitted by universities and by princes.[16]

Treating expectancies as forms of papal provision will prove helpful in understanding the Constance reforms. In his recent ground-breaking study Andreas Meyer does so, and is able to draw some important conclusions about the effects of these reforms. The picture that will emerge after our analysis of the reforms will be strikingly similar to that found in the case of the tax reforms.

2. The reform committee deliberations concerning provisions

The records of the first reform committee in E and S contain a schedule which appears to be a combination of two earlier schedules, one submitted by the English nation, the other by Alemanno Adimari, the Cardinal of Pisa.[17] Out of the twenty-four paragraphs

---

[15] Weiss, "Expektanzen," 149; Baix, *Libri*, cxciv.

[16] On the university *rotuli*, see Rashdall, *The Universities of Europe in the Middle Ages*, ed. F.M. Powicke and A.B. Emden (Oxford, 1936), 1:555–558; for English rotuli in this period, see E.F. Jacob, "Petitions for Benefices from English Universities during the Great Schism," *Royal Historical Society Transactions*, 4th ser., v. 27 (1945), 41–59.

[17] Each of these two earlier schedules was a comprehensive list of specific reforms; all of these were included in the composite schedule, but the preamble of the English proposal, which offered theoretical justification for the reforms, was dropped, and six additional sub-paragraphs of specific reforms were added, the source of which is uncertain. The composite schedule, which consists of twenty-

of this composite proposal six deal directly with either papal rights of provision (Para. 11 and 12) or expectancies (Para. 5–8). The remainder (with the exception of Para. 13 on the common services) deal chiefly with the promotion of graduates to office. The measures concerning provisions and expectancies were all part of the proposal originally submitted by Adimari early in the deliberations of the first reform committee (August 28, 1417) and were referred to subsequently as the proposals made by the cardinals of the first reform committee. Adimari wanted to retain the reservations of *Ad regimen* but not allow any others outside the *ius scriptum* (such as those of the chancery rules.) He wanted to eliminate some of the abuses connected with expectancies by having them granted more moderately and excluding expectancies to priories and elective dignities (the highest offices in cathedral and collegiate churches). Monasteries and cathedral chapters with revenues of less than 100 fl. were to be guaranteed the right to elect their abbots and bishops. The reform committee strengthened these latter measures considerably when it included them in the composite proposal[18] (See Table 1).

The German nation took a much more extreme position[19] than Adimari's; they called for an end to all reservations not included in the *corpus iuris*, restoration of all rights of election with confirmation to be made by immediate superiors, and no use of expectancies for elective benefices. And they demanded that any future general reservations be made only with conciliar "declaration, authority, consent, and approval." Indeed, these reformers demanded an exception even to the reservations of the corpus iuris: collation of

---

four sub-paragraphs, does not appear as a separate chapter in E or W, but is added without rubric after the chapter concerning parish priests unable to speak the vernacular language of their parishioners (the point at which C ends). The marginal notes indicate considerable disagreement and debate within the committee concerning many of the specific reforms in the schedule. At the beginning of the schedule in E and W appears a note which Finke did not edit: "XIII Septembris conclusum quod tota ista materia referatur ad nacions (!)". Hardt printed this note in his edition, but for "nacions" he has "vacationes". Some of the specific reforms listed in the composite schedule also appear in D.

[18] Even though it dropped his restriction on expectancies to poorer benefices. These differences are not apparent in Finke's edition because he does not edit Adimari's proposal or give the alternate readings from Adimari's proposal in his edition of the composite proposal, even though Adimari's proposal appears as part of the reform deliberations in D and S!

[19] *Hardt*.1.Prolegomena.32. Finke's inclusion of the German nation's demands among the reform committee deliberations is somewhat puzzling, since there is no evidence that they were submitted to the reform committee; they do, however, provide a good benchmark for the strength of the German nation's opposition to reservations and expectatives.

TABLE 1

Proposals for reform of papal provisions

	Adimari	Composite	Concordats
Reservations	Ius scriptum+ *Ad regimen*	Same as Adimari	Ius scriptum+ *Ad regimen* w/ modifications+ *Exsecrabilis*
Elections	Free election in bishoprics and abbacies w/revenues <100 fl.	Free election in all bishoprics and abbacies	Free election to all **non-reserved** bishoprics and abbacies
Confirmations	Pope confirms all elections	Ordinaries confirm elections for bishoprics and abbacies w/ revenues <100 fl.	Ordinaries confirm elections to poorer abbacies (<200 fl. in France; <100 fl. in Spain); pope confirms elections to other abbacies and to bishoprics
Expectancies	Moderation Only to one benefice Limit on early dating Not to elective dignities or benefices <10 marks revenue	Same; except that no restriction on expectancies to benefices with <10 marks revenue	Not to certain monastic offices or to offices in charitable institutions (different for each concordat)
Other			*Ius alternativum*—pope has right to grant one-half of all non-reserved benefices (with some exceptions)

the benefices of cardinals, even of those dying in Rome, would revert to the ordinaries.[20]

This strong divergence of opinion must have prevented any further action in the first reform committee on any of the measures;

---

[20] They complained that the cardinals were trying to establish the custom that such benefices could only be granted out to other cardinals. At the same time they asked that each cardinal be guaranteed an annual income of between three and four thousand florins from the papal chamber.

the word "expeditus" does not appear next to any of them in W[1]. The marginal notes on the paragraphs concerning expectancies in the composite proposal in manuscripts E and W[1] are indicative. "The opinions were varied. Some (the majority) liked the text; some wanted them limited, others that the matter not be discussed. Finally it was concluded to defer the matter."

The second reform committee took up all the points in the composite program again and appears to have recommended their approval after making some important modifications.[21] Papal confirmation of episcopal elections was restored, but other collegiate churches and monasteries with revenues less than 500 fl. (rather than 100 fl. as before), as well as all nunneries, were to be guaranteed their rights of election.

Let us glance ahead to the results of the negotiations as they were concluded in the concordats of 1418. I have summarized these very briefly in the third column of Table 1. Though some of the reforms emerged stronger than in Adimari's original proposal,[22] they were still quite far from what the German nation, for example, had wanted. Also, a new factor had entered the equation—the *ius alternativum*, which gave the the pope the right to fill one-half of all non-reserved benefices.[23] Was this the price for the strengthening of other reforms? If so, past judgments of the overall failure of these reforms would appear to be largely justified.

3. The significance of the ius alternativum

The recent study of the operation of papal provisions in Zurich by Andreas Meyer is of great value because it considers the effects of papal provisions over the entire period from 1316 to 1523 as part of the larger picture of appointments to all the benefices in the two major Zurich collegiate churches. By looking at each recipient of a papal provision to see whether or not the provision resulted in his obtaining a benefice, Meyer is able to give reliable data on the success rate of the different kinds of papal provisions. Between 1316 and 1448, the success rate for expectancies was 28.1% (55 of the

---

[21] The evidence for the deliberations is found only in W[2] (fol. 2v) in two short schedules which deal with major and minor benefices respectively. It is possible, but unlikely, that these stem from the third, rather than the second, committee.

[22] For example, the number of curial officials whose benefices were subject to reservation was limited by placing limits on the numbers of these officials. This was, in effect, at the same time a reform of the curia; see below p. 124 n. 57.

[23] It was introduced in one of the two short schedules presented to the second reform committee; see above, n. 21 and below, p. 97.

196 recorded). This was less than half the success rate of provisions made on the basis of reservations (62.3%).[24] (On the other hand, it was more than twice as great as that for provisions made *iure concursus* on non-reserved benefices [13.6%]; in fact, only three benefices were obtained in this latter manner during the entire 150 year period, a clear indication of the extraordinary nature of such provisions noted in the canonistic theory discussed above.)[25] Meyer also analyzes the reasons for failure of provisions. In the case of expectancies, the largest number failed when they were annulled by the next pope; i.e., the holder of the expectancy was unable to use it before the pope who granted it had died because more expectancies had been granted than could be used during his pontificate.[26] This helps explain why the reformers were so concerned about moderating the number of expectancies.[27]

The greatest anger against expectancies may well have come from those whose expectancies failed. Of course, a person who obtained an expectancy relatively late in a given pontificate must have known that his chances of failure were greater than for others with earlier dates. However, by means of an *anteferri* clause or other special prerogative one could be advanced ahead of those who actually held earlier dates. Clerics with a special relationship to the curia or with greater knowledge of the law had an advantage in obtaining such prerogatives.[28] Those passed over by such string-pulling must have been triply angry. The whole process must have seemed to them more and more like a rigged lottery.

Because Meyer treats papal expectancies as a type of provision, he is thus able to measure their importance in comparison with the other forms of collation, papal and otherwise. His results are very significant for our understanding of the effects of the Constance

---

[24] Pp. 86–87.

[25] P. 91.

[26] Expectancies *in forma pauperum* seem to have been granted more sparingly (although Meyer acknowledges that the records of such expectancies have not been as well maintained as those for other types), and thus enjoyed a much greater success rate (13 were recorded between 1316 and 1365; of these 8 or 61.5% were successful). The cost of obtaining an expectancy *in forma pauperum* was also much less (8 as opposed to 20 grossi). However, it became increasingly difficult to use expectancies *in forma pauperum* for the highest offices because they were taken by those holding expectancies with *anteferri clauses*. See p. 81.

[27] In her article on expectancies, Weiss cites a sobering statistic reported by Diener: Pope John [XXIII] issued between 14,000 and 15,000 expectancies in the first year of his pontificate alone. See Heinrich Diener, "Rubrizellen zu Kanzleiregistern Johanns XXIII. und Martins V.," *QFIAB* 39 (1959) 123, cited by Weiss, 143.

[28] Pp. 87–88. "Suppliken um Prärogativen sind also ein Kennzeichen für 'Insider'".

TABLE 2

Zurich provisions

Benifices granted on basis of:	No/Yr
1. Papal provision *iure reservationis* (except by resignation *in manibus papae*):	1.3
2. By resignation *in manibus papae:*	.7
3. Permutations	2.4
4. Expectancies	4.0

reforms: Almost twice as many benefices in Zurich were filled by expectancies (*iure praeventionis*) as by provisions based on reservations (*iure reservationis*). Because so many of the papal provisions were made by expectancies and because their method of application was so subject to abuse and resulting outrage, the reforms of expectancies at Constance were of crucial importance. And here Meyer's study also makes it very clear that the institution of the *ius alternativum* in the Constance reforms was aimed precisely at the benefices touched by papal expectancies; moreover, he shows that this reform measure together with subsequent papal enactments based on it did significantly reduce the number of offices obtained by expectancies in Zurich, thus helping to restore the collation rights of the ordinaries there.[29]

Meyer calculates the number of benefices filled per year by the major types of extra-ordinary collation; Table 2 summarizes his findings.[30]

Meyer's records show that during the 207-year time span of his study a minimum of 1093 collations were made, and of the 324 cases in which the basis for collation is known, 149 were made by papal provision.[31] Since it is safe to assume that few of those benefices for which the basis of collation is not known were made by papal provision, it seems likely that the ordinaries had control of more than three-quarters of the collations. However, the papal provisions affected disproportionately the benefices with the

---

[29] Pp. 172–173. See also his more general comments about the effects of the concordats in "Das Wiener Konkordat von 1448—eine erfolgreiche Reform des Spätmittelalters," *QFIAB* 66 (1986) 108–152 at 123.

[30] Compiled from data on pp. 102 and 156.

[31] Pp. 158–160.

greatest revenues; Meyer shows that a full 55.4% of the canons in the Grossmünster received their benefices through papal provisions during the 207 year period.[32] In fact, during the period of the Avignon papacy and the schism almost all the canonries were filled by papal provisions (mostly expectancies), with two brief exceptions—the pontificate of Benedict XII (who was known for his austerity and reform) and that of Urban VI (when the ordinaries were able to benefit from the uncertainty of conditions at the beginning of the schism).[33] The papal provisions changed the composition of the chapter greatly. Meyer shows that during the period 1320 to 1400 the percentage of canons who belonged to families of Zurich's ruling class (Ratsfähige) shrank from 58% to 8.7%.[34]

We might suspect that most of the newcomers were curial officials, but Meyer shows that this is not the case.[35] His finding is important, because it shows that for Zurich the effects of *Ad regimen* were not so marked as they were in France, for example.[36] As a result of that decretal, the granting of benefices to curial officials through papal provisions virtually insured that those benefices would remain the pope's to grant in the future. Reformers from churches like those of Zurich would have been much less concerned about attacking *Ad regimen* than reformers from churches with high numbers of benefices in the hands of curial officials.

There were other things about Zurich which may have made it less than typical. Not only were there relatively few benefices in the hands of curials (Meyer mentions none in the hands of cardinals) to provoke anti-Roman sentiment; but also there was no papal-episcopal tension involved in the filling of benefices. Since Zurich had no cathedral church, its chief benefices were found in its two collegiate churches. Its diocesan bishop was the bishop of Constance, and he filled very few of the benefices in the Zurich collegiate churches. Overall, the "benefice chase" in Zurich seems to have been much more sedate than in many other places. Meyer shows

---

[32] Pp. 168–169 and Table 19.

[33] Pp. 163–4.

[34] Pp. 169–170. Meyer observes that the proportion of canons drawn from ruling class families did not rise steadily until after 1450, since the vast majority of the canons in the years following the Constance reforms were still of non-Zurich origin and thus would not be inclined to choose new canons from the Zurich ruling class.

[35] On the number of canonries held by curial officials, see pp. 75–78.

[36] This leads Meyer to underestimate the importance of the reservations of *Ex debito* noted by Mollat; see *Zurich*, 36–37. *Ex debito* was the decretal which initially established the reservation of benefices of curial officials who died outside Rome or who resigned their benefices.

that in Zurich the canon law with regard to ecclesiastical appointments was observed scrupulously; there were relatively few irregu-
lar activities and few disputed successions and trials compared with
many dioceses.[37] The scrupulousness with which the law was
observed at Zurich makes it possible for the historian to observe the
system working as intended; it also reminds us that we cannot
assume that the Zurich situation is representative of the wider state
of the church. Unfortunately, there are no other studies of the
operation of papal provisions that are comparable to Meyer's. The
works of Baix and Weiss suggest, however, that the situation was
quite different in other areas.[38] The differences remind us that
reformers from these different areas shared correspondingly different interests.

The study of Françoix Baix of the operation of papal provisions
in the Low Countries during the pontificate of Martin V reveals a
very intense competition for benefices.[39] Recipients of papal provisions often had great difficulty in making effective use of them. The
candidate of the ordinaries often took possession first and thus had
a much more favorable position in any legal battle. Moreover, even
if a papal providee was successful in court, it was difficult for him to
have the favorable judgment enforced against a candidate already
in possession. Baix's study shows how often papal provisions were
issued as *novae provisiones*, i.e. confirmations of rights already
granted, in cases where these rights had been contested. Sometimes
such *novae provisiones* were acquired by persons who had already
received a papal expectancy or other provision but had found
themselves confronted by one or more other claimants to the benefice. Sometimes clerics collated by the ordinaries actually sought
a *nova provisio* from the pope for the same benefice in order to
obviate all possible contest from rival claimants. As many as six or
eight contestants might struggle for the same benefice. In such
contests the rival claimants would often relinquish their claims
through composition (often in exchange for a pension from the benefice's revenues). In such instances a remaining claimant might seek
a papal provision *per modum surrogationis* (in which the cleric receiving
the provision was substituted for the one who relinquished his rights,
but must still pursue his rights against other competitors).

---

[37] Meyer, *Zurich*, 111–114.
[38] The conciliar reform documents themselves suggest this; note the stark
contrast of the situation in the Rhineland described in the documents discussed
below, p. 93.
[39] Baix, cxxii–clxxxvi; see also Weiss, 147–148.

The studies of Meyer, Baix, and Weiss thus suggest that, in the reforms of provisions just as in the tax reforms, part of the difference in interests among reformers was regional; i.e., the reformers had different interests according to the different ways in which provisions operated in their regions. Peter Pulka's report on the deliberations also suggests this. He noted an interesting split in the negotiations concerning reservations that became evident after the papal election. The German and French nations still wanted to limit reservations to those of the *ius scriptum*, but the English, Italian, and Spanish nations now joined in opposing such a limitation. The German and French Avisamenta confirm their common front here. The split among nations on this crucial issue is strikingly different from the earlier North-South split which Hübler had observed. Pulka's explanation of the divergent stances[40] suggests that the English abandoned their effort to achieve a general reform of reservations and had come to rely instead on the "observations of their own kingdom"—i.e., the statute of provisors, which—as recent studies show—worked quite effectively in preventing papal reservations in England.[41] Other regional differences help explain the split. The revenues of Spanish and Italian benefices were much smaller on the average than those in Germany and France and thus not as much was at stake in the reservations there.[42] On the other hand, the strong interest in reform of reservations in France reflects

---

[40] Pulka, Letter of December 27, 1417, p. 62: Volente natione Italica ut omnes collationes remanerent apud papam sicut hucusque ab editione Sexti et Clementinarum, quibus consentiebant Anglici salvis tamen observationibus sui regni et Hyspani simpliciter. Sed natio Gallicana et nostra volebant eas reduci ad ordinarios juxta jura antiqua quemadmodum etiam mater nostra universitas ante censebat processu tamen temporis Gallici fuissent et hodie essent contenti, quod 3^{tia} pars collationum apud ordinarios libere remaneret. Cardinales concordabant cum Italicis addentes reservationes certas ultra comprehensas in corpore juris videlicet omnium ecclesiarum cathedralium et aliarum praelaturarum valentium anno ultra 300 florenos omnium secundariarum post pontificales dignitatum et certorum canonicatuum etc.

[41] Margaret Harvey, "The Benefice as Property: An Aspect of Anglo-Papal Relations During the Pontificate of Martin V (1417–1431)" in *The Church and Wealth*, ed. W.J. Sheils and Diana Wood. (Oxford, 1987), 161–173, at 163, who cites the study of Robin L. Storey, "Clergy and the Common Law in the Reign of Henry IV," *Medieval Legal Records edited in Memory of C.A.F. Meekings*, ed. R.F. Hunnisett and J.B. Post (London, 1978), 342–408.

[42] Twice in the deliberations Spain and Italy are treated differently on the basis of the smaller revenues of their benefices. In Adimari's proposal (also later in the Responsio) that expectancies be granted to only one benefice, they may be granted to two benefices in parts of Italy and Spain. Also in the Responsio elections in monasteries with revenues less than 150 livres tournois in France, but less than 60 liv. in Spain and Italy, were exempted from papal confirmation. In the concordats these limits were further modified to 200 liv. in France and 100 in Spain.

the situation we have already observed above—that papal reservations and the taxation associated with them had grown faster there
during the Avignon papacy and the Schism than almost anywhere
else.

It was natural for the divergent interests among the reformers to
become expressed as "national differences" during the Constance
negotiations, since the council fathers were organized by nations.
However, what appear to be national differences were really regional ones, having to do with the different functioning of the papal
provisions in different regions; and the regional differences were
intertwined with other differences of interests, chiefly those of the
prelates and universities. Here again Pulka offers keen insight. In
both the French and German nations the prelates and universities
clashed on the reform of provisions; however, the clash was different in each nation.[43] The French universities, especially Paris, did
not want to limit expectancies, because they deeply distrusted the
prelates and believed the university rotuli were the best way to
secure benefices for graduates. Many of the German university
members regarded the expectancies as very unreliable (the studies
of Weiss and Meyer suggest why) and preferred to require that a
certain quota of benefices in each church be filled by graduates.
This would be "a better and more stable provision because it would
rest on certain law and not purely on grace." The introduction of
the *ius alternativum* into the negotiations complicated the situation.
Pulka tells us that the German prelates were able strongly to resist
the quotas, saying that they would only agree to them if the papal
expectancies were much more sharply limited—to no more than
two expectancies affecting the collations of each ordinary collator,
as the German nation had originally proposed. Pulka's picture of
the deliberations shows that the universities increasingly lost
ground in the negotiations. The expectancies they had often
counted on would not be worth as much in the future. Fewer
benefices would be subject to them, both because the effort to limit

---

[43] Pulka, 62–63: Nam Galliae repugnantes suis praelatis suadent expediens
fore collationes remanere apud papam juxta voluntatem Italicorum etc. sibi
consentaneorum, et Parisienses dicunt se hoc habere in suis capitulis et instruc-
tionibus juratis et ideo non posse in alium modum consentire; allegantes se prius
sensisse, quod praelati non servaverint eis promissa de quotis collationum in
synodo Gallicana assignatis. Aliquibus vero de universitatibus Germaniae apparet
hoc reformationi ecclesiae plurimum derogare. Nec pro promotione universitatum
expediens attento quod hucusque per rotulos et gratias expectativas modicum
nimis est ipsis provisum, sed quod si deputaretur 6ta pars in kathedralibus et 4ta in
aliis, esset provisio melior et stabilior, quia certo jure subnixa et non pure de
gratia.

other kinds of papal provisions had been blunted considerably and because the *ius alternativum* had returned to the ordinaries one-half of the collations subject to expectancies.[44] The universities also lost ground in their effort to enact the reforms that would directly support the promotion of graduates.

4. Promotion of graduates

Interestingly, the initial and in some ways the most persistent support for the promotion of graduates came from the cardinals. Adimari's proposal contained a number of paragraphs on this matter, which were debated and refined by the first reform committee. Even after these had been abandoned by the nations in their Avisamenta they were revived, almost verbatim, in the papal Responsio. Adimari's proposals sought to advance graduates in two ways: 1) by requiring a minimum level of learning for each of the higher church offices and 2) by insuring that a certain quota of offices in cathedral and collegiate churches would be filled by graduates. The English proposal also sought to advance graduates, in a somewhat different and vaguer manner.[45] The deliberations of the first reform committee consisted of refinement of these rules.

In the second reform committee the promotion of graduates was addressed in a separate schedule (*Licet divina*, S[2], c.5) which had the form of a proposed final decree. Though graced with an elaborate preamble, the specific provisions of the decree were much weaker than the earlier efforts. All that remained were the minimum education requirements for bishops and for only those abbots who were heads of orders. The provisions concerning minimal requirements for the other major dignities in cathedral churches and minimum quotas of graduates in these churches were quickly added back in, but there was no mention of collegiate or parish

---

[44] Letter of March 1, p. 68: Verum multis apparet quod expectativae gratiae sint minus quam antea valiturae. Nam ordinarii habebunt medietatem suarum collationum libere [as a result of the *ius alternativum*] ... Ex qua alternatione aestimantur lites multiplicandae etc. Sunt etiam certa beneficia pro graduatis deputata sed pauciora quam alias potuissemus obtinuisse si tunc non fuissemus inixi gratiis expectativis; sunt etiam reservationes multae gratiis expectativis derogantes.

[45] It called on the pope and the ordinary collators to advance graduates, according to the principle that, other things being equal, a graduate should be preferred to a non-graduate (and a local boy to an outsider); and it showed special concern that graduates so appointed reside and impart their learning by teaching and administering. Specifically, it called for one out of every four vacant benefices to be conferred upon graduates who as yet had not been promoted.

churches, and the mandatory quota of graduates in cathedral
churches was now one-sixth instead of one-fourth. Even this watered-
down version encountered fatal opposition. The German nation
voted it down; the only changes it requested in the existing canon
law were the one-sixth quota of graduates in cathedral churches,[46]
and the general statement that, other things being equal, *doctores*
should be favored in promotion. The reasons for their opposition to
further change were not stated, but several qualifications added to
the original decree in the reform committee suggest clues. One
stated that for benefices without care of souls literate non-graduates
were acceptable, *especially nobles* (emphasis mine). Another made
exception for all reasonable rules laid down by the founders of the
benefices and all rights of lay patronage. Most revealing is a
qualification (Postilla) which allowed for the promotion of literate
non-graduates even to episcopal or higher dignities if they were of
royal, ducal, or comital blood. Hermann Heimpel has argued
persuasively that Job Vener was the author of this "Postilla."[47] Not
that Job was himself such a blue-blood; though his family were
comfortable "urban aristocrats," they were hardly among the feudal *potentes*. According to Heimpel, Job was motivated rather by
pragmatism, by a sense of tradition, and by his personal friendship
for Bishop Hraban of Speyer, a shining example of the kind of
literate, noble non-graduate for which Job had made exception in
his postilla. I would stress the first motivation. The practically
minded reformer was almost certainly trying to blunt the opposition which he foresaw in the German nation.

Heimpel's argument is buttressed by his very fine analysis of a
related reform avisamentum presented to the second reform committee, an avisamentum which we know certainly to be the work of
Job himself (D^2, c.7). It appears immediately preceding *Licet divina*
in D^2 and, as *Licet divina*, deals with the lack of sufficient education
of the higher clergy. Job laments that this is a particular problem in
Germany because there "one's lack of learning is not made up for
by the perfection of one's charity, but by the nobility of one's blood
and the power of one's friends." Heimpel explains the felicitous
irony of this wording which plays upon the the words of Innocent
III in the decretal *Nisi cum pridem* (X 1.9.10). Innocent, citing 1
Cor. 8,1 ("Whereas knowledge inflates, love upbuilds"),[48] had
stated the principle "Completeness of love can make up for incomplete learning." Job was also acutely aware, however, that it was

---

[46] For the German nation, *baccalaurei formati* could qualify as graduates.
[47] Heimpel, *Vener*, 2:736–743.
[48] Scientia inflat, caritas autem aedificat.

unrealistic to expect too sweeping changes. He remarked that the pivotal decretal concerning educational standards (X 1.6.19 *Cum nobis olim*) had spoken in a somewhat lax manner, and that the decretalists had explained that it is permissible to dispense with the requirement for learning in a powerful noble appointee, if otherwise the temporalities of the church might be placed in danger. Job's language is again ironic and understated.

What Job really means is probably this: Only appointees with sufficient feudal clout could protect the rights and possessions of many German churches against the predatory rapaciousness of their fellow nobles. A revealing passage in a letter written by Cologne University's envoys reflects the very real dangers: Powerful nobles extort the promotion of their family and friends by the ordinaries. If such noble appointees find themselves rejected in favor of non-noble graduates, they and their powerful friends and families immediately avenge themselves against the temporalities of the church by arson, plunder, and pillage.[49] Job does not mention such activities in his avisamentum, but he does list other characteristics of these noble bishops which disturb him greatly (and here his understatement is expressed only in the qualifying words "in aliquibus partibus" and "nonnulli"):

> Some are totally illiterate, not ordained, always engaged in war and military activities; many seldom or never exercise their pontifical duties, celebrate orders, preach or make visitations, as they are bound to do, but they commit the first duties of their office to titular bishops, even to lightweight persons and officials or vicars, and they do personally that which is accessory to the office and which ought to be done by others or not at all. Day and night they strain after profane and secular pleasures and activities and never remember that they have been set apart to be holy by the profession which they have made.

---

[49] Martène and Durand, *Thesaurus* 2:1686: "Si ordinarii collatores haberent collationes [beneficiorum] tot ad eos venirent preces armatae dominorum, nobilium et ruterorum, quod non possent de eis disponere ad utilitatem ecclesiarum, nec conferre ea dignis et bene meritis; sed oporteret condescendere precibus eorum, nec in hoc satisfacerent: quia ubi complacerent uni, displicerent aliis; et illi statim se vindicarent incendiis, rapinis, et bona ecclesiarum et maxime collegiatarum et monasteriorum in brevi funditus destruerentur." The Cologne envoys use this argument to support the maintenance of papal provisions. A set of reform proposals from the summer of 1417 at Constance presents a similar picture of the intimidation of the church by powerful noble patrons who present "pro rectoribus seu vicariis perpetuis instituendis et investiendis milites, nobiles, armigeros, puros laicos, puros inhabiles, indoctos, illiteratos, ymmo aliqui eorum ignotos, profugatos, distulos, apostatas et discurrentes. Et nisi episcopus tales sic investiat, dicti patroni laici per potenciam [et] tyrannidem eorum dicto episcopo et ecclesie sue minas imponunt et lites ac guerras movere nituntur . . ." (ACC.4.740–741).

What does Job's proposal present as a solution? Simply a conciliar decree that bishops must perform the principal duties of their
office personally and that in the future only suitable persons be
advanced to the episcopal office, their suitability to be determined
by the inquiries required by canon law. These measures are to be
enforced by severe penalties to be prescribed by the council, and
the decree is to be published two or three times each year, and
especially just before any election. As Heimpel points out, Job does
not insist here on any explicit educational requirement for bishops;
he merely insists that they be "suitable" (*ydonee*). But I believe
Heimpel goes too far in saying that Job accepts the "Adelsprinzip"
here, that "Job's ideal is the bishop who is qualified through both
noble ancestry and suitability—and, by virtue of suitability, also
through education." The proposal contains no such statement; in
fact, its opening words suggest strongly that the bad bishops are the
ones who have been advanced through their noble blood and
powerful connections. If Job did not insist upon educational qualifications here, it was not because of his approval of the "Adelsprinzip," but because he was in the employ of a secular prince and
because his practical sense told him that the German nation at
Constance would not accept the preferment of graduates over
nobles in promotions to the highest offices. It was for the same
reasons that he sought to add the postilla to *Licet divina eloquia*.[50]
The postilla was voted down by the majority of the reform committee. In turn, *Licet divina* was voted down by the German nation.

We have no record of the debate on *Licet divina* in the French
nation. But we know that a similar struggle between nobles and
non-noble graduates eventually prevented that nation from enacting any measures concerning educational requirements for the
clergy in their final concordat with Martin.[51] The conflicts between
graduates and other providees in the French kingdom are very

---

[50] See the letter of the envoys of the University of Cologne to their university,
Martène and Durand, *Thesaurus*, 2:1686. The envoys say that they cannot openly
support the opposition of the University of Paris to the collations made by the
ordinaries; to do so would be too dangerous.

[51] See Hübler, 200: "Quia circa qualitates graduatorum nobiliumque et liter-
atorum ad effectum promotionis eorum ad dignitates honores et beneficia ecclesiastica, quorum suffragiis indigere noscitur ecclesia, nondum haberi potuit plenaria
concordia, dominus noster cum deputandis ad hoc per nationes singulas quantum
fieri commode poterit providebit." This passage is the interim draft of the French
concordat published by Hardt and Mansi from a transcription made by Schelstrate of the copy in Paris, BN lat. 14457—the same collection of Plumetot which
contains the French Avisamenta and the *Instructiones*. The note is not found in the
manuscripts of the final concordat. See above, p. 46 n.61.

clearly revealed in the arrangements established after the withdrawal of obedience in 1398 and after the neutrality legislation of 1407.[52] In the first case, the ordinary collators were instructed to provide vacant benefices alternately to candidates of the universities and candidates of the king and princes. In 1408 this was modified so that the ordinary collators would name a university candidate one out of every three times; one of the other two times, they had to appoint candidates of the king or princes, but the third time they could name their own candidates. The failure of the Constance reform committee's efforts to guarantee the promotion of graduates must have played a substantial role in the opposition of the universities at Constance to the more extreme reform measures for returning collation rights of the bishops. The poor spiritual qualities of the noble bishops in Germany, as outlined in Job's avisamentum, certainly dampened the enthusiasm of the German universities.

Conversely, the prelates opposed the reforms which would have guaranteed offices to graduates. This is probably why there is no mention of them in the Avisamenta of either the French or German nation. As if confirming the commitment of the Holy See to advance graduates, the cardinals on the reform committee and the new pope Martin V were the leading advocates of the reforms concerning educational requirements of the clergy. Even after the nations had abandoned these, Martin V revived them in his *Responsio*. With one exception, the nations again abandoned them in the concordats. The one exception was the German concordat. Peter Pulka relates the intense struggle of German graduates to salvage as much as possible of these reforms.[53] They had requested one-sixth of the benefices in cathedral churches and one-quarter of benefices in collegiate churches, but they had to settle for only one-sixth in both categories. They had also wanted important parish churches to be conferred to graduates and here they even had to haggle over the size of the churches; the prelates said only churches with more than 3,000 communicants, the universities finally won approval for churches with more than 2,000. Further struggles occurred concerning how the quotas were to be reached.

---

[52] On these matters, see Joseph Sznuro, "Les origines du droit d'alternative bénéficiale," *Revue des sciences religieuses* 5 (1925) 1–13, 389–415; 6 (1926) 1–25. On the 1399 arrangements, pp. 8–9; on the 1408 revision, p. 394.

[53] Pulka, 69–70.

5. *Outcome of the negotiations*

All this intense haggling was only part of even more complicated interlocking negotiations concerning the whole package of reforms on provisions. In the end, the nations all allowed the reservations of *Ad regimen* to remain; however, limits were placed on the benefices subject to *Ad regimen* by specifying the maximum number of curial officials of each type whose benefices would be subject to papal reservations when vacated. In particular, the benefices of honorary chaplains (unless these were graduates) were totally excluded. The popes of the Schism had often vastly increased the numbers of such officials. The reservations of *Exsecrabilis* were also allowed. These had been reintroduced in the papal *Responsio*, not in the article on reservations but in the article on dispensations, where Martin expressed his intention to combat pluralism by enforcing *Exsecrabilis* more strictly. Baix's study suggests, however, that reservations resulting from *Exsecrabilis* were used very seldom during Martin's reign, despite numerous examples of the kind of pluralism which *Exsecrabilis* was intended to remedy.[54]

The reformers also compromised on elections. They did not restore elections in all prelacies, but only in the non-reserved ones. And they conceded to the pope extensive confirmation rights over these elections. The pope could review the elections and set them aside if questionable; even if they were legally correct, the pope could replace the electee with his own candidate (but only if he was especially worthy and then only with the approval of the cardinals). Those confirmed by the pope did still have to swear oaths of loyalty to their ecclesiastical superiors; and many abbots (and all abbesses of non-exempt abbeys) were not required to receive papal confirmation and were thus spared the journey to Rome and the expense of the annates or services.[55] But this was still a long way from the goals of many reformers to restore all election rights and eliminate all reservations not included in the *ius scriptum*.

---

[54] Baix, *Libri*, clxvi–clxxvi; see also p. ccii where Baix notes that out of Martin's desire to enforce *Execrabilis* expressed in the *Responsio* at Constance "il n'est guère sorti que prétextes à intervention pour la Curie romaine, et à son profit."

[55] The German concordat is somewhat vague in this matter: "In monasteriis autem, quae non sunt immediate subjecta sedi Apostolicae, nec non in aliis beneficiis regularibus, super quibus pro confirmatione seu provisione non consuevit haberi recursus ad Sedem Apostolicam, non teneantur venire electi, seu illi quibus providendum est, ad curiam, ad habendam confirmationem seu provisionem." In the final French and Spanish concordats non-exempt abbots with less than 200 *livres petits tournois* revenue (100 livres in Spain) would not be required to receive papal confirmation or to pay services. This represented an improvement

Perhaps the concessions were made in partial exchange for the pope's concession of the *ius alternativum*. The idea of the 50–50 division of collation rights first appeared in a proposal from the second reform committee which Hübler did not know, since it appears only in MS W.[56] It was probably one of the French members of the second reform committee who introduced the idea into the deliberations. The "Instructions of the Gallican church" mention a *ius alternativum*, but as a purely temporary measure.[57] The Instructions also make it clear that the papal quota of appointments would go to the *familiares* of the pope, the king, the princes, and the cardinals, and to the universities. The groups who had competing interests in the granting and receiving of expectancies are here clearly delineated. Much negotiation must have gone on

---

over the limits offered in the *Responsio*, which were 150 and 60, respectively. On the value of the *livre petit tournois*, see Baix, xxviii–xxix; Martin V's constitution of September 1, 1419 declared that it was equal to one florin of the chamber for the purposes of papal accounting. In his note on this matter (p. 132 n.13), Hübler argues that the *livre* had fallen drastically in value by the time of the council, but the currency he refers to in his evidence is not *livres tournois*, but money used in the region of Constance.

[56] Hübler (p. 199 n.13) mistakenly suggested that the earliest source of the idea of the *alternativum* was the 1407 neutrality legislation of the Gallican church. On the history of the *alternativum*, see Sznuro (as in n. 52 above). Sznuro shows that the legislation of 1408 which followed upon the neutrality legislation reestablished with modifications an *alternativum* of 1398. (On this see above, p. 95.) However, it was an *alternativum* of the candidates to be advanced by the ordinary collators; the pope was not involved. The first appearance of an *alternativum* between the pope and ordinaries was a proposed reform offered by Alexander V at the Council of Pisa. It appears in Martène and Durand, *Thesaurus*, 7:1131 (cited by Sznuro, 400 n. 1): "Ad articulum de multitudine gratiarum expectativarum respondetur: Placet domino nostro, quod praelati et alii collatores, patroni ecclesiastici habeant facultatem conferendi et praesentandi usque ad certum numerum beneficiorum, scilicet usque ad quartam partem numeri collationum seu praesentationum quae ad eos spectant, gratiis expectativis apostolicis non obstantibus. Ita videlicet, quod postquam duo apostolici fuerint provisi in virtute gratiae expectativae, ordinarius facultatem habeat conferendi seu praesentandi auctoritate apostolica tertium beneficium vacans et sic successive, donec numerus quartae partis sit consumtus." Sznuro shows that the idea of an *alternativum* was not new, even in 1399; it had been used at least since the thirteenth century by various kinds of co-patrons (bishops and chapters, canons within a chapter, clerical and lay patrons, etc.) and had even been recommended by a canon of the Council of Vienne included in the *Clementinae*—Clem. 3.12.2 *Si plures*. On these matters, see Helmrath, "Reform," 109 n.120.

[57] Paris, BN lat. 14457, fol. 332v, ed. ACC.2.681 : Item tolerandum videtur, quod per modum tractatus et ad tempus d.n. papa omnia reservata ex iuris communis scripti dispositione conferat et de aliis pro prouidendo familiaribus suis et regum, principum, et d. cardinalium et uniuersitatibus studiorum mediam partem conferre possit et ualeat alternatisque uicibus ordinarii aliam partem mediam conferant ita, quod prouisus auctoritate apostolica primo preferatur et post per ordinarium [ACC: ordinem] prouisus et sic deinceps.

behind the scenes among these groups, as well as between the French nation and the pope. Such separate negotiation is implied by the preamble to a statement concerning provisions which follows the French Avisamenta in Plumetot's collection: "Concerning the collation of benefices, the ambassadors of the king and the prelates and other collators and patrons (?) of benefices of the Gallican church are in agreement on this matter, that they want to stand with our lord [the pope], who knows their mind and the intention of the university."[58] The statement clearly implies the conflicting interests between the king and collators on the one hand and the universities on the other. It goes on to express the demand of the king and the collators that certain classes of well-endowed benefices not be subject to papal expectancies. Mainly these were the highest offices in cathedral and collegiate churches and other high monastic offices identified in a now lost draft from the third reform committee;[59] however, the text also adds a group of offices specially founded for singing masses. This latter addition may well reflect the concern of secular lords that their chantries not be staffed with absentee benefice-gatherers. This entire text appears to reflect negotiations which took place after the submission of the Avisamenta; under the article on collations in the Avisamenta all that had appeared was a statement that the nation had not yet deliberated the matter. The further negotiations did finally lead to the exemption from expectancies of the major dignities in cathedral and collegiate churches as well as priories and deaneries, but not the other offices.

Pulka had suspected that the *ius alternativum* would multiply legal trials, and his premonition proved prophetic. Meyer and Baix have shown that the *ius* introduced great uncertainty about titles to benefices received through expectancies. The result was a signi-

---

[58] Paris, BN lat. 14457, fol. 332v, ed. ACC.2.679: "De beneficiorum collacione ambaxiatores regis et ecclesie Gallicane prelati et alii collatores et patroni (?) [ACC: collatorum ac parte] beneficiorum sunt super hoc in concordia, cui stare uolunt cum domino nostro, qui scit mentem eorundem et nouit intentionem uniuersitatis.

[59] "maiores dignitates in cathedralibus et principales [princ. *om.* ACC] ac alie dignitates ellective, prioratus conuentuales, officia claustralia, necnon alia beneficia regularia et secularia, de quibus latior fit mentio in articulo reformatorii et etiam uicariatus perpetui seu capellanie perpetue et officia cathdralium uel collegiatarum ecclesiarum, quorum seu quarum beneficiati ex speciali fundatione, statuto, uel consuetudine tenentur in ecclesiis huiusmodi personaliter officiare et missas magnas uel alias cum uota [ACC: votis] singulis diebus uel alterius uicibus per se ipsos celebrare et horas canonicas diurnas pariter et nocturnas incipere, continuare, perficere . . . "

ficant increase of legal trials and of persons visiting the curia to seek a *nova provisio*, a provision *Si neutri*, or a *surrogatio in ius*.[60]

Nevertheless, Meyer believes that the concordats did return to the ordinaries some of their power over appointments. True, its duration was only five years. After May 2, 1423, the chancery rules went back into effect; but, on April 13, 1425 Martin V issued a new chancery rule in which he stated that during the next five years, the benefices which became vacant in the months of March, June, September, and December would be filled through ordinary collation; he reserved to himself the right to fill the benefices which became vacant in the other months. He renewed this measures for five years in 1430, and it was confirmed by Eugene IV in 1431 and Nicholas V in 1447.[61] Moreover, Martin had introduced a significant improvement by converting the *ius alternativum* into an *alternativum mensuum*. The determination of whether a given appointment fell to the pope or to the ordinary was now much clearer, since it depended only on the date on which the benefice became vacant. The Council of Basel took up a more radical attack on expectancies. In their decree of 1438 they ordained the total cessation of them, but at the same time they attempted to guarantee appointment of graduates. During Lent each year graduates were to register with the ordinaries; presumably the ordinaries were then to prefer them to office, although the exact procedure was not specified. Both measures proved unworkable, and were replaced in the Empire by the Concordat of Vienna in 1448, which returned to the *alternativum mensuum* adopted by Martin V in 1425, but increased the ordinaries' months from four to six.

Thus the Constance reforms enacted a limitation on papal expectancies which, when extended and improved, did in the long run restore to the ordinaries significant collation rights. A further very important concession of the pope regarding expectancies appeared suddenly in the concordats under the article on annates: No annates were to be paid on benefices acquired through expectancies. This concession underlines the intimate connection between reform of provisions and the reform of papal taxation. It is one of the successful aspects of the tax reforms, of particular importance because of the large proportion of provisions made through expectancies, and in France it formed the counterpart for lesser benefices

---

[60] Baix, ccxx.
[61] See Meyer, *Concordat*; this chancery rule is not found in Ottenthal but is edited by Döllinger, *Beitrage* 2:335–344.

to the reduction of the services tax on consistorial benefices. Both were of special importance to the universities.

6. Conclusion

Thus, in the case of the reforms of provisions, like those of papal taxation, what emerged was a complex compromise of competing interests of different groups of reformers. Partly these differences were regional, since papal provisions operated differently in different areas of Europe. The benefices likely to be touched by provisions were the wealthier ones, since applicants eschewed the time, money, uncertainty and frustration involved in pursuing poorer benefices. The richest benefices other than prelacies were the canonries in cathedral and collegiate churches in France, central and Eastern Europe, and England. The English benefices were insulated from papal interference by the Statute of Provisors, so the major demands for reform of provisions came from the clergy of the French and German nations at the council. In each of these nations, however, powerful conflicting interests existed between the local ordinaries and university graduates.

As in the case of papal taxation reforms we had to look at the new owners of revenues, so in the case of provisions we must look at the new patterns of patronage. In most chapters the ordinaries were the canons, and, although in theory they elected their candidates, in practice the candidates were most often nominated by individual canons according to a system analogous to that of the papal expectancies.[62] In the case of non-reserved bishoprics and abbacies, free and uncontested elections were also a relative rarity; kings, princes, town governments, and lay nobles as well as capitular and monastic factions all competed with each other; and one or another of them often sought papal intervention.[63]

---

[62] Meyer, *Zürich*, 115–125 and "Wiener Konkordat," 117–123.

[63] See the studies of Dieter Brosius, "Päpstlicher Einfluss auf die Besetzung von Bistümern um die Mitte des 15. Jahrhunderts," *QFIAB*, 56 (1976), 199–228; and Franz Kummer, *Die Bischofswahlen in Deutschland zur Zeit des grossen Schismas, 1378–1418* (Jena, 1892). See also the study of Adriano Prosperi, "'Dominus beneficiorum': il conferimento dei benefici ecclesiastici tra prassi curiale e ragioni politiche negli stati italiani tra '400 e '500," in *Strutture ecclesiastiche in Italia e in Germania prima della Riforma*, ed. Paolo Prodi and Peter Johanek (Bologna, 1984), 51–86 at 79–81, who discusses the arrangements in Italian city-states. In Milan, e.g., the duke generally nominated candidates to the archbishopric and many other high offices, and the pope conferred the benefice on his nominee; this practice arose out of a struggle between John XXII and the Visconti family in 1311. For the attempts of Alfonso the Magnanimous in Aragon and Sigismund in

From one point of view the *ius alternativum* was a classic compromise: a fifty-fifty split of collation rights. If we look at it only this way, however, we miss its true significance made clear by Meyer. Short of abolishing papal provisions entirely, it was the only way effectively to break the tendency toward papal monopoly on the wealthier benefices in any place where the pope competed with the ordinaries. This is because, as the frequency of papal provisions increased, a candidate tended to seek these provisions rather than the collations of the ordinary. Those who held out for the ordinary's collation had to wait longer and longer, and even they usually ended up seeking papal provisions. Thus, the ordinaries' collation to the wealthier benefices became effectively closed out. The *ius alternativum* made the ordinaries' collations again desirable.

It also involved a major shift in the policy of papal provisions and was closely coupled with the other major shift observed in the last chapter by which benefices received through expectancies were freed from payment of annates. The results of these changes were moot. In the short run, they probably introduced new abuses by bringing new uncertainty, resulting in increased litigation and competing claims, and often making it necessary for recipients of expectancies to seek *novae provisiones*, making them subject to payment of annates after all. Ironically, the substitution of the *ius quatuor mensuum* for ordinaries in 1425 by Martin V, though it might appear to have been a setback, since it allowed the pope to provide in eight months out of the year, was probably a distinct improvement because it eliminated this uncertainty.

In the long run, the changes set in motion by the Constance reforms did restore to the ordinaries a good deal of their powers of collation. The effects of this were generally to favor the local powers and families, and in most places, especially in Germany, this meant the nobility. In one sense we can say the reform was definitely successful; it was a large step in the direction of what reformers had been urgently demanding, especially in Germany. But on closer view, we must note that the reformers themselves had mixed motives. The result for graduates was thus particularly ambivalent. It probably meant that their chances of receiving a benefice were lessened, especially if they were not nobles. True, the reform was coupled with the reform requiring promotion of graduates; but this reform, like the similar ones at the Council of Basel later, was difficult to enforce. As Meyer observes, the situation of graduates was probably helped most by the numerous foundations of new universities in the fifteenth century, making it possible to study nearer home and thus have better opportunities for securing benefices in one's own home territory.

For all the above reasons, we cannot view the reforms of provisions as such a clear success as the reforms of taxation. This is mainly because the compromise involved such complex interests and because the reformers themselves had mixed motives, especially in Germany, where the power of the nobility over the church was so great and often so deleterious. Why did reformers like Job Vener, who bitterly criticized the unspiritual and downright lawless activities of noble prelates and clergy, favor so strongly reforms that ultimately enhanced the control of the nobility over the church? One clear answer would hinge on the localism of such reformers, which outweighed their objections about the nobility. Another reason is the disproportionate anger felt by those who had been disappointed in their effort to secure a benefice through a papal provision. We shall return to these questions in Chapter 7.

In a wider sense, the problem of provisions was insoluble; it was too inextricably linked to the whole system of ecclesiastical benefices, which was from so many perspectives anything but beneficial. For insight into the wider problem, let us recall the significant proportion of benefices in Table 2 which were made by permutation and resignation *in manibus papae* (the latter was a form of permutation officially monitored by the curia.) These methods of securing benefices were much preferable to papal provisions in at least two senses: 1) the choice of the recipient was made locally; and 2) they gave the recipient much greater prospect of peaceful possession—to put it in Meyer's terminology, their success rate was close to 100%. However, they shared with provisions two disadvantages: 1) They circumvented the ordinary collator; and 2) they resulted in appointment of persons whose motivations for holding their offices were at least questionable (one wonders how much money passed hands unofficially in such permutations, not to mention the questionable morality of officially sanctioned resignations in exchange for receipt of a pension.)[64] This last point was

---

Hungary see above, Chapter 2, nn. 42 and 57. For the English situation see Harvey, "Benefice as Property," and, most recently, *England, Rome, and the Papacy, 1417–1464: The Study of a Relationship* (Manchester, Engl., 1993).

[64] On this question in the related area of permutation of curial offices, see Brigide Schwarz, *Organisation kurialer Schreiberkollegien von ihrer Entstehung bis zur Mitte des 15. Jahrhunderts* (Tübingen, 1972), 173–74 and n.41. She cites Hinschius, *Kirchenrecht* (3:282, 285f.) on permutations of benefices. Simony could be avoided in two ways in such permutations: 1) in a resignation *cum pensione*, if the amount of payment was officially set by the higher church authority; and 2) in a simple permutation, if the terms of agreement were made known to the higher authority. She says that in the case of permutations of curial offices where no reason is stated,

crucial, especially when we recall the frequent complaints of German reformers that scarcely anyone had attained his office without the taint of simony. In Germany temptations were greater because the benefices there were so lucrative.

On the other hand, the system of benefices had positive uses. The revenues from wealthier benefices supported the work of royal and higher church officials who held these benefices in absentia.[65] They supported universities and their students. In any event the system was so deeply locked into the entire social and political structure of medieval Europe that there was no thought of replacing it in any thoroughgoing way. No one, not even the most radical of reformers seriously considered this. Yet, that would have been the only way to remedy the abuses in a thorough manner. All other reforms were doomed to be only palliatives. Still, palliatives were important, and could be far-reaching. The Constance reforms of provisions, especially as they were enhanced by the tax reforms, did go a long way toward alleviating what abuses they could. In the next chapter we will again turn to reforms that were still more unqualified successes.

---

we must assume some sort of financially beneficial agreement, but we will never see any direct evidence of such agreements because they were regarded as simoniacal.

[65] See William Pantin, *The English Church in the Fourteenth Century* (Cambridge, Engl., 1955; repr. Toronto, 1980), 39–46.

CHAPTER FIVE

REFORM OF THE HEAD

Hübler believed that the Constance reforms which sought to limit the power of the pope were based on theories that in the Middle Ages would have been regarded as "the sheerest heresy." Thanks to the studies of Congar, Tierney, Buisson, and others,[1] we will be able to see, as we turn to analyze these reforms more closely, that they were in fact founded on many orthodox theological and canonistic theories of the Middle Ages. Perhaps too many. I will argue that competition among different theories kept a number of these reforms from being enacted. Yet the ones which were enacted were impressive indeed. The council's success here follows the same pattern observed in Chapters 3 and 4 on the two most important reforms of the head. In fact, there was much more widespread early agreement on these reforms than there had been on the annates and services. This agreement, together with the sense of urgency of these reforms, explains why they were the first to be deliberated and approved by the reform committee; they form the first six reforms of the Common Collection: c.1, requiring decennial celebration of general councils; c.2, a papal oath of office sharply circumscribing papal power; c.3, tougher legislation against simony, in the Roman curia and elsewhere; cc.4 and 6, reform of the college of cardinals and the curial administration; and c.5, a declaration that a pope could be deposed by a council for notorious crimes. Despite early agreement on all of these except c.6, all were considerably modified in the course of further deliberations and some were ultimately never enacted. I will argue, however, that even the ones that were not enacted had a strong effect, and that the overall successes in these reforms were among the greatest achieved by the council.

1. Decennial celebration of general councils

This reform (*Quoniam ex obmissione*) was the first of all the reforms and the most important, indeed the epitome of the conception of

---

[1] See Chapter 1 above, pp. 8 and 14.

conciliar reform. It gave rise to the first two reform decrees of the thirty-ninth session, *Frequens* and *Si vero*. *Si vero*, which dealt with conciliar actions to be taken in the event of future schisms, formed the second part of the decree which began with *Frequens*. The decree's incipit had changed because *Quoniam ex obmissione* had by then received a different arenga. In fact, the proposal went through no less than four arengas in its different versions, and the final arenga does not even appear in any of the extant reform committee drafts, but turns up suddenly in the final decree. Its beautiful language captures the central idea of the earlier arengas and relates it to one of the central patterns of reform imagery at the council, as we shall see in Chapter 8.

The first portion of *Quoniam ex obmissione* is also beautiful in the simplicity of its one provision, especially by contrast to the legalistic and complicated specificity of *Si vero*. The one provision was just this: that henceforth general councils would be held at regular intervals of no longer than ten years. The language was progressively honed during the reform committee deliberations to make this one provision automatically enforceable, and the conceptual elegance was maintained through the final draft.

In his study of *Frequens-Si vero*, Walter Brandmüller helpfully points to earlier discussions at Constance which linked the ending of schisms with the holding of regular councils; he especially signals a chapter in the *Capitula agendorum*.[2] However, one could gain from this the impression that *Frequens* was only an appendage of *Si vero*. I believe this would be quite wrong. The logical relationship between the decrees even in the earliest reform committee draft was just the reverse: Because general councils have been omitted, "errors, schisms, intimidations, and scandals" have grown horribly; therefore councils will from now on be held regularly. If, however, (*si vero*), a schism should break out anyway, it should be solved by a general council in the way explained by the rest of the decree. Thus the need to solve a schism represents only the exceptional case; the decree really deals with the ways to *prevent* not only schisms but all manner of ills. The errors, intimidations, and scandals mentioned in the arenga refer to heresies and abuses of power, especially papal power. The very terse wording implies the fundamental idea spelled out much more fully in the later arengas.

Brandmüller stressed that *Frequens-Si vero* was the product of a crisis situation during the tumultuous summer of 1417. The final

---

[2] Walter Brandmüller, "Das Konzil, demokratisches Kontrollorgan über den Papst?" *AHC* 16 (1984) 328–347.

form, especially of *Si vero*, was influenced by that crisis, as Brand-müller nicely shows; but the substance of both decrees was hammered out soberly and methodically by the first reform committee in 1415 to deal with future councils and (God forbid!) schisms. The reformers were thinking of the events of the Great Schism and especially looking back to its fatal outbreak in 1378. They carefully tailored *Si vero* to prevent each element which contributed to that disaster.

Si vero falls into two main sections, the first dealing with schisms in general and the second with elections made under duress, which, if not remedied, could easily lead to schisms (as in 1378).[3] In each case the primary remedy is the judgment of the next general council (since regular meetings of general councils will have been established through the provisions of *Frequens*); however, if its meeting is more than a year away, the meeting date will automatically be rescheduled one year from the date when the schism began or when the election took place under duress. In the former case those claiming to be popes are to convoke the council; in the latter case, the cardinals. But if they fail to convoke it, the participants must assemble on their own.

Marginal notes in the first committee's draft specify that the papal claimants are not to preside in the council. Those claiming to be popes are suspended *ipso iure* from administration of the papal office, and no one is to obey them (Manuscript S entitles this section "On the subtraction of obedience.") There is no language here of automatic deposition, only suspension. Then, when it meets, the council will render judgment. How it will do so is not specified, but presumably and if need be it will depose one or both claimants, but might equally confirm that the election was valid, or that one of the papal claimants is legitimate.

With an eye to 1378, the reformers, in their draft prepared in the first reform committee, commanded the cardinals under pain of the severest penalties not to proceed to a second election if their first election occurred under duress. However, they also considered the possibility that the cardinals might ignore this injunction. So they declared that any such second election was null *ipso iure*. The second reform committee added that "in this case the council will provide concerning the election, for this time only," but without specifying how.[4] Suddenly the context of the decree had shifted

---

[3] In D² these are divided into two separate decrees, the second with the rubric "De remedio electionis pape facte per metum."

[4] This is the situation of crisis that Brandmüller is talking about as the context for the whole decree; but this context really applies only to these provisions added

from 1378 to 1417. The addition of this phrase must have been bitter medicine for the cardinals. The cardinals were at that very time involved in a tense unresolved struggle about the mode of election at Constance. Small wonder that the decree's specificity stopped short here! But the committee did consider the frightening possibility that a disputed election might occur at a council itself— a possibility all too plausible in the summer of 1417. The committee's concern was evidently that the cardinals might claim after the council was over that the election had been made under duress. The second reform committee therefore added a provision stating that any such fear or duress had to be alleged by the electors during the council. If they alleged it after the council was over they would not be given an audience. This whole enigmatic passage was finally dropped from the decree. But another provision added during this period of crisis did remain in the final decree; it threatens severe punishment for anyone who tries to influence an election through intimidation as well as anyone who abets such a person or any authority (including the emperor) who is negligent in punishing such offenders. Any city that was guilty in these ways was subject to interdict and loss of its dignity. The reformers referred to Rome as an example, but they were talking about Constance.

When I studied *Frequens-Si vero* earlier in my doctoral dissertation, I was struck by the apparent lack of enforcement measures in *Frequens* by contrast to the very rigorous measures directed against cardinals and even against papal claimants in *Si vero*. It appears that *Frequens* contains no provision in case a pope fails to call a council at the end of the ten-year interval, whereas *Si vero* makes the meeting of a council automatic in case a schism should arise. Closer examination reveals, however, that *Frequens* made the formal convocation of a council by the pope otiose, since the meeting time was fixed by the decree (ten years from the close of the preceding council) and the place of the council was to be chosen in the preceding council. In fact *Frequens* requires the pope to name the place there, with the approval of the council, and if he fails to do so, the council will do so itself. The only need for further convocation is if the pope decides to have the council meet sooner or in some other place. He can only do these things for weighty cause and then only with the consent and subscription of two-thirds of the cardinals. (Under no circumstances can he delay the meeting date beyond the ten year interval.) He is bound to announce such changes one year in advance of the meeting time, and the participants are bound to attend in any new place just as they had been bound to attend in the former one. Thus the meeting of councils became automatic; in the words of the decree, thus "the council will always be ruling (*vigeat*) or will be awaited because of the set date." The decree was very tightly drawn indeed.

William Durant the Younger would seem to have been the first to propose the automatic decennial celebration of general councils. Constantin Fasolt has underlined the revolutionary nature of Durant's proposal, distinguishing it from Durant's other demand that a general council be called "if and only if there was any doubt about the validity of law."[5] The latter demand, stated in the main body of Durant's *Tractatus maior*, was supported by canon law, chiefly D.20 c.3. Durant realized that there was no exact canonical precedent for requiring decennial meetings of councils, so he placed this demand in the summary section of the treatise, which contains no canonistic citations. The Constance reformers, or at least some of them, surely had Durant's proposal in mind. They were not following it rigidly, however, since they at first suggested other intervals between councils besides ten years.[6] The difficulty of finding exact legal precedents for *Frequens* was reflected in the multiple attempts at drafting a preamble. The final preamble, with its striking agricultural imagery, was evidently not drafted until the very last minute; it does not appear in any of the reform committee drafts.[7] In Chapter 8 below, I will argue that the Constance reformers nevertheless saw the decennial celebration of councils as the enactment of a conception of conciliar tradition that was thoroughly grounded in Scripture and church legislation from the earliest times. The agricultural imagery of *Frequens* is imagery of correction. It pictures the ongoing, continuing reform of the universal church; when *Frequens* refers to the prevention and removal of heresies and scandals, it implicitly ascribes to the council power to reform all persons, even the pope.

---

in this time period. For some reason Brandmüller says that it was the third reform committee that deliberated these measures; but even the latest changes were made by the second committee (the third committee was not formed until after this decree had been enacted.)

[5] Fasolt, *Council*, 242. I am indebted to Dr. Fasolt for the interpretation of Durant's proposals in this paragraph.

[6] See Brandmüller, "Konzil," 332–33. Dietrich of Niem proposed five year intervals between councils (ACC.4.588, 595); the "Italian proposal" (see below, n.7) called for councils every "ten or twenty-five years"; Pileus, Archbishop of Genoa, suggested that each pope be required to hold a council within the first five years of his pontificate (*Informationes*, ed. Döllinger, *Beiträge* 2:303).

[7] The final two drafts (W[2], cc. 11 and 12a) are among the group which contains final corrections and additions in W[2]; out of this group only these two drafts and the reform of the Sacred College (c.5) do not contain notation of approval by the Spanish nation on October 1 or 2 (one week before enactment of *Frequens* in Session 39); see below, p. 287.

2. *The cardinals and the* reformatio in capite
(Common, cc. 2, 4, and 6)

The *Capitula agendorum,* which Brandmüller mentioned as a source
of the idea for *Frequens-Si vero* is only one of a number of reform
platforms circulated in the early months of the council which
included many of the reforms *in capite* to be discussed in this
chapter. The "Italian proposal" of late 1414 is in many ways the
most interesting.[8] Some have argued that this proposal represents
the work of the cardinals, just as others have argued that the
Capitula agendorum was the work of Cardinal D'Ailly.[9] I would argue
instead that both the "Italian proposal" and the *Capitula agendorum*
represent broad platforms that contain reforms desired by a wide
consensus of reformers. Among them were quite a few in which the
desires of reforming cardinals converged with those of other reformers. It is interesting that the "Italian Proposal" is identified in the
famous "Petersburg manuscript"[10] used by Finke as the work of
Jean de Rochetaillée, the French Patriarch of Constantinople, and
that Cerretano, who included it in his journal of the council,
attributed it to D'Ailly. Heimpel considers it to be a proposal of
Italian prelates after all.[11] The fact that its provenance has been so
diversely ascribed to Italian and French sources may well indicate
that it represents the results of sharing of ideas, especially among
Italian and French adherents of John [XXIII]. The fact that
extensive portions of the *Capitula agendorum* appear also in the
reform proposals of Pileus of Genoa may be another example of
such sharing. I would argue further that the *Capitula* themselves
were probably the result of group deliberations in which prelates
and cardinals met together, as was probably also the *Italian proposal*
itself.[12] Such is probably also the case with three collections of

---

[8] Mansi 27:541C and H.2.23; Hardt took them from Bzovius, who edited them
from Cerretano's journal. On this, see ACC.3.42 No. 8, and Heimpel, *Vener,*
3:1029– 32.

[9] See Francis Oakley, "Pseudo-Zabarella's *Capitula agendorum*: An Old Case
Reopened," *AHC* 14 (1982) 111– 123. Oakley reviews the past arguments for
D'Ailly's authorship and concludes against them.

[10] See ACC.4.xcix, which cites this manuscript as Petersburg, Staatsbibliothek,
Nr. 321.

[11] Heimpel, *Die Vener,* 3:1029.

[12] The *Capitula agendorum* are based heavily on the reform proposals of the
University of Paris in 1411 for the Roman Council of 1412 (ACC.1.131–48). In a
similar fashion, the proposals of the University of Oxford from 1408 contain the
reforms introduced by the English nation in the first reform committee; see below,
p. 148, n.19.

curial reform proposals which were circulated in the first month of
the council and which are particularly important because many of
their demands were taken up in c.6 of the Common Collection.[13]

There was also abundant friction between cardinals and prelates. The ways in which Cerretanus and Pulka report Zabarella's
famous sermon on reform July 24, 1415, are illuminating. On that
occasion Zabarella apologized that reform had been delayed for so
long and expressed the strong desire of the cardinals that reform
now begin and that it begin with the head and extend downward
through the body. Cerretano says that after Zabarella's speech,
Jean Mauroux, the Patriarch of Antioch, stood up and applauded
the speech, pointing out stingingly all the ranks of the curia which
needed reform, most of all the cardinals themselves. After this,
Cardinal Pierre d'Ailly retorted, says Cerretano, "with some comments about hypocrisy."[14] It is interesting that all three of the
prelates in this interchange were members of the first reform
committee.

Mauroux and the prelates had thrown down the gauntlet. The
cardinals picked it up and introduced many of the reforms in the
first reform committee. As we saw in the last two chapters Cardinal
Adimari introduced the reforms of provisions (including the first
reforms of annates) August 28. September 3 he introduced another
weighty package of reforms of the curial administration (c.6),
which we shall consider at some length below. The first five reforms
in the Common Collection must have been introduced in the period
before this, during the first few weeks of the committee's meeting,[15]
and I would argue that at least two of them (cc. 2 and 4), were first
introduced by cardinals. (Schedules 1, 3, and 5, on the other hand,
were most likely framed first by non-cardinals.) The cardinals
probably introduced cc. 2, 4, and 6 to the committee because they
shared an interest in these reforms and because in this way the
reforms would receive their first consideration in the shape that

---

[13] These were the proposals collected by Stefano di Geri del Buono, bishop of
Volterra and papal registrator, circulated between December 4 and 17, 1414. See
ACC.3.2–3,41. They are edited in "Gli avanzi dell'archivio di un Pratese vescovo
di Volterra," *Archivio storico Italiano*, ser. 4, 13 (1884) 339–359. Though one of
them bears Geri's name, all three probably represent compilations of desiderata
from numerous individuals inside and outside the Curia.

[14] ACC.2.252: omnes gradus et status Romane curie et maxime d. cardinalium
pupugit, eis symonias et alia inhonesta improperando. Semper tamen in genere
loquutus est. Cui rev[mus] d.d. Petrus miseracione divina tituli sancti Grisogoni
presbyter cardinalis Cameracensis vulgariter nuncupatus respondens et eum in
suis dictis impugnans plura de ypocrisi loquutus est.

[15] See below, p. 277.

best suited the cardinals' particular interests.

However, we should not try to draw too many conclusions on this basis. For c. 6, where we have Adimari's original draft and the record of the deliberations that followed, we can see that the finished draft looks very different in many ways. Thus, it is safe to assume that cc. 1–5 looked different in their original, no longer extant versions, and that each now reflects the product of diverse contributions from both cardinals and non-cardinals. Still, it will be valuable here to precede our detailed analysis of these reforms by some reflections about the possible interests of the cardinals in reform.

Hübler tended to assume that the cardinals' interests coincided with those of the papacy. In fact, however, the cardinals were engaged in an often intense power struggle with the pope, as we saw in Chapter 3 above in the discussion of reforms of the tenths and the spoils. Jean Lulvès and Walter Ullmann have studied this power struggle by examining late medieval oaths, or capitulations, required of popes at the time of their elections.[16]

Ullmann has even claimed that the struggle between the pope and cardinals was the chief cause of the Great Schism.[17] Interestingly, he identified one of the cardinals' chief reasons for the deposition of Urban VI as their recalcitrance to his attempts to bring about reforms of them. But then Ullmann dismissed this motive as merely "ancillary to the eventual rupture," citing Urban VI's nepotism as evidence that he did not take a "single step . . . in the direction of the radical reform." But the reform of papal nepotism would not have endangered the cardinals' interests; if anything it would have enhanced them by making the pope more dependent on themselves. On the other hand, the cardinals had good reason to believe that Urban sought to bring about reforms which, even if perhaps not "radical," would have seriously prejudiced their interests. As Delaruelle has perspicaciously observed, Urban had never been a cardinal and did not share in their interests; he lived a life of personal austerity, presented himself as a reformer, and reproached the cardinals severely for their simony and extravagance.[18]

---

[16] See especially Jean Lulvès, "Die Machtbestrebungen des Kardinalkollegiums gegenüber dem Papsttum," *MIÖG* 35 (1914) 455–483 and "Päpstliche Wahlkapitulationen," *QFIAB* 12 (1909) 212–235; and Walter Ullmann, "The legality of the papal electoral pacts," *Ephemerides iuris canonici* 12 (1956) 246–278.

[17] Walter Ullmann, *The Origins of the Great Schism: A Study in Fourteenth-century Ecclesiastical History* (London, 1948), 7–8, 187.

[18] Delaruelle, 905–906.

Ullmann chose to see the struggle between pope and cardinals chiefly in terms of a struggle between two political conceptions, the papal one, which was monarchical or autocratic, and the cardinalitian one, which was oligarchic and sought to limit and control the monarchical power of the pope. Friedrich Merzbacher in a 1953 article suggested that in the later Middle Ages an oligarchic ecclesiological conception formed a *tertium quid* between papalism and conciliarism.[19] Brian Tierney developed the discussion further, calling attention to Johannes Monachus as an important source for the cardinalitian oligarchic ideas and suggesting Francesco Zabarella as one of the most important exponents of them during the Schism.[20] He further argued that Zabarella successfully synthesized the cardinalitian concept with the conciliar one. This is of particular relevance here since Zabarella was one of the members of the first Constance reform committee, and he had recently become a cardinal himself. All three cardinals on the first reform committee had, in fact, been elevated recently, by John [XXIII]. Zabarella's oligarchic theories had been enunciated before he became a cardinal.[21] There has been considerable debate about how much D'Ailly modified his episcopalist reforming views to reflect the interests of his new estate.[22]

Zabarella was probably the leading authority of his day on canon law, and D'Ailly was one of the two leading theologians (the other, Gerson, was D'Ailly's student.) Their reforming stances had already been well-articulated before they became cardinals. The third cardinal on the committee, Alamanno Adimari, Cardinal of Pisa, had experience as cardinal legate in France, which had made him aware of the depth of anger of the Gallicans.[23] Thus the reforming stance of all three cardinals on the committee was shaped strongly by factors other than their interest as cardinals.

However, those interests did also have a strong influence on their stances in the Constance reforms. They were particularly willing to support reforms which would have enhanced their position in their power struggle with the pope. Let us now review those interests as they may have affected the specific reforms in cc. 2, 4, and 6.[24] This

---

[19] Friedrich Merzbacher, "Wandlungen des Kirchenbegriffs im Spatmittelalter," *ZRG Kan.* 39 (1953) 274–361.
[20] Tierney, *Foundations*, 180–191, 220f.
[21] Tierney, *Foundations*, 220–237.
[22] See Tschackert, 259–260; Oakley, *Political Thought*, 250–252 and 346–349.
[23] See Valois, *Schism*, 4:220–222.
[24] The principal secondary literature dealing with the Sacred College and its interests during this period is to be found in the studies of Guillaume Mollat,

struggle manifested itself in every area in which pope and cardinal
shared the prerogatives of the Roman Church. The Sacred College
claimed the right to one-half of all the seigneurial revenues of the
Roman Church[25] as well as one-half of the *servitia* (See Chapter 3).[26]
The cardinals shared also in the curial administration, in the
exercise of the jurisdiction of the Roman Church, in the governing
of the lands of the Papal States and Avignon, and in the administration of the universal Church, through their roles as papal counsel-
lors and legates. Their position of rank and honor in the Church
was directly below that of the pope, above even the patriarchs.

During the Schism the popes were too weak to cut off the cardinals' share of the seigneurial revenues of the Roman Church, a step
apparently taken by Martin V after the Schism.[27] But even during
the Schism the popes effectively denied to the cardinals certain
seigneurial revenues when they alienated or mortgaged lands and
rights of the Roman Church in exchange for liquid capital or when
they granted these lands and rights to their relatives, friends, and
servants.[28] The cardinals had an interest in preventing such practices and in ensuring that the pope appoint only cardinals to
administer lands of the Roman Church.[29] This interest extended
beyond that of recovering lost revenues in which they had a share.
By limiting the pope's personal expedients for raising liquid capital
to meet immediate political needs, the cardinals could force the
pope to rely upon their agreement, even on their own offers to lend
him money to support important actions; they thus limited his

---

"Contribution à l'histoire du Sacré Collège de Clément V à Eugène IV," *RHE* 46
(1951) 22–112, 566–594, and Paul Maria Baumgarten, *Untersuchungen and Urkun-
den uber die camera collegii cardinalium fur die Zeit von 1295 bis 1437* (Leipzig, 1898).
Somewhat outdated but still of use are M. Souchon, *Die Papstwahlen in der Zeit des
grossen Schismas.* Entwicklung und Verfassungsgeschichte des Kardinalates von
1378–1417, 2 vols. (Brunswick, 1898–99) and J.-P. Kirsch, *Die Finanzverwaltung
des Kardinalkollegiums im XIII. und XIV. Jahrhundert* (Münster, 1895). See also W.
Decker, "Die Politik der Kardinäle auf dem Basler Konzil," *AHC* 9 (1977)
112–153 as well as Norman Zacour, "Papal Regulations of Cardinals' Households
in the Fourteenth Century," *Speculum* 50 (1975) 434–55. For the cardinals' stance
at the council, see Karl Gatzemeier, *Stellung und Politik der Kardinäle auf dem
Konstanzer Konzil nach der Absetzung Johanns XXIII* (Mosbach, 1937).
[25] This practice had been established by the constitution of Pope Nicholas IV,
July 18, 1289; see Mollat, "Contribution," 71.
[26] Favier, 342. The one-half of the common services received by the Chamber of
the Sacred College was divided among the cardinals who were present at the
consistory at which the prelate who paid the services had been approved.
[27] Decker, 128.
[28] Favier, 603–608.
[29] See p. 117 below.

maneuverability in power struggles with themselves.[30] Preventing the pope from rewarding his personal servants with lands and revenues would have had a similar effect. And for analogous reasons the cardinals would have had an interest in curial reform which would have reduced the number and powers of these officials personally loyal to the pope.

The proposal for the reform of the curial administration submitted by Cardinal Adimari to the reform committee called for limiting the number of curial officials and for enforcing more rigorous standards in their selection.[31] It also demanded that certain of the most important officials, the protonotaries and auditors, be appointed only with the counsel of the cardinals.

Even the Constance reform measure for the reform of the Sacred College itself (c.4, *Quia plerumque*) would have in fact strengthened the role of the cardinals in the Church.[32] The key provision of the article, which secured the role of the existing cardinals in the naming of new cardinals, betrays the real thrust of the measure. This provision stated that in the future the election of new cardinals was not to be made by auricular vote (*vota auricularia*), but rather only with the collegiate counsel of the cardinals. Hübler explained that according to the method of the *vota auricularia* each cardinal had approached the papal throne separately and whispered in the pope's ear his recommendation; and that the pope then made his choice, presumably on the basis of these recommendations.[33] The reform measure made it necessary for the pope to base his choice on the collegiate opinion of the cardinals and not only on their private recommendations.[34] By making this counsel common knowledge to the pope and all the cardinals it provided a control that the pope would in fact follow the cardinals' advice.

---

[30] Baumgarten records several sizeable loans of the Sacred College to the apostolic chamber and argues that such loans were probably not infrequent; see p. clxviii, and especially the document edited on pp. 357–359, in which the apostolic chamber assigns to the chamber of the Sacred College certain assets which it possesses as surety for a loan of 3,000 gulden made at papal request. Sometimes the pope relied on the cardinals to advance the surety for loans which he sought from secular bankers. Cf. also Mollat, "Contribution," 74–75.

[31] ACC.2.644–652. This set of proposals should be seen in parallel to the proposals for reform of the English royal household in the mid-fifteenth century; cf. A. R. Myers, *The Household of Edward IV* (London, 1959). The latter proposals were supported by the powerful nobles of the realm, whose role was similar in many respects to that of the cardinals in the Church.

[32] Hübler, 73–77.

[33] *Ibid.*, 129, n.3.

[34] Common, c.4 required consent and written subscription of the majority of existing cardinals; this was diluted in the second committee (S², c.11) to "counsel of the cardinals given collegially and verbally".

The other provisions of the article for reform of the Sacred College may be similarly interpreted as efforts to strengthen its role vis-à-vis the pope. The limiting of the number of cardinals ensured that each individual cardinal would receive a greater proportion of the revenues of the curia. This provision and also the requirements concerning age, education and moral stature of candidates for the cardinalate, would help to ensure that new cardinals would be mature, powerful, and above all independent figures, and not the creatures as well as the creations of the pope. Likewise, the requirements that candidates should be chosen in proportionate numbers from all parts of Christendom and that they should not be closely related to any existing cardinals would have helped to prevent the Sacred College from falling under the control of any national or familial clique and thereby under control of a pope elected by such a clique.

The interests of the cardinals would have been similarly enhanced by c.2 (*Professio Bonifacii*), which required the pope to swear an oath prior to his coronation.[35] It had long been a custom for popes to make professions of faith at the time of their coronations, but these had not contained any promises about the manner in which the pope would administer the Church. Then, in the mid-fourteenth century the cardinals of Innocent VI required him to swear an oath in which he promised to follow certain rules of government.[36] The reformers at the Council of Constance called attention to another papal coronation oath with promises concerning administration which purported to be even older; it had allegedly been sworn by Boniface VIII at his coronation. Scholars now generally agree that this document was in fact forged in the early fifteenth century.[37] The bulk of it is, however, formed by the papal profession of faith found in the *Liber diurnus*, reworked to include some administrative provisions. The reformers knew that the oath was based on that in the *Liber diurnus* and they seem to have had no doubts that it was the authentic oath sworn by Boniface VIII. In the administrative provisions attached to the oath we can surely see the cardinals' hand at work. They call upon the pope to preserve "undiminished" and "to the letter" all the

---

[35] See Hübler, 69–70; and see especially the articles cited in notes 16–17 and 24 above by Lulvès, Ullmann, Souchon, etc.

[36] The text appears in Raynaldus, *Annales ecclesiastici*, ed. A. Theiner (Bar-le-Duc, 1872), v. 25, ad annum 1352, n. 26, pp. 540–541.

[37] ACC.2.569–570 and Heinrich Finke, *Aus den Tagen Bonifaz VIII.* (Münster, 1902), 54ff. See also G. Buschbell, "Die professiones fidei der Päpste," *RQ*, 10 (1896) 251–97, 421–50.

statutes, rites, customs, and properties handed down from their predecessors. One clause in particular is remarkable: With respect to "whatever emerges contrary to canonical discipline among my sons, the cardinals of the holy Roman church (with whose counsel, consent, direction and reminding I exercise and perform my office)" the pope is to swear that he will "either amend [it] by counsel or patiently tolerate [it], (except for grave offenses to the Christian faith or religion). . . . "

Following the oath in the Common Collection are two schedules (2a and b) which could stand as separate decrees, but the first of which (*Cum antiqui*) was clearly drafted as a set of additions to the oath, and the second of which (*Quia decet*) seems to have originated as an alternate to *Cum antiqui*. *Cum antiqui* consists of a long list of weighty business of the Roman church which the pope is not to undertake without the "counsel, consent, and subscription of the brothers." At the end of the schedule appears the statement linking it to the oath: "Or let the above constitution be made in the manner of an addition to the oath of Boniface VIII which appears just above, with the verbs changed into the first person. And this would perhaps be more fitting (*honestius*) than a constitution."[38] The final clause is quite striking, especially for the profound lack of historical consciousness which it reveals.[39] The modern historian cringes when he or she reads this. How can one fabricate clauses and attach them to this supposedly historical oath, implying they were actually sworn by Boniface VIII, and call this *honestius*? It is important to see here that *honestius* does not mean "more honest."[40] What it does mean is of great interest, and I shall return to it at the end of this chapter.

This list of weighty business in *Cum antiqui* included the following items: decisions concerning matters of faith, canonizations of saints, reduction of the amount of time between years of jubilee, erection of new sees or suppression or divisions of old ones, unions of cathedral churches and monasteries, promotions of cardinals,

---

[38] W^2, c.13a in fact contains a fragment of a schedule which appears to be an effort to carry out these suggestions. It contains some of the clauses of *Cum antiqui* placed in the first person.

[39] In this regard it is interesting that the date of Boniface VIII's accession is given as 1214 in every extant manuscript.

[40] The real thrust of this clause was to advocate making these provisions part of an oath rather than a decree, so that the pope is binding himself, rather than being bound. It may well be that the author of this clause was D'Ailly, and he may have also had a hand in the original forgery of the oath or at least have been privy to the forgery. If so, it would have been but a small step to add additional requirements in the oath.

removal of prelates from their sees or the transfer of them between sees without their consent, new concession of exemptions and re-vocation of old ones, the establishment of vicariates or rectorates of lands of the Roman Church, the conclusion of peace treaties, declaration of war, and appointments of legates and nuncios; in general, all serious business or business pertaining to the general welfare of the Church. This list represents a good summary of those areas of Church administration in which pope and cardinals strug-gled with one another for assertion of power.[41] We will observe a whole series of other reforms at Constance which required the pope to receive the counsel, or the consent, or the consent and subscrip-tion "of his brothers the cardinals."

Thus we may conclude that, although some of the reforms at Constance prejudiced the cardinals' interests, other reforms would have enhanced their role in the Church and given them greater leverage in their power struggle with the pope. To further their interests the cardinals could thus join with other groups at the Council in supporting many reforms.[42]

3. Reforms of the Sacred College (Common, c.4)

The interests of these other groups were nevertheless distinct from those of the cardinals. These groups had an interest in the appoint-ment of qualified and responsible personnel because they had to deal with such persons when they had business in the Roman Curia. They desired the reduction of the number of curial officials, including cardinals, in order to reduce the expenditures of the Roman Church which they were called upon to support financially through their payment of the various taxes assessed by the pope. And they wanted the composition of the curia, especially of the Sacred College, to better reflect the regional diversity of Christ-endom.

The reforms of the Sacred College (Common, c.4) addressed these three main areas: 1) reducing the total number of cardinals to twenty-four;[43] 2) establishing moral and educational qualifications

---

[41] At the end of *Cum antiqui* one further proposed addition requires the pope to swear that he will not appoint anyone to govern lands of the Roman church who is not either a cardinal or a prelate.

[42] See H.4.24.

[43] Many reformers desired an even lower maximum of eighteen; the Instruc-tions of the Gallican church requested this, and the French *Avisamenta* also expressed preference for this number, as did the German nation in its deliberations (See ACC.2.680 and 673 and the marginal notes to S^2, c.11.)

of cardinals; and 3) attaining more equal representation of regions in the Sacred College.[44] Next to the reforms of the sacred college in W² appears the word *Prima*, indicating that they were the first on the list of reforms to be enacted in the second reform committee (see below, p. 296). However, they did not emerge among the decrees of the 39th session, but became rather the first item in the list established by the *cautio* decree of Session 40 and thus the first item in the Avisamenta and Responsio. Still they did not reach enactment in the decrees of Session 43, but rather became the first item in all the national concordats. The wording of this article is, in fact, almost identical in the German, French, and Spanish concordats; it is thus difficult to see why a conciliar decree was not enacted.

In implementing these reforms, Martin V gave first priority to the provision limiting the size of the Sacred College, and he thus exercised great restraint in the creation of new cardinals, reformers, especially in Germany. He gave first priority to the provision limiting the size of the Sacred College and thus exercised great restraint in the creation of new cardinals. At the beginning of his reign there were already thirty-three cardinals (the result of uniting the existing cardinals of the former three obediences). Thus Martin denied the explicit requests of Sigismund for the creation of two German cardinals. His actions left many reformers, especially in Germany, dissatisfied. When he finally created cardinals, Martin did make an effort to observe the *equalitas regionum*, although to many reformers it seemed too little too late. Martin's new cardinals consisted of six Italians, four French, three Spanish, one English, one Bohemian (thus from the German nation at Constance), and one Cypriot.[45] And by the end of his reign Martin had brought the total number of cardinals below the maximum of twenty-four established by the Constance reforms, even though he was technically no longer bound by the concordats, which had lapsed.

---

[44] This was expressed as *equalitas regionum*; the cardinals were to be drawn from all parts of Christendom proportionately, as far as possible. Job Vener, in his reform *Avisamentum* of 1417, had made the interesting suggestion that there be seventy-two cardinals, one from each of seventy-two provinces; however, such a number would have been totally unacceptable to reformers who wanted the size of the college limited to twenty-four or even eighteen. See Heimpel, *Vener*, 2:798–808.

[45] See John Broderick, S.J., "The Sacred College of Cardinals: Size and Geographical Composition (1099–1986)," *Archivum historiae pontificiae* 25 (1987) 7–72 at 36; also see Alfred Strnad, "Konstanz und der Plan eines deutschen 'Nationalkardinals.' Neue Dokumente zur Kirchenpolitik König Siegmunds von Luxemburg," in *Das Konzil von Konstanz*, 397–428.

4. The reforms of the curia (c.6)

In his study of the history of curial officials in the later Middle Ages, Walter Hofmann viewed the Constance reforms as a watershed, however generally not in a favorable sense.[46] Beginning with the council, according to Hofmann, successive generations of reformers missed their opportunity effectively to eliminate the abuses which had proliferated during the disorder and financial exigency of the Great Schism. Even at the time of their drafting the curial reforms considered by the first reform committee had been weakened because the cardinals who proposed them had yielded to resistance from the curial bureaucracy. Besides this the reformers did not have sufficient direct knowledge of the actual practices of the curia; moreover, their conception of reform as exact restoration of past practices, even though conditions had changed drastically, could not solve the most pressing problems. Though the Constance reforms were thus fatally flawed and were never enacted at the council, Martin V tried to put them into effect, but only halfheartedly. Ironically, every successive curial reform effort for more than a century took those reforms as their starting point, repeating their errors and thus inevitably failing.

Even though Hofmann carefully qualifies his statements much more than this brief summary can indicate, his judgments amount to a devastating indictment. However, I believe that the Constance curial reforms and their results can be viewed differently. The starting point is a reassessment of the first reform committee's deliberations, for which we have a better manuscript record than that available to Hofmann in Hardt's edition. The information in V shows that Cardinal Adimari was the one who drafted the proposed reforms of the curia in c.6, thus vindicating Hofmann's hypothesis that the cardinals played a leading role in introducing the reforms. However, Hofmann took the three tracts collected by Bishop Geri of Volterra (see above, n. 13) as the best index of the cardinals' reform desires and argued that these were compromised in the reform committee deliberations by the resistance of the numerous curial officials on the reform committee. But we can now identify the earliest version of the reforms in c.6 as the cardinals' program itself and not already a dilution of it. And although the changes introduced to the reforms in the committee did sometimes weaken

---

[46] Walter Hofmann. *Forschungen zur Geschichte der kurialen Behörden* (Rome, 1914), 1:5–17. On the operation of the curia in this period, see also the very helpful introductory sections to the volumes of the *Repertorium germanicum*.

them,[47] they more often strengthened them.[48] New information in C and V about para. 29 in c.6 reveals much about the power struggles within the committee.

Paragraph 29 (*De sessionibus et locis ordinandis*), concerned the organization of sessions of the curia, especially questions of rank and protocol. It recorded a hot dispute which took place in the committee concerning these matters. It is one of the few cases in which the results of a roll call vote of the committee are recorded. The main point at issue was whether the apostolic protonotaries would take precedence before the prelates in curia. All committee members agreed that outside the curia they should not, and that in the curia they should, as long as they were carrying out their official duties. The intense division arose over the question of precedence when the protonotaries were not conducting official business. A majority of eighteen to ten voted that in this case the prelates should precede, just as outside the curia; the minority said they wanted to follow the *mos antiquus*. The discord became so great that the president proposed sending the matter to the nations to get their opinion, and everyone favored doing so.[49] A marginal note in C suggests the animosity of the curial minority to the vote when it observes that the measure was not executed because it was "scandalous."

This dispute reminds us of the presence of a third, larger group in the committee alongside the cardinals and the curial officials. The individuals in this third group often wanted to strengthen proposals in order to eliminate abuses of particular concern to them, perhaps even because they had personally suffered as a result of these abuses. The changes made by the committee to the proposals presented by Adimari probably resulted more from this group than from curial officials on the committee, as Hofmann thought.

The concerns of this group are especially apparent in the para-

---

[47] As, for example, in Para. 4, noted by Hofmann, where the consent of the cardinals for choice of auditors is weakened to require only their counsel and the auditors are required to have taught law in a university for only two years instead of three prior to assuming office.

[48] For a specific counter-example to Hofmann's cited in the preceding note, see Para. 15, where the provision requiring counsel of the cardinals in the selection of referendaries is strengthened to require their *consent*.

[49] On similar strong feelings concerning relative precedence of prelates and protonotaries, see Fasolt, *Council*, 201 and n.114, for William Durant the Younger's views; see also the later dispute recorded in a letter of Aeneas Sylvius Piccolomini in *Der Briefwechsel des Eneas Silvius Piccolomini*, ed. Rudolf Wolkan (Vienna, 1912) 2:193–194 (For this latter reference I am indebted to Thomas Izbicki.)

graphs which deal with ordinations made in curia and with the awarding of honorary academic degrees by the pope (para. 21 and 27). Para. 21 declares that only curial officials may be ordained in curia. Curial ordinations were a circumvention of the rights of ordinaries. Moreover, they were the door of entry to the priesthood; reformers concerned about the large numbers of unqualified clergy wanted to guard this door carefully. Thus, even for curial officials ordained in curia they demanded a rigorous examination. Adimari had included this requirement in his initial proposal, but the committee strengthened the measure by strictly forbidding any money whatever to be paid for such ordination or for letters confirming it. Such payments were part of the whole pattern of payments made in curia which smacked of simony, payments which had grown so enormously during the Schism.

The measure against academic degrees awarded by papal bull was considered so important that the committee commissioned Cardinal Adimari to draft it into a separate constitution. His draft (*Eo iam multos*) appears as c.8 of the Common Collection. Its preamble evokes the ambition of those who want to be called "Rabbi" and acquire the "highest places in the synagogue without the work required to attain the knowledge upon which such honors should be based." At issue were chiefly degrees awarded outside the curia by legates and others through powers given them by the pope. The measure makes it clear that it is not attacking degrees awarded for academic study undertaken in the curia itself, which had acquired the status of a university (*studium*).[50] But the degrees could only be given there after due course of rigorous study completed by an examination. If anything, the committee wanted to strengthen the curial *studium*; para. 23 of c.6 called for maintaining the studies there of arts, theology, both laws, and Latin, Greek, Hebrew, Arabic, and Chaldean (Aramaic) letters which had been instituted by the Council of Vienne (Clem. 5.1.1)

In such sensitive areas we can see the anger of the prelates, the secular clergy, and the universities at the curial practices which circumvented their powers. However, the great bulk of curial reforms dealt with the wider effort to rid the curial administration of

---

[50] However, the measure also did not refer to the *generale studium* at Rome, which was a separate university distinct from the Studium of the Curia. See the study of D. S. Chambers, "Studium Urbis and *gabella studii*: the University of Rome in the Fifteenth Century," in *Cultural Aspects of the Italian Renaissance: Essays in Honour of Paul Oskar Kristeller*, ed. Cecil Clough (Manchester, 1976), 68–110. Chambers describes the Studium of the Curia as "migratory" (p. 68) and "amorphous" (p. 87).

abuses and to make it more efficient and fair. Many of these reforms
focused on reducing the numbers of officials and setting qualifications and standards for them to insure they would be knowledg-
able, impartial, efficient, and speedy in the performance of their
office. In all these areas the other reformers on the committee
generally wanted to be more stringent than the cardinals; in fact,
they tried to return to the greater stringency of the demands set
forth in the earlier reform tracts which Hübler took as his index for
the cardinals' reform plans.

Adimari's proposal called for restoring the good practices of
earlier popes. They called for returning to the exact numbers of
former officials in each category and the exact amount of former
fees. In Para. 17, Adimari called for the legislation of John XXII to
be carried out to the letter (*ad unguem*) in the chancery and the
Rota. The wording is very similar to that in the papal oath noted
above. Here we are reminded of Hofmann's criticism that the
reforms did not take adequate concern for changed needs and his
comments about the inadequacies of the medieval concept of reform as literal restoration. Let us look more closely at how the
committee handled these matters. When it started to deliberate this
paragraph, the committee realized it did not even have a copy of
John XXII's legislation. Even the curial members of the committee
must have been unaware of its contents, so the committee commissioned Michael Bolosonis to go to the vice-chancellor and obtain a
copy of it. Significantly, Bolosonis was also to procure the legislation of Gregory XII; it would have reflected the most recent practices of the Roman obedience. The committee also appointed a
sub-committee to review the legislation and report to the full committee. The sub-committee was composed of one representative
from each nation; and two of the four were also curial officials—
Nicholas Lubich, bishop of Merseberg, a referendary; and Angelo
Baglioni, an auditor of the camera.[51] Thus the committee was
trying to draw on officials who had knowledge of the functioning of
the curia; and they were not simply trying to restore old laws
without looking at changed conditions in the more recent past.[52]

---

[51] See Hofmann, 1:240; on Nicholas Lubich, see Hans Schmiedel, *Nikolaus
Lubich (1360–1431): Ein deutscher Kleriker im Zeitalter des grossen Schismas und der
Konzilien, Bishof von Merseburg, 1411–1431* (Berlin, 1911, repr. 1965), 81–100.
Lubich had been appointed referendary just eight months earlier by John
[XXIII], but had also had extensive earlier experience in the curia.
[52] This sub-committee was also consulted on other matters covered by the
legislation; see Para. 19, deliberation on salaries of notaries.

It is, in fact, striking how serious and practical all the reforms were. Above all the reformers sought to deal with the critical problem of poorly qualified officials. They established high educational qualifications for the top officers.[53] Not just those in the papal penitentiary, as Hofmann says, but also the protonotaries and auditors were required to be in holy orders (the last named had to take orders within a year of assuming office); in fact, all the chief officials of the penitentiary, including its scriptors, were to be priests, and the scriptors of the chancery, though not required to be priests, were required to be celibate. In addition, rigorous examinations were required for auditors and abbreviators.

The reformers also sought to insure the impartiality of the officials by forbidding them to be directly financially dependent on the pope or any cardinal; by insuring that auditors, penitentiaries, and clerks of the chamber were drawn from diverse geographical regions; and by decreeing that auditors, penitentiaries, and scriptors be provided with adequate and independent sources of income.

The serious problem of sale of offices, which had begun under Boniface IX,[54] was attacked directly by forbidding the sale of scriptors' offices. The reforms tried to limit the venality which was invited by the custom of giving tips (*propina*) to officials for their services. Strict limits were placed on the amounts that could be received, and all payments were to be gifts freely offered, not sums extorted by the officials. Penitentiaries in particular were threatened with loss of office if they even hinted at a desire to receive gifts from penitents. It is interesting that almost none of these provisions against venality were included in Adimari's original proposal; they were all added during the course of the deliberations.

The reforms sought above all fairness and efficiency. Officials were to be serious and professional and always to wear the proper dress. Notaries and others were not to pad documents or make more documents than necessary (in this way increasing the amount they could charge). Documents were to be produced accurately by those responsible, not by stand-ins, and were to be properly

---

[53] The corrector, auditor litterarum contradictarum, and the auditor of the camera, as well as all the auditors of the Rota were to have their doctorates (Rota auditors were to have taught for two years beyond the doctorate in a university). Protonotaries, penitentiaries, and clerics of the camera, as well as the pope's chaplains and the subdeacon, were all to be masters of law or theology.

[54] See Brigide Schwarz, "Die Entstehung der Ämterkäuflichkeit an der Römischen Kurie," in *Ämterhandel im Spätmittelalter und im 16. Jahrhundert* (Berlin, 1984) 61–65.

authenticated. Officials were enjoined under penalty to issue documents speedily and diligently. Those who lost supplications were to receive no compensation for their services. Procedures for the important court of the Rota were especially carefully regulated to insure that the auditors and notaries did their jobs, and to prevent bribery and conflicts of interest.

For all their weaknesses, these amount to an impressive set of reforms. It is not surprising that each successive reform movement in the fifteenth century returned to them as a starting point.[55] Even though most of them were not enacted in the final decrees or concordats at Constance, Martin V made efforts to carry out virtually every one of them. This latter point Hofmann also concedes, but he dismisses Martin's efforts as half-hearted and ineffectual. A more recent and intensive study by Thomas Frenz has yielded quite different conclusions on one of the central reforms—the reduction of the number of chancery scriptors.[56] (This was one of the few parts of c.6 that was actually enacted as legislation by the Council.)[57]

Frenz shows that Martin issued no less than eleven constitutions to deal with this problem. One of the difficulties was that, as the curia had been forced to travel over the years, many of the scriptors had simply drifted away, but still officially retained their office, title, and privileges. Martin's return to Rome did much to lessen this problem in the future. And, in 1423, Martin issued a decree requiring the absentees to return within a year or lose their office. The numbers even of active scriptors were quite high in the early years of Martin's reign because the scriptors from the three former obedience were now combined into one college. Reducing the numbers of functioning scriptors was difficult because they were organized collegially and were able to stage very effective resistance to dismissal.[58] In spite of all these difficulties, by using great restraint

---

[55] The record of the reform committee deliberations in M was probably one used by a reform commission established by Martin V in 1423; see below, p. 293.

[56] Thomas Frenz, "Zum Problem der Reduzierung der Zahl der päpstlichen Kanzleischreiber nach dem Konzil von Konstanz," in *Grundwissenschaften und Geschichte: Festscrift für P. Ach*, ed. W. Schlögl and P. Herde (Kallmünz, 1976), 256–273.

[57] It was enacted in the concordats (except the English Concordat), but interestingly, as part of the article on papal reservations; see above, 84, n.22; see Hübler, 169–71.

[58] See Schwarz, "Ämterkäuflichkeit," 62. See also her *Organisation*, 182–83. Individual scriptors generally granted (sold) their offices to successors. Thus the granting of these offices was largely removed from the hands of the popes. Schwarz

in the appointment of new scriptors, Martin was able to reduce by attrition the total number of active scriptors from 110 to 81. Frenz estimates that the overall total (active and inactive) was reduced from ca. 250 to ca. 150, i.e. from 250% above the limit down to 50% above the limit of 100.

All this indicates that Martin's actions in executing the Constance legislation were neither half-hearted nor ineffectual. Moreover, our survey of the manner in which the Constance reforms of the curia were drafted shows that they were much more carefully and practically constructed than Hofmann and others have thought. The most serious abuses set in later in the century when the curia again departed—in quite extreme ways—from the standards which the Constance reforms had tried to establish.[59]

5. The papal oath of office (cc.2, 2a, and 2b)

Similar success is observable in the results of negotiation on the papal oath. Here, however, reforms were more seriously threatened by rivalry between conciliar and cardinalitian views. Nowhere is this rivalry more apparent than in the two proposed constitutions appended to the oath. The first (*Cum antiqui*), as we have seen, required the pope to secure the cardinals' consent before undertaking any serious action. In the second (*Quia decet*) a similar (and overlapping) list of actions is drawn up, but in this case it is the consent of the council that he must receive.

For the cardinals *Cum antiqui* was a logical extension of the oath itself. Significantly, that alleged oath of Boniface VIII was sworn, not to God, but to St. Peter. St. Peter is the patron saint of the Roman church, and according to medieval tradition the possessions of a church belong to its patron saint.[60] (The oath implies limitations on papal power even here, by also invoking the co-patron saint of Rome, St. Paul, who of course on one occasion in the New Testament (Gal. 2,11) had openly rebuked St. Peter.) The principal concern of the cardinals was to protect these possessions

---

shows that the inability to reduce the numbers of scriptors led to a large increase in the gratuities demanded by the scriptors for their work.

[59] On these later practices, see the works by Partner cited in the bibliography, especially *The Pope's Men: The Papal Civil Service in the Renaissance* (Oxford, 1990); also John Thompson, *Popes and princes, 1417–1517: Politics and Polity in the Late Medieval Church* (London, 1980), 95–113. See also Schwarz, *Organisation*, 216.

[60] Otto Gierke, *Das deutsche Genossenschaftsrecht*, 4 vols. (Berlin, 1868–1913, repr. Graz, 1954), 2:526–32.

against alienation and misuse because they shared in the privileges
of the Roman church and in its governance. It was also very much
in their interest to prevent the pope's unrestrained disposal over
these possessions which gave him a freedom of action and thus
power over against themselves. As Hübler already noted without
realizing the full import of this concept for conciliar canonists,[61] the
cardinals were in fact offering to act as the episcopal chapter for the
bishop of Rome.

By requiring the pope to swear that he would take no action in
these areas without their written consent, the cardinals were offering their oversight to prevent such abuses in the future. This
method of preventing abuses had two great advantages for the
cardinals. First, it enhanced their powers in the church, as indicated above; and second, it promised to foreclose conciliar action in
these matters. Such conciliar action would have placed legal limits
on the powers of the Roman church, powers which the cardinals
shared. Now according to the prevailing canonistic theory, it was
lawful to break an oath if the higher demands of love (*caritas*)
demanded it.[62] (This same canonistic teaching had been used by
reformers to justify withdrawal of obedience from a schismatic
pope.) In some ways the oath could allow a flexibility desirable
even in some reformers' eyes. A clarification to the clause concerning transfer of prelates in *Quia decet* suggests the problem. The pope
must not transfer prelates unwillingly until the next council, it says,
*although where "scandal and danger for the church would threaten if he
waited until the meeting of the next council, the pope is allowed with the
counsel and consent of the majority of cardinals to provide for this scandal, but
without making a transfer."* In other words, the authors of the decree
realized that by denying the pope power to transfer prelates, except
in a general council, they were taking away disciplinary power that
might be needed in the meantime for the purposes of reform. The
word "scandal" here is important; we shall return to it.

For many reformers, even an oath not to act without conciliar
consent would have been too weak, not least because it would have
been so difficult to enforce. Conciliar reformers had different
reasons and interests in seeking to control the administration of the
Roman Church than did the cardinals. Indeed, for them the Roman Church itself meant something quite different. It was not
chiefly the local church in which St. Peter had been bishop, but the
universal Church. True, they had an indirect interest in the way in

---

[61] Hübler, 145 n.66. See Tierney, *Foundations*, 68–84.
[62] Buisson, 237–269.

which the local Roman church was managed; if the pope could not support himself, they would ultimately have to pay the price of supporting him through taxation. But for most reformers the squandering and mismanagement of the material possessions of the Church were subsumed under the larger question of the pope's faithful stewardship of the Christian religion. And thus it is no accident that the changes made to the oath in the second reform committee (S², c.3, *Quanto Romanus*) limited its scope (perhaps we should rather say broadened it) to deal with this stewardship alone. These changes also represented an important victory for the conciliar conception of reform: In the new oath, the councils of the Lateran, Lyons, and Vienne are added to the list of general councils whose decisions the pope must swear to obey. Significantly, the oath is to be sworn not only to St. Peter, but also to God; and the church which the pope is to rule is not called the church of St. Peter, but the Church of God.

6. *The clauses salvaged from Quia decet*: Transfers of prelates and alienations

Not only was the oath itself transformed, but *Cum antiqui* and *Quia decet* were dropped. This might suggest that the reformers won a conceptual victory at the cost of the practical defeat of those measures which promised to restrain papal practices such as transfer of prelates against their will. This was not the case, because the most important clauses in *Quia decet* were erected into separate reform proposals.

Early in its deliberations, the reform committee had already removed the clauses on transfer of prelates and on alienations from *Cum antiqui* and placed them in *Quia decet*, making conciliar rather than cardinalitian consent necessary for these papal actions.[63] Moreover, it appears that the committee had already decided in August, 1415,[64] to make a separate decree on transfer of prelates.

---

[63] The third matter transferred from *Cum antiqui* to *Quia decet*—shortening of the year of Jubilee—appears to have been lost in the further deliberations, although it is interesting that the major fragment of the revised papal oath found among the second reform committee's deliberations in W² (see n. 38 above) contains as its major provision a promise not to shorten the interval between years of jubilee. In my reconstruction of the proceedings in this entire section I am making assumptions about the relationship of the manuscripts which are explained in the Introduction to the Edition below, p. 277.

[64] The evidence for this in MSS E and W of the Common collection at c. 37 does not specify the year. It is conceivable, but unlikely, that this occurred in 1416.

The draft of this decree appears in the manuscripts of the Common Collection as c.37, *Translationes invitorum*. A separate decree on alienations, on the other hand, does not appear to have emerged until the second reform committee, whose membership did not include cardinals.

The outcry against transfer of prelates against their will was great at Constance. This demand appears prominently in almost all the reform tracts at the council. The reformers were convinced that the popes of the schism had used such transfers as a fund-raising technique.[65] Although the actual use of such transfers for this purpose was probably less frequent than reformers thought, a single transfer of a powerful prelate could create an enormous amount of bad will. Such was the case with Élie de Lestrange, bishop of LePuy, whom John [XXIII] had attempted to transfer against his will in 1412.[66] Lestrange was a member of the first reform committee. Reformers also believed that John [XXIII] had transferred prelates to punish them for his opposition to them; it was with this thought that they nullified all his transfers of unwilling prelates in one of the paragraphs of *Haec sancta*, in April, 1415.[67]

The wording of the first draft of the separate decree, Common, c.37, is almost exactly the same as that of the clause in *Quia decet*. It includes a ban on transfers of abbots which had been added already in the marginal notes to *Quia decet* in some manuscripts. It is not until the second reform committee that we find a formal decree with arenga (S², c.6, *Cum ex prelatorum*). There the arenga stresses the suffering of the churches whose prelates are transferred and, significantly, also of all churches whose prelates defend their liberty (*libertas*) less vigilantly out of fear of being transferred. This is one of the few times in the reform deliberations when we observe the famous Gallican watchword "liberty," of which Haller made so much. And there is not a word here about the fiscal motives for transfers, although the arenga suggests that the pope, who is, after

---

[65] In fact there was an official document in the Avignon chamber under Clement VII which called for filling vacant sees through transfers (involving several sees if possible), in order to multiply the services which could be collected on this occasion; see Favier, 374–378. However, Favier also finds that in practice such transfers were not particularly frequent. On the other hand, Giulio Silano points to consistent use by popes of transfers for fiscal purposes beginning in the thirteenth century. See his "Episcopal Elections and the Apostolic See. The Case of Aquileia: 1251– 1420," in *Diritto e potere nella storia europea: Atti in onore di Bruno Paradisi* (Florence, 1982), 163–194 at 174, 182–83, and 194. I am indebted to Thomas Izbicki for this reference.

[66] See Paris, Archives Nationales, 65A, no. 7, cited in ACC.4.lvii–lviii.

[67] Mansi 27:591A-B.

all, only a man, might be unaware of the tawdrier motives of those who try to persuade him to make such transfers. The execution clause of the decree contains a surprise. Instead of forbidding the pope to make transfers except in a general council and with its consent, as in *Quia decet*, it returns to the idea of cardinalitian oversight. And this draft was the work of a reform committee from which cardinals had been excluded! Returning to the requirement for cardinalitian consent and subscription enabled the committee to provide for the situation in which a transfer was urgent for the sake of reform. It shows that successful syntheses of conciliar and cardinalitian solutions were possible when practical needs dictated.

The negotiations concerning alienations followed a similar pattern. The first clauses concerning alienations in *Cum antiqui* had been very broad and general. They simply required the cardinals' consent and subscription for all alienations of what we would today call real property (*immobilia*) and of permanent rights of the Roman and other churches, as well as of precious movable property of the same churches; similar approval was required for remissions or postponements of payments due to the same churches in perpetual taxes or other obligations. In *Quia decet* these clauses were expanded and made much more specific. The committee added a long list of types of property which now could not be alienated without conciliar approval: property (*res*), rights, revenues, possessions, castles, cities, towns, manors, taxes, pensions, and canons. Moreover, not only permanent alienations required conciliar approval, but so did other arrangements which transferred property to other parties for long periods (ten years or more); these would include leases, mortgages, and enfeoffments.[68] And in the clause about delays in payments, the committee specified a two year limit.

The first separate draft on alienations included in the records of the second reform committee (*Ut Romanus*, S[2], c.7) returns to the idea of an oath to be sworn by the pope prior to his coronation that he will not alienate possessions or rights of the Roman or other churches. In one sense the measure is stronger than earlier ones; it calls on the pope not to make any alienations at all. A list of specific examples very similar to that in *Quia decet* is included. Another new clause also greatly expands the measure's scope: the pope is also to promise that he will recover the things that have been alienated in the past, as far as he is able. Here the measure begins to parallel

---

[68] Later the German Avisamenta placed special emphasis on the pawning of lands.

contemporary legislation in secular governments requiring rulers to revoke alienations. However, the word used is *recuperare* rather than revoke and is of special interest to the present study since it is a verb of reform. Because the measure calls on the pope to forswear all alienations it makes no requirement for consent, either conciliar or cardinalitian. We have seen that canonistic theory allowed oaths to be broken if *caritas* demanded it; and this measure left it up to the pope to decide when such demands existed.

A much more incisive measure dealing with past alienations (*Cum post obitum*, S², c.9) was submitted to the committee August 15 (record of deliberation in W², c.4). As the incipit signals (the death in question, as so often, was that of Gregory XI), the measure revokes alienations made during the Schism. In place of the word *recuperare* it uses the word *reuocare* to refer to the gaining back of the lost property (*proprietas*), and in an extraordinarily strong statement the decree annuls, cassates, and abrogates all the grants by which the alienations had been made, even if they were made *motu proprio de plenitudine potestatis*. The arenga refers to the grants as extortions, made under false pretenses by "diverse schemes and plots under the cloak of favor and assistance or some other necessity or utility." It finally simply calls them usurpations.

In the deliberation of the measure August 15, committee members fastened on this latter terminology, but made a distinction between alienations and usurpations. They concluded unanimously that both alienations and usurpations of property of the Roman church should be revoked. But as for the property of other churches, while all usurpations were to be revoked, only alienations made unduly (*indebite*) would be so handled.

The reforms in *Cum post obitum* were soon abandoned in the deliberations. When alienations were listed in Article 12 of the *cautio* decree of the 40th session, only future alienations were specified. Both the French and German nations expressed approval for the reform committee article in their Avisamenta. The Germans even wanted the pope to punish bishops and abbots by deposition if they alienated their churches' lands; likewise, episcopal chapters which gave their assent to such alienations. The papal *Responsio* expressed willingness to go very far indeed—revocation of all alienations made by popes during the Schism and of illegal alienations made by prelates and others. It even resurrected the cardinals' request from the first reform committee that only cardinals or prelates be sent to govern lands of the Papal States. And, when none of this was enacted in the decrees or concordats, Martin nevertheless made regaining the alienated possessions one of his highest priorities.[69]

7. *Deposing a pope*

Romanus pontifex (c.5 of the Common Collection) is the most striking of all the reforms presented to the reform committee at Constance, both in its language and its scope. The rubric alone sets the tone: "That the pope may also be deposed for other crimes besides heresy, if they notoriously scandalize the church." Its highly polemical arenga brings together and harmonizes in felicitous language all the major orthodox theoretical traditions, both canonistic and theological, which supported the limitation of absolute papal power. The polemics must be seen against the background of the council's recent successful deposition of John [XXIII], who was not a heretic, but who had done a great deal which notoriously scandalized the church. All his notorious deeds (along with many things he did not do) had been rehearsed in lurid detail in his trial just two months earlier. In some ways *Romanus pontifex* can be seen as a ratification of that proceeding.

It had two more practical aims as well. First, the council faced the likelihood that it would need to depose another pope in the near future—Benedict XIII, who showed no sign of giving up his office voluntarily, as Gregory XII had recently done. A conciliar decree like *Romanus pontifex* could pave the way for that deposition by removing any remaining doubts about the council's authority in such matters. Many reformers also wanted a clear statement about one particular papal crime that would remove a different set of doubts. They wanted the decree to declare that a pope could be guilty of simony, particularly when he demanded payment for the granting of benefices. They hoped in this way to attack the very real simony which had occurred in the curia during the Schism (this had been one of the charges against John [XXIII], e.g.), and many also hoped in this way to attack the annates and services. Thus the decree acquired a second aim. This aim became more urgent as it became apparent that the decree against simony (*Contra labem,*

---

[69] See Peter Partner, *The Papal State under Martin V: The Administration and Government of the Temporal Power in the Early Fifteenth Century* (London, 1958), 43–94.

Common, c.3) would not contain an explicit reference to papal simony.[70]

All the indications are that *Romanus pontifex* was approved early by the committee and sent on to the nations.[71] However, by the time of the second reform committee circumstances had changed. Benedict XIII had already been deposed, not for notorious crimes but for heresy: through his stubborn persistence in schism, he had denied the fundamental article of faith concerning the unity of the church.[72] On the other hand, the reforms of the annates and services were being debated more hotly than ever. Thus, in some ways the second aim identified above came to outweigh the first. The decree was radically truncated, the arenga was dropped, and in the new decree (*Ne sancta mater*, S², c.4), a correspondingly greater stress was placed on the statement that the pope could be deposed for simony. The new very brief arenga used the significant word *laberetur* to refer to the crime for which the pope could be deposed, thus evoking the decree against simony, *Contra labem* (Common, c.3). But above all the decree contained a new clause which specifically clarified that the simony in question might be involved in the granting of ecclesiastical benefices, as well as in the dispensing of sacraments (*tam circa sacramenta quam circa beneficia ecclesiastica*). This phrase in fact appears first in a copy of *Romanus pontifex* itself which is found in W² (although the first seven words of the decree are replaced with a slightly longer opening, so that the new incipit becomes *Et quoniam decet Romanum pontificem*). The fact that this draft was retained among the deliberations of the second reform committee in W² (which also contains the later draft *Ne sancta mater*) shows that there was still interest in the remarkable arenga of *Romanus pontifex*.

Let us now return to that arenga. Its central focus was the *scandalum*. The pope was to be deposed for crimes that notoriously *scandalize* the church. Ludwig Buisson has demonstrated the importance of this term in the development of theological and especially canonistic thought about the papal *plenitudo potestatis*.[73] Over the century and one-half before the Council of Constance an *opinio*

---

[70] See above, Chapter 3; see also the two marginal notes on *Contra labem* in C which suggest this explicitly (although it is very possible that one or both notes were added at the time of the Council of Basel; see above, p. 75.)

[71] The marginal note "Expeditus" appears next to it in W, and it was among the five proposals in P sent to the French nation (See below, pp. 277–78.)

[72] Harald Zimmermann, "Die Absetzung der Päpste auf dem Konstanzer Konzil," in *Das Konzil von Konstanz*, 113–137 at 129–135.

[73] Buisson, 125–165.

communis had developed among canonists in strong opposition to Innocent IV's claim that the *plenitudo potestatis* is unlimited because anything is allowed (*licet*) to the pope. Building on Augustine's teaching concerning the *exemplum caritatis* (the example of love which the prelate is to offer), the canonists had argued that though everything is possible (*licet*), not everything is fitting (*decet*) or expedient (*expedit*). Thus they added to the criterion of power (*potestas*) the criterion of decency (*honestas*) and love (*caritas*). If an action of the pope causes scandal (literally, a stumbling block) to one of his followers, he must refrain from it; even though it is lawful for him according to the *plenitudo potestatis*, it is not expedient according to the demands of love (*caritas*). Buisson shows how this *opinio communis* came to be applied more and more directly to concrete situations as a result of the very real scandals which people experienced through the actions of the popes during the Schism.

At the Council of Constance, the concept was in fact used as a practical guide to determine which papal privileges, dispensations, and unions granted during the Schism should be revoked. If such papal grants were scandalous, they should be revoked; sometimes, however, for grants which had already gone into effect, scandal would have resulted from their revocation, and they should be allowed to remain (see Chapter 6 below, p. 147). These were not the kinds of scandalous acts for which a pope would be deposed; *Romanus pontifex* speaks of notorious crimes. Simony was such a crime. So were many of the other acts for which John [XXIII] had been deposed.

Such actions committed by the person who was supposed to be the pastor of pastors constituted a very real scandal. *Romanus pontifex* calls attention to this again and again by stressing the supreme position of the pope in the hierarchical conception of the church. The pope is the shepherd of shepherds, the leader not just of one people, but of all people; an example (*exemplum*) not just for people, but for prelates. The proposed decree exalts the pope to the heights of heaven using pseudo-Dionysian terminology.[74] The ecclesiastical hierarchy is compared to the angelic one; the pope, as the sun, purges, illumines and perfects the prelates as though they were stars. The pseudo-Dionysian imagery of light pervades the arenga. All this underlines the absurdity and scandal of such a person committing public crimes, and the arenga reinforces this

---

[74] On the pseudo-Dionysian terminology, see below, pp. 211–212 and 248ff.

with its use of irony. It refers to the ironic difference between name and deed ("let him be holy in fact as well as name"). This was of utmost importance for the mimetic tradition of reform[75] and the *exemplum caritatis* that the prelates were to provide for their flock. In referring to Christ's commission to Peter, the arenga selects the text in which Jesus tells Peter to confirm his brothers after he himself has been converted (Luke 22,32), thus alluding to Peter's denial of Christ. Then it ironically sets Peter's conversion against the possible conversion of the pope from celestial things to terrestrial, and it turns the Pseudo-Dionysian angelic hierarchy upside down by quoting a gloss on a canon in the *Decretum* (C.9 q.3 c.14 *Aliorum*) which reminds the pope that Lucifer, because he was the highest angel was "punished all the more irreparably" when he fell.

This passage not only completes the irony, but also takes us to the heart of the substantive issue involved. The decree is in fact a direct answer to *Aliorum*. A passage in the anonymous annate tract *Ad ostendendum*, written at Constance, demonstrates the connection.[76] *Aliorum* is, in fact, all too relevant to *Romanus pontifex*; an excerpt from Ps.-Symmachus, its main point is that God has reserved to himself judgment of the pope.[77] *Romanus pontifex* answers this apparently insuperable obstacle to the conciliar deposition of a pope quite directly: "And let him not take confidence that he has been reserved only to the divine and Last Judgment . . . because God also exercises his judgments in this world through the church which is the body of Christ; and general councils represent the universal church."

---

[75] Karl Morrison, *The Mimetic Tradition of Reform in the West* (Princeton, 1982).

[76] ACC.2.592–600. Finke omitted this passage from his edition (and also omitted almost all of the scores of canonistic citations in this tract.) For a more detailed analysis of this tract, see Chapter 7 below. Finke edited it from Paris, BN lat. 14644; another copy is found in the same Augsburg manuscript which contains a copy of the reform committee deliberations (manuscript A of the edition below; see p. 289). The relevant passage (Augsburg 2° 226, p. 381) reads as follows: " . . . cum symonia sit prohibita de iure diuino ut infra dicetur ad illud obligatur papa ymo fortius et strictius quam alius et hoc respectu dicit glosa in c. Aliorum ix q. iii [C.9 q.3 c.14] quod papa peccans sine spe venie puniri debet ad instar dyaboli qui prout dicit beatus Gregorius in moralibus loquens de Lucifero inter ceteros angelos sublimiori inquit idcirco peccans sine venia dampnatus est quia magnus sine aliorum comparatione fuerat creatus, de quo De pe. di. ii c. Principium [De pen. D.2 c.45 fin.] et in hoc non insisto quia iste dominus Jo. XXIII ex isto crimine symonie per generale concilium nuperime et merito dampnatus est multis ad hoc racionibus et auctoritatibus sacrum mouentibus concilium."

[77] On the use of *Aliorum* by Johannes Falkenberg, O.P. to oppose judgment of a pope for simony, see Hartmut Boockmann, *Johannes Falkenberg, der Deutsche Orden und die polnische Politik: Untersuchungen zur politischen Theorie des späteren Mittelalters* (Göttingen, 1975), 138.

In a skillful manner, the person or persons who drafted *Romanus pontifex* combined the canonistic discussion with the Pseudo-Dionysian imagery of the angelic hierarchy as archetype for the earthly one. The conclusion concerning the council's power to judge the pope is clearly based on the belief that the council represents the universal church and may have been influenced by Gerson's teaching that the council represents all the ranks of the ecclesiastical hierarchy.[78] However, its principal thrust is to synthesize this idea with the gospel teaching concerning fraternal correction (Matt. 18,15–18) in which the sinning brother is first to be warned and then to be denounced to the community for judgment.[79] The text of *Romanus pontifex* goes on to specify the procedure for warning the pope. It starts with the most obvious choice, warning by the cardinals, but it specifies that this must be done collegially by two-thirds majority (an addition in W² says it must be done publicly before a great multitude). Then as a sufficient alternative it proposes warnings by three provincial councils in three different nations under three different kings. One manuscript even suggests warnings by three different universities. The emphasis in all of these is clearly on the public nature of the scandal.

However, the council abandoned *Romanus pontifex* and finally never enacted any decree on the deposition of a pope. The German Avisamenta expressed the desire for a decree, but the French, who had pursued it so ardently, finally said simply that they did not like the decree of the reform committee (i.e., *Ne sancta mater*); however, they expressed willingness to go along with whatever the other nations could agree on. The papal *Responsio* observed drily that there did not seem to be any need for further statements on this matter. In one sense there was not a need. The council had already deposed a pope for notorious crimes. The legitimacy of Martin's throne depended on the legitimacy of that act. Some reformers also saw such a decree as a way to attack the annates, but most must have realized that the result would have been a clumsy effort to fuse very different types of legislation.

I believe there may be a further explanation for the abandoning of both *Quia decet* and *Romanus pontifex*. It takes us back to the word

---

[78] See Pascoe, *Gerson*, 39–48; strikingly absent from *Romanus pontifex* are Gerson's references to the presence of the Holy Spirit at the council which gives the council its authority. The decree *Haec sancta*, which is another intertext for *Romanus pontifex*, was much more careful in this respect.

[79] Panormitanus made a similar synthesis later; see Buisson, 191–192.

honestius in *Cum antiqui*. The authors of the note at the end of that draft had said it might be more fitting to express these limits on papal power as oaths rather than as decrees. In many ways the criterion of *honestas* (*quid decet*) turns out to be more important at Constance than Buisson's study might suggest. Several decrees, including *Quia decet* itself,[80] apply this standard quite specifically to the pope's exercise of his plenitude of power. However, conversely, when the council was frankly acknowledged to be above the pope in the ecclesiastical hierarchy, then the council's exercise of its *plenitudo potestatis* with respect to the pope became subject to this same criterion of *honestas*. This is one reason why the decree *Frequens* was so important for the Constance reformers. The frequent meeting of general councils offered the prospect of exercising the council's power in a way that would limit abuses of papal power without injuring the criterion of *honestas*. Instead of binding the pope by inflexible legislation, it would hold up papal actions to the continuous scrutiny of reason. The council would use restraint in the exercise of its own power towards the pope according to the same standard of *honestas* which it expected the pope to use in dealing with the lower ranks in the hierarchy. The legislation on the deposition of a pope may have been dropped, not because the council had doubts about its power in this matter, but because it deemed the legislation not to be fitting.

8. Conclusion

The reforms of the head considered in this chapter, like those in Chapters 2 and 3, enjoyed marked success. In those chapters the reforms were mainly pragmatic efforts to deal with specific practical abuses. The reforms discussed in this chapter also involved practical matters, such as the operation of the curia, the transfer of prelates, and the alienation of church lands. Reformers also attempted to lay the basis in theory for correcting, and above all preventing, papal abuses of power in general. They enjoyed success in both spheres.

Reforms were enacted in the concordats which set limits on the numbers of curial officials. Martin V made major efforts to carry

---

[80] See especially the decree "*Decet Romanum pontificem*" (W2, c.18), dealing with spoils and fruits during vacancies. This schedule invokes the famous Roman law text *Digna vox [C.1.14.4]*, which had applied the same standard of *honestas* to the use of the emperor's absolute power. See Stump, "Taxation," 80–82 for a fuller discussion of this schedule.

out these reforms and did achieve impressive results. Beyond this, the reform committee, in an exemplary process of thoughtful deliberation, developed an entire program of sensible and well-crafted measures which, though not enacted at Constance, became the model for all future efforts at curial reform down to the Council of Trent. Martin V attempted to carry out these reforms as well, even though the council did not officially enact them. He pursued the unenacted reforms of alienations of Roman church property even more aggressively. The conciliar decree restricting transfer of prelates against their will seems to have been observed for many years; and the final version of the decree reflects a successful synthesis between the conciliar and cardinalitian models for preventing papal abuses of power. Extraordinarily finely crafted measures for preventing future schisms were honed by the committee and enacted in *Si vero*. And finally, the greatest success of all, *Frequens*, inaugurated the frequent celebration of general councils. Like *Si vero*, it was exceedingly well crafted, in this case to carry out the reformers' intent to make councils permanent, automatic, and universal.

Frequens was the greatest single success in the areas of both reform theory and practice. Combined with the final version of the papal oath, it built on generations of canonistic and theological thought to take the proposal first made by William Durant the Younger a century earlier and create from it a strong new theory of ongoing conciliar reform of the church. The magnitude of this achievement and its significance will become apparent in the rest of this study. In the next chapter we shall see that *Frequens* was, in some ways, even more important for the reform *in membris* than for reform *in capite*.

CHAPTER SIX

REFORM OF THE MEMBERS

Historians have consistently underestimated the extent to which
the reformers at Constance dealt seriously with the reform of the
members alongside the reform of the head. Hübler concentrated all
his attention on the reforms which were finally enacted in the
decrees and concordats. In tracing the development of these he did
sometimes shed light on the broader reform program of which they
were a part, but only in a manner incidental to his main theme.
Reforms which were not enacted in any form, and this includes
most of the reforms of the members, escaped his attention entirely.
Finke compounded the problem in his edition by re-organizing the
record of the reform deliberations, wrenching them out of their
context in the manuscripts in order to group together the reforms
that led to each of the final decrees or major articles in the concordats. Almost all of these were primarily reforms of the head. Most
of the other reforms he simply listed after these; indeed, for most of
them he did not even provide texts, instead referring the reader to
Von der Hardt's edition. The manuscripts themselves provide a
much more accurate view of the *reformatio generalis* undertaken by
the reformers. It is true that the reformers did give priority to
reform of the head, but this was because they saw it as a vital
prerequisite to the reform of the members; according to the prevailing hierarchical view reform would extend down from the head to
the members. Moreover, reformers saw abuses of the head as
deeply intertwined with those of the members; it was in the context
of papal dispensations, for example, that they discussed the serious
problems of pluralism, absenteeism, and lack of sufficient qualification of the clergy. Part of the reason for the reformers' failure to
enact more of the reforms of the members was the need they felt to
concentrate energy first on the apparently more serious abuses of
the head. But this was only part of the reason. I will suggest others,
above all problems of enforcement and the different regional situations which made a *reformatio generalis* increasingly difficult.

1. *Clerical* mores

Reform of the members involved three main areas: the morality (*mores*) of the clergy, their qualifications, and their performance of duty (i.e. pastoral care). Infractions in these areas had long been targets of conciliar legislation, so much so that many reforms at Constance were prefaced by a statement that the reformers were renewing the good laws of the past. Yet these same matters were still among the leading problems in the church on the eve of the later Protestant Reformation. The urgency of reform in these areas was heightened by the efforts of the clergy to set itself apart from and above laymen, coupled with the clergy's own critique of clerical worldliness from the pulpit. In this way, they unwittingly accentuated their own hypocrisy just when laymen's expectations for the clergy were rising.

The council sermons were replete with reprovals of clerical worldliness, the attempt of clerics to live like laymen. Clothing was one of the prime symptoms. Ambitious persons sought to show that they had risen to a higher social position through their mode of dress. Peter Pulka delivered a scathing satire of clerics who tried to dress modishly, with indecently decorated garments, stylishly tailored and luridly colored; whose sleeves were so full that their owners looked more as though they wished to fly like vultures than to walk like men.[1] These clerics were chimeras, Peter said, their clerical heads (with their tonsure, the true crown of a cleric) monstrously joined to the torsoes of knights and the feet of actors. Other reformers attacked the clergy's pursuit of other lay status symbols—castles, horses, retainers, and hunting birds and dogs,[2] which they mentioned under the general label of pomp and luxury. They detected such pomp especially at the papal court and among the cardinals but also in many monasteries and courts of prelates.[3] The attacks varied in their acerbity; the most bitter even struck tones of a certain anarchism: "O future pope, cardinals, and others, you are all brothers and you are not to call anyone father on earth," cried one preacher, who warned the future pope that he was a man, not an angel. He might be about to be pope, but he might also die

---

[1] Peter Pulka, Sermon, September 6, 1416, ACC.2.465.
[2] Anonymous sermon, January 12, 1416, ACC.2.428.
[3] Cf. Johannes de Vincelles, Sermon, July 11, 1417, ACC.2.500f.; also Johannes Zacharie, Sermon, September 29, 1415, Stuttgart Landesbibliothek, Theol. et phil. Fol. 50, fol. 7v.

tomorrow like any other human and would then be eaten by vermin, which were generally unimpressed by royal or princely dignity.[4]

The existing records of the reform committee focus on three areas of clerical morals—dress, sexual *mores* (specifically concubinage), and simony.[5] The first two were addressed in three proposals which were among the additions to the Common Collection—cc. 39 on concubines, 40 on clerical vestments, and 48 on prelates who enter church without proper tonsure or dress. Proposed decrees on these matters are found in the additional schedules in V overlooked by Finke and in the Augsburg manuscript. V also includes a draft of the decree on vestments finally enacted in the forty-third general session.

The proposal on concubines in Common, c.39 was very stringent; it called upon all clerics including bishops who were living with concubines to give them up within one month or to suffer *ipso facto* privation of all benefices. However, there was debate in the committee about whether the parishioners of such clerics should avoid them, i.e., not receive sacraments from them. The committee decided that they should be avoided only if their superiors had warned the people specifically to do so; private decisions in such matters could lead to scandal. As if following up on this discussion, the proposed decree in the Augsburg manuscript[6] required bishops to search out clerics who were cohabiting and to warn everyone in the diocese not to hear mass or receive sacraments from them.[7] The

---

[4] Anonymous sermon, 1417 (?), ed. Schneyer 115 (1967) 125: "Nec modo laetentur, quia forsan cras morientur nec aliquis ipsorum est tam tortis, cui parcant vincula mortis. Cur nunc caro laetatur quia vermibus esca paratur, jam rex et princeps apud ipsos modicum reputatur. O summe future pontifex, quando considerabis te esse summum pontificem, consideras te esse vilissimum vermem. Reformetis igitur praefati domini et corrigatis statum clericorum tantae superbiae et praelatorum vanae gloriae ad debitum statum pro reformatione ecclesiae."

[5] On simony, see below, p. 150.

[6] This proposed decree may have been drafted by the humanist Pier Paolo Vergerio; see below, p. 276.

[7] This was a matter of continuing importance, particularly in Germany and Eastern Europe, where reformers around John Hus demanded similar and much harsher measures against immoral clergy. The provision in the German concordat known as *Ad vitanda*, which established a new and more moderate rule in this matter, and which otherwise seems to have had no basis in the prior reform deliberations of the council, may in fact have been a spinoff of this discussion of avoiding priests who hold concubines. For *Ad vitanda*, see the exhaustive discussion in Hübler, 186–191 and Excurs I., 333–359. *Ad vitanda* stated that people should not avoid a priest until he had been formally denounced by a judge. At the Council of Basel the earlier, harsher practice was re-instated; i.e. that mere notariety was sufficient reason to avoid the priest. See Helmrath, "Reform," 114–114 and n. 140.

wording of the decree suggests the difficulties of enforcement. Bishops were admonished to deprive guilty clerics of their benefices if they did not give up their concubines within a month *or if they moved them from place to place to elude the mandate. If the bishop himself was negligent* in these matters, he could be deprived of his see by the pope, but also by a provincial council (by two-thirds vote).

There was a radical solution available to prevent the scandal of concubinage: allow married priests.[8] Reformers were aware that this was the custom in the Greek church and had also been practiced in New Testament times. William Durant the Younger had proposed this solution in his *Tractatus* one hundred years earlier.[9] Reformers at Constance also broached the question, sometimes tongue-in-cheek, as in the case of one who added to his proposal an ironic parenthesis: "And the earth will thus be multiplied."[10] In the final event, the council passed no legislation concerning concubines, and this matter was left for the Council of Basel to take up again.[11]

The Constance fathers did enact a decree on clerical dress, however, an area where rules were probably as flagrantly evaded as those regarding concubines. The final Constance decree actually opens with an acknowledgment that such excesses were among the most inveterate of clerical faults. The earlier draft (Common, c.40) had begun by invoking a decree of the Council of Vienne one hundred years earlier (Clem. 3.2.2 *Quoniam*), which had outlined very similar abuses. In fact, large parts of the wording of that decree were taken over verbatim into c. 40 and into the final

---

[8] See Martin Boelens, "Die Klerikerehe in der kirchlichen Gesetzgebung vom II. Laterankonzil bis zum Konzil von Basel," in *Ius sacrum: Klaus Mörsdorf zum 60. Geburtstag*, ed. Audomar Scheuermann and Georg May (Paderborn, 1969), 600–614; and N. Grévy-Pons, *Célibat et nature: Une controverse médiévale* (Paris, 1975). On the actual practice at the local level, see Louis Binz, *Vie religieuse et réforme ecclésiastique dans le diocèse de Genève pendant le grand schisme et la crise conciliaire (1378–1450)* (Geneva, 1973), 357–88.

[9] Fasolt, *Council*, 238.

[10] Anonymous reform tract, ACC.2.580–592 at p. 589: " . . . uel ad uitandum scandala, quod omnes [clerici] habeant [uxores], ut Greci habent, ut in antiquo testamento et in nouo beatus Petrus, sanctus Agricola episcopus et plures alii, qui fuerunt sanctiores nobis. Et mundus multiplicabitur, yronice loquendo." For the suggestion of permitting clergy to marry cf. Matthew Roeder, Sermon, January 24, 1417, ACC.2.485: "Habemus enim malum carnis, quod sic multos effeminat, ut paruum uideretur malum, unumquemque talium uxorem ducere propter fornicacionem . . ."; also *Capitula agendorum*, ACC.4.570: "Alias sic negligendo (to deal effectively with concubinage) prestaret permittere coniugium clericis. Et de hoc eciam disputetur."

[11] For later reform efforts at the Council of Basel, see Helmrath, "Reform," 113–114, and idem, *Basler Konzil*, 336f.

Constance decree—the same references to red and green colors, to clothes that are striped and slit, to the tabard that is lined beyond the cuff; even the same penalties appear in the final Constance decree—donation of the offending tabard to the poor (!) and, for other violations, six months suspension from collection of revenues. The earlier drafts had suggested stiffer penalties—one year's suspension (V, c.27), even privation of benefices (c.40, V, c.27 for repeat offenders), but these were dropped in the final decree.

A final decree which did little more that re-enact earlier measures might seem a disappointment. But from another point of view it was quintessential conciliar reform—the maintaining of the good traditions established by past councils. And if the stress on dress might seem literally and figuratively superficial, the wording of the Constance decree, like that of the Vienne decree before it, made the deeper significance clear. The observation of the Vienne decree that external appearance (*extrinsecus*) is a reflection of the internal state (*intrinsecus*) touches closely on a central theme of Pauline reform.[12] The Constance decree (Extrav. 4) further evokes this theme by observing that what clerics do with their minds, they profess with their dress, linking this idea with another central Pauline reform theme: All too many clerics delight to be *de*formed (*deformes*) and want to *con*form (*se conformare*) to lay society by dressing like laymen. Speaking all the more loudly by its absence is the Pauline conclusion: "Be transformed (Vulgate: *reformamini*) by the renewal of your mind . . ."[13]

2. Dispensations and privileges of clergy

And yet the Constance reformers had to deal with far more urgent clerical failings than inappropriate dress. Too many clergy were unqualified in the most fundamental ways: They were not in holy orders, they were under age, they lacked learning, and worst of all they were pluralists, clerical bigamists, absentees who all too often did not even reside in their benefices or perform their duties. The reformers attempted to deal with all these matters. In their view a breakdown in discipline had caused the abundant ecclesiastical legislation on these abuses to go unenforced. At fault were negligent superiors and cunning subordinates, but above all papal privileges

---

[12] See 2 Cor. 4,16. In the Pauline ideology, the decay of the external body is set in contrast to the renewal of the inner man; see Ladner, *Idea of Reform*, 54.

[13] Rom. 12,1–2; see Ladner, *Idea of Reform*, 53.

and dispensations. Thus the reform committee's effort to deal with the problem of unqualified clergy began with reforms of papal dispensations.

Table 1 summarizes the reforms concerning dispensations introduced in the first reform committee (Common Collection, cc. 10–16). These schedules are not proposed decrees, but rather reports of deliberations with terse lists of diverse remedies. The reforms were a two-pronged effort. On the one hand, they attacked relaxation of existing legislation caused by papal privileges and dispensations; on the other, they tried to make enforcement of the legislation more rigorous, mainly through stiffer penalties.

In dealing with each class of papal privilege the reformers made a tripartite distinction among future ones and past ones which had and had not yet taken effect. Past privileges considered especially abusive were revoked even if they had gone into effect; these included privileges for "infants" to hold office and privileges granted to mendicants to hold secular benefices. For future grants, the reformers demanded as a minimum that a reasonable cause for the privilege be stated in writing; in some cases they specified acceptable causes. For some dispensations granted to prelates, the reformers required consent and even subscription of the cardinals. They generally placed limits beyond which the pope could not dispense, even with reasonable cause. In invoking the legislation of Lateran IV against pluralism, the reformers acknowledged the exceptions stated there for those of noble birth or great learning. They also added a third exception—the case when the revenues of the benefices were small—and they placed limits on the maximum number of benefices which could be held even with dispensation. Significantly, they specified different maximum numbers according to regions.

To enforce the existing legislation against pluralism, the reformers required pluralists to give up all but two benefices within one year, and they specified stern penalties for non-residence: Bishops and abbots lost their offices if absent more than six months. An interesting alternate draft (V, c.28) softened this penalty to suspension of one-third of annual revenues for each year of non-residence; probably more enforceable than outright privation, this penalty found its way into the papal *Responsio*, but was never enacted. In a more positive vein, the reformers tried to define adequate residence in terms of being present for the major feast days.

In the final event neither the positive measures nor the penalties were enacted because nothing was enacted concerning residency; indeed, the final decree on dispensations dealt only with dispensations

TABLE 1

Limits on Papal Privileges and Dispensations
First Reform Committee

("Cause" = Reasonable cause must be stated in writing)

Dispensation or privilege for:	Future	Past, in effect	Past, not taken effect
1. Delay of ordination a. Bishops and abbots	Cause; consent of cardinals; only for one year	Revoked	Revoked
b. Students	Only one year past end of study; study unbroken	Revoked	Revoked
2. Waiving age requirements for office a. Bishop	Cause; not below age 27		Revoked, if person still under age
b. Abbot	Cause; not below age 22		
Dispensations "for infants" all revoked because against natural law			
3. Pluralism a. Bishops or abbots to hold other benefices	Only if revenues small; counsel, subscription of cardinals		
b. Priests for holding incompatible benefices	Cause (see examples); not above two (see exceptions)[1]	Excess benefices surrendered w/in year	All revoked
c. Canons to hold more than one prebend	No more than two without cause		
d. Religious to hold benefices outside order	Not to be granted; if granted, null	All revoked, even if *per modum commendarum*	
1) Friars	As above	Allowed	Revoked
2) Monks	————	to	
3) Canons regular	(Unclear)	remain	Revoked[2]
4. Non-residence a. Bishops	Cause (e.g. need to serve in curia or royal court)	Not stated	Not stated
b. Abbots	Cause (not for study, teaching, or royal counsel)		

[1] Invokes legislation of Lateran IV (X. 3,5, c.28 De multa)
[2] In later deliberation this revocation was dropped.

granted for delaying ordination. It revoked all such dispensations granted during the schism, and for all offices, not just the higher ones (but students were explicitly excepted). Those already holding offices requiring orders must take them within six months or lose their offices. Interestingly, the decree makes no mention of future dispensations.

Some of the earlier reforms of dispensations were retained in the concordats. The German, French, and Spanish concordats retained the revocation of dispensations of age requirements and also a blanket statement that major dispensations should be made only with counsel of the cardinals. Measures concerning dispensations for non-residence were retained only in the English concordat, which enjoined strict enforcement of the legislation of Lateran IV; the wording suggests that the main offenders were clergy serving in the courts of nobles and prelates (especially chantry priests).[14] Pluralism seemed a greater abuse in England because the benefices there were wealthier than in other regions. In Common, c.12, the reform committee had been willing to allow dispensations for up to four incompatible benefices in Apulia and parts of Spain, but they stated categorically that in England the maximum was two. As for past dispensations, we encounter again in the English Concordat the striking grant of power to a commission of the ordinaries to judge these and to revoke any which it finds to be scandalous. (See above, Chapter 3, p. 71, for similar commissions regarding indulgences.) Another commission of ordinaries was ordered to review past dispensations for non-residence and for archdeacons to make visitations by procurator.

The English concordat also revived an earlier measure against dispensations for religious to hold benefices outside their order. The first reform committee had decided that no future such privileges should be granted to monks or friars; if any were granted, they would be invalid.[15] As for past privileges, those for mendicants were revoked without distinction; those for monks were not (although the statement here remained vague). This measure disappeared in the further negotiations and only resurfaced in the English concordat. There it in fact assumed an even stronger form: it applied to both past and future grants, revoking the former and prohibiting the latter, and to grants made both to mendicants and other religious. On matters of concern to them, the English achieved potent reforms indeed.

---

[14] See Hübler, 212 n. 27, for further evidence in Ullerston, c. 12 (H.1.1161).
[15] See Common, c.23a, 35; see also Introduction to Edition, p. 283.

3. Unions and incorporations

The matter of greatest concern to the English was probably unions
and incorporations of benefices, especially appropriation of parish
churches by monastic houses. This was the abuse whose reform
Ullerston had depicted as ushering in the "new Jerusalem."[16] The
council enacted reforms of unions and incorporations in one of its
decrees of the forty-third session. However, the English found these
insufficient and revived large parts of the reform committee measures in their concordat.[17] The first reform committee had made a
tripartite distinction similar to that in the reforms of dispensations.
Again the chief criterion was reasonable cause stated in writing.
Future unions and incorporations were not to be made without
such cause; past ones made without cause were to be revoked even
if they had gone into effect. Past unions which had not taken effect
were all to be revoked, as were all unions of perpetual vicariates.
The reforms dealt with unions granted by the pope as well as those
granted by the ordinaries. When the committee voted on all these
provisions, there was agreement about future unions, but difference
of opinion on the past ones. Most agreed with revoking those made
without reasonable cause, and a subcommittee was elected, one
member from each nation, to give advice about what constitutes a
reasonable cause. On the basis of this deliberation and the sub-
committee's advice, Cardinal Zabarella drafted a proposed conciliar decree. In this decree the legal requirements for valid unions
were made much stricter: the interested parties had to be summoned, and the reasonable causes had to be inserted into the public
documents; failure to do so nullified the union. Unions made
during the schism by reputed popes without following this proce-

----

[16] See E. F. Jacobs' very helpful effort to arrive at an estimate of the numbers of
incorporations during the schism. He believes it may have been as high as 275,
and that the numbers of grants *motu proprio* (i.e., bypassing the ordinaries) by the
papacy, especially during Boniface IX's reign, were abnormally high; E. F. Jacob,
"A Note on the English Concordat of 1418," in *Medieval Studies presented to A.
Gwynn*, ed. J.H. Watt, et al. (Dublin, 1961), 349–58 at 356–58.

[17] The manuscript record of these deliberations presents some problems. V,
c.19 says that Zabarella presented a proposed conciliar decree to the committee
October 8 and gives the incipit of the decree (*Diuinum cultum volentes*), but not the
text. Then it records the results of deliberations, supposedly of Zabarella's proposed decree. The text of *Diuinum cultum volentes* is found in M, c.44. Strangely,
however, the substance of the discussion recorded in V, c.19, relates more directly
to c.23 of the Common collection than it does to Zabarella's decree. Therefore, I
believe that Common, c.23 represents an initial proposal presented to the committee in late September; on the basis of the discussion of this proposal (recorded in
V, c.19) Zabarella drafted the decree *Diuinum cultum volentes* and presented it to the
committee October 8.

dure were likewise all nullified (but an element of doubt was injected by adding "especially those which had not gone into effect"). Zabarella's draft identified two reasonable causes for unions: 1) enlarging the chapels of kings and princes, and 2) for erecting new collegiate churches and university colleges. Reference to unions made by ordinaries disappeared in Zabarella's draft.

No further record of deliberation of unions in the reform committee exists. In the eighteen points for reform established in the fortieth general session, unions and incorporations were lumped with exemptions (Article 9). A new proposed decree must have been drafted in the third reform committee, since the French Avisamenta refer to passages which do not exist in Zabarella's draft. The German Avisamenta made a renewed effort to distinguish between reasonable and unreasonable unions, and shifted the focus back to pastoral care and the divine cult. Incorporations diminished revenues so much that suitable persons could not be found to fill the offices, complained the Avisamenta; moreover, when monks live in parish churches, their zeal for the monastic observance wanes.

The interests of those who benefitted from unions, especially monasteries and secular lords, must have made it difficult for the committee to reach agreement on the troublesome issue of unions granted during the schism, even though the new pope was surprisingly willing to revoke any and all of these (but with moderation, for the sake of justice). The final decree revoked the ones made without reasonable cause but retained the strangely uncertain language of the papal Responsio ("since a secure rule cannot be given for [resolving] the disputes of those who have an interest" in the unions). The Responsio and the decree dropped all reference to the future unions, even though there had been general agreement earlier on limiting these. It was again only the English concordat which salvaged these measures on future unions, at least as far as they affected parish churches. Appropriations of these in the future were not to be made *motu proprio*; instead requests were to be screened by commissions of ordinaries and allowed only if reasonable. Unreasonable ones granted in the past were to be revoked by such a commission unless scandal would result from the revocation. There is good evidence that Martin V followed this provision in practice; research in Vatican records for Scotland, for example, has revealed a series of instances in which planned unions were rejected by the pope with specific reference to the Constance concordat.[18]

---

[18] See *Calendar of Scottish Supplications to Rome*, 3d series, vol. 23 (Edinburgh, 1934), ed. E.R. Linsdsay and A.I. Cameron, pp. 212 and 286 for examples of

4. Further "English" reforms; exemptions

The reforms of unions were probably among a series of measures introduced by members of the English nation in the reform committee in late September.[19] Four of these measures were introduced by Nicholas Bubwith, the bishop of Bath, when he was committee president: After measures concerning indulgences on September 25 (See Chapter 3 above), he brought three measures on September 27, the first two of which, like the measure concerning unions, reflected struggles between the secular and religious clergy. One forbade abbots and other regular clergy to wear pontifical insignia. Again, this measure ultimately found enactment only in the English concordat. An interesting addition to this schedule which disappeared in the final version makes it clear that some abbesses also wore such bishops' insignia.

The other measure attacked exemptions granted during the schism for religious houses or persons; all without distinction which had been granted without the approval of the ordinary or without cause were to be revoked. The measure was approved by the committee with some exceptions (exemptions for students, for universities, and for houses newly founded under the condition that they be exempt.) The English concordat did not resurrect this draft; it did not need to, since the draft was accepted by Martin V and enacted by the council in the forty-third session with few substantial changes. In fact, the main change strengthened it considerably by dealing with future exemptions as well; they were to be made with cause and consultation of the affected parties (*vocata parte*) in keeping with an addition proposed by the German Avisamenta. In some ways this positive result was remarkable. Exemptions had been a cynosure of the papal plenitude of power for critics like William Durant the Younger;[20] but in the interim more

---

unions revoked with specific reference to the Constance legislation.

[19] These are all reforms which had been requested earlier in the proposals prepared for the Council of Pisa by the University of Oxford (ed. Wilkins, *Concilia*, 3:361–65), as follows:

> 20. Appropriation of parochial benefices for episcopal mensae and monasteries (cf. Common, c.23)
> 21. Tiny portion of revenues allowed to vicars (Cf. Common, c.32)
> 22. Exemptions of religious houses (Cf. Common, c.23a, 35)
> 26. Against abbots who wear miters (Cf. Common, c.21)
> 27. Against taking away the goods of converts when baptized (Cf. Common, c.19)
> 28. Against mendicants taking away young children (Cf. Common, c.28)

[20] Fasolt, *Council*, 171–176.

serious grievances had eclipsed them. Durant might have been surprised to see exemptions treated at Constance among the reforms of the members, but that is exactly the way the second reform committee categorized them.[21] The main opposition to the measure probably came from the religious who had received or hoped to receive such exemptions. Even they found it difficult to support the very questionable exemptions made by rival popes during the schism. Martin V himself in the final decree refers to the multitude of importunate ones who had sought questionable exemptions in those days. We are reminded, however, that the decree explicitly preserved the exemptions made before the schism. As so often, the reformers' intent was not to attack papal power in general, but to remove the abuses of that power during the schism. In this case they were singularly successful.

5. *Pastoral care and the divine cult: Reforms of the secular clergy*

The reforms discussed in this chapter can and should be viewed from several angles. In the last chapter we viewed some of them as part of a long struggle between pope and prelates. In this chapter we have seen that a number of them also involved struggles between secular and regular clergy. The reformers themselves, however, tended to stress that the reforms were efforts to enhance and restore pastoral care and the divine cult.

Those responsible for direct pastoral care were now more and more the vicars, especially since absentee rectors had become an increasingly accepted part of a system by which the revenues of more well endowed parish churches were siphoned off to support university students and the higher levels of ecclesiastical and civil administration (see above, p. 103). This is why the English reformers attacked unions of vicariates so intensely and ultimately restored to their concordat the clause abolishing the ones granted during the Schism, even if they had taken effect.[22] In fact they expanded the clause into a paragraph on vicars, incorporating material from another unenacted proposal considered by the first reform committee (Common, c.32). Following the model of this proposal, the concordat declared that each parish church should

---

[21] Next to the first committee's draft in W appears the word "Membra"; see Introduction to the Edition, p. 286.

[22] The papal *Responsio* had also included such a revocation of unions of vicariates, along with revocation of appropriations of the *ius patronatus* by laymen during the Schism (unless the laymen were the endowers of the churches in question).

have one vicar who was adequately endowed with revenues to perform the duties of his office (pastoral care, divine cult, maintaining hospitality, etc.) Any countervening papal letters, or compositions made with the ordinaries were declared invalid. In doing so, the concordat effectively outlawed future unions of vicariates. A further measure on vicars considered by the first reform committee (Common, c.49) was more general; it sought to establish that all vicars acting on behalf of any prelate or ecclesiastical person should be unmarried clerics who were literate and knowledgeable in the law. Common, c.30 (*Quia a longis temporibus*) attacked the simony of unqualified, grasping stand-ins acting in place of prelates. It recognized the spiraling structural problems created by pluralism. Vicars or assistants without adequate revenues were likely not only to neglect the *cura animarum* but also to extort money for spiritual services and visitations. Simoniacal ordinations were particularly dangerous because they were likely to usher in clergy who were either corrupt or had guilty consciences or both.

Ordination was the crucial door of entry to the clerical order. We saw in the last chapter how reformers attacked ordinations made in curia and tried to insure that those ordained there would be adequately examined. A similar measure for examination of ordinands by local prelates was proposed in the first reform committee (V, c.18; summarized in Common, c.34); it was in fact the third of the measures proposed by the bishop of Bath on September 27, again reminding us of the English concern about pastoral care. The schedule complained that examiners had become negligent, allowing ordination of persons unsuitable in learning and "merits of life" and other things required by law. If other people than the ordinary have acquired special (papal?) privileges to examine, the ordinary must still oversee their examinations, and if he has any doubts about the suitability of the persons they admit he should re-examine these before ordaining them. This measure apparently got no further than the first committee.

The sums charged for ordinations by the impoverished stand-ins in *Quia a longis temporibus* paled by comparison with the sums which wealthy prelates and chapters extorted, especially from new canons and priests. Interestingly, the reform measures which attacked these payments (see cc. 43–44) never mentioned the word simony, but they spoke of the payments as grave oppressions of the poor ("poor" here probably meant poorer members of well-off or once well-off families).[23] According to the schedules, some new canons

---

[23] See Richard Trexler, "The Bishop's Portion: Generous Pious Legacies in the

had to pay their prelates the entire revenues of their benefices for one or more years (V, c.22 says even up to eight years or more, so that such canons sometimes died poor, having never been able to collect any of the regular revenues of their prebends.)

When we place these alongside the other reforms of the secular clergy which entered the deliberations of the first reform committee, we see that the committee dealt with a range of the most serious abuses. Most of these reforms unfortunately did not emerge from the first committee, including one reform not yet mentioned which could have been the key to enforcement of all the rest: the regular celebration of provincial councils. This reform had appeared frequently among the desiderata of programs voiced before and during the council.[24] Provincial councils could have worked hand in hand with general councils to implement the reforms enacted in the latter. Abuses identified at provincial councils could be referred to the general council or to the pope for punishment. (See Common, cc.14 and 24 for examples.) Only one proposal on provincial councils from the Constance reform committee deliberations is extant (Common, c.29). It stresses the correction of *mores* which is to occur at such councils and calls for them to be held triennially (and diocesan synods annually). Strong penalties are assessed on metropolitans who fail to convoke councils and on suffragans who fail to attend; metropolitans who delay four years and bishops two years in calling councils can even be deprived of all their benefices by the next general council.[25]

Late Middle Ages in Italy," *Traditio* 28 (1972) 397–450; repr. Richard Trexler, *Church and Community, 1200–1600: Studies in the History of Florence and New Spain* (Rome, 1987), 289–353 at 300, 321–335.

[24] See the excellent study of Silvio Bonicelli, *I concili particolari da Graziano al concilio di Trento* (Brescia, 1971), which traces the history of these reform efforts. Bonicelli (pp. 106–109) cites the major reform tracts published at Constance which strongly urged triennial meetings of provincial councils—Dietrich of Niem's *Avisamenta* (ACC.4.608–9), Pileus of Genoa's *Informationes* (Döllinger, *Beiträge* 2:307), and D'Ailly's *Tractatus* (H.1.409–413)—and he notes the major role of provincial councils in the *Decretales reformationis*. (see below, p. 164).

[25] Helmrath suggests that the stiff opposition of the prelates at Basel to similar penalties might have prevented enactment of the decree on provincial councils and synods at that council if the prelates had not had such a small proportion of votes (55 to 300); see Helmrath, "Reform," 113 and n.135. The greater weight of prelates at Constance may help explain that council's inaction. It is important to note, however, that Martin V took up this reform again during his pontificate and on April 13, 1425 issued a constitution similar to the proposed Constance reforms (ed. Döllinger, *Beiträge* 2:340–42; Martin's constitution in fact occurs among the reforms in V which are labelled "ex concilio Constanciense.") Unfortunately this constitution was not widely followed (see Bonicelli, 112–115), but it in turn became a model for the Basel reformers; see *Concilium Basiliense* 8:120 and n.6.

Some reformers even wanted the Council itself to begin reforming abuses of the members directly, starting in the diocese of
Constance. Von der Hardt published two proposals to this effect
from one of his Leipzig manuscripts.[26] The first called for the
election of a prelate who would police the morals of the secular and
regular clergy at the council, with full power to arrest, incarcerate,
and fine offenders for actions which scandalize the clergy, such as
wearing inappropriate vestments, gambling, or frequenting nunneries. The second called for the visitation of the diocese of Constance by deputies of the council who would investigate the types of
abuses in order to present them to the future pope so that he could
appoint visitors to correct such abuses throughout the world.
Further, the council would appoint prelates "powerful in word and
deed" to visit the city and diocese of Constance and correct the
exempt and non-exempt.

6. Reforms of laymen

The latter proposal appears also at the end of a petition submitted
to the council probably in 1417 and found in Stuttgart iur. Fol. 130,
fol. 109–112 (in the same manuscript S which contains the most
complete copy of the reform committee deliberations). The petition
lists the most egregious abuses (*enormitates*) of the secular and
regular clergy in southwest Germany and warns that if they are not
remedied the churches, especially the see of Constance, will be
reduced to nothing. Among the abuses are the familiar ones we
have reviewed—unqualified, unlearned, non-resident prelates and
secular clergy, apostate monks, and benefices incorporated to religious houses. Behind all these abuses the petition sees the influence
of powerful lay patrons, mostly nobles, who fill the abbeys and
benefices with their own family members, intimidate and threaten
bishops, incorporate all the richer benefices to their monasteries,
fine and tax the clergy and take over into secular courts matters
which belong to ecclesiastical jurisdiction, such as cases involving
marriage and usury law.

We know that this manuscript belonged to Siegfried Gerlacher,
abbot of Ellwangen in southwest Germany and friend of Job
Vener's uncle, Nikolaus Vener.[27] Gerlacher was the only non-noble

---

[26] H.1.1090; the opening words "Placuit dominis reformatoribus" suggest that
these measures were approved by one of the reform committees; however they do
not appear in any of the manuscripts of reform committee deliberations.
[27] Heimpel, *Vener*, 2:917–926.

abbot for many years in this almost exclusively noble and quite dissolute abbey; he attempted to reform it, but without success. The complaints in the above petition reflect the concerns of many like Gerlacher and the Veners and the representatives of the University of Cologne (see Chapter 4, p. 193) about the lawless robber barons of the late Middle Ages.

These concerns are expressed in a number of the reforms considered by the first reform committee. The German avisamenta even suggested that one reasonable cause for a union was to keep a benefice from falling into the hands of such laymen. However, the monasteries which absorbed benefices in such unions were themselves often exclusively dominated by nobles. C.42 of the Common Collection was directed against monasteries and collegiate churches which had rules excluding non-nobles. Erasmus later said of such churches that Jesus himself could not have been admitted to them.[28] Common, c.42 called for abolishing such restrictions unless they were required by the charters which founded the churches; even in this case the schedule held that advanced academic degrees (doctorate or licentiate) could be considered the equivalent of nobility.

The reformers were above all disturbed by the way in which such nobles, seldom literate, often violent, monopolized the wealthiest ecclesiastical offices. In Chapter 4 I referred to complaints about the undue influence of lay nobles on elections and collations. This matter was raised in the first reform committee September 11, 1415 (See Common, c.38). Cardinal Adimari and Jean Mauroux, patriarch of Antioch, were commissioned to draft a proposed decree ("Statutum Innocentii III"). There is some confusion in the records of the first reform committee here, because the decree, which was presented September 20, is referred to at that point in V as written by Zabarella. Perhaps all three men worked on the draft. In any event, the decree reinvigorated legislation of Lateran IV (X 1.6.43 *Quisquis*), which punished those who secured their election through the intimidation (*preces*) of the electors by lay lords. During the deliberations which followed, Adimari's draft was strengthened by increasing the penalty from suspension to excommunication and by broadening the definition of undue pressure. Then an alternate draft (Common, c.9a *Si quis uocales*) was proposed which went still further, claiming that such pressure smacks of simony. This draft also forbade clerics to move a trial concerning a benefice from an

---

[28] See Barraclough, *Provisions*, 59 n.1.

ecclesiastical to a secular court. The German complaints of summer 1417 similarly railed against secular courts taking over ecclesiastical matters, such as trials for usury.

Other concerns about lay encroachments were set forth in a number of the schedules among the additions to the Common Collection. Common, c.46 attacked burdens placed on clerics by princes and towns, especially their efforts to tax the clergy in the same way as the laity, thus "trampling all reverence" and gravely injuring ecclesiastical liberty. A further measure (c. 45) complained of lords who took excessive advantage of the hospitality of religious houses, making the monks keep dogs and hunting birds for them, even pigs and cows to be fattened.

Almost all the reform measures at Constance dealing with the laity were directed against such oppressions of the church by lay nobles, princes, and towns. These measures were thus more aimed at protecting the liberty of the church than at reforming the morals of laymen. Constance also did not consider any reforms dealing with Muslims or Jews, except for one which sought to protect the property of Jewish and other non-Christian converts from confiscation.[29] This appears to have been among the measures submitted by the English nation to the first reform committee. Two different versions exist, one in the Common Collection (c.19) the other in V, c.13. The original proposal in V records a vote in the committee which determined that absolutely none of their goods are to be confiscated by the church or lay lords. As for those goods acquired through usury, their disposition was left to the consciences of the converts. The version in Common, c.19 is not quite as clear but appears to say the same. The proposal was not enacted.

7. Monastic reform

The reform committee also considered relatively few measures that dealt directly with the *mores* of monks or friars. This does not mean that monastic reform did not occur at Constance. The observant movements that became so important in the later Middle Ages found powerful stimulus in the Franciscan and Benedictine reforms which took place at Constance under the council's authority. According to Duncan Nimmo, the approval by the council of the

---

[29] On this see S. Grayzel, "Jews and the Ecumenical Councils," in *The Seventy-fifth Anniversary Volume of Jewish Quarterly Review*, ed. A.A. Neumann and S. Zeitlin (Philadelphia, 1976), 287–311 at p. 303; and Helmrath, "Reform," 109. Grayzel believes the measure was intended to promote conversion of Jews.

Franciscan observant movements associated with the monastery of Mirebeau in France and with the reformer Peter of Villacreces in Spain was a watershed in the development of the order.[30] It set a pattern of separation within the order between Conventuals (unreformed) and Observants that would last for the next century until the permanent double division of the order which occurred in 1517 and 1528.

Reforms of great significance within the Benedictine Order were set in motion by the provincial chapter at Petershausen (a suburb of Constance, just across the bridge over the Rhine), held under the auspices of the council from February 28 to March 19, 1417.[31] Most of the reforms enacted at the chapter were efforts to insure a stricter observance of older legislation; in this sense they form a close parallel to the Franciscan and other observant movements. They particularly invoked the famous bull of Benedict XII ("Summa magistri," 1342, better known simply as the "Benedictina") which in turn invoked the legislation of the Fourth Lateran Council and of Pope Honorius III. All of these had called for annual provincial chapters for the purpose of reform, but this observance had fallen into disuse. One of the most important Benedictine reformers from France at Constance, Louis de la Palud, abbot of Tournus, had begun to revive the provincial chapters in France.[32] He played an important role in organizing the Petershausen chapter. He and Abbot Thomas Spofford of St.-Mary-without-the-Walls, York,[33] were two of the four presidents elected for the Petershausen chapter. The chapter was for the province of Mainz and the exempt diocese of Bamberg; this is because the diocese of Constance was part of the province of Mainz. Mainz and Bamberg together had more representatives at Constance than all the other German

---

[30] Duncan Nimmo, "The Franciscan Regular Observance: The Culmination of Medieval Franciscan Reform," in *Reformbewegungen und Observanzbestrebungen*, 189–205, at 199–202; see also his earlier studies: "Reform at the Council of Constance: The Franciscan Case" in *Renaissance and Renewal in Church History* (Studies in Church History, vol. 14, ed. Derek Baker; Oxford, 1977), 159–174; and *Reform and Division in the Medieval Franciscan Order, from Saint Francis to the Foundation of the Capuchins* (Rome, 1987).

[31] See Joseph Zeller, "Das Provinzialkapitel im Stifte Petershausen im Jahre 1417: Ein Beitrag zur Geschichte der Reformen im Benediktinerorden zur Zeit des Konstanzer Konzils," *Studien und Mitteilungen zur Geschichte des Benediktinerordens und seiner Zweige* 41 (n.s. 10, 1921/22) 1–73.

[32] Copies of proceedings from provincial councils held recently by him in France are found in Stuttgart iur. Fol. 130, 103r–106v; see Zeller, 17 n.42.

[33] On Spofford, see Allen Breck, "The Leadership of the English Delegation at Constance," *University of Colorado Studies* ser. B, Vol. 1, No. 3 (1941) 289–299 at 291.

provinces combined. Benedictines from other provinces were also invited to attend.

One who views the decrees of the chapter is struck initially by their emphasis on what seem to be external matters, such as clothing and tonsure. As in the case of the general reforms of clerical dress discussed above, however, we should recall that, for the reformers, extrinsic matters were close reflections of inner states. The *opus dei* of course assumes the central position; the monks must be present for the office on time each time during the day. But then the decrees go on to specify rules about other more external matters—common meals and readings, appointed times of silence, sleeping (preferably in a common dormitory; if monks have separate rooms their doors must have windows; no feather beds or sheets are allowed), stationing of a guard at the gate to prevent monks from leaving without permission and to keep out unnecessary visitors, especially women. Great stress was placed on the absolute ban on individual possessions.

From one point of view, this stress on particular infractions and punishments may appear overwhelmingly negative. Abbots who failed to attend the chapter were fined and their houses subjected to special visitations. The procedures established for visitation of all the houses also stressed inquisition and punishment. The chapter produced a list of questions which the visitors were to ask in order to search out infractions. We have records of several visitations that took place as a result of the Petershausen chapter. The most famous was that of St. Gall, conducted by Abbots Louis of Tournus, Siegfried Gerlacher of Ellwangen, and Conrad of Pegau themselves.

In other senses, however, the stress of the Benedictine reforms was highly positive. First, they were enormously successful and influential—the famous Melk Abbey reform movement grew directly out of the reforms of the Peterhausen chapter, for example.[34] The apparent negativity of their proceedings is outweighed by the solemn, public example which they set and the expectation of renewal which this produced. Richental and Gobelinus Persona tell of the dramatic procession of 373 monks who walked out two by two across the bridge to attend the chapter. The common counsel which took place in the chapter concerning abuses helped encourage the self-reform of those present. This solemn, corporate reform activity was then mirrored in the visitation of individual houses.

[34] See Zeller, 3.

The expectation of renewal is also expressed in the striking language of the bull issued by the council to summon the Benedictines to the chapter. The ringing sound of the Savior's trumpets of salvation awaken the monks from sleep, causing them to rise and run to works of justice. Christ calls them by secret inspirations, by the teachings of Holy Scripture, by the instruction of his own actions, and by the professed religion of their own father, who is in name and fact "Benedictus." Finally, they are called by the council itself.[35] Here the bull returns to the negative tone of warning, correction, and punishment. "The ax is placed at the roots" (Luke 3,9); if the authority of the council did not spare three who occupied St. Peter's throne, how will it ignore monastic abuses?[36]

Thus, the hope for renewal is a sober one, seen always against the background of correction and judgment. I will argue in Chapter 8 that this view is characteristic of the central reform ideology of the council in general. The language of the bulls convoking the Petershausen chapter explicitly evoked the parallels between the chapter and the council; it is echoed in the preliminary drafts of the decree *Frequens*. The past omission of chapters, like that of councils, has led to many dangers and abuses, because the celebration of these chapters results in the correction of depraved things, the reform of *mores*, the avoiding of many evils, and the promotion of multiple good.[37]

One document from the council, the *Decretales reformationis*, contains an impressive package of twenty-five reform proposals on the

---

[35] Zeller, 50: "Quanto salutarium tubarum a negligentie sopore excitamur clangore, tanto somnolentia nostra si surde aure transierit reprehensionis censebitur durioris obnoxia, proinde metuendum nobis est et summo studio providendum, ut ad Salvatoris nostri vocantis nos tubas apertis oculis assurgamus et eidem iustitie operibus occurramus. Vocat quippe nos inspirationibus occultis, vocat et sacre scripture doctrinis, vocat nos actionum ipsius instructio, vocat insuper nos preelecti famuli sui re et nomine Benedicti patris nostri . . ."

[36] *Ibid.*: "'Securis ad radicem arboris posita est.' [Luc. 3,9] Nam si tribus sedem beati Petri occupantibus huius concilii auctoritas non pepercit, monachalis pernicitatis (!) abusiones quomodo dissimulabit?"

[37] Zeller, 49–51, and especially the language of the council's bull ordaining the meeting of the Petershausen Chapter, pp. 47–48: "Que quidem capitula provincialia necnon generalia in regionibus quam plurimis raro a longis temporibus executioni mandata feruntur, ex quorum obmissione multa in spiritualibus et temporalibus incomoda et fere irrecuperabilia detrimenta religioni huiusmodi provenerunt. Cum itaque ex huiusmodi capitulorum celebratione depravatorum correctio, morum reformatio, plurium malorum vitatio et multiplicis boni promocio non dubium soleant evenire . . ." Note especially the parallels to the wording of Common, c.1. On the affinities between Benedictine structure and the conciliar structure that prevailed *sede vacante* in the years 1415–1417, see Dieter Mertens, "Reformkonzilien und Ordensreform im 15. Jahrhundert," in *Reformbewegungen und Observanzbestrebungen*, 431–457, at 444–445.

monastic life grouped together under Book 3, Title 10, *De statu monachorum et aliorum religiosorum*; they include eight proposed canons concerning mendicants and five concerning nuns.[38] Some canons parallel proposals considered by the reform committee—canons on payments required of new monks (3.10.5); revocation of privileges for abbots to wear bishops' insignia (3.10.10) and to serve in the courts of princes (3.10.4), and generally revocation of all privileges and exemptions granted to monastic houses during the schism (3.10.8); concern about violations of residence requirements (3.10.14) and about monks holding secular benefices or other benefices outside their orders.[39] These could all reflect concerns of the secular clergy about abuses in the religious orders. Other proposed canons in this title, especially the first three, seem to reflect more the observant tendencies within the orders themselves. The first canon sets the agenda for all the rest by calling on each order to follow its rule, since this is so important for conserving the *status regularis*, especially the three substantial things of each religion—obedience, chastity, and poverty. The stress in the collection is clearly on the last of these three since "the abdication of property is so closely bound to the monastic profession that not even the pope can dispense from it." (3.10.2) Very similar views are expressed by Job Vener in a treatise on the "depravity" of monks' owning property composed by Job Vener at the Council of Constance in 1415, which enjoyed a wide circulation in later years. Vener and Gerlacher must have had occasion to work together within the German nation, especially because of their converging reform interests. Job's uncle Nikolaus, as noted above, had been a close friend of Abbot Siegfried. Heimpel has pointed to the probable influence of Nikolaus's work "On the Cases of Excommunication of Monks" *via* Siegfried on the list of questions which the Petershausen chapter drew up to be used in visitations.[40] I will

---

[38] Dieter Mertens has called attention to the provisions of the *Decretales* concerning the religious, particularly the mendicants, and notes that the author does not merely regard the orders as an outsider would (he contrasts the *Decretales* here to D'Ailly's reform writings); see "Reformkonzilien und Ordensreform im 15. Jahrhundert," in *Reformbemühungen und Observanzbestrebungen*, 431–457 at 442.

[39] See the interesting canon on monks in more lenient orders who receive papal dispensations to obtain places in more strict orders (because they covet the revenues), but then obtain licenses not to live according to the strict rules; going out allegedly to serve as parish priests, they end up wandering throughout the world (3.10.6); the canon refers to them as wolves in sheeps' clothing.

[40] Heimpel, *Vener*, 2:933–961, especially 936–939. The treatise (*Compendium de vicio proprietatis*) is edited by Heimpel, 3:1257–87. On the possible influence of Job's uncle Nikolaus's work on the Petershausen Chapter's visitation formulary, see 2:931–933.

suggest below that Job and Siegfried probably belonged to a group of reformers in the German nation which was responsible for many of the proposals which went into the *Decretales*.

The second canon in the title on the monastic life in the *Decretales* describes in vivid detail the contemporary abuses which were often quite sophisticated methods of evading both the letter and the spirit of the rules. Such abuses contribute to the downfall of "the entire regular observance (*totius regularis obseruantie*)" and cause "envies, strifes, rancors, scandals . . . and infinite other exorbitant practices (*exorbitantie*)." The failure to hold provincial councils is attacked in c.3; at such councils abuses should be "visited, corrected, and emended."

The canons dealing with friars and nuns show much less sympathy. Rather they reflect a paternalistic concern to prevent abuses which lead to scandal. With regard to friars, the *Decretales* call for the disbanding of the regular tertiary orders; they should return to work and give up their scapula. One canon proposes a peaceful resolution of the issue of pastoral care by mendicants along the lines of the legislation of the Council of Vienne. The canons on nuns attempt to limit their contact with men more strictly ("because it leads to indecent things"). They seek to protect the nuns by insuring that they do not take vows too early (the age of profession is to be set at twenty years for women "since the female sex is less able to resist carnal impulses because of its fragility") or without adequate means of material support ("so they will not be compelled to seek food or clothes in an unseemly way"). Male priors and business agents are to be appointed, and the nuns are to be disciplined by the superiors of their order rather than the secular clergy. These measures all reflect the sexism inherited especially from Aristotelian and Patristic views of women.

8. *The vision of the* reformatio in membris *in the* Decretales reformationis

The *Decretales reformationis* deal more fully than any other document from the Council of Constance with all the above issues pertaining to reform of the members. They are especially expansive on the monastic reforms and the measures for protection of the freedom of the church from the inroads of predatory local nobles. Most of the measures cited above from the reform committee deliberations concerning oppression by lay nobles exist in parallel texts in the *Decretales*, including the alternate version of c.9, on lay efforts to influence elections by intimidation. The *Decretales* also contain further similar measures, including a very carefully conceived and practical remedy for dealing with local nobles who try to seize and plunder church property. This remedy, originally proposed by William Durant the Younger in his *Tractatus* one hundred years earlier, called for excluding from ordination and from ecclesiastical offices local nobles *and their sons and grandsons*, if the nobles have oppressed the church in this way. Through this reform, as Constantin Fasolt has observed, the church used its power to insure that lay nobles would find their own best interests served by honorable behavior toward the church.[41]

Despite the richness of the *Decretales* on all these matters pertaining to reform *in membris* (or perhaps sometimes because of this richness) they have been largely neglected, ever since Hardt first edited them from the Elstraviensis manuscript of the Vienna Hofbibliothek in Volume 1 of his great collection.[42] Although Hardt held them to be a collection of the reform decrees passed by the council, Hübler not only rejected this idea, but went on to argue that the text does not represent any direct record of the reforms considered by the reform committee. He regarded it as a purely private set of proposals, and thus of little wider interest.[43] A more decisive reason for Hübler's lack of interest was probably that the text contains none of the "constitutional" measures which he regarded as central to the council's reform program. Following Hübler, Finke also regarded the text as a "private" work and neglected it even more fully than Hübler.[44]

However, the manuscript evidence suggests a close connection with the council's reform deliberations. Four of the manuscripts Finke used for his edition of the reform committee deliberations

---

[41] See Fasolt, *Council*, 239 and n.60. The passage in the *Tractatus maior* is 2.94 (3.25) fols. 58^{ra-b}. Professor Fasolt has reminded me that a similar provision was enacted at the Council of Vienne and included in the *Clementinae* (Clem. 5.8.1 *Religiosi*) and that the author(s) of the *Decretales* could have taken their idea from it rather than directly from Durant. See Fasolt, *Council*, 304 n.48. The provision in the *Decretales reformationis* differs substantially in wording from both Durant's proposal and the canon of Vienne; however, it is closer to Durant's proposal. Its practicality has been further honed beyond that of William's version, since it envisions the systematic questioning of ordinands at their examination to insure that the ban is enforced.

[42] Recently, however, Mertens has called attention to the collection of proposed reforms of monastic life mentioned above; see "Reformkonzilien und Ordensreform," 442.

[43] Hübler, *Reformation*, 23–25. Yet, Hübler does make reference fairly often to the *Decretales* in the course of his analysis of the deliberations of individual measures; he even treats them at times as reflecting a stage in the deliberations.

[44] ACC.2.563–564.

contain the *Decretales*, three of them (A,E, and W) either just before or just after the records of the committee's deliberations. And six of the proposals from the *Decretales* appear also in the committee's records with large portions of text so identical that the overlap cannot be accidental.[45] It is possible that the author of the *Decretales* drew these texts from the reform committee and included them in his collection. But I would propose the hypothesis that the *Decretales* represent instead a refined and fully elaborated later draft of a comprehensive reform program probably submitted to the reform committee in the early stages of its deliberations. Only some of its suggested reforms entered the existing records of the committee's deliberations. The authors of the *Decretales* then organized the initial proposals in a collection and equipped them with arengas and execution clauses. I believe the measures represent a collection of reforms desired by the German nation, or perhaps by a group within it. If so, it would be the counterpart to similar platforms of the English, French, and Italian nations discussed above. Its compilers seem to have borrowed widely from reforms that circulated at the council, also among the other nations. Thus, for example, a number of the items among the English nation's desiderata (e.g., the measure against abbots wearing *pontificalia*—3.10.10—and against confiscating goods of *conversi*—5.5.1. We have already observed the distinctive reform of William Durant the Younger concerning nobles who plunder churches, which turns up in 5.6.1.

Whoever borrowed Durant's text retained the basic concept of the measure, but gave it his own wording. That person may have been Job Vener, whom we know to have been familiar with Durant's *Tractatus*.[46] The other reforms of lay nobles and the monastic reforms also closely reflect Job's interests. He may well have been one of the contributors to the collection, or even its compiler. Possibly Siegfried Gerlacher worked with him. Some of the canons from other nations may have been gathered through the network of Benedictine abbots, such as Thomas Spofford, or the eminent canonist Caspar of Perugia in Italy, or the reform minded Portuguese abbot Andreas of Escobar.[47]

---

[45] See below, p. 285 for details.

[46] Constantin Fasolt, "Die Rezeption der Traktate des Wilhelm Durant d. J. im späten Mittelalter und in der frühen Neuzeit," in *Das Publikum politischer Theorie im 14. Jahrhundert*, ed. Jurgen Miethke (Munich, 1992), 69; and Heimpel, *Vener*, 3:1297–1299.

[47] See António Sousa Costa, "Due 'sermones' sui Concili Ecumenici dei teologi portoghesi del secolo XV: Fra Andrea Dias e Fra Andrea do Prado," in *Proceedings of the Seventh International Congress of Medieval Canon Law* (Città del Vaticano, 1988), 385–403 and *Mestré André Dias de Escobar* (Rome, 1967).

One of the reforms in the *Decretales* gives clues as to dating. Canon 3.10.8 addresses the problem of the religious orders which had been divided by the schism; it says that these orders have now been united, but are to be still more perfectly united, and calls on the future single, true pope to concede to the entire orders privileges which had been granted to religious in only one obedience. This wording strongly suggests a date after the resignation of Gregory XII, but probably prior to the deposition of Benedict XIII, i.e., during the time in which the first reform committee was deliberating.

The *Decretales* are testimony to a widespread interest in reform *in membris* and the consideration by one important group of reformers at the council of a quite comprehensive program of reform *in membris*. What makes them even more striking is that they also are informed by a deep conviction that the proper governance of the church is conciliar.

They did not neglect reforms *in capite*. In this regard they addressed some of the major reform issues, as follows:

1.   Reservations (1.3.1): They should be limited to those of the *ius scriptum*.

2.   Services (1.3.5): The may be collected, but only after peaceful possession, in two annual installments, and with moderation (no more than one-third of first year's revenue, consideration for ability to pay); such payment is to be considered only a temporary charitable subsidy, until the meeting of the next council.

3.   Confirmation of elections (1.3.5): To be made normally by immediate superior; if pope confirms, he must not delay confirmation.

4.   Papal exemptions and privileges (3.10.8): All those granted since the schism are revoked.

5.   Papal privileges for mendicants (3.10.12): All those which go beyond the privileges in the *Clementinae* are revoked.

6.   Summoning of person outside their dioceses for trials (1.1.1): Prohibition of all such papal summons which go beyond those allowed by Boniface VIII's decretal *Statutum, quod circa* (VI. 1.3.11).

These reforms are representative of those favored by large groups of reformers. However, they comprise only a small fraction of the contents of the collection. The other reforms all deal with ills in the members of the church, which are enumerated in amazing detail and shed interesting light on some of the local practices of the late medieval clergy.

Some were abuses at the local level which paralleled those of the Roman curia. We have observed a number of these, mostly concerned with extortion of money, which entered the reform com-mittee deliberations (3.12.1, 3.12.3, 5.2.1). Laws which forbade collection of spoils and fruits during vacancies, by prelates, were to be more strictly enforced (3.8.un, 1.3.7). Extortion of subsidies and procurations without visitation were outlawed (5.8.1). Alienated church property was to be recovered (*reuocatum*) (3.7.un). Chapters and monasteries were forbidden to charge money for admission of new members. (3.10.5). Prelates were not to allow sale of abusive indulgences (5.10. un.)

The reforms show intense concern about the major ills of the clergy discussed at the beginning of this chapter—pluralism, absenteeism, immorality and lack of education. They attacked these ills directly, but within a traditional clerical framework, inveighing against unconsecrated bishops (1.3.8), untonsured cler-gy (3.1.1), child canons (3.3.2), and priests who spent their days gambling in taverns clad in the latest modish dress (3.1.1–3). They did not primarily blame papal reservations and the annates for the ills, as did many reformers, but they showed acute awareness of the increase of abuses during the schism. They focused their attention above all upon venality at all levels, lamenting that during the schism virtually all spiritual things were set out for public sale (5.9.un.).

Of special interest are a number of measures directed against the seemingly endless variety of unscrupulous methods of fund-raising used by some local prelates and clergy. Ecclesiastical judges en-riched themselves during disputes over benefices by collecting the disputed revenues themselves and sometimes after the trial did not even turn the benefice over to the winning party (2.2.1). Chapters restricted the number of canons so that each canon would receive a larger revenue (3.3.3). Individual canons pocketed the revenues of suspended canons (3.3.4). Senior canons in chapters set aside certain large blocks of revenues for themselves, so that junior canons remained poor, without any hope of becoming seniors (3.3.5). Prelates attempted to appoint their own successors and made pacts with them to share the revenues during their lifetime (5.3.3). Other prelates sold and leased their jurisdiction in legal matters (5.5.un.). Kickbacks and rebates were charged when be-nefices were conferred (3.6.un.). Clerics forged papal letters and then sold the forgeries for money (5.7.un.). Some particularly un-scrupulous clerics would lodge suits against persons who had peacefully occupied their benefices for years, asserting their own rights to these benefices. They did so particularly when such an incumbent was old and near death, so that when he died they would already have a claim against any new beneficiary (3.4.un.).

Again and again the text rails against the rampant avarice of its time; one of the most frequent words is *imbursare*. There are constant complaints against clerics who themselves pocket the revenues intended for others, especially revenues which belong to the church itself. The authors lament that even the measures earlier intended to correct abuses—especially visitations—are misused as fund-raising activities. The *Decretales* instruct visitors not to use fines as penalties unless absolutely necessary, and then to convert the moneys collected either to pious uses or to common or public use.

The primary enforcing authority for the ecclesiastical reforms is the council—diocesan synods, provincial councils, and ultimately the general council itself. In several cases the text says that offenders will be punished in the next council to be held. It is also the general council that carries through the reforms. The council commands, ordains, and disposes (2.1.2, 1.3.1, among many examples); it nullifies and revokes (elections, privileges, etc.—1.3.2, 1.5.un., again among many examples); it strengthens papal penalties (1.3.7); it dispenses and absolves from oaths (1.2.un., 1.3.8). The council establishes the lists of matters to be heard in ecclesiastical and in secular courts (2.1.1). The council passes its decrees *non obstantibus* papal constitutions (1.3.6); and it forbids the pope to establish any new reservations without its consent (1.1.1).

This stress on the role of the council in reform is all the more striking when we note that the *Decretales* contain none of the references to the consent of the college of cardinals for papal actions which appear often in reform committee proposals. In other words, the *Decretales* conceive of an exceedingly broad program of reform *in membris* to be executed primarily by the council and the pope working together. The haunting question returns: Why was so little of this program enacted?

9. *The problem of enforcement*

The enforcement measures included in the proposed canons provide some clues. They are very well thought out and calculated both to meet the nature of the offence and to be effective. However, the authors of the *Decretales* betrayed profound doubts about this enforcement. They knew that abundant previous legislation existed on most of these matters which had been evaded or ignored. In part, this was because the penalties had proven to be ineffectual.

Thus, one strategy of the reformers was to make the penalties more stringent. In a few cases they even envisaged incarceration as a penalty (e.g., for the flagrant, continuous violation of monastic vows, especially for monks who live outside established communities (1.3.1, 6, and 7). While the reformers believed that the "atrocity of the punishment should serve to heal offenders and be an example to others (3.10.1)," they still must have wondered how penalties could be atrocious enough to produce their desired effects. Excommunication was already seriously overused. One measure in the *Decretales* (5.8.4) is in fact specifically aimed against prelates who use excommunication for minor offenses.

For serious offenses, the *Decretales* called for removing the offender from office, especially when he had not heeded an earlier sentence of excommunication (3.8.un., e.g.). But who would enforce this? The sentences of privation of office usually added that the office became *ipso iure* vacant and the ordinary collator could freely grant it out to another. But would the ordinary do so? And would the offender surrender the benefice to the new appointee? Many of the reforms of illegal acts of prelates simply nullified those acts and freed the subordinates from obligation to obey them. But what would keep the prelate from forcing subordinates to obey? And did not this whole approach threaten to undermine the very discipline that the reformers were seeking to restore? Suspension from revenues offered itself as a less harsh but more enforceable, and therefore more effective penalty than removal from office (1.4.1, 1.8.2, 3.1.1, among numerous examples). Yet so great was the avarice of the time that the collection of suspended revenues by a superior led to even worse abuses, new taxes and new oppressions. One measure called for the prelate to appoint two honest priests to collect suspended revenues (2.2.un.); another even proposed that suspended revenues be collected by the papal camera— one can imagine what some reformers would have thought of that!

In spite of all the uncertainties about enforcement, the authors of the *Decretales* seem to have believed strongly that the council provided the best hope of reform. The canons often specified that further penalties for an offense would be decided in the next general council (1.6.2, 3.1.2, 5.7.un., 5.8.2–3). Moreover, they presupposed that the council, like the provincial chapter of the Benedictines, would bring abuses to light and demonstrate the opposition of these abuses to reason and decorum. Reformers were not entirely naive in hoping that in this manner offenders would be induced to reform themselves. This hope surely lies behind the ironic statements used in the *Decretales* to point out the absurdity of the abuses.

Of prelates who threaten their subordinates with heavy penalties for absenteeism and then extort money from them for licenses to be absent: "They now say something is lawful which they had before thundered against as unjust" (3.2.1). Of customs which set aside revenues of collegiate churches for older canons (*seniores*), thus keeping the younger canons poor: "The avarice of the old is made youthful by the oldness of the times." (3.3.5) Of monks who act as judges in parish churches: "It is unseemly (*inconueniens*) that a monk should act as pastor and judge of many people, when the duty of the religious life he has assumed requires him, strictly speaking, to take charge of one person only." (3.10.7). Of the prelate who collects a subsidy for his "joyeuse entrée" and then excommunicates the clergy who are too poor to pay: "Thus the joyous entry is converted to penal sadness." (5.11.un.)

Here we see the canonist succumbing to the humanist strategy of combatting abuses with satire. Yet he is also harking back to a world view in which reform could be brought about simply by demonstrating that the desired change was congruent with reason. This view underlay a number of Constance reforms that in place of execution clauses contained simple statements that the reform in question was "fitting" or "consonant with reason."[48]

Reason also provided an alternative to papal *auctoritas*, as we saw especially in the demand of reformers that papal dispensations and privileges be justified by "reasonable" cause stated in writing. The council was almost synonymous with reason for many reformers because of the connection between the council and counsel, in the sense of good counsel or reasoning together. The words *concilium* and *consilium* were used fully interchangeably in the documents to mean either "council" or "counsel."[49]

---

[48] One very important and successful reform contained the phrase "consonant with reason (*ratione fore consentaneum*)"—the reform of spoils and procurations—see S², c.10 and the discussion in Chapter 3 above, p. 176; see also S², c.7 on alienations. On this matter see the very helpful discussion of such ideas in William Durant the Younger by Fasolt, *Council*, 212–216. It is interesting that many of the bulls issued by the council during the period after the deposition of John [XXIII] began with the phrase "Rationi congruit" or "Rationi congruit et conuenit honestati"; (these phrases had been used in the past in bulls issued by the chancery *sede vacante*.) The council's bulls begin August 17, 1415 in Reg. Lat. 186 of the Vatican Secret Archive; see ACC.4.xxxi–xxxii and Emil Göller, "Zur Geschichte der apostolischen Kanzlei auf dem Konstanzer Konzil," *RQ* 20 (1906) 205–213; also Hans Schneider, "Die Siegel des Konstanzer Konzils: Ein Beitrag zur Geschichte der spätmittelalterlichen Reformkonzile," *AHC* 10 (1978) 310–345 at 332.

[49] See Michaud-Quantin, *Universitas*, 135–41. These terms were interchangeable throughout the period from the eleventh to the fifteenth century. Despite the close connection of *consilium* with reason, a veritable mystique surrounded the term.

And yet there was a gap between reason and reasons. The council/counsel may have been synonymous with reason, but it did not have enough reasons. There was a good reason for dispensations for pluralism in the early fifteenth century. The demographic and economic conditions of the time had reduced the revenues of benefices in some regions to such a degree that the revenues from one benefice no longer sufficed to support one priest. The reformers did cite "exiguity of revenues" as a reasonable cause for a dispensation from the laws against pluralism, but of the demographic and economic causes they were unaware and spoke not a word.

10. Conclusion

Yet, the authors of the *Decretales*, just as the Constance reformers in general, did make an impressive effort to deal with the diversity of time and place. They considered the impact of geographical differences, and they did not simply try to restore ancient laws to the letter. They usually looked to the relatively recent past. They showed a special preference for recent conciliar legislation—that of Lateran IV, Lyons II, and Vienne—but they also freely invoked papal legislation. Even this recent legislation they sought to adapt to changing circumstances. This is the importance of the discussion of dispensations, where the reformers seemed willing to allow the pope to deviate a considerable degree from the letter of the law when the situation warranted it.

Nevertheless, the reformers were deeply aware of how seriously power had been abused for fiscal purposes by the popes of the Schism. They focused on the ways in which abuse of the power of the head had made possible abuses in the members through dispensations, exemptions, unions, and incorporations. They struggled hard with the question of how to limit that power effectively. In doing so, they turned to the criterion of the *scandalum* to prohibit new papal grants that would cause scandal, but also to prohibit revocation of past grants if the revocation might cause scandal. In their efforts they achieved some striking successes, particularly in England, where the reforms gave the ordinaries power to monitor and revoke papal grants. The reformers required the pope to formally summon and listen to those who would lose their rights as a result of the papal privileges, and above all they demanded that he justify all these privileges by stating in writing the reasonable cause for them. In serious matters they required the consent of the cardinals to insure the reasonableness of the cause. But in all these actions they presupposed a still more important enforcer of reason—the council itself, which embodies good counsel or reason. This is why all these reforms were so integrally linked to the concept of regular general councils established in *Frequens*. The regular meeting of councils would insure that papal power would not be abused. It would do so, not by enforcing the letter of the old laws, but by holding up the use of papal power to the standard of universal reason.

It is interesting that the ordinaries in England struggled as much against the powerful abbeys as against the pope, and here the alliance of a reforming abbot at the council (Thomas Spofford of York)[50] was of much help. The reforming abbot Siegfried Gerlacher played a similar role in the Benedictine reforms of the Peterhausen chapter and seems to have been much involved in the reforms desired by the secular clergy of Germany at the council as well.

Gerlacher moved in the circles that produced the *Decretales* and may have contributed to them himself. The *Decretales* capture much better than most documents a conception of truly conciliar reform, reform in which the pope and council together would coordinate, oversee, and enforce a general reform that was carried out at the provincial and diocesan level through parallel and interlocking reforms of secular and regular clergy. It is quite remarkable that the *Decretales* make no mention whatsoever of the counsel or consent of cardinals as a way of enforcing the reforms. The *Decretales* provide an exact complement to the idea of conciliar reform *in capite* found in *Quia decet* (Common, c.2b; see above, p. 125)—an extraordinarily thoroughgoing concept of reform *in membris* conducted jointly by pope and council. The authors of this document were not in any way denying papal authority; rather they were looking all the more earnestly to the pope to enforce the reforms which they knew would encounter intense resistance from the local nobility.

In this study of the Constance reforms, the nobles, the cardinals, and the princes have emerged as the leading obstacles to effective conciliar reform. This result is ironic because each of these groups had its own reform agenda at Constance; doubly ironic because these agendas have often been taken by various modern scholars as the essence of conciliar reform.

We must frankly acknowledge that conciliar reform was less successful in reforming the members than in reforming the head.

---

[50] Interestingly, Thomas became a bishop soon after the council; see Breck, 291.

However, past scholars have often overlooked the comprehensive efforts, and the successes, of the reform of the members because these scholars have been so interested in the reforms of the head. And the truth is that the conciliar reformers themselves placed their first emphasis on reform *in capite*. They did so, however, because they believed that it was the most urgent and would in turn make possible true reform *in membris*, to be enacted at future councils which would meet regularly according to the decree *Frequens*.

PART III

THE IDEAS AND IMAGES

CHAPTER SEVEN

ARGUMENTS CONCERNING PROVISIONS, ANNATES, AND SIMONY

After having reviewed the specific negotiations concerning the reforms, we turn now to examine more closely the terms, images, and arguments with which the reformers conceived their reforms. In Chapters 8 and 9 we will focus primarily on the terms and images. In the present chapter we will examine arguments about the two principal reforms: those concerning papal provisions to benefices and the taxes on those benefices (annates and services). The arguments are primarily academic discussions of the simony which reformers saw in these papal practices. They appear principally in ten tracts or pamphlets. Through a series of tables I would like to show the parallel places where arguments appear in the tracts. The tables are not meant to be exhaustive, but I have tried to include the more important arguments and especially citations of legal and theological sources. The following are the tracts and the sigla by which I shall identify them.

A = Anon. annate tract "Ad ostendendum"[1]

F = Pons Simonet, "De annatis non solvendis"[2]

G = Jean Gerson, "De simonia," (*G*.6.167–173)

M = Mateusza z krakowa [Matthew of Cracow] "De praxi Romanae Curiae"[3]

S = Paulus Vladimiri, "Speculum aureum de beneficiis ecclesiasticis"[4]

---

[1] Augsburg, Stadt und Staatsbibl. 2° 226, pp. 381–409; Paris, BN lat. 14644, fols. 361r–369v; partially edited ACC.2.592–600. Pp. 406–409 in the Augsburg manuscript contain additions to the tract as it appears in P. See n. 12 below for my conjectures about authorship. References in the tables are to the page numbers in the Augsburg manuscript.

[2] Response written on behalf of the French nation to the *appellatio* of the fiscal procurator during the annate debate in November 1415 (H.1.761–91); see Stump, "Taxation," 85 n.47 and 86. Simonet's response is included in the record of the French nation's annate deliberations.

[3] Ed. Wjadyslaw Senko (Wroclaw, 1969).

[4] In Christian Wilhelm Walch, *Monimenta medii aevi* (Göttingen, 1757–1764, repr. 1966), 2.1.69–216.

V = *Idem*, "'De annatis' I and II"[5] (De annatis I=pp. 299–304; De annatis II=305–312)

B = Anon. annate tract II (ACC.2.600–602)

L = Élie Lestrange, Annate tract (ACC.2.602–605)

R = Maurice Rvačka (Maurice of Prague), interchange with Cardinal Zabarella, 1416[6]

Of these, four are major tracts and six are shorter ones.[7] The four major tracts fall into two groups, AF and MS. On a number of important questions, they show quite different emphases, even different answers. V belongs with MS, since its author is the same as the author of S (Paulus Vladimiri). The two tracts in V were written for the council—the first during Vladimiri's journey to Constance, the second at the council, probably in 1416[8]—whereas S was written considerably earlier, in 1404/5. Matthew's work was written about the same time as S (1403), but its arguments were still very much alive at the council Constance, especially since its co-author, Job Vener, was in attendance and played a major role in the reform deliberations.[9] A and F were written at the council.

F, and almost certainly A as well, were written by members of the French nation at Constance; M and S were written by people from the lands that composed the German nation at the council. Do their divergent opinions reflect national differences or even

---

[5] Ed. M. Bobrzynski in *Rerum publicarum scientiae quae in S. XV in Polonia viguit, monumenta litteraria (Staradwne prawa Polskiego pomniki* 5) (Cracow, 1878), 299–312.

[6] Recorded by Cerretanus ACC.2.325–328, with Zabarella's response 328–333. An additional unedited response of Rvačka is found in Augsburg, Staats- und Stadtbibliothek, 2° Cod 226, pp. 378–80. This response is in the form a twelve conclusions which form a reprise of his earlier statements. Zabarella's statements in his reply to Maurice refer to a still earlier exchange between the two, for which there is no extant record.

[7] I am deliberately not considering here the reform tract of the canonist Johannes Cardinalis von Bergreichenstein, because it did not play any discernible role in the reform negotiations. See František Bartoš, "Das Reformprogramm des Mag. Joh. Cardinalis von Bergreichenstein, des Gesandten der Karls Universität in Prag für das Konzil zu Konstanz," in *Festschrift Heimpel zum 70. Geburtstag* (Göttingen, 1972) 2:652–85. Cardinalis composed the tract for the council and brought it with him when he arrived as an envoy of the University of Prague and as a friend of John Hus (see Bartoš, 661). Bartoš reminds us that the attacks on simony launched by Cardinalis and indeed by Hus himself show some striking similarities to those found in tracts M and S (see 665–68.) Many Catholic and Hussite reformers were products of the same late-fourteenth century Bohemian reform movement inspired by Milič (666–67). A detailed comparison and contrast of the views analyzed in this chapter with those of Cardinalis, Hus, and other writers in Hus's circle would be of great interest, but is beyond the scope of this study.

[8] See Belch, 132, 161–62.

[9] On these matters, see Heimpel, *Studien*, and p. 14 above.

nationalism? To both questions the answer is "No." The nations at
Constance were highly artificial. The "German" nation included
many East European peoples, including Poles, Czechs, and Hunga-
rians. In fact, the leading tracts, A and S, were written by Polish
reformers; and R, which belongs also to this same group in its
general viewpoint, was written by a Czech, Maurice Rvačka.[10] The
German reformers generally shared these views as is clearly indicated by Job Vener's co-authorship of the *De praxi*. The same views
were shared by some members of the Italian nation. We saw in
Chapter 1 Hermann Heimpel's idea of a reform rectangle linking
Prague, Cracow, Heidelberg, and Padua. Klaus Wriedt's study
(see above, p. 14 and n. 43) shows, however, that reformers in all
these places were also linked by their loyalty to Gregory XII,
which often continued even after the Council of Pisa. Heimpel
included Zabarella in the reform rectangle, but by the time of the
council, Zabarella had become a cardinal of the Pisan pope John
[XXIII]. It is revealing that R is in fact the record of a confrontation between Maurice and Zabarella, who appears at Constance as
a defender of the annates and services.

I will argue that the characteristic views of the reformers in M,
R, and S were shaped strongly by their historical experiences as
part of the Roman obedience during the Schism, just as those in A,
L, and F were shaped by historical experiences in the Avignon
obedience. I believe that the latter tracts also represent a distinct
sub-set of views within the Avignon obedience, indeed within the
French nation itself at Constance. They particularly represent the
views and historical experiences of the clergy within the kingdom of

---

[10] On Maurice Rvačka, see the article of J. Kadlec in *Dictionnaire de Spiritualité*
10:833–34, and especially the article of Bohumil Kvapil, "Mistr Mařík Rvačka,"
in *Sborník J.B. Novákovi* (Festschrift J.B. Novák) (Prague, 1932), 192–99. I am
indebted to Ms. Virginia Dunn of the Lynchburg College Library for translating
this article for me. Maurice was born about 1365 in Bohemia and entered the
monastery of Holy Cross in Prague. He received his M.A. at Prague in 1387 and
taught philosophy there for three years. He studied theology at the papal curia in
Rome and received an M.Th. before leaving Rome in 1402, having been appointed
visitor of his monastic order in Bohemia and Poland by Pope Boniface IX, whose
favor he had won through his care for the ill and aged former Archbishop of
Prague, Jan of Jenstein, while in Rome. While visitor in Poland, Maurice lectured
in theology at the University of Cracow; Paulus Vladimiri was among his students
(see Belch, 119). He also sought to teach theology at Prague upon his return about
1405, but was not granted a license. Maurice was active in the following period as
a pro-papal theologian and appears to have served for a time as an inquisitor. At
the Council of Constance, he wrote two tracts against the Utraquist teaching of
Jacobus de Misa (ed. Hardt.3.799–83), and he supported the Polish representatives in their struggle with the Teutonic Knights. There is evidence (though not
conclusive) that after the council he lived in France.

France. The kingdom of France was by no means coterminous with the French nation at Constance. In the annate deliberations of the French nation we detected a clear difference in the stance of the prelates inside and outside the French kingdom; and in the French Concordat it was prelates only in the kingdom of France, not the entire nation, who won the fifty percent reduction in services. On the basis of these considerations, I am going to label the distinct points of view in A, L, and F "Gallican," and those in M, R, and S "non-Gallican." This is purely a matter of heuristic convenience, and I want to stress that it represents a deliberate oversimplification. Above all, "Gallican" here should not be understood to represent the later position of the Gallican articles. Rather it refers to the Gallicanism which Victor Martin spoke of as being born at the Paris Council of 1406/7, and which, to shift metaphors, had strong roots in the "Gallicanisme parlementaire" traced by Guillaume Mollat.[11]

All the "Gallican" tracts were written at the council. F is directly connected with the annate deliberations of the French nation in October/November 1415; it was a reply to the appeals of two curial supporters of the annates, written at the request of the nation by Pons Simonet. These two appeals, written by Johannes Ponceti and Johannes de Scribanis, form our best evidence for the curial arguments in support of the taxes, alongside Zabarella's statement in his reply to Maurice Rvačka (R). The final portion of the anonymous annate tract A also gives curial arguments and then replies to each of them; it is, however, a far less reliable source for the curial arguments, since it produces them second-hand. The authorship of A is still uncertain; however, a progressive narrowing of the field points strongly to Jean Mauroux, the patriarch of Antioch.[12]

---

[11] See above, p. 12; and Guillaume Mollat, "Les origines du gallicanisme parlementaire au XIVe et XVe siècles," *RHE* 43 (1948) 90–147.

[12] Finke already identified a number of the clues in the introduction to his edition, ACC.2.548–49, but without suggesting Mauroux's authorship: the author's loyalty to Sigismund, his enmity towards the cardinals, and his knowledge of the functioning of the curia (Mauroux was acting papal camerarius at Constance). Finke argued that the loyalty to Sigismund was not unusual for a Frenchman in late 1415, when Finke assumed the tract was written, in spite of the author's statement that the Schism had lasted already for about 38 years (which would place the tract in 1416). Finke said the author's words here were only approximate, but a date of 1416 would be further evidence for Mauroux's authorship, since he stayed loyal to Sigismund far longer than most of the French nation. One final indication is the close connection between one passage in the tract and the reasoning behind the text of *Romanus pontifex*, as noted in Chapter 5 above, p. 134. This strongly suggests that the author of the tract was a member of the reform committee, which Mauroux was. On Mauroux's role in the French

Gerson's tract on simony seems to have been written in 1416. His name does not appear as one of the participants in the French annate deliberations of 1415; however, he was heavily occupied at the time with the Jean Petit affair, which consumed so much of his energy at the council.[13] The treatise of Élie Lestrange (L) is in the form of a brief summary of the major arguments against the simony involved in annates and services. The fact that both of the extant copies of Lestrange's tract as well as a second, somewhat longer copy of A unknown to Finke are found in German manuscripts suggests that the Gallican arguments found a ready audience in the German nation at the council. Indeed, the arguments of Gallicans and non-Gallicans often converged. The reformers generally agreed about the negative effects of the provisions and annates. Sometimes it even seems they were using an old set of stock arguments about these effects. Reformers also converged in their rejection of stock papal arguments in support of provisions and annates, above all the argument about papal lordship over all benefices. Let us turn first to these broad areas of convergence.

1. Arguments about effects

Table 1 shows the arguments concerning effects. The tracts complain of both moral and physical results. Papal provisions result in the appointment of unsuitable officials, they say; unsuitable because they are mercenaries (having purchased their offices), foreigners (who do not know or care about the people subjected to their rule), unlearned and non-noble. Papal taxation results in the impoverishment of the churches, both physical destruction (dilapidation of buildings, etc.) and diminished resources for alms and hospitality. Both the unsuitable appointees and the diminished revenues in turn result in the decline of pastoral care, the detriment of the divine cult, the diminution of the orthodox faith, the declining devotion of the people, and the lost legal rights of the churches. Sometimes these arguments have the distinct ring of slogans — stock phrases, even clichés, relatively independent of context, capable of being used and reused as the need arises.

To these clichés the fifteenth century reformers add many nuances from their own experience. When Matthew of Cracow

---

annate deliberations, see Stump, "Taxation," 85–96. esp. 90–91 n.60; on Mauroux in general see most recently Heribert Müller, *Die Franzosen, Frankreich, und das Basler Konzil (1431–1449)* (Paderborn, 1990), 543–573.

[13] See his speech delivered in this matter during this period, ACC.2.423.

TABLE 1

Arguments concerning effects

	A	F	M	S	V	B,L,G,R
1. Appointment of unqualified persons	384	774	85	100		
Grantor thinks about money rather	384					
than qualifications of grantee						
D.39 c.1 Petrus diaconus	384					
Cod. 1.3.30 Si quamquam	384					
Wrong state of mind of those seeking			83,	101		
benefices: Avarice			109			
Expectancies make people hope for			84			
death of another person						
Exclusion of poor			109			
Pope cannot be better informed than			79			
local ordinaries						
Appointees are illiterate, no one will			774	94		
want to study any more						
2. Scandal and oblocutio in populo	385	768	81			B601
	397		85			
Worse to smack of simony—causes						B601
scruples in consciences						
Also among unbelievers	385					
C.1 q.7 c.27 fin. Patet	385					
X 5.3.32 Per tuas	385					
3. Damage to souls (*damnatio animarum,*	384	768	81	96		B601
detrimentum animarum)	388					
X 1.6.41 Ne pro defectu intended to			81			
prevent such damage						
Periurio		768				
Meretricium because of venality	385		83			
	397					
C.1 q.1 c.20 Cum omnis			83			
C.6 q.1 c.21 Quero			83			
4. Destruction of churches, ruin	385	769	95	101		B601
Churches endowed by founders			95			B601
Money intended for expiation of their		772	109			
sins, etc.						
Reduction of number of ministers in		770	95			
such churches because of annates						
5. Defrauding of endowers		772	109			
X 2.19.1 De probationibus			109			

TABLE 1 cont.

	A	F	M	S	V	B,L,G,R
6. Violence and injury, oppression		769	109	101		R326
X 5.39.21 A nobis			109			
X 3.38.28 Cum dilectis			109			
Vilification of clergy by reducing it to such servitude			109			
Expenses, long absences			81			
Active more than contemplative life favored						B601
8. Uncertainty about identity of rightful pastors because of competing collations of pope and ordinaries	82					
9. Schism has been caused and/or prolonged by the annates						B601
10. Special abuses during schism	388					
Payment before possession	388	767	89		299	
This is simony	388	767	89			
Much more than tax charged	388	774	89		301	
More in four ways—thing, place, time, cause (X 2.11.un. Consilium)					301	
Benefices sold in curia	387		89			
Public auction (*licitatio in spiritualibus*)	387					
Ecclesiastical censures	387	770				R326
Benefices sold to more than one person	387					
Trials	387		84	101		
Money borrowed	387					
Beneficiary is made into passive		775				
usurer Whoever has best banking connections is most likely to receive benefice		775				
Annates paid twice in one year if benefice becomes vacant twice			108			
John XXIII's abuses; must be prevented in future	388	773				
Pope's wars; rights of church should be defended by humility, not violence		771				
11. All curial officials who participate in simoniacal granting of benefices are guilty of mortal sin			188			
			–			
			201			

mentions the declining devotion of the faithful, he specifically laments that the Hussites' criticisms of papal appointees weakened the people's loyalty to the clergy. When Matthew of Cracow talks about the unsuitable papal providees he mentions specifically cooks and pimps; such catalogs of unsavory appointees proved so quotable, however, that they in turn became stock arguments repeated by reformers. Paulus Vladimiri and Nicholas of Clémanges both show similar lists (and in the sixteenth century the theme received renewed fame through the citation of Matthew's list by the Magdeburg Centuriators.)[14] Matthew (p. 82) also cites very specific dangers to the *cura animarum* caused by the uncertain title to ecclesiastical offices when papal provisions competed with the collations of the ordinaries; long absences resulted from the litigation in curia over benefices. When Pons Simonet speaks of diminution of the divine cult, he refers specifically to the interruption of divine services caused by papal censures imposed on prelates who had not paid their services.

Some of the bitterest complaints involve the fraud and deception which resulted from the provisions, especially from the mushrooming grants of expectancies. All too often two or more persons are named to the same office simultaneously. Appointees are required to pay their annates or services before they were able to take peaceful possession of their benefices. They would have to borrow money from bankers to make the payments, since they have not yet collected any revenues from the benefice. When they try to take possession, they often face an "intruder," a rival claimant to the benefice elected or appointed by the ordinaries. They might find themselves unable to oust the intruder and still faced with the dilemma of paying the bankers although they can collect no income from the benefice. All this might delay for years, and sometimes forever, the providee's enjoyment of the benefice he has struggled to obtain. In these circumstances the demand for payment of annates or services prior to peaceful possession could very clearly smack of fraud, violence, or extortion, not to mention simony. Matthew says it makes the clergy the laughing stock of the people; small children make fun of the way their priests were thus duped. The Hussites gain more supporters.

Moreover, even when the providee takes possession, he might find that the previous incumbent has already used up that year's revenues; even if that incumbent had held the benefice less than a

---

[14] Heimpel, *Vener*, 2:710.

year and had paid the annates, the new providee has to pay them again out of the now non-existent revenues. Even if revenues have accrued during the vacancy, the new providee is probably unable to collect either these or the accumulated capital of his predecessor, because these too have been reserved by the pope (See above, Chapter 3, p. 57.) Worse still, if his predecessor has not paid his annates, the new providee might find himself charged twice, once for his predecessor's annates and once for his own; indeed, he is liable for all the accumulated debts of all his predecessors for annates.

The tracts show remarkable agreement in their identification of the ill-effects;[15] when we turn shortly to examine their analysis of the causes of those effects, we shall see important differences of emphasis. Before doing so, however, let us examine another set of arguments in which there was broad agreement: the arguments reformers made to refute curial efforts to justify the papal provisions and taxes.

2. Response to papal arguments

After hearing the tirades about oppressive effects, it is surprising to see that the main curial arguments were based on the need to support the pope and cardinals because of the services they rendered to Christendom! The arguments grouped under Number 3 and 4 all hinge on scriptural passages which justify the material support of God's ministers, and the curia stresses its neediness rather than its prerogatives. The analogy of the Roman church to a parent in Argument 1 alludes to this nurturing rather than to parental authority, and even Argument 2 about primacy stresses historical primacy rather than fulness of power. The strongest appeal to prerogative comes ironically from Zabarella in his interchange with Maurice Rvačka.[16] When other curial supporters talk of maintaining the pope's material status, they underline the pope's vulnerability to rebellion and attack (Argument 5). Using the reformers' own language the supporters of annates recall that if the head is weak the whole body suffers.

The Gallican tracts are richer in counter-arguments than the

---

[15] However, S shows a special focus on the guilt and consequent damnation of curial officials and cardinals involved in the simoniacal granting of benefices.

[16] See ACC.2.330. Zabarella says that like many exactions of money from lower prelates by higher prelates, they are paid as tribute, because they are an affirmation of subjection: "Ideo tributa prestantur, quia sunt protestatio subiectionis."

TABLE 2

Refutation of papal arguments (R:=Response)

	A	F	M	S	V	B,L,G,R
1. Provide for parents, Roman church is mother of all		Cf. 777				R325
R: Only when parent is needy; parents should support their children rather than vice versa; 2 Cor. 12,14						R326
2. Roman church is first and others have their origin from it		777* = 667				
R: This doesn't give it the right to tax; it should live from it own income, like St. Paul; the Greek, not the Roman church was first; it should be recognized as first only because of its virtues		777				
3. Old Testament example of Levites paying tenth to high priest; Numbers 18,19; Deut. 1,15						R326, 378; G168
R: Ceremonial law, no longer valid, according to St. Jerome; payment of first year's income is more damaging than annual tenth; the high priest in O.T. was not otherwise provided for.						R326
4. Workman worthy of hire, Matt. 10,24, 1 Cor. 9,13			108			G168–9 R329, 378
X 2.26.16 Cum ex officio			101			
X 1.31.15 Inter cetera			101			
a. Owed to pope for his solicitude for the churches						R326
R: This is his obligation; he is sufficiently provided for; he should not take money from the particular churches since these revenues were provided by founders						R326
b. Payment for pope's officiating			97 103			R328
R: Is purely spiritual act because for eternal felicity of souls			103			
c. Because of pope's and cardinals' service to the community and republic		781				R330
R: Pope's government is only for the		781				

TABLE 2 cont.

	A	F	M	S	V	B,L,G,R
salvation of souls						
d. Cardinals should be provided for		778 –				R330
since they govern with the pope		779				
R: They have their own revenues,		778 –				
too; they have two roles, and have		779				
lost the revenues from their first						
roles; they do not govern with the						
pope, only advise him						
5. Annates necessary to protect from	401		87,	162		R326,9
adversaries, maintain status, prevent			111	168		
rebellion						
R: Vice of annates led to this						R326
opposition						
R: Imitators of Christ cannot be						R327
harmed 1 Pet 4,14						
R: Pope can only receive revenues						
through good means, not through						
violence, rape, simony						
C.15 q.6 c.1 para. 6						
X 5.22.1 Scripta						
6. To abolish annates is *subversio totius*		785				
ordinis clericalis						
R: Supporters of annates are trying		782				
to make an order out of *inordinato et*						
vitioso ordine						
7. There is such a multitude of people			Cf.	Cf.		R329;
who would be guilty of simony if			73	106		cf.
annates are simonical that this cannot						G170
be true.						
8. What pleases prince has force of law:	398					
Inst. 1.2.6 Sed quod principi	–99					

non-Gallican ones. This is probably because most were written at the council in response to concrete opponents, whereas M and S were both written over a decade earlier. On the other hand R was written in direct response to Zabarella's curial arguments at the council and thus has the fullest panoply of refutations found in any non-Gallican tract. A is interesting because its author presents the curial side hypothetically at the end of his tract after having given pride of place to the anti-curial position. However, the ease with which he shifts from one side to the other suggests that he is prepared to argue either side (again, this would fit quite precisely what we know about Mauroux.)

Haller would say that the widespread consensus among the tracts shows that the Gallicans had spread their gospel of liberty throughout Europe (and Haller believed the French derived their gospel from the experience of the English church, which he found epitomized in a set of statements he called the "English slogans.")[17] Indeed, he provided his book with a handy appendix which presented the "English slogans" drawn from English documents of the fourteenth century.[18] These slogans do appear often, especially among the arguments about ill effects. However, I would stress that the large consensus represented an *opinio communis* which had developed over many preceding centuries and which was much broader than the English slogans. Its other and more important proximate sources were, from the earliest to the most recent, Bernard of Clairvaux's *De consideratione*, the theological arguments concerning hierarchy in the secular-mendicant controversy, the ideas of William Durant the Younger's two *Tractatus*, and the canonistic *opinio communis* in reaction to Innocent IV's extreme position on the *plenitudo potestatis*, as traced by Buisson.[19] The more important remote sources, this time working backward in time, were the legislation of the eleventh century reformed papacy against simony, the Pseudo-Isidorian decretals, the letters of Pope Gregory I, and certain passages from the Bible relating both to simony and to the exercise of power within the church.

---

[17] There is some evidence in F to support Haller's position about the English example; Simonet points to the English resistance to the annates in his treatise as evidence that the taxes did not receive the consent of the clergy.

[18] Haller, 543–552: "Englische Schlagworte zur Begründung der Gallikanischen Freiheiten."

[19] See below, pp. 245–249.

3. *Papal* dominium *refuted*

The curialist argument which all the reformers attacked with greatest zest was the argument that the pope was lord of all benefices. (See Table 3.) It is not surprising that few curial supporters of provisions and annates dared to invoke it at Constance. It had, however, been used by curialists in the past, and reformers set it up as a "straw man" to attack. They deployed an arsenal of Biblical and canonistic terminology which referred to the pope not as dominus, but as minister, as pastor, procurator, steward, faithful servant, and dispensator. They invoked the Pauline dictum that all power in the church is given for edification, not for destruction. The reformers complained that, instead of acting in these ways, the popes had usurped the election and collation rights of the ordinaries, chapters, and monasteries.

The complaints summarized in Table 3 do not echo the English slogans; their antecedents lie more likely in the arguments used by the Paris theologians during the preceding two centuries supporting the rights of the ordinaries against the encroachments of the mendicants secured through papal privileges.[20] Echoing these, the reformers complained that the excessive provisions enervated the power of the ordinaries and threw the entire ecclesiastical order into confusion. They were usurpations which were contrary to the common law of the church, the most salubrious decrees of the councils, and the traditions of the most holy fathers. Again, such terminology is not characteristic of the English slogans.

All these arguments have to do with the distribution of power in the ecclesiastical hierarchy. They emphatically did not deny the position of the pope at the apex of that hierarchy, but they sought to insure that each rank in the hierarchy would likewise retain its full powers and functions. We shall return to these ideas in Chapters 8 and 9. They found valuable support in the canon law in statements made by popes themselves about their own powers. Job Vener gathered some quite potent ones for Matthew's treatise.[21] He used them to show that the pope was to follow the same principles of justice, love, and good faith that the laws bound his subordinates to follow; indeed all the more so since his example and leadership role were so important.

Excerpts from letters of Gregory I were central. "One should not

---

[20] See above, p. 13.

[21] It is quite likely that Job drew a number of these ideas from William Durant the Younger's two *Tractatus*; see Fasolt "Rezeption," 69.

TABLE 3

Refutation of papal dominium

	A	F	M	S	V	B,L,G,R
1. Pope is not lord of all benefices		769	97, 104		300	
2. Distinction among different kinds of lordship; all lordship except God's is limited, D.8 c.2 Que contra			105			
Pope's power over benefices like that of king over goods of vassals, X 3.20.1 Insinuatione, X 3.20.2 Ex parte tua			107			
3. Pope does not have ordinary responsibility for particular churches			81			
4. He is minister, *dispensator* (Luke 22,25–26)	383		100 104	159	300	R327
Not *retentor, imbursator*			108			
1 Cor. 4,1–2	383		100			
Matthew 23	383					
Pope is procurator			104		300	
Pope is faithful and prudent servant					300	
Fidelis: doesn't usurp authority; *prudens*: receives moderately only for urgent necessity						R327–8
Servus servorum dei					300	
Pope is vicar			104			
5. Power in church given for edification, not destruction		769	104 107			R327, 378
6. Pope is not the usufructarius, the intitulati are					300	
Clem. 5.8.3					300	
7. Limits on papal power			107	94–		
a. Power only valid when he acts reasonably; cf. St. Augustine; C.11 q.3 c.62 Tunc vera			–8	95		
b. Pope cannot change what was reasonably ordained by his predecessors				96		
c. Pope is to preside for common good, not for himself		769				
d. Pope cannot administer entire world directly: X 2.23.6 Mandata		81				
e. God's limits on bad rulers, so they won't damage church: C.6 q.1 c.13 Ex merito; C.8 q.1 c.18 Audacter; X 2.27.8 Cum causa; X 2.27.18 Cum Bartholdus			106 107			
f. Pope must use due process			107			
8. Usurpation of the rights of ordinaries and chapters by pope			77			
Injury to ordinaries, C.11 q.1, c.39 Pervenit; X 5.1.17 Qualiter et quando; X 1.10.3 Licet; X 2.13.7 Conquerente; D.56 c.7 Satis peruersum			77– 78			
No mechanism like devolution for correcting bad papal appointments			79			
Pope should not desire honor by which honor of others is lessened: C.11 q.3, c.13 Si quis non; D.99 c.4 Nullus; D.99 c.5 Ecce			88			

desire an honor by which the honor of another is diminished," Gregory wrote to the Patriarch of Constantinople, explaining why the patriarch should not to address him as "universal pope." (D.99, c.5 *Ecce*) Gregory added that his real honor was the full power of his brothers. The passage was ideally suited to support the reformers' defense of the rights of ordinaries against papal encroachments. Even more important was Gregory's statement in the canon *Pervenit*: "For if each bishop's jurisdiction is not maintained (*servatur*) for him, what is this but the confounding of the ecclesiastical order by us who are obligated to safeguard it?" (c.11 q.1 c.39 *Pervenit*) The word *confundere*, like the related verb *turbare*, was used often in the hierarchical arguments of the reformers.

A dictum of Gregory included in the canon *Mandata* in the *Liber extra* (X. 2,23, c. 6) provided support for the reformers' arguments that the ordinaries were better suited than the pope to make appointments in their dioceses since they were better acquainted with local conditions and since the pope would be impossibly overburdened by taking over the collations which belonged to the ordinaries: "We execute the celestial order more efficaciously if we share the burdens with our brothers." This argument was stated by Pierre LeRoy at the Paris synod in 1398 and greatly elaborated by Matthew of Cracow.

Job was even able to extract supports from the decretal law. "Injuries should not arise from whence the laws take their origin." (X. 2,13, c.7 *Conquerente*) Job cited this principle from a decretal of Innocent III; in the letter Innocent was addressing a commission conducting an inquest under papal mandate, exhorting it not to act unless its accusations were well-founded. "It is not fitting to despoil of their benefices those whom you are held to counsel by paternal provision." This principle, stated by Alexander III with reference to an action of an archbishop of Canterbury, was boldly applied by Vener to the pope's own "usurpations" of the rights of the ordinaries through the general reservations of benefices.

Job frequently borrowed principles and terminology which the popes had applied to limit abuses of lower prelates in order to apply them to abuses of power by the papacy itself. These principles were especially important when linked with another set of canonistic arguments—those which prohibited the pope from changing laws reasonably established by his predecessors. The most important of these established free capitular elections of bishops. Paulus Vladimiri cited these in S. He cited also the law establishing the election of the pope by the cardinals. If this law is reasonable, so are the laws for capitular election of bishops.

4. Simony

In a similar manner, once it was clear that the pope could commit simony, papal simony could be attacked with all the legislation of the Gregorian reform period, as well as the copious decretist and decretalist literature. Thus the main thrust of their arguments was to show that the pope committed simony when he required papal providees to pay annates and services on benefices. For this reformers found strong support in theology, in law, and in the council's own actions. In Thomas Aquinas they found a very powerful authority who had declared unequivocally that the pope could commit simony: "The Pope can be guilty of the vice of simony, like any other man; indeed the higher a man's position the more grievous is his sin. For although the possessions of the church belong to him as chief dispenser, they are not his as master and owner. Were he to accept money from the income of any church in exchange for a spiritual thing, he would not escape being guilty of simony. . . ."[22]

The Council of Constance itself had in effect corroborated this theoretical statement by its actual condemnation of a pope for simony. Simony had been among the charges against John [XXIII]. Reformers even tried to associate this simony with heresy; however, if challenged most would have admitted that simony usually did not involve a depravity of the intellect and therefore could not strictly be called a heresy.

In Arguments 1–3, the reformers again showed overall agreement. Table 4 reflects significant divergence on Argument 4, however. Before we examine this, let us look at some further complications.

5. Answers to curial objections

John [XXIII] had blatantly sold offices, so his condemnation for simony at Constance carried no necessary implications about the annates. On the other hand, Thomas's statement about taking the revenues of a church might seem to fit the collection of annates

---

[22] *Summa theologiae*, 2ª2ᵃᵉ, 100,1, Resp. ad Obj. 7: "Ad septimum dicendum quod papa potest incurrere vitium simoniae, sicut et quilibet alius homo: peccatum enim tanto in aliqua persona est gravius quanto majorem obtinet locum. Quamvis enim res Ecclesiae sint eius ut principalis dispensatoris, non tamen sunt ejus ut domini et possessoris. Et ideo si reciperet pro aliqua re spirituali pecuniam de redditibus alicujus ecclesiae, non careret vitio simoniae. . . ."

rather precisely. The matter was not quite so simple, however. Supporters of annates had developed a sophisticated set of distinctions to show that no simony occurred in their collection. These distinctions are summarized in Table 5. The first was the most audacious. Earlier canonists had made a distinction between acts that are simoniacal because forbidden by law and acts that are simoniacal absolutely. They said that the pope had legally defined the annates as not simoniacal. Vladimiri vented his greatest anger against this "false distinction" and said that his whole *Speculum aureum* was devoted to its refutation.

He traces the distinction back to its *locus classicus* in the *Glossa ordinaria* on X 1.29.12 (v. Illicite pactiones),[23] and laments that the canonists commonly accepted this distinction.[24] Their reasoning was that benefices were introduced by positive law[25] since they didn't exist at the time of the apostles; therefore, buying and selling them is simoniacal only because the church has prohibited such purchase and sale. Vladimiri then calls this a "superficial and damnable distinction which has sent a multitude of souls to hell." He expresses his amazement that so many famous doctors agreed in this error, even though it is unsupported by any canonical text.[26]

Defenders of this distinction also invoked the support of civil law concerning the *lex Iulia de ambitu*, which forbade sale of offices; specifically they cited the passage in Dig. 48.14.un. which declared that the *lex Iulia* did not have force in the city of Rome because the "creation of magistracies pertains to the oversight of the prince, not to the favor of the people." Hostiensis said that in Rome the magistrate is selected by the prince, who is not bound by the law. Goffredus and Iohannes Andreae repeated this dictum. The absolutist tone of such argument was driven home still more strongly by the citation of Inst. 1.2.6 *Sed quod principi* ("What pleases the prince

---

[23] On these canonistic theories see Hubert Jedin, "Kann der Papst Simonie begehen?" in *idem, Kirche des Glaubens—Kirche der Geschichte* 2 (Freiburg, 1966) 264–284. Jedin (265 n.4) cites the gloss from the Lyon 1543 edition: "Secus in simoniacis, quia prohibita, secus in prohibitis, quia simoniaca. Prohibita, quia simoniaca, sunt illa quae in veteri testamento novoque simoniaca erant in sui natura, ut vendere sacramenta, ut praedicto c. Qui studet et c. Sicut eunuchus. Simoniaca, quia prohibita, sunt illa, quae per constitutionem ecclesiae facta sunt simoniaca, quale est hoc, et etiam pastum dare receptionem in canonicum, et in istis non sufficit sola voluntas, nec in aliis, dum tamen sit contenta suis terminis." At the time of the Council of Trent, Pope Paul IV dismissed the distinction as an "old wives' tale."
[24] *Speculum,* pp. 140ff. Vladimiri also cites glosses on X 1.35.4 *Cum pridem* (v. Quedam) and X 2.24.26 Etsi Christus and C.1 q.3 c.8 *Saluator* (v. iudicem).
[25] Vladimiri refutes this; *Speculum,* 186.
[26] *Speculum,* 172:

TABLE 4

Simony in papal provisions and annates

	A	F	M	S	V	B,L,G,R
1. Biblical definition of simony	381			147		G169
Acts 8,9–24 Simon Magus						
C.1 q.1 c.11, Qui studet	384					
2 Kings 5,20–27 Giezi	381			147		G169; R 379
Numbers 22 on Balaam				146 –7	306– 7	
Example of Jesus cleansing temple, John 2, etc.	384			144		
2. Simony of pope	381		97			L603,
Pope can commit simony.						G169
Thomas Aquinas, *Summa theol.* 2ᵃ 2ᵉ,	384					
Art. 1, Resp. ad obj. 7	395					
D.40 c.6 Si papa	381					L603
John XXIII condemned by council	381					Cf.
for simony						G171
Apostolic see can sell sacrament of			97			
body of Christ, just as one apostle sold						
Christ.						
Pope should be punished more	381					Cf.
harshly since he is more exalted						G169
Like Lucifer	381					
De pen. D.2 c.45 fin.	381					
C.9 q.3 c.14 Aliorum, Gloss	381					L603
Because pope abuses power of keys						L603
and gives pernicious example.						
Prelates of higher status—bishops						L603
and cardinals should be punished more						
harshly.						
3. Footnote: Simony and heresy	384		90	150		
Simony is heresy						
C.1 q.1 c.19 Petrus; C.1 q.1 c.20				150		
Cum omnis; C.1 q.1 c.21 Eos qui						
C.1 q.7 c.27 fin. Patet			90			
Because it shows disrespect for	384					
spiritual things						
Forces people to become heretics,		767–				
declaring spiritual things can be bought		8				
4. Simony connected with benefices	381		91			
Benefices are the gift of God						

TABLE 4 cont.

	A	F	M	S	V	B,L,G,R
C.1 q.3 c.8 Salvator	381		91			
Benefice is what is given by God to men or by men to God (Augustine)			98		300	
Dona dei should be given freely Mt. 10,8: Gratis accepistis	382		100	143	302	G169; R379
Payment of money connected with benefices is simony		766			302	
C.1 q.3 c.9 Ex multo	394					
C.1 q.3 c.15 fin. Si quis prebendas						
X 3.12.un. Ut nostrum			108		302	
Payment is price, commercio					302	
Mediator equally guilty as parties who buy and sell, C.1 q.1 c.8 Si quis episcopus			91			
Tacit purchase and sale, C.1 q.5 c.2 Eos					302	
Facts speak louder than words, X 2.28.1 Dilecti filii, Glo. 1					302	
Benefices are spiritual by nature and therefore cannot be bought or sold.			98, 100			R380
Benefices spiritual because annexed to spiritual offices	Cf. 383		99–100	142		
X 3.40.3 Quod in dubiis			99			
C.12 q.2 c.3 Nulli			99	300		
C.1 q.3 c.7 Si quis obiecerit			100			
Benefices are spiritual because they principally serve for the perfection of the human spirit				153		
See also cases where temporal things can be given for maintaining sustenance of minister w/o simony			101 –2			
Spiritual things belong to God.						
Spiritual things are in the possession of no individual; cannot enter into commerce.	382			142		
Dig. 1.8.1 In princ. Para. Summus rerum	382					
Dig. 1.8.6 In tantum, Para. Sacre	382					
Benefices, as spiritual things, are of inestimable value			98	142		
Just as grace cannot be bought or sold (Rom. 11,6)			100			
Whoever takes away spiritual things commits a sacrilege: C.12 q.2 c.3 Nulli liceat; C.12 q.2 c.5 Que multotiens; X 5.41.7 in glossa 2ª					300	

TABLE 5

False distinctions refuted

	A	F	M	S	V	B,L,G,R
1. Simony because forbidden vs. simony absolutely			97, 103	73, 172		L602 G172
R: Pope can dispense from positive law penalties, but not take away sin of simony			103			L602 G172
2. Whether payment is for consecration or promotion: C.1 q.1 c.10 Sanctorum patrum; C.1 q.3 c.7 Si quis obiecerit	382					
R: Parallel case: if marriage prohibited, engagement also: D.23 c. 16 Oratio	382					
3. Granting of orders vs. promotions to benefices						L602
4. Benefices with cura vs. benefices without cura	382					
C.1 q.3 c. Res que ex consecratione	382					
5. Between office and benefice						
R: *Propter officium dat beneficium*						G167
VI 1.3.15 Quia per ambitionem				79		
Right of receiving temporalia because of obligation to spiritual office						G169
6. Whether because office is vacant or because pope confers	389	766				
R: He doesn't collect from all vacant benefices		766				
R: Only cardinals present in consistory share in the services		766				
7. Whether by payment or by obligation made before peaceful possession						L604–5
R: It is simony if the curia withholds bulls until payment made						R327, 379
8. Whether anything transferred or not— intention alone is simony	389					L602
9. Whether intentional or not	389					
R: X 3.12.un. Ut nostrum	389					

has the force of law.") and the statement that the will of the prince is sufficient to abrogate the law.

Most of these arguments were strikingly absent from the curial defense of annates at Constance. Curialists knew the reformers were unanimous in attacking them vehemently. Reformers also found little trouble in exposing the speciousness of Nr. 2–5 in Table 5. However, it is also with Nr. 5 that we find the reformers beginning to diverge in important ways.

In Argument 5 the curialists tried to distinguish between paying for the benefice and paying for the spiritual office; they said the payment was made for the benefice, whereas the spiritual office was conveyed freely. All the reformers flatly rejected this by saying that the benefice was given because of the office, that it was attached inseparably to the office, and that it is a gift of God (and gifts of God should be freely given, freely received). They could point to clear statements in canon law which said payment of money in connection with receipt of benefices was simony. However, the non-Gallicans tended to go much further.

6. The nature of the benefice

For the non-Gallicans the benefice was not merely annexed to a spiritual office, but it in fact became spiritual itself by attraction, even by nature. The Gallicans, invoking Roman law from Justinian's codification (See Table 4, No. 4), observed that spiritual things cannot enter into commerce, because they are in the possession of no individual. But for the non-Gallicans, the benefices could not be bought or sold because they were of inestimable value, just as grace itself was. Indeed, they cited canons which had to do with sacrilege, to show that sale of benefices was tantamount to sacrilege because collection of annates amounted to the removal of sacred objects.

Matthew of Cracow's idea of reform here is found frequently at Constance; it consists of restoring sacred things to their sacred state and preserving them from profanation. In using Mircea Eliade's terms "sacred" and "profane,"[27] I am using words which occurred repeatedly in the reformers' writings. Eliade tells us that for the religious mind sacred things are manifestations of a higher reality and partake of that reality which they thus represent. Gold and silver, in the minds of many council fathers, manifested and

---

[27] Mircea Eliade, *The Sacred and the Profane*, ed. W. Trask (New York, 1957).

partook of permanence, purity, strength, richness, beauty, internal warmth and spirituality. For these reformers the use of gold and silver as money was quite literally a profanation. It made these sacred things dirty, debased, and dishonest. When such reformers objected to the buying and selling of Church offices, they did so not only because such commerce was simoniacal but also because the sacred offices were thus profaned; for many reformers, any buying and selling, any use of money was to some degree a profanation. For them it was not only the love of money that was evil, but money itself. On the other hand, it was not the gold and silver that were evil, but the profanation of them, in their use as money.[28] For such thinkers morality was in a very real way incarnated in things. Justice is in things themselves, said Maurice Rvačka; injustice is an unjust exchange of spiritual for temporal things,[29] i.e., the profanation of the spiritual. A cleric who paid for an ecclesiastical office would be similarly profaned, by the very act of his payment for it. His inner intention would be quite secondary; indeed, it would be itself defined or fixed by his very act with regard to the things.

Let us briefly note Gerson's position here by way of contrast. For him it was not the benefice but rather the right of receiving it which was spiritual.[30] This right, no matter how temporal it might appear, was spiritual because of the purpose for which it was to be used: the eternal felicity of those to whom the holder of the benefice ministered. For Gerson, since the benefice itself was not sacred, simony did not always occur when an exchange of money accompanied the conferring of a benefice; it became necessary to consider the intentions of the persons who conferred and received the benefice.

Gerson's position here did not, however, fall into line with the view of the more extreme Gallicans either.[31] Their primary concern was the total abolition of the annates, and they wanted to equate

---

[28] On the problematic nature of money for many reformers, see especially Helmrath, "Reform," 82–84 and the literature cited there. Helmrath shows the link between simony and usury and asks if the simony tracts do not reveal the "Inbegriff einer tiefen Hilflosigkeit, mit dem Faktor Geld fertig zu werden."

[29] Maurice Rvačka, Sermon, July 26, 1416, Tübingen, Universitätsbibl., Mc 282, fol. 84v.–85r: "Omnis justitia consistet in equitate ... in communicacione symoniaca spiritualis pro temporali nulla est equalitas.... Iustitia consistit in medio rei ad rem." On the subject of the reaction against the growing influence of money in relation to critiques of papal power, cf. John Yunck, "Economic Conservatism, Papal Finance and the Medieval Satires on Rome," *Mediaeval Studies* 23 (1961) 334–351.

[30] Gerson, *De simonia*, G.6.169: "Ius suscipiendi temporalia, quantumcumque temporale videatur, sit pure spirituale, ratione finis et objecti."

[31] See article of Bruno Bertagna below, p. 201 n. 36.

the annates with simony without any consideration of intent. A decretal of Innocent III (X. 3,12, c. un. *Ut nostrum*) offered the prospect of doing so. It categorically established that simony occurred whenever any prelate, upon conferring a benefice, held back part of its revenues for himself (provided he was not the one who had formerly had the right to collect the revenues). The canon was particularly apposite because it established that acts analogous to the collection of annates were simoniacal regardless of place, time, cause, means of payment, or mental state of the parties. This last point was most crucial because it removed the issue of intent. Reformers like Matthew of Cracow and Paulus Vladimiri had already largely removed the question of intent by regarding the payment of annates as a sacrilege. The differences between Gallicans and non-Gallicans should not be too sharply drawn, however. Matthew too cited *Ut nostrum*; and Vladimiri spoke of the right of receiving the benefice, rather than the benefice itself, as spiritual. The author of A also cited the texts which referred to the sale of benefices as a sacrilege.

7. The "Gallican" arguments

For those who opposed the taxes, *Ut nostrum* was not a panacea. It did not outlaw as simoniacal the payment of a portion of the revenues of the benefice after the benefice had been conferred. And, in fact, virtually none of the tracts questioned the right of the popes in cases of necessity to reserve part of the revenues of the benefices to which they would make future provisions. They thus accepted on this ground the initial reservation of the annates by John XXII in *Cum nonnulle* (See below, p. 197.) But they also stressed that the necessity had to be clearly established and was by nature temporary, not permanent. In his first annate tract, written on his journey to Constance in 1415, Vladimiri went so far as to say that it was acceptable for providees to promise formally prior to receiving their benefices that they would pay the annates. However, in his second tract, which was written at Constance in 1416, Vladimiri, having been rebuffed by Zabarella and others, took a firmer stance and rejected categorically such obligations as simoniacal. In this his reasoning was generally similar to that found in A, pp. 389–90, although Vladimiri's argument used different canonical references and relied more on Aristotelian reasoning.

The bulk of Vladimiri's argument was dedicated to showing that the payment of annates, even the signing of an obligation to pay them, was in effect the purchase of a benefice and of the right to

TABLE 6

The "Gallican" arguments

	A	F	M	S	V	B,L,G,R
1. History of annates; refutation of prescriptive rights						
a. Custom does not create right in this case	396			Cf. 175		B601
Cum nonnullae temporary	385	762				
Imposed for limited time for recovery of holy land; since cause has ceased, so should effect						B601
Pope changed obligation into a real and actual payment					299	
Origins of servitia as a free gift; gifts don't create custom		764, 766				
b. Smacks of simony; is also alienation of church's property		765				
c. Bad faith precludes prescription, VI 5.12.2 Possessor	386					
d. Annates not paid for more than ten years without resistance		764				
e. Those who paid did not have faculty to resist	386					
g. Collected by violence	386	767				
Penal constitution, Extrav. comm. 1.3.1 Iniuncte; beneficiaries forced to pay amount stated in books		767				
Violent entry; *fures et latrones*	388					
C.1 q.3 c. Res que ex consecratione, glossa	388					
Before schism delays allowed, remissions given	386					
h. Scandal involved	397	769				
C.14 q.3 c.3 Plerique, glossa						
Collection is vitiosus, inhonestus, continens speciem mali						
i. Simoniacal provision does not confer title				103		
Footnote: Failure of Council of Vienne to deal with services						B601
Joh. Andreae's gloss concerning this						
Council of Constance must not be blamed in same way						B601
2. Pope has no real property right in the annates						
Seven reasons why the obligation is not *realis*		786				
Freedom of the churches						B601
Church should be free from all exactions and burdens	392 – 396					B601
Footnote: Support of civil law						
Punished simony by privation of priesthood and infamia	391					
Auth. De sanctissimis episcopis, para. Sed neque clerici and Sed neque xenodochium	391					

administer the sacraments; it was thus simoniacal by nature. Thus, he did not pay much attention to two curialist arguments which occupied much of the Gallicans' attention: 1) that the Roman church had developed a customary, or prescriptive right to the collection of these taxes; and 2) that the obligation to pay the annates demanded by the curia was not a personal one of the beneficiary, but rather a real property obligation owed as a sort of attachment on the revenues of the benefice itself (hence no simony could be involved in the payment.)

The curial arguments the Gallicans sought to refute might be summarized as follows: The annates and services are not personal taxes, but are reserved from the first years' fruits of benefices filled by papal provision. They were reserved to support urgent needs of the Roman church and had been collected without opposition, thus with tacit consent, for a time that exceeded human memory. Therefore, they could continue to be collected by customary right according to all the canon and civil laws which established that right.

These are the arguments which the Gallicans spent so much of their energy refuting. It is striking that the non-Gallicans gave so little attention to these arguments, and still more striking that on one them the position of Vladimiri was diametrically opposed. Vladimiri held very strongly that the debt for annates and services was "real" rather than personal. Let us turn first to the Gallican arguments, then return to consider Vladimiri's reasoning.

Since F was composed as part of the annate discussion in the French nation in October-November 1415, the argument in F is closely tied to the substance of those discussions. It starts by tracing the course of the deliberations on annates within the council, focusing particularly on reform committee's effort to research the origins of the annates and services. This research revealed that these taxes were never formally enacted by legislation. The annates began with a temporary three year assessment made by John XXII (*Cum nonnulle*).[32] The services began with an early custom of gifts freely given by prelates who received their offices in curia, but the gifts were converted into a tax and official tax rates drawn up in a

---

[32] F does not identify *Cum nonnulle* (Extrav. comm. 3.2.11) by name; A does and also notes that it presupposed an earlier such decree: "..... dominus Jo. xxii fecit unam constitutionem que incipit Cum nonnulle et supponit aliam prius fecisse ad quam se reffert ..." Augsburg, 2° 226, p. 385, ed. ACC.2.593. The earlier constitution referred to must have been the bull of Clement V, now lost, which levied annates in England in 1306. See Baix, cdviii–cdxi for complete bibliography on this question.

book.[33] This research shows the remarkable degree of historical analysis which the Constance reformers could exercise when it served their purposes. F uses this information to show that there was no legal basis for the annates and services, since they had only been collected by customary right. The entire section of the tract which follows consists of twenty-four reasons to show that this custom had produced no legally binding right to the continued collection of the taxes, especially no prescriptive right, according to civil or canonistic definitions of prescription. The final section of the tract then answers twenty specific arguments made by the supporters of annates in their appeals.

The tract *Ad ostendendum* (A), on the other hand, does not make specific reference to the French nation's annate deliberations and is more discursive. It is not an intellectually rigorous work, but does provide a very handy compendium of the current legal arguments concerning annates and services in the French nation, and especially of the legal texts cited in support of these arguments. The section which refutes the existence of a "real" right to collection of the taxes is of particular interest because of the ways in which it relates liberty to property and consent. It also shows the clearest contrast to the "non-Gallican" positions.

I have edited this section in Appendix 2 below (see, p. 000). Here I will briefly summarize the argument, which is in three parts. The author attempts to show why the curia has no legal claim to any "real" right to collect the annates from papal providees, from three standpoints: 1) the standpoint of the one from which the right is said to have been acquired (i.e., the providee) 2) the standpoint of the one for whom the right has allegedly been acquired (i.e., the curia); 3) the standpoint of the thing itself (i.e., the benefice). The author's awkward circumlocution results from his obvious discomfort in referring to the providees as the owners of the benefices. However, his argument in fact treats them in this manner, even though its ultimate thrust is to show that the benefices are by nature free of any lordship. This thrust is evident from the beginning of his argument, which contains a remarkable statement concerning the origin of property rights. God originally created all people *and all things* free, declares the author, but he subjected

---

[33] The "book" to which F refers must be the series of *Obligationes et solutiones* registers, whose real purpose according to Favier, was to make a record of the amount of the tax, which was often still imprecisely defined, and to help establish papal right to collect the taxes. See Favier, *Finances*, 343–345, and the older literature cited there, in particular the studies of Göller and Clergeac.

things to the dominion of men. In the rest of the first two sections of his argument the author proceeds to treat the benefices as though they had come to be owned by the clergy, but he vacillates between assumption of individual ownership and collective ownership. He says that "no one can acquire a right in something that is mine without my true and express consent or at least the presumption of it." With regard to the clergy taken collectively, he argues that their true and express consent has not occurred. Express consent is required because "servitude is repugnant to nature and to liberty." There can be no presumption here because "by the presumption of law and nature no one can be presumed to want his property to be subjected to another," and especially here, where the beneficiary is sworn to uphold the liberty of the church, and contrary behavior leads to the detriment of his soul.

From the standpoint of the curia, there has not been consent to impose the burden on the churches perpetually. The original exaction of annates was for a three-year period only, in a situation of emergency (*necessitas*). Necessity can and does cease. The most telling evidence that the burden was on the beneficiary rather than the benefice was the curia's practice of collecting the annates from the providee prior to peaceful possession. There can be no real property action against someone who is not in peaceful possession. The actions of the curia demonstrate its *de facto* recognition that the burden to pay annates is a personal rather than a real property obligation. One's will is demonstrated more by one's deeds than by one's words.

The third and final standpoint is the most interesting and most crucial. From the standpoint of the benefice itself, no real property right can be acquired to collect the annates, because no new taxes or burdens are to be imposed on the churches. Therefore, any oath or obligation signed by the providee to pay them is not binding. The argument is supported with a veritable barrage of texts drawn from canon and civil law. All the arguments about resistance to unlawful commands of superiors and the freedom of the churches from burdens are set forth here.

Now let us return to Vladimiri's contrasting view. In the first of his two treatises composed for the Council of Constance, Vladimiri stated categorically that the debt owed for annates and services was "real," not personal. In fact, this view corresponded with the actual practice of the curia, which required new providees to take over any accumulated unpaid annates and services on the benefice (i.e. from previous incumbents of the benefice. If the debt had been personal, it would have expired with the death of the previous incumbent, or, if he had been transferred, it would have followed him.)[34] However, other, more recent practices of the curia could not be squared with this view, above all the practice mentioned above of requiring payment prior to assumption of office. If the providee had to pay the tax before assuming office, it was clearly not being taken out of the first year's revenue of the benefice. Vladimiri called this practice "detestable," and it was in the course of attacking it and related practices that he made his categorical statement about the "real" nature of the debt.

In discussing these practices, Vladimiri moved from theoretical objections to the actual concerns of the clergy. They are the same ones discussed above which were also voiced by Matthew of Cracow and Dietrich of Niem, above all the fraud, the uncertainty, and the loss incurred, and the effective payment of much more than the tax, all greatly exacerbated by the necessity of paying in Rome, which exposed the providee to the dangers of the road, the wiles of money-changers, and the high interest rates of money-lenders. Significantly, Vladimiri notes that the annates had earlier been collected locally by official collectors. During the Schism the Roman popes had ceased this practice which had been observed during the Avignon papacy and which the popes at Avignon still continued during the Schism. This proved to be a very significant difference between the two obediences. A person in the Roman obedience had to go to Rome (or send a procurator) in order to get an office, and increasingly he had to pay the amount of the annates (and more) there in the curia before he could return to his locality and try to take possession of his office. It was hard to look at this as anything else but an intentional act undertaken for the express purpose of buying an office. On the other hand, in the Avignon obedience, the annates had become much more customary and acceptable. They were owed on a much larger proportion of benefices in France than elsewhere, and they were collected locally according to a regular process.

However, during the Schism they had been collected much more rigorously, not to say ruthlessly, by the popes at Avignon, especially in times of increasing economic distress. Moreover, what had been acceptable when the papacy and its patronage were located in France became less so as it appeared increasingly certain that the papacy would return permanently to Italy.

There was a final sense in which the experience of the Gallicans was different from that of the non-Gallicans. That was the experi-

---

[34] Zabarella affirms this in his reply to Maurice Rvačka, ACC.2.331.

ence of the common action of the clergy of the realm of France during the subtractions of obedience in the years preceding the council. This withdrawal of obedience in opposition to papal absolutism was based on a theory of resistance firmly grounded in the canonistic *opinio communis* traced by Buisson. The clergy in the French kingdom had put this theory into practice; in doing so they never intended to create a separate Gallican church, but rather to reunify the universal church by compelling Benedict to resign. The Gallicans saw their action as fully compatible with the role and authority of the general council, and they even acknowledged the pope's universal authority, as long as the exercise of that authority did not scandalize the church.

However, in practice, the doctrine of resistance which the Gallican theorists developed on the question of the annates and services invited them to see their resistance as a collective action of the clergy of the kingdom, and it required them to continue to resist until the annates and services were completely abolished. That continued resistance was the best evidence that a prescriptive right to their collection had not in fact been established. This is why the French nation was so insistent in its Avisamenta that any provision of revenues for the curia would be only temporary and *per modum tollerantie*.[35]

8. Gerson's position

After the polemics of the other treatises, Gerson's little tract offers a refreshing combination of common sense and uncommonly fine distinctions. Although Gerson accepts most of the distinctive Gallican positions,[36] his focus is clearly on genuine and intensely practical reform of the problems created by simony and the appearance of simony.

Gerson accepts that the pope can commit simony, as proven most recently by John [XXIII]'s condemnation by the council for simony. Papal simony is all the more serious because of the pope's high position. If the pope forces providees to pay money before they can exercise their offices (i.e., annates and services), simony occurs. Gerson in fact goes beyond the other Gallicans in one sense by

---

[35] ACC.2.674.
[36] See Bruno Bertagna, "Il problema della "plenitudo ecclesiasticae potestatis" nella dottrina ecclesiologica di Giovanni Gersone (1363–1429)," *Apollinaris* 43 (1970) 555–612 at 606–609; Bertagna argues that Gerson had normally distanced himself from other Gallican positions.

tackling two curialist arguments that they shied away from:

1) First, to the curialist argument that payments similar to annates were demanded of new appointees by prelates and cathedral chapters, Gerson first argues that in these cases, payment is often licit because it is made after the person takes peaceful possession; but then he takes the bull by the horns and acknowledges that simony does often occur in these other cases. Both this simony and the pope's simony must be eliminated; evil should be reproved wherever it occurs.

2) The second curialist argument was one made by Zabarella in his reply to Maurice Rvačka: If simony does indeed occur when annates and services are paid, then vast numbers of clergy would be guilty of simony and would have to give up their benefices, leaving their people without pastoral care.[37] Again, Gerson faces the argument head on: We must not be deterred by such considerations from doing what is right. However, he also expresses his conviction that fewer people are in fact guilty of simony in the payment of annates than might be thought.

And, for those guilty of simony through payment of annates and services in simoniacal manner, Gerson has a fascinating answer: They can continue to administer their offices and retain their benefices, because the pope has freed them from the penalties of simony established by positive law![38] In this one sense, the simony of the pope in conferring benefices is less dangerous than that of the ordinaries, because he can excuse the recipients from the positive law penalties, while the ordinaries cannot. For Gerson, this emphatically does *not* mean that the pope can excuse them from the *guilt* of simony. That is a matter of divine, not positive law. The bulk of Gerson's argument concerns ways to deal with this guilt itself.

His strategy is two-fold, according to past and future simony. First, by subtle casuistry he shows that many who might think they are guilty are not. He suggests the appointment of confessors by the council to counsel and absolve them (as the reform committee itself had proposed; Common, c.27). His explanation suggests clearly the ways in which the confessors would have proceeded. Many persons could be excused because of a lack of knowledge of the laws and the facts involved. It may be possible to argue that they paid the money, not to buy the office, but to "redeem the vexation" of the

---

[37] See Table 2 above, and ACC.2.330.

[38] With his usual reasonableness, however, Gerson declares that a person should give up his benefice if he has caused another more worthy person to lose the benefice. Compare this with the position of Vladimiri in *Speculum*, 103–119.

person conferring it, as when the parents of a child pay a priest to baptize her when the priest refuses to do so otherwise, not because they are trying to buy the sacrament of baptism, but because they want to provide for their child. The remedy for simony may be a rectification of the intention. The wrong intention would be to receive the *temporalia* as a price for the granting of spiritual things (in the manner of *do, ut des*; this involves a simoniacal exchange.) A right intention would be to have necessary physical sustenance for performing one's office.

As to future simony, Gerson says that the council should oppose simony by renewing, changing, or interpreting existing laws concerning collation of benefices, by both head and members. This should be done with moderation: not too strict, but not so lax as to give rise to real simony or the scandalous appearance of simony. The council has the power to prescribe these laws, especially for the pope, without injury to his plenitude of power; in this way, God willing, the papal plenitude of power would be harmonized with the same plenitude of power of the general council.[39]

Thus, Gerson acknowledged the power of the council to enact laws which deal with simony involved in the collection of annates and services. He was not any more specific here. Later he warns against making too strict a restriction on simony "under the pretext of reformation," and in this way introducing greater scandal and danger to souls. Finally, Gerson says that simony is first to be eliminated in men's hearts, and is better to be rooted out in both head and members by leading men back to the fear of God, than by penalties alone. The best solution of all would be to appoint worthy people to office.

9. Conclusion

The two tracts of Vladimiri composed for Constance resemble Gerson's tract in the fineness of their intellectual distinctions and

---

[39] *G*.6.174: "Simoniaca labes poterit pro futuro praeservationem habere per hoc sacrum Concilium, ne passim et licenter ut hactenus introeat; constituendo leges debitas vel jam institutas renovando, mutando vel interpretando circa collationem omnium spiritualium tam a capite quam a membris, cum tali moderamine quod neque fiat strictior prohibitio temporalium quam oportet, in capite vel in membris, sicut factum esse plures existimant in quibusdam; neque rursus permittatur talis laxatio quae vel veram simoniam vel scandalosam simoniae speciem introducat. Haec autem particulariter aperire sit eorum qui ad hoc particulariter commissi sunt. Ceterum generale concilium in qua potestate possit leges huiusmodi praescribere, praesertim Summo Pontifici sine laesione plenitudinis potestatis, utilis est practicatio de qua si annuerit Deus alias et alibi videbitur, concordando plenitudinem potestatis papalis cum ipsa plenitudine potestatis Concilii generalis."

the depth of their concern for practical reform of the simony connected with annates and services. Both thinkers came very close to
one another in their discussion of the problem of intent involved in
the payment of the taxes. Both were willing to accept the idea that
payment of annates and services could be free from the taint of
simony if the payment was not extorted. Both agreed, though for
somewhat different reasons, that most persons who had received
benefices through simoniacal payment of annates in the past could
legally retain their benefices. But both remained deeply troubled by
the simony committed by the pope in extorting these payments. In
their concern for the consciences of those who had received their
benefices in this manner they reflected the deep and widespread
concern of the clergy at Constance. Their tracts also represented
the penetrating analysis of the most well-informed theologian and
canonist who commented on these matters. The inability of both to
arrive at a successful conceptual resolution of these issues shows the
intractability of the problems.

The council's actions did little to lessen these conceptual difficulties. It finally accepted the Gallican argument that the obligation
was personal, even though this involved a major change in the way
the curia collected arrears of annates and meant that the appearance of simony would be even more difficult to avoid. It sought to
avoid these appearances in the future by insuring that payment
would be made only after peaceful possession and by eliminating
annates altogether on benefices obtained through expecantancies.
However, it did nothing about eliminating the troublesome requirement to sign obligations to pay the annates prior to peaceful
possession, nor did it abolish the ecclesiastical censures for those
who were late in payment. And it abandoned all action on the
crucial issue of those tainted by simoniacal payment of annates in
the past.

The results of the conciliar action were thus a palliative, not to
say a *pis aller*. Although they did provide some relief from the worst
practical problems, they did not provide a satisfying conceptual
resolution. Such a resolution would have been most difficult because of the decided differences in approach between the Gallicans
and non-Gallicans, which in turn betrayed their very different
historical experiences and different conceptions of the nature of the
benefice and of property in general. The historical experience of the
non-Gallicans caused them to direct the brunt of their attack
against what they saw as an effort to sell sacred things. The
historical experience of the Gallicans made their chief strategy a
refutation of the curia's prescriptive right to collect the taxes. It

invited and indeed required them to continue to resist the payment of those taxes in theory, even while they agreed to pay them in practice as a temporary concession.

The inability to resolve the conceptual issues involved in the annates and services must rank as the most significant single failure of the council; it was to have ominous results for the future of conciliar reform.

In Chapters 5 and 6 I showed the development of the concept of conciliar reform in practice. Now in Chapters 8 and 9 we will turn to the ways in which the reformers imagined this reform, imaginations which held great promise.

CHAPTER EIGHT

IDEAS AND IMAGES OF REFORM AS CHANGE

Ideas of reform are ideas of change. Like the Roman god Janus they guard the threshold, looking forward and backward at once. Modern historians find this ambivalence toward change disconcerting; they much prefer the unilinear change we call progress. Haller dismissed the conservative terminology of the reformers by saying that every revolutionary movement has always paraded itself under the banner of restoring the past. He saw the reforms as a revolution of national churches struggling under the banner of the freedom of the church against the centralizing monarchy of the pope. There is irony in his analysis, since these reformers used much of the same reform terminology, imagery, and ideology as the earlier Gregorian reformers who had set in motion the process of papal centralization of power. Some have said that the Gregorian reform itself was a revolution which used ideas of antiquity and tradition for merely polemical purposes.[1] I propose that the ambivalence of reform terminology is not revolution masking itself as conservatism, but is instead an accurate reflection of the ambivalence of reformers toward change itself, of their mixed desires to restore and renew.

1. Restoration and reform

Gerhart Ladner treats reform ideas as a species within the larger genus of ideas of renewal. He thus distinguishes them not only from restoration but from at least three other closely related categories: 1) renascence, which generally involves cosmological or vitalistic change; 2) revolution, which involves a complete turning, or revolving, and seems to appear first in the sense of historical change in Villani's *Chronicle* in the early fourteenth century; and 3) rebellion, which first appears in the Roman Empire and then reappears in the later Middle Ages in the context of revolutionary move-

---

[1] Karl F. Morrison, *Tradition and Authority in the Western Church, 300–1140* (Princeton, 1969) 346, cited by Heiko Oberman, "'Et tibi dabo claves regni caelorum': Kirche und Konzil von Augustin bis Luther. Tendenzen und Ergebnisse II'," *Nederlands Theologisch Tijdschrift* 29 (1975) 97–188 at 97–98.

ments.[2] With one exception, all these other categories overlap at some points with reform ideas at Constance. The exception is revolution; *pace* Figgis and Haller, there is virtually no evidence in the sources that anyone at Constance regarded the work of the council as a revolution. The relative infrequency of ideas of renascence at Constance is more surprising since the council occurred during the first blush of the *Quattrocento* and was attended by prominent humanists.[3] The most extensive overlap is with ideas of restoration. Ladner has argued that ideas of restoration in the Middle Ages were frequently linked with the renewal of the Empire.[4] The reunion of the schism-torn church at the council provided an interesting parallel to the idea of imperial renewal. Terms such as *redintegrare* and *resarcire* (literally, to patch up) were used frequently alongside *restaurare* to refer to this goal; also the old phrase *reformatio pacis*, which had long been employed to refer to the end of hostilities between warring groups. This phrase, exceedingly current at Constance, clearly shows the overlapping terminology of reform and restoration. It also suggests why we should not expect to find much evidence at Constance of Ladner's final category of reform ideas—rebellion.[5] The council fathers were attempting to "re-form the peace", not to "go to war all over again." However, the more peaceful counterpart to rebellion—resistance—did play a significant role at the council, where there was often talk of

---

[2] Gerhart Ladner, "Terms and Ideas of Renewal in the Twelfth Century," in *Renaissance and Renewal in the Twelfth Century*, ed. Robert Benson, *et al.* (Cambridge, Mass., 1982), repr. in *Images*, 2:687–726, at 687. On the early uses of the Latin word *reformare*, see also the lexicographic study of Adolf Lumpe, "Zur Bedeutungsgeschichte des Verbums 'reformare' und seiner Ableitungen," *AHC* 14 (1982) 1–12. Using the archive of the *Thesaurus linguae Latinae* Lumpe shows that the word *reformare* first appears in Ovid and that early authors used it to denote a change in form, usually in the sense of restoration of an earlier form. However, it was also used in the sense of change to something new, usually something better, but also sometimes something worse.
[3] On humanism at the council, see Paul Lehmann, "Konstanz und Basel als Büchermärkte während der grossen Kirchenversammlungen," *Zeitschrift des deutschen Vereins für Buchwesen und Schrifttum*, 4 (1921) 6–11, 17–27, repr. in Paul Lehmann, *Erforschung des Mittelalters* (Stuttgart, 1961) 1:253–280. The most prominent humanists at Constance were Poggio Bracciolini and Pier Paolo Vergerio.
[4] On the links between Reichsreform and church reform in this period see Heinz Angermeier, *Die Reichsreform, 1410–1555: Die Staatsproblematik in Deutschland zwischen Mittelalter und Gegenwart* (Munich, 1984), 51–63.
[5] Excluding the advocates of secular tyrannicide Jean Petit and Johannes Falkenberg. Two of the leading reform thinkers at the council, Gerson and Vladimiri, spent much of their energy in trying to have these teachings condemned. See Alfred Coville, *Jean Petit: La question du tyrannicide au commencement du XVe siècle* (Paris, 1932) and Belch, *Vladimiri*.

resisting tyranny or abuse of power by the pope or any other authority in the church.[6]

The overlap with ideas of restoration is the most problematic. For many, restoration meant only "back to normalcy" and was doomed to disappoint because conditions had changed so profoundly. I believe the most promising way of approaching this conceptual problem is first to recall that ideas of reform by their very nature look backward and forward at once; they seldom express an attempt to reproduce exactly the conditions of the past. Then we can shift our focus away from the tension between restoration and reform, concentrating instead on the tensions within the reform ideas themselves between restoration and newness.

In doing so, we shall be asking about the reformers' view of past and future history.[7] What did they foresee for the future? How did they look to the past? In what ways did they want to go back, and how far back? We shall also be looking at the images with which they pictured this change, asking how the reformers "imagined" the effects of their reforms.

2. Reform and history

The tension between restoration and amelioration pervades the entire history of reform ideas. The very concept of reform in the Pauline teaching offered possibilities for both developments. On the one hand, it was the re-forming in the individual of the image-likeness of God which had been damaged by the Fall. But on the other hand, this reformation was also a transformation, a new creation, the emergence of a new man. Both aspects were further developed during the patristic period. Whereas the Greek Church fathers in their reform conceptions placed greater emphasis on the

---

[6] See Chapter 9, note 34 below and the discussion of resistance in Chapter 7. See also ACC.3.116, where Dietrich Kolde says a pope "qui tyrannus est bonos sibi resistentes exterminabit directe uel indirecte siue sint cardinales siue prelati inferiores et creabit cardinales sibi similes." The most developed idea of resistance among the writings which played an important role at the council is found in Matthew of Cracow, De praxi, 116–121, which discusses the hypothetical case of the resistance of a monastery against a bad abbot. Heimpel, Vener, 2:724–725) argues convincingly that this entire chapter is primarily the work of Matthew's canonistic collaborator, Job Vener, who was present and played an important role at Constance. Vener's presentation of this theme, says Heimpel, reflects his involvement with Benedictine monastic reform in his time.

[7] On this subject, see Peter Stockmeier, "Causa Reformationis und Alte Kirche: Zum Geschichtsverständnis der Reformbewegungen," in Von Konstanz nach Trient, ed. Remigius Bäumer (Munich, 1972), 1–13.

restoration of man to his original state of perfection, it was especially the Latin fathers who developed the idea of a *reformatio in melius* or *reformatio ad meliora* (amelioration), a reform to the better, an improvement of the present condition. It is important to note that even in this limited sense the *reformatio ad melius* was different from the ideas of restoration because it was not directed chiefly toward the past. But in another sense the concept of *reformatio ad melius* transcended that of restoration; by referring to the reform of man to an even better state than he had known in paradise, it captured the eschatological implications of the Pauline reform teaching.

For minds trained in medieval scriptural exegesis, the eschatological and the historical were intimately connected. According to the four senses of Scripture, history was the literal sense of a passage which could be applied allegorically to conditions in the present but whose anagogical sense lay in the realm of eschatology.[8] A remarkable statement of Richard Ullerston captures these levels, at the same time evoking the golden age of Greco-Roman myth: "Let the vessels of exile be returned and let a new Jerusalem be made, and let the Golden Age return, just as it was instituted from the beginning."[9] Only more surprising than the grandiose imagery is its prosaic context. The vessels of exile (*vasa transmigrationis*; cf. Ez. 12,9) whose return would usher in the golden age were in fact parish churches which had been removed from the control of their bishops and placed under the control of monastic houses. When Richard Ullerston spoke of building a new Jerusalem, he united his concrete historical situation with all the exegetical meanings of Scripture. The Constance reformers saw their work of re-union as the rebuilding of Jerusalem after the Babylonian captivity of the church. Time and again they invoked the image of restoring the temple which had been desecrated.

3. Restoration as reconsecration

The image of restoring and reconsecrating the temple appeared especially apt as reformers viewed the devastation of churches around them which resulted from the economic crisis exacerbated

---

[8] See Henri de Lubac, *Exégèse médiévale: Les quatres sens de l'Écriture* (Paris, 1959–1964).

[9] Hardt.1.1143: "Reducantur ergo vasa transmigrationis et fiat nova Jerusalem et redeat aureum seculum, sicut fuit ab initio institutum." Ullerston was a professor of theology and later chancellor of the University of Oxford. He wrote the tract from which this passage is drawn (the *Petitiones quoad reformationem ecclesiae*

by the fiscal abuses of the papacy. In their concrete reform proposals they called often for the restoration of religious objects and
buildings which had fallen into disrepair or which had even been
sold or pawned. Dietrich of Niem also demanded the restoration of
the proper ceremonies when the temple was rebuilt.[10] He was not
referring to the literal divine cult, whose restoration he and other
reformers also demanded, but rather to proper administrative practices in the curia. The image of the temple was the central image in
a wider pattern of imagery of reform as reconsecration—the restoration to their sacred state of holy things which have been profaned.

Reformers spoke not only of sacred things—churches, religious
objects, and ceremonies, but also metaphorically of sacred persons,
and of the sacred Person of the Church considered as body of Christ
or bride of Christ. All had been profaned and must be restored to
their sacred state. The clergy was to be washed clean of its filth;[11]
the council fathers were to be refined by fire as silver in a furnace.[12]
The Church, which had fallen from the purity of her primitive
beauty into the filth of multiple deformity, was to be purged and
reformed.[13] Such ideas often reflect a genuinely conservative frame
of mind, one that had not accomodated itself to the growth of
wealth and worldliness. Similar views had been expressed by satires directed against papal centralization of power over the preceding two centuries.[14] They often found expression side by side with
more sophistocated critiques of papal encroachments on the freedom of local churches.

---

militantis) in preparation for the Council of Pisa; through Robert Hallum it
exercised a strong influence at Constance. See E.F. Jacob, *The Fifteenth Century,
1399–1485* (Oxford, 1961) 93.

[10] *Avisamenta*, ACC.4.594–95.

[11] See, for example, Pontius Fengeronis, Sermon, September 12, 1417,
ACC.2.516: "quo purgetur ipse clerus sentine spurcicia."

[12] D'Ailly, Sermon, December 25, 1414 (?), H.1.444–445, 446 (quoting Ez.
22,18–22): "Pro eo quod versi estis in scoriam, congregabo vos et conflabo, et
succendam vos igne furoris mei. . . . Utinam ad expurgandam Ecclesiae scoriam
accendatur in nobis ignis boni furoris, id est, zelus divini fervoris . . . 'Et conflabi-
mini, sicut constatur argentum in medio fornacis'. . . . Christus afflatu suo nos
inflammet in fornace charitatis . . . 'Ignem veni mittere in terram.' (Luke 12,19)"

[13] *Ibid.*, 445: "Ut . . . ecclesiam, quae a puritate sui primitivi decoris versa est in
scoriam multiplicis deformitatis, purgare et reformare valeamus. . . ."

[14] See Yunck, "Economic Conservatism"; see also above, 194.

4. Restoration of liberty and hierarchy

The ideas which surround this theme of restoration of freedom are those usually identified as the "Gallican liberties," but at the council they concerned the liberty of the whole church in general. In this context reformers frequently used the verbs *restituere* and *reddere*. Reformers demanded the return of powers which they claimed the pope had usurped from the ordinaries and the lower clergy.[15] They listed the negative results of this usurpation: destruction of churches, diminution of the divine cult, danger to souls, and impoverishment of the Christian people.

The same catalog of ills occurs in other contexts where it is attributed to the bad quality of prelates in general.[16] Like the Gregorian reformers three and one-half centuries earlier, the Constance reformers linked freedom of the church with restoration of high standards for the clergy, and they blamed lay interference with the church's freedom for the clergy's poor state. Unlike the Gregorians, they also blamed the pope himself. In this sense, it might at first seem doubly contradictory that the Constance reformers, often in the same context, called for restoration of the hierarchical order of the church.[17] Such ideas drew heavily on the terminology and imagery of pseudo-Dionysius. The very words used by pseudo-Dionysius to describe the hierarchical activity of the clergy were words of reform and renewal—*purgatio, illuminatio,*

---

[15] See especially Dietrich of Niem, *De modis*, 15, 19: "potestatem usurpatam diu a capite ecclesie, sc. summis pontificibus. . . . et dico quod tantam fraudem in administracione huius papatus fecerunt aliqui antiqui, qui cum multis viris peritis, imo maliciis imbutis, Deum non habentes pre oculis, multa iura sibi usurparunt, et pro se fecerunt, et meliorem partem sibi attribuerunt, et de re publica non curarunt." See also the sermon of Andreas of Escobar, August 9, 1416, ACC.2.456, which says if the popes take more than is rightfully theirs, "sacrilegium committunt et sacrilega crudelitate subripiunt . . . et mortaliter peccant et tenentur ad restitutionem. . . ."; also the anonymous sermon, May 10, 1416, ACC.2.443, which asks that the "ablatum [cultum] restituatur" and that "cause minores remittantur ad patres, scilicet ad ordinarios" and predicts that in this manner "magna tranquillitas redderetur ecclesie . . ."

[16] See the sermon of Johannes Huguonetti, March 7, 1416, ACC.2.439, who presents the usual catalog of bad results mentioned above, but sees them as a result of bad priests in general: "propter que et alia gravamina innumera, quot sunt ecclesie desolate ac destructe, quot monasteria et alia pia loca a pastoribus derelicta, quot vagi per mundum sacerdotes, quot excommunicationi per abusum clavium innodati, quot inde pericula imminent animarum, quot decedunt sine baptismi sacramento, quantaque sit cultus divini diminucio et populi christiani depauperacio. . . ."

[17] On the importance of hierarchy in the reform thought of Gerson, see Louis Pascoe, *Gerson: Principles*, 17–48. See also the fuller discussion of ideas of hierarchy in Chapter 9 below.

perfectio, and above all, *reductio*, in the sense of leading back.[18] "The lowest things are to be led back to the highest things through the intermediate things," ran the famous pseudo-Dionysian dictum.[19] The Constance reformers borrowed these words to refer to historical changes, such as the reduction of schismatics.[20]

The secular theologians of the University of Paris, had used pseudo-Dionysius in their dispute with the mendicants during the thirteenth century, as Yves Congar has shown.[21] The Paris theologians at Constance revived all these arguments in a complaint submitted to the council against Alexander V's recent bull, *Regnans in excelsis*.[22] Like their thirteenth century predecessors, they claimed that the papal privileges granted to mendicants undermined the secular clergy and usurped its powers.

Not only theologians, but also canonists, had contributed to the development of such ideas. Using terms and concepts borrowed from Gratian's *Decretum* and from the pseudo-Isidorian decretals, conciliar reformers demanded the restoration of the hierarchical order of the church and the re-establishment of discipline. Theologians and canonists used the words *turbatio*, *confusio*, and *enervatio* to describe the disturbance of proper order and discipline.[23] Sometimes it was heretics, other times it was opponents of papal authority who were said to be causing the *confusio*.[24] But increasingly the reformers had come to point the finger of blame for abuses of authority at the pope himself. They argued that the church had

---

[18] This is clearly spelled out in the complaint of the seculars from the University of Paris against the bull *Regnans in excelsis* mentioned below; see ACC.2.694–95. See also Anon. Sermon, December 13, 1416, ACC.2.477.

[19] G.7.981: "Infima reducuntur ad summa per media." On this phrase, see Pascoe, *Gerson: Principles*, 35, n.75. See below, p. 248.

[20] See Dietrich of Niem, *Avisamenta edita in concilio Constanciensi*, ACC.4.622: "Romana curia prius ad ipsos veteres mores et consuetudines laudabiles reducatur." Note also the interesting formula "Reformatio sonat quasi in priorem formam reductio" in Anon. Sermon, Vienna, Österreichische Nationalbibliothek, MS lat. 4292, fol. 14v.

[21] Congar, "Quérelle," 58–62, 72.

[22] ACC.2.690–98.

[23] See below, p. 249 and n. 68, for example.

[24] The citation of Bohemian nobles by the council spoke of the Hussites as "contra structuram totius ecclesiastici edificii molientes euertere fidem Catholicam cum legibus et ecclesiasticis moribus a sanctis patribus traditis; super hierarchiam militantis ecclesie se suasque traditiones laborantes extollere . . ." Mansi 27:920B. For criticism of opponents to papal authority see anonymous tract against annates (see ACC.2.592–600), Paris, BN, MS lat. 14644, fol. 368r: "totus Israel id est ecclesia militans turbatur ex inobedientia ad summum sacerdotem per subditos si et quando fiat. . . ." (The author of this annate tract cites this as a counter-argument given by papal supporters.) On the pope as supreme hierarch, see below, p. 244 n. 45.

been brought into disorder by papal reservations, dispensations, and exemptions which circumvented the intermediate levels of the hierarchy.[25] Reformers like Pierre d'Ailly even asserted that the council, since it represented the universal church, could act as a supreme hierarch and remove anyone, even a pope, who through his persistence in error perturbs the state of the universal church.[26] Thus we arrive at the paradoxical result: The Constance reformers, using terminology developed by the popes of the Gregorian reform, called for restoring the lost freedom of the church. However, using even more venerable terminology, they equated that restoration of freedom with the restoration of hierarchical order and discipline, and they identified the actions of the papacy as the principal threats to both the freedom and the order.

5. Restoration and tradition

When reformers spoke of restoration they often spoke of restoring good customs and good practices of the past. In these contexts they made frequent use of the adjectives *pristina, prisca, antiqua,* and the nouns *primordia* and *vestigia.*[27] Some spoke of the reforms as restoring a *seculum aureum*[28] or the practices of the *ecclesia primitiva.* However, the "venerable ancient customs," on closer inspection, usually prove to be specific practices interrupted in the recent past. Reform proposals often call for return to good customs observed under popes of the recent past. Even the allegedly radical Dietrich of Niem seldom speaks of the abuses as more than two hundred

---

[25] See Dietrich of Niem, *Avisamenta,* ACC.4.600: "Preterea per istas pessimas reservaciones totus status ecclesiasticus a capite usque ad membra turbatur et pervertitur. Fiunt enim illis causantibus mercancie pessime et excluduntur electores ordinarii." See also Archbishop Pileus of Genoa, *Informationes:* "exemtiones turbant clerum et scandala producunt et magnos contemptus ordinariorum . . ." Döllinger, *Beiträge,* 2:310.

[26] See Mansi 27:560C: "ecclesia universalis quae vere vel interpretative et virtualiter consistit in concilio generali, potest quemlibet etiam summum eiusdem ecclesie ministrum, per cuius persistentiam status universalis eiusdem ecclesie turbaretur, et per cuius admonitionem ad statum debitum reduceretur, etiam sine culpa ministri amovere."

[27] The use of such terms was extremely common at the council; for example: "iocunda sanitatis primordia" in Matthew Roeder, Sermon, January 24, 1417, ACC.2.486.

[28] *W.*1.2.36–37, 48: "Si diebus vestris aurea secula reuiuiscant"; elsewhere he refers to the church's youth "cum fiebant lignei calices et aurei sacerdotes" (Sermon of Matthew Roeder, December 27, 1415); ACC.2.469: "O utinam ista [the sycophancy and duplicity of flattering office seekers] cito cessarent et redirent illa aurea ecclesie secula in quibus illi modi, qui iam defenduntur ut liciti et honesti, fuissent abhominabiles." (Sermon of Dietrich Kolde, October 11, 1416).

years old. Like most reformers, he calls most often for return to the pristine morals and venerable customs observed prior to the Schism.[29]

The reformers who defended the venerable and pristine old customs and traditions also attacked bad new customs. We have observed that they distinguished customs (*consuetudines*) from corruptions (*corruptele*), attempting to prove that the recent customs of the papacy had no validity. It is striking to note the degree to which the papal curia argued against these reformers on their own grounds, seeking to show that its recent practices were based on venerable traditions. The historical analysis of the French reformers was in fact an attempt to answer the claims of curial lawyers that the papacy had acquired a prescriptive or customary right to the collection of annates.[30] And Cardinal Adimari claimed that the papal reservations established in the constitution "Ad regimen" were "ita moderata et consueta" that they could be reputed to be law.[31] Such arguments stand in strange counterpoint to the manifesto of the Gregorian reformers: "The Lord says, 'I am the truth and the life.' He does not say 'I am custom', but truth."[32]

6. Three approaches to tradition

Faced with the dilemma of distinguishing good customs from bad ones, one group of reformers found an incisive criterion. Rather than equating reform with tradition, they drove a wedge between the two. While other reformers called for the return to the "salu-

---

[29] See Dietrich of Niem, *De modis*, 81, and *Avisamenta*, ACC.4.617–18, 622 ("pristini boni mores, prout fieri consuevit antiquitus tempore unionis, antequam scisma illud inchoaret . . ."); see similar statements in the protest of the German nation from 1417, H.4.1421. See also Haller, 22–23. However, note the interesting use of such terms to refer to a negative past state which is to be reformed into something new and better: "ut de antiqua conversatione in novam innocentiam reformatus. . . . status ecclesiae pristini calamitas dolorosa reformatio. . . . Edicanturque statuta sanctissima contra pristinas abominationes." (Vitale Valentin, Sermon, March 28, 1417 (=1416? cf. H.4.1360–62) in Hardt, *Hist. litt. ref.*, 20–24.)

[30] See above, p. 197.

[31] "Quae ita moderata est et consueta ut pro jure satis reputari possit"; see above, p. 80.

[32] ". . . Dominus dicit: Ego sum veritas et vita. Non ait: Ego sum consuetudo, sed veritas." Cited by Gerhart Ladner, "Two Gregorian Letters: On the Sources and Nature of Gregory's Reform Ideology," in *Studi Gregoriani* 5 (1956) 221–42. Gregory took this statement from Tertullian. Ladner argues, however, that Gregory's statement was not quite as radical as it sounds, since the Gregorians had also distinguished bad new customs from good old customs, which they sought to revive.

brious tradition of the most holy fathers," this group demanded
that divine law be followed and castigated the "pontiffs who greatly
prefer their traditions to divine commandments."[33] For purposes of
nomenclature, I would like to label these two approaches as "uncritical" and "critical," respectively. Later I will identify yet a
third approach, which I will call "conciliar." The three most
prominent spokesmen for the critical approach—Nicholas of Cla-
manges, Pierre d'Ailly, and Jean Gerson—were all friends who
had much in common. All had at one time been professors of
theology and chancellors of the University of Paris. We know that
they influenced each other mutually, and their influence at the
council was great, especially because of the key reforming roles of
D'Ailly and Gerson there.

The approach of these reformers to tradition is intimately bound
to their view of the past, a view which differed markedly from the
Golden Age of the uncritical approach. When they spoke of an age
of primitive simplicity, purity and goodness it was more with
nostalgia than with any thought of return.[34] Nicholas' view in some
way forms a bridge with the uncritical approach; he also depicted
scenes of a mythical state of innocence quite similar to the Golden
Age—a state in which the faithful spurned earthly wealth to seek
heavenly gold.[35] But this mythical age which Nicholas evoked was
not to be restored by the reform of abuses; its evocation was a
literary foil to highlight the evils of the present age. For Nicholas
the ideal conditions of the primitive Church had not been interrupted only recently by the new papal practices. To be sure,
Nicholas virulently attacked these practices, despite his intense
personal loyalty to Pope Benedict XIII, and he warned that the
lust for power—*libido dominandi*—is all the more consuming in
popes than in other men because of their high position. The current
decay was not the result of recent papal innovations alone, but
rather of the lust for power and its twin, avarice. These ills began
very early, when the Church first received temporal possessions,

---

[33] *De praxi* 83: "Et quid plus quaeso sanctissimorum patrum abhorret salubris
traditio quam avaritiam . . ."; *De ruina*, 128: ". . . pontificibus qui suas tradiciones
divinis longe mandatis anteponunt".
[34] See Glenn Olsen, "The Idea of the Ecclesia primitiva in the Writings of the
Twelfth-Century Canonists," *Traditio* 25 (1969) 61–86; Louis Pascoe, "Jean
Gerson: The 'Ecclesia Primitiva' and Reform," *Traditio* 30 (1974) 379–409; John
O'Malley, "Fulfillment of the Christian Golden Age under Pope Julius II,"
Traditio 25 (1969) 265–338; and Arthur Lovejoy and George Boas, *Primitivism and
Related Ideas in Antiquity* (New York, 1965).
[35] *De ruina*, 112–116.

and ever since had infected all levels of the clergy not only the pope. For Nicholas, this historical development was an ironic result of divine grace. The more purely the early fathers lived, the more land and goods were donated to them because of their piety; but the possessions led to greed, envy and other moral decay. Gerson and D'Ailly took a different stance here. While lamenting the impossibility of recovering the rigor of the ancient discipline and purity,[36] they also acknowledged that the acquisition of temporal goods which had caused it was irreversible and had even in part been helpful to the Church in accomplishing its mission of world-wide expansion.[37]

This view of the past made possible a much more critical evaluation of custom and tradition. Posthumus Meyjes has analyzed Gerson's discussions of the development of law in the Church enunciated in his important treatise entitled *De vita spirituali animae*. Gerson argued that the primitive Church was governed by divine law alone because it had no temporal possessions. Christ left no instructions for the government of these *temporalia*, but rather gave the prelates the power to make these rules when they became necessary.[38] But the rules made by the prelates governing *temporalia* are traditions, that is to say, they are not divine law. In his *Tractatus de materia*, D'Ailly developed this distinction in the context of a debate on the restoration of obedience to the pope, which the French clergy had withdrawn in order to pressure the pope to end the Schism. D'Ailly argued that obedience should be restored *in spiritualibus*, since the *spiritualia* are immutable and should be protected by recourse to a single head. The *temporalia* on the other hand are regulated by human traditions, which are variable according to time, place, people and rite; therefore they should be determined by recourse to more than one person, and it might be wise to postpone restoration of obedience *in temporalibus* pending a general council.[39] Gerson honed more finely the distinction between divine law and traditions. Divine law is distinguished from other laws primarily by

---

[36] *De ruina* 142–3; Pierre d'Ailly, *Canones reformationis*, H.1.417, 420–21.

[37] See Pascoe, *Gerson: Principles*, 53–56, for summary of relevant arguments in Gerson's writings.

[38] *DuPin* 3:22: "Christus legislator perfectissimus volens concedere legem dignissimam et beatificativam omnes tales leges ordinantes hominem ad finem humanam et politicam, reliquit ad arbitrium prelatorum et principum, ita tamen ut semper meminisse potestatem eis datam pro veritate . . ."

[39] *Tractatus* 262: "Sed de traditionibus humanis pro regimine temporalium Ecclesiae totaliter oppositum invenitur, quoniam secundum varietatem temporum, locorum, et gentium, et rituum, variandae sunt decretales et ordinationes super collationibus et regimine talium temporalium."

its supernatural goal—eternal beatitude. According to this potent distinction, which Posthumous Meyjes suggests may be original with Gerson, not even all laws revealed directly by God can be called divine laws, since many such laws, especially those of the time before Christ were established by God to promote man's temporal felicity, not his eternal beatitude.[40] Gerson charges that the canonists have obscured the distinction between divine and human law by multiplying their traditions and then equating them with divine law.[41]

The distinctions of Gerson and D'Ailly had quite practical consequences for reform. D'Ailly stressed the need to remove many superfluous and excessive statutes which were merely human traditions and impeded reform.[42] Gerson said that excommunication should be used to punish transgressions of divine law only; it should not be applied, for example, to a prelate who fails to pay his annates.[43]

It is important to note that for D'Ailly and Gerson the traditions were not necessarily bad nor were they simply to be abolished because they were not divine law but they did not enjoy the same authority and immutability as divine law. The law of the primitive Church on the other hand did enjoy this authority, partly because of venerability, partly because of apostolic tradition but also because of the simplicity of the primitive Church—it was ruled solely by divine law. This law of the primitive Church was also tradition in a sense; it consisted of the "leges immediate a Christo traditae" which were not known through Scripture but from the apostles by successive narration (*relatio* is the word he uses.)[44] Paulus Vladimiri

---

[40] *DuPin* 3:17–21; Posthumus Meyjes, 198–202.
[41] *DuPin* 3:16–17. On these matters, see the further comments of Posthumus Meyjes in his recent article "Exponents of Sovereignty: Canonists as Seen by Theologians in the Late Middle Ages," in *The Church and Sovereignty, c. 590–1915: Essays in honour of Michael Wilks*, ed. Diana Wood (Oxford, 1991), 299–328.
[42] *Tractatus* 254–5: "reformatio Ecclesiae universalis fieri non potest in moribus sine abolitione multorum statutorum super excommunicationibus et ceteris traditionibus nimis multiplicatis, quia nec observantur nec observari possunt rationabiliter ubique propter varietatem morum et temporum.
[43] *DuPin* 3:17.
[44] *DuPin* 3:23–24: "In tertio gradu reponentur leges diuinae immediate a Christo traditae . . . quae per successiuum relationem Apostolorum et aliorum ad nos aequiualentum scripturae canonicae notificatae sunt." What Gerson is talking about here is the extrascriptural tradition accepted by adherents of the position that Heiko Oberman has called "Tradition II"; see *The Harvest of Medieval Theology: Gabriel Biel and Late Medieval Nominalism*, rev. ed. (Grand Rapids, 1967), 371–387. Tradition I held that all truths of the faith were included in the Scripture and that the only ongoing tradition was one of scriptural interpretation (*per modum doctrinae*) by a *successio doctorum*; at the time of the Council of Constance

spoke of the *successiones patrum* in the same way and in a similar sense of a *traditio clavium*.[45] In these cases what was transmitted through tradition was not specific customs, but orthodox faith and authority. Vladimiri's statements represent a third approach to tradition, one which joins the "critical" and "non-critical" approaches. I would like to call it the "conciliar" approach to tradition. It was also an approach which could join ideas of newness and amelioration with ideas of restoration and conservation.

7. Newness

Ideas and images of newness include ideas of individual and ecclesiastical transformation as well as visions of cosmological change and vitalistic concepts of birth and rebirth, fertility, growth, and flourishing. Prominent here are patterns of vegetative symbolism and symbols involving light. The change envisioned in such ideas and images is generally spontaneous change, not brought about by human plan and action.[46]

The major cosmological ideas of newness at Constance were eschatological. There was talk of the approaching evening of the world, of the last judgment, the millennium, even of the heavenly pastures where the sheep will graze when the reforms are completed.[47] Such images were usually part of the hyperbole of

---

it was mainly the Hussites and Wycliffites who adhered to Tradition I. Tradition II accepted truths established *per modum auctoritatis* alongside those established *per modum doctrinae*. Oberman shows that conciliarists as well as papalists adhered to Tradition II. For conciliarists, however, the leading authority would be conciliar, rather than papal pronouncements. The three approaches to tradition which I have identified in this chapter have to do with broader uses of the word "tradition"; but the third approach which I have identified and labelled "conciliar tradition" comes very close to the conciliarist version of what Oberman calls Tradition II. On Oberman's conception of Traditions I and II see Hermann Schüssler, *Der Primat der heiligen Schrift als theologisches und kanonistisches Problem im Spätmittelalter* (Wiesbaden, 1977) 67–71. Schüssler's work deals only indirectly with the question of tradition, since he is concerned with the late medieval understandings of the relationship between church and scripture. Concepts of tradition at Constance were not generally directly related to questions of approbation of Scriptural interpretation through church authority.

[45] *Speculum* 94: "sunt duae claves, vicario Christo et cuilibet praelato ecclesiae traditae . . ."

[46] Such terminology of renovation has been discussed by Ladner in *Idea of Reform*, 16–26 and "Die mittelalterliche Reform-Idee und ihr Verhältnis zur Idee der Renaissance," *MIÖG* 60 (1952) 31–59; cf. also his article "Vegetation Symbolism and the Concept of Renaissance," in *Essays in Honor of Erwin Panofsky: De artibus opuscula XL*, ed. Millard Meiss (New York, 1969), 1:303–332.

[47] John of Almaria in his sermon December 16, 1414, ACC.2.385, speaks of the approaching evening of the world ("vergente mundi vespere") and the judge of

sermons, however, and they were part of the standard themes of advent sermons. At the council, the negative image of judgment predominated in them.

Likewise the imagery of spontaneous growth which Ladner shows to be so characteristic of ideas of renascence was often used at the council in a negative or ironic sense. It was vices which flourished, evils which pullulated.[48] Even the central image of birth as used by the council fathers stressed the pain of birth due to God's judgment.[49] Images of vegetative growth were usually images of agriculture—of growth produced by human action and volition—and thus lacked precisely that spontaneity which we would look for in ideas of renascence.[50]

The closest thing to vitalistic spontaneity in the reform thought of the council is the description of the renewal wrought by the Holy Spirit. Reformers cited Biblical texts which refer to the renewal of the individual by the Holy Spirit, extending them to describe renewal of the whole church. One Pentecost sermon spoke of the transformation of Peter and the other apostles, who had become such fully new men that people were astounded to see them now

---

truth, who is at hand ("ecce astat veritatis indagator"); Dietrich Kolde, Sermon, February 16, 1416, in W.1.3.97f., is full of eschatological terminology, such as "hic autem circa horam diei ultimam operarios vocat pro mercede . . ." (p. 98). See also Peter Pulka, Sermon, end of November/December 1414, ACC.2.383: "ovesque pascue domini per virtutum prata tam salubriter deducantur, ut ad superna pascua divine visionis ac fruicionis una cum sanctitate vestra nostroque pastore feliciter inducantur."

[48] Vitale Valentin, Sermon, January 6, 1416, W.1.2.68–71: "turpe tugurium carnalis appetitus"; see also, Anon. Sermon, January 12, 1415, ACC.2.427: "Florent iam nunc venditores spiritalis gracie." See also Anon. sermon, March 29, 1416, Tübingen, Universitätsbibl., Mc 282, f. 45v: "errores undique pullulare cernimus."

[49] Hugonetti de Metis Avignonensis, Sermon, August 3, 1417, W.1.3.217: "Vitiorum horribilium crebris flagellationibus atteratur ipsa ecclesia more parturientis, uterinos cruciatus experta, et ad quantum etiam, per filios sceleratos, qui omnia mala noverunt, redacta sit gemebundae confusionis opprobrium . . ."; see also Anon. Sermon, September 18, 1415, W.1.2.135–136: The Church has lost her consort; whereas before she conceived holy apostles and martyrs, "nunc vero intuear eius pristinam maternitatem foecunditatem turbatam sterilitate, cassatam debilitate, impeditam adversitate . . ."; see also Henricus Abendon, Sermon, October 27, 1415, W.1.2.201–202: ". . . ut fructibus vestrae iustitiae vestros mortuos spiritualiter suscitetis. Numquid stolidi creditis, hoc facere absentes? . . . Elisaeus misit Gehasi cum baculo ad filium mortuum suscitandum. Et tu Elisaeus, tantum nomine, tuum mittis Geziacum, ignarum sacerdotem, ad ecclesiam tuam, qui baculo percutit filium tuum mortuum; . . . sed non suscitat, quin potius mortificat."

[50] For a good example of the stress on the human effort involved in this flourishing, see Dietrich Kolde, Sermon, February 16, 1416, W.1.3.105: "vinea haec colenda requiritur, quae tantorum Patrum laboribus olim floruit . . ."

boldly addressing kings and great men despite their own humble origins (Acts 3,13).[51] The preacher stresses the totality and the newness of the change and its spontaneity, in that it was wrought by the Holy Spirit. Such a change is more a *transformatio* than a *reformatio*; other preachers described such changes using biblical language of transformation[52] and newness: "Let us walk in the newness of life." (Rom. 6,4)[53] "We shall be remade with good fruits and we will be transformed, receiving new forms." (cf. 2 Cor. 3,18).[54] "Make new (*innoua*) the Holy Spirit within me" (cf. Ps. 51,12) and "Renew the spirit of your mind." (Eph. 4,23)[55]

The last two passages are from a particularly rich anonymous sermon preached on the text "Facite homines discumbere" from the story of the feeding of the five thousand (John 6,10). The preacher uses the refreshment of the people by Jesus's preaching and feeding to evoke the renewal of the church. The terminology is exuberant. Through the three-fold activities of *recreatio*, *refocillatio*, and *renovatio*, the members of the Church will be bound together in unity and revived (*vegetative vivicentur*).[56] The preacher goes on to evoke the renewal of the entire creation, citing Psalm 104,30: "Thou breathest forth Thy Spirit and they are created (*creabuntur*) and Thou renewest the face of the earth."[57] Restoration of the church's unity will enable the Spirit to pour love into the body of

---

[51] Anon. Sermon, June 7, 1416, W.1.3.203–205.

[52] The idea of tranformation is also captured by terminology of conversion; see the sermon of Vitale Valentin, January 6, 1415, W.1.2.53f. which refers to the conversion or turning of the Magi to Christ. This was only the beginning of their total transformation; they are a figure of the council or the Church, which is to be similarly transformed. See also the anonymous sermon, September 18, 1415, W.1.2.140f., for an interesting discussion of conversion, and whether the action of the Holy Spirit precedes the decision of the human will. The individual terminology is applied to the whole Church through the use of the passage in Jeremiah 3,22: "Convertimini filii revertentes."

[53] Anon. Sermon, undated, in Schneyer, 115 (1967) 134: "In novitate vitae ambulemus."

[54] Vitale Valentin, Sermon, Epiphany 1415, W.1.2.53f.: "Nos ergo a spiritu sancto in unum congregati et ad unum ordinati, postposito obiecto et dimisso turpi et foetido tugurio, transeuntes per angustam portam, quae est poenitentia, intremus supradictum et declaratum viridarium, in quo persistentes reficiemur fructibus novasque formas recipientes transformabimur . . ."

[55] Anon. Sermon, March 29, 1416, Tübingen, Universitätsbibl., MC 282 fol. 47r: "Spiritum Sanctum innova in visceribus meis . . ." and "Renovamini spiritus mentis vestre spiritu scilicet caritatis."

[56] Anon. Sermon, March 29, 1416, Tübingen, Universitätsbibl., MC 282 fol. 45r: "Corpus ecclesie misticum opus habet spirituale, quo similiter membra S. Matris Ecclesie unitiue consolidentur et vegetative uiuicentur."

[57] *Ibid.*, fol. 47r: "Emitte spiritum tuum et creabuntur, et renovabis faciem terre."

the Church, binding the members together with one another and with the head (both Christ and the pope are implied here), renewing, recreating, feeding, and strengthening that body.[58] Words of newness and of spontaneous growth and flourishing, were thus spoken at Constance, but not frequently. They appeared most often in Pentecost sermons or in anonymous sermons invoking biblical terminology of transformation, usually in the context of the working of the Holy Spirit. Even here the element of human cooperation with the Holy Spirit is sometimes stressed, as in the the fascinating injunction of one anonymous preacher: "Therefore let everyone strive to reform himself, changing his life for the better. Cast off all your lies and make for yourselves a new heart and a new spirit."[59] Nevertheless, the hopeful waiting for the Holy Spirit to bring renewal through the council, especially by bringing unity, was an important theme at Constance, expressed most eloquently in Gerson's sermon "Spiritus domini," preached on Pentecost, 1416.[60]

8. Amelioration

Most of the Constance reform ideas which looked toward the future did so in a restrained and cautious manner; Ladner would call them ideas of amelioration. They fall into three main categories: ideas of healing, ideas of building up or edification, and ideas of vegetative growth (but guided, not spontaneous). Healing and health were associated with the central idea of reform in head and members—the healing of the church as a body. The decrees of general councils were often called most healthful (*salubres*).[61] The

---

[58] *Ibid.*, fol. 47v: "Unio, qui habet nutrire et renouare in corpore S. Matris Ecclesiae et ejus membris Spiritum caritatis . . ." and just above this passage: "Renouationem influxus caritatis, que . . . habet uiuere ciuiliter et conglutinare membra Christi cum suo capite et inter se inuicem . . ."; and 45v: "Spiritum vitalem fidei virtualiter recreando, spiritu caritatis membra Christi concorditer uniendo."

[59] Anon. Sermon, September 15, 1415, W.1.2.157–158: "Eapropter unusquisque studeat se ipsum reformare, vitam suam commutando in melius. Proiicite a vobis omnes praevaricationes vestras, quibus praevaricati estis, et facite vobis cor novum et spiritum novum [Ez. 18,31] . . . ."

[60] G.5.520–538; on this sermon, see André Combes, "Facteurs dissolvants et principe unificateur au Concile de Constance," *Divinitas* 5 (1961) 299–310 at 305–306.

[61] See the draft of the reform decree on the deposition of popes (see below, p. 329, Common, c.5): "Unde super premissis salubriter providere cupientes . . ." See also the argument of the Paris seculars against the bull *Regnans in excelsis* which they found intolerable "propter non obstantem illius saluberrimi statuti editi in

imagery of building up (edification) was closely associated with the
dictum of St. Paul that all power in the church is given for
edification.[62] Several reformers, including D'Ailly and Gerson, used
it as a test by which the exercise of papal power could be measured
and limited.[63] Reformers pointed often to the ways in which papal
actions had brought destruction to the church, most obviously the
alienation of the lands and rights of the Roman church, but also the
destruction caused by taxation,[64] by the granting of monasteries in
commendam, and by the incorporation of parish churches with
monasteries. By removing these abuses, the council would build up
the church. As one reformer put it, the "destruction of destruction
is construction." In a similar manner, the removal of abuses would
cause the church to grow and flourish again. Thus, the vegetal
image of growth and flourishing was tied closely with images of
pruning and weeding.[65]

---

concilio generali "Omnis utriusque sexus"..." ACC.2.694. See also Dietrich of
Niem, ACC.3.106, who says that many general councils have been held in which
"semper reperi aliqua singularia et ualde utilia pro bono statu uniuersalis ecclesie
et eius membrorum statuta et ordinata que sepe protulerunt salutares effectus."
    [62] 2 Cor. 10,8; 13,10; see the argument of the Paris seculars, ACC.2.694:
"Preterea summus pontifex derogare non potest talibus, presertim in hiis, que
pertinent ad ordinem ierarchicum ecclesie a Christo salubriter institutum. Quia,
sicut habetur II^a ad Corinthios X: non est data potestas ad destruccionem sed ad
edificacionem." See also Dietrich Kolde's tract from February 1415 which uses the
word *construere*: The pope's power was given him so that "per illam potestatem
construeret ecclesiam in unitate et sanctis moribus..." (ACC.3.121). The word
edificatio was also used at the council in the sense of education or instruction of the
people; see the draft of the reform decree for the provision of learned clerics (see
below, p. 364, Common, c.36, para. 24): "Item prouideatur quod per illam
provisionem graduatorum diuinus cultus et edificatio populi crescat et augeatur."
    [63] See Louis Pascoe, "Theological Dimensions of Pierre d'Ailly's Teaching on
Papal Plenitude of Power," *AHC* 11 (1979) 357–365 at 359.
    [64] Archbishop Pileus of Genoa, for example asks that there be no more annates
"quia per illas destruuntur ecclesie..." Döllinger, *Beiträge*, 2:306. See also the
recurring words to the same effect in the treatise prepared for the annate discussion in the French nation in November "De annatis non solvendis," Hardt 1:769
and *passim*. (See above, Chapter 7, p. 173 and 177.)
    [65] For a clear expression of this idea see the sermon of Johannes Zachariae,
O.E.S.A., Sermon, December 26, 1415, W.1.3.85, which cites St. Jerome's commentary on Jeremiah 1,10 to show that the prelate "aedificet et plantet.... Nec
poterant inquam aedificari bona, nisi eradicarentur pessima... vt in ea, quasi in
horto frugifero et irriguo cresceret triticum fidei et botrus morum ac sanctitatis."
See also, Jacobus de Camplo, Sermon, August 15, 1416, ACC.2.460: "[hereses
and errors] que, nisi lima correctionis et condempnacionis sarculo praescindan-
tur..." and Dietrich of Niem, Avisamenta, ACC.4.605: "Gravamina [reserva-
tions, etc.]... sunt... aut totaliter resecanda vel saltem ad tempus congruum
suspendenda..." Ladner in "Vegetation," 304 n. 4, points out the important
development of this imagery of pruning in the ideas surrounding Justinian's
codification of the Roman law, especially the prefatory constitutions to the Digests

Images of pruning and weeding are images of correction or emendation. Ladner has shown their importance as renewal ideas, especially in the context of legal reform, from Justinian's compilation of Roman law to the Gregorian reformers' similar efforts with respect to canon law. Terms of correction occurred often at the council—*corrigere, corripere, emendare*, and, less often, *arguere*, in the sense of reproving. One might say that in the strictest sense they are not reform terms, since they do not imply in their very structure the idea of change that looks forward and backward at once. But the ideas of change they express are clearly ideas of reform; indeed, I would argue that the terms, and above all the images, of correction are central to the Constance reform ideas. The two major patterns of corrective imagery at the council, were tied to the two central images of forward-looking change. The first was agricultural imagery, one example of which—weeding and pruning—we mentioned above. The second was imagery involving the medical correction of the human body—the healing of disease and surgical intervention—and the restoration of the body's health.[66]

The medical imagery was often extreme and forceful, indeed violent. Not just the light syrups, plasters, and ointments of physicians are needed to heal the disease of simony, observed Maurice Rvačka, but also the harsh incisions and cauterizations of surgeons.[67] The most extreme form of surgery, amputation, conjured up a well known image of individual corporeal reform in the teachings of Jesus, which Dietrich of Niem, Jean Gerson, and other reformers applied to the living body of the church. "If your hand or foot offend you, cut it off and throw it from you." (Matt. 18,8) The word "offend" here appears in the Vulgate as *scandalizare* and means to cause offense or to lead into sin; it was used very frequently at the council to refer to abuses of power by persons in authority,

---

("Deo auctore," "Omnem," and "Tanta") and the Codex ("Cordi nobis est," "Haec," and "Summa rei publicae") in *Corpus iuris civilis* ed. Th. Mommsen and P. Krueger (Berlin, 1954[11]).

[66] See, for example, S², c.5, p. 389 below: "Volentes itaque detestabili huic morbo possibili occurrere cum medela ultra priores sanctiones specialibus duximus remediis . . . expressius providendum . . ."

[67] Maurice Rvačka, Sermon, July 26, 1416, ACC.2.455: "En morbus symoniacus continuatus per annos XXXVIII perniciosi scismatis eget non solum levibus medicorum syrupis et emplastris et glysderiis, set acerrimis insuper cyrurgicorum inscissuris et cauteriis, qualem expertissimi medici in hoc sacro concilio spiritu sancto congregati curam conantur apponere . . ." See also the schedule presented November 14, 1414, by the doctors in theology of the obedience of John [XXIII], Mansi 27:535D: Those who refuse to resign are considered "destructores ecclesie et acriter coercendi. Quia in morbo pestilentico est etiam cum cauterio prouidendum."

including the pope.[68] "If your foot, your hand, or even something from your head, scandalizes you, cast it away from you," said Gerson in his treatise on ecclesiastical unity.[69] Dietrich went further: "In the church the member which does most harm . . . should be the most quickly removed and amputated. Therefore, a bad pope is to be most quickly deposed. . . ."[70] If one could imagine amputating the head in such a way that the man would still remain alive, it ought to be done most quickly, observed Dietrich, lest the whole man be lost. Dietrich was keenly aware of the inherent limitations of the image. For him, as for the other reformers, the illness in the head was so devastating precisely because the head was so important and powerful.[71]

Other reformers attempted to moderate the extremes of the corrective imagery. One conciliatory anonymous preacher asked that the illness be cured without destroying the patient.[72] How does one distinguish between illness and patient? "Take away the infirmity and let each retain his power" was his answer. Some council fathers warned against tearing out all the weeds indiscriminately, citing Jesus's parable about the grain and the tares which the Lord

---

[68] See Pileus of Genoa, *Informationes*, ed. Döllinger, *Beiträge*, 2:303: "contra statuta per se [papa] in eodem [concilio] uenire non ualeat: ac declaretur et decernatur, Papam ex heresi simoniaca et abusu plenitudinis potestatis ac quolibet uitio notorio, per quod scandalizetur ecclesia, posse iudicari et deponi per concilium . . ."

[69] Jean Gerson, *Tractatus de unitate ecclesie* G.6.144: "Si pes tuus, aut manus, et ita de capite scandalizat te, projice abs te."

[70] Dietrich of Niem, *De modis*, 17–18: " . . . in corpore mystico universalis ecclesie membrum, quod amplius nocet, occasionaliter sive effectualiter, est cicius dirimendum et amputandum. Ergo papa malus cicius deponitur, quia est membrum validius quam quicumque alius prelatus . . . Quod si per imaginacionem amputari posset, homine manente, amputari cicius deberet, ne totus homo perdatur." The reformers often viewed the ills of the church as a disease which had spread downward from the head; see, for example, Nicholas of Clémanges, *De ruina*, 115: "Sed ut nos istius pestis nepharie ab ipso summo vertice usque ad infimos pedes originem et progressum videamus." They quoted Isaiah 1,6 (see below, Chapter 9, n.24): "A planta pedis usque ad verticem vix est in ea sanitas"; see Johannes de Almaria, Sermon, December 6, 1414, ACC.2.384.

[71] Dietrich quotes often the aphorisms "Dum caput egrotat, cetera membra dolent" and "a capite edenda est ratio"; see below, p. 245, nn. 50–51; see also the words of Pierre d'Ailly in a tract he circulated at the council, ACC.3.58: "Secundum dictamen iuris naturalis in quolibet corpore ligandum est capud et modis omnibus cohercendum, si in membra cetera furore niteretur seu tyrannicam rabiem exerceret."

[72] Anon. Sermon, December 16, 1416, ACC.2.477: "Tollantur abusus, auferatur morbus, salvis semper subiectis, et erit pax. Quomodo autem distinguatur morbus a subiectis, quadam brevi consideracione deduco. . . . Tollatur, queso, infirmitas et cuique maneat sua potestas . . ." The author appears to have been a mendicant attempting to propose a middle way between pope and prelates, seculars and mendicants.

allows to grow together in the field until the harvest. The response of Johannes Zacharie to this argument was blunt: "The harvest is now!" he declared.[73] The agricultural images of pruning and weeding gave way to the extreme images of eradication—tearing out by the roots: *evulsio, eradicatio, exstirpatio,* and also *destructio, dispersio, dissipatio.*[74] Reformers cited the words of the prophet Jeremiah which, as Ladner has shown, had a long history of use by Gregory VII and other reformers: "This day I set you over nations and kingdoms, to root up and to tear down, to destroy and to demolish, to build and to plant."[75] The image of the lord's field choked by thorns, briars, and thistles had also appeared frequently in the context of the struggle against the Albigensian and other heretics at least since the twelfth century. Reformers at Constance used this imagery to refer to the elimination of heresy—Hussite and Wycliffite—as well as to the termination of the schism and the rooting out of vices and abuses, especially simony.[76]

The use of the terminology and imagery of correction to refer interchangeably to elimination of heresy and reform of abuses at Constance is no accident. Reformers saw the manifold abuses in the church as the chief causes of heresy and schism, and in the early months of the council it seemed to many that the abuses emanated chiefly from the curia of John [XXIII]. In those months action against John proceeded simultaneously with action against the alleged heretic Hus; and John's deposition occurred precisely because he had proved himself "incorrigible," as the sermons,

---

[73] Sermon, December 26, 1415: "Vel dico, quod iam est messis, et quod colligi debent zizania . . ."

[74] Dietrich Kolde, Sermon, February 16, 1416, W. 1.3.119: "Vos vineam Domini omni genere culturae laborandam suscepistis. Et nunc a vobis, herbas nocivas evellendi, haereses exstirpandi ac capiendi feras vineam depascentes, tollitur potestas. Attamen ad vos obnixe clamitat ecclesia: Capite vulpeculas, quae demoliuntur vineas." (Cant. 2,15) Cf. also Peter Pulka, Sermon, late Nov./Dec. 1414, ACC.2.383: "ut perniciosorum errorum spine in quibus misere versatur mundus, evellantur . . ."; and Johannes Zacharie, OESA, Sermon, December 26, 1415, *W.*1.3.84–85: "Dilectus in hortum suum [Cant. 2,3], id est rite electus in hortum ecclesiasticum, non ut fruatur deliciis voluptuosis . . . sed ut in horto ecclesiastico evellat et destruat, disperdat et dissipet, aedificet et plantet [Jeremiah 1,10]. . . . Quam necessaria esset iam in ecclesia Dei evulsio zizaniorum, haeresis et discredentiae, destructio loliorum, hypocrisis et fraudulentiae, dissipatio raphanorum, gravaminis et iniustitiae . . ."

[75] Jeremiah 1,10, *New American Bible.* For the use of this terminology by Gregory VII, see Ladner, "Gregory," in *Images,* 2:653.

[76] See its use by Archbishop Pileus of Genoa to refer to the elimination of reservations: "reseruationes, quae non sunt in corpore juris clausae, exstirpentur . . ." Döllinger, *Beiträge,* 2:306.

pamphlets, and official acta themselves from this period constantly reiterate.

The preamble to the central reform decree *Frequens* draws together in a remarkable way the terminology and the agricultural imagery of correction. The decree grew out of deliberations for the prevention of future schisms, and it called for the regular meeting of general councils. "Frequent celebration of general councils is the best method of cultivating the field of the Lord. It extirpates the thorns, briars, and thistles of heresies, errors, and schisms; it corrects excesses, reforms the things which are deformed, and brings the Lord's vineyard to the fruits produced by richest fertility. The remembrance of times past and the consideration of present things places this before our eyes."[77]

Here there is no thought of restoring the past. The reformers looked to the past to identify abuses, and they were impressed by past examples of conciliar reforms which had eliminated such abuses. They did so because their focus was on the present and the future. By present reforms they wanted to avoid future abuses. They also envisaged future health, growth, and fruit, but it would be the fruit of hard labor and cultivation, not of spontaneous, exuberant growth. Such cultivation would come above all through correction. The ideas of correction were the most radical at the council, and they were the ones that prevailed. Theirs was not the radicality of a utopian future or an atavistic past; it was the radicality of attacking at the roots the enormous abuses of a church rent by schism. The Constance reforms were rooted in the present, a living present which they linked to the past and future through the tradition of the regular celebration of councils.

9. Reform and conciliar tradition

This conception of conciliar traditions is expressed most clearly in the proposed conciliar reform establishing a papal oath of office. In the proposed oath, the pope, after referring twice to the faith and the keys which Christ gave over (*tradidit*) to St. Peter, is to promise

---

[77] *Conciliorum oecumenicorum decreta*, ed. J. Alberigo, *et al.*, (Bologna 1973³) 438–439: "Frequens generalium conciliorum celebratio, agri dominici praecipua cultura est, quae vepres spinas et tribulos haeresium, errorum et schismatum exstirpat, excessus corrigit, deformata reformat, et vineam Domini ad frugem uberrimae fertilitatis adducit, illorum vero neglectus praemissa disseminat atque fovet. haec praeteritorum temporum recordatio et consideratio praesentium ante oculos nostros ponunt."

the saint that he will conserve all those things which he received from him by tradition for the rectitude of the orthodox faith.[78] Gerson's understanding of faith here would have been clear-cut: purely spiritual matters which had only to do with man's eternal beatitude. But other reformers sought to expand the idea, working from the "uncritical" approach to tradition. Thus, they sought to append to the oath an entire series of papal promises concerning "ancient and laudable customs" of administration. These proposed expansions of the oath were dropped again from the final version of the decree, but the oath was expanded there in another way.[79] Now the pope was to promise to conserve not simply those things pertaining to the faith which he received by tradition from Peter, but rather the Catholic faith according to the traditions of the apostles, of the general councils and of the other holy fathers; and to the list of the eight ecumenical councils this version adds the general councils of the Lateran, of Lyons (probably it meant Lateran IV and Lyons II) and of Vienne.[80] The Council of Vienne (1311) was the last undisputed general council held prior to the Council of Constance; the clear implication was that Constance would in turn take its place in the list.

In this conception of tradition, the traditions of the councils continued from Christ and the primitive Church to the present. The continued role of councils in the Church was one of two ways in which both the "critical" and the "uncritical" approaches to tradition could agree in seeing continuity with the primitive Church; the other way was the collegiality or equality of the bishops gathered in these councils as successors of the apostles. Both Dietrich of Niem and Gerson cited the example of St. Paul's correction of St. Peter as a precedent for the correction of the pope by the council.[81] The decrees of the early councils did not read "It pleases Peter", notes D'Ailly, but rather "It pleases us who are united here together."[82]

---

[78] See below, p. 322, Common, c.2: "id est, quecunque ad rectitudinem vere nostreque orthodoxe fidei a te traditionem accipiunt conservare . . ."

[79] *Conciliorum oecumenicorum decreta* 442.

[80] See below, p. 388, S[2], c.3. See also the interesting statement in the gloss on the oath of Boniface VIII, ACC.2.686A: "Usque ad unum apicem: Argumentum, quod a simili potest papa obligari ad immutilatam id est integram observacionem quorundam aliorum conciliorum, quia licet illa fuerint priora et principalia, tamen sequencia generalia concilia universalis ecclesie auctoritate firmata non minoris videntur esse roboris.

[81] *De modis*, 87. Cf. Pascoe, "Ecclesia Primitiva," 390.

[82] H.1.449: "Nam in primo concilio Hierosolymis celebrato, de quo in actibus Apostolorum legitur, Jacobus presente Petro protulit sententiam, ubi non ait: 'Placuit Petro,' sed 'Placuit nobis collectis in unum. . . .'"

D'Ailly was citing the *Acts of the Apostles*. Conciliar reformers considered the meetings of the apostolic community recorded there to be the first Church councils.[83] In his *Tractatus* D'Ailly refutes the arguments of those who claim that the council only deliberates and gives counsel but does not judge or make definitions; as proof he cites the wording of earlier conciliar decrees found in the Decretum, the Decretals, and the Book of the Councils.[84] The third source he names here is one he cites quite often in the *Tractatus* and refers to as "most useful and necessary";[85] what was the *Liber conciliorum*? Francis Oakley recognized it to be none other than the Pseudo-Isidorian decretals,[86] and I would like to suggest here that this is a source to which historians have generally given too little attention in the context of conciliar reforms.

This collection of legal materials forged in a ninth-century Frankish workshop has perhaps gained most fame for its apocryphal letters of the popes of the first centuries after Christ.[87] But at the core of their work the forgers placed a quite genuine canonical collection known as the *Hispana*. This collection contained a very extensive chronological sequence of the texts of early Church councils, general, regional, and provincial, together with genuine papal letters of the fourth through the sixth centuries. The conciliar texts were emended by the forgers for their own ends, but their basic substance remained. Even the apocryphal letters were to a considerable extent constructed from genuine papal letters and other early documents, so that it is quite difficult to draw the line between the false and the genuine in the forgers' final product. An expanded manuscript of the Pseudo-Isidorian collection in fact formed the core of the first printed collection of conciliar texts made by Merlin in 1524, and thereby also of all the subsequent editions through Mansi's.[88] The Pseudo-Isidorian texts probably exercised their greatest influence on conciliar reformers through the extensive

---

[83] See, among many examples, D'Ailly in H.1.410–412 and 449; W.1.3.66, and anon. sermon, March 29, 1416, Tübingen, Universitätsbibl. Mc 282, fol. 45r.

[84] *Tractatus*, ed. Francis Oakley, *The Political Thought of Pierre d'Ailly: The Voluntarist Tradition* (New Haven, 1964), 305: "Legitur in multis locis Libri Conciliorum et etiam Decreti et Decretalium, ubi sic dicitur: 'Placuit sancto concilio . . .'"

[85] *Ibid.*, 338; for Job Vener's reference, cf. ACC.3.630.

[86] *Ibid.*, 266 n.2 *bis*. Job Vener also cites a *Liber conciliorum*, but Heimpel and Fasolt argue that this is William Durant's *Tractatus* rather than Pseudo-Isidore; see Heimpel, *Vener*, 3:1297–1299 and Constantin Fasolt, "Rezeption," 69.

[87] Horst Fuhrmann, *Einfluss und Verbreitung der pseudoisidorischen Fälschungen*, (Stuttgart 1972). He mentions the use by D'Ailly; cf. 1:59 n. 139.

[88] Henri Quentin, *Jean Dominique Mansi et les grandes collections conciliaires* (Paris 1900).

excerpts from them which appear in Gratian's *Decretum*. But the comments of D'Ailly show his direct knowledge and use of them, even though D'Ailly notes with regret at one point that copies of the collection had become most rare.[89] We do know of one copy of the collection made in the year the Council of Constance ended.[90] A number of Pseudo-Isidorian ideas and phrases also entered the conciliar reform discussions through another and more proximate intermediate source: the two *Tractatus* written a century earlier by William Durant the Younger to set forth a reform program for the Council of Vienne.[91] Durant's work shows the influence of Pseudo-Isidore almost at every turn, as suggested by the parallel between its title and the Pseudo-Isidorian *Ordo de celebrando concilio*, the text of which Durant copies verbatim from Pseudo-Isidore into his work.[92]

The Pseudo-Isidorian collection has often been cited as one of the prime pillars in the edifice of papal primacy erected by medieval popes; what was its appeal to conciliar reformers? We have touched already on two important aspects—its role as a book of councils *par excellence* and the view it provided of the *ecclesia primitiva*. It was the most complete collection of councils which reformers knew; as D'Ailly remarks, it contained in full texts found only piecemeal and in truncated form in Gratian.[93] Moreover, it offered a treasury of precedents for the authority and reforming activity of councils. Not only the conciliar texts, but also the fictive letters of the early popes (whose genuineness was scarcely doubted at that time) formed one of the most significant sources of the understanding of the primitive Church for fifteenth century reformers. Its appeal was enhanced for many of them by the convenient little treatise which the pseudo-Isidorian forgers provided in their collection to explain and justify the manner in which certain aspects of

---

[89] *Tractatus* 338.

[90] Prague, Narodni a Universitni Knihovna IV.B.12; cf. Shafer Williams, *Codices Pseudo-Isidoriani* (Monumenta iuris canonici, Series C, III; New York 1971) 50.

[91] William Durant the Younger, *Tractatus de modo generalis concilii celebrandi* (Lyons, 1531). This is the *editio princeps*; see Constantin Fasolt, "The Manuscripts and Editions of William Durant the Younger's 'Tractatus de modo generalis concilii celebrandi,'" *AHC* 10 (1978) 290–309. The most readily available edition is a Gregg reprint of the Paris, 1671 edition done in London, 1963 (?). However, it is less accurate than the *editio princeps*, and both editions contain significant deviations from the manuscripts.

[92] *Ibid.*, fol. 19v: "Item ordo iste de celebrando concilio assumptus est ex libro ab Isidoro edito".

[93] D'Ailly, *Tractatus* 271: "Librum Conciliorum, ubi ad plenum legitur quod a Gratiano truncate diversis in locis recitatur."

the primitive Church, especially the community of goods among believers, had ceased to exist.[94] Though the value of Pseudo-Isidore was thus moot for the small minority of reformers at the Council who desired that the whole Church return to the *vita apostolica*, the Pseudo-Isidorian view of apostolic succession was quite congenial to reformers occupying episcopal sees (e.g., D'Ailly and Durant, at the time they wrote their treatises). The Pseudo-Isidorian texts positively exalted the bishops as the successors of the apostles.[95] Congar has pointed to the use of these texts by the secular clergy in its disputes with the mendicants; the seculars sought to show that the claims of the mendicants threatened the hierarchical order of the Church established by Christ.[96]

The pseudo-Isidorian texts stressed not only the Church's essential hierarchical structure, but also the continued role of councils in the Church's government. On both these points the "critical" approach to tradition could agree with the "uncritical" approach in seeing continuity of tradition reaching back to the primitive Church. But on both points the view of the primitive Church was more historically accurate than the idealized Golden Age conjured up by the "uncritical" approach. The language of the council's official reform pronouncements seems to agree better with the views of the "critical" approach. We have seen how the council dropped the version of the reform decree on papal oaths which contained the language concerning ancient and venerable traditions of the fathers. The official decrees looked to the past less as a condition to be restored than as a teacher. "In consideration of past losses, wishing to avoid the same in the future", reads a typical preamble to a decree.[97] The reforms are grounded upon experience, reason, and expediency.[98] The reformers speak often of framing their measures to achieve a certain end; they cite past measures which, though carefully thought out, did not achieve their desired end, and they point to abuses which have obstructed such ends in the past. The language does agree with the accurate tracing of historical abuses which characterized even the "uncritical" approach. But

---

[94] "De primitiva ecclesia et sinodo Nicena", *Hinschius* 247–49.

[95] Fuhrmann, 1:145–47.

[96] Congar, "Quérelle," 60–62. Against the mendicants the seculars used arguments which had been developed by the pseudo-Isidorian forgers against the claims of the chorbishops; the key point was that Christ established only two essential orders in the Church's hierarchy, bishops and priests.

[97] Preamble to *Quia decet* (Common, c.2b, see below, pp. 325): "futuris dispendiis consideratione preteritorum ecclesiam dei scandalizantium obuiare . . ."

[98] See below, pp. 389–391, 326 and 375 (S², c.5 and 6; Common, c.3; and V, c.18a).

the reforms themselves seem on the whole to fit better with Gerson and D'Ailly's definitions of human traditions as positive law which is mutable and framed to meet specific human ends.[99] On the other hand we should recall that, according to Gerson and D'Ailly, the power to make and change these human traditions was based on the divine tradition of conciliar authority. In Gerson's words, the council itself was the "regula a Christo tradita".[100]

---

[99] Cf. note 39 above; cf. also *DuPin* 3:16–17: "Lex humana siue positiua praeceptiua pure et appropriate describitur quod est signum verum humana traditione et auctoritate immediate constitutum, aut quod non infertur necessaria deductione ex lege diuina et naturali ligans ad aliquid agendum vel non agendum, pro consecutione finis alicuius humani."

[100] *G*.5.44: "Ecclesia vel generale concilium eam representans est regula a Spiritu Sancto directa, tradita a Christo . . ."

CHAPTER NINE

AGENTS AND OBJECTS OF REFORM

The decree *Frequens* marks the most celebrated use of the agricultural pattern of reform imagery. In it the council acts as the agent of reform, bringing reform throughout the entire vineyard. The other pattern of reform images, the corporate one, is more multivalent in its evocation of the power relationships involved in reform. There were many corporations which offered themselves as models for this reform. Alongside, indeed, over-arching these was the concept of universal reform, not of a corporation, but of a *corpus*, of the church as the living body of Christ, em-bodied on earth in the general council. The reform in head and members is a *reformatio generalis*. It does not single out individual deformities, but surveys the ills in all the members in order to correct them and promote the common good or public utility. To some extent these are "horizontal" conceptions of reform, which seem to run counter to the "vertical" conception of the church as an ordered hierarchy in which reform starts from the top and diffuses downward through the hierarchy. The great beauty of the concept of a reform in head and members for the Constance reformers was that it so effectively synthesized the vertical and horizontal, the hierarchical and collegial views of reform.

1. Historical background of the concept

First let us survey very briefly the major developments in thought concerning the church as Body of Christ, beginning with the Pauline epistles in the New Testament. In those epistles the principal focus was on the unity of the body, but with a significant difference of emphasis in two groups of letters. In the *Letter to the Romans* and the *First Letter to the Corinthians* the emphasis was on the mutual unity of the members with one another, i.e., their interdependence and mutual sympathy, parallel to the organic unity of a natural body. In the *Letter to the Ephesians* and the *Letter to the Colossians*, often called deutero-Pauline, the stress is on unity of the members with the divine head of the Body, Christ.[1]

---

[1] On these matters, see especially Hoffmann, *Repräsentation*, 121–25, and the literature cited there. On the Pauline letters, see Emil Mersch, *Le corps mystique du*

In the former letters St. Paul spoke of the unity of the body which exists in spite of the diversity of the national origin and worldly status of the members; Jew, Greek, slave, and freeman are all members of one body.[2] There is also unity in the diversity of their functions in the church. Like the different organs or senses of a body they have different activities since they have been given different gifts by God's grace.[3] Yet all are dependent on one another, and no member can say to another that it doesn't need it. Quite the contrary, explains Paul, enigmatically: The members which appear weaker are in fact the more necessary; those which we think to be most ignoble receive the greatest honor.[4] Therefore, although the Pauline teaching in these letters strongly implies a hierarchical ordering among the members, it does so in such a way as to emphasize the paradoxical nature of this order: the "higher" members need the "lower" members as much as, if not more than vice versa. The head cannot say to the feet, "I don't need you."[5] Not only is the relationship among the members one of mutual dependence, it is also one of mutual caring and feeling. This compassion or sympathy, the sharing of suffering and joy,[6] is not only a desideratum but a fact, because the members are connected in an organic way. These members are not only parts of the same group but are "individually members one of another."[7]

Even though a number of the same themes recur in the letters to

---

Christ (Louvain, 1933), 1:61n. and 109–130. Mersch accepts all the letters as genuine letters of the Paul and argues that the letters to the Ephesians and the Colossians were written at a relatively late period in the apostle's life, during his imprisonment, and that they therefore reflect a more mature and profound conception of the Church as Body of Christ than do the letters to the Romans and the Corinthians. Many scholars, of course, believe that the letters to the Colossians and the Ephesians cannot be attributed to St. Paul; and the Bultmann school argues that these letters were influenced by Gnostic savior myths.

[2] 1 Cor. 12,13: "etenim in uno Spiritu omnes nos in unum corpus sumus . . ."

[3] Rom. 12,5: "ita multi unum corpus sumus in Christo singuli autem alter alterius membra habentes autem donationes secundum gratiam quae data est nobis differentes . . ."

[4] 1 Cor. 12,22–24: "quae videntur membra corporis infirmiora esse necessariora sunt et quae putamus ignobiliora membra esse corporis his honorem abundantiorem circumdamus et quae inhonesta sunt nostra abundantiorem honestatem habent honesta autem nostra nullius egent sed Deus temperavit corpore ei cui deerat abundantiorem tribuendo honorem . . ."

[5] *Ibid.*, v. 21: "non potest dicere oculus manui opera tua non indigeo aut iterum caput pedibus non estis mihi necessarii."

[6] *Ibid.*, v. 25–26: "pro invicem sollicita sint membra et si quid patitur unum membrum conpatiuntur omnia sive gloriatur unum membrum congaudent omnia membra . . ."

[7] *Ibid.*, v. 27: "et membra de membro"; cf. Rom. 12,5: "ita multi unum corpus sumus." English translation is from *The New American Bible* (New York, 1970).

the Ephesians and the Colossians, the emphasis there is different. Whereas in the former letters Paul spoke of ministries as gifts given by the Spirit,[8] in the letter to the Ephesians the various ministries of the members are said to be derived from the head, and it is Christ's fullness rather than the Spirit which is depicted as filling the entire body.[9] The letter to the Ephesians also speaks of ministry in the context of the growth or building up of the body of Christ.[10] God has provided the apostles, pastors and others for the "perfection of the saints in the work of ministry in the edification of the body of Christ." This ministry is compared to the joints of a body through which the growth of each member contributes to the growth of the whole body in love. The members thus grow up to one perfect man whose stature is that of the fullness of Christ.

Many later reformers came to expect reform to emanate from the pope, whom they regarded as vicar of Christ, the head of the church. Paul's concept of the plenitude of Christ certainly helped to shape the later conceptions of the papal plenitude of power.[11] Other reformers, basing their demands on the Pauline teaching that the body is to grow in love, demanded that all members of the hierarchy, including the pope, act according to love. Such reformers called attention to Paul's teaching in the Second Letter to the Corinthians (10,8 and 13,10) that all power in the church is given for the church's edification, and they called for the reform of those abuses of power which did not build up the church.[12]

Thus the Pauline ideas provided the foundation for diverse ideas concerning the reform of the church as the Body of Christ, in particular through the two different conceptions of the body. They were further enriched by developments in Greco-Roman Patristic and medieval corporate thought. These developments occurred

---

[8] 1 Cor. 12,11: "haec omnia operatur unus atque idem Spiritus dividens singulis prout vult sicut enim corpus unum est et membra habet multa omnia autem membra corporis cum sint multa unum corpus sunt ita et Christus etenim in uno Spiritu omnes nos baptizati sumus . . . et omnes unum Spiritum potati sumus."

[9] Eph. 4, 15–16: "in caritate crescamus in illo per omnia qui est caput Christus ex quo totum corpus conpactum et conexum per omnem iuncturam subministrationis secundum operationem in mensuram uniuscuiusque membri augmentum corporis facit in aedificationem sui in caritate."

[10] Eph. 4, 11–12, 16: "et ipse dedit quosdam quidem apostolos quosdam autem prophetas alios vero evangelistas alios autem pastores et doctores ad consummationem sanctorum in opus ministerii in aedificationem corporis Christi . . ."

[11] See Robert Benson, "Plenitudo potestatis: Evolution of a formula from Gregory IV to Gratian," *Studia Gratiana* 14 (1967) 193–218 at 198–199; also Ladner, "The Concepts: Ecclesia, Christianitas, plenitudo postestatis," *Miscellanea historiae pontificiae*, 19 (1954) 49–78.

[12] See above, p. 234 n. 12. This was the central theme of the *opinio communis* shared also by canonists whose development Buisson traced in *Potestas und Caritas*.

above all in three areas: philosophy, sacramental theology, and law. Although the second Pauline conception clearly posits Christ as the divine head of the body which is the church, the first conception compares the church to any living body in a way similar to Stoic conceptions.[13] Analogies between the human body and the cosmos (microcosm-macrocosm) were quite widespread . in antiquity.[14] Greek thinkers at least from the time of Socrates had compared the polis (city-state) to the human body. The Stoic philosophers combined the two analogies in their doctrine of cosmopolitanism. Especially in thinkers like Poseidonius the cosmos and the state take on the organic characteristics of the human body. Like the body they are held together by a unifying spirit which "animates" them. Their members are interdependent, feeling a relationship of mutual sympathy, so that the joy or suffering of each member affects the whole body. Roman writers eagerly borrowed Stoic concepts, comparing the Roman Empire to the cosmos on the one hand and to a human body on the other and thus referring to Rome or to the emperor as the *caput mundi*, the head of the world. These conceptions were not lost when the Roman Empire became Christian; and in Western Europe they came to be applied to the Roman church, especially by popes who were confronted very directly with the necessity of assuming duties which a weakened empire could no longer perform.[15] Leo I, who had to defend Rome against the threat of the Huns, played a key role in this development, as did many popes of the eighth and ninth centuries, who were faced with the declining power first of the Byzantine, then of the Carolingian Empire. Two centuries later popes would vie with emperors for the role of *caput mundi*, and as the vicars of Christ they could even claim support from the Pauline doctrines discussed above.

The medieval western emperors in turn regarded themselves as successors of the Roman emperors and called upon the same Roman legal and Stoic ideas of the emperor as the head of the world or of all humanity.[16] As the leaders of *Christianitas* they could also draw

---

[13] The extent to which it also helped shape the Pauline teaching itself has been much discussed but lies outside the scope of our study; see Arnold Ehrhardt, "Das Corpus Christi und die Korporationen im spät-römischen Recht," *ZRG Rom.* 70 (1953) 299–347.

[14] On the Greek and Roman ideas, cf. Ehrhardt, 305–329; on the medieval ideas see Marian Kurdziałek, "Der Mensch als Abbild des Kosmos," in *Der Begriff der repraesentatio*, 35–75, and the works cited there.

[15] Yves Congar, *L'ecclésiologie du haut moyen age* (Paris, 1968).

[16] Otto von Gierke, *Das deutsche Genossenschaftsrecht* (Berlin, 1881) 3:548ff. By the fifteenth century there was direct knowledge of the classical antecedents; cf. G.5.44 and ACC.2.391.

on the Pauline ideas of the church as body of Christ. Similarly kings came to regard themselves as emperors in their own kingdoms and thus as the heads of the bodies politic in those kingdoms. By the fifteenth century comparisons between living, natural bodies on the one hand and the church or secular governments on the other hand had become quite common. The authors of such comparisons spoke on the one hand of the *corpus naturale* or *animale* and on the other of the *corpus mysticum*, and they used the latter term indiscriminately to refer both to the universal church and to secular governments.

Corpus mysticum had earlier been used to denote the host in the Eucharist. Henri de Lubac has traced the curious semantical "chassé-croisé" by which it was transferred to the church.[17] On the one hand, by the thirteenth century the Eucharistic body had ceased to be identified by the usual appellation *corpus mysticum* and had become regularly referred to as *verum corpus* or simply *corpus Christi*, without any qualifications (mainly to reinforce the doctrine of the real presence). On the other hand, the church, which had usually been called simply *corpus Christi* came more and more to be identified by the term *corpus mysticum*, which was no longer used to refer to the Eucharist.

Developments in canon law were as important as those in theology. At least from the twelfth century, canonists began to treat individual churches and monasteries as corporations, groups of persons which continued to exist even when new members of the corporation replaced old ones.[18] It might seem at first that legal corporation concepts were similar to the Stoic teaching concerning the state as a living body. The canon lawyers worked out the legal technicalities necessary to allow the corporation to act as an individual person in the eyes of the law, so that it could hold property and receive testamentary bequests, for example. But with increasing intellectual rigor the canonists also insisted that the person whose rights were so defined was a juridical fiction, a *persona ficta*. This person had neither soul nor body, they declared. They of course spoke of it as having both in order to explain the corporate will or to account for the relationship between head and members; but they always insisted that such analogies were only legal con-

---

[17] *De Lubac, Corpus*, 89–135; cf. 88: "Par quel curieux chassé-croisé le 'corpus quod est ecclesia' en vint à prendre à son tour, et précisément dans son opposition au corps eucharistique, le nom de *corpus mysticum* . . ."

[18] See the classic, still much debated study of this development in Gierke, *Genossenschaftsrecht*, 3:198ff.; on the debate see the overview in Hofmann, *Repräsentation*, 126–148 and Tierney, *Foundations*, 132ff.

veniences. The canonists' treatment of churches and monasteries as corporations, as *personae fictae*, had important consequences. The marriage of a bishop to his church lost much of its mystical significance.[19] And for them the corporate whole was often no more than the agglomeration of its parts; it was not a living body as in the Stoic teaching concerning the state and the cosmos or as in the Pauline doctrine of the church. Ehrhardt showed that a similar doctrine of corporations as fictitious bodies in classical Roman law continued alongside the Stoic doctrine of the Empire as a living body.[20]

The earliest use which I have observed of the phrase "reform in head and members" was in the context of the canonistic corporation teaching applied to cathedral churches. It appears in the decretal *Qualiter et quando* of Innocent III, which was included in the Decretals of Gregory IX. The letter, written in 1206, was addressed to the Bishop of Modena who was trying to solve a dispute between the Bishop and cathedral chapter of Novara.[21]

---

[19] J. Trummer, "Mystisches im Kirchenrecht," *Österreichisches Archiv fur Kirchenrecht* 2 (1951) 62–75; Tierney, *Foundations*, 133–134. Trummer and Tierney show how the canonists converted the symbol of the marriage of the prelate and church into a legal fact, applying principles of marriage law in their discussion of the prelate's rights, duties, and status with regard to his church. But in the twelfth and thirteenth centuries their discussions were limited to the relationship of bishops to their diocese and priests to their churches. The relationship of the pope and the universal Church, on the other hand, was viewed in terms of the Pauline conception of the Church as the bride of Christ, since the pope came to be viewed as the vicar of Christ. Congar ("Quérelle," 105–107) has shown how thirteenth century theologians, especially mendicant theologians, came to place much greater emphasis on the pope as spouse of the Church than on bishops or priests as spouses of their churches. In the fourteenth and fifteenth century theologians like Gerson in turn subjected this mystical image of the marriage of the pope and the Church to a more detailed and rational, even legal analysis, similar to that undertaken earlier by the canonists with respect to the marriage of prelates to their churches. It was through such analysis that Gerson was able to propose the idea that the Church could be divorced from its spouse, the pope, in certain cases (see his tract "De auferabilitate sponsi ab ecclesia," G.3.300ff.) See also Matthew of Cracow, *De praxi*, 120.

[20] Ehrhardt, 331ff. He stresses that classical Roman lawyers carefully avoided applying Stoic doctrines to corporations.

[21] X 5.1.17: "Formam vero iuramenti, quam a clericis Novariensibus super inquisitione facienda in hoc negotio recepistis, in similibus volumus observari, ut videlicet iurent clerici, quod super his, quae sciunt vel credunt esse in sua ecclesia reformanda tam in capite quam in membris, exceptis occultis criminibus, meram et plenam dicant inquisitoribus veritatem." I am indebted to Michael Phelps, who called my attention to similar uses of the phrase in letters of Gregory IX dealing with reform of the heads and members of monasteries and cathedral chapters; his references led me to the earlier ones in Innocent's letters. Reformers who used the phrase may have been influenced also by the passage in Isaiah 1,6 (see above, p. 224 n. 70.)

Two years later Innocent took similar action concerning the abbot and canons of the abbey of St. Denis in Rheims; this decretal (*Cum I. et A.*) is included also in the *Liber extra*, where it is erroneously ascribed to Alexander III.[22] In his commentary on *Qualiter et quando*, Pope Innocent IV stressed that the words "tam in capite quam in membris" refer to a general inquisition rather than the specification of a certain crime of an individual which is to be investigated.[23]

William Durant the Younger was almost certainly the first to apply the phrase to the reform of the universal church (in his *Tractatus maior*, 1308/11).[24] However, the first application of the phrase in a universal sense may have been that of Nicholas IV to refer to his reform of the Cluniac order.[25] Durant used the phrase as a summary or watchword for his entire program of reform, which called above all for the redressing of the balance of powers between papacy and episcopate by requiring the pope to seek the consent of the general council for all legislation. The path of transmission of this motto from Durant to the conciliar thinkers of the later fourteenth century is still unclear.[26] However, it is virtually certain that they borrowed it and probably other corporate ideas from him. One important example is the phrase "a capite sit edenda ratio." This maxim had occurred first in Roman legislation concerning the lending of money;[27] it meant that the conditions of the loan must be made public at the beginning of the loan, not at the time of

---

[22] X 2.27.22: " . . . ut ad ecclesiam ipsam personaliter accedentes, tam in capite quam in membris appellatione postposita corrigerent corrigenda, et statuerent quae statuenda viderent."

[23] Innocentius IV, *In V. libros decretalium commentaria*, ed. L. Rosello and M. Leonardus (Venice, 1570), 585.

[24] Fasolt, *Council*, 1, 116, 129–132. Durant probably borrowed the phrase from its use in the *Liber extra*; however, both he and the popes who had used it earlier may have been influenced by the image in Is. 1,6, which Durant cites in the same context with *reformatio in capite et in membris*: "A planta pedis usque ad verticem vix est in ea sanitas." (Durant, TMI 1 (3.1), fol. 52ra; TMA 2.96 (3.97), fol. 58va); see Fasolt, *Council*, 296 n.21 and Haller, 8 n.2.

[25] Letters no. 1556 (September 5, 1289) and 1772 (December 10, 1289): "Ad statum pacificum et tranquillum Cluniacensis ordinis paternis studiis intendentes, quamplura statuta pro reformatione ipsius tam in capite quam in membris intendentes, quamplura statuta pro reformatione ipsius tam in capite quam in membris edidimus," cited by F. Neiske, "Reform oder Kodifizierung? Päpstliche Statuten für Cluny im 13. Jahrhundert," *Archivum historiae pontificiae* 26 (1988) 72–118 at 74 n. 118; and Fasolt, *Council*, 1 n. 2.

[26] See Fasolt, "Publikum," 67–69. It is very difficult to establish direct uses of William by later writers; however, it is certain that Vener and D'Ailly knew and used the *Tractatus*. See also p. 245 below for use of Durant's terminology by Dietrich of Niem and the *Capitula agendorum*.

[27] *Dig.* 2.13.10.2 (lex Argentarius) and 3.5.18.1 (lex Ad quin) ed. Theodor Mommson and Paul Krueger (Berlin, 1954), 56, 75.

repayment. In its original context, the word "ratio" meant something like calculation, chiefly the reckoning of the interest rate; the words *"edenda sit"* referred to the publication of the agreement; and *"a capite"* meant "from the beginning." The phrase had come to be used by canonists in different contexts, usually with similar meaning. But Durant used it to express the totally unrelated idea that reason in the church should be established by the head of the church, i.e., by the pope or Roman church.[28] And so the phrase became associated with the teachings concerning the church as body of Christ.

2. Hierarchical aspects

A very complex heritage of ideas concerning the church as body of Christ thus converged in the reform ideas of the Council of Constance. Already the Pauline teaching had offered two fundamental alternative reform concepts according to the two-fold Pauline conception of the church as body of Christ. On the one hand, if one thought of the church as head and members together, animated by the Holy Spirit, then reform could be thought of as the restoration of the proper relationship and harmony among the members, the head being considered as one of the members. On the other hand, if the church was considered to consist of the members, and Christ to be the head of the body, reform would involve the hierarchical activity of the head acting upon the members. According to the second concept the head was the agent of reform; according to the first, the head might be one of the objects of reform. In the first conception the apostle did not ever equate any members of the body with particular offices in the church. His lack of explicitness coincided well with the paradoxical nature of the concept of ministry in the New Testament: those who exercise authority in the church do so by serving. This sense of paradox was lost in the often banal and mechanical medieval anatomies of the body politic or the church. Such had been John of Salisbury's description;[29] that of Gérard du Puy in a sermon at the Council of Constance was quite similar.[30]

---

[28] Durant, TMI 1 (3.1), fol. 52ra; TMA 2.96 (3.97), fol. 58va; see Fasolt, *Council*, 296 n.21. See below, p. 245 n. 50.

[29] John of Salisbury, *Policraticus*, Bk. 5, c. 1, cf. Gierke, 3:548ff. See the detailed discussion such anatomical imagery in Marie-Christine Pouchelle, *Corps et chirurgie à l'apogée du Moyen Age: Savoir et imaginaire du corps chez Henri de Mondeville, chirurgien de Philippe le Bel* (Paris, 1983).

[30] Gérard du Puy, Sermon, March 11, 1415, ACC.2.404–405. The imperial

Though such identifications of offices with parts of the body had become almost clichés, there remained fundamental unresolved ambiguities. Gérard du Puy depicted the body as consisting of all Christians; but increasingly from the eleventh century, it had been thought of as a clerical corporation. If it included all Christians, what was the position of laymen, especially of the emperor and other secular rulers? Gérard said that the laymen were the arms and legs; the peasants and craftsmen were the feet, the princes and nobles the hands and secular rulers were the arms. We are reminded of the expression "secular arm (*brachium seculare*)" which was often used to speak of the secular power which enforced the decrees of the church and executed capital punishment for it so that the clergy would not have to shed blood. Gérard's image would thus appear to give laymen a lower hierarchical role than the clergy. The Carmelite Bernard Vaquer, in complaining of the usurped authority of laymen, said that the proper order of the body had been inverted; the feet had come to be placed above the head.[31] On the other hand the same image could be used in a way much more favorable to laymen, to justify their intervention in ecclesiastical affairs to bring about reforms. Dietrich of Niem cited the duty of the arm to come to the aid of the head when it was ailing, meaning thereby that the arm should reform the head.[32] The same image was taken up in this sense a century later by Luther in his reform tract addressed to the German nobility.[33]

Other thinkers had assigned an even higher position to the secular ruler in the body—that of the heart, for example.[34] Sometimes the heart was referred to as the ruling member of the body; it was often identified with the will, whereas the head was identified with reason.[35] Boniface VIII had inveighed against such claims,

---

and royal authorities are the arms; the princes and nobility the hands, the city dwellers the knees and the peasants and craftsmen the feet.

[31] Bernard Vaquer, O. Carm., Sermon, August 18, 1415, W.1.2.116: "Et ideo talium excessus tantam deordinationem et confusionem induxit, quod terra est sursum et caelum deorsum, pedes sunt supra et caput infra, dorsum ante et facies retro. Interiora sunt extra."

[32] Dietrich of Niem, *De modis*, 10.

[33] Luther, *An den deutschen Adel* (in *Ausgewahlte Schriften*, ed. H. Borcherdt, et. al., 2:89): "Nun sieh, wie christlich das gesetzt und gesagt sei, weltliche Obrigkeit sei nicht über die Geistlichkeit, solle sie auch nicht strafen. Das ist ebensoviel gesagt wie: die Hand soll nichts dazu tun, ob das Auge grosse Not leidet. Ist's nicht unnatürlich, geschweige unchristlich, dass ein Glied dem andern nicht helfen, seinem Verderben nicht wehren soll: Ja, je edler das Glied ist, je mehr die andern ihm helfen sollen."

[34] Henricus Abendon, Sermon, October 27, 1415, W.1.2.188: "Videmus in omni corpore membra cordi, quasi domino non resistere; sed obedire."

[35] Vitalis Valentini, Bishop of Toulouse, Sermon, Epiphany, 1415, W.1.2.75:

alleging that they were dualistic and declaring that there could only be one head of the body—Christ himself, because a two-headed body would be a monster.[36] There was expectedly no reference to the emperor or any other secular ruler as head of the body on the part of the Constance reformers. On the other hand, conciliar reformers did on occasion place a different accent on Boniface's dictum that the body had but one head, Christ; they argued that therefore the pope was not head of the body.[37] Gerson expressed the *via media*, which went back at least to Innocent III: the body had one head Christ; but the pope was a "secondary head (*caput secundarium*)."[38] Such terminology was very helpful in explaining how a pope could be deposed without decapitating the ecclesial body.[39]

We have discussed the growing tendency in the Middle Ages to refer to the pope or the Roman church as the head of the church. The "or" in this statement betrays a further ambiguity which by the fifteenth century still remained unresolved. On the one hand, the head of the earthly church was the papal monarch alone; on the other hand it was the Roman church, consisting of pope and cardinals, which was the head of all the churches. This ambiguity is related to the one observed earlier by which the cardinals were at the same time members of the church and parts of the head, and

---

"Per cor enim, quod movet alia membra, intelligitur voluntas, quae movet alias potentias ad agendum." Gérard du Puy identified the cardinals as the heart of the Church, while he named the Roman Church as head. See ACC.2.404. Gérard also cited the fable about members of the body rebelling against the stomach, which Livy had placed in the mouth of Menenius Agrippa addressing the Roman plebeians at the time of their secession in 494 BC; on this fable see Hofmann, *Repräsentation*, 122 n.14 and the literature cited there. On fol. Ir of Manuscript D of the reform deliberations (Vienna lat. 5113, the Dorre manuscript; see below, p. 291) appears the following inscription, probably from the time of the second reform committee at the council: "Receptum pro stomacho sancti Petri et reformationi totali eiusdem data in concilio Constantiense: Recommendatio: XXIIII cardinales, C archiepiscopos et prelatos totidem de qualibet natione et de curialibus quantum habere poteris et immergantur in aqua Reni et ibidem submersi per triduum permaneant et erit bonus pro stomacho sancti Petri et totali eius corruptione remouenda."

[36] De Lubac, *Corpus*, 130–131; cf. Yves Congar, *Die Lehre von der Kirche von Augustinus bis zum Abendländischen Schisma*, in *Handbuch der Dogmengeschichte*, v.3, fascicle 3c (Basel, 1971), 179.

[37] See Dietrich Kolde, Sermon, April 5, 1416, W.1.3.169; and on the other hand Gerson, who in his sermon March 23, 1415, speaks of "unum caput Christus" and a "caput secundarium," the pope, G.6.44. On the use of this term by Conrad of Gelnhausen and Henry of Langenstein see Hofmann, *Repräsentation*, 278 n.155.

[38] Cf. Congar, "Quérelle," 42, who cites the use of the term by Innocent III, Gregory IX and Innocent IV.

[39] See Chapter 8 above, pp. 223–224.

therefore simultaneously reformers and persons to be reformed. Thus "head and members" could be pope and cardinals, or pope and curia, or pope and bishops, or Roman church and other churches, or pope (or Roman church) and the rest of the clergy, or pope and all of Christendom. Although the same thinker often used the phrase in more than one of these senses at various times,[40] the different senses reflect to a considerable extent the rival conceptions of the council fathers concerning the proper structures of ecclesiastical authority. The two chief alternatives were a church governed by pope and cardinals versus a church governed by pope and council.

These ambiguities ought not to obscure several important broader facts. First, the corporate image in general strongly emphasizes the indispensable role of the head as the leading member of the body. The Constance reformers often stressed the necessity that there be only one head with authority to insure unity in the church. They quoted the maxim *Tot capites quot rationes*: "There will be as many opinions as there are heads."[41] Furthermore, the image of reform in head and members in particular presupposes an earthly head of the body, whether it be the pope alone or the Roman church. We have observed that the identification of this head of the ecclesial body with the pope or Roman church had its chief bases in Stoic philosophy and Roman law, but that it was quite consonant with the Pauline doctrine. In fact, it made possible a harmonization of the two Pauline conceptions of the ecclesial body. The head was an earthly member of the body like other members and thus fit the first Pauline conception; but it also stood in the place of Christ the divine head as his representative or vicar and in this sense also fulfilled the role of the head in the second Pauline conception. In this second sense it was amplified by neo-Platonic ideas of hierarchy in which all being emanated from the One. Especially impor-

---

[40] See, for example, *Capitula agendorum*, ACC.4.551; "in capite cum cardinalibus et officialibus Romane curie et in membris . . ."; cf. Dietrich of Niem, *Avisamenta*, ACC.4.616: "expedit igitur, quod ipsa curia in suis membris in ipso instanti concilio reformetur" but also just above in this passage: "cum . . . in capite ita . . . infirmitas . . . quod eciam per istos [excessus] membra languescant . . ." (Here Dietrich is speaking of the members in all of Christendom.)

[41] Anon. Sermon, September 15, 1415, W.1.2.178: "Nam si ultima resolutio in regimine ecclesiae dei esset ad rationem; et non ad autoritatem, nunquam in ecclesia pacifice regeretur. Tum quia vox est nimis aequivoca, tum quia tot capites, tot rationes, tum quia in eodem secundum variationem adsensus, diversis rationibus variantur rationes et adparentiae. Ideo merito autoritas lata, limites suae potestatis non excedens, in regimine ecclesiastico supra rationem tenet locum supremum."

tant were the ideas of pseudo-Dionysius according to which the ecclesiastical hierarchy was patterned after the angelic hierarchy in heaven.[42] Along this hierarchy a two-way action took place, a going out (*egressus*) and a return or leading back (*reductio*). Power and love descended from the summit of the hierarchy through the intermediate levels to the lowest levels. In this way the lowest members were led back to the highest through (or by means of) the intermediate members: *Infima reducuntur ad summa per media*, as medieval thinkers expressed it.[43]

On these bases the idea of a reform of the church emanating from its head could be fully developed. The Gregorian reform culminated in a concept of reform initiated by the head. This reform came increasingly to be described in pseudo-Dionysian terms. But as early as St. Bernard, Christians who supported fully this hierarchical reforming activity of the earthly head began at the same time to insist that this activity should be effected through the appropriate intermediate members of the hierarchy. St. Bernard thus warned Pope Eugenius III: "Nothing is more unworthy of you, father, than that you should mutilate the churches in their members. It is a monster, if the finger hangs directly from the head."[44] And he warned the pope that this would happen if he arranged the members of the body of Christ differently than Christ himself had ordained. Later critics, like Bernard, found considerable support for their demands in the same pseudo-Dionysian description of the hierarchical order which was used to support papal reform. They, like Bernard, stressed that hierarchical activity is always to be exercised through the intermediate ranks of the hierarchy and never to circumvent them. Bernard's epigram concerning the finger hanging from the head shows clearly how well-adapted the corporate image is to illustrate the pseudo-Dionysian dictum that *infima reducuntur ad summa per media*. Like that dictum it could be used to stress the authority of the head but at the same time to protect the functions of the intermediate members of the hierarchy.

Reformers at Constance exploited both aspects of the image. One preacher combined the corporatist and pseudo-Dionysian terminology in the following quite typical way: "The pope is the hierarch

---

[42] Congar, "Quérelle," 108–138, cf. Pascoe, *Gerson:Principles*, 17f.
[43] See above, p. 212 n. 19. On this phrase, see also Pascoe, *Gerson*, 35 n. 75.
[44] Bernard of Clairvaux, *De consideratione*, III, iv. 17–18, in *Oeuvres*, ed. J. LeClercq (Rome, 1963) 3:444–445: "Nihil pater, tibi indignius, quam sic ecclesias mutilare suis membris . . . Monstrum est, digitum pendere de capite. Hoc facis, pater, si in corpore Christi aliter disponas membra, quam disposuit ipse." See Henricus Abendon, Sermon, October 27, 1415, W.1.2.191–92.

of the entire church militant; from him there is a descent and distribution and operation of powers in all the members. In the church, just as in every body, there is a distribution of gifts from the head."[45] Henricus Abendon, on the other hand, cited Bernard's image in the context of his attack on papal exemptions, which he felt deformed the body by removing clerics from the jurisdiction of their prelates.[46]

And so the concept of reform of the ecclesial body involved not only the emanation of reform from the head, but also the restoration of the proper hierarchical order among head and members. The Stoic and Pauline teaching (especially the first Pauline conception of the ecclesial body) had left the door open for such developments, but, as we have observed, the crucial steps were the coining of the phrase "reform in head and members" to refer to the reform of episcopal churches and then the application of the phrase to the reform of the universal church. This phrase was acceptable to strong supporters of the authority of the Roman church or of the pope because it strongly emphasized the leading role of the head in the body.[47] Cardinal D'Ailly interpreted it in this sense when he said that the Roman church should first reform itself and then reform the other churches.[48] In turn the high view of the role of the head was important to many conciliar reformers, especially to stress the contrast between the role the head should play and the actual shortcomings of the pope and cardinals. Matthew of Cracow proposed a quite remarkable list of functions which the Roman church as supreme hierarch should perform, including those of "founder of laws, propagator of spiritual things, corrector of evils, leader of the wandering, persecutor of vices, prosecutor of justice and virtue, defender of the oppressed, uplifter of the poor, rectification and reformation of things wrongly ordained. . . ."[49] Such ex-

---

[45] Anon. Sermon, September 15, 1415, W.1.2.171: "Summus pontifex est totius ecclesiae militantis hierarchia a quo est dissensio et potestatum distributio et operationum in omnibus membris quae sunt in ecclesia, sicut a capite in omne corpus est donorum perfusio prout habetur dist. 19. Ita dominus [D.19 c.7]."
[46] Henricus Abendon, Sermon, October 27, 1415, W.1.2.192f.
[47] See Michele Maccarrone, 'Vicarius Christi': Storia del titolo papale (Rome, 1952).
[48] Pierre d'Ailly, Capitula agendorum, ACC.4.557: "Expediret Romanum ecclesiam, que caput est omnium, se prius in iusticia et moribus reformare ac deinde ad reformacionem ceterum membrorum procedere."
[49] Matthew of Cracow, De praxi, 75: "Iurium conditrix, propagatrix spiritualium, correctrix malorum, directrix errantium, . . . persecutrix uitiorum, iustitiae et virtutum prosecutrix, oppressorum defensio, relevatrix pauperum, rectificatio et reformatio deformiter ordinatum, doctrix errantium, morum exemplar, magistra et ministra omnis boni, regula agendorum."

pectations were frequently expressed in the context of the corporate imagery. We have noted William Durant the Younger's co-opting of the Roman law phrase *A capite sit edenda ratio* (Reason is to emanate from the head), a phrase used often by conciliar reformers, including Dietrich von Niem and the authors of the *Capitula agendorum*.[50] Dietrich often applied to the church another proverb concerning the body, which he may have also borrowed from Durant: "When the head is ailing the members suffer (or grieve)."[51] The image implies that the head stands in need of reform; but it also implies that the reform is to be a process of healing which could also be thought of as a strengthening. The same phrase was used by a papal supporter at the Council of Basel to warn against weakening the Roman church by the elimination of the annates.[52]

3. The secular-mendicant controversy revisited

In Chapters 5 and 7 above, the use of hierarchical arguments in the context of reforms of provisions, taxes, dispensations, and judicial reforms was discussed. However, by far the most concentrated occurrence of these arguments at Constance occurred in the same context in which they had developed most fully during the preceding two centuries: the struggle between the new mendicant orders and the secular clergy, with whose powers the mendicants' activities came into increasing conflict. This conflict was still quite important at the time of the Council of Constance; in fact, it had gained a heightened actuality through the recent promulgation of the bull *Regnans in excelsis* by Alexander V (1409) which reasserted the right of mendicants to hear the confessions of laymen without the permission of the parish priests of those laymen.[53] The secular

---

[50] See above, n. 28; see also Dietrich of Niem, *Avisamenta*, ACC.4.622; Dietrich asks how heresy can be eradicated unless the Roman curia is first brought back to its old ways and customs: "Quod a capite edenda est racio. Et dum caput egrotat, cetera membra dolent"; cf. also *Capitula agendorum*, ACC.4.551, where the phrase stresses the importance of good government of the Church as a prerequisite for ending the Schism.

[51] Dietrich of Niem, *De modis*, 17–18: "Cum caput egrotat, cetera membra dolent." This saying occurs several times in the council writings. Heimpel has traced its use as a proverb, as seen in Werner, *Sprichworter und Sinnspruche des Mittelalters* (Heidelberg, 1912) d 152 and Otloh, *Proverbia* (PL 146:307).

[52] Anon. Annate Tract (from Council of Basel, falsely identified as from Constance by Finke in *Forschungen und Quellen*, ed. Finke, 283–284; cf. Zwölfer, v. 28, p. 206 n. 240; "ne capite languescente facilius membra corporis inficiantur." Cf. ACC.2.599 for similar ideas expressed at Constance.

[53] *Bullarium Franciscanum*, v. 7, ed. C. Eubel (Rome, 1904) 420–423.

masters of the University of Paris, and especially their chancellor Jean Gerson, were very disturbed by this bull; at Constance they submitted to the reform committee a proposal which denounced the bull and called for its total revocation.[54]

The Paris masters stated succinctly the epitome of their complaint against the bull: "it tends to disturb the peace and the whole status of the church, and it tends greatly to weaken the hierarchical order of the church militant."[55] This is evident, claimed the masters, from a consideration of the effects of the bull on the groups (*status*) concerned, i.e. the mendicants, the secular clergy and the subject laymen.[56] In explaining how the bull perturbed the mendicants the university drew on the distinction between the passive acquiring of perfection which was proper to the mendicants and the active exercise of perfection which was proper to the prelates. They claimed that the bull gave the mendicants the opportunity to turn from their proper function and take over the function of the prelates, by preaching, for example; or even to presume to correct the prelates ("corrode" would be a better word, punned the masters). The bull perturbed and disquieted the prelates because it led the mendicants to accuse and calumnify them, thus also confusing and perturbing the whole clergy and the people. It raised up the mendicants above the prelates, who had been instituted by Christ to exercise authority over them.

The authority of the priests over their parishioners was very important for the masters; the themes of discipline and local lordship of the clergy recurred very strongly in their argumentation. They compared the bond of mutual obligation between priest and parishioner quite explicitly to that between lord and subject. It was a bond of protection in exchange for obedience.[57] But again for them the understanding of the obligation and function of the priest was sacramental. He was to feed his flock, purge them and wash away their sins through confession, and to administer to them the other sacraments.[58] The masters complained especially that the power given to the mendicants broke this mutual bond; it removed the obligation of the parishioners to be obedient without removing

---

[54] ACC.2.690–698.
[55] *Ibid.*, 690: "cum sit intollerabilis et pacis ac ordinis ierarchici ecclesie a Christo saluberrime instituti turbativa."
[56] *Ibid.*, 695–696.
[57] *Ibid.*, 695: "item iura non debent claudicare, ut obligetur dominus servo, non autem servus sive subditus vel inferior domino suo set mutuam omnem esse obligacionem, ut quemadmodum dominus subditum protegere et tueri, ita subditus domino obedire illum revera et amare tenetur."
[58] *Ibid.*: "pastor obligatur oves suas pascere et a sordibus viciorum purgare . . ."

the obligation of the priest to care for them when they were in need.[59] We have observed that the struggle between mendicants and secular clergy was in part a competition for power. The demands of the secular masters attempted to protect the boundary of the secular clergy's authority upon which the mendicants were encroaching. They evoked the principle of *suum cuique* when they inveighed against the mendicants who were not only selfish— *querentes, que sua sunt*—but also ambitious—*eciam non sua concupiscentes.*[60]

Competition for financial support between priests and mendicants was an implicit factor here; the masters complained that the mendicants greedily sought the money of the people in order to enrich themselves. The mendicants had from their inception posed a threat to the established economic order of the church because they did not fit within the system of support according to which each office was to be accompanied by a benefice which would provide for the physical sustenance of the cleric who filled it.[61] The secular clergy had often invoked against them the Biblical maxim against "putting one's scythe into the harvest of another."[62] "Who can tolerate that these men who wantonly beg bread from the people take away from their superiors the dignity of their rights and preeminence?"[63] The masters' injured pride caused them to evoke the honor of their university and city in this same context. At the same time there is a poignancy in their observation that "the priests are always obligated to their parishioners at every hour when they are in need; they cannot desert them in time of plague without providing for them to make confession of their sins."[64]

Alongside these practical arguments stood those considerably more theoretical. When the masters distinguished between the mendicants' function of acquiring perfection and the prelates' and priests' function of exercising perfection they were drawing upon

---

[59] *Ibid.*: "Nec rationabile aut iustum esse potest, ut solvatur vinculum obligacionis in uno et non in altero.

[60] *Ibid.*, 690: "querentes, que sua sunt, affectione comodi et ceca ambitione eciam non sua concupiscentes . . ."

[61] Congar, "Quérelle," 54–58.

[62] Dietrich of Niem, *De modis*, 80. On this maxim and its Biblical source (Dt. 23,26), see Congar, "Quérelle," 73.

[63] ACC.2.696: "Quis tolerare . . . posset, homines ultro mendicare panem a populis et a superioribus auferre iurium suorum preeminenciarumque dignitatem."

[64] *Ibid.*, 695: "Cum igitur curati semper obligentur in omni hora in necessitate suis parrochianis, quos nec possunt tempore pestis deserere sine provisione confessionis . . ."

pseudo-Dionysian ideas of hierarchy. *Perficere* was one of the words Pseudo-Dionysius had used to describe the three-fold hierarchical activity by which the higher members of the ecclesiastical hierarchy acted upon the lower ones. It was the final stage of the activity, the initial stages being purgation and illumination. The mendicants had sought to establish their special role in the church by referring to their status as a state of perfection (*status perfectionis*). The secular masters had countered with the clarification that this was a "state of perfection to be attained" (*status perfectionis acquirendae*) in contrast to the prelates' "state of perfection to be exercised" (*status perfectionis exercendae*).[65] The distinction between passive and active perfection was rooted in pseudo-Dionysius's ontological ideas. According to these each grade in the ecclesiastical hierarchy, like each grade in the angelic hierarchy was suited by its nature to be the agent and/or recipient of hierarchical activity. The highest levels of the hierarchy were agents only and the lowest level, in which the masters placed the mendicants along with other laymen, was only the recipient of hierarchical action exercised upon it by the higher grades. The intermediate levels were both agents and recipients. Each level was acted upon only by the level immediately above it and in turn acted only on the level immediately below it. The direct commissioning of the mendicants by the pope to exercise his powers was contrary to the usual medieval understanding of the pseudo-Dionysian maxim that *infima reducuntur ad summa per media*.

Congar has demonstrated how the pseudo-Dionysian terminology of hierarchy, which had originally had been so favorable to the role of the pope as supreme hierarch, was gradually borrowed to meet the needs of the prelates in asserting their local authority and power against papal encroachments.[66] That it could still be used to support the papal claims is shown by the argument of one clever preacher at the council who modified it to support exemptions on the grounds that God revealed some things to the lower angels that he kept secret from the higher ones.[67] However, the most frequent

---

[65] For pseudo-Dionysian ideas of hierarchy, see Pascoe, *Gerson: Principles*, 17–48; and Congar, "Quérelle," 58ff.

[66] Congar, "Quérelle," 51ff.

[67] Anonymous sermon, March 29, 1416, Tübingen, Universitätsbibl., Mc 282 fol. 49: For good and just reason the pope can and should in exceptional cases grant privileges and exemptions, thus exercising direct hierarchical control over the lowest members of the hierarchy, skipping over the intermediate ones. This occurs not only in the angelic hierarchy, but also in secular governments. "In iure enim positiuo et humano papa derogare potest uel abrogare concedendo priuilegia et exceptiones circa monasteria et personas, presertim cum subest iusta et rationabilis causa . . . nec hoc est, cum reuerentia loquor, aliquorum ordinem ierarchi-

use of the pseudo-Dionysian terminology and hierarchical arguments in general at the council was to support the rights of intermediate members against papal abuses of power. We have
observed it in many contexts. The hierarchical arguments are
signalled especially by the appearance of certain verbs and phrases
that express the ill effects of the breakdown of order: *maculare*,
*turbare, confundere, scandalizare, destruere, mutilare in suis membris, eccle-
siasticam ordinem enervare*.[68] It is interesting to note that all these
verbs are closely related in one way or another to the corporate
imagery.

4. Collegial aspects: The bonum commune *and the* respublica

The idea of the common good was part of the classical heritage of
political ideas. Aristotle had identified the common good as the
final cause or purpose of a political community or state, and for him
it thus became the chief standard for judging the actions of rulers.[69]
He identified six types of states. First, he classified them according

---

cum ecclesie ledere uel turbare, quia licet regulariter infima debeant reduci in
suprema per media ad instar celestis ierarchie, non tamen sequitur; quoniam pro
iusta et rationabili causa supremus ierarcha possit et debeat ierarchisare aliquos
singulares infimos, obmissis mediis, et ita reperitur fieri quandoque in celesti
ierarchia, ubi supremus ierarcha frequenter illuminat et docet reuelando aliqua
secreta sua angelis inferioribus, nescientibus superioribus et mediis, ut patet de
misterio incarnationis, quod ignorantibus multis superioribus et mediis apertum
est et revelatum Gabrieli et aliis. Quinymmo hoc idem experimur in politiis
secularibus et temporalibus . . ." See also the anonymous sermon, December 13,
1416, ACC.2.478–479: An exemption is like a miracle in which an effect is
produced directly by a primary cause, without secondary cause. It is not contrary
to divine law when the pope through exemptions reserves certain persons to be
illuminated directly, especially when they are specially suited by their status to
receive this light. But to perform miracles daily would perturb the order established by God.

[68] For *turbare*, see Leonardo Dati, Sermon, February 28, 1417, ACC.2.489, who
cites some of the arguments against the mendicants which make use of this term;
he also admits that if the pope is a *turbator* he should be deposed; cf. Dietrich of
Niem, *Avisamenta*, ACC.4.600; for *confundere*, see Dietrich of Niem, *De modis*, 76,
and Leonardo Dati, Sermon, September 15, 1415, ACC.2.418: "quod possit
introductam ecclesie confusionem in debitum ordinem reformare. For *scandalizare*,
among very frequent references, ACC.2.444, 460; also Pons Simonet, *De annatis non
solvendis* H.1.769–772; and *destruere*: Dietrich of Niem, *De modis*, 73 (laws of earlier
councils destroyed by reservations) and Matthew of Cracow, 95, 105 (in context of
destruction caused by the annates.) *Mutilare in suis membris*: Henricus Abendon,
Sermon, October 27, 1415, W.1.2.191–92 (citing Bernard of Clairvaux; see above,
n. 44); cf. also *ibid.*, 195: sathanas adeo macerauit ecclesiam . . . quod ipsa
languens . . ." *ecclesiasticam ordinem enervare*: See p. 389 below (S², c.5): "neruus
ecclesiastice discipline dissoluitur . . ."

[69] Aristotle, *Politics*, 3.5; *Ethics*, 8.9; cf. de Lagarde, 2:19.

to whether they were ruled by one person, by a few, or by many.[70] But within each of these three classes two different kinds of governments resulted according to whether the rulers in each case sought the common good or their own private good. And whereas Aristotle considered the rule of one person for the common good (monarchy) to be the best form of government, he considered the rule of one person for his own private good (tyranny) to be the worst.[71] The common good was among the Greek political concepts borrowed by the Roman philosophers, especially Cicero, and was taken over in turn by Roman lawyers and by the church fathers, especially Augustine.[72] In classical and Patristic writers the concept was sometimes expressed in somewhat different words. Sometimes *bonum* (good) was replaced by *utilitas*, and sometimes *commune* by *publicum*. The private good to which the public good was contrasted was alternatively identified as the good of a single individual (*bonum alicuius*) as opposed to the good of all (*bonum omnium*). The term also entered the canon law; it was used in a decretal of Pope Leo I which was taken into the *Decretum Gratiani*.[73] As soon as Book V of Aristotle's *Ethics* and his *Politics* had been translated in the Middle Ages (ca. 1230 and 1260 respectively)[74] the Aristotelian use of the term came to exercise considerable influence on medieval thought. For example, Thomas Aquinas, Godfrey of Fontaines and Henry of

---

[70] Cf. Gerson's variation on the Aristotelian teaching, G.6.225. He argues that the best form of government would be a *politia mixta*, a combination of monarchy, aristocracy and timocracy. This would, he feels be the best way of ruling the Church.

[71] Cf. Pierre de Bruxelles, Sermon, March 25, (year unknown), H.1.857: "Tyranni proprietas est quaerere non commune bonum subditorum, sed proprium. Cf. also Dietrich of Niem, *Avisamenta*, ACC.4.603 Gloss**: "Philosophus dicit: Quicunque politice intendunt communem utilitatem, boni sunt et iusti, qui autem intendunt utilitatem propriam, sunt viciosi. Set absit, quod hoc ascribatur d. pape." Cf. de Lagarde, 2:22–23.

[72] Cf. the quotation from Augustine by Henricus Abendon, Sermon, October 27, 1415, W.1.2.194: "Cum ergo est vel esse debeat optimus in ecclesia nostra, utinam attenderet ipse ad hanc regulam, tunc enim propter bonum alicuius non faceret malum omnium, nec propter malum alicuius dimitteret bonum omnium." A convenient summary of the important classical Roman, patristic, and medieval uses of the common good is provided by I. Th. Eschmann, "A Thomistic Glossary on the Principle of the Preeminence of a Common Good," *Mediaeval Studies* 5 (1943) 123ff. See also Winfried Eberhard, "'Gemeiner Nutzen' als oppositionelle Leitvorstellung im Spätmittelalter," in *Renovatio et reformatio: Wider das Bild vom "finsteren" Mittelalter: Festschrift für Ludwig Hödl*, ed. Manfred Gerwing and Godehard Ruppert (Münster, 1985).

[73] For Roman law usage, cf. Dig. 41.3.1 and Dig. 9.2.51.2, for example. The decretal of Leo I in the *Decretum*, C.25 q.1 c.3: "Que ad perpetuam generaliter ordinata sunt utilitatem nulla conmutatione varientur, nec ad priuatum trahantur commodum que ad bonum sunt conmune prefixa . . ."

[74] De Lagarde, 2:13–15.

Ghent explored the complex philosophical issues which this principle evoked.[75]

In the writings of the council fathers it is seldom possible to determine to what degree their use of the concept presupposed a familiarity with such philosophical complexities. Generally they argued more on the basis of historical example or practical experience. Thus they claimed that the tyranny of the Roman Empire had brought its downfall,[76] they pointed out the injury to the common good which had resulted from the failure to hold provincial councils,[77] and they invoked the experience of cities which had learned that they must often let one house burn in order to save the entire city's good.[78] And further, they used the argument of the common good to support specific reform demands. The above example of letting one house burn for the common good of the town was cited by Henricus Abendon in the context of an argument for the revocation of exemptions. He contended that though the individuals who had benefited from the exemptions would be injured by their revocation, the common good of all would be served thereby. Similarly reformers argued against dispensations for age and other qualifications in appointees to ecclesiastical offices on the grounds that the good of the churches rather than that of private persons should be considered first.[79]

In their arguments the reformers cited the common good interchangeably with other similar arguments, some of them of more specifically Christian origin. The pope or prelate who placed his

---

[75] *Ibid.*, 175f.; for St. Thomas' position, cf. Eschmann, "A Thomistic Glossary," and id., "Bonum commune melius est quam bonum unius," *Mediaeval Studies* 6 (1944) 62–120.

[76] Dietrich of Niem, *Avisamenta*, ACC.4.612: "Preterea non est obmittendum, verbi gracia, quamdiu veteres Romani more regio bonum commune fideliter procurarunt, per eorum studium Romana res publica adaucta et conservata est. Set quia post hoc plurimi eorum in subditos quidem tiranni, ad hostes vero facti desides et imbelles, Romanam rem publicam ad nichilum redigerunt."

[77] *Ibid.*, 609, Gloss*: "Numquid salubrius est, quod sic fiat et reparetur templum Domini in hoc tamdiu neglectum, quam sic turpiter et negligenter torpere in preiudicium animarum et boni communis etc."

[78] Henricus Abendon, Sermon, October 27, 1415, W.1.2.193–194: "Videmus enim ex lege ciuium, quod facta valida combustione in ciuitate aliqua, domus quandoque proxima deiicitur funditus, vt cesset incendium et saluetur ciuitas."

[79] Dietrich of Niem, *Avisamenta*, ACC.4.610. After demanding that bishops and other prelates who had not yet taken orders do so within one year, Dietrich added: "Quod si non fecerint, quomodocunque sedes ipse propterea vacent eo ipso et non promoti omni iure sibi competenti in eisdem sedibus eo ipso sint privati, ab eis nulla obtenta et forsan in futurum per eos super hoc impetranda dispensacione papali in aliquo suffragante, quia in talibus providendum est ecclesiis et non personis."

own private good above the common good was compared to the shepherd who cared more about himself than his sheep, or to the wolf who sought to enter the sheepfold by violence and devour the sheep.[80] Dietrich Kolde reminded the fathers that although the gifts of the Holy Spirit were given to individuals, they were given for the good of all.[81] We have discussed these arguments in the context of preferring the good of the whole body to that of any of its members; proponents of these arguments found support in the injunction of Christ to cast aside any member of the body which caused scandal to the whole body.[82]

The common good is also often referred to as the good of the *respublica*.[83] One tract called upon the rival popes to follow the example of Christ, and like a good soldier not avoid giving up their lives for the republic.[84] One of the council's decrees gave the participants at the council the right to collect the revenues of their benefices *in absentia* since they were "absent for the sake of the republic." Zabarella spoke often of the *respublica* and regarded the cardinals as the *senatus* of the *respublica*. The frequent use of this term by Italian council fathers probably reflects the medieval political experience of the Italian city-republics, above all Florence (Zabarella was the Cardinal of Florence).[85] A more frequent synonym for the *bonum commune* among the other council fathers was the *status ecclesiae*.

5. Hierarchy and collegiality combined:
The status generalis ecclesiae

Alongside the rich concreteness of the body image, the term *status* seems pale and abstract. Yet the great strength of this term was its abstractness, its generality, and above all its multivalence. The

---

[80] Peter of Brussels, Sermon, March 25 (year not known) H.1.857. Immediately following his definition of tyranny cited in note 3 above, Peter added: Tales sunt pastores, qui non pascunt gregem domini sed semetipsos."
[81] Dietrich Kolde, Sermon, July 4, 1415, W.1.2.87: "Et saepe contingit, quod uni soli datur aliquod tale donum ad vtilitatem omnium."
[82] Henricus Abendon, Sermon, October 27, 1415, W.1.2.193–194: "Sic enim pes laeditur, vt totum corpus sanetur"; see above, pp.223–224.
[83] See above, p. 76.
[84] Mansi 27:553: "tenetur non euitare mortem pro republica"; the statement is found in manuscripts of Fillastre, dated January 30, 1415. Probably Fillastre himself was the author; see ACC.3.7 and 81.
[85] See David Peterson, "Conciliarism, Republicanism, and Corporatism: The 1415–1420 Constitution of the Florentine Clergy," *Renaissance Quarterly* 42 (1989) 183–226.

same word was used regularly and fully interchangeably to mean government, constitution, welfare, common good, way of life, status, and estate (in both the sense of hierarchical rank and of social-occupational group). The modern concept of the State in French, German, English, and Italian vernacular grew out of a long and complicated historical evolution which involved interplay of all these meanings.[86]

The political meanings are the ones which seem most immediately relevant to the idea of reform in head and members. These meanings have also captured the most interest of scholars. Gaines Post and Yves Congar have shed much light on these in both secular political theory and ecclesiology of the later Middle Ages. *Status* had been used in classical times, especially by Cicero to mean government, in the phrase *status reipublicae* and alone simply as *status*. The Middle Ages took over this usage and applied it to kingdoms, talking both about the *status regis* and the *status regni*. In all this, there was no clear distinction between the rulers and the ruled. If the government of the ruler in the sense of lordship were to be stressed the word *dominium* would be used. Whatever extreme papalists might have said in the fourteenth century, at the Council of Constance there was general agreement that the pope did not exercise this kind of dominion over the church; rather he was the chief minister. *Status* could even be used to talk about a form of government, such as monarchy or oligarchy, although *politeia* was a more likely word for this purpose.[87] Post has shown that *status* could be used alternately to refer to the governing authorities or to the common weal (*status, id est magistratus* or *status, id est utilitas publica*).[88]

The special development of this concept within the church has been illuminated by Congar. He demonstrates that the term *status ecclesiae*, though used interchangeably with the common good as a criterion for judging the papal government of the church, was also used as a basis for asserting and extending that power. Papal dispensations could be justified, for example, on the basis of the common good or *status ecclesiae*.[89] Congar traced the development of

[86] For a general overview see the article by Reinhart Koselleck, "Staat und Souveränität," in *Geschichtliche Grundbegriffe*, 6 (Stuttgart, 1990), 1–154 and the literature cited there.

[87] See Yves Congar, "Status ecclesiae," *Studia gratiana*, 15 (1972), 3–31 at 29.

[88] Gaines Post, *Studies in Medieval Legal Thought* (Princeton, 1964), 379f.; see also Paul-Ludwig Weinacht, *Staat: Studien zur Bedeutungsgeschichte des Wortes von den Anfängen bis ins 19. Jahrhundert* (Berlin, 1968), 58 (who cites Post) and Tierney, *Foundations*, 50f.; also J. Hackett, "State of the Church: A Concept of the Medieval Canonists," *The Jurist*, 23 (1963), 259–290 and Congar, "Status ecclesiae," 3f.

[89] Congar, "Status ecclesiae," 30–31 ; see also Post, 264, n.49.

the term *status ecclesiae* through several changes of meaning.[90] It
meant successively 1) ideal state or condition of health; 2) actual
condition, concrete situation; 3) structure or order of public powers. He felt that the decisive changes of meaning from 1) to 2) and
from 2) to 3) both took place during the course of the thirteenth
century. I would stress that none of the meanings was lost; they
continued to coexist, and we observe them all at the Council of
Constance.

When *status ecclesie* is used as a criterion for limiting papal power,
for example in the teaching that the pope could not grant dispensations against the decrees of the first four Ecumenical Councils, it
has the meaning of "constitution" or "fundamental structure or
nature" of the church. I will examine this meaning further below in
the context of specific usage at Constance.

Alongside and interacting with these political meanings of *status*
are a set of social meanings which Congar and Post did not system-
atically investigate. *Status* was used in the fifteenth century to
refer to any group which shared a common condition and was often
so used by reformers to refer to the reformation of various groups.
This sense of the word parallels the meaning of the equivalent
vernacular words—*estate, état, Stat* (or *Stant* or *Stand*). The concept
of estates in society at large has undergone intense research.[91]
However, I know of no systematic study of the use of the word *status*
in the sense of estates in the church. Most of what has been written
on this matter has been part of wider studies of hierarchical order in

---

[90] Congar, "Status," 7–22; cf. also Hackett, 260–290; Eschmann, 5, 65–76;
and J. Brys, *De dispensatione in iure canonico* (Bruges, 1925).
[91] For the best survey of research and literature see the article Rudolf Walther
"Stand, Klasse," in *Geschichtliche Grundbegriffe*, 6 (Stuttgart, 1990), 155–284, especially parts I–VI, by Otto Oexle (158–200). For English estate literature, see
especially Ruth Mohl, *The Three Estates in Medieval and Renaissance Literature* (New
York, 1933; repr. 1962) and Jill Mann, *Chaucer and Medieval Estates Satire: The
Literature of Social Classes and the General Prologue to the Canterbury Tales* (Cambridge,
1973). For French estate literature, the leading expert is Jean Batany, but his thèse
d'état, *Les Origines et la Formation du thème des "états du monde"* (Paris, Sorbonne,
1979) still exists only in typescript; see his article "États du monde (revues de)" in
the *Dictionnaire des Littératures de la Langue Française*, ed. J.–P. Beaumarchais, *et al.*
(Paris, 1984) 774–775. For the eleventh and twelfth centuries, when the fundamental idea was one of orders rather than estates, the fundamental work is
Georges Duby, *Les Trois Ordres ou l'Imaginaire du féodalisme* (Paris, 1978). For
German estate literature, see especially Wolfgang Heinemann, "Zur Ständedidaxe
in der deutschen Literatur des 13.–15. Jahrhunderts I–III," *Beiträge zur Geschichte
der deutschen Sprache und Literatur* 88 (1967) 1–90; 89 (1967) 290–403; and 92 (1970)
388–437; on the uses of the word *Stat-Stant* in the sense of estate, see Weinacht,
Staat (as in n. 86 above). See also especially the studies of Pierre Michaud-
Quantin, *Études sur le vocabulaire philosophique du moyen âge* (Rome, 1971).

the church. Several excellent studies exist here,[92] but they have
focused on earlier periods. Most of the ecclesiastical studies have
also paid relatively little attention to the vernacular estate literature, which was influenced by ecclesiastical ideas concerning
estates (Indeed, the vernacular estate literature may have grown
out of the *Sermones ad status* of twelfth-century preachers.) To do so
is important because there are illuminating parallels, which in
some cases may even be the result of a complementary influence of
the vernacular ideas on the ecclesiastical conceptions. I believe that
such a systematic study of the idea of estate in the church (starting
with a close contextual study of the changes in the use of the word
status in this sense) will shed much light on wider questions of
political and social theory as well as on evolving ideas of hierarchy
in the church. My own study here cannot address these wider
questions; it must of necessity be limited to the concept of estate in
the Constance reforms themselves.

It was a central concept there, and it differed significantly from
earlier ideas of hierarchy. The word *status* does have a hierarchical
sense, but it is less univocally hierarchical than other terms such as
gradus, dignitas, ordo or *praeeminentia*.[93] It stands between them and
the not specifically hierarchical *conditio*, which is often used as a
synonym for *status*.[94] All six of these words appear frequently in
various combinations in legal formulas which state the universal
applicability of laws to all persons regardless of their *status*. In this
sense the equivalent vernacular word Stat was taken over into
charters in Germany, where it represents one of the earliest vernacular uses of this word.[95] It appears first in urban documents of
the 14th century, and in the imperial chancery under Sigismund in
1437 (the latter timing may reflect a direct influence of the usage at
the councils.)

Because it was not univocally hierarchical, *status* was a convenient term to refer to groups such as monks, friars, and laymen,

---

[92] See the studies of Congar and Fasolt cited above; see also Luise Manz, *Der
Ordo-Gedanke: Ein Beitrag zur Frage des mittelalterliche Ständesgedankens* (Stuttgart/
Berlin, 1937).

[93] On the development of the use of this word in the *sermones ad status* to refer to
different social groups, see Michaud-Quantin, *Vocabulaire*, 180–184; he says that,
used in this sense, it is a new word, which had no place in the ancient world or
even the early Middle Ages. It carries an idea of stability and refers above all to
the functions of the groups, their roles in the *corps social* (Michaud-Quantin
underlines its connection with the corporate imagery); finally he observes that
status in this sense connotes the common good much more than hierarchy.

[94] *Ibid.*, 41–47; in its earliest usage to describe a social condition, however,
conditio referred to the specific condition of a slave.

[95] Weinacht, 72–74.

who did not fit neatly into the hierarchy. In this sense it referred more to a "way of life" than to a rank in society.

Its hierarchical sense, however, meant that it could often be used to mean "a high status." Probably it was this usage that gave rise to one of the most frequent meanings of the word at the council: the expense needed to maintain a level of wealth and display that was appropriate to a high status. Thus it could refer to the pomp and ceremony of a cardinal's court. As applied to an individual rather than a group, this *status* becomes the possession of the prestige which can be further increased by acquisition of further offices, honors, and revenues. It is in this sense that Kaminsky speaks of it as one the principal preoccupations of prelates like Simon de Cramaud.[96]

The persons of a *status* shared the same condition; they thus had similar interests which they were often called upon to defend. Thus, traditional arguments of self-definition and self-justification for each *status* had been developed, especially to defend its rights with regard to other *status*. In much of the vernacular estate literature, there is a strong sense of struggle among the estates; it appears most strongly in the *Quadriloge invective* of Alain Chartier, where the estates hurl mutual recriminations at each other.[97] In the English estate literature, the convenient rhyme of *estat* and *debat* is used often to stress the confrontations among estates. At Constance the struggle forms a strong undercurrent in the reform deliberations. It sometimes surfaces, most notably perhaps in the decision of the French nation in the midst of their heated annate debate to appoint a committee with one member from each major *status* to discuss the reforms.[98]

6. Uses of the word status *in the reform committee deliberations*

In the reforms considered by the reform committee at Constance, most of the above meanings of the world *status* appear, and in several cases the usage either combines or falls between two of the different meanings. By far the most frequent appearance of the term

---

[96] Howard Kaminsky, *Simon de Cramaud and the Great Schism* (New Brunswick, N.J., 1983), 66–68.

[97] Alain Chartier, *Quadriloge invectif,* ed. E. Droz, 2d ed. (Paris, 1960).

[98] *Thesaurus,* 2:1552,1553,1560: "Quod super hoc deputentur de quolibet statu duo, videlicet de Episcopali, Abbatiali, Capitulorum, et Rectorum, qui cum Deputatis per DD. Cardinales tractent et concordent de modo providendi D.N. Papae et Cardinalibus." On this, see Stump, "Taxation," 90.

is as a synonym for rank or dignity in the formulas enumerating the groups to which a measure applies; usually the effect is to show that no matter how high one's rank he is subject to the measure's sanctions. In this sense *status* is clearly the possession of an individual, and in some cases the reform calls for the possible removal of this status from the individual. *Si vero* (Common, c.1a) says the cardinals will be deprived of their dignity, honor, and *status* if they proceed to a double election, and they will be considered unfit to hold such *status* in the future. Gerson's distinction between papal power considered absolutely, and papal power as held by this or that individual is closely related; it has often been described as a distinction between person and office, but could equally be seen as a distinction between person and *status*. At about this same time Gerson also made a similar distinction in secular government between the *vita personalis* of the king and his *vita civilis*.[99]

The reform concerning expectancies (Common, c.36, para. 6) says that those with the earliest dates are to be granted to people according to their merits and *status*; here *status* may well refer to ranks in secular society. On the other hand, when Common, c.6 (para.21) calls for ordinands to be examined especially concerning their *status*, it probably means less their rank in society than their way of life (in particular its celibate nature or lack thereof). Thus *status* can be a way of living that is observed in a certain group. When Job Vener's *avisamentum* (D², c.7) talks about the lamentable *status* of the bishops we realize from the qualifiers *modernus* and *in aliquibus partibus* that Vener is talking about the way some members of the episcopate are living. Thus, those who temporarily share a certain condition can form a *status*. For example, in *Quia a longis temporibus* (Common, c.30) it is those who have received their orders with taint of simony; the council will provide concerning them and their *status*. It can be seen that in all these senses the meaning of the word is very fluid, referring interchangeably to hierarchical rank in church or society, to ways of life, and even to temporary conditions shared by a group.

The word is also applied to the government of the church, or its constitution. The classic use of the word in this sense was in canonistic corporation theory, where a bishop was forbidden to take actions which affected the *status* of his church without the consent of the chapter. Thus we shall not be surprised to find the word turn up in *Cum antiqui* (Common, c.2a) in the general definition of those papal actions which require approval of the cardinals.

---

[99] See Koselleck, 9 and n.15.

A preliminary draft of *Frequens* (W², c.12) expresses the desire to
provide for the status of the universal church in the sense of its
welfare or health, but it interestingly replaces the expected *statui
ecclesie* with *statui ecclesiastico multitudinique fidelium*. This may well
represent a transition toward the two *status*, lay and clerical, of the
later Gravamina movement.

The idea of providing for the *status ecclesie* in the sense of welfare
reflects a more ameliorative conception of reform, whereas that of
conserving the *status ecclesie* in the sense of its constitution represents
a more restorative conception. *Status* is also used in both senses in
the Constance reform deliberations to refer to reforms concerning
particular churches and monasteries; in both examples the two
meanings are combined. The first (Common, c.42) attacks the poor
administrators of monasteries, who do not conserve them in their
being and status (*esse et status*), but squander their rights and
possessions. Both the monastery's constitution and its welfare are
meant here. The other measure (V, c.24) calls for conserving and
directing the *statum* and *immunitatem* of ecclesiastical persons and of
ecclesiastical goods and property. The pairing of *status* and *immuni-
tas* is significant. The goods, properties, rights, and immunities of a
church or monastery were all part of its fundamental nature or
constitution. Often they were established by a real or putative act,
even a charter of foundation. There is thus here a curious connection with later constitutionalism. One of the earliest uses of *Stat* in
the German vernacular in this sense of "constitution" was in fact
found in the description of the mutation of the *Stat* of the Benedictine abbey of Ellwangen into a secular collegiate church.[100]

This use of the word *status* to refer to the constitution of particular churches sheds light on the ways in which conciliar reformers
may have understood the *status* of the universal church. The founder of the universal church was Christ. Many conciliar reformers
regarded not only the four gospels but also the *statuta* of the first
four ecumenical councils as tantamount to a foundation charter for
the church; in doing so they were building on the long tradition
traced by Congar. Earlier writers had even used the words *status
generalis* and *statutum generale* interchangeably when referring to the
statutes of the first four councils.[101]

---

[100] Weinacht, 102. Ironically, this was the same monastery that Siegfried
Gerlacher had tried so hard to reform (see above, p. 153); the conversion to a
secular institution was the final result of his inability to overcome the noble monks'
resistance to reform.

[101] See Tierney, *Foundations*, 50f.; Post, *Studies*, 140ff.; and Congar, "Status
ecclesiae."

7. Status *and reform in the other conciliar documents*

The patterns we observed above are those which recur in the sermons, tracts, and official acta of the council. Additionally we find in these documents more frequent reference to the *status* collectively, i.e., to reform of all the *status* and to the relationships among the *status*. We will also observe frequent explicit and implicit connections with corporate imagery.

The reformers called for all the *status* to be reduced to their due *status*.[102] In other words, they clearly saw the inherent conflict between the widespread pursuit of *status*, as Kaminsky describes it,[103] and the idea of *status* as the honor and wealth appropriate to a given rank. This conflict is evident in the abundant sumptuary legislation enacted by secular governments in the later Middle Ages. In a similar sense the Augustinian hermit Dietrich Vrie rebuked the clergy for not wearing clothing suitable to its *status*.[104]

In the frequent references to reforms of the *status* of the pope and the Roman church, the ambiguity of the word does not always make it possible to determine whether the word means "wealth and display," "government," or simply "hierarchical rank." The suggestion that the rival popes of the Schism be induced to resign by guaranteeing them, among other things, a "notable and secure *status* in the church"[105] clearly falls under the first sense. An anonymous mendicant preacher cleverly plays on the ambiguity between the first and second meanings in his felicitous demand that "the Roman church so temper (*temperare*) its *status* by reason that faithful Christians can reasonably obey it (*ei obtemperare*) and be under its rule (*regimine*)."[106] Opponents of annates and services saw these taxes being used to support exorbitant standards of living in the *curia*. On the other hand, supporters of these taxes argued that the

---

[102] See the anonymous sermon, 1417 (?), Schneyer, 125: "omnes status clericorum effectualiter reformetis et ad debitum reducere statum." See also Theobald of Saxony, Sermon, August 23, 1416, H.1.859: "Oportet quemlibet facere, quae ad suum pertinent statum."

[103] See above, p. 256 and n. 96.

[104] Sermon of Dietrich Vrie, preached June 24, 1416 (or 1417), ed. Adolar Zumkeller, "Unbekannte Konstanzer Konzilspredigten des Augustiner-Theologen Gottfried Schale und Dietrich Vrie," *Analecta Augustiniana* 33 (1970) 5–74 at 72: "Per hoc reprehenduntur, qui portant vestes eis non competentes secundum status suos vel in scissura vel in colore."

[105] Anon. proposal, ACC.3.80: "eidem provideretur de notabili et securo statu . . ."

[106] Anonymous sermon, September 15, 1415, W.1.2.157: "ut Romana ecclesia suum statum sic ratione temperare studeat, ut ei rationabiliter obtemperare et suo regimini subesse Christi fideles possint."

members would only harm themselves in the long run by dimi-
nishing the *status* of the head.[107] The church needed an imposing
head in order to protect against the depredations of the secular
powers. Here again we see curialists using corporate imagery.
According to natural reason, they argued, in all bodies the members come to the aid of the head. And they cited a letter of
Ps.-Symmachus found in Gratian which declared that the pope had
been designated head of the whole body by Christ. The words of
the prophet Isaiah (10,3) seemed to speak of the dignity of this
head, observed Symmachus, when they said "If it is humiliated, to
whom will you flee for refuge? And where will you abandon your
glory?"[108] Ironically, this is precisely the canon (C.9 q.3 c.14
Aliorum) whose gloss was cited in *Romanus pontifex* to prove that the
pope, because of his exalted position, is to be punished all the more
severely if he falls.

The word *status* is used often to refer to reform of the universal
church in both the restorative and the ameliorative senses discussed above (restoring the constitution, improving the welfare, etc.).
The restorative senses generally outweigh the ameliorative ones
when *status* is used for the universal church. The term appears
especially often in the idea of maintaining the established hierarchical order against threats of upheaval. The corrective verbs *ser-
vare* and *conservare* are set against the disruptive verbs *turbare* and
confundere, and it is the *exorbitantia*, especially of papal power, that
are cited as causes of the upheaval. Sometimes *status ecclesiae*
appears metonymically for the phrase "reform in head and members" itself. In this case it has an ameliorative sense as well. We
find this ameliorative usage also in several authors, most notably

---

[107] Curial arguments cited by the anonymous author of Annate tract A (See
chapter 7, p. 176), Augsburg, p. 400 (Paris, fol. 367v): "Item membra subuenire
debent suo capiti ratio naturalis s. ymo et ipse instinctus etiam ex inopinatino
impetu et etiam in brutis hoc demonstratur in aperto. Igitur et nos pape et ratione
ecclesie que sunt aliarum ecclesiarum capud xxii di. c. Sacrosancta Romana [D.22
c.2]. Item ista ratio magis uiget quando subuentio que sit capitis tendit de directo
ad fomentum membrorum quia tunc talis conseruatio redundat in ipsosmet sub-
uenientes et membra. Si enim status pape non sit magnificus et presertim hiis
diebus habens (?) magis reueretur et timetur ecclesia et pro communis omnes uiri
ecclesiastici cum presidens in ea et eius status est magnificus quo stante sic
protegit et tuetur membra ab emulorum uiolentiis et iacturis et in hac ratione
fundatur tex. ix q. iii. c. Aliorum [C.9 q.3 c.14] nisi ubi dicitur ad litteram loquens
de ecclesia rationa si hoc humiliatur ad cuius fugietis auxilium et ubi reliquetis
gloriam uestram."
[108] In fact, the quote was taken out of context from Isaiah; the first four words
do not appear in the original text, which concerns divine retribution for statutes of
the Israelite authorities which oppress the poor.

Dietrich of Niem, whose reform terminology is otherwise overwhelmingly restorative. In general councils, "very useful things are always decreed and ordained for the good *status* of the universal church," observes Dietrich.[109]

Almost all the uses of the term *status* discussed so far were fairly traditional ones. The newer and more interesting uses at Constance were those which referred to the reform of the *status*, i.e., the estates. In the *Capitula agendorum* and D'Ailly's *Canones reformationis*, the estates of the church pass in review before the reader; the abuses in each are catalogued and remedies for appropriate reform suggested.[110] Such was precisely the format in which vernacular estate literature usually dealt with the "estates of the world." In the secular society of the time, just as in the church, there was not yet a fixed number of three estates. There were four estates in Philippe de Mézière's *Songe du vieil Pélerin*, "twelve estates which govern" in the *Lay des douze estas*, a full one hundred estates in the most elaborate of the estate satires, *Des Teufels Netz*.[111] The last named work, though anonymous, was probably written by a Beghard in the region of Einsiedeln in the time of the Council of Basel, and is especially fascinating in that the highest estate named is the general council, placed above the pope. But for this satirist, the council was also the greatest sinner![112] The four estate schema of Philippe de Mézières is also interesting because the additional estate there is formed by the inchoate *noblesse de robe*—the lawyers and officers of the king. It corresponds remarkably well in fact to the group which George Huppert has identified as *bourgeois gentilhommes* in this period.[113] This was probably the main group behind the *gallicanisme parlementaire* which sometimes agreed with but also sometimes

---

[109] See Chapter 8, n. 61. In another example, he asks that simony be eliminated by the conciliar deliberations and that "alia fiant instanter pro bono et salubri statu ipsius [ecclesie] quomodolibet oportuna." ACC.3.122 (reform pamphlet from February 21– 27, 1415).

[110] ACC.4.558–561 (*Capitula agendorum*; here the word is used more in the sense of condition). In the rubrics and text of his *Tractatus de reformatione* (ed. H.1.409f.), D'Ailly spoke of the *status papalis, status episcopalis, status religiosorum, status inferiorum ecclesiarum et ecclesiasticaorum virorum* and the *status laicorum*.

[111] Eustache Deschamps, "Le lay des douze estas du monde," *Oeuvres complètes* (Paris, 1880) 2:226f.; Philippe de Mézières, *Le songe du vieil pélerin*, ed. G.W. Coopland (Cambridge, Mass., 1969); *Des Teufels Netz*, ed. K.A. Barack (Stuttgart, 1863).

[112] *Teufels Netz*, 93–98: "So das hopt is krank und bloed/ Soltent denn die glider nit sin oed?/ Das concilium wil sich nit reformieren."

[113] See George Huppert, *Les Bourgeois Gentilhommes: An Essay on Development of Elites in Renaissance France* (Chicago, 1977).

clashed with the position of the other university graduates among the clergy in the realm of France.

The vernacular literature often represented the various estates as part of the body politic, underlining the way in which terminology of estates jibed with corporate imagery and with political thought. Gérard du Puy's sermon noted above (p. 240) was really estate literature, an exact parallel to its vernacular counterparts. Indeed, it may well have been influenced by one of the greatest works of estate literature, the *Livre du Corps de Policie* of Christine de Pizan, composed between 1406 and 1409.[114] Christine and her writings were well known in the French court, especially to Gerson, who supported her in her attack on the *Roman de la Rose*.[115]

The estate terminology at Constance paralleled very well the imagery of corporate reform at the council—a general reform in head and members. Again and again the reformers called for the reform of all the estates, especially the self-reform of the estates.[116] Peter Pulka punned on the root meaning of the word *status* (to stand) when he lamented that the whole ecclesiastical order lay fallen (*collapsus*) from its *status*, and all ecclesiastical discipline languished.[117] The same ironic juxtaposition of standing and reclining appears a few years later in the vernacular estate satire of Alain Chartier.[118] We saw above how the estate terminology could be used along with the corporate imagery to support a hierarchical view of the church. It could lend itself also to the horizontal theme of the common good, the public utility. Dietrich Vrie called upon

---

[114] Christine de Pisan, *Le livre du corps de policie*, ed. R.H. Lucas (Geneva-Paris, 1967).

[115] See Charity Cannon Willard, *Christine de Pizan: Her Life and Work* (New York, 1984), 78–89, 156.

[116] See, among many examples, Dietrich Kolde, Sermon, April 5, 1416, W.1.3.177–178: "Si quilibet status in ecclesia vellet suos defectus recognoscere veraciter . . . ac etiam ad suam reformationem se inclinare . . ."; and Johannes Rocha, Sermon, September 29, 1415, Stuttgart, Landesbibl. Cod. theol. et phil. 50, fol. 57 (with alternate readings from Karlsruhe, Landesbibl. Rei 23, fol. 83r): "Ex prima conclusione sequitur quod de quolibet statu illi qui nouerunt speculatiue etsi non pratice deformitates suorum statuum de necessitate congrua sunt uocandi. Non enim cecus de coloribus potest iudicare . . ."

[117] Peter Pulka, Sermon, Nov/Dec 1414, Vienna lat. 4300, fol. 197r-199v at 198r: "Mundus iste peruenit, deuoluitur ut non sola cuiuslibet siue secularis siue ecclesiastice ordo a suo statu collapsus iaceat, sed etiam ipsa ecclesiastica disciplina solotenus ut ita dixerim reclinata ab assueta illa celsitudinis sue auctoritate languescat . . ."; see also Jacobus de Camplo, Sermon, August 15, 1416, ACC.2.460: "ac eciam de reformacione ecclesie et turpissimus moribus ecclesiasticorum severius arguendis, quoniam in omni statu, gradu et ordine lapsa est, proch dolor, omnis ecclesiastica disciplina . . ."

[118] Chartier, 10.

each estate not to exceed its *status* by ambition and self-interest; it should seek not so much to dominate (*praeesse*) as to be useful (*prodesse*).[119] When the council fathers argued in defense of their rights and position in the church, they did not see themselves as pursuing their own self-interest. Rather they thought of themselves as defending the interest of their *status*, and only insofar as not to conflict with the public utility.

In the church, however, the concept of utility was still intimately bound with the idea of brotherly love, especially because of the evangelical and Pauline teaching concerning the *scandalum*, which had been taken over into the canonistic *opinio communis* concerning the exercise of power in the church. The "quia expedit" was the criterion of love. This love was often seen in the context of hierarchy, but into that concept of hierarchy in both the gospel and the Pauline letters was built the fundamental paradox discussed above. The master is minister in the gospel; and in the Pauline teaching the lower members of the body receive the greater honor.[120] The paradoxical nature of this hierarchy was often forgotten in the church. However, the preachers at Constance did often called for harmony and mutual love among the estates. An anonymous Premonstratensian preacher called for love among the *status*, since they are members of one mystical body. "Nor should member oppress member; nor *status statum*. But whatever is in them to be corrected, let the abuse be removed and let the *status* be preserved, with love of men and hatred of vices."[121]

8. Corpus, *corporations, and representation*

Canon and civil law dealing with corporations provided some conceptual models for the reformers. It allowed them to imagine the church working together as an individual, and invited them to consider the common good of the whole; moreover it permitted

---

[119] Dietrich Vrie, in Zumkeller, "Konzilspredigten," (see above, n. 104), 66: "Videant ergo dominationes vestrae, quatenus notabilis in omni statu fiat reformatio, ut promoveantur, qui prodesse possint et non tantum praeesse, qui sint iusti servantes aequalitatem, qui sint viri 'prudentes sicut serpentes et simplices sicut columbae.' [Matt. 10,16] Alias enim, quanto clerus exaltatus fuerit, tanto in imum deprimetur."

[120] On these ideas see Yves Congar, *Power and Poverty in the Church* (Baltimore, 1964).

[121] Anon. Sermon, February 2, 1416, *W*.1.2.209–232 at 231: "Nec [membrum] membrum deprimat, nec status statum; sed quod in eis corrigendum fuerit, tollatur abusus et seruetur status, cum dilectione hominum et odio vitiorum. . . ."

visualization of the distinction between the whole church conceived distributively and collectively. This latter distinction was of fundamental importance in establishing that the pope, although superior to each individual member, could be subject to the judgment of the council because the council represented the universal church.

Yet few reformers seem to have imagined the council as a corporation. The cardinals did of course emphatically regard the Roman church as a corporation whose head was the pope, and they associated the Roman church with the universal church, but in practice they imagined themselves and not the council as the members of corporation. The closest the reformers came to imagining the council as a corporation was in the alternate version of the additions made to the papal oath in *Quia decet*. This would have required the pope to obtain consent of the council, rather than the Sacred College, before taking action in weighty matters.[122] This measure was abandoned, probably not because the council fathers had difficulty with it conceptually, but because of the unwieldiness of requiring approval by a body which met at intervals of only ten years. Similar considerations undoubtedly resulted in the modification of the requirement of conciliar approval for all papal tenths.[123] It may well have been the princes who chiefly opposed this, since they were so often the ones who received the revenues from tenths levied by the pope. In the final decree the requirement for conciliar consent for tenths was replaced with the requirement for consent of the cardinals and of those prelates whose counsel could readily be obtained. This measure, however, applied only to universal tenths, whereas the vast majority of papal tenths were territorial ones. For territorial tenths the final decree require consent of the territorial clergy (and this strengthened the papal Responsio, which called only for consultation rather than consent). In this provision the decree treated the clergy of a territory or realm as a *de facto* corporation. It is interesting that the first appearance of this provision in the surviving records is found in the Instructions of the Gallican church, from which it entered the French Avisamenta.[124]

---

[122] See Chapter 5 above, pp. 125–127.

[123] For a fuller account of this matter see Stump, "Papal Taxation," 76–78.

[124] *COD*, 449: "Nec specialiter in aliquo regno vel provincia, inconsultis praelatis illius regni vel provinciae et ipsis non consentientibus, vel eorum maiori parte . . ." The wording in the French Avisamenta, taken almost verbatim from the *Instructions* called for tenths not to be levied "nisi in casu necessitatis et causa significata et racionabili, indicata seu approbata per prelatos vel maiorem partem ipsorum illius regni vel provincie, ubi indicetur . . ." The papal Responsio (Hüb-

The English prelates acted in a similar *de facto* manner as a corporation in a number of provisions in the English concordat in which commissions of ordinaries were to review papal actions and reject those that were scandalous.[125] The concordats themselves were the most striking example of the clergy of a region acting as a *de facto* corporation. However, none of these pragmatic experiments with corporate action appears to have been supported by arguments drawn from existing corporation theory.

Historians have shown the importance of corporation theory for the development of representative government and ideas of representation.[126] The idea of corporate representation had long been intertwined with the functioning of councils; according to the medieval understanding of councils the persons attending the council had full power to act on behalf of their churches (corporations) and to bind them to obey the decisions of the council. When the reformers spoke of the council representing the universal church, they undoubtedly understood it partly in this way. Another explanation was needed for the representative role of other significant groups at the council—university professors, representatives of secular princes, and individual curates, canons, monks, and friars—and for the special representative role of the cardinals. The explanation which would have agreed with the understanding of most council fathers was that expressed most succinctly by Gerson: The council represented the whole hierarchical order of the church with all its different estates and ranks. Those present who were not bishops or abbots were representing their *status*; however, *status* here emphatically did not mean a closed corporation in the sense of the later secular Estates.

The cardinals and the *doctores* represented the church in still further ways that were implicit in some of the most fundamental conceptions of the late Middle Ages. The cardinals represented the Roman church, which was often identified with the universal

---

ler, 157) had only "nec specialiter in aliquo regno vel provincia inconsultis praelatis illius regni vel provinciae."

[125] See above, Chapter 3, p. 71 and Chapter 6, pp. 145, 147.

[126] See Adalbert Podlech, "Repräsentation," in *Geschichtliche Grundbegriffe*, 5 (Stuttgart, 1984), 509– 549 and the literature cited there. See especially Hasso Hofmann's thorough study cited above; also Adolf Lumpe, "Zu repraesentare und praesentare im Sinne von 'rechtsgültig vertreten,'" *AHC* 6 (1974) 272–90.; and Werner Krämer, *Konsens und Rezeption: Verfassungsprinzipien der Kirche im Basler Konziliarismus* (Münster, 1980). The best overview of these complex developments in in Jeannine Quillet, "Universitas populi et représentation au XIVe siècle," in *Der Begriff der repraesentatio*, 186–201.

church. The pope acting alone could also represent the universal church, but the cardinals preferred to have him represent it collegially with them. The *doctores* represented the continuity of received interpretation of Scripture, *per modum doctrinae* alongside the *per modum auctoritatis* of the pope and episcopate. This representation was of particular importance because the consent of the universal church for conciliar decisions had ultimately to be confirmed by reception.[127] Medieval thinkers were not clear about how this reception was to be registered, but the large role of university graduates at late medieval councils may have been in part an effort to insure this reception.

We cannot probe further these important ideas, except insofar as they relate directly to reform at Constance. They are very directly related in one sense: The council claimed to represent the universal church in its power to correct the pope and in this manner to regulate the exercise of his *plenitudo potestatis*. The two main official documents which expressed this power were *Haec sancta* and *Romanus pontifex*.[128] In some ways *Romanus pontifex* should be read as an attempt implement the power of the council posited by *Haec sancta* in the area of reform. Both these documents base the corrective power of the council on the fact that it represents the universal church. The representation here is not that of consent based on corporation theory, but is rather representation of the sovereign power of the universal church to act as the agent of reform.

Whence came this power of the universal church? Different rationales existed. One was the power of the keys committed to the episcopate as successors of the apostles; this was not invoked by the decrees even implicitly, although many reformers surely understood it as a basis. *Haec sancta* did strongly invoke, however, the image of the body with the phrase *reformatio in capite et in membris*. This image evoked both the Body of Christ, which is identical with the church, and the metaphor of the natural body, which is superior to any of its individual members; here the body's right to self-preservation figured prominently.[129] *Romanus pontifex* evoked

---

[127] See Schüssler, 153–158; for ideas of reception at Basel, which were much more explicitly developed, see also Johannes Helmrath, *Das Basler Konzil, 1431–1449: Forschungsstand und Probleme* (Cologne, 1987), 475–77 and Werner Krämer, *Konsens und Rezeption: Verfassungsprinzipien der Kirche im Basler Konziliarismus* (Münster, 1980).

[128] See above, p. 131.

[129] See, for example, D'Ailly's statement, ACC.3.48 that it is silly to say that the authority of one member of the body is greater than that of the whole body ("Concilium presente papa a quo ipsum concilium uocatum est uelut unum

both senses when it referred to the acts of the pope which scandalize the church. In the gospel Jesus warned against those who caused scandals (stumbling blocks) for the faithful. He also told the disciples to remove from their bodies any member which caused scandal, so that their entire body might be saved. It was easy to transfer this teaching concerning the individual body to the body of the church.[130] An important school of canonistic theory came to treat scandalous acts of a pope as tantamount to heresy and therefore grounds for deposition of the pope by the council. This theory became intensely practical during the Schism, and was frequently reiterated during the early months of the council, culminating in the council's actions against the scandalous acts of John [XXIII]. *Haec sancta* was the most famous of those actions. In the discussions surrounding John's deposition, there was frequent reference to a pope who had become "incorrigible". This brings us to the principal justification for the corrective action of the universal church: the evangelical teaching concerning fraternal correction (See above, Chapter 5, p. 135). The point was that God exercises his judgments through the universal church.

In the council's discussion of the scandalous acts of John [XXIII] and Benedict XIII, the main focus fell on those acts which prolonged the schism, and particularly those acts of Benedict XIII in defiance of conciliar authority which prolonged the schism. These acts caused very real scandals for believers, in the most original sense of the word in the Gospels, the Pauline letters, and Saint Augustine. Most reformers believed strongly that the simony involved in papal provisions and taxes caused widespread and dangerous scandals in the same sense. *Romanus pontifex* was an effort to deal with those scandals.

It was only in these extreme cases when the reformers spoke explicitly of the council representing the universal church in the sense of sovereign agent of reform. This concept of representation needed to be made explicit in these cases in order to refute possible arguments based on canonistic teaching that the pope was immune

---

corpus mysticum cuius papa est caput et alii sunt membra. Et ideo secundum aliquos non solum falsum sed fatuum esset dicere quod maior sit auctoritas unius partis quam tocius corporis". See also the assertion of D'Ailly during the early days of the council that according to the teaching of natural law, the head is to be tied up by the other members if it goes mad and tyrannizes them: "Secundum dictamen iuris naturalis in quolibet corpore ligandum est caput, modis omnibus coercendum per membra cetera, si nitentur tyrannidem et rabiem exercere." ACC.3.58.

[130] See above, 223.

from human judgment. In other cases the other concept of representation discussed above prevailed (representation in the council of all hierarchical status, including the papal status). The reformers appear generally to have assumed that under normal circumstances the pope would work with the council, as presiding officer of the council, to bring about an ongoing general reform.[131] Although Martin V and the council did practice such cooperation during the final months of the council, the reformers did not develop any clear theoretical definitions of procedures to be followed in the cooperation. Individuals made numerous statements attempting to explain the role of papal power within a council. Brian Tierney has examined many of these and argued that they are conceptions of divided sovereignty.[132] Here I only add a few additional examples which focus on the interaction of papal and conciliar power in the area of reform.

The most striking is still that of Gerson cited in Chapter 7 in the context of reforms concerning simony. In dealing with simony, the council can make laws regulating papal actions "without any injury to the papal plenitude of power"; Gerson speaks of "harmonizing . . . the papal plenitude of power with the plenitude of power of the council."[133] Another French reformer, Gérard du Puy, reports the opinion of "some great men" that the "authority of the council is greater as far as the disposition and conclusion of the agenda, while the pope is greater as far as the execution and dispensation of those things which have been concluded."[134] Finally, a statement of

---

[131] Hofmann calls this "Mitregierung"; see *Repräsentation*, 280.
[132] Brian Tierney, "'Divided Sovereignty' at Constance: A Problem of Medieval and Early Modern Political Theory," *AHC* 7 (1975) 238–256.
[133] See above, Chapter 7, p. 203.
[134] Gérard du Puy, Sermon, March 11, 1415, ACC.2.406: "Audiui aliquos magnos viros et fortassis non minus bene dicentes quoad ordinacionem et conclusionem agendorum auctoritatem concilii maiorem, sed quoad execucionem et dispensacionem deliberatorum et conclusorum pape. Concilii enim generalis deliberacio, eciam si papa solus vel cum paucis eciam cardinalibus contradicat, est omnino tenenda et pape voluntati preferenda." The date of this statement, in the critical negotiations with John [XXIII] concerning his abdication, may help to explain its unusual specificity about power relationships between pope and council. It is interesting that du Puy also mentions discussions he has heard which clearly involve the application of corporation theory to the relationship between pope and council: "Ymmo multi asserunt in conciliis generalibus papam esse sicud episcopum particularis ecclesie. Aliqui autem dicunt, quod tamtam vim et auctoritatem habet vox pape in concilio generali, sicut episcopi vox in capitulo sue ecclesie, ubi de negociis arduis ecclesie agitur, quod effective est in idem reincidere." It is also interesting that he states the basic principle of *Haec sancta* several weeks before that document was drafted: "Firmissime autem tenendum est, quod quoad raciones heresis et scismatis et que universalem statum et reformacionem

an anonymous preacher draws together felicitously most of the themes in this chapter: "The reunion of the church is to renew the spirit of love in the holy mother church and its members; concerning this Cato said that 'Harmony nourishes love.' It is not enough for the renewal of this spirit of love that the individual members all recognize one unique vicar of Christ and obey him, but there must also be a most perfect and unanimous harmony between head and members, and of the members with each other, as in the *ecclesia primitiva*. . . . But, alas, experience has taught us how many discords and scandals have arisen from the head in the past. . . . It is necessary to quell these scandals, and it is apparent that this is the responsibility of this general council which represents the universal church."[135]

9. Conclusion

Just as the image of the body synthesized the hierarchical and collegial dimensions of reform, it offered possibilities for harmonizing the power of the pope and council in effecting that reform. The hierarchy involved was made far less rigid by associating the members with the different *status*, according to the very flexible early fifteenth century usage of the word *status*. The idea of *status* as the possession of an individual facilitated the separation of an incorrigible pope from his *status*, or, in corporate imagery, the removal of the *caput secundarium* from the church. The reformers envisioned reform as a cooperation between head and members under normal circumstances. But in the event of scandals originating from the head, the council itself could act as a sovereign agent of reform to reform even papal actions. This reform was primarily a restoration of order within the body, which would re-establish the harmony among the estates of the church.

---

ecclesie concernunt, maior est auctoritas concilii quam pape, et concilii, non pape deliberacioni in hiis obediendum est . . ."

[135] Anonymous sermon, March 29, 1416, Tübingen, Universitätsbibl., Mc 282 fol. 47v–48r: "Hoc est unio, que habet nutrire et renovare in corpore sancte matris ecclesie et eius membris spiritum caritatis, propter quod ait sapiens Cato, 'Concordia nutrit amorem.' Non sufficit itaque pro renouatione huiusmodi spiritum caritatis in ecclesia dei quod singula membra recognoscunt unicum uicarium Christi ei obediendo, sed opus est, quod inter huiusmodi membra et ipsum caput et membrorum inter se sit perfectissima et unanimis concordia quamadmodum in ecclesia primitiua. . . . Quante autem ex hoc capite nuper et alias in ecclesia dei exorte sint dissonantie et scandala satis et nimis proch dolor docuit experientia. . . . Necessarium est huiusmodi sedare scandala. Constat quod hoc spectat ad hoc presens generale concilium sanctam uniuersalem ecclesiam representans. . . ."

CONCLUSION

In this study I have chosen to stress the success of the conciliar reform efforts at Constance. I could have instead emphasized the failures, especially in the reform of the members, where the failure to achieve comprehensive reform was in part the result of the clergy's own lack of attention to the needs of the laity they served and of their unwillingness to deal with the obscene disproportions of wealth within the church. These failures had much wider repercussions, because they made conciliar reformers reluctant to expose curial abuses to the full light of reason for fear of also exposing their own abuses. The greatest single failure occurred in the area which most reformers regarded as central, the reform of provisions and taxation; here the council failed to arrive at a conceptual resolution concerning the nature of benefices and of annates and services, and it failed to assuage many consciences tainted with the guilt of simony.

These were failures to meet goals the reformers had set for themselves. Historians have often charged the reformers with failure to meet other goals which represent more nearly the conceptions of these historians than those of the reformers themselves. In this way the very real successes of the council in the area of reform have been downplayed or overlooked. My major thesis in this study has been that the reforms of the Council of Constance were much more successful than past historians have admitted. The council did successfully remove the worst fiscal abuses, and it achieved a compromise on papal provisions that went a good way toward redressing the rights of the ordinaries. It reformed the operation of the curia, limited the burgeoning number of officials, and reversed the practice of granting monasteries to cardinals in commendam. It enacted effective reforms of exemptions and incorporations. And it fostered reforms in the Franciscan and Benedictine orders which formed watersheds in their development.

More important than all these practical results, however, was the success of the council in developing a conception of conciliar reform and putting that conception into practice through truly collegial deliberation. The concept of continuous conciliar reform defined above all by *Frequens* and *Quanto Romanus* realized the vision of William Durant the Younger of a reform that would hold up the actions of the papacy to the standard of universal reason embodied in the council. Such a concept avoided the temptation to which William ultimately succumbed of conceiving reform as the integral restoration of ancient law. Moreover, it forged a working conceptual relationship between the pope and council in legislating and executing reforms, one which Martin V and the council practiced with considerable success in the deliberations that led to the final decrees and concordats. Far from being failures, the concordats were striking successes in the effort to take account of regional differences in the enactment of universal reform. The reformers' implementation of the concept of conciliar reform enabled them to bridge many gaps between competing reform conceptions — between the local and universal, the papal and conciliar, the canonistic and theological, the restorative and ameliorative, the hierarchical and republican, and the oligarchic and episcopalist.

This conception of conciliar reform forged at Constance was profoundly different from the reform ideas which Haller posited as the dominant ones in the fifteenth century. Hübler's characterization of the Constance reform ideas was much closer to the historical reality than Haller's. However, Hübler had little inkling of how deep a foundation for the concept of conciliar reform lay in the orthodox canonistic and theological theories of the period. Challenged by the scandals of the Schism, the Constance reformers put these theories into practice. Hübler also underestimated the depth of commitment of the Constance reformers to a real reform of the members. Conciliar reform envisioned a continuous, ongoing reform of both head and members. The truth is that Hübler himself was not much interested in the reforms of the members.

Most of my chapters have begun with criticisms of Hübler's model. However, I want to say here strongly that much of Hübler's analysis remains still valid after well over a century. My book is intended as a supplement to, rather than a replacement of Hübler's study. I have interacted chiefly with Hübler's model rather than Haller's because I find much of Haller's analysis is irrelevant to the central concepts of reform at Constance.

Not suprisingly, Haller's model is most helpful in understanding the conceptions and actions of the reformers I have called "Gallicans." We cannot simply call them "French" reformers, because their conceptions prevailed only within the borders of the kingdom of France. Even there, these conceptions were less a common ideology than a set of shared interests and above all shared historical experiences during the period of the Avignon papacy and the Schism. The actions of the "Gallican" church during the Schism, culminating in the subtraction of obedience and above all the neutrality legislation of 1406/7, were supported by a theory of resistance that was quite different from the conciliar conception of reform expressed in *Haec sancta* and *Frequens*. The conciliar conception clearly posited the council's sovereign power of reform based on the council's claim to represent the whole hierarchical order of the universal church guided by the Holy Spirit. Ironically, however, it was the practice of resistance which had made possible the full development of this concept of conciliar reform and its implementation at the council. And when the council failed to reach a satisfactory conceptual resolution on the critical reform of annates, the Gallicans could withdraw to this theory of resistance. Their historical experience invited and indeed compelled them to do so, since they needed to prove that they had never consented to the payment of the taxes.

A fundamental tension between sovereignty and resistance was embedded in the conception of conciliar reform. That tension is reflected in the decree *Haec sancta*. *Haec sancta* declared the council's sovereign authority to reform the entire body in head and members; but the head of that body—the pope—was at the same time a sovereign agent of reform himself. The Constance reformers never explicitly resolved this tension. However, a careful reading of the reform deliberations and the records of the trials and depositions of John [XXIII] and Benedict XIII suggests that the central criterion was the *scandalum*. If the pope's actions were unfitting, i.e, contrary to the criterion of *honestas*, they were to be resisted by exposing them to the common counsel of the church. If they were scandalous, they were tantamount to heresy and subject to the council's sovereign reforming power. If the council did not act, the right of resistance still freed the members from obedience to the pope's scandalous acts.

Under normal circumstances reform was to be enacted by the collegial activity of head and members working together. The Council of Constance was a bold and successful experiment in collegiality. Those who participate in collegial bodies today can still learn lessons from studying its reform deliberations. It is too easy to say that the ultimate failure of this experiment in the fifteenth century was the inevitable result of the rise of the nation-state. The causes of that demise must be sought in a close analysis of the reform deliberations of the Council of Basel and in the actions of the pope who was conspicuously absent from that council.

EDITION OF THE CONSTANCE REFORM COMMITTEE DELIBERATIONS

INTRODUCTION

1. The earlier editions: Hardt and Finke

Hardt had discovered three records of the reform committee deliberations in two Vienna manuscripts (5113 and 5069), to which Finke assigned the sigla D and E, after their original owners, Johannes Dorre and Nicholas Elstraw.[1] Hübler suggested that the record in E and one of the records in D were protocols of the first reform committee, and that the other record in D was a protocol of the second reform committee.[2] In E, Hardt had found another document which he also believed to be a product of the reform deliberations; it was a much longer set of decrees, organized according to the books and titles of the Decretals of Gregory IX. Hardt thus dubbed it the *Decretales*, and I shall refer to it by that name.[3] Finke discovered four new manuscripts with collections of reform committee deliberations, which he labelled C, S, V, and W respectively, according to the libraries in which they are found— Cues, Stuttgart, Vatican, and Vienna (Wien).[4] On the basis of these new manuscripts, Finke's collaborator in the edition of Volume 2 of the *Acta*, Johannes Hollnsteiner, attempted to revise Hardt's and Hübler's earlier analyses of the manuscript record.[5] He argued that the records in D and E are semi-private collections

---

[1] Two of the specific reforms have also received separate editions. The reform of the papal penitentiary was edited by Emil Göller, *Die päpstliche Pönitentiarie von ihrem Ursprung bis zu ihrer Umgestaltung unter Pius V.* (Rome, 1907–1911), 1.2.132f. Job Vener's reform proposal in Vienna, ÖNB, lat. 5113 (D^2, c.7 below) has been edited separately by Heimpel, *Vener*, 3:1288–90.

[1] Hardt.1.485 (*recte* 578)–583; ACC.2.550.

[2] Hübler, 11–16. He referred to the record in E as the first recension (*Elaborat*) of the protocol and to the record in D as the second recension.

[3] H.1:664–754.

[4] Bernkastel-Kues, St. Nikolaus-Hospitalbibliothek 168, fol. 178r–187v; Stuttgart, Württembergische Landesbibliothek, iur. Fol. 130, fol. 70r–90r; Vat. lat. 12572, fol. 372r–378r; and Vienna, Österreichische Nationalbibliothek, cod. lat. 5094, fol. 1r–25v.

[5] ACC.2.550–554.

and not protocols (a protocol being minutes of the committee's proceedings kept by notaries). He deemed the *Decretales* to be a totally private work which could be ignored in a consideration of the reform committee deliberations.

As for Finke's new manuscripts, Hollnsteiner judged that two of them (C and S) present collections parallel to those in E and D, but that they often display *"a completely different ordering of the proposals"* (italics mine). On the other hand, V contains the only collection which resembles a protocol, since it is chronologically organized and provides reports on the committee's actions. W is a composite, with two sets of proposals: 1) a copy of the collection found also in E, and 2) a set of new proposals. In general, Hollnsteiner concluded that no collection except that in V can be identified exclusively with either the first or second reform committee and that we cannot even establish a chronological relationship among the collections. Each collection contains proposals from various stages of the deliberations; in a single collection the text of one proposal may be earlier, the text of another proposal later, than the corresponding texts in another collection.

Finke and Hollnsteiner believed that by comparing the wording of drafts of the same proposal in the different manuscripts one could trace its evolution through the successive stages of deliberations. They decided to facilitate the tracing of this evolution by grouping all the texts pertaining to each particular reform together in their edition and arranging the texts within each group in chronological order. The whole edition is constructed looking backward from the vantage point of the final decrees and concordats in order to show how those documents took shape.

2. Rationale for the New Edition

In my re-edition of the reform committee documents below I have chosen instead to retain the order of the manuscripts, for two main reasons. First, Finke's re-ordering suggests patterns of development which may not have in fact existed and prevents the reader from trying to determine the true patterns. Second, Hollnsteiner grossly exaggerates the extent of divergence in the ordering of the proposals in the manuscripts. I believe that six manuscripts present essentially the same collection of proposals from the first reform committee; the composition and sequencing of this collection shows sufficient uniformity that it is possible to talk of a "Common Collection" (See Tables 1 and 2 at the end of this introduction).

Three new manuscript records of the committee's deliberations which have surfaced since Finke's edition help to shed light on this process.[6] The first is found in Paris, BN lat. 9514 (= P), and is a copy of the first five proposals in the Common Collection; its chief interest lies in the fact that it is the only extant, clearly identified copy of a set of proposals sent from the reform committee to one of the nations (in this case the French nation) for deliberation. The second record, found in Augsburg, Staats- und Stadtbibliothek, cod. 2° 226 (= A), is valuable as an independent record of the Common Collection as it appears in D and S. The third record is in many ways the most interesting. It is found in Vat. lat. 3884 (= M), a manuscript which Finke already knew to contain a copy of one reform measure considered at Constance. But he and others overlooked the extensive collection of Constance reforms found at the beginning of this manuscript, a collection which appears to have been used by a later reform commission convened by Pope Martin V. I am indebted to Dr. John Sawicki for calling this collection to my attention. The collection is the third most complete, after those in D and S, and it provides a valuable independent witness to the series of additions to the Common Collection hitherto known only from those two manuscripts. It also provides a second copy of most of the drafts hitherto known only from Finke's manuscript V.

Vat. lat. 3884 in fact contains the text of one proposed decree announced in V, but not reproduced there; it is the schedule "Divinum cultum volentes," on unions, drafted by Cardinal Zabarella (see ACC.2.625).[7] The Augsburg manuscript also contains a hitherto unknown proposal dealing with priests holding

---

[6] Augsburg, Staats- und Stadtbibliothek, cod. 2° 226, pp. 579–604; Vat. lat. 3884, fol. 1r–14v (See John Sawicki and Phillip Stump, "New Evidence of the Reform Committee at the Council of Constance in Vat. lat. 3884," *Bulletin of Medieval Canon Law*, 8 (1978) 50– 55); Paris, Bibliothèque Nationale, lat. 9514, fol. 166r–171v (Finke edited the diary of Guillaume de la Tour from this manuscript, but he overlooked the copy of the reform committee deliberations in it.)

[7] V contains a number of reform proposals scattered through its earlier folios which are labelled "Ex concilio Constantiense"; one of these is almost identical with the text of the reform decree of Session 43 on clerical decorum; I have edited it as Extrav. 4 below, p. 413. Three others (fols. 52v and 56r) are in fact texts which appear as paragraphs within Martin V's reform constitution of May 16, 1425, ed. Döllinger, *Beiträge* 2:339–40 (*Preterea quilibet archiepiscopus . . . absentandum*), 340–41 (*Porro ut per frequentem . . . compelli*), and 342 (*Et quia, dum ecclesiarum . . . eo ispo*); could Martin V have drawn these from Constance drafts? A further proposal in V (fol. 47v, *Consulta Romani pontificis*) is edited tentatively below as Extrav. 5; however, it may in fact not be from Constance.

concubines and is of interest because its author apparently was the humanist Pier Paolo Vergerio.[8] The new copy of the Common Collection in A brings the total to six—A,C,D,E,S, and W—of which three (D,S, and W) also have separate collections of schedules from the second reform committee (identified in the edition as D^2, S^2, and W^2.) Hollnsteiner's description of the records in the important manuscript W is particularly confusing and needs to be clarified. In W, the record of the second reform committee is found in the first eleven folios (and continued on fols. 46r-v and 156r, which at some time in the manuscript's history became separated and interpolated among later, totally unrelated, materials in the manuscript). I have identified this record using the siglum W^2 (or in a few cases W^3, where there is more than one successive draft of the same measure); an incipit-explicit analysis of it is found below, pp. 396–407. The record of the first committee (Common Collection) in W is found on fols. 13r–26r and is analyzed in Tables 1 and 2 below (siglum: W).[9]

3. The records of the first reform committee:
Relationships among the manuscripts

In Tables 1–3, I have shown the sequence of the proposals from the Common Collection in all the manuscripts. Table 1 follows the order of the whole collection in S (the most complete version). Table 2 shows the order in E and W for cc.23–39 and makes clear the major divergences in sequencing of proposals in the manuscripts. For cc.1–29, A and D follow almost exactly the order of S,[10] while C agrees with the order in E and W (although C lacks cc.10a–14). The sequence of proposals in the two Vatican manuscripts deviates extensively from that of the other six manuscripts; however, the table shows that even here there are important parallels.

The sequence of proposals in the manuscripts of the Common Collection roughly parallels the chronological order of the deliberations in the summer and fall of 1415. Within the period from July to

---

[8] On Vergerio's activities at the council, see ACC.2.112, 3:617–618, 667–670. His proposal is edited as Extrav. 1 below.
[9] Changes made in W by a later hand at the time of the second reform committee are also identified by the siglum W^2 in the critical apparatus for the Common Collection below.
[10] Thus the order in my edition parallels closely that of Hardt's edition, which used D for its base manuscript.

late November, 1415, we can distinguish several sub-phases, in which different groups of proposals were considered. The main differences in the composition of the manuscripts of the Common Collection cluster around the breaks between these phases, as follows:

Dates	Chapters in Common Collection
Jul – Aug 1415	cc. 1–5
Sep 3–7	c. 6, para. 1–24; c. 36
Sep 7 – Oct 10	c. 6, para. 25 – c. 22
Oct 11 – Nov 19	c. 23–29
Nov 20, 1415 – Oct 8, 1416	c. 30–51

These breaks are reflected in Table 1 (See also Table 3 for the break which occurred in early September between the second and the third phase, which is reflected in the different sequence of sub-paragraphs 24–31 in the proposal for reform of the curia (c.6). Table 4 compiles in chronological order all the notes in the manuscripts which give dates of deliberation of individual measures. The discussion which follows is based on these notes.

4. The first five (August 1415)

The first five proposals in the Common Collection form a distinct group. They all are worded as formal final decrees, and they must have been made ready in this form to be sent to the nations. Manuscript P in fact contains these five decrees copied separately for this exact purpose. Conversely, they do not appear in the two Vatican manuscripts, probably because of the distinct purposes for which these later copies were made.[11]

Already in these five proposals we can see a division of the manuscript tradition into two distinct groups: C, E, W (and P) in one group, and A, D, and S in the other. Not only are these groups distinguished by the similarity of the variants in their manuscripts, but in the text of two of the proposals entire sections appear in manuscripts of one group that are missing in manuscripts of the other, as follows: 1) In c.2a *Cum antiqui* (papal oath additions), a number of clauses are found in ADS, but not in CEWP. 2) Also, C and P are lacking two clauses (concerning transfer of bishops and shortening of the year of Jubilee) that are found not only in ADS,

---

[11] See below, pp. 293–294.

but in EW as well; however, in W they are underscored (indicating deletion). 3) A and D have additional clauses in c.2b (*Quia decet*) that roughly duplicate other clauses in 2a (on matters of faith, exemptions, etc.). 4) Finally, in c.4, A and S lack most of the elaborate arenga; the long missing section is replaced by the words "etc. Nos".

Here I will attempt an explanation of these divergences based on the following hypotheses: All the clauses in 1) and 2) above were matters that were transferred to c.2b (i.e., they were to be subjected to the control of the control of the council rather than the cardinals; see Chapter 5 above, p. 125); in ADS they already appear in c.2b also, but they have not yet been deleted from c.2a. In a similar manner, the two clauses in 2) above must not have been deleted from the archetypes of E and W as yet, since E and W retain them; however, the scribe of W later went back and deleted them by underscoring.

As for the additions in 3) above, they probably reflect an effort to transfer these items, like those listed in 2) above, from control of the cardinals to control of the council. This effort was ultimately rejected by the committee, and so the clauses do not appear in CEWP.

Finally, A and S probably omitted the long passage from the arenga in c.4 (no. 4 above), either because the final text of this passage had not yet been agreed upon when the exemplar of A and S was made, or because those who copied A and S already had a copy of the schedule.

If these hypotheses are correct, it would appear that C and P present the latest versions of c.2a, c.2b and c.4. This would agree with the fact that P contains the version of the first five schedules which was sent to the French nation for deliberation. Then E and W would represent the penultimate version and ADS would reflect still earlier versions; the additional passages in c.2b in A and D might reflect changes desired by the groups in which those manuscripts circulated.

5. *Possible provenance of records in A, D, and S and of C and W*

We know that D and S belonged to members of the German nation at Constance (D to Johannes Dorre and S to Siegfried Gerlacher; see description of manuscripts below). A was probably also associated with the German nation. S may have even been used by a member of the reform committee in his communications with the German nation, since its record of the second reform committee deliberations contains marginal notes on the response of the German nation to particular measures (see below, p. 287).[12] S also presents extensive marginal glosses on c.1 of the Common Collection which record suggested additions, some of which were adopted in later versions, others not. It is possible that these, as well as the additions in c.2a, reflect changes desired by the German nation. A, D and S may have all been copied from a semi-official or official record maintained by members of the German nation on the reform committee. A and S present very similar readings but neither can be a copy of the other, so it is likely they are both direct copies from a single exemplar. On the other hand, D has many idiosyncratic qualities, all the earmarks in fact of a personal copy that may have acquired some of its readings from other versions of the Common Collection alongside the archetype of A and S. Its readings are on the whole not as reliable as those in A and S.

The manuscripts in the other main group—C, E, and W—were also associated with Germany or Eastern Europe. E was copied for Nicholas Elstraw, secretary of Duke Ernst of Austria; C belonged to Nicholas of Cusa;[13] and W, although its provenance remains enigmatic, has a transmission history centered in Eastern Europe, and its spelling variants would also suggest a Central or East European scribe. The readings in C and W are very close and on the whole the most accurate in any manuscript. (On the other hand, E is a much less accurate copy made from the same source.) I will suggest below that W was used in the second reform committee as an official or semi-official record. The copy of the Common Collection in W was probably made directly from an official record, but not the same record as the exemplar of ADS; most likely the exemplar of CEW was an official record maintained by the committee itself, a record which was constantly updated as the deliberations of the measures continued.

6. Reforms of the Curia (c.6)

The first five proposals in the Common Collection were probably introduced, deliberated, and largely finalized during late July and

---

[12] See the marginal note to S^2, c.5, which reports that the decree was read ("lectum") and then records what appears to be the response of the German nation.

[13] The record of the reform deliberations in C may have been copied from an Italian manuscript, since it was collected for Cardinal Cesarini (see below, p. 290.)

August.[14] Then in late August and early September a large number of proposed reforms were placed on the table. First, Cardinal Adimari submitted two long texts each containing multiple proposals, one set August 28 (concerning collations and provisions) and the other September 3 (concerning reform of the curia). Deliberation of the first set seems to have been postponed.[15] Manuscripts V and M begin with copies of Adimari's proposals for curial reform, which also became c.6 in the Common Collection.[16] V contains marginal notes and notes in the text concerning deliberation of these measures. They were discussed and amended on September 3, 4, and 6; on September 4, Adimari introduced two additional schedules on curial reform which became incorporated into c.6 as cc.25–26. As Hollnsteiner observed, the notes concerning deliberations in V suggest that its archetype (V itself dates from the mid-fifteenth century) had many of the characteristics of a protocol. However, the numerous errors and irregularities in the text are not indicative of a direct copy; and its archetype was also probably not the official committee protocol, but possibly a record kept by the Italian nation or a cardinal.[17]

C.6 shows remarkably divergent readings in all the manuscripts. For some paragraphs almost every manuscript has a unique text. The base text—the proposals submitted originally by Adimari—seems to be reproduced consistently only by C, a further indication that C was made directly from an official committee record. Even V, which in most cases has the earliest version of proposals in its texts and subsequent deliberation in the margins, presents texts for some paragraphs of c.6 that already incorporate the results of the deliberations (e.g., Para. 4, where a marginal comment notes that "Reformatus fit iste articulus pro ut nunc iacet . . .") Most of the paragraphs of Adimari's proposal received extensive discussion and revision in the committee. In one case (para. 17) a sub-

---

[14] See the note on c.37 in E and W which refers to a decision made concerning c.2 on August 20 (the year is not specified, and it is of course possible that it could have been 1416, but this is most unlikely.)

[15] This schedule appears later as the first portion of c.36; however, D interpolates it in the middle of c.6; See Table 3 below.

[16] To be precise, the record in M begins with a fragment, the last part of the proposal concerning the number of cardinals; i.e., one of the initial five proposals in the common collection (=Common, c.4, but with some major textual differences). An older foliation reveals that the first three folios of this collection are missing; they may well have contained the other four proposals.

[17] See the note concerning deliberations on future dispensations, November 4: "Circa futuras uero dispensationes *fuit obtentum* quod non fierent nisi de consilio cardinalium" (italics mine); this is not the language of an official protocol.

committee was appointed to get further information (see above, p. 122); later seventeen additional paragraphs were added to c.6 (para. 30–46) on the basis of that sub-committee's research. The fact that c.6 in V does not contain these additional paragraphs suggests strongly that its archetype was copied before the sub-committee completed its research. The extensive deviation in sequencing of paragraphs 25–29 (just prior to the added paragraphs) occurred partly because para. 25–29 were themselves additions at the end of Adimari's original proposal, which was still being debated. CEW present the same sequencing, and here S also joins them, even against A and D. In fact, A would also have the same sequence if it did not lack para. 25, on the clerks of the papal chapel. S also originally lacked para. 25, but added it later in the margin at the correct point.

The most unusual sequence of proposals within c.6 is found in D. Not only does it have the paragraphs in a different order, but it also introduces into c.6 several totally new proposals, including the full text of a formal decree which was commissioned by the committee in deliberations recorded in Para. 25 of c.6, which prohibits the granting of academic degrees by papal fiat. The formal decree (*Eo iam multos*) was drafted by Cardinal Adimari and presented to the committee September 19. In the other manuscripts it appears as a separate chapter, c.8; but in D it follows Para. 25 in c.6. Following it are three more proposals that do not occur at this point in any other manuscript: 1) a proposal against curial concubinage which is unique to D;[18] 2) the proposal of Adimari on collations and provisions presented on August 28 which the committee had decided to refer to the nations;[19] and 3) the proposal *De casibus reseruatis* which appears again below in D as a separate proposal (c.31). The compiler of D may well have been a member of the committee who was particularly incensed by curial abuses.[20] The dispute concerning precedence in the curia[21] possibly spurred him to make a collection of the reform committee's deliberations for his own private record and for communicating with other like-minded reformers.

---

[18] Edited below as Extrav. 2, p. 411.
[19] This is the proposal which Hardt edited separately, H.556–57.
[20] See above, p. 240 and n. 35.
[21] See above, p. 120.

7. The First Committee's Further Work

The copyist of V observes, following para. 27, which is its last full paragraph in c.6, that on September 6, "since many schedules have been submitted and many things proposed, there has been no deliberation of any of them except the schedules on dispensations" (cc.10– 17). The order of proposals in V follows the chronological order in which the proposals were first formally deliberated (not the order in which their deliberation was concluded). Marginal notes in V record deliberations of the measure and give the text of the resulting amendments. These amendments have in most cases already been incorporated into the texts of proposals as they appear in the Common Collection.

In a number of cases, the initial deliberation of a proposal ended with a decision to commission one or more persons (usually cardinals) to draft a proposed decree. Two such decrees, one on the awarding of doctorates by papal bull (drafted by Adimari; see above, p. 281) and the other on elections made by *preces* (drafted by Zabarella) appear as cc.8 and 9, following c.7, a proposed decree on spoils, which may have been similarly commissioned in earlier deliberations. An alternative decree on elections made by *preces* (c.9a) is added after Zabarella's draft, and then follow seven reforms concerning dispensations (cc.10–16), which we know had been laid on the table in early September (see above, p. 282), to which is appended a short proposal on litigants in the papal curia (c.17). Then on September 20 and 24, measures on tenths and on *conversi* were proposed (cc.18 and 19). During the next three days, the English Bishop of Bath introduced several measures,[22] only two of which became part of the Common Collection at this point. The measures concerning exemptions for religious houses and privileges of abbots and others to wear pontifical insignia were taken up as cc.20 and 21, but two elaborate decrees on indulgences and examination of ordinands proposed on September 25 and 27 were apparently dropped (they appear only in V and M at this point.)

C.22 is a proposal requiring priests to know the vernacular language of their parishioners; it was discussed (*repetita*) October 3, but probably introduced a few days earlier. It is also likely that c.23 on unions, deliberated October 7–8, had also been introduced somewhat earlier, probably also under the presidency of the Bishop

---

[22] I believe that c.19 and cc.22–23 were also submitted by the English nation; they would seem to have been derived from the Oxford proposals; see above, p. 148 n. 19.

of Bath. It and the four other measures mentioned above were of considerable importance to the English representatives, as evidenced by their re-appearance in the English concordat in the final months of the council.[23] This hypothesis about introduction of cc.22–23 in late September would also fit well with the fact that A, D, and S append to the schedule on unions a short schedule on privileges of mendicants (c.23a), which we know to have been concluded September 30.

Between c.23 and 23a, E and W insert brief descriptions of deliberations of the two of the measures introduced by the Bishop of Bath but tabled on September 27. These descriptions appear later in S as cc.33 and 34. It is in fact at this point, before and after c.23, that the major divergence in the sequencing of proposals between ADS and EW occurs (See Table 2). Between c.22 and 23, E and W insert, anachronistically, three schedules which are records of earlier deliberations: the proposals concerning reform of collations which had been introduced August 28 (but expanded now to include other proposals), the ban on transfers of prelates which the committee had decided to make into a separate measure on August 20, and the initial deliberation of elections involving *preces* on September 11. These are all included in S as additions to the Common Collection (cc.36–38).

After c.23 E and W insert the other two schedules (cc.33–34) mentioned above, followed by a fuller version of c.23a, which also appears in S as c.35; then EW and ADS agree in sequence through c.29, which is the last schedule in the main body of the Common Collection. Schedules 24–29 deal with non-residence of lower clergy, reductions of tax rates, reform of simoniacs, the custom of German collegiate churches of collecting first years' revenues from new canons, the age for religious vows, and finally the regular holding of provincial councils. We know that the last three were introduced on October 1, 9, and 10 respectively, again suggesting the overall chronological order of the Common Collection.

Though the last measure in the main body of the Common Collection was introduced October 10, deliberation on many of the measures continued well into November. This further deliberation is reflected as marginal notes in E and W, whereas A, D, and S already include the more advanced texts. All of this suggests again that there were at least two working records of the committee maintained in the chronological order reflected in the Common

---

[23] C.23 and the parallel texts in V and M present a number of problems. See above, p. 146 n. 17.

Collection and that the records in CEW and ADS were made at different times from these working records. C was finished earliest and thus does not contain the schedules on dispensations, upon which deliberation was not yet complete.

E and W contain notes which seem to refer to the disposition of the measures. "Expeditus" appears to mean that an official final copy of it had been prepared and forwarded to the German nation for consideration. "Detur" would then seem to indicate approval by the nation. (Some measures in W have the abbreviation Po. or Po ̃, next to them; I take this to stand for "Ponitur" and to mean that the measure was referred back to committee.) The first use of the marginal "Detur" and "Expeditus" actually occurred in manuscript C in the context of the dispute about precedence in the curia mentioned above and is an index of the visceral feelings that dispute evoked: "Non detur, quia scandaloza et non expedita."

8. Additions to the Common Collection

We have seen that before and after c.23 a number of schedules which did not fit clearly into the chronological order were interpolated into the collection in E and W, but appended as additions in S, and omitted altogether by A and D. Marginal notes and signs in S show that a person who used this manuscript compared it to a manuscript of the type of E and W (or possibly to the prototype of E and W) noting the places where S's sequence of proposals diverged from the other sequence. The signs are letters from "a" to "h" (except for the note leading to c.36 which is a ⸶†|†⸷). If one follows these notes in alphabetical order, they lead one through the sequence of proposals in E and W.

E is the only text which records its date of completion: "Finitum VIII. Octobris Anno MCCCCXVI° per familiarem Nicolai Elstraw, etc." (at the end of the last proposal in the Common Collection in E).

The additional proposals cc.30–32 and 39–51 are shared by S and D and (with one exception, c.31) by M. The fact that they are included in M before the later stages of deliberations of cc.19–27 suggests that they may well have been submitted to the committee (perhaps among the large group aired in early September), but not yet deliberated.[24] If this is true, some quite significant reforms were lost in this way. Among them are five, cc.30 and 42–45, of particu-

---

[24] However, c.31 does appear in E; and c.30 appears also in A.

lar interest because they are also found in the *Decretales reformationis*. There is in fact a parallel text for one measure from the *Decretales* in the main body of the Common Collection itself. It is the alternate text on elections made by *preces* (c.9a) Large portions of it agree almost verbatim with portions of (1.3.3) in the *Decretales*. All this makes it evident that the *Decretales* were not a purely private collection.

In fact, the *Decretales* are found accompanying the reform committee deliberations in manuscripts A, E, and W, either directly before or directly after the records of the reform committee. They also appear in S, at the very beginning of the manuscript, where they are accompanied by brief marginal notations which suggest that they were given consideration in some public forum, perhaps the German nation, or even the reform committee itself. Proposals 42–45 in the Common Collection all present impressive arengas which identify problems that need reform, followed by brief requests for remedies in the form "Petitur super hiis prouideri". In place of these requests for remedies the *Decretales* offer elaborate execution clauses. The execution clause of one of the five *Decretales* proposals in the Common Collection (c.30, "Quia a longis temporibus") does also appear in the reform committee version, suggesting that at least this one measure (as well as c.9a) was approved by the committee. It may well be that the German nation continued to seek consideration for the other proposed reforms in the *Decretales*. Comparison of the parallel texts suggests that they represent different adaptations of texts drawn from a common source, possibly a comprehensive catalog of reforms desired by members of the German and Italian nations.

9. The Records of the Second Reform Committee (S², D², W²)

Table 4 below shows the comparative sequence of the measures in the three manuscripts; the final column in the table shows the relationship to drafts from the first reform committee. If the second committee's draft was a rewording of a draft from the first committee, the first committee's draft is identified in the final column by its number in the Common Collection; if the second committee substituted a new draft on a topic dealt with by the first committee, reference is made to the schedule in the Common Collection which dealt with that topic (e.g., "cf. c.7"). The word "New" in this column indicates that no schedule from the first reform committee dealt with the topic.

Relatively few measures from the second committee were totally new. (And some of the "new" schedules in W^2 may have in fact been drafted in the first reform committee and gathered here for consideration by the second committee.) Even the proposed reforms of alienations had been dealt with before, but as part of the additions to the papal oath; now they received their separate schedules. It is interesting that the reforms concerning cardinalitian revenues and benefices appear not to have been introduced at all until the second committee, which included no cardinals among its members.

As noted above, S appears to have been used in communications with the German nation, and W may have been used as a working document in the committee itself.[25] In its record of the Common Collection, two proposals (cc.1a and 3)[26] are marked with extensive corrections and additions in a different hand and darker ink. These changes appear incorporated into the text of the second reform committee's later drafts of these proposals. Moreover, as Finke also observed, the new proposal concerning expectancies in the second reform committee (W^2, c.3) refers the reader to "infra fol. 23", i.e., to fol. 23 of the same manuscript. This folio indeed contains that portion of the record of the Common Collection which deals with expectancies (c.36, para. 5). However, Finke did not note an interesting set of marginal notations in the record of the Common Collection in W used to indicate the disposition of the specific measures. In part these are simply copies of the same "Expeditus" and "Detur" notations which appear in the parallel manuscript E and probably date from the first reform committee. But a second set of "Expeditus" notations also appears, written in the different hand and the darker ink mentioned above; this set has no parallel in E. It must surely refer to action by the second reform committee, especially since the same hand and dark ink also annotate other measures with the words *Respicit membra*, or *Membra* (members), in order to distinguish them from the reforms of the head—*in capite et curia Romana*—which, according to the agreement between Sigismund and the cardinals in July 1417, were to be enacted prior to the election. Because of that agreement these reforms of the mem-

---

[25] See above, p. 276 and below, p. 295, concerning composition of W.

[26] W^1 c.1a, an intermediate draft of *Si vero* (on prevention of future schisms), was then again further amended in W^2, c.13 and c.15. W^1, c.3 (on simony) in its amended form agrees generally with the draft found in S^2 and D^2; no version of it appears in W^2. (See Table 4).

bers were given lower priority in the deliberations of the second reform committee.

Of the three collections D^2, W^2, and S^2, D^2 generally presents the texts of the proposals in their earliest versions, and S^2 in their latest. However, for several proposals in W^2, even though the base text presents an earlier version than S^2, further marginal and interlinear amendments represent changes not yet found in S^2; indeed, as Finke observed, the final readings produced by these amendments usually bring the drafts into agreement with the wording of final decrees.[27] The schedules in question are W^2, cc.5,6,9,10,11,12a,15. With the exception of c. 5 (*De numero et qualitate dominorum cardinalium*), the decrees in question are those which were enacted in the Thirty-ninth Session, as follows:

c.6: Spoils and procurations (39.4 *Cum per papam*)

c.9: Transfers of prelates (39.5 *Cum ex prelatorum*)

c.10: Papal oath (39.3 *Quanto Romanus*)

c.11 and 12a: Meetings of general councils (39.1 *Frequens*; but here in two successive preliminary versions with different preambles; the relevant text following the preambles begins with *Hoc perpetuo decreto*)

c.15: Provisions against future schisms (39.2 *Si vero*)

W^2, cc.6, 9, 10, and 15 contain marginal notes which record the approval of "the Spanish."[28] Both W^2 and S^2 also contain marginal notations which record the reception of proposals in the German nation ("Placuit nationi", etc.)

10. Conclusion

The Common Collection represents an official collection from the first reform committee which formed the basis for deliberations of both the first and second reform committees. Its main core of twenty-nine schedules is organized in roughly chronological order according to the dates when each measure received its initial deliberation. Six manuscripts are extant, along with an additional manuscript P which contains the first five decrees only, in the form sent to the French nation for deliberation. The manuscripts fall into

---

[27] See ACC.2.553. The amendments appear in the same hand and the same darker ink as texts, i.e. the same hand and ink as the "Expeditus" and "Membra" comments in the common collection in W mentioned above.

[28] c.6: "Placuit etiam Hispanis II Octobris"; c.9: "II Octobris, placuit Hyspanis"; c. 10: "Concordatum etiam per dominos Hispanos"; c. 15: "Prima Octobris concordatum est etiam per Hispanos".

two main groups—C,E,W in one group and A,D,S in the other. Manuscripts C and W were probably copied directly from the committee's official record. They generally provide the best readings of any manuscript. E is a poorer copy of the same version. Manuscripts A, D, and S were probably copied from a record maintained by members of the German nation on the committee. Manuscripts V and M provide an independent witness of the schedules in the Common Collection and also a few additional schedules that individuals apparently introduced, but that the committee did not approve. V is a mid-fifteenth century copy of a chronologically organized collection with protocol-like comments which was probably maintained by members of the Italian nation or cardinals; M was copied from several different sources; it has copies of texts found otherwise only in V and other texts found otherwise only among the additions to the Common Collection in D and S; some of its readings are better than the readings in those manuscripts.

There are two main sets of additions to the 29 schedules which form the core of the Common Collection: 1) six schedules interpolated into the main collection in E and W before and after c.23, and in S added after the end of the main collection (cc.33–38). 2) In S these additions are preceded by three other additional schedules and followed by thirteen further schedules (cc.30–32 and 39–51), most of which are also found in D and in M. These latter additions, which were probably not approved by the committee, include a number of texts which closely parallel or duplicate portions of texts found in the *Decretales reformationis*, a set of texts much more closely connected to the Common Collection than most scholars have thought.

The second reform committee seems to have used W's copy of the Common Collection as a working base manuscript, annotating it with indication of the disposition of measures (whether expedited, tabled, or relegated to the reforms *in membris*). In a few cases W indicates the second committee's changes directly in the text of schedules from the Common Collection, using corrections, erasures, and marginal additions; more often it provides copies of the new drafts with which the second committee replaced the earlier measures; these new measures (identified below with siglum W^2) are collected in the folios which in W precede the Common Collection. Two other manuscripts which contain the Common Collection (D and S) also contain collections of drafts from the second committee (identified as D^2 and S^2.) S^2 generally gives the most recent version, except for a few schedules in W^2 which have corrections leading to the final decrees.[29]

The collections from the first two committees appear to represent a rather full record, although additional proposals that have already turned up in new manuscripts suggest that there may be some other proposals yet to be discovered. The existing record is generally quite accurate and allows a relatively complete reconstruction of the deliberations of those committees. No record remains from the third reform committee.

Many other questions remain unanswered, particularly concerning the external history of the manuscripts, above all Manuscript W. However, the internal evidence suggests reliable conclusions about the ways in which the record was constructed. I have endeavored to construct the new edition in a manner that will facilitate further conclusions and discussion on the basis of this internal evidence.

MANUSCRIPTS

A = Augsburg, Staats- und Stadtbibliothek, 2° Cod 226
      Paper, II + 694 pages, Southwest Germany, S. $XIV^{1/4}$
For complete analysis, see *Handschriftenkataloge der Staats- und Stadtbibliothek Augsburg* (Wiesbaden, 1974), 1:252–258. The manuscript bears the signature 170 of the library of Eichstätt. It contains an autograph copy of Dietrich of Niem's *De convocatione generalium conciliorum* (pp. 1–26).

The reform committee deliberations are found on pp. 580–604, following the *Decretales reformationis* (pp. 517–579). The committee deliberations begin in the middle of a sexternion the first part of which contains the final pages of the *Decretales*; they continue through a second gathering which consists of a quinternion (pp. 585–602) with an additional binion glued on (pp. 603–606). On p. 603–604 appears a second copy of c.26, *Contra simoniacos*; after the first sentence the wording is virtually identical with the first copy.

---

[29] The most notable example is the decree on transfer of prelates (S^2, c.6; W^2, c.9). Even here, the base text in W^2 is earlier than that in S^2. Some of the additions and corrections to this base text in W^2 have been incorporated into the text in S^2. However, a second set of corrections and additions to the text in W^2 does not appear in S^2 but does appear in the final decree. In his edition of a number of the reforms, Finke reproduces the texts of the final conciliar decrees, giving variants from the most recent versions of the reforms. I have not done so here, mainly because no critical edition of the conciliar decrees exists.

On p. 579 appears an additional schedule not found in other
manuscripts of the reform committee deliberations; it is edited
separately below, p. 410. This proposal is copied in a different hand
from the other proposals, which are all in a single hand. Spelling
irregularities are few, but note *intrepite* for *intrepide* and consistent
use of terminal y (with two dots) for terminal ii. In the margin a
modern hand has added paragraph numbers next to each schedule,
beginning with 158 for the schedule on p. 579, followed by 159
through 190 for the schedules in the Common Collection. On pp.
44–46 is found a copy of the schedule W², c.16 (Prolocuta et
aduisata per dominos deputatos. . . ; see below, p. 400). In addition, the manuscript contains copies of the German Avisamenta
(pp. 38–43) and the forged papal oath of Boniface VIII with
glosses (pp. 247–249).

C = Bernkastel-Kues, St. Nikolaus-Hospitalbibliothek 168
    Paper, 212 fols., Germany, S. XV²ᐟ⁴,
    For analysis, see J. Marx, *Verzeichnis der Handshriften-Sammlung des
Hospitals zu Cues* (Trier, 1905), 155–157. See also Constantin
Fasolt, "The Manuscripts and Editions of William Durant the
Younger's 'Tractatus de modo generalis concilii celebrandi,' " *AHC*
10 (1978) 290–309 at 294–295 for further analysis and bibliography. The manuscript belonged to Nicholas of Cusa and, it contains,
following Durant's *Tractatus,* a set of texts collected by Cardinal
Cesarini for the reform deliberations at the Council of Basel.[30] The
Constance reform committee deliberations are found on fols. 178–
188, in a separate gathering of eleven folios (a sexternion with the
last folio cut away). The text shares most of the same marginal
notations which appear in E and W, but the schedules on simony
(Common, cc. 3 and 26) have additional notations unique to this
manuscript; they are written in a different hand from both the text
and the other marginal notations, and at least one was clearly
written after the Council of Constance.[31] All the remaining notes
and the text are written in a single hand. Spelling peculiarities
include frequent *y* for *i* (*layci, byennium*), some irregularity in double
and single consonants (*gramatica,* but also *peccunia*; several times the

---

[30] See "Die Handakten des Konzilspräsidenten Cesarini," ed. Heinrich Dan-
nenbauer, in *Concilium Basiliense* 8 (Basel 1936) 3–31 at 4–5; and Gerald Christianson, *Cesarini, The Conciliar Cardinal: The Basel Years (1431–1438)* (Sankt Ottilien,
1979), 131– 133.
[31] The hand is neither that of Cesarini nor that of Cusanus, but the notes
probably were made at Basel.

scribe wrote *electus* as *ellectus*, then corrected it to *electus*), retention of *b* in verbs with prefix *ob-* (*obstentare, obmiserint*), and *w* for *uu* and sometimes for *u* (*wlgare, lingwas*, but *u* in *guerre* and *unguem*, where S and W have *gwerre* and *ungwem*).

D = Vienna, Österreichische Nationalbibliothek, MS lat. 5113
Paper, I + 214 + II, Southern Germany, S. XIV$^{1/4}$
This manuscript belonged to Johannes Dorre, licentiate in decretals and prebendary in the Speyer cathedral chapter, who was present at the Council of Constance (See Heimpel, *Die Vener*, 1:367 n. 174, 2:971 n. 18, and the literature cited there; see esp. the study of Erich Meuthen.[32] Two of Heimpel's remarks must be corrected, however. The Vienna 5094 manuscript bears the siglum W, not D, in the Finke edition; and more importantly, Stuttgart iur. Fol. 137 does *not* contain a record of the reform committee deliberations.) According to Heimpel, Dorre's manuscript was in the imperial Hofbibliothek in Vienna by the later sixteenth century.

Hermann von der Hardt edited many texts out of this manuscript in his *Magnum oecumenicum Constantiense concilium*. See his note, v. 2, p. 3 (transcribed also by Heimpel). Hardt also transcribed a note found on the original fly-leaf of the manuscript (which has since been lost) concerning Dorre's claim to a vacant benefice in Worms acquired through a papal expectancy granted by Martin V at the Council of Constance. In his edition Hardt refers to Vienna lat. 5113 as the Codex Dorreanus or the "quartum volumen actorum Concilii Constantiensis."

The record of the Common Collection with additions is found alone in a separate hepternion, fols. 140r–153v (size of page: 227 x 293; size of written portion: 144 x 221). There are two different hands, fol. 140r–150v and 150v–153v respectively; the break comes at the beginning of the additions (c.31). A record of the second reform committee's deliberations is found fols. 1–4. Here again there are two hands. The first (fol. 1r, cc.2–3, and fol. 4r–v, cc. 9–10) seems to be the same hand which adds the rubrics and colophons for major divisions in the manuscript. The second hand (fol. 1r and 2r–4r, cc.1, 4–8) is a hand which appears identical with that found on fols. 140–150v. Spelling peculiarities include occasional *w* for *v* and *y* for *i*, especially in place names (*Wiennensis, Nycenum*); *exst* for *ext* (*exstinguendum*); frequent, but not uniform *k* for *c* in *cathedralis, cisma* for *scisma, proch* for *proh*.

---

[32] *Das Trierer Schisma von 1430 auf dem Basler Konzil: Zur Lebensgeschichte des Nikolaus von Kues* (Münster, 1964), 3–9.

The manuscript has three sets of foliation. On fol. 22 of the most recent foliation an older foliation begins, with fol. 67. The older foliation for fols. 140–153 is 167–181 (skipping 177 with no missing text). New folios 1–8 carry only the most recent foliation.

E = Vienna, Österreichische Nationalbibliothek, MS lat. 5069
    Paper, 120 fols., 1415–1417
For analysis see Dietrich von Nieheim, *Historie de gestis Romanorum principum*, ed. K. Colberg and J. Leuschner (MGH Staatschriften 5,2, 1980), xxxi f. See also ACC.4.lxvii–lxviii and *Tabulae codicum manuscriptorum . . . in Bibliotheca Palatina Vindobonensia asservatorum* (Vienna, 1870) 4:12. The manuscript is part of three continuously numerated manuscripts (5069, 5070, 5071) copied for Nicolas Elstraw, secretary to Duke Ernest of Austria at the Council of Constance. At the time of the Council of Basel they were in the hands of Leonhard Huntpichler, O.P., who apparently made a gift of them to the emperor; see Alphons Lhotsky, *Quellenkunde zur mittelalterlichen Geschichte Österreichs* (*MIÖG Erg.* 19; Graz/Cologne 1963), 368–370.
The records of the Constance reform committee deliberations are found on fols. 85–96. They are written in a single hand. Spelling peculiarities include retention of *b* in words with prefix *ob-* (*obmiserunt*) and *cotidianus* for *cottidianus*.

P = Paris, Bibliothèque Nationale, MS lat. 9514
    Paper, I + 171 fols. France, S. XV^{med}
Shelf mark, fol. [I]r, 1r: Supp. lat. 165. Ex libris, fol. 1v: Bibliothecae Sedanensis.
This manuscript contains the journal of Guillaume de la Tour, portions of which are edited in the ACC.2.349–365 (see ACC.2.12 and 4.lii). The last item in the journal is "Acta in sessione die xvii^a mensis Augusti celebrata . . . Nuper sacrosancta uniuersalis . . ." It breaks off with the words "Sacroscancta Constantiensis sinodus mittit ambasiatores suos . . ." Colophon: "Diligenter etiam collationata est de uerbo ad uerbum per me prothonotarium Ianuen. cum originali propria manu. Hec acta concilii generalis Constantiensis sunt domini Guillelmi de Turre archidiaconi sancti Flori in ecclesia Claromontensi que fecit constitutionibus dum ibi erat." The record of the reform committee deliberations is found on fols. 166r–171v as part of a separate gathering of sixteen (fols. 158r–171v, with a folio cut away between 163 and 164). The copy of the five decrees is relatively clean, without additions or changes (other than the scribe's correction of his own copying errors); there

are no indications of the nation's response or other marginal annotations. C.3 appears to have been copied after c.4, since it is squeezed into a space left for it in the manuscript; the space was not large enough, so the copyist still had to continue the text into the lower margin of the page.

The section containing the reform proposals is written in three hands—fols. 166r–169v, 170r–v, and 170v (upper one-third of page; remainder reverts to second hand).

M = Vat. lat. 3884
    Paper, Italy, S. XVI^{in}

On this manuscript, see the article by John Sawicki and Phillip Stump, "New Evidence of the Reform Committee at the Council of Constance in Vat. lat. 3884" and the literature cited there, especially, Michael Tangl, *Die päpstlichen Kanzleiordnungen* (Innsbruck, 1894) lxxiii, 361–362.

The manuscript is a collection of the records of the most important attempts of the fifteenth century popes to reform the curia and was probably compiled in its present form during the reign of Julius II. The collection of reforms from Constance, found on fols. 1–14, is all written in a single hand and may have been compiled in conjunction with a program of reform drafted at Martin V's behest prior to the Council of Pavia-Siena.

S = Stuttgart, Landesbibliothek, Cod. iur. Fol. 130
    Paper, 179 fols., Southwest Germany, S. XV$^{1/4}$

This manuscript almost certainly belonged to Abbot Siegfried Gerlacher of Ellwangen, a close friend and associate of Nikolaus Vener (uncle of Job Vener);[33] see above, p. 158. Stuttgart iur. Fol. 130 contains a number of texts pertaining to monastic reform, including, fols. 116r–209v, parts of a commentary on the Benedictine rule with German translation. See Johannes Zeller, "Das Provinzialkapitel im Stifte Petershausen," *Studien und Mitteilungen zur Geschichte des Benediktinerordens und seiner Zweige* n.s. 10 (1921/22) 1–73 at 17 n. 42 and 19–20 n. 49, where the manuscript is incorrectly cited as iurid. Fol. nr. 120. See also Wolfgang Irtenkauf, "Alte Bibliotheken in Ellwangen," *Ellwanger Jahrbücher* (1962–64) 54–77, at 55–56 and 67.

---

[33] Heimpel, *Die Vener*, 1:370 n.183. But the work Heimpel mentions here on fol. 40r as possibly a reform treatise of Andreas of Escobar is in fact simply Pierre d'Ailly's *Canones reformationis* (or *Tractatus de reformatione*), ed. H.1.409–33; on this work see Oakley, "Capitula agendorum," 113 n.17 and 122 n. 57; and Oakley, *Political Thought*, 250–252 and 346–49.

The text of the Common Collection with additions is found on fols. 70r–82v; fols. 71 and 72 form the last two folios of a sexternion and fols. 73–84 form a second sexternion (with two blank folios at the end).[34] The record of the second reform committee's deliberations is on fols. 85r–90v, a separate ternion (with two blank folios at the end.) Each set is written in a single hand with marginal notes in the same hand as text. Spelling peculiarities include *ngn* for *gn* (*congnitio, pungnandum*) frequent doubling of consonants (*nunccupatur, parrochialis, uiccarius*), *w* for *uu* (*wlgare*), occasional *y* for *i* (*extyrpare*) and *k* for *c* (*kathedralis*); *dextre* for *dextere* and *diuoluatur* for *deuoluatur*.

V = Vat. lat. 12572

    S. XV^med, Italy, paper, II + 435

This manuscript belonged to Domenico Capranica (see note of ownership, fol. 2r: Liber domini Dominici Reuerendissimi cardinalis Firmani.) It later passed into the Vatican Secret Archive, where it bore the signature "Extrauagantes modernae, Armarium XXXII, vol. 50. In 1920 it was transferred to the Vatican Library, along with a series of other manuscripts, which now bear the signatures Vat. lat. 12345–12847.[35]

The manuscript is written in several mid-fifteenth century humanist hands. It contains a collection of papal decretals and conciliar decrees. The six different series of foliation which appear in the manuscript suggest that different portions of it were written at different times and then later assembled in the current order by Capranica. On the folio following the reform deliberations (379r) appears a statement apparently by Capranica, explaining to the pope that he had gathered together a collection of texts for the purpose of compiling a *liber octavus* of the canon law; it is possible that the collection to which he refers is that found in this manuscript.

The table of contents (new fol. 2r–17r) is keyed to the most recent of the older foliations.[36] The collection of the Constance

---

[34] Between fol. 71 and 72 appears a strip of paper whose width is that of the other folios, but whose height is only about one-quarter that of the others. It bears the folio number 71ᵃ; the recto is blank and the verso contains an addition (in a different hand) to the schedule on fol. 71v.

[35] Information taken from the handwritten inventory maintained in the Vatican Library, v. 36: Codices ex archivio in Bybliothecam Vaticanam translati anno 1920.

[36] The table agrees with the contents of the volume up to new fol. 424 (old 462); on this folio is found a new table of contents, in which the first item is the Pragmatic Sanction of Bourges, which follows on the next folio in the manuscript

reform committee deliberations used by Finke for his edition is found on new fols. 372–378 (old folios 400–406).[37] It is identified in the table of contents as "Quedam determinationes super reformatione Curie etc." The folios 372–378 are part of a larger gathering in which a binion (375–378) and a quaternion (379–386) are embedded within a ternion, as follows:

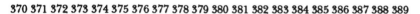

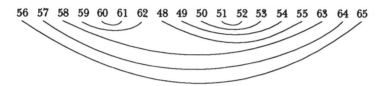

W = Vienna, Österreichische Nationalbibliothek, MS lat. 5094, Paper, 164 fols., Southern Germany, S. XV[1/4]

See *Tabulae codicum . . . Vindobonensia* (as above, p. 292), 4:20 for analysis of the other contents, which chiefly include excerpts from St. Thomas Aquinas's *Summa theologiae*, the *Epigrammata* of Prosper of Aquitaine and of Aurelius Prudentius, a treatise *De gradibus superbiae*, unidentified sermons, a Latin-German epistolary formulary, and miscellaneous hymns, some with musical notation. See also Kurt von Fischer, "Repertorium der Quellen tschechischer Mehrstimmigkeit des 14. bis 16. Jahrhunderts," *Essays in Musicology in Honor of Dragan Plamenac*, ed. Gustave Reese and Robert Snow (Pittsburgh, 1969), 59.

The reform committee deliberations are found in the first three gatherings: II[2] + X[12] + XII[25] (except for some scattered proposals from the second reform committee on fol. 46r–v and 156r). They are followed by the *Decretales reformationis*, fol. 26r–57v. Fols. 1r–11v contain the record of the second committee; fol. 12r–v is blank; and fols. 13r–25v contain a copy of the Common Collection (see

---

(the Pragmatic Sanction is also listed in the original table of contents as being on this folio.) The text of the Pragmatic Sanction is followed, fol. 469v, by a summary of the Sanction's contents; then the rest of the manuscript consists of blank folios, even though the original table of contents lists eleven further items.

[37] On these folios two other sets of foliation also appear (struck out): 56–62 and 67–73.

above, p. 274). An older foliation appears on some of fols. 1–11, as follows:

Old: 2 3 4 – 8 – – – – 9 10
New: 1 2 3 4 5 6 7 8 9 10 11 12

(The old numbers 8 and 10 have been struck out.) Fol. 10 is only half the height of the other folios (153 rather than 311 mm.). It and folio 9 form a binion pasted to folio 8 in the original gathering. Fols. 4 and 5 are also somewhat shorter (300 mm.) and also must be a separate binion, in this case pasted to the stub of a folio which once followed fol. 3 but has been cut away. The stitching of the gathering 2–11 is between fols. 7 and 8.

Numbers appear in the margins next to some of the schedules, as follows:

c.1 (*Licet diuina*, on educational qualifications): 2
c.5 (*Statuimus ut deinceps*, on number of cardinals): *Prima*
c.6 (*Cum per papam*, on spoils): 6
c.7 (*Ut Romanus*, on alienations): 9
c.8 (*Ne sancta mater*, on deposition of pope): 10
c.9 (*Cum ex prelatorum*, on translations): 3
c.10 (*Quanto Romanus*, on papal oath): 8
c.24 (*Cum post obitum*, on alienations): 4
W^1,c.3 (*Contra labem simoniace*, on simony): 5

At least fifteen different hands appear in the texts in W^2, as well as three other different hands in the marginal notes. The text in W^1 is written in a single hand; concerning the marginal notes and corrections, see above p. 286.

EXPLANATION OF EDITION

For the Common Collection my readings in most cases represent the *consensus codicum*. However, in the case of cc. 10–22 the manuscripts clearly present two distinct recensions, an earlier one in the text of V (and sometimes also in the text of C, E, and W) and a later one in the text of the other manuscripts. When these two recensions differ widely I have presented the recensions in parallel columns; otherwise I have presented V's text as the main text with variants from the other manuscripts in the apparatus. For paragraphs in c.6 which appear in more than two distinct recensions I have given each recension separately.

Since V and M do not follow the order of the Common Collection, I have provided incipit-explicit analyses of these manuscripts. Texts of schedules which are unique to V and M are presented in full at the appropriate places in these analyses. For the six manuscripts of the Common Collection, I have shown the deviations in sequencing by means of Tables 1 and 2. The center columns in Table 1 present the sequences in the two Vatican manuscripts for comparison.

For the second reform committee's deliberations I have provided a complete edition of S^2 and incipit-explicit analyses of D^2 and W^2. Variants for schedules common to S^2 and the other manuscripts are given in the text of S^2. For schedules unique to W^2 and D^2 I have edited the texts in full within the incipit-explicit analyses at the appropriate places. A concordance is provided in Table 4.

The chapter numbers preceding each proposal have been added by me and do not appear in the manuscripts.[38] (In addition, I have used sub-paragraph numbers for the paragraphs in the long proposals on curial reform and reform of provisions and collations (c.6 and c.36)[39] The numbering of proposals in V and M in Tables 1 and 2 and in the edition has likewise been assigned by me.

The numbers in square brackets following the chapter numbers (I 1, I 2, etc.) are the numbers which Finke assigned to the proposals in the ACC. A concordance of my numbers with Finke's numbers is provided in Table 6. Table 6 also doubles as a concordance between the reform committee's drafts and the final legislation of the council.

Several proposals which were almost certainly considered by the reform committee do not appear as part of any of the collections. They are edited as *Extravagantes*, pp. 411–414 below. Extrav. 1 and 2 are the proposals in A and D discussed pp. 276 and 281 above; Extrav. 3 is the proposal associated with Jean Mauroux in Paris, BN 1485, which Finke edited ACC.2.672–73 [XLIV]. (However, he overlooked the second page of the proposal in the manuscript; the complete proposal is edited below.) Finally, Extrav. 4 appears to be a copy of the draft decree of the 43d session on clerical decorum; no other draft of this decree appears in any of the Constance reform deliberations. See above, n. 7.

---

[38] See my remarks above, p. 290, about the overall numeration of proposals found in manuscript A, which is not usable for this edition.

[39] Contemporary numeration of the sub-paragraphs in c.6, De reformatione curie, is found in manuscripts A, C, and D. In numbering these sub-paragraphs I used the numeration found in manuscript C. The sub-paragraphs in c.36 are not numbered in any manuscript, so I have again supplied my own numbers in square brackets for convenience of reference.

Rubrics of the collections

A, p. 500: Auisamenta in loco reformatorii Constantiensis

D, fol. 140r: Auisamenta per XXXV cardinales, prelatos et doctores in loco reformatorum Constantiense

D, fol. 141r: Incipit materia reformationis cleri concepta in concilio Constantiense

D^2, fol. 2r: Auisata in reformatorio per XXV prelatos et doctores

E, fol. 85r: Auisamenta reformatorum concilii Constantiensis

M, fol. 1r: Cedule date nationibus pro mundatis

P, fol. 166r: Articuli aduisati super reformatione per deputatis in hac parte et lecti ad deliberandum in natione gallicana

S, fol. 70r: Capitula aduisata in reformatorio

S^2, fol. 85r: Secuntur auisata per quinque nationes

V, fol. 372r: Cedule exhibite coram dominis reformatoribus super constitutionibus faciendis et determinate per ipsos sequentur ut infra

W^2, fol. 1r: Decreta proposita reformatorii

TABLE 1

Manuscripts of the First Reform Committee

Rubric	S[1]	A	D[1]	M	V	C	E	W[1]
[c.1][I 1] Meetings of general councils *Quoniam ex obmissione*	70r	580	140r				178r 85r	13r
[c.2][III 1] Papal oath of office *In nomine sancte*	71r	582	141r				179r 86r	14r
[c.3][IX 2] Simony *Contra labem*	72r	586	142v				180v 87r	15v
[c.4][XII 1] Qualifications of cardinals *Quia plerumque*	72v	587	142v	1r c.1			181r 88r	16r
[c.5][XIX 1] Deposition of pope *Romanus pontifex*	72v	587	143r				181r 88r	16r
[c.6][XV 1] Reform of curia *Littere apostolice*[1]	72v	588	143r	1r c.2	372r c.1	181v 88v	16v
[c.7][V 1] Spoils, procurations, and fruits during vacancies *Dudum fuit*	74r	592	146v	4r c.5			184r 90v	19r
[c.8][XV 1a] Doctorates awarded by papal fiat *Eo multos*	74v	593	[2]	3v c.3	375r −v c.10	184v 91r	19v
[c.9][XXIII 2] Elections made by *preces Statutum felicis*	75r	594	147r	4r c.4	375v c.11	184v 91v	19v
[c.9a][XXIII 3] Elections made by *preces Si quis vocales*	75r	594	147r			—	91v	20r
[c.10][X 1] Dispensations for orders *Intentio quod papa*	75v	595	147v		373v c.2	—	92r	20v

[1] See Table 2 for more detailed analysis of this long proposal.
[2] Rubric only appears in D at this point, struck out.

TABLE 1 cont.

Rubric	S¹	A	D¹	M	V	C	E	W¹
[c.11][X 2] Dispensations for incompatible benefices *Ex nunc reuocentur*	75v	595	147v	10v c.29	373v – 374r c.3	—	92r ³	20v
[c.12][X 3] Dispensations for pluralism *Quod papa non*	75v	596	147v	10v c.30	374r c.4	—	92r	20v
[c.13][X 4] Dispensations for incompatible benefices *Reuocentur ille*	75v	596	148r	11r c.31	374r c.5	—	92v	21r
[c.14][X 7] Dispensations for non-residence *Quilibet summus pontifex*	75v	596	148r	11r c.32	374r -v c.6	—	92v	21r
[c.15][X 8] Dispensations *Quod prelati*	76r	597	148v	11v c.33	374v c.7	185r	93r	21v
[c.16][X 9] Dispensations for age of prelates *Non dispenset*	76r	597	148v	11v c.34	374v – 375r c.8	185r	93r	21v
[c.17][XXIV] Trials in curia *Non imponat papa*	76r	597	148v	12r c.35	375r c.9	185v	93r	21v
[c.18][XXII 1] Tenths *Quod papa non*	76r	598	148v	12r c.36	375v c.12	185v	93r	21v
[c.19][XXV 1] Property of *conversi Quod bona illorum*	76r	598	148v	Cf. c.37	Cf. c.13	185v	93v	21v
[c.20][VI 1] Exemptions *Quod omnes exemptiones*	76v	598	149r	6r c.13	375v c.16	185v	93v	22r
[c.21][XXVI 1] Privileges to wear pontifical attire *Quod omnia priuilegia*	76v	598	149r		Cf. c.17	185v	93v	22r

³ In E, the last sentence of this schedule is separated from the rest to form an independent schedule with the rubric "De facultatibus religiosorum habes xix Octobris sed non conclusione."

TABLE 1 cont.

Rubric	S¹	A	D¹	M	V	C	E	W¹
[c.22][XXVII 1] Priests ignorant of vernacular *Item nulli*	76v	598	149r		Cf. c.20	185v – 186r ⁴	93v	22r
[c.23][VII 2] Unions *Uniones de beneficiis*	76v	598	149r	4v c.6	Cf. c.21	186v	95v	24r
[c.23a][XXXV, para. 2] Privileges for religious *Reuocentur omnes*⁵	76v	598	149r	4v c.7	Cf. c.19	——	See [c. 35]	See [c. 35]
[c.24][XXVIII] Non-residence *Quod omnes habentes*	76v	599	149r	4v c.8		186v	95v	24v
[c.25][XIII 6] Reduction of taxation *Fuit propositum*	77r	599	149v			——	96r	25r
[c.26][IX 1] Simony *Conclusum quod expediens*	77r	600	149v	5r c.9		186v	96r	25r
[c.27][XXIX 2] Payments required of new canons *De oneribus*	77r	600	150r	5v c.10	Cf. c.22	187r	96r	26r
[c.28][XXX] Age for religious vows *Fuit conclusum*	77v	603⁶	150r	6r c.11	377r c.18 ⁷	187v	96v	26r
[c.29][XXXI] Provincial councils *Fuit conclusum*	77v	603	150r	6r c.12	378r c.23 ⁸	187v	96v	26r
[c.30][XXXIV] Money charged for pontifical acts *Quia a longis temporibus*	77v	601	150v	7r c.32	c.19	——		

---

⁴ The remainder of fol. 186r is blank.

⁵ This text in A,D,S, and M is essentially the same text as the second paragraph of [c.35] below; in S the text is struck out. See Introduction, p. 283.

⁶ The pages of this manuscript have been inverted; the correct order should be 600, 603, 601, 602, 604.

⁷ This proposal appears in V as a marginal note in the proposal concerning examination of persons to be ordained, (V, c.18.)

⁸ Rest of 187v and 188r are blank.

TABLE 1 cont.

Rubric	S¹	A	D¹	M	V	C	E	W¹
[c.31][XXXII] Reserved penitential cases *Propositum fuit*	78r		150v c.30 [9]				96v	
[c.32][XXXIII] Perpetual vicars *In singulis ecclesiis*	78v		150v c.31	6v c.14				
[c.33][VI 2] Exemptions *Item quod omnes*	78v						95v	24r
[c.34][XXXV 1] Examination of ordinands *Fuit dictum quod*	78v				Cf. c.40 -41	Cf. c.18 -18a	95v	24r
[c.35][XXXVI] Privileges for religious *Conclusum quod facultates*[10]	78v						95v	24v
[c.36][XIII 4] Collations *In collatione beneficiorum*	79r		145r - 146v [11]				93v	22r
[c.37][IV 1] Translations of prelates *Translationes inuitorum*	80v						95r	24r
[c.38][XXIII 1] Elections made by *preces XI Septembris*	80v						95r	24r
[c.39][XXXVII] Concubines *Ad arcendum concubinatus*	80v		151r c.32	8r c.20				
[c.40][XI 1] Clerical dress *Statutum felicis recordationis*	81r		151v c.33	8v c.21				
[c.41][XIII 5] Promotion of graduates *Ad episcopatum*	81r		152r c.34	9r c.23				

[9] Another copy of this proposal is also found in D on fol. 145v, within the draft of c.6 (See Table 2)

[10] See c. [23a] above.

[11] In D only Para. [1]–[13] of this composite proposal appear, and they are found within the proposal on the reform of the curia (Common, c.6; see Table 3 below and Introduction above, p. 281)

TABLE 1 cont.

Rubric	S¹	A	D¹	M	V	C	E	W¹
[c.42][XIII 9] Chapters which exclude non-nobles *Quia in ecclesiis*	81v			152r c.35	9v c.24 [12]			
[c.43][VIII 1] *Annalia* charged by prelates *Aduersus dampnabilem*	82r			152v c.36	10r c.25			
[c.44][XXIX 3] Entrance fees charged by chapters *Quoniam nonnulla ecclesiarum*	82r			153r c.37	10r c.26			
[c.45][XXXVIII] Secular princes' taxation of clergy *Quoniam nonnulla*	82r			153r c.38	10v c.27			
[c.46][XXXVIII] Ecclesiastical freedom *Quia per diuersa*	82r			153r c.39	10v c.28			
[c.47][XXXIX] Auditor at Avignon *Conclusum quod reuocetur*	82r			153r c.40	6v c.15			
[c.48][XI 2] Clerical decorum *Fuit conclusum*	82v			153v c.41	9r c.22			
[c.49][XL] Qualifications of vicars *Et fuit conclusum*	82v			153v c.42	6v c.16			
[c.50][XLI] Election capitulations of chapters *Propositum fuit*	82v			153v c.43	6v c.17			
[c.51][XLII] Prelates who wage war *Item omnes conuenerunt*	82v			153v c.44	7r c.18			

The following schedules are found only in the two Vatican manuscripts. In most cases they are parallel versions (usually earlier) of schedules found in the common collection; after the rubrics, I have indicated the related schedules in the common collection.

| [XXV 2] Property of *conversi* See Common, c.19 | | | | 12r c.37 | 375v c.13 | | | |

---

[12] The second part of this proposal (Ad idem. Omnes constitutiones . . .) is not found in M.

TABLE 1 cont.

Rubric	S[1]	A	D[1]	M	V	C	E	W[1]
[XXI 1] Indulgences				12v c.38	376r c.14			
[XXI 2] Indulgences *Ad succidendas ambitiones*				12v c.39	376r c.15			
[XXVI 1] Privileges to wear ponifical attire See Common, c. 21					376v c.17			
[XXXV 2-3] Examination of ordinands *Quoniam diligenter* See Common, c.34				13r c.40 -41	376v c.18 -18a			
[XXXVI para.2] Privileges of religious See Common, c. 35				13v c.42	377r c.19			
[XXVII 2] Priests ignorant of vernacular See Common, c. 22				13v c.43	377r c.20			
[VII 2] Unions *Diuinum cultum volentes* See Common, c. 23				13v c.44	377v c.21 [13]			
[XXIX 1] Payments required of new canons See Common, c. 27				14r c.45	377v c.22			

[13] V lacks the text of the schedule (text appears only in M).

TABLE 2

Schedules 22–39, Showing Order in MSS E and W

Rubric	E	W	S	A	D
[c.22][XXVII 1] Priests ignorant of vernacular	93v	22r	76v	598	149r
[c.36][XIII 4] Collations	93v	22r	79r		145r–146v[1]
[c.37][IV 1] Translations of prelates	95r	24r	80v		
[c.38][XXIII 1] Elections made by *preces*	95r	24r	80v		
[c.23][VII 2] Unions	95v	24r	76v	598	149r
[c.33][VI 2] Exemptions	95v	24r	78v		
[c.34][XXXV 1] Examination of ordinands	95v	24r	78v		
[c.35][XXXVI] Privileges for religious	95v	24v	78v	599	149r
[c.24][XXVIII] Non-residence	95v	24v	76v	599	149r
[c.25][XIII 6] Reduction of taxation	96r	25r	77r	599	149v
[c.26][IX 1] Simony	96r	25r	77r	600	149v
[c.27][XXIX 2] Payments required of new canons	96r	26r	77r	600	150r
[c.28][XXX] Age for religious vows	96v	26r	77v	603	150r
[c.29][XXXI] Provincial councils	96v	26r	77v	603	150r
[c.30][XXXIV] Charges for pontifical acts	—		77v	601[2]	150v c.32
[c.31][XXXII] Reserved penitential cases	96v		78r		150v c.30
[c.32][XXXIII] Perpetual vicars			78v		150v c.31
[c.39][XXXVII] Concubinage of priests			80v		151r c.33

[1] In D only Para. [1]–[13] of this composite proposal appear, and they are found within the proposal on the reform of the curia (Common, c.6; see Table 3 below and Introduction above, p. 281)
[2] Pages out of order in manuscript; see Table 1, Note 4

TABLE 3

Divergent Sequencing of Paragraphs in
De reformatione curie (Common collection, c.6, para. 24–29)

NOTE: Three of the manuscripts place numbers at the beginning of the
paragraphs. Those in A were added much later, while those in C and D
are contemporary with the hand of the manuscripts. For the manuscripts
with unnumbered schedules, the numbers in square brackets were added
by me to show the sequence of the proposals.

Rubric	A	C	D	ESW	V	M
Et habeant maliscallum	23	24	24	[24]	[24]	[23]
Item clerici capelle		25	25	[25][1]	[25]	[24]
Item examinator curie	24	26	27	[26]	[27][2]	[26]
Item quod deinceps non fiant magistri	25	27		[27]	[3]	
Magister hospitii	26	28	26	[28]	[26]	[25]
Eorum multos produxit ambitio			[28]			
Item officiales curie Romane non permittantur publice nutrire concubinas (Not found in any other manuscript; edited p. 411 below)			[29]			
In collatione beneficiorum (=Common, c. 36, para. [1]–[13])			[30]			
De casibus reseruatis (=Common, c. 31)[4]			[31]			
De sessionibus et locis ordinandis	27	29	[32]	[29]	[5]	[6]
Circa constitutiones Jo. xxii	28	30		[30]		[27]
[Item quando uadunt equitando] (part of preceding paragraph in other MSS)	29					
Item quod auditores non sint familiares	30	31	[33]	[31]		[28]

---

[1] Appears in margin rather than text of S.
[2] V lacks the remaining paragraphs in c.6.
[3] V lacks this paragraph, but has a note in the text saying that the constitution
follows below.
[4] The text appears a second time in D in the normal order of the Common
collection (fol. 150v; see Table 1)
[5] V has a marginal note which reports the deliberation of this paragraph, but
lacks the paragraph.
[6] In place of this schedule M has only the following short statement:
Ordinentur sessiones in curia et interea hoc plenius deliberetur.

TABLE 4

Second Reform Committee
Concordance of Manuscripts

Rubric	S^2	W^2	D^2	Common
Meetings of general councils (*Quamuis ex sacrorum*) [I 4]	c.1	c.11	c.4[1]	c.1
Prevention of future schisms (*Si vero*) [II]	c.2	c.13,15	c.5–6	c.1
Papal oath of office (*Quanto Romanus pontifex*) [III 3]	c.3	c.10, 13a[2]	c.1	Cf. c.2
Deposition of pope (*Ne sancta mater*) [XIX 2]	c.4	c.8	c.3	Cf. c.5
Educational qualifications for clergy (*Licet diuina*) [XIII 7]	c.5	c.1	c.8	Cf. c.36
Transfers of prelates (*Cum ex prelatorum*) [IV 2]	c.6	c.9	c.9	Cf. c.37
Alienations of property (*Ut Romanus pontifex*) [XVIII 1]	c.7	c.7	c.2	Cf. c.2b
Simony (*Contra labem*) [IX 3]	c.8	Cf. W[1], c.3	c.10	c.3
Alienations (*Cum post obitum*) [XVIII 3]	c.9	c.24		Cf. c.2b
Spoils and procurations (*Cum per papam*) [V 2]	c.10	c.6		Cf. c.7
Cardinals (*Statuimus ut deinceps*) [XII 2]	c.11	c.5		c.5
Elections made by *preces* (*Statutum felicis recordationis*) [XXIII 2]	c.12			c.9

---

[1] The arenga is lacking in D^2; the decree begins with the words "Hoc perpetuo decreto".

[2] This fragment is probably the final lines of a schedule on the papal oath of office. I agree with Finke (*ACC*.2.555) that the schedule was an attempt to convert the schedule "De grauibus" into additions to the papal oath (See Common collection, [c.2a]: "Vel fiat supradicta constitutio per modum additionis ad professionem Bonifatii VIII supra proxime positam mutatis verbis in primam personam. . . .")

TABLE 4 cont.

Rubric	S²	W²	D²	Common
Dispensation for age requirements (*Non dispenset papa*) [X 9]	c.13			c.16
De causis tractandis in Curia et remittendis a penis friuole appellantium [Rubric only] [XIV]	c.14			
Poor qualifications of clergy in Germany [Job Vener's proposal] (*Quia proch dolor*) [XLIII]			c.7	New
Confirmations of elections (*Vacantibus ecclesiis*) [XVII]		c.2		Cf. c.36
Collations and reservations (*De beneficiis vacantibus*) [XIII 8]		c.3		Cf. c.36
Alienations (*Congregatis dominis*) [XVIII 2]		c.4		New
Meetings of general councils (*Quantis iam quasi*) [I 2]		c.12		Cf. c.1
Deposition of pope (*Et quoniam decet*) [XIX 1]		c.14		c.5
Commendams (*Primo dimittent*) [XX 1]		c.16		New
Revenues of cardinals (*Primo, nullus*) [XX 2]		c.17		New
Spoils and fruits during vacancies (*Decet Romanum*) [VIII 3]		c.18		Cf. c.7
Tenths (*Videtur sancte synodo*) [XXII 2]		c.19		Cf. c.18
Revenues of cardinals (*Primo infra annum*) [XX 3]		c.20		New
Dispensations (*Primo quod tollantur*) [X 10]		c.21		Cf. cc.10–15
Indulgences (*Item reuocentur omnes*) [X 10]		c.22		Cf. V, cc.14–15
Papal privileges (*Item inhibeatur*) [X 10]		c.23		New
Fruits during vacancies (*Vacantibus ecclesiis*) [VIII 2]		c.25		Cf. c.7

TABLE 5

Information from Reform Committee Manuscripts Concerning Dates of Deliberation of Reform Proposals

Actions: I = Introduced C = Concluded D = Deliberated G = General comment R = Repetita The schedule listed is the version discussed on the given date; the manuscript listed is the one which contains the date.

Date	Reform	Action	Schedule	MS
August 20, 1415	Translations of prelates (*Hec est in constitutione iam data que incipit Quia decet; xx augusti fuit determinatum quod non nisi in concilio fiant et quod sic statuatur.*)	D	Common, c.2 (Part 2)	EW, c. 37
August 28, 1415? (die Augustini)	Reforms concerning provisions	I	Common, c.36 (D, fol. 145r)	D
August 30, 1415	Educational requirements for abbots	C	Common, c.36, para. 2	EW
Tuesday Sep 3, 1415	Reforms of curia introduced by Adimari	I	Common, c.6, para. 1–24	V
Sep 6	Reforms of curia	D	"",15–24	V
No date	Additions to reforms of curia, Adimari; clerici capelle and examinator curie	I	"",25–26	V
Sep 4 ?	Reforms of curia, para. 25–26	D	"",25–26	V
Saturday Sep 7	Fuller discussion of Sessiones in curia, whether prelates should precede protonotaries	D	"",29	C W? V
Sep 11–12	Constitution to be drawn up against use of *preces* in elections, etc.; concluded Sep. 12	I	Common, c.9	EW, c. 38
Sep 13	Provisions—Decided to refer all these matters to the nations	G	Common, c.36	EW

TABLE 5 cont.

Date	Reform	Action	Schedule	MS
Sep 14, 16	Dispensations for bishops and abbots not to take orders	C	Common, c.10	EW
Before Thursday, Sep 18 (!)	Many schedules presented, much proposed, so that nothing discussed except dispensations	G	Common, cc.10–16; V, preceding c.2	V
Thursday Sep 19	*Eo iam multos* introduced by Adimari	I	Common, c.8	V
Friday Sep 20	Zabarella's schedule against use of *preces* in elections (See Sept. 11–12 above.	I	Common, c.9	V
Friday Sep 20	Measure on tenths	I	Common, c.18	V
Tuesday Sep 24	Measure on conversi (Deliberated on second day)	I	Common, c.19 V, c.13	V
Wednesday Sep 25	Indulgences (V says it was discussed Sep 20, prob. error)	I	M, c. 38–39	V M
Sep 27	Three measures presented by Bishop of Bath:		V, cc.16–18a	V
	1. Exemptions for religious houses (Commission formed to draft measure)	I	V, c.16; cf. Common, c.20	V
	2. Privileges of lesser prelates to wear pontifical insignia	I	V, c.17; cf. Common, c.21	V
	3. Examination of persons to be ordained	I	V, c.18–18a; cf. Common, c.34	V
Sep 30	Privileges of religious to hold benefices	C	Common, c.35, para. 2	EW V M
Oct 1	Statutes of cathedral chapters which require new canons to surrender first years' revenues	C?	Common, c.27 V, c.22	CEW

TABLE 5 cont.

Date	Reform	Action	Schedule	MS
Thursday Oct 3	Dispensations for those ignorant of the vernacular	R	Common, c.22	V M
Mon–Tues Oct 7–8[1]	Schedule of Zabarella on unions	ID	M, c.44 V, c.21	V M
Wednesday Oct 9	Examination of ordinees (includes initial discussion of c.27, which is concluded November 9 below)	D	V, c.18–18a	V
Oct 10	Provincial councils	?	Common, c.29	CEW
Oct 18	Tenths (deliberation of schedule prepared by Adimari and Zabarella?)	D	Common, c.18	V
Oct 19	Examination of those to be ordained		Common, c.34	EW
Saturday, Oct 19	*Eo iam multos*, second deliberation	RD	Common, c.8	V
Oct 20	Privileges for religious; not concluded yet	D	V, c.19 Common, c.35	EW
Oct 28	Privileges granted to lower prelates	D	Common, c.21	V
Nov 4	Privileges for religious and dispensations	D	Common, c.11 23a, c.35 V, c.19	V
Nov 5	Incompatible benefices	D,C?	Common, c.12–13	EW
Nov 7	Dispensation for incompatible benefices	D	Common, c.11	EW

---

[1] Both V and M have the wrong day of the week for the introduction of the measure (Monday, October 8); but V says the proposed decree was deliberated Tuesday, October 8, which is correct.)

TABLE 5 cont.

Date	Reform	Action	Schedule	MS
Nov 7	Residency of prelates	C	Common, c.14, 28	CEW
Nov 9	On age for making religious profession	C	V, c.18^2 Common, c.28	CEW
Nov 16	Simony	C	Common, c.26	CEW
Nov 18	Collations, concerning residence of bishops who are doctors of theology	D	Common, c. 36 Para. [15]	EW
Nov 19	Unions Beginning of notations "Detur"	C	Common, c.23	CEW
Nov 22	Material on exemptions hasn't been discussed yet	G	Common, c.33	ESW
Nov 27	On penitential cases reserved to Holy See	C	Common, c.31	E
Aug 14, 1416?	Incompatible benefices	C	Common, c.12	W

---

[2] Substance appears as extensive marginal note on c.18 in V

TABLE 6

Concordance of *ACC* with this edition

I. SCHEDULES RELATING TO REFORM ARTICLES OF 39TH SESSION

39.1   Meetings of general councils *De conciliis generalibus*
 I 1   Common, c.1
 I 2 W^2, c.12
 I 3 D^2, c.4
 I 4 S^2, c.1
 I 5   Reform decree
39.2 Prevention of future schisms *Aduersus futura scismata*
 II S^2, c.2   Si uero
39.3   Papal oath of office *Professio pape*
 III 1   Common, c.2
 III 2 W^2, c.13a
 III 3 S^2, c.3
39.4   Transfers of prelates *Ne prelati transferantur inuiti*
 IV 1   Common, c.37
 IV 2 S^2, c.6
39.5   Spoils and procurations *De spoliis et procurationibus*
 V 1   Common, c.7
 V 2 S^2, c.10

II. SCHEDULES RELATING TO REFORM ARTICLES OF 43D SESSION

43.1   Exemptions *De exemptionibus*
 VI 1   Common, c.20
 VI 2   Common, c.33
43.2   Unions and incorporations *De unionibus et incorporationibus*
 VII 1   V, c.21
 VII 2   Common, c.23
43.3   Fruits during vacancies *De fructibus medii temporis*
 VIII 1   Common, c.43 [Really deals with money extorted by prelates
             from clergy]
 VIII 2 W^2, c.25
 VIII 3 W^2, c.18
43.4   Simony *De simonia*
 IX 1   Common, c.26
 IX 2   Common, c.3
 IX 3 S^2, c.8
43.5   Dispensations *De dispensationibus*
 X 1   Common, c.10
 X 2   Common, c.11
 X 3   Common, c.12
 X 4–5   Common, c.13
 X 6–7   Common, c.14
 X 8   Common, c.15

X 9   Common, c.16; S^2, c.13
X 10 W^2, c.21–23
43.6   Papal tenths *De decimis*: See 40.18 below (The *ACC* deviates here from its proposed order)
43.7   Clerical attire and decorum *De vita et honestate clericorum*
XI 1   Common, c.40
XI 2   Common, c.48

III.   SCHEDULES RELATING TO ARTICLES IN THE REFORM *CAUTIO* OF
       THE 40TH SESSION AND TO THE CONCORDATS
       (Key: F1 = Article 1 of French concordat, etc.)

40.1   Number and qualifications of cardinals *De numero, qualitate et natione dominorum Cardinalium* (F1, S1, G1, E1)
XII 1   Common, c.4
XII 2 S^2, c.11
40.2,3,4   Reservations, provisions and annates *De reservationibus sedis Apostolice. De annatis, communibus servitiis et minutis. De collatione beneficiorum* (F2–3, S2–3, G2–3) (See also 40.10 below)
XIII 1–2   ¹
XIII 3   ²
XIII 4   Common, c.36
XIII 5   Common, c.41
XIII 6   Common, c.25
XIII 7 S^2, c.5
XIII 8 W^2, c.3
XIII 9   Common, c.42
40.5   Trials in the Roman Curia *De causis in Romana curia tractandis vel non* and 40.6 Appeals to the Roman curia *De appellationibus ad Romanam curiam* (F4, S4, G4)
XIV S^2, c.14
40.7   Reform of the curia *De officiis cancellarie et penitentiarie* (E7)
XV 1   Common, c.6
XV 1   Common, c.8; D, c.6,
                para 28³
XV 2   Extrav. 4
[40.8   *De exemptionibus et incorporationibus tempore scismatis factis* and 40.9 *De commendis* See 43.1–2 above and 40.16 below] (F5, S5, G5, G9, E3, E5)
40.10   Confirmations *De confirmationibus electionum* (See also measures under 40.2–4 above)
XVII W^2, c.2
[40.11   *De fructibus medii temporis* See 43.3 above]
40.12   Alienations of property *De non alienandis bonis Romane ecclesie et aliarum ecclesiarum*

---

¹ Proposals of German and English nations; not part of reform committee deliberations.
² D, c.6 para. [30] (See Table 3); variants from this text are included in the edition of Common, c.8.
³ See Table 3

XVIII 1 S^2, c.7
XVIII 2 W^2, c.4
XVIII 3 S^2, c.9
40.13   Deposition of pope *Propter que et quomodo papa possit corrigi vel deponi*
    XIX 1 W^2, c.14
              [=Common, c.5]
    XIX 2 S^2, c.4
[40.14   *De extirpatione simonie* and 40.15 *De dispensationibus* See 43.4 and 43.5 above]
(F7, S7, G6, G8, E7)
40.16   Provision for status of pope and cardinals *De provisione status pape et cardina-lium* (F5, S5, G5, G9)
    XX 1 W^2, c.16
    XX 2 W^2, c.17
    XX 3 W^2, c.20
40.17   Indulgences *De indulgentiis* (F6, S6, G10, E2)
    XXI 1   V, c.14
    XXI 2   V, c.15
40.18   Papal tenths *De decimis* (See 43.6 above)
    XXII 1   Common, c.18
    XXII 2 W^2, c.19

IV. PROPOSALS NOT LINKED BY THE *ACC* WITH ANY DECREE OR ARTICLE IN THE REFORM *CAUTIO* OF THE 40TH SESSION

Elections made by *preces*
    XXIII 1   Common, c.38
    XXIII 2   Common, c.9; S^2, c.12
    XXIII 3   Common, c.9a
Litigants in curia (Belongs with 40.5–6 above)
    XXIV   Common, c.17
Non-confiscation of possessions of *conversi*
    XXV 1   Common, c.19
    XXV 2   V, c.13
Privileges to wear pontifical attire (See English concordat, c.4)
    XXVI 1   Common, c.21
    XXVI 2   V, c.17
Priests ignorant of the vernacular
    XXVII 1   Common, c.22
    XXVII 2   V, c.20
Non-residence (Belongs with 43.5 above)
    XXVIII   Common, c.24
Payments which collegiate churches require new canons to make
    XXIX 1   V, c.22
    XXIX 2   Common, c.27
    XXIX 3   Common, c.44
Minimum age for taking religious vows
    XXX   Common, c.28
Provincial councils and synods
    XXXI   Common, c.29
Penitential cases reserved to the Holy See
    XXXII   Common, c.31

Perpetual vicars (See English Concordat, c.3)
XXXIII   Common, c.32
Simony in pontifical acts (Belongs with 43.4 above)
XXXIV   Common, c.30
Examination of ordinands
XXXV 1   Common, c.34
XXXV 2   V, c.18
XXXV 3   V, c.18a
Privileges of religious to hold benefices outside their order
XXXVI   Common, c.35; V, c.19
Concubinage of priests (Belongs with 43.7 above; see also German concordat, art. 7)
XXXVII   Common, c.39
Payments demanded by princes from the clergy
XXXVIII   Common, c.45–46
Auditor of the camera at Avignon
XXXIX   Common, c.47
Qualifications of vicars (See English Concordat, c.3)
XL   Common, c.49
Oaths required by chapters of collegiate churches
XLI   Common, c.50
Against prelates declaring war on each other
XLII   Common, c.51
Poor qualifications of clergy in Germany (Job Vener's proposal)
XLIII D^2, c.7
Proposal of Jean Mauroux for reform *in capite*
XLIV   Extrav. 3

FIRST REFORM COMMITTEE

COMMON COLLECTION

A = Augsburg, Staats- und Stadtbibliothek, 2° Cod 226
C = Bernkastel-Kues, St. Nikolaus-Hospitalbibliothek 168
D = Vienna, Österreichische Nationalbibliothek, lat. 5113
E = Vienna, Österreichische Nationalbibliothek, lat. 5069
M = Vat. lat. 3884
P = Paris, Bibliothèque Nationale, lat. 9514
S = Stuttgart, Landesbibliothek, Cod. iur. Fol. 130
V = Vat. lat. 12572
W = Vienna, Österreichische Nationalbibliothek, lat. 5094

[c.1][I 1] De conciliis generalibus et aduersus futura scismata
  Quoniam ex obmissione generalium conciliorum errores et scismata, impressiones et scandala in ecclesia dei dampnabiliter hactenus succreuerunt, volentes futuris obuiare periculis hoc perpetuo
decreto statuimus ut deinceps saltem de decennio in decennium   5
generalia concilia, exceptis duobus primis futuris conciliis, quorum
primum a fine huius concilii usque ad quinquennium, secundum
vero a fine sequentis concilii usque ad septennium, et deinceps de
decennio in decennium celebrentur, in locis que summus pontifex
in fine cuiuslibet concilii, approbante et consentiente concilio, vel   10
in eius defectum ipsum concilium deputare et assignare teneatur;
ut sic per quamdam continuationem semper aut concilium vigeat
aut per termini pendentiam expectetur. Quem terminum liceat
summo pontifici de fratrum suorum consilio ob emergentes forte
casus abbreuiare sed nullatenus liceat prorogare. Locum autem   15
deputatum non mutet nisi forte ex euidenti necessitate et de fra-

---

1 De conciliis . . . scismata] *om.* P; Aduersus futura scismata S; Auisamenta per
XXXV cardinales prelatos et doctores in loco reformatorum Constantiense *add.*
D   2 Quoniam] Primus punctus: De concilii [celebratione?] *rubric add. in marg.*
S   3 dampnabiliter] et fere irreparabiliter *add. and underscored* S   4 hoc per-
petuo] ac perfecto D   6 conciliis *om.* E   7 fine] vel ante finem *add. in
marg.* S   12 sic] *corr. from* sicud S   14 suorum] aut duarum partium *add above
line* S   ob] *corr. from* aut P   ob emergentes] obmergentes EW   15 ab-
breuiare] breuiare EPW; *corr. from* breuiare S (ab *add. above line*)   locum] *above
line* S, *in text* DEW   autem] aut E   16 deputatum] deputet A

trum predictorum aut duarum partium consensu atque subscriptione; quam mutationem vel abbreuiationem per annum ante prefixum terminum publicare et intimare teneatur.

[c.1a][I 2] Si vero, quod absit, nouum scisma oriri contigerit, ita quod duo vel plures pro summis pontificibus ex quacumque causa se gerant, a die quo ipsi duo vel plures insignia pontificatus publice assumpserint seu administrare ceperint, intelligatur ipso iure terminus concilii tunc forte ultra annum pendens ad annum proximum breuiatus. Ad quod omnes prelati et ceteri qui ad concilium ire tenentur sub penis iuris et aliis per concilium imponendis absque alia vocatione conueniant; necnon imperator ceterique reges et principes vel personaliter vel per sollempnes nuntios tamquam ad commune incendium extinguendum per viscera misericordie Iesu Christi ex nunc exorati concurrant. Et quilibet ipsorum pro Romano pontifice se gerentium infra mensem a die qua scientiam habere potuit alium vel alios assumpsisse papatus insignia vel in papatu administrasse, teneatur sub interminatione maledictionis eterne et amissione iuris si quod forte quesiuit in papatu, quam ipso facto incurrat, et ultra hoc ad quaslibet dignitates actiue et passiue sit inhabilis, concilium ipsum ad terminum anni predictum indicere et publicare ac per suas litteras competitori vel competitoribus ipsum vel ipsos prouocando ad causam et ceteris prelatis ac principibus quantum in eo fuerit intimare, necnon termino prefixo ad locum concilii personaliter se transferre, nec inde discedere donec per concilium causa scismatis plenarie sit finita.

Qui sic electi seu papatum tenentes a die predicta in papatu nullatenus administrent nec interim eisdem a fidelibus, nisi quo ad conueniendum ad concilium sub interminatione diuini iudicii, quomodolibet obediatur.

---

1 aut *om.* P   3 teneatur] singulis prouinciis. Additio: Quod statuatur pena [si] non fecerit vel iuret [in] professione sua se facturum singulis prouinciis *add. in marg.* S   4 vero] Secundus punctus: De scismate *rubric add. in marg.* S   8 ultra] *corr. from* infra P   12 personaliter] *corr. from* principaliter S   14 Et] Additio: Nichilominus *add. in marg.* S   16 potuit] potuerit P   17 administrasse] administrare P   18 quam] quem P   19 et *(second)*] vel D   22 ac] et EW   26 Qui] De subtractione obedientie tempore scismatis *rubric add. in marg.* S   tenentes] Additio: Pretextu electionis facte ab hiis ad quos ius pertinet eligendi. *add. in marg.* S   27 administrent] administretur C; Additio: Sic tamen quod nullus illorum contendentium in concilio presidebit nec vocem habebit in discussione [sue] cause. *add. in marg.* S   28 iudicii] Additio: Et pena fautorie schismatis *add. in marg.* S   29 obediatur] Additio: Cardinales vero et alii quicumque eligentes medio tempore nichil recipiant de camera necque de beneficiis que obtinebunt sed eos camerarius colligere teneatur diligenter restitutendos et distribuendos prout deliberauerit concilium. *add. in marg.* S

Quod si forte electionem Romani pontificis per metum seu impressionem fieri contingat, ipsam nullius decernimus efficacie vel momenti. Nec posse per sequentem consensum etiam metu cessante ratificari vel approbari. Non tamen liceat cardinalibus sub pena amissionis cardinalatus et omnium beneficiorum quam ipso facto incurrant ad aliam electionem procedere nisi ille sic electus forte renunciet vel decedat, donec per generale concilium de electione illa fuerit iudicatum. Et si procedant, nulla sit electio ipso iure. Sintque sic eligentes et electus, si se papatui ingesserit, omni dignitate, honore et statu, etiam papali, cardinalatus et pontificali, ipso iure priuati et inhabiles de cetero ad easdem.

[W², *in marg.*: Et eo casu concilium de electione pape prouideat, illa vice. Nec aliquis eidem secundo electo ut pape sub pena fautorie scismatis obediat quoquomodo.]

Sed liceat, immo et teneatur collegium totum aut saltem maior pars ipsorum, nam paucioribus in hoc casu audientiam ad euitandam scandalum decernimus denegari, quam cito sine periculo personarum poterunt, etiam si periculum omnium bonorum immineat, retrahere se ad locum tutum et metum predictum allegare, nec ultra proximum futurum concilium ullo modo possint differre.

Teneantur insuper, postquam se retraxerint et metum allegauerint modo predicto prouocare sic electum ad concilium, quod si ultra annum pendeat a die prouocationis huiusmodi intelligatur ad annum ut supra ipso iure terminus breuiatus. Et nichilominus teneatur electus ipse sub penis predictis et cardinales prouocantes sub pena amissionis cardinalatus et omnium beneficiorum suorum,

(marginal line numbers: 5, 10, 15, 20, 25)

---

1 metum] qui caderet in constantem *add. above line* W² (*corr. from* in constantem cadentem)   3 sequentem] consequentem D   metu] predicto *add. above line* W²   4–6 sub pena . . . incurrant *om.* CD, *underscored* W; *bracketed* S   9 sic] secundo *add. above line* W²   et] Additio: secundo *add. in marg.* S   ingess.] ingesserint D; ingresserit E; inexerit (?) P   11 easdem] eosdem P; et etiam ad papalem *add. in marg.* W²; Additio: Quo casu pape electio penes concilium plenarie remaneat. *add. in marg.* S.   12 pape] *add. above line*   13 vice] Prout sibi videbitur expedire *add. and struck out.*   eidem] *add. above line*   14 quoquomodo] quo casu d. Maiori parte licet reclamare sed in concilio maior pars tertie licet reclamare et audietur in concilio *add. and struck out.*   16 ipsorum] eorum AS casu] causu (!) P   16–17 nam . . . denegrari] *underscored* W   19 retrahere] *struck out,* transferre *add in marg.* W²   allegare] Coram notariis publicis et notabilibus personis (in loco insigni *add. and struck out*) ac multitudine populi in loco insigni *add. in marg.* W²; Additio: Coram notariis publicis et notabilibus personis et si in loco insigni fuerint coram multitudine populi et sub penis suprascriptis. *add. in marg.* S   20 ullo] nullo D   differre] differere D; deferre P   21 Teneantur] Terminus concilii propter metum *rubric add. in marg.* S   retraxerint] *struck out,* transtulerint *add. above line* W²   22 quod] concilium *add. above line* W   23 prouocationis huiusmodi] *struck out* W², allegationis preterite *add. above line, but also struck out* W², prouocationis huiusmodi *add. in marq.* W²   26 suorum] Additio: Si que forsitan tunc habeant *add. in marg.* S

quam ipso facto incurrant, infra mensem a die prouocationis concilium ipsum ut supra dicitur indicere et publicare et quam citius poterunt intimare, et ad locum concilii tempore conuenienti personaliter se transferre et usque ad finem cause expectare. Teneantur quoque prelati et ceteri ut supra ad conuocationem cardinalium tantum, si forte electus conuocare cessaret, accedere. Qui sic electus post prouocationem predictam nisi in conuocando concilium ut prefertur administrare in papatu non valeat nec sibi a Christi fidelibus sub interminatione diuini iudicii interim nisi quo ad conueniendum ad concilium quomodolibet obediatur.

Quod si infra annum ante diem indicti concilii contingant supradicti casus, vel quod plures se gerant pro papa vel quod unus per metum eligatur, censeantur ipso iure tam gerentes se pro papa quam electus per metum et cardinales ad dictum concilium prouocati, teneanturque in ipso concilio comparere personaliter, causam exponere et iudicium concilii expectare.

Sed si dictis casibus contingentibus contingat forte casus aliquis quo necessarium sit locum concilii mutare, ut obsidionis vel guerre aut pestis aut similis, teneantur nichilominus tam omnes supradicti quam omnes prelati ceterique qui ad concilium ire tenentur ad locum proximiorem qui sit habilis ad concilium conuenire. Possitque maior pars prelatorum qui infra mensem ad locum certum declinauerint illum sibi et aliis pro loco concilii deputare, ad quem ceteri conuenire teneantur ac si a principio fuisset deputatus. Concilium autem ut prefertur conuocatum et congregatum de huiusmodi scismatis causa cognoscens et incontumatiam electorum seu

---

2 et (*first*)] *om.* EW   et (*second*)] *om.* ACPS   citius] totius S   2–3 indicere . . .
intimare] indicere, publicare, et intimare quam citius poterunt. P   6 forte] sic
add. above line–W² conuocare] conuenire (?) A   7 conuocando] in concilio ipso
non presideat; quinymo sit a [die] nuntiandi conci[lii] ipso iure ab administratione papatus suspensus. *add. in marg.* W²   8 nec] Additio: Nec in concilio
presideat neque vocem habeat.*add. in marg.* S   sibi] sibi quoque *add. above line* W
9–10 conueniendum] conuocandum S   7–10 post prouocationem . . . concilium *struck out* W²   11 Quod *om.* P   indicti] interdicti (!) P   12 pro]
Additio: vel pro Romanis pontificibus *add. in marg.* S   13 metum] seu impressionem *add. above line* W²   eligatur] allegatur D; *corr. from* alligatur C; Additio:
vel impressionem *add. in marg.* S   censeantur] *struck out, but added again*; electus
interdicitur *add. above line and struck out* W²; vel impressionem *add.
above line* W²;   14 metum] seu impressionem *add.
above line* W²   15 comparere] compare
E   17 Sed] De mutatione loci *rubric add. in marg.* S   contingentibus] *struck
out,* occurrentibus *add. in marg.* W²   21 proximiorem] Additio: Et aptum ut
supra conuenire. *add. in marg.* S; ut premittitur *add. in marg.* W²   qui] quis (!)
P   24 a] *corr. from* in P   26 incontumatiam] incontumationem W; Additio:
seu absentiam *add. in marg.* S

gerentium se pro papa seu cardinalium si forte uenire neglexerint, litem dirimat causamque diffiniat ac culpabiles in scismate procurando seu nutriendo, vel in administrando aut obediendo vel administrantibus fauendo, seu contra interdictum superius eligendo vel calumpniosos in allegando metum etiam ultra predictas penas cuiuscumque gradus, status, seu preeminentie existant ecclesiastice vel mundane sic puniat, ut vindicte rigor transeat ceteris in exemplum. Additientes quod in fine cuiuslibet concilii generalis hoc decretum sollempniter legatur et innouetur.

[c.2][III 1] Professio Bonifacii VIII, que hic ponitur ut de cetero per assumendos in pontifices summos fiat, additis illis de quibus in sequentibus constitutionibus et que videbuntur addenda.

In nomine sancte et indiuidue trinitatis Amen. Anno dominice incarnationis Millesimo CC^{mo} XIIII° (!) indictione octaua ego Benedictus Gaytanus sancte Romane ecclesie dyaconus Cardinalis et electus, ut fiam per dei gratiam huius sancte et apostolice sedis humilis minister, profiteor tibi, beate Petre, apostolorum princeps, cui claues regni celestis ad ligandum atque soluendum in celo et in terra creator atque redemptor omnium Iesus Christus tradidit, inquiens, "Quecumque ligaueris super terram erunt ligata et in celis, et quecumque solueris super terram erunt soluta et in celis,"[1] sancteque ecclesie tue quam hodie tuo presidio regendam suscipio, quod, quamdiu in hac misera vita constitutus fuero, ipsam non deseram, non derelinquam, non abnegabo, nec abdicabo aliquatenus neque ex quacumque causa et cuiuscumque metus vel periculi occasione dimittam, vel me segregabo ab ipsa; sed vere fidei rectitudinem quam Christo auctore tradente per te et beatissimum

5

10

15

20

25

---

1   Mt. 16,19

---

1 pro *om.* D   papa] propria E; Additio: vel summis pontificibus *add. in marg.* S   si] se S venire] venit E   2 culpabiles] inhominabiles (?) E   5 in] aut C   7 puniat] puniant D   9 hoc] ob D   10 Professio] *This schedule begins on a new folio in D and is preceded by the rubric* "Incipit materia reformationis cleri concepta in concilio Constantiense"   12 sequentibus . . . addenda] consequentibus constitutionibus videbuntur. C; addenda *om.* EPW   15 Gaytanus] Gagetanus D; Gauetanus P   16 et (first) *om.* DW   17 beate] sancte D; patre *add.* E   22 tuo] toto P   suscipio] accipio C   23 ipsam] papatum (?) P   25 neque] utque C   27 Christo] ipso D   per te] partem C

coapostolum tuum Paulum que per discipulos et successores vestros usque ad exiguitatem meam perlatum in tua sancta ecclesia
reperi totis conatibus meis usque ad animam et sanguinem custodire; tam de sancte et indiuidue trinitatis ministerio, que unus est
deus, quam que pro dispensatione que secundum carnem facta est
unigeniti filii domini nostri Iesu Christi et de ceteris ecclesie dei
dogmatibus sicut in uniuersalibus conciliis et constitutionibus
apostolicorum pontificum probatissimorumque ecclesie doctorum
scriptis sunt commendata, idest quecumque ad rectitudinem vere
nostreque orthodoxe fidei a te traditionem accipiunt conseruare;
sancta quoque octo uniuersalia concilia id est Nicenum, Constantinopolitanum, Ephesinum primum, Calcedonensem, quintum quoque et sextum item Constantinopolitanum, et septimum item Nicenum, octauum quoque item Constantinopolitanum, usque ad
unum apicem immutilata seruare et pari honore et reuerentia digna
habere, et que predicauerunt et statuerunt omnimode sequi et
predicare, queque condempnauerunt condempnare ore et corde;
diligentius autem et viuatius quamdiu vixero omnia decreta canonica predecessorum apostolicorum nostrorum pontificum, quecumque vel sinodaliter statuerunt et probata sunt, confirmare et indiminuta seruare et sicut ab eis statuta sunt in sui vigoris stabilitate
custodire, quemque vel quosque condempnauerunt vel abdi-
cauerunt simili sententia condempnare vel abdicare; disciplinam et
ritum ecclesie sicut inueni et a sanctis predecessoribus meis canonice traditum reperi, quamdiu michi vita comes fuerit, illibata
custodire et indiminutas res ecclesie conseruare neque alienare seu
in feudum aut censum vel emphiteosim dare quomodolibet ex
quacumque causa; et, ut indiminute custodiantur, operam dare
nichil de traditione quam a probatissimis predecessoribus meis
traditam et seruatam reperi diminuere vel mutare aut aliquam
nouitatem admittere, sed feruenter ut eorum vere hic discipulus et
sequipeda totis mentis mee conatibus que tradita canonice comperi
obseruare ac venerari; si qua vero emerserint contra canonicam
disciplinam filiorum meorum sancte Romane ecclesie cardinalium,
cum quorum consilio, et consensu, directione et rememoratione
ministerium meum geram et peragam, consilio emendare aut

2 perlatum] perlatam S, et perlatum C   6 de ceteris] *corr. from* de certis
D   9 ad *om.* P   10 a] et P   11 sancta] Nota que sint octo concilia un-
iuersalia *add. in marg., but struck out* D   12 primum] *corr. from* quintum
D   13 et (*first*) *om.* S   14 item *om.* S   13–14 et septimum . . . . Con-
stantinopolitanum] *add. in marg.* S   15 inmutilata] in mutilate S, in mutilata
E   18 vixero] vixere E   19 nostrorum] meorum P   22 quemque] queque
E   22–23 abdicauerunt] applicauerunt P   24 sicut] sint S; sicud CE   et
add. CDE

patienter excepta fidei aut Christiane religionis graui offensione tua
et beatissimi coapostoli tui Pauli patrocinante intercessione tolle-
rare; sacrosque canones et canonica instituta pontificum ut diuina
et celestia mandata deo auxiliante custodire, utpote deo et tibi
sciens me redditurum de omnibus que profiteor et quamdiu vixero   5
egero, vel obmisero districtam in diuino iuditio rationem, cuius
sanctissime sedi diuina dignatione te patrocinante presideo et
vicem intercessionibus tuis adimpleo.

Eris autem michi in illa terribili die propitius hoc conanti et
diligenter seruare curanti. Adiutorium quoque ut prebeas obsecro   10
in hac corruptibili vita constituto, ut irreprehensibilis appaream
ante conspectum iudicis omnium domini nostri Iesu Christi dum
terribiliter de commissis aduenerit iudicare, ut facias me dextre
partis participem et inter fideles discipulos ac successores tuos esse
consortem.   15

Hanc autem professionem meam per notarium et scrinearium[2]
sancte Romani ecclesie me iubente scriptam propria manu subscripsi, et tibi beate Petre et apostolorum omnium princeps pura
mente et deuota conscientia super sanctum corpus et altare tuum
sinceriter offero. Actum Rome mense, anno et indictione quibus   20
supra, presentibus etc.

[c.2a] De grauibus per papam non faciendis nisi modo infrascripto
Cum antiqui et laudabilis moris fuerit ut maiores ecclesie cause
per summum pontificem sine cardinalium sancte Romane ecclesie
consilio et assensu disponi non deberent unde etiam cetus cardina- 25
lium in hac quasi possessione esse dinoscitur quod eorum consilio
sunt per Romanos pontifices ardua negotia tractanda et terminan-
da, ad quod etiam iudicandum vetusti moris fuit assensum ipsum
subscriptionibus declarare. Ideo presenti decreto morem ipsum
laudabilem renouantes statuimus ut Romanus pontifex sine con-   30
sensu et subscriptione saltem maioris partis cardinalium collegialiter facta infrascripta de cetero non disponat: ut causarum fidei
decisiones, sanctorum canonizationes, anni jubilei reductionem,
seu de nouo indictionem, erectiones, extinctiones, seu suppres-

---

2 Cf. Hübler, p. 126.

---

3 ut *om.* P   4 celestia] ecclesiastica E   6 obmisero] obliuissero (?) P   8
vicem] vitam E   12 ante] autem E   16 scrinearium] scribeanum D;
scrinearium AE; *corr. from* scrinerium W; scrinearum (?) C; scrinearium *altered to*
scribeanum S.   22 grauibus] et arduis *add.* EW   infrascripto] ut sequitur
add. DEW   26 hac] hoc E   27 ardua] parua A; *corr. from* parua
S   tractanda] pertractanda D   28 iudicandum] iudicandi D   moris]
morum S   ipsum] ipsius E   33–34 anni . . . indictionem] *om.* CP; *underscored* W

siones, diuisiones, subiectiones, uniones ecclesiarum kathedralium et monasteriorum, promotiones cardinalium, priuationes, translationes inuitorum patriarcharum, archiepiscoporum, episcoporum, et abbatum saluo iure constitutionum suorum ordinum; priuilegiorum perpetuorum et realium nouas concessiones; exemptionum hactenus per Romanos pontifices ecclesiis, monasteriis, collegiis, et aliis locis concessarum reuocationes. Exemptiones etiam nouas et perpetuas ecclesiis, monasteriis, seu capitulis usque ad proximum futurum concilium non concedat sine cause cognitione et vocatis ordinariis (quod tamen locum non habeat in ecclesiis, monasteriis, seu capitulis de nouo edificandis seu constituendis que possit eximere.) Exemptiones ante presens scisma factas, alienationes bonorum immobilium vel mobilium preciosorum Romane ecclesie vel aliarum ecclesiarum et aliorum locorum ecclesiasticorum et piorum, priuilegia perpetua, immunitates, censuum et quorumcumque iurium et prouentuum perpetuorum remissiones seu dilationes, vicariatus et rectoratus terrarum ecclesie Romane, constitutiones, federa, paces, bella, legationes de latere, seu vicariorum et nuntiorum auctoritate legatorum de latere fungentium deputationes, et quecumque ardua seu pertinentia ad statum uniuersalis ecclesie; decernentes ut gesta preter vel contra formam premissam sint nulla ipso iure nec eis a katholicis in aliquo pareatur.

Vel fiat supradicta constitutio per modum additionis ad professionem Bonifacii VIII supra proxime positam mutatis verbis in primam personam, et hoc forte esset honestius quam per constitutionem. Et posset addi ad professionem etiam quod sequitur, videlicet: "Rectores ad regendum prouincias vel ciuitates ecclesie Romane nisi Cardinales aut prelatos non mittam; vicariatum alicuius terre ecclesie nisi ad triennium non concedam. Et ad custodiendum castra vel arces (rockas) ecclesie Romane non mittam aliquem consanguineum vel affinem nec aliquos alios ultra triennium duraturos."

---

1 subiectiones] subgessiones P   2–3 translationes inuitorum *om.* CP; *under-scored* W   3 inuitorum] inimicorum (!) E   4 constitutionum] constitutioni C   ordinum] Vicariatus et rectoratus terrarum ecclesie Romane constitutiones *add. and struck out* E   6 monast.] monachis E   7 reuocationes] renouationes (?) C   10 quod] quidem D   5–12 priuilegiorum . . . eximere] *in marg.* DW (*in a different hand* D)   12–15 Exemptiones . . . piorum *om.* P   15–17 censuum . . . dilationes *om.* P   12–17 Exemptiones ante . . . dilationes *om.* CEW   19 et *om.* EW   18–19 seu . . . latere *add. in marg.* D (*homoiotel.*)   24 supradicta] predicta D   29 aut *om.* P   31 arces (rockas)] arces ACP; rockas *add. above line* S; arces *om.* D; *in W* rocchas *appears in the text but is underlined and arces written above* (E *has* "ac rocchas" *with* "arces" *above line and no underlining.*)   32 aliquem *om.* P   ultra] ad C

[c.2b] Ad idem.

Quia decet Romanum pontificem ministerium suum cum discretione, que mater est omnium virtutum, peragere, fratrumque suorum cardinalium in magnis, et concilii generalis in maioribus, consilio et consensu uti, intendens sacrosancta generalis Constantiensis sinodus Romane et aliarum ecclesiarum, monasteriorum et aliorum locorum piorum futuris dispendiis consideratione preteritorum ecclesiam dei scandalizantium obuiare, statuit, diffinit et ordinat, quod deinceps ipse Romanus pontifex, sine consilio et assensu generalis concilii, res, iura, redditus, possessiones, castra, ciuitates, villas, oppida, census, pensiones, canones seu alia bona quecumque immobilia vel mobilia preciosa Romane et aliarum ecclesiarum monasteriorum seu aliorum locorum ecclesiasticorum predictorum in perpetuum seu ad tempus magnum, quod intelligatur decem annorum contra iuris formam non alienet nec inpignoret seu de nouo infeudet aut in emphiteosim vel afficctum assignet. Nec pensiones, census, aut canones ecclesiarum monasteriorum et locorum predictorum remittat aut ad solutionem eorum terminum ultra biennium proroget seu concedat. Erectiones, suppressiones, diuisiones, uniones ecclesiarum cathedralium et monasteriorum ac prioratuum qui sunt principales dignitates, translationes inuitorum patriarcharum, archiepiscoporum, episcoporum non faciat usque ad proximum futurum concilium. (Ubi tamen immineret scandalum et periculum ecclesie expectando celebrationem futuri proximi concilii generalis, licitum sit Romano pontifici cum consilio et consensu cardinalium seu maioris partis eorum absque translatione facienda de inuito scandalo huiusmodi prouidere.) Annum etiam iubileum seu plene remissionis non mutet, sed perduret fixus anno quinquagesimo ut alias fuit statutum, nec mutari possit nisi in concilio generali. Et si contrarium premissorum vel eorum cuiuslibet fecerit id sit ipso facto auctoritate huius sancte sinodi irritum et inane.

5

10

15

20

25

30

---

1 idem] Expedita *add. in marg.* W² 4 maioribus] moribus P 11 ciuitates] ciuitas C 13 seu] et E 16 aut] et E afficctum] afficctam DEW; officium C nec] ut E 19 Erectiones] Electiones A 20 diuisiones] subiectiones *add.* DS (*in marg.* S) 21 qui] que A 19–21 Erectiones . . . dignitates *om.* CEPW 22 archiep.] seu *add.* CDP episc.] seu abbatum saluo iure constitutionum *add.* D; seu abbatum ordinum *add.* EW 22–23 usque . . . concilium] *om.* CP; *underscored* W; licet *add.* DE, *add. and underscored* W 23 tamen] *om.* D 24 expectando] spectando D 25–26 et consensu *om.* P 28 plene] *om.* E; plene *add. above line* (along with word "uacat") W; maioris partis eorum *add. and expunged* W remissionis] remissionem D 31 facto] *corr. from* iure A

[DS *in text*: Nec liceat etiam ipsi Romano pontifici sanctorum canonizationes, priuilegiorum perpetuorum et realium nouas concessiones, exemptionum hactenus per Romanos pontifices ecclesiis, monasteriis, collegiis et aliis locis concessarum reuocationes sine consilio et consensu ac subscriptione dictorum Cardinalium, seu maioris partis eorundem, facere seu expedire. Exemptiones etiam nouas et perpetuas ecclesiis, monasteriis, seu capellis usque ad proximum futurum concilium non concedat sine cause congnitione et vocatis ordinariis, quod tamen locum non habeat in ecclesiis, monasteriis seu capellis de nouo edificandis seu constituendis que possit eximere.]

[c.3][IX 2] Contra simoniacos

Contra labem simoniace pestis, qua decor ecclesie plurimum denigratur, multa remedia per apostolicos patres ac sacra concilia hactenus excogitata fuerunt salubriterque prouisa, que tamen temporum excrescente malitia, ut experientia docet, optatum non attulerunt effectum. Volentes igitur quantum possumus radicem pestis huius penitus extirpare hoc perpetuo decreto statuimus, quod quicumque ecclesiasticus, cuiuscunque status, gradus, ordinis seu preeminentie fuerit, etiamsi episcopali, archiepiscopali, patriarchatus vel cardinalatus dignitate prefulgeat qui de cetero simonie crimen, in Romana Curia vel extra, siue dando siue recipiendo, siue promittendo siue paciscendo, siue mediando commiserit

---

7 capellis] capitulis D   10 capellis] capitulis D   1–11 Nec liceat . . . eximere] DS *only (in S this material is found on separate fol. 71ᵃᵛ inserted at this point (71ᵃʳ blank); see Table 1*   11 eximere] Et si contrarium premissorum vel eorum cuiuslibet fecerit id sit ipso facto auctoritate huius sancte synodi irritum et inane. *add.* D   14 denigratur] denigatur A   ac] et DE   15 salubriterque] salubriter S   15–16 temporum excrescente] excrescentes P (!)   17 attulerunt] obtulerunt E   19 quicumque] de cetero *add.* P   gradus] Videtur etiam papalis exprimenda, ut etiam eis via precludatur, sed fiat per speciale capitulum ut infra: Romanus pontifex. *add. in marg.* C (*See Common, c.5 below*) 19–21 ecclesiasticus . . . qui *om.* S   21 de cetero] *struck out* W; circa beneficii ecclesiastici electionem, postulationem, impetrationem, collationem, prouisionem, presentationem, siue dispositionem qualemcumque *add. in marg.* W. Videtur addendum pro clarificatione: que de cetero circa beneficii impetrationem, collationem, prouisionem, presentationem, inuestituram, installationem siue aliam dispositionem qualitercumque, unionem, etc., (dispensationem *add. and struck out*), electionem, permutationem. *add. in marg.* C   22 extra] per conuentionem aut pactionem [aut *add. and struck out*] *add. in marg.* W; Videtur specificandum clarius dando per conuentionem aut pactionem *add. in marg.* C   siue *struck out* W   siue *struck out* W   23 promittendo] siue [*struck out*] remittendo *add. in marg.* W   siue *struck out* W; *om.* E   paciscendo *om.* E   mediando] ultra summam taxandam per generale consilium *add. in marg.* C

ipso facto omni dignitate, officio ecclesiastico et omnibus beneficiis suis perpetuo sit priuatus. Possintque beneficia sua tamquam vacantia libere conferri et impetrari. Prelati vero, qui ad custodiam gregis ad purgandam vitiis ecclesiam dei positi sunt, cogitent quantum excedant, si in executione huius decreti negligentes extiterint. Et 5 nichilominus, ne talis negligentia sine debita pena pertranseat, cum ex hoc videantur aliena crimina sua facere, statuimus ut de tali negligentia contra prelatos huiusmodi procedi possit et debeat etiam ad priuationem si qualitas negligentie id exposcat. Laici autem qui in huiusmodi culpabiles fuerint excommunicationem 10 incurrant ipso iure.

[C, *in marg.*: Ibi videretur addendum ut ab ea non nisi a summo pontifice preterquam in mortis articulo absoluatur.]

[W², *in text.*: Constitutionibus aliis contra symoniacos editis in suo robore duraturis.] 15

[W², *in marg.*: Ceterum uniuersis et singulis ordinariis districte precipiendo mandamus, quatenus cum omni solertia circa punitionem sic delinquentium taliter intendant, quod de negligentia minime redargui valeant. Qui si negligentes extiterint, per suos superiores prout facti qualitas exposcit sic puniantur, quod ceteris 20 cedat in exemplum.]

---

1 ipso facto] Hoc videtur durum; videtur non propter ipsum committentem symoniam, sed propter subditos suos, qui in casu quo eum ullus expelleret a beneficio, a non suo iudice et non pastore iudicaretur et regeretur ipsis etiam insciis et innocentibus. Ideo forte cautius ageretur, si superioribus auctoritas concederetur ymmo iniungeretur priuandi, et alys facultas denunciandi vel accusandi et eorum beneficia impetrandi et acceptandi. Item ad euitandum difficultatem probandi symoniam addi posset quod sufficeret de eius commissione habere indicia verisimilia vel famam publicam, cui saltem opus esset expurgatione. *add. in marg.* C   officio *om.* P   2–3 vacantia] Declaratione tamen per prius legitime facta super commissione predicti criminis vocatis euocandis *add. in marg.* W   8 negligentia] Statuimus: Declarandum videtur: Quando prelati censentur negligentes; et pena negligentium posset exprimi determinatius per quem, videlicet quod pro illa vice ad superiores collatores collatio beneficii symoniace collati vel acceptati deuoluatur ut quod ille priuet et conferat. Vide consequenter capitulum "Romanus pontifex." [*Common, c.5 below*] Vide infra circa finem capitulo conclusum. Vide in sexterno domini abbatis c. Martinus ubi papa alias videtur penas apponere. *add. in marg.* C   possit] ubi etiam per quem *add. above line* C   debeat] per executores concilii *add in marg.* C   3–9 Prelati . . . exposcat] *circled and underscored* W   11 iure] *struck out,* facto *add. above line* W²   17 mandamus] *corr. from* precipiemus

[c.4][XII 1] De numero et modo assumptionis cardinalium et qualitate assumendorum

[*Portion of earlier draft in M (See above, p. 280 n.16)*]:. . . assistant, non de una tantum mundi regione, sed de omnibus nationibus saltem principalibus assumantur; quod etiam ad seruandum pacem et unionem in ecclesia maxime perutile uidetur, ne una natio per ambitionem summum et uniuersalem presulatum sola teneat, nec ne sanctuarium dei iure hereditario possidere uideatur, ex quo discensiones et scandala plurimum orientur et]

Quia plerumque multitudo superflua confusionem inducere consueuit, statuimus ut deinceps numerus cardinalium sancte Romane ecclesie in futurum assumendorum decem et octo non excedat. Sint autem viri in scientia, moribus et rerum experientia excellentes, qui non minores sint triginta annis, doctores in theologia, iure canonico vel ciuili, preter admodum paucos qui forte de stirpe regia vel ducali aut magni principis oriundi existant, non affines seu attinentes alicuius cardinalis viuentis usque ad quartum gradum inclusiue, nec de eadem stirpe, familia seu domo vel agnatione; nec de uno ordine religionis ultra unum, non illegitime nati, non corpore vitiati, non alicuius criminis aut infamie nota respersi. Nec fiat eorum electio per auricularia vota solummodo, sed illi solum eligi et assumi possint in quos facto vero scrutinio ac publicato maiorem partem cardinalium per subscriptionem manus proprie constiterit collegialiter consensisse. Et apostolice littere conficiantur exinde. Qui etiam modus scrutinii et subscriptionis obseruetur quando aliquis ex cardinalibus vel alius in episcopum cardinalem assumetur. Et aliter celebrata cardinalium assumptio ipso iure non subsistat.

[c.5][XIX 1] Quod papa etiam pro alio crimine quam heresim si notorie scandalizat ecclesiam possit deponi [*variants from W², c.14 (record of second reform committee) are included.*]

---

1 et] de *add.* DE   6 perutile] per uere (?) MS   7–8 nec ne] nene MS
12 assumendorum] assumendi EW; Expedita *add. in marg.* W²   in futurum
assumendorum *om.* D   13 scientia] conscientia M   14 theologia] saltem
quattuor, reliqui *add.* CDP   iure] in iure C   16 affines] consanguinei
EW   16–17 seu attinentes *om.* EW   18 familia *om.* A   seu *om.*
DEW   ordine] *in marg.* S   24 consensisse] concessisse D   littere
om. EW   25 subscriptionis] obscriptionis M   27 assumetur] assument C
aliter celebrata] si aliter celebretur M   29 Quod] Sequitur quod CD   heresim] heresi CD; heresis P   30 ecclesiam] non *add.* P; et monitus non desistat
add. W²   deponi] Expedita *add. in marg.* W²

Romanus pontifex, quanto ceteris ecclesie rectoribus presideret, tanto debet sanctiori vita et clariori fama fulgere. [Si enim qui singulis plebibus superintendunt tales esse debent ut eorum estimatione populus grex dicatur, qualem se exhibere debet qui non uni populo sed uniuersis, nec solum populis sed ipsis pastoribus pastor   5 est positus, dicente domino Petro: "Et tu aliquando conuersus confirma fratres tuos."[3] Exhibeat se ergo presul ille qui iam sanctissimus ex officio nominatur, sicud nomine ita re sanctum. Consideret quam difficile sit tenere sedem Petri, cum non solum populis, sed prelatis sit positus in exemplum; docere debeat non discipu-   10 los sed vel magistros. Eleuet lumen suum in excelso qui lumina cetera debet illustrare sic sol in mundo qui in ecclesia populos ut tenebras, prelatos ut stellas purgare debet, illuminare atque perficere. Teneat mentem suam mundissimam semperque Christo coniunctam in celestibus, cuius vicariatus officio fungitur in terris.   15 Si autem, quod absit, vita et moribus sit peruersus, si oblitus dignitatis sue et relictis celestibus conuersus ad terrena dampnabilibus et capitalibus criminibus se inmisceat, considerat quod Lucifer quanto ceteris angelis clarior et perfectior est creatus, tanto ex peruersitate sua seuerius et irreparabilius est punitus. Nec confidat   20 solum diuino ac ultimo iudicio reseruari, quod tamen quanto certius atque seuerius, tanto debet humilius trepidantiusque formidari, quia et per ecclesiam que corpus est Christi deus iudicia sua etiam in hoc mundo exercet, et concilia generalia uniuersalem ecclesiam representant. Unde super premissis] salubriter prouidere   25

---

3 Luc. 22,32

---

1 presideret] presidere DE; presidet ACP et *om.* ACPS   1-2 Romanus . . . fulgere] Et quoniam decet Romanum pontificem, in quem cunctorum respiciunt oculi, quanto pluribus ecclesie ministris et rectoribus prelatus est, tanto sanctiori vita et celebriori fama fulgere et non solo verbo sed conuersatione et exemplis gubernare subiectos et totius semetipsum imitatorem virtutis ostendere. W[2]   3 superintendunt] super D   3-4 estimatione] CP, extimatione DEWW[2]   4 populus grex dicatur] ceteri grex dicantur   W[2]   qualem] igitur   et *add.* W[2]   5 populo] *corr. from* paulo W[2]   6 Petro *om.* P   7 confirma] confirmas W[2]   9 quam] qua W   sit tenere] sic tenetur D   10 exemplum] difficile *add.* D; et *add.* W[2]   debeat] debet W[2]   non] solum *add.* DW[2]   11 vel] etiam D; etiam et W[2]   12 sic sol] sit sal E   ut] ac D; et P   14 mundissimam] nudissimam E   17 relictis] derelictis W[2]   18 capitalibus] capitabilibus (!) W   19 angelis] *om.* EW   22-23 formidare] sed etiam *add. above line* C   et *om.* W[2]   2-25 Si enim . . . premissis] *om.* AS; etc. Nos *add.* AS (*See above, p. 278.*)

cupientes, hoc decreto perpetuo declaramus ac diffinimus quod summum pontifex non solum de heresi sed et de simonia et quocumque alio crimine ecclesiam dei notorie scandalizante, de quo et sollempniter monitus saltem per annum post monitionem incorrigibilis appareat, possit per generale concilium puniri etiam per depositionem a papatu. Monitionem vero non quamlibet sed si per duas partes cardinalium collegialiter siue per tria diuersa concilia prouincialia diuersarum trium nationum sub diuersis tribus regibus consistentium, moneatur monitio canonica ac sufficiens intelligatur. Teneanturque sic monentes monitionem suam infra mensem sollempniter publicare.

[c.6][XV 1] [V, *in text*: Cedula oblata per dominum Pisanum die martis III Septembris] De reformatione curie et officialium eius

Primo. Littere apostolice tam de gratia quam de iustitia expediantur per cancellariam nec eis adhibeatur fides in iudicio vel extra nisi in cancellaria sint expedite, quod appareat per signa consueta, exceptis dumtaxat concernentibus negotia camere apostolice ut consuetum est, que tamen iudicentur in eadem camera, et signa habeant consueta.

2°. Item quod in bullis ubi dicitur de fratrum consilio etc. debeat esse subscriptio saltem trium priorum collegii ad probandum consilium.

3°. Prothonotarii de cetero assumantur de consensu maioris partis cardinalium, et sint magistri in sacra pagina, vel doctores in iure, aut illustres et in sacris ordinibus constituti; et non ultra septem sicut antiquitus consueuerunt.

---

2 simonia] tam circa sacramenta quam in beneficialibus ecclesiasticis [eccl. *add. in marg.*] commissa *add.* W² 3 et] etiam EWW²; *om.* D 4 monitus *om.* AS saltem] semper EW 5 per *om.* D 6 non] nostro (!) S si *om.* E sed si] censemus reputari canonicam sed si W² 7 collegialiter] et publice coram populi multitudine facta *add.* W² tria] concilia *add.* P diuersa *om.* D prouincialia *om.* EWW² 8 diuersis] sub duobus vel *add. in marg.* C 9 consistentium] existentium D; vel per tria studia generalia similiter sub duobus regibus vel tribus consistentia. *add. in marg.* C; siue per tria diuersa concilia diuersarum prouinciarum unico contextu aut etiam successiue *add.* W² 9–10 monitio . . . intelligatur] *om.* D 10 sic] sicut S 13 Septembris] Deliberata super ipsa cedula die martis III Septembris. *add. in marg.* V De reform . . . . Rubrica *om.* V; et officialium eius *om.* M; Rubrica *om.* AS 14 Primo C; *numbering of paragraphs in c.6 in ACD only (see above, p. 297.)* de (*second*) *om.* D; *add. above line,* W 15 per] in M 18 ut . . est *om.* MV 19 consueta] Articulus fuit approbatus pro ut iacet. *add. in marg.* V 20 quod *om.* MV 21–22 consilium] Deliberant quod ad probandum consilium fratrum tres priores dominorum cardinalium se subscribant. *add. in marg.* V 25 aut] vel V; *om.* M 26 consueuerunt] Placet textus. *add. in marg.* V

[Version in AS]:

4. Auditores etiam assumantur de consensu maioris partis cardinalium et qui per biennium post doctoratum legerint in aliquo studio generali vel per annum in curia, et quod examinentur cum assumuntur.

Nec sint ultra XVI neque pauciores XII et iurent non recipere post sententias esculenta et potulenta ultra valorem trium florenorum. Habeant quoque stipendia de camera vel de beneficiis coniunctim vel diuisim florenos CCC. Et quod non stent cum cardinalibus in domo, et sint de diuersis prouinciis et in sacris ordinibus constituti.

5. Scriptores litterarum apostolicarum et penitentiarie assumantur cum diligenti examine et non nisi prius facta reductione ad numerum consuetum qui erat centum et unus quo ad grossam et XXIIII quo ad penitentiariam; et non sint coniugati, nec scribant per alios nisi causa necessitatis vel infirmitatis, que necessitas declaretur per vicecancellarium vel penitentiarium, et non possint ista officia vendi, nec unus habeat duo officia talia.

[CEW, in text:

4. Auditores etiam assumantur de consensu maioris partis cardinalium et qui per triennium post doctoratum legerint in aliquo studio generali. Tunc quod morentur ad liberatam pape, nec sint ultra sedecim nec pauciores duodecim. Et iurent non recipere post sententias esculenta et potulenta ultra valorem trium florenorum.]

[CEW, in marg.: Placet cum hoc quod ubi dicitur de consensu dicatur de consilio. Et loco triennii ponatur biennium vel annus in curia. Et quod examinentur etiam cum assumuntur. Et quod habeant stipendia de camera vel de beneficiis coniunctim vel diuisim florenorum III C. Et quod non stent cum cardinalibus in domo. Et quod sint de diuersis prouinciis. Et in sacris ordinibus constituti.]

[CEW, in text:

5. Scriptores litterarum apostolicarum et penitentiarie assumantur cum diligenti examine et non nisi prius facta reductione ad numerum consuetum qui erat centum et unus quo ad grossam et XXIIII quo ad penitentiariam.]

[CEW, in marg.: Placet quod sint centum quo ad grossam et XXIIII quo ad pentitentiariam, nec possint vendi, nec sint coniugati, nec scribant per alium, nisi ex causa necessitatis vel infirmitatis que necessitas declaretur per vicecancellarium vel pentitentiarium; et quod unus non habeat duo officia.]

5

10

15

20

25

30

35

40

3 consensu] *corr. from* consilio S   4 per biennium *struck out* S   6 generali] et quod morentur ad liberatam pape *add in marg.* S   6–8 vel . . . assumuntur *struck out* S   13 florenorum] Placet cum hoc quod ibi dicitur de consensu dicatur de consilio et loco triennii ponatur biennium vel unus in curia, et quod examinentur cum assumuntur. *add. in marg.* S   26 Penitentiariam] Placet quod sint centum quo ad grossam et XXIIII quo ad penitentiarium nec possint vendi. *add. in marg.* S   et non] *corr. to* nec S   28 vel infirmitatis *struck out* S   31 non possint . . . uendi *struck out* S   32 talia *om.* A

5 aliquo] universitate *add and struck out* C   5–6 studio generali] *corr. from* uniuersitate C   tunc] et EW   7 liberatam] libratam EW   13 quod *om.* EW   36 ex *om.* W   40 non . . . officia] scriptor duo officia non habeat. EW

[D, *in text*:

4. Auditores etiam assumantur de consilio maioris partis cardinalium et qui per biennium in aliquo studio generali vel in curia per annum post doctoratum legerunt. Qui habeant stipendia de camera vel de beneficiis coniunctim vel diuisim florenos CCC. Et quod morentur ad liberatam pape. Non sint ultra sedecim nec pauciores duodecim, et iurent non recipere post sententias esculenta vel proculenta (!) ultra valorem trium florenorum, nec stent cum cardinalibus, et sint de diuersis prouinciis et in sacris.

5. Scriptores litterarum apostolicarum et penitentiarie assumantur cum diligenti examine et non nisi prius facta reductione ad numerum consuetum. Et quod non sint coniugati et non locent, sed per se exerceant cessante infirmitate, et non habeant duplex officium scriptorie, et quod huiusmodi officium non vendatur, non donetur nec permutetur nisi pro simili officio.]

[D, *in marg*.: Placet ille numerus, utique nec possit vendi, nec sint coniugati, nec scribant per alium nisi ex causa necessitatis vel infirmatitatis, que necessitas declaretur per vicecancellarium vel penitentiarium; et quod unus non habeat duo officia.]

[MV, *in text*:

4. Auditores etiam assumantur de consilio maioris partis cardinalium et qui per biennium post doctoratum legerint in aliquo studio generali vel per annum in curia, et examinentur etiam cum assumuntur.

Et habeant in beneficiis dandis sibi infra annum vel in stipendiis l de camera vel inter beneficia et stipendia prouentus CCC florenos. Et non sint ultra XVI nec pauciores XII. Et iurent non accipere post sententias esculenta et l potulenta ultra valorem trium florenorum. Et non morentur in domo vel ad expensas alicuius Cardinalis. Et sint de diuersis nationibus ac teneantur infra annum 2 promoueri ad sacros ordines.

5. Deliberata die mercurii in Septembris. Scriptores litterarum apostolicarum et penitentiarie assumantur cum diligenti examine et 2 non nisi prius facta reductione ad numerum consuetum.]

[M, *in text*; V, *in marg*.: Addatur in fine quod erat centum quo ad scriptores litterarum apostolicarum 3 quo ad scriptores penitentiarie XXIIII. Nec possint vendere officia. Nec de cetero assumantur coniugati. Nec scribant per alium nisi ex causa infirmitatis vel ali- 3 cuius necessitatis que declaretur per vicecancellarium vel penitentiarium. Item quod unus non habet duo officia.]

9 in *om*. M   20 teneantur] Alii dixerunt "Et sint in sacris." *add. in marg*. V   21 ordines] Reformatus fit iste articulus pro ut nunc iacet et sic placet et approbatus fit pro ut reformatus est. Quidam habent istam particulam sic et habeant stipendium de camera vel de beneficiis coniunctim vel diuisim florenorum CCC *add. in marg*. V 22–23 Deliberata . . . Sept.] V *only*   28–29 Addatur in fine *om*. M   29 quod] que MV   quo] que (?) V   30 apostolicarum] et *add*. M   31 scriptores] scriptorum V   34 Nec scribant] Neque scribantur M   35–36 vel alicuius necessitatis *om*. M

10 pape] Non in domibus cardinalium, et sint de diuersis prouinciis et in sacris ordinibus constituti. *add. in marg*.

6° Abbreuiatores etiam cum examine assumantur et non ultra numerum XXV.

7° Scriptores et procuratores penitentiarie sint sacerdotes cum secreta delicta debeant audire.

[AS, *in text*: Et idem volumus intelligere de auditore, sigillatore, registratore eiusdem penitentiarie.]

[EW, *in marg.*: Et addatur: "Idem de auditore, sigillatore et registratore."]

[D *alternate text*: 7ᵃ Et Auditor sigillator et Registrator. § Scriptores ac procuratores penitentiarie sint sacerdotes cum secreta delicta debeant audire.]

8°. Clerici camere non sint ultra sex et doctores vel licentiati in iure. Et in fine addatur quod sint de diuersis nationibus.

9°. Corrector litterarum apostolicarum sit unicus et doctor excellens in studio generali et bene expertus in cancellaria.

10. Auditor contradictarum sit etiam unicus et excellens doctor et assumatur de rota vel etiam aliunde dum modo excellens sit in scientia iuris.

11. Auditor camere similiter doctor sit et probatus bone scientie et expertus in curia.

12. Acoliti non sint ultra octo sed et sint honesti viri. Placet quod sint sex.

13. Subdiaconus sit unicus et magister in theologia vel doctor in iure attento quod magne cause sibi committi consueuerunt.

---

1 etiam] procuratores penitentiarie sint sacerdotes cum secreta delicta *add. and struck out* A   2 XXV] Abbreuiatores placet textus. *add. in marg.* V   4 delicta . . . audire] debeant audire peccata V; Scriptores placet textus et addatur idem de auditore, sigillatore et registratore. *add. in marg.* V; Placet et addatur "Idem de auditore, sigillatore et registratore." *add. in marg.* CEW, *add. in space at end of line* S   12 camere] tamen V   13 iure] Placet. Nisi reperiatur alius numerus ordinatus ante scisma. Et in fine addatur. *add.* C; Placet quod non sint ultra sex nisi repereatur alius numerus ordinatus ante scisma et in fine addatur "Et sint de diuersis nationibus." *add. in marg.* V; placet nisi reperiuntur alius numerus ordinatus ante scisma et in fine addatur quod sint de diuersis nationibus. E   quod sint] et D; et sint A   Et . . . nationibus] *om.* V   quod . . . nationibus] ADS *only*; Sic placuit articulus nisi reperiretur alius modus ordinatus ante scisma *add.* A; *add. and struck out* S   14 Corrector] Placet textus. *add. in marg.* V   doctor] famosus et *add.* D   14–15 exc.] qui ad minus legerit per tres annos *add.* D   17 rota] Placet. Et in fine addatur *add.* CEW   etiam *om.* CEVW   excellens sit] sit bene excellens D   17–18 vel etiam . . . iuris] Placet et in fine addatur vel aliunde dummodo sit excellens in scientia iuris *add.* C; V, *in marg.*: Placet textus et similiter de auditore camere.   19 Auditor . . . probatus] Et idem de auditori camere sit doctor probatus D   bone] bene S   20 curia] Placet *add.* CV   21 octo] *corr. from* sex S   sed et sint] et CDEW   viri] Placet quod non sint ultra sex et residuum placet. *add. in marg.* V   21–22 Placet . . . sex] *om.* ADV   23 subdiaconus] Placet. *add. in marg.* V

14. Cappellani commensales stent in domo pape et ad liberatam et incedant in habitu honesto. Cappellani vero qui dicuntur honoris reuocentur vel saltem priuilegia ipsorum, etiam si habeant processus, quia sub illa spe pretendunt eximi a prelatorum.

[ADS, *in text*: Nisi sint magistri vel in theologia vel in iure seculares nec sint exempti etiam si habeant processus qui eximant]

[V, *in marg.*: Capellani: Placet usque ibi: "vel saltem". Quod totum residuum tollatur usque in finem et addatur "nisi sint magistri in theologia vel doctores in iure et seculares, nec sint exempti etiam si habeant processus. Et de cetero processus non dentur eis in camera.]

[E, *in text*; CW, *in marg.*: Placet articulus usque ibi "vel saltem." Quod tollatur illa verba usque ad finem et addatur "nisi sint magistri in theologia vel in iure seculares nec sint exempti etiam si habeant processus in camera qui eximant."]

15. [V, *in text*: Deliberata die VI Septembris] Referendarii non sint ultra sex homines excellentes et in iure famosi et integerrime vite, et assumantur cum consilio maioris partis cardinalium. Sintque de diuersis nationibus.

16. Penitentiarii sint magistri in sacra pagina vel bene periti et digni magisterio, etatis quadraginta annorum adminus, et distribuantur per linguas secundum exigentiam, et nichil exigant, nec ad dandum alliciant directe vel indirecte pro confessionibus, sub pena priuationis officii. Et habeant de camera stipendia consueta, et teneantur predicare populo diebus consuetis.

---

1 liberatam] CV; libratam ADEW; *corr. from* libratam S; libertatem (!) M   2 cappellani] *A new paragraph (15) begins here in* D.   3 reuocentur] Placet usque ibi quod tollantur illa verba usque ad finem et addatur *add. in marg.* S   4 prelatorum] prelatis W   3–4 vel saltem . . . prelatorum] *only in* CEVW, *underscored in* CW   11 camera] quibus examinantur *add. and underscored (as though a lemma)* V   5 mag . . . . theol.] doctores in sacro pagina D   iure] iures et D   6 nec] et declaretur de nouo quod non D   processus] in camera *add. in marg.* S   qui eximant] *om.* D; et quod de cetero non dentur eis processus de Camera. *add.* D   12 articulus] *only in* E   13 sint] sunt C   14 iure] iures W   17 et (*first*) *om.* E   et (*second*)] *add.* CEV   18 cum consilio] de consilio D; cum assensu CEW; cum consilio *altered to* cum consensu S   cardinalium] Placet sed addatur quod sint de diuersis nationibus. *add. in marg.* V   18–19 sintque] Placet usque ibi "cum assensu"; diceris consilio et in fine addatur quod sint C   sintque . . . nation.] et de omni natione. D; *om.* EVW; *underscored* S   20 periti] experti V   et] etiam D   22 nec] vel CDEV   22–23 ad dandum] *om.* ADV; addendum E   23 confessionibus] et *add.* DV   24 officii] V *only*; Maior pars stat cum textu nisi quod ante verbum alliciant ponatur verbum "ad dandum" et addatur in fine: "Et habeant de camera stipendia consueta et teneantur predicare populo diebus conseutis." *add. in marg.* V   et habeant] Placet; et in fine addatur quod habeant C   priuationis . . . camera] Sed a camera habeant D   et] quod *add.* C   25 teneantur predicare] predicent ACS   populo] in *add.* C   consuetis] scilicet dominicis et festiuis. *add.* D   24–25 Et habeant . . . consuetis] *om.* EW; *underscored* S

17. In audientia contradictarum et sacri palatii apostolici causarum seruentur ad unguem constitutiones Johannis XXII et similiter in cancellaria et addantur pene grauiores. [CEW, *in marg.*: Commissum est quatuor, uni pro natione, qui examinent constitutiones predictas et quod hic legantur. Nomina   5
sunt episcopus Mersburgensis, auditor camere, abbas Vandrigii, et Robertus Appelton.]

18. In registro litterarum apostolicarum nichil recipiatur nisi pro litteris taxatis et pro illis nichil ultra taxam et fiat expeditio cita et sub pena et scriptores etiam habeant salarium de publico sicut   10
consueuerunt.

19. In registro supplicationum nichil recipiatur pro supplicationibus registrandis. Et si in manu registratorum perdatur supplicatio nichil recipiat de sumpto et fiat expeditio cita et votiua sub pena.   15
[CESW, *in marg.*: Placet sed quoad salarium notariorum se informent illi quatuor de quibus in c. xvii.]

20. Item fiat reductio taxe litterarum apostolicarum et sacre penitentiarie ad solitum.

21. Item nullatenus teneantur promotiones ad ordines in Curia   20
nisi pro officialibus curie et qui continue residerint in curia per annum cum bono examine maxime super statu nisi sint forte aliqui habentes litteras dimissorias a suis ordinariis vel promoti in Curia ad episcopatus vel abbatias.

[D, *in text*: Vel ad beneficia requirentia ordinem et nichil re-   25
cipiatur de ordinibus. Nec dentur dimissorie in curia vel extra quattuor tempora fiat. Nec dentur duo vel plures sacri ordines simul nisi promotus ad episcopatus vel abbacias vel pro litteris aliquid detur in curia vel extra.]

---

2 XXII] Commissum est Michaeli Bolosonis qui vadat ad dominum vicecancellarium pro constitutionibus d. Johannis XXII et Gregorii XII et deputati sunt certi qui eas aduisent. *add. in marg.* V   3 cancellaria] camera V   11 consueuerunt] Placet *add.* C; Placet omnibus textus *add. in marg.* V   13 registratorum] registratoris V   14 recipiat] recipiatur V   expeditio] expeditur (!) A   cita] cito D   14–15 sub pena] et *add.* D; Maiori parti placet textus, sed tantum quo ad salarium, deputati super premissis et auisandis constitutionibus auisent etiam super hoc. *add. in marg.* V   16 se] si S   18 Item] et D; *om.* CESW; *in A, the text of this paragraph is included within the preceding paragraph without break.*   19 solitum] solidum S; solitum iuxta constitutiones D; Placet textus sed tamen stetur predictis constitutionibus si quod in eis super hoc determinetur. *add. in marg.* V   20 promotiones] *corr. from* ordinationes D   prom. ad ord.] ordinationes V   21 et V *only*   residerint] resideant V   22 maxime *om.* C   super] de D   cum . . . statu] factis informationibus de statu V

[E, *in text*; CW, *in marg.*: Placet et in fine addatur vel beneficia requirentia ordinem et nichil omnino recipiatur pro ordinibus sub pena. Et non dentur dimissorie in curia, nec extra 4^{or} tempora fiant, nec dentur duo vel plures sacri simul alias eadem die nisi promotis ad episcopatus vel abbatias nec pro litteris aliquid detur in curia vel extra.]

[AS, *in text*: Nec pro litteris aliquid detur in Curia vel extra vel beneficia requirentia ordinem, et nihil omnino recipiatur pro ordinibus sub pena. Et non dentur dimissorie nec fiant ordines extra 4 tempora, nec dentur duo vel plures sacri simul vel eadem die, nisi promotis ad episcopatus vel abbatias, nec pro litteris aliquid detur in Curia vel extra.]

[V, *in marg.*: Placet textus nisy quod ubi dicitur "teneantur ordines," dicatur "celebrentur ordines" vel "promotiones ad ordines". Et ibi "de statu": Apponetur "cum bono examine et maxime de statu"; et addatur in fine "et ad beneficia requirentia ordinem et nihil recipiatur omnino pro ordinatione nec pro litteris sub pena. Et non dentur dimissorie in curia nec possint ordinari extra quatuor tempora. Nec dentur duo sacri ordines eadem die nisi forte promotis ad episcopatus vel abbatias.]

22. [V, *in text*: Deliberata] Officiales Curie, ut scriptores, abbreuiatores, procuratores, aduocati et ceteri incedant induti daphardis ut antiquitus consueuerunt. Et sub pena.

23. Item in Curia continue vigeat studium tam in artibus quam in theologia quam etiam in utroque iure et in litteris latinis, grecis, hebreis, arabicis et caldeis iuxta Clementinam[4] et habeant stipendia a camera.

24. Item habeant maliscalkum nobilem, iustum et honestum, non capientem lucra ignominiosa sicut aliquando consueuerunt. Nota de magistro hospitii et de clericis capelle.

25. [V, *in text*: Cedula additamenti ad <. . .> exhibita per dominum Pisanum] Item clerici capelle alias cerimoniarum

---

4 Clem. 5.1.1 *Inter sollicitudines*

22 et ceteri *om.* V   23 daphardis] tabardis CVW   pena] Placet *add. in marg.* CV   24 Curia] Romana *add.* DV   tam in artibus quam] quam D; in artibus tam V   25 etiam *om.* DV   27 a] de V   26–27 stipendia a camera] stipendium de camera. Et prouideatur de executione. D; stipendia a camera. Et fiat executio in isto. A; Placet et prouideatur (V: addatur) de executione. *add. in marg.* CV   28 Item] Et V; *corr. from* Et S   habeant] habeat curia V   maliscalkum] marescallum V; maliscalcum EW   29 non] nec ACD; ac non V   consueuerunt] Placet prout iacet. *add. in marg.* V   31 ad] *Blank space of 3 cm. follows.*   32 Item *om.* CEW   capelle] capella (!) EW alias] siue CD

sint tantum duo qui sint presbiteri et probi ac experti in cerimoniis curie et cognoscant prelatos et sciant eos bene locare in sessionibus, satis litterati et diligentes in officio suo.

26. [V, *in text*: Deliberata die martis 4a (!) Septembris] Item examinator curie sit prelatus honestus et doctor, qui non querat 5 lucra sed qui diligenter et fideliter examinet beneficiandos, ne promoueantur indigni. Et detur sibi iuramentum duplex, unum super diligentia examinis, aliud quod non recipiat pro examine ultra certam taxam, etc.

[D, *in text*: Et caueatur ne unus pro alio examinari se faciat. De 10 taxa videri debet constitutio, si aliquid de hoc caueatur. Sin autem detur pro quolibet unus carlinus, quorum decem faciunt unum ducatum.]

[E *in text*; CSW, *in marg.*: Placet et addatur quod sit doctor et quod adhibeatur diligens cautela in examinandum, ut unus non 15 faciat se examinari pro alio. Et quod examinator per se ipsum et non per alium exerceat officium et subscribat se propria manu in cedula. Et de ista taxa solutionis examinis respiciantur constitutiones et si reperiantur diuerse taxe recipiatur minor.]

[V *in text*: Ordinentur sessiones in Curia ut materia hec plenius 20 deliberetur. Nota hic de doctoribus non fiendis in Curia quia super hoc facta est constitutio que incipit "Eo iam multos" et infra sequitur.

Cum multe cedule fuerunt oblate et multa proposita de nullo sint deliberatum nisi quod die iouis XVIII Septembris super cedula de 25 dispensationibus que sequitur.]

---

2 curie *om.* C   et] qui *add.* CESW   eos bene] bene D; *om.* CEW   3 et] etiam AS   suo] Placet textus. *add. in marg.* V (*See above, p. 281*)   4 Item] S *only*   5 et doctor] *om.* CEVW; doctor in iure rigidus D   6 beneficiandos] bene faciendos (!) EW   7 indigni] Et qui adhibeat diligentem cautelam in examinandis ut unus non faciat se pro alio examinari: Ipse quoque examinator per se ipsum et non per alium exerceat officium suum et se subscribat propria manu *add. and struck out* S; per se et non per substitutum et cedulam examinis subscribat manu sua. *add.* D   Et detur . . . duplex] Detur quoque ipsi examinatori duplex iuramentum S   unum] primo V   8 aliud] alterum DV   9 certam *om.* V certam taxam] taxam etc. V   11 caueatur] *corr. from* videatur   14 et] ut S   15 examinandum ut] examinando ne S   non *om.* ESW   16 se *om.* E   18 Et] quod *add.* CEW   ista *om.* CEW   respiciantur] *corr. from* recipiantur SW   21 deliberetur] debberetur V   23 sequitur] Nota hic: Positum in deliberatione utrum prelatos debeant precedere prothonotarii. Omnes concordarunt quod extra curiam nullo modo precederent. In curia vero maiori parti placuit quod non precedentur nisi in exercitio officii sui. Aliquibus vero placuit quod precedentur secundum morem antiqum. Sed dominus patriarcha presidens videns discordiam ad nationes que super hoc determinent quid eis videatur et huic dicto omnes consenserunt. *add. in marg.* V (*See Table 3, p. 306; c.6 in V ends here.*)

27. Item quod deinceps non fiant magistri vel doctores per bullam apostolicam sine examine sed in studiis generalibus per rigorem examinis. Et si studium fiat in curia sicut ordinatum est, possint fieri doctores sicut in aliis studiis generalibus. Sed fiat examen per cancellarium studii quem papa deputabit adhibita sollempnitate magistrorum et doctorum in examine sicut in aliis studiis est de more.

28. Magister hospitii sit miles grandeuus nobilis et deo deuotus, qui sciat honorare dominos et nobiles venientes ad curiam et tenere ordinatam domum quo ad laycos cum omni honestate. Placet quod remaneat in dispositione pape de sua familia.

29. De sessionibus et locis ordinandis in curia Romana. Disputatum fuit de loco prothonotariorum; et, auditis votis, inuentum fuit quod fuerunt vota XXIX. Et concordauerunt in hoc quod extra curiam prothonotarii non precedant prelatos. In curia vero cum prothonotarii sunt in exercitio sui officii precedant. Si autem non sunt in exercitio officii sui tunc X vota fuerunt quod adhuc seruaretur mos antiquus; reliqui dicebant quod prelati precedant.

[CEW, in marg.: Sic fuit deliberatum die sabbati VII Septembris 1415.]

30. Circa constitutiones Johannis XXII quo ad audientiam Rote videbantur addenda infrascripta: Quo ad cappam et rochetum portandum semper in publico per auditores, locum habeat quando vadunt ad Rotam vel audientiam vel consilia seu missas et officia alia papalia vel exequias et sermones et alios actus in Curia publicos; item quando vadunt equitando in Curia post papam vel dominos cardinales. Hec tamen intelligenda sunt dummodo non est tempus pluuiosum aut alias lutosum quod eis uti non possint.

---

1 fiant] corr. from faciat S, fiat A   magistri . . . ex nunc om. A   2–3 in studiis . . . rigorem] in studio cum rigore S   6 magistrorum et doctorum] et magistrorum S   6–7 aliis studiis] generali studio S   4–7 Sed . . . more.] in marg. S   7 more] Placet. add. in marg. C   9 et nobiles om. W, underscored S   10 honestate] Placet textus nihilominus dixerunt plures quod sit in dispositione pape de familia sua. add. in marg. V   10–11 Placet . . . familia om. A; add. in marg. CSW (in S, in empty space at end of paragraph)   12 et locis om. EW   De sessionibus . . . Romana underscored S   15 precedant] corr. from pretendant S; procedant A   vero om. EW   16 prothonotarii] si add. E; add. above line W   precedant] corr. from pretendant S   17 officii sui] om. CW; officii E   18 dicebant om. CEW   precedant] Non detur quia scandaloza et non expedita. add. in marg. C   19 fuit deliberatum] sint deliberati W   20 1415 om. E   21 Johannis] pape add. D   22 videbantur] videatur C; videnda EW   infrascripta] infra D   24 et] corr. from vel S   26 vadunt om. CEW   26–27 dominos om. EW   27 Hec tamen . . . sunt underscored S   dummodo] dum AD   28 alias om. A   27–28 hec tamen . . . possint] Placet, dummodo non sit tempus pluuiosum vel alias lutosum quod eis non possint uti. CEW (E in text; CW, in marg.)

31. Item quod auditores non sint familiares dominorum cardinalium nec debeant ad eorum expensas morari extra Cardinalium domus.

32. Quod cause auditorum vel notariorum suorum vel aduocatorum aut procuratorum non committantur auditoribus nisi de 5 utriusque partis assensu.

33. Quod causam non audiant in qua scienter consilium dederunt nisi de consensu utriusque partis hoc scientis.

34. Quod esculenta et poculenta vel propinas post sententias tantum mera liberalitate oblatas et non fraudulenter recipere 10 valeant, prout consuetum est hactenus, licet non dicatur in constitutionibus. Et non recipiant ultra quam superius in una constitutione fuerat expressum.

35. Quo ad notarios quatuor auditoris etc. addendum videtur quod duos eligat auditor alios vero cancellarius, et in manus came- 15 rarii iurent in camera auditor et notarii.

[CW, *in marg.*; E, *in text*: Placet quod tollatur de camerario quia non est de antiqua consuetudine.]

36. Quod de dictis notariis auditor non teneat in domo nisi unum pro commissionibus recipiendis, et faciat inter notarios distribu- 20 tiones causarum more solito.

37. Quod notarii non scribant per alios nisi in casu infirmitatis et tunc per alium consocium et non per substitutum.

38. Quod officium notarii audientie Rote et notarii audientie camere siue auditoris non possint per eundem haberi simul nec 25 unus notarius coram duobus auditoribus scribere in causis nec possint notarii dominorum Cardinalium esse in Rota ad scribendum coram auditore.

39. Quod notarii examinentur per vicecancellarium presente decano et duobus antiquioribus Rote et approbati per eos admit- 30 tantur tantum.

---

2 morari] etiam *add.* D   3 domus] domum CEW; Placet. *add. in marg.* C 5 aut] seu C   6 assensu] Placet. *add. in marg.* C   8 scientis] Placet. *add. in marg.* C   10 liberalitate] libertate D   oblatas et] oblata EW   12–13 Et non . . . expressum *om.* CEW; Placet dummodo [non recipiant *add.* C] ultra quam constitutum est supra c. IIII. *add.* E, *add. in marg.* CW   15 manus] *corr. from* manibus S   15–16 et . . . camerarii] vel unum cancellarius et alium camerarius in cuius manibus CEW   19 dictis] 4ᵒʳ *add.* CEW   20 recipiendis] etcetera *add.* CEW   21 solito] Placet. *add. in marg.* C   23 et *om.* CEW   substitutum] Placet. *add. in marg.* C   28 auditore] Placet. *add. in marg.* C   30 duobus] de *add.* W   31 tantum] Placet. *add. in marg.* C

40. Quod notarii in faciendo registra non extendant in registro aliquod instrumentum procurationis vel aliud vel citationem, inhibitionem aut eorum executionem nisi semel tantum et alibi in registro referant se ad illud primo extensum; et in executione seu relatione executionis, citationis et inhibitionis similiter. Nec faciant prohemium in productione instrumenti in quo interserant tenorem vel partem tenoris etc., sed dicant "cuius tenor infra sequitur".

41. Quod auditores non consulant scienter in causis in Rota vertentibus vel que verti sperantur pro consanguineis usque ad tertium gradum vel etiam pro ecclesiis in quibus huiusmodi consanguinei sunt beneficiati et tunc exeant Rotam.

[CEW, *in marg.*: Placet usque ad tertium gradum pro consanguineis.]

42. Quod auditores vel notarii causas non sollicitent seu procurent in Rota etiam pro consanguineis vel aliis.

43. Quod auditores pronunciantes male appellatum et bene processum per aliquem in Curia in casu in quo de iure fienda esset remissio remittent ad iudicem a quo.

44. Quod citationem et inhibitionem faciant in eadem littera et pro una taxentur.

45. Quod non sint veloces ad inhibendum vel absoluendum ad cautelam in causis de curia tantum.

46. Sequitur videre de auditore camere et eius notariis.

[c.7][V 1] De spoliis prelatorum, de procurationibus, de fructibus medii temporis per papam nec inferiores prelatos capiendis Rubrica

Dudum fuit prouide dispositum quod non reseruarentur de cetero spolia prelatorum ac clericorum decedentium nec fructus medii temporis ecclesiarum seu beneficiorum vacantium nec procurationes que ratione visitationis debentur episcopis et aliis pre-

---

1 registra] registrari AS; etc. *add.* EW   2 procurationis] procurationem DEW aliud] aliquod E   3 aut eorum] vel earum EW   5 inhibitionis] inhibitorie CEW   7 sequitur] etc. *add.* C   9 sperantur] nisi *add.* CEW   9–10 usque . . . gradum] tertii gradus CEW   10–11 etiam . . . consanguinei] ecclesiis in quibus CEW   15 aliis.] Placet *add. in marg.* C   17 casu] causa E 18 quo] Item quod auditores non viuant de sallario notariorum. *add. in marg.* W² 19 citationem . . . faciant] citatio et inhibitio fiant CEW   20 una] vino (!) E   21 absoluendum] ad soluendum A   23 Sequitur . . . notariis] CMW *only*   24 de (*third*)] et W   25 nec] *corr. from* et S   capiendis] cupiendis C 25–26 nec . . . rubrica] *om.* AD   24–26 De . . . rubrica] De spoliis prelatorum non auferendis M   27 Dudum] Expedita ad partem. *add. in marg.* W²   quod *om.* M   reseruarentur] seruari M   28 ac] et M   30 et aliis] aut M

latis. Verum quia dicte dispositiones hactenus non fuerunt plene
obseruate et a nonnullis possint in dubium reuocari an fuerint
personales vel perpetue, volentes ecclesiarum ac prelatorum dispendiis prouidere, declaramus dispositiones ipsas fuisse ac esse
perpetuas et per quoscumque summos pontifices inuiolabiliter   5
obseruandas. Et nichilominus de nouo statuimus, ne spolia cardinalium, que etiam inferioribus prelatis penitus interdicimus, nec
fructus aut prouentus, qui vacantibus ecclesiis, monasteriis aut
quibuscumque dignitatibus, beneficiis, administrationibus aut locis
piis medio tempore obuenerint, nec procurationes supradicte, que   10
ratione visitationis prelatis vel aliis quibuscumque debentur, possint de cetero, etiam per commissiones seu concessiones eis forte
iam factas, quas tenore presentium reuocamus, nomine summorum
pontificum camere apostolice reseruari, leuari aut quomodolibet
participari; adicientes quod de cetero prelatis et aliis qui ex officio 15
visitare tenentur facultas siue licentia visitandi per procuratorem
nullatenus per sedem apostolicam aut alium concedatur, nisi forte
ex causa infirmitatis aut alia necessaria personaliter visitare non
possint, que specialiter in litteris exprimatur; alias concessio nullius
sit roboris vel momenti. Et concessas hactenus tenore presentium   20
reuocamus, constitutionibus que circa fructus huiusmodi con-
seruandos et procurationes ac taxationes ipsorum per alios retro
pontifices et generalia concilia prouide facte sunt in suo robore
duraturis.
    Et nota quod quibusdam visum fuit quod circa spolia etc. adi-   25
cienda esset pena, ut scilicet tam diu curia Romana quo ad officia
sua remaneat suspensa donec per summum pontificem huiusmodi
spolia fuerint plenarie restituta; dicta vero suspensione durante,
officia sua exercentes excommunicationis sententiam incurrant ipso
facto.   30

---

1 dicte] *corr. from* directe E   plene *om.* EW   2 possint] possit C   3 vel]
aut M   4 ac] et EW   6 obseruandas] Etiam ab instato (?) actis reseruatur
articulus de prelatis inferioribus. *add. in marg.* W² statuimus] Et bonum forte
est adicere penam, ut scilicet (*as in lines 25–30 below*) . . . facto *add.* CDEW (E *in
text,* CDW *in marg.*)   ne] in M   6–7 cardinalium] prelatorum aut clericorum quorumcumque in curia vel extra decedentium *add.* ACEMW   8 qui]
per M   ecclesiis] aut *add.* EW   10–11 supradicte . . .prelatis] supradictis
prelatis M   11 quibuscumque] dignitatibus beneficiis *add.* DS   debentur]
debent E   13 factas] concessas CEMW   15 prelatis] archidyaconis *add. in
marg.* W²   18 necessaria] legitima *add. in marg.* W²   20 concessas] concessa EMW   22 ac] et EW   taxationes] per *add.* DEMW   per *om.* EMW   23
prouide facte] pro fide facta E   facte] facta C   sunt] sint M   26 Roma-
na] pro *add.* S   25–30 Et nota . . . facto] AS *only (See above, line 6* Statuimus)

[c.8][XV 1] Quod per sedem apostolicam nulli detur facultas de cetero licentiandi aliquos ad gradum magisterii seu doctoratus
Rubrica

Eo multos iam produxit ambitio ut qui primas cupiant cathedras in synagogis gradum scientie non labore et studio per scientiam querant sed a summo pontifice per ambitionem impetrant. Cupientesque vocari Rabbi satis habeant, si per bullam apostolicam magisterii sui signum valeant ostentare. Ex quo contemptibilis multiplicatio magistrorum et doctorum exoritur, scientie margarita vilescit et sermo dei ex ore prolatus ignorantium populi indeuotione contempnitur.

Volentes igitur huic morbo salubriter prouidere statuimus ut nec legatis nec nuntiis apostolicis seu generalibus ordinum aut alteri cuicumque persone preter cancellarios in generalibus studiis ordinatos detur per sedem apostolicam facultas aliquos ad gradum magisterii seu doctoratus in quacumque facultate de cetero licentiandi vel assumendi. In curia vero Romana, que priuilegium studii generalis censetur habere, ita demum ad gradum predictum licentiari et assumi possint, si in studio dicte curie cursum consuetum auditionis et lectionis repetitionum et disputationum in illa facultate perfecerint, vel si extra curiam in aliquo studio generali, de quo et eorum sufficientia in vita et moribus eiusdem studii cancellarius et doctores seu magistri facultatis per suas autenticas litteras prestent sufficiens documentum, et tunc non per bullam seu commissionem specialem, sed alias per consuetos officiales et doctores studii dicte Curie cum rigoroso etiam examine tales ad licentiam vel doctoratum seu ad magisterium assumantur. Aliter autem licentia vel assumptio huiusmodi per bullam, commissionem siue facultatem apostolicam facta non valeat, nec recipientes licentiati, doctores aut magistri de cetero reputentur, et idem intelligatur de doctoribus secularibus.

1–2 Quod . . . doctoratus] Cedula exhibita per dominum Pisanum die iouis XIX Septembris de doctoribus et magistris non creandis per bullam apostolicam V   3 Rubrica *add. in marg.* V   4 Eo] Eorum D   iam *om.* DM   produxit] produxit CDEV   cupiant] copiant D; capiant V   5 studio] studiose D   6 querant] querat EW   8 ex] et V   9 et doct. *om.* D   10 prolatus] prelatus DV   12 Volentes . . . prouidere *om.* D   nec] aut V   14 cuicumque] cuiuscumque V   cancellarios in] cancellariis et D   14–15 ordinatos] ordinatis D   15 facultas] aut quos ad quos gradum magisterii seu doctoribus detur per sedem apostolicam facultas *add. and struck out* S   aliquos] aut quos S   17 priuilegium] priuilegia V   18 demum] domum A   18–19 licentiari] licentiati D   20 et lectionis *om.* V   20–21 facultate *om.* V   22 eorum] eius V   cancellarius] cancellarii D; cancellarios E   25 alias per] per alios CEV   26 etiam *om.* V   tales] etiam *add.* D   27 vel] et A; et *struck out* C   doctoratum] doctorum V   ad *om.* DV   magisterium] magistratum DM   27 aliter] alter E   30 intelligatur] etiam *add.* CEW   30–31 Et idem . . . secularibus] *om.* ADV; Et ista cedula placet ut est deliberata. *add. in marg.* V

[V, *in marg.*: Super cedula presenti de doctoribus factis per bullam domini reformatores concluserunt quod qui si facti sunt doctores vel magistri a quinquenio citra per bullam et non fecerunt cursum suum in studiis generalibus non gaudent priuilegiis que habent alii magistri in suis ordinibus et hoc si sint religiosi nec 5 precedant alios expeditos secundum formam studiorum generalium.

Repetita dicta cedula cum secunda deliberatione, placuit sed deliberatis.

Et idem de doctoribus secularibus et laycis. 10

Die sabbati XVIIII Octobris. Deliberata.]

[c.9][XXIII 2] [Constitutio de impressionibus et precibus exhibita per dominum Florentinum deliberata die veneris XX Septembris] Quod electiones et prouisiones de cetero non fiant per preces Rubrica 15

Statutum felicis recordationis Innocentii pape III editum in concilio generali⁵ contra electiones, eligentes ac electionibus consentientes per secularis potestatis abusum locum habere decernimus in prouisionibus quibuscumque etiam per summum pontificem faciendis quo ad prouisiones ipsas ac prouisionibus 20 consentientes. Et nichilominus decernimus [et declaramus] electionem seu prouisionem per secularis potestatis abusum factam censeri debere non solum si expressa uis aut metus fiat [pro] electoribus ⌜aut⌝ prouisori.[Si quis tales preces pro electione sua aut prouisione inpetrauerit, usus fuerit per se vel alium vel appro- 25 bauerit aut electionem seu prouisionem ad tales preces per se factas acceptauerit, et electionis et prouisionis commodo careat. Etiam inhabilis ipso iure fiat ad episcopatum et omnes ecclesiasticas dignitates.] ⌜Sed etiam preces litteratorie vel vocales sint tales et a tali

---

5 X 1.6.43 *Quisquis*

---

1 factis] facta MS   12–13 Constitutio . . . Septembris] V *only*   14–15 Quod . . . Rubrica] ACDESW   17–18 ac electionibus consentientes] et electos concentientes V   19 prouisionibus] promissionibus E   20 ac] et V   21 et declaramus] V *only*   23 censeri] censere A; conscire (?) E   debere] deberi CV   pro] V *only*   24 aut *om.* V   26 aut] *corr. from* vel   24–29 Si . . . dignitates] V *only*   28–29 dignitates] V, *in marg.*: Placet, sed addatur post verbum prouisori: "Sed etiam sy preces letteratorie vel vocales [*corr. from* vocalis] sint tales et a tali vel talibus emanantur, quod sy non pareatur possint electores seu prouisores dampna seu incommoda non modica in personis suis vel suorum vel rebus aut ecclesiis verisimiliter formidare. [*Second note*] Et addatur procurans tales preces ultra penas predictas sit excommunicatus ipso iure. [*Third note*] Et publicetur hec constitutio <in> singulis sinodis et capitulis <prouin> cialibus vel regularibus <et> alias ubi videbitur exp<edire> cum ad electionem <fuerit> procedendum.

vel talibus et taliter emanent quod si non pareatur, possint electores vel prouisor seu prouisores dampna vel incommoda in personis suis vel suorum vel rebus vel ecclesiis suis verisimiliter formidare. Et publicetur hec constitutio in singulis sinodis et capitulis prouincialibus vel episcopalibus vel regularibus et alias ubi videbitur expedire, et specialiter cum fuerit ad electionem vel prouisionem procedendum. Et ubi in capitulo "Quisquis"[6] dicitur de suspensione, dicatur "ipso iure," et procurans preces ultra penas predictas sit excommunicatus ipso iure.]

[c.9a][XXIII 3] Alia constitutio de eodem

Si quis vocales aut litterales preces quorumcumque secularium que aut propter consanguineitatem vel alias simoniam sapiant aut propter potentiam deprecantium impressionem pro sua electione aut promotione ad episcopatum vel abbatiam aut prouisione cuiuscumque beneficii ecclesiastici impetrari, uti, aut approbare, immo non expresse contradicere, et statim cum poterit electoribus seu promotori aut prouisori contradictionem suam non intimare presumpserit, electio, promotio vel prouisio nulla sit et ipse ad episcopatum ipsum seu abbatiam vel beneficium ea vice sit inhabilis ipso iure. Sapiunt enim ut plurimum tales preces vitium simonie, et cum a potentioribus ingeruntur metum et tacitam impressionem inducunt. Si quis etiam ecclesiam quamcumque seu beneficium post rem contra ipsum in foro ecclesiastico in possessorio seu petitorio iudicatam et contra executorium iudicati per solam facti resistentiam per mensem a die scientie detinere presumpserit, omni iure quod in illo vel ad illud sibi fore competebat et ceteris beneficiis suis sit ipso facto priuatus. Sit preterea inhabilis ad omnes alias dignitates et ecclesiastica beneficia obtinenda. Eadem etiam pena ipso iure pellatur si quis super episcopatu, abbatia vel beneficio quocumque ecclesiastico litem in foro seculari super petitorio seu possessorio mouere presumpserit, nisi forte post rem iudicatam in

---

6 X 1.6.43

---

1 vel] a add. C.   emanent] emanetur EW   et . . . emanent] underscored W
2 incomoda] commoda EW; incommodo   5 alias] alios E   7 in capitulo]
nec C   9 ipso] ipse D   p. 343 line 29–p. 344 line 9 Sed . . . iure]
ACDESW   10 Alia...eodem] Ad idem. EW; Ad abbreuiandum lites add. in
marg. W   12 que] qui D   14 aut (second)] vel EW   15 impetrari]
impetrare AEW   16 statim] statum E   20 tales] ceteros S   cum] tum
S   23 possessorio] possessoris D   petitorio] petitoris D   24 executorium]
executoriam EW   25 mensem] mensam (!) E   26 illud] aliud E   fore]
forte EW   suis om. EW   29 pellatur] precellatur EW   31 presumpserit]
presumpsit EW; persumpserit (!) A

foro ecclesiastico in vim executorie impetret brachium seculare ab ecclesiastico iudice inuocatum. Non tamen prohibemus, quin iudex seu dominus secularis in dictione sua, etiam inter ecclesiasticas personas in rebus ac beneficiis ecclesiasticis, vim fieri vetet, sed solum ut de facto vim arceat, scandala prohibeat, causas ipsas tam   5 possessorias quam petitorias ad ecclesiasticum iudicem iudicandas remittat.

[c.10][X 1] De non dispensando cum promotis ad episcopatus et abbatias, quod non teneantur ad sacros ordines promoueri

[V, *in text*: Deliberata] Intentio quod papa non dispenset cum   10 aliquo promoto ad episcopatum vel abbatiam quod non teneatur ad sacros ordines promoueri vel ad sacerdotium vel consecrari infra tempus iuris sine consensu maioris partis cardinalium et causa rationabili in litteris specialiter expressa, et tunc non ultra annum dispenset. Et quod omnes tales dispensationes in preterito facte per   15 papam reuocentur. Et currat tempus iuris a fine presentis concilii.

[EW, *in marg.*: De hac materia habes conclusionem XIV. et XVI. Septembris.]

[c.11][X 2] De dispensatione ad incompatibilia [cum promotis ad maiores dignitates vel diuersarum regionum]   20

[Intentio quod] ex nunc reuocentur omnes concessiones facte episcopis vel abbatibus ⌈a tempore scismatis⌉ de beneficiis tenendis ultra episcopatum vel abbatiam nisi forte episcopatus vel abbatia esset adeo exilis quod non posset de ipso sustentari.

[EW, *in marg.*: Si tempore schismatis citra in futurum fiant per   25 papam nisi ex causa euidenti que in literis exprimatur et cum consilio et subscriptione dominorum cardinalium, ut habes VII^{ta} Nouembris.]

---

1 executorie] executorim E; executorem W   3 etiam] unam E   7 remittat] remittit W   8–9 et abbatias] vel abbatiam EW   9 sacros] sanctos sacros E; promoueri *om.* EW; Rubrica *add.* EW   8–9 De . . . promoueri EVW *only; see above, Table 1.*   10 Intentio] Placet omnibus capitulum siue articulus. *add. in marg.* V   Intentio quod *om.* ADMS   12 consecrari] Non dicitur usque ibi quod prelati. *add. in marg.* EW   15 preterito] preteritum EVW   16 per papam reuocentur] reuocentur per papam V   19 incompatibilia] Rubrica *add.* EW   19–20 cum . . . regionum] MV *only*   21 Intentio] Placet omnibus similiter. *add. in marg.* V   intentio quod] EMVW *only*   22 a . . . schismatis.] *om.* EMVW   tenendis] retenendis V   23 nisi . . . abbatia] *om.* DS (*sign in text of S for marginal addition, but none appears*); nisi *add. in marg.* D   24 de ipso] de ipsis EW; ex eis V   sustentari] Placet omnibus similiter *add in marg.* V.

⌐Item tales concessiones in futurum non fiant per papam nisi ex causa euidenti que in literis exprimatur et cum consilio ac subscriptione dominorum cardinalium.⌐

Item quod nullus monachus habeat beneficia in diuersis religionibus et reuocentur concessa ita quod remaneant in beneficiis sue religionis. [Idem in canonicis regularibus.]

[c.12][X 3] [De dispensatione ad incompatibilia cum secularibus de parrochialibus ecclesiis et dignitatibus et ceteris curatis] ⌐De pluralitate beneficiorum Rubrica⌐.

Quod papa non dispenset nisi ex causa rationabili expressa specifice in litteris, scilicet propter scientiam vel nobilitatem vel exilitatem beneficiorum ut in c. De multa.⁷ Ad tria autem non dispenset nisi ex eminenti sciencia vel magna nobilitate et quia illustris, nisi forte in partibus ubi essent exigua beneficia ut in Apulia et in certis partibus Hispanie et ibi non ultra quatuor. In Anglia vero omnino caueat ut non nisi ad duo ad plus dispenset, et hoc etiam ex magna causa.

Item quod nullus possit habere ultra duas prebendas ecclesiarum cathedralium, ⌐non obstante quacumque consuetudine, nec possit dispensari per papam nisi ex causa specialiter expressa in litteris, que sit rationabilis et vera.⌐ Et quod non possint lucrari eadem die cottidianas distributiones nisi in uno beneficio.

[EW, *in marg.*: De hac materia habes quinta Nouembris quod quis non possit habere ultra duas prebendas ecclesiarum cathedralium non obstante quacumque conswetudine nec possit dispensare per papam nisi causa specialiter expressa in literis et que sit vera et rationabilis.]

10

15

20

25

---

7 X 3.5.28

1–3 Item tales . . . cardinalium] ADS *only*   4 quod] EMVW *only*   in] de V   4–5 religionibus] *corr. from* regionibus V   5 concessa] concessis EW; concessiones V   remaneant] maneat V, maneant EW   4–6 Item . . . religionis] De facultatibus religiosorum habes XIX Octobris, sed non conclusiue. *add.* EW (W *in marg.*; E, *in text, as rubric of separate schedule*)   6 Idem . . . regularibus] V *only*; Illud fuit reuocatum per reformatores IIII die Nouembris. Circa futuras vero dispensationes fuit obtentum quod non fierent nisy de consilio dominorum cardinalium vel maioris partis et ex causa rationabili que in dispensatione exprimatur. *add. in marg.* V   7–8 De . . . curatis] MV *only*. De incompatibus (!) secularibus alias de pluritate beneficiorum Rubrica EW; Conclusa 14ᵗᵃ Augusti. *add. in marg.* W   8–9 De plur. . . . Rubrica] ADS   11 specifice] specificate E   12 non *add. above line* V   13 vel] et V   et] ut V   14 illustris] illustres ADS   exigua] exilia ADS   15 non] ad *add.* V   17 etiam *om.* W   causa] Idem conclusum est quod de aliis *add. in marg.* V   19– 21 non . . . uera *om.* EMVW   21 non] nullus MV   possint] possit AMV

[c.13][X 4–5] De preteritis dispensationibus ⌐quo ad incompatibilia reuocandis⌐.

Reuocentur ille ⌐ex toto⌐ que non sunt sortite effectum; sed
sortite effectum reducantur ad duo tantum. Ita quod liceat habenti
plura incompatibilia infra annum eligere duo que malit. Nec possit   5
⌐alia⌐ cum aliquo permutare.

[EW, *in marg.*: Similiter de isto habes quinta Nouembris quod
dispensationes de incompatibilibus secularibus si non sunt sortite
effectum reuocentur ex toto. Sed sortite effectum rediri ad duo et
instituti teneantur infra annum eligere que duo velint, nec possint   10
permutare.]

[c.14][X 6–7][De dispensatione de non residendo] ⌐De residentia
episcoporum et superiorum prelatorum Rubrica⌐

[EW, *in marg.*: De hac materia habes conclusionem VII. Nouembris et incipit rubrica de episcopis et superioribus prelatis et abbati-   15
bus non residentibus in suis ecclesiis.]

Quilibet summus pontifex in principio assumptionis sue pro-
ponat edictum, quod omnes archiepiscopi ⌐et⌐ episcopi similiter et
abbates ⌐iurent in promotionibus suis⌐ et alii exempti, ⌐quod⌐
teneantur in propriis ecclesiis [et] monasteriis et dignitatibus,   20
curis et administrationibus residere. Et si steterint per sex menses
absentes ab ecclesiis suis ⌐vel monasteriis⌐ absque expressa licentia
sedis apostolice, sint ipso iure priuati episcopatibus et abbatiis suis.
Nec det papa licentiam nisi ex rationabilibus et iustis causis [ac] in
⌐ipsorum⌐ litteris specialiter expressis, ut puta [quod] Romana   25
Curia indiget de presentia sua vel quia tenentur prosequi causam
ecclesie sue in Curia vel alibi vel quia est de consilio alicuius regis

---

1 De . . . dispensationibus] *Part of paragraph, not rubric* V   1–2 quo . . . reuo-
candis] *om.* MV; Rubrica *add.* AEMW   3 ex toto *om.* EMVW   3–4 sed . . .
reducantur] in totum. Alie autem reuocentur EMVW   4 liceat habenti] licet
habeant EW   5 infra . . . eligere] possit eligere infra annum EW   4–5
liceat . . . malit] qui plura incompatabilia elegere (!) teneantur infra annum que
duo malit V   6 alia *om.* EMVW   7 isto] ista W   8 si] sed E   9 re-
diri] *corr. from* reuocentur W   10 teneantur] teneant E   11 permutare] per
auctoritate E   12 De . . . residendo] MV *only;* Placet omnibus. *add. in marg.*
V   12–13 De . . . Rubrica] *om.* MV   18 et (*first*) *om.* EV   similiter et] ac
etiam MV; iurent: similiter et abbates iurent in promotionibus suis quod *add. in
marg.* V   19 iurent . . . suis] *om.* V; iurent M   quod *om.* MV   20 et
(*first*)] MV *only*   et (*second*)] ac MV   21 curis] iuris V   per] preter
ADS   22 suis] ab ecclesiis suis: addatur vel monasteriis *add. in marg.*
V   vel monasteriis *om.* MV   23 sint] *corr. from* fuerit S   24 rationabilibus . . . causis] rationabili et iusta causa MV   ac] MV *only*   25 ipsorum
om. MV   literis] libris D   specialiter expressis] limitata MV   quod] quia
AEMW   25–26 Romana . . . sua] indiget presentia sua in Romana curia vel
alibi MV   27 de] in V

vel principis ⌜sui⌝; hoc tamen adiecto quod pro consiliis ⌜regum et⌝ principum ⌜sint deputati ad certum et determinatum numerum.⌝
Intelligantur tamen esse presentes si morantur in castris vel aliis locis vicinis ⌜ecclesie sue⌝ infra diocesim, ita tamen quod ⌜saltem⌝ in precipuis festiuitatibus et diebus sollempnibus scilicet natiuitatis domini, circumcisionis, ephiphanie, quadragesima, pasce, ascensionis, penthecostes, in natiuitate ⌜sancti⌝ Johannis Baptiste, in assumptione nostre domine, et in aliis festis principalibus, ut consecratione seu dedicatione ecclesie sue sint presentes in ecclesia et missas celebrent si possint. Similiter episcopi teneantur sub pena ponere simile edictum omni anno in ecclesia sua pro abbatibus non exemptis et aliis curatis ⌜et⌝ habentibus beneficia requirentia residentiam de iure, consuetudine vel statuto. Nec dent licentiam non residendi nisi ex causa iusta et expressa, ut supra. Nec aliquid capiant pro tali licentia sub pena.
Item quod abbates non possint abesse a monasterio [suo] causa studiorum, quia debent esse scientes, nec immo ut legant in aliqua facultate, quia utilius est ut suscepta monasteria [sua] gubernent, quam quod scolaribus legant. Item quod non possint esse in officiis secularibus vel consiliis principum nec propterea habere absentiam, quia mortui sunt mundo. In conciliis prouincialibus habeatur diligens inquisitio ⌜et relatio⌝ de subditis ipsorum, ut puniatur. Et de episcopis et exemptis qui per semestre non residerint vel negligentes fuerint [in] compellendo subditos ad residentiam, ut per concilium referatur pape.

1 sui] MV *only*   regum et *om.* MV   2 ad] et EW   determinatum] deputatum EW   sint . . . numerum] limitetur V; limitetur etiam numerus M   3–4 vel . . . infra] ecclesie sue seu aliis locis infra MV   4 saltem *om.* MV   5 precipuis] principibus E   et . . . sollempnibus *om.* A   natiuitatis] in natiuitate MV   6 pasce] pascha EW; pascathe MV   7 sancti *om.* V   7–8 in assumptione] assumptionis EVW, assumptione M   8 in aliis] ceteris MV   ut] videlicet in MV   10 missas] missam MV   missas celebr.] missa celebrentque EW   12 requirentia] requirentibus ASW   13 vel] et E   dent] det EMVW   13–14 non residendi] de non residendo V   14 nec] ne V   cap.] capiat EW   16 suo MV *only*   17 quia] qui V   nec . . . legant] vel quia legent MV   18 est ut suscepta] quod MV   sua MV *only*   16–19 Item . . . legant *om.* EW   20 consiliis] officiis V   21 In] Et in EMVW   22 diligens *om.* EW   et relatio *om.* MV   ipsorum] episcoporum MV   puniatur] puniantur EW; et puniantur M   23–24 negligentes] negligenciis EW   24 in] MV *only*   ut] ac MV   25 referatur] referat EW; efferatur (?) M

[c.15][X 8] De dispensatione ad ordines ⌐Rubrica⌐

Quod prelati seruent capitulum "Cum ex eo."[8] ⌐Item⌐ quod in litteris exprimant, quod nisi studium continue prosecutus fuerit cessante studio dispensatio cesset. Et de facto reuocent dispensationem si habentes relicto studio vel intermisso abutantur ipsa. Et idem in litteris de non residendo causa studii vel alia quacumque papa etiam non det dispensationem quod non teneantur ad sacros [ordines] vel ad sacerdotium intra annum promoueri, nisi ex iusta causa et specialiter in litteris expressa; nec tunc [etiam] ultra annum ⌐concedat⌐, et in preteritum concesse reuocentur, ita quod remaneant ad annum tantum.

[c.16][X 9] [De dispensatione super defectu etatis] ⌐De dispensatione etatis episcoporum, abbatum, curatorum et ordinum Rubrica⌐

Non dispenset papa nisi in tribus annis infra etatem iuris, ut in episcopo si expleuit XXVII annum, in abbatibus et curatis etc. si XXII annum attigerunt, et similiter in ordine presbiteratus, etc. Et tunc ex causa rationabili et specialiter in litteris expressa. ⌐Preterite⌐ dispensationes ⌐reuocentur⌐ que non sunt sortite effectum. Si habentes ⌐ipsas⌐ hodie sint infra dictas etates dispensabiles sint reuocate; hoc adiecto quod dispensationes que dicuntur facte cum infantibus ad dignitates suprascriptas, etiam si sint effectum sortite, sint reuocate, quia contra ius naturale [sunt]. In prebendis ecclesiarum cathedralium stet regula cancellarie quod non possint conferri nisi existentibus in XIIII [anno]; possit tamen papa conferre existenti in XII facta mentione de etate.

5

10

15

20

25

---

8 VI 1.6.34

1 Rubrica] *om.* MV; Similiter placet omnibus. *add. in marg.* V; Respicit membra *add. in marg.* W[2]   2 capitulum] ADV (*corr. from* casum) D; casum S; c. CEW; D, *add. above line:* libro sexto   Item *om.* V   3 exprimant] exprimatur MV   4 dispensatio] ipsa *add.* CMV   4–5 reuocent dispensationem] reuocetur dispensatio MV   5 intermisso] intermissio A   7 dispensationem] dispensationes MV   8 ordines MV *only*   ad *om.* EW   intra] ultra CEW   intra . . . promoueri] vel ad tempus MV   9 etiam] MV *only*   10 concedat] DS *only*   in . . . concesse] preterite dispensationes MV   11 remaneant] non maneant (!) V; maneant M   12 De . . . etatis] MV *only*   12–13 De . . . rubrica] ADESW   14 annis *om.* E   ut] et V   15 expleuit] expleat MV; 27 *add. in marg.* E   annum] annos MV   abbatibus] abbate V   etc. *om.* DS   16 annum] annis M; annuum C; *om.* DEW   attingerunt et similiter] attingerit et sit MV   etc. *om.* DS   et] ex (!) A; *om.* E   17 tunc] hoc non nisi DS; hoc non fiat nisi A   expressa] *Blank space of 3 cm. follows.* V   17–18 Preterite *om.* MV   18 reuocentur *om.* MV   sunt] fuere C; sint MV   19 ipsas *om.* MV   19–20 sint reuocate] reuocentur MV   20 adiecto] addito C   21 suprascriptas] supradictas C; vel ecclesiam curatam V   22 sint reuocate] reuocentur MV   23 cancellarie] canonum M   possint] possit EVW   24 anno *add.* MV   papa *om.* ADS   25 mentione] intentione E; inuentione (!) W   etate] Placet omnibus. *add. in marg.* V

[c.17][XXIV] ⌈De litigantibus in Curia⌉

Non imponat papa silentium litigantibus, nec extinguat litem nisi causa cognita per sententiam, nec restituat contra rem iudicatam nisi ex causa legitima et ⌈causa⌉ cognita.

[c.18][XXII 1] De decimis per papam non imponendis ⌈Rubrica⌉ [propositum die veneris XX Septembris de mane]

[Conclusum est] quod papa non imponat decimam clero ⌈vel⌉ toti vel ⌈eius⌉ parti nisi in concilio generali ⌈et cum consensu concilii.⌉ Possit tamen [ei] postulare caritatiuum subsidium cum caritate quando res exigit. [Et super hoc fuit constitutio in forma oportuna per dominos Pisano et Florentino.]

[W³, *in marg., gloss on* caritatiuum: Ex euidenti et necessaria causa. Innouetur capitulum Aduersus⁹ non minus quocumque priuilegio non obstante.]

[c.19][XXV 1] De conuersis ad fidem quod etc. Rubrica

Quod bona illorum qui conuertuntur ad fidem non confiscentur per ecclesiam vel principes seu dominos seculares sed eis remaneant nisi sint de usuris vel alias male ablatis et tunc incerta eis libere remaneant.

[c.19] Version in MV:

De infidelibus conuersis ad fidem recipiendis ad baptisma propositum die martis XXIIII Septembris

Dominus Bathoniensis presidens proposuit de Iudeis et aliis infidelibus ad fidem Christi conuersis recipiendis ad sanctum baptisma absque eo quod oporteat eos sua bona dimittere utrum videatur honestius uel fauorabilius uel utilius.

Et tandem scrutatis votis conclusum est per omnes quod bona baptizandorum non confiscentur nec ullo modo accipientur ab eis per prelatos uel dominos seculares. De

9 X 3.49.7 (?)

1 De . . . Curia] *om.* MV; Romana *add.* EW; Rubrica *add.* A   2 litem] lites MV   3 cognita] Placet ut supra. *add. in marg.* V   5 Rubrica] *om.* MV; aut aliquam quottam aut exactionem *add.* W   6 propositum . . . Septembris] MV *only*   de mane] V *only*   7 conclusum est] MV *only*   decimam] decimas MV   vel *om.* MV   8 eius *om.* MV   generali] Post verbum generali addatur et cum consensu consilii. *add. in marg.* V   8–9 et . . . concilii *om.* MV   9 ei] V *only*   postulare] postulari MV   10 caritate] et de consensu concilii *add.* CE; *add. and underscored* W   exigit] exigerit V; exiget C; et reuocentur facultates leuandi et percipiendi predicta quibuscumque *add. and struck out* W²   10–11 Et . . . Florentino] V *only*; Deliberata XVIII Octobris. *add. in marg.* V

15 De] Sequitur de C   16 quod etc. *om.* CEW   Rubrica] Membra *add. in marg.* W   20 eis] eius E   20–21 remaneant] De ceteris relinquatur [relinquantur C] eorum conscientie. *add.* CEW   19 Bathoniensis] Bartholomeus M *om.* CEW   27 uotis] uitis (!) V   28 bona *om.* M

[c.20][VI 1] De exemptionibus religiosis concessis Rubrica

Quod omnes exemptiones quibuscumque religiosis domibus aut aliis locis vel personis quibuscumque a tempore scismatis per Romanos pontifices concesse preter consensum ordinariorum aut sine cause cognitione indistincte reuocentur, cassentur, irritentur et annullentur exceptis ecclesiis vel locis nouiter fundatis sub conditione exemptionis, etiam a tempore scismatis, exemptionibus tamen studentium et generalium studiorum semper saluis.

[c.21][VII 1] De priuilegiis inferiorum prelatorum ipsis concessis Rubrica

Quod omnia priuilegia et indulgentie a tempore scismatis concesse inferioribus prelatis de utendo pontificalibus sicut mitris, sandaliis, rocheto de benedicendo populo et dando indulgentias et huiusmodi ad dignitatem pontificalem pertinentibus reuocentur; et idem intelligatur de abbatissis.

male ablatis bona, incerta sibi remittantur uel dantur in elemosinam; de certis oneretur eorum conscientia sed ab ipsis nihil penitus auferatur.   5

[c.20] Version in V: De exemptionibus

Quod omnes exemptiones quibuscumque religiosis domibus aut locis vel personis a tempore scismatis citra per Romanos pontifices vel pro Romanis pontificibus se gerentes preter consensum ordinariorum et sine causa concesse indistincte reuocentur, cassentur, irritentur, annullentur.   15

[c.21] Version in V:

De priuilegiis concessis inferioribus prelatis de utendo pontificalibus

Item quod omnia priuilegia et indulgentie concesse inferioribus prelatis de utendo pontificalibus sicut mitris, sandaliis et huiusmodi ad dignitatem pontificalem pertinentibus, ab obitu felicis recordationis Gregorii citra indistincte reuocentur.   25

Conclusum est quod indistincte a tempore felicis recordationis Gregorii XI citra omnes concessiones indulgentie et priuilegia de signis episcopalibus ferendis concessis minoribus prelatis reuocentur.   30

10   20

---

2 Rubrica] Membra add. in marg. W   4 aut] ac E   5 a] corr. from et S   7 concesse] concessis C   10 annullentur] annichilentur E   12 fundatis] et add. E   14 exemptionis] emptionis EW   13-16 etiam . . . saluis ADS only; Et fuit dictum quod habeatur aduertentia de exemptionibus pendentibus ex necessaria causa orta ante scisma et de exemptionibus studentium in studiis generalibus. add. in marg. W   18 prelatorum om. D   ipsis om. CEW   19 Rubrica] Membra add. in marg. W   25 dando] de D; corr. from do S   27 et] et ad E; corr. from ad W   27-28 intelligatur] intelligantur E

6 exemptionibus] Deliberata die XXVII Septembris add. in marg. V   9 personis] Habeatur aduertentia de exemptionibus pendentibus ex verisimili causa orta ante scisma [et?] de exemptione studiorum generalium. add. in marg. V   15 annullentur] Maiori parti placuit quod omnes exemptiones indistincte reuocarentur, aliquibus quod personales tantum; sed conclusum quod deputetur unus pro natione qui cum cardinali Pisano et Florentino concipiant formam constitutionis. Fuit correctus articulus ut nunc iacet, nisi quod in fine sit postea additum. Item addatur in fine: "exceptis ecclesiis et locis nouiter fundatis sub conditione exemptionis." add. in marg. V   19-21 Item . . . utendo] See V, c.17 below concerning misplacement of these words. marg.   26 reuocentur] Declaratum: Diliberatum (!) die XXVIII Octobris. Addatur de [blank space of 2 inches] de populo et dandi indulgentias de abbatissis. add. in marg. V

[c.22][XXVII 1] De ignorantibus ydeoma Rubrica
Item nulli ad ecclesias parrochiales promoueantur in aliquo
regno nisi ydeoma uulgare eiusdem patrie sufficienter intelligant et
loquantur. Et ibi conclusum fuit quod innouetur constitutio Gregorii XI et extendatur ad ordinarios.
[Version in MV:
Domino Aniciensi presidente prefato fuit repetita materia de non
dispensando super idoneitate die iouis III Octobris
Et super hoc fuit constitutio domini Gregorii XI que sequitur.]
[c.23][VII 2] De unionibus   1(
Uniones de beneficiis cuiuscumque status siue etiam de ecclesiis
secularibus vel regularibus deinceps non fiant per summum pontificem nisi ex causa rationabili et causa cognita et aliter facte ipso
iure sint nulle; idem et fortius in ordinariis. Facte autem in preteritum que nondum sortite sunt effectum indistincte intelligantur   1.
cassate et penitus reuocate, et idem de unionibus factis de vicariis,
que intelligantur reuocate, etiam si effectum sortite sint. Que vero
de aliis beneficiis, siue per summos pontifices siue ordinarios facte
sunt, et effectum sortite a tempore huius nephandi scismatis citra,
causa rationabili non subsistente, indistincte habeantur pro nullis   2(
et sint ipso iure reuocate.
[c.23a][XXXVI, para.2] [See above, p. 283]
[Domino Aniciensi presidente propositum fuit die ultimo Septembris de religiosis habentibus litteras facultatis ad beneficia.]
⌐Item⌐ [conclusum fuit scrutatis votis quod] reuocentur omnes   2⌐
littere facultatum concesse mendicantibus [de obtinendis beneficiis
per ipsos ecclesiasticos] etiam per modum commendarum, etiam si
sortite sint effectum et similiter concesse aliis religiosis pro
[obtinendis] beneficiis extra suum ordinem, si [tamen] non sunt
sortite effectum, ⌐indistincte reuocentur⌐. Secus si effectum sortite   3(

---

1 De] Sequitur de C   Rubrica] Membra add. in marg. W² 2 Item] quod
add. CEW   ad . . . parrochiales] om. C; ad beneficia ecclesiastica curata
EW   4 Et ibi om. CEW   fuit om. CEW   innouetur] mouetur E   4–5
conclusum . . . ordinarios] appears in marg. CEW; Sequitur in tertio folio de translationibus [with sign and letter a] add. S (See Introduction, p. 284)   9 fuit] allegata
add. M   que sequitur] om. M; Conclusum est quod innouetur et extendatur ad
ordinarios. add. in marg. V   10 unionibus] Detur. Ista conclusio fuit facta XIX
Nouembris [1415 add. C] add. in marg. CEW.   11 Uniones] in marg. C   14
sint om. D   16–17 et idem . . . revocate] om. C (homoiotel.)   23–24 Domino . . . beneficia] V only; De litteris facultatum concessis mendicantibus et
aliis religiosis ad beneficia secularia et extra suum ordinem. M   25 Item] om.
V; quod add. MS   conclusum . . . quod] V only   26 concesse] concessis
M   26–27 de . . . ecclesiasticos V only   27–28 etiam . . . similiter] etiam si
sortite sint effectum, et etiam si per modum commendarum, sed ADSM   28
pro om. M   29 obtinendis] V only   sunt om. M   indistincte reuocentur om. V

sunt. [Et] in futurum [autem] indistincte non concedantur, et ⌜si concedantur⌝ non valeant.

[c.24][XXVIII] De beneficiatis citra episcopos et abbates non residentibus Rubrica

Quod omnes habentes beneficia requirentia residentiam de iure, consuetudine vel statuto vel alia speciali ordinatione resideant, et moneantur per edictum publicum quod faciant episcopi et alii prelati iurisdictionem habentes in principio sue institutionis, et repetatur hoc in sinodis et conciliis prouincialibus. Et si absque causa rationabili et superioris licentia fuerint absentes per sex menses, exequantur prelati penas iuris contra ipsos et ultra hoc dixerunt aliqui de specialibus penis imponendis. De licentia autem que datur pro absentia quod nichil recipiatur pro ipsa, et non detur nisi causa rationabili et expressa, nec habeatur pro rationabili si stant in curia regis vel principis pro officiis voluntariis in quibus stant propter lucrum. Et si episcopi et alii iurisdictionem habentes fuerint negligentes in premissis, fiat super hoc inquisitio in conciliis prouincialibus et generalibus ad effectum ut in primis redarguantur et in generalibus puniantur. Item etiam papa in principio assumptionis faciat edictum publicum in Romana Curia de residendo ut supra. Et dispensationes facte contra premissa ex toto sint reuocate, nec in futurum concedantur, nisi ex causa rationabili et euidenti et in litteris specialiter expressa, et specialiter habeatur aduertentia quod non dispensetur cum illis qui sponte iurauunt residere, et quod habentes dignitates principales post pontificales teneantur ad residentiam.

[c.25][XIII 6] De taxis ecclesiarum reducendis ad debitum modum Rubrica

Fuit propositum et dictum quod materia in se erat bona et necessaria sed tamen differanda usque quo per dei gratiam habeatur unio et unicus pontifex in dei ecclesia.

[c.26][IX 1] Contra simoniacos (A²=second draft; A, p. 602; ends with word ignorantiam, line 23; see Introduction, p. 289)

Conclusum quod expediens est, quod per concilium procedatur contra aliquos, saltem illos qui sunt de hoc publice diffamati, et

1 Et] V   futurum autem indistincte] futuris aut distincte M   2 valeant] valent ADS; Sequitur de exemptionibus in 3° folio add. in marg. S   4 Rubrica om. M; Hanc conclusionem habes VII Nouembris 1415 add. in marg. C   6 et om. M 9 conciliis om. M   11 hoc om. M   13 datur] dicitur M   16 et] vel EW 18–19 ad ... generalibus om. M   19 in (second)] a M   20 de om. M   21 premissa] premissis C   22 causa] rationabili add. EW   rationabili] om. S   23 et (first) om. E   24 iurauunt] iurauerunt A; iurauerint M   28 Rubrica] Non detur. add. in marg. EW   30 differanda] deferenda D; defferenda S; differandam EW quo om. EW   34 quod om. M   procedatur] concedatur M   35 aliquos ... illos] cardinales, patriarchas, archiepiscopos, episcopos, et contra omnes et singulos cuiuscumque conditionis et preeminentie existant et alios A²

dentur iudices zelatores veritatis et affecti ex conscientia contra hoc crimen, qui contra predictos constanter intrepide procedant, etiam summarie et sine strepitu et figura iudicii; et hoc vel ad instantiam volentium agere ciuiliter vel criminaliter, vel etiam ex officio et omnibus modis iuridicis, etiam per denunciationem vel inquisitionem, et hoc quoad forum iudiciale. Sed quoad penitentiale, quia multi dicuntur hiis turpibus illaqueati, tam clerici quam laici, et nonnulli etiam creduntur esse qui forte faciunt sibi conscientiam, existimantes se hoc crimine contaminatos esse etiam ultra quam sint. Ideo ad hoc, ut facilius inducantur ad penitentiam super hoc agendam, volens hoc sacrum concilium prouidere saluti animarum, statuit quoad tempora preterita quod quicumque tales voluerint penitere, liceat eis eligere sibi confessorem discretum qui sciat bene talibus consulere prout fuerit expediens. Et, ne contingat confessores in hoc per ignorantiam errare, decernatur quod sint vel magistri in sacra pagina vel in sacris canonibus. Et istis sic electis conferatur a concilio plena potestas, ita quod possint secundum qualitatem criminis et deuotionem confitentis et aliis circumstantiis attentis, huiusmodi confitentes plene absoluere imposita penitentia salutari et sufficienter consulere et prouidere predictis et eorum statui, habentes in hoc omnimodam potestatem quam potest tribuere concilium; intelligendo semper quod quamquam per predictos in premissis gestum fuerit valeat quoad dictum forum penitentiale tantum, sine preiudicio fori iudicialis. Et iudices predicti deputentur per nationes, unus pro natione et unus de collegio cardinalium, quem ipsum collegium voluerit deputare.

[CEW, *in marg.*: Detur. Hanc conclusionem habes XVI. Nouembris.]

[c.27][XXIX 2] De iniquis statutis

[CEW, *in marg.*: De hac conclusione vide prima Octobris.]

---

1 ex] de C   2 constanter] et *add*. CM   5 modis] modum A   6 quoad (*first*)] forum *add*. EW   7 turpibus] temporibus A²CEMW   8 faciunt] fuerint A²   12 statuit] statuat C   13 penitere] Videtur solum (debere *add. and struck out*) concedi occultis eo quod in consilio (*corr. to* concilio) Constantiensi satis sunt premoniti ne publice peccent aut symoniam committant. *add. in marg.* (*in new hand*) C   sibi *om*. C   15 sint] doctores *add*. E   vel *om*. M   17 secundum] solum M   18 confitentis] plene absoluere *add*. M (*homoiotel.*)   20 prouidere] de *add*. M   22 quamquam] quidquam DE; quamquid A; quidquid W; quicquid M   22–23 predictos] dictos W   23 quoad] ad A   dictum] suorum *add*. AS   25 per nationes *om*. M   de] pro E   26 collegium . . . deputare] collegium deputet CEW; deputat M   deputare] Sequitur "Quia a longis temporibus" *add. and struck out* S   29 De . . . statutis] *in marg*. DS

De oneribus seu solutionibus pecuniarum quas habent subire hii
qui recipiuntur ad canonicatum vel prebendam in ecclesiis cathedralibus vel aliis collegiatis, et specialiter de statutis vel iuramentis
propter que recipiendi stant per multos annos quod nichil perci-
piunt; et de littera "Vidimus".   5
Conclusum erat varie, tamen communiter inclinarunt in hoc,
quod onera que sunt ad cultum diuinum, ut quod recipiendus
soluat pluuiale, vel quid simile, stent. Sed prouideatur quod solutio
fiat de fructibus prebende et illud fiat cum effectu ad utilitatem
publicam. Si autem soluitur pecunia que distribuitur inter canoni-   10
cos, illud prohibeatur. Et si est consuetudo de faciendo pascum,
non cogatur recipiendus ad hoc, et si etiam velit facere non possit
excedere florenum. Item si consuetudo habet quod fructus primi
anni debeantur fabrice et secundi anni alteri loco vel persone et sic,
non extendantur talia ultra duos annos. Distributiones autem cotti- 15
diane sine aliqua exceptione debeantur a die receptionis si receptus
deseruit in diuinis. De receptionibus vero que fiunt per expectatiuas, quod etiam tunc nichil exigatur, cum tunc non consequatur
prebendam, que non vacat, vel forte si vacat alii concurrunt cum
eo, ita quod inter eos est lis quis potior.   20
[c.28][XXX] De tempore professionis fiende Rubrica
[CEW, *in marg.*: De hac conclusione vide IX. Nouembris.]
Fuit conclusum, quod in religionibus, licet possint recipi pueri,
tamen ad professionem non admittantur nisi plene puberes, scilicet
qui sint in decimo octauo anno et maxime quo ad puellas; nec   25
eciam obligentur ex professione tacita ante dictam etatem. Et quod
nouitii non admittantur ad professionem nisi sciant competenter
legere et cantare, nisi in religione militari, ut sancti Johannis vel
simili; nec ad sacros ordines admittantur nisi sint professi et sint
competenter in grammatica instructi.   30
[c.29][XXXI] De conciliis prouincialibus et synodis episcoporum
Rubrica
[CEW, *in marg.*: Hanc conclusionem habes X Octobris non
tamen discussam, prout habetur in fine.]

2 recipiuntur] recipiunt C   5 et . . . "Vidimus"] *om.* M, *underscored* D *and rubric*
add. in marg.: "De littera 'Vidimus'"   6 conclusum] Detur. *add. in marg.* EW
erat *om.* CEMW   7 ut] et D   8 quid] quod E; *corr. from* aliquid C   solu-
tio] solummodo (?) A   10 Si] Sed M   inter] in CEMW   18 conse-
quatur] consequantur AC; exsequatur E; exequantur W   21 Rubrica] *om.*
M   23 religionibus] conclusionibus M   24 professionem] prouisionem EW
plene *om.* V   scilicet *om.* V   25 qui] que (!) S   anno] annos   constituti V
nec] neque M   28 militari *om.* V   vel] et EV   29 ordines admittantur *om.*
EMW   31 conciliis] spoliis (!) A   31-32 et . . . Rubrica] *om.* MV   34
habetur] habes EW

Fuit conclusum quod concilia prouincialia fiant saltem de triennio in triennium, et sinodi episcoporum singulis annis, in quibus agatur de correctione morum et aliis, ut est iuris. Et teneantur archiepiscopi et episcopi per se ipsos si non sint legitime impediti. Et si omiserint sint suspensi ab omni iurisdictione, et deuoluatur ad capitulum cum emolumento ipsius, quod conuertatur in utilitatem publicam ecclesiarum et non priuatam ipsorum de capitulo. Et si metropolitanus per quadrennium, et diocesanus per biennium, differant, tunc in sequenti concilio generali possint, si videbitur concilio, priuari dignitatibus episcopatus vel archiepiscopatus. Et episcopi teneantur ire ad concilium prouinciale sub pena excommunicationis, quam incidant ipso facto nisi habeant causam rationabilem, que discutiatur in concilio, vel sint suspensi a collatione beneficiorum per annum et deuoluatur ad capitulum suum. Et de loco concilii prouincialis statuatur in precedenti concilio prouinciali et duret saltem octo diebus vel decem; aliqui dixerunt de mense. De sinodo vero, quod duret saltem quinque diebus. Nichilominus fuit dictum quod illa materia latius tractaretur in sequenti die. Postea tamen nichil fuit mutatum.

[c.30][XXXIV] De actibus pontificalibus, scilicet de ordinatione clericorum vel consecratione ecclesiarum et ceteris nichil recipiatur, etc.

Quia a longis temporibus humani generis hoste procurante nonnulli immo multi pontificali dignitate sublimati, quibus ex debito incumbebat pontificalis officii sacrorum et inferiorum ordinum ministeria necnon consecrationes et alia pontificalium actuum exercitia per se gratis sine quarumcumque pecuniarum exactione

---

3 iuris] moris EW   4 sint] *om.* DS   6 conuertatur] conmitatur V   7 et (*first*) *add.* EV   8 metropolitanus] metropolitani V   quadrennium] quadrigenium (!) S; quatreniis V   et] in V   9 in sequenti] inconsequenti A   concilio] continuo D   11 episcopi] ipsi D   12 quam] quod V   incidant] incident E   16 octo . . . decem] VIII vel X diebus et V   17 vero] Nota ita V   quinque] *corr. from* III D   18 illa] ista CEM   19 die *om.* A   18–19 in sequenti die] die sequenti CEM   17–18 Nichilominus . . . die *om.* MV   19 mutatum] concordatum C   postea . . . mutatum] CDES *only* (*in new hand* D, *in marg.* C); nichil fuit S (*other words excised by trimming*).   20–22 De . . . etc.] Quod pontifices ordines, consecrationes, et alia pontificalia, per se vel substitutos, gratis sine quacumque exactione pecuniarum, celebrare teneantur. Et quod non dispensent cum ordinatis per simoniam. Rubrica DM   24 immo *om.* D   27 quarumcumque] quacumque DM

celebrare, huiusmodi exercitia aliis episcopis titularibus, pauperibus, et aliunde unde viuerent non habentibus interdum annua
pensione ex pacto seu alias soluta commiserunt exequenda; qui
differenter secundum differentias ordinum aut rerum consecratar-
um implicito vel explicito pacto ab ordinatis, vel de consecratis, aut 5
reconciliatis rebus pecunias nedum receperunt, sed et satis inhu-
maniter extorquendo exigerunt, vicium symoniace prauitatis mis-
erabiliter et satis impudenter, nedum exercendo sed et alios
recipientes huiusmodi ordines ac de consecrationibus aut recon-
ciliationibus paciscentes dampnabiliter maculando; idcirco hec 10
sacrosancta sinodus, volens tale vitium tam euidenter ecclesiam dei
scandalizans inquantum potest extirpare, statuit et decernit quod
quilibet archiepiscopus vel episcopus prefatos suos quoslibet actus
pontificales, vel per se ipsum, si poterit, alioquin per substitutum
pontificem catholicum, gratiam et communionem sancte apostolice 15
sedis habentem, gratis absque omni datione aut exactione pecuniarum preuia vel sequenti ipsi pontifici, ianitoribus, intitulator-
ibus, examinatoribus, scriptoribus vel seruitoribus quomodolibet,
cum pacto vel sine pacto soluendarum, exerceat aut faciat (litterarum testimonialium que formate nuncupantur, pro quibus unus 20
solus papalis grossus aut euis valor tam pro sigillo et cera quam
scriptura solutione, vel, si archiepiscopum vel episcopum ad ex-
tranea remotiora loca pro consecratione aut reconciliatione ecclesie, monasterii, cimiterii, altaris vel capelle profiscisci contingat,
precise moderatarum et supportabilium expensarum et non ultra, 25
procuratione dumtaxat exceptis); et cum ordinatione et dispositione, quod episcopo ordinanti, consecranti aut reconcilianti substi-
tuto de redditibus mense sui principalis taliter et tam sufficienter
prouideatur, ne egestate grauatus sibi in huiusmodi actibus forsitan
symoniace questum querat. Quod si secus actum fuerit, ut quod 30
pecunie ultra id quod promittitur exigantur, dentur aut recipiantur, sit ipse ordinans vel alium actum pontificalem exercens, tam

---

1 titularibus] secularibus M   5 ab] vel D   de om. D   6 reconciliatis]
de conciliatis D   7 exigerunt om. D   9 recipientes] recipiendos D; recipiendo M   ac om D   aut] et D   10–11 hec sacrosancta] sacra D; hec
sancta M   13 quoslibet om. D   15 pontificem] et add. DM   16 gratis]
et add. DM   omni datione] ordinatione S only   17 vel sequenti] om. DM
18 examinatoribus om. D   19 exerceat aut faciat] exerceat. Et faciat D   fa-
ciat] taxa add. DM   22 solutione, vel] solui debet. Vel D; solui debetis vel
M   vel (second) om. M   23 aut] et D   25 moderatarum] moderatum
A   mod. et supp.] om. DM   26 procuratione] et solutione add. D   excep-
tis] excepta M   et cum om. DM   26–27 dispositione] dispensatione
M   27–28 substituto] corr. from restituto D   29 forsitan om. DM   30 ut] et
D   ut quod] om. M

principalis quam substitutus, ultra alias penas iuris eo ipso sua dignitate pontificali priuatus et inhabilis ad eandem; et taliter ordinatus ab officio suo suspensus tam diu donec a solo summo pontifice aut generali concilio a tali suspensione relaxari mereatur. Et nichilominus, quia hactenus talis dampnate corruptionis abusus nimium inualescens quasi totum ordinem ecclesiasticum ministrorum dei simplicium per symoniacam suorum ordinum receptionem hinc inde per diuersas infecit mundi partes, ita ut paucissimi inueniantur qui non sint hoc vicio maculati seu decepti, idcirco hec sancta synodus errantium multitudini compatiens velut pia mater omnes taliter promotos aut qui aliter commode promoueri non poterant a singulis excommunicationum et suspensionum sententiis quas taliter ordinati usque ad presens incurrerunt aut inciderunt ipso iure postquam eorum taliter commissa aut delicta suis confessoribus in foro consciencie et confessionis exposuerunt, accepta secundum modum culpe penitentia salutari ex nunc prout ex tunc absoluendos et relaxandos decernit; necnon presenti constitutione absoluit et relaxat. Super irregularitate seu inhabilitate quacumque in officiis ordinum suorum ministrando quomodolibet hactenus contracta pie et misericorditer dispensando non obstantibus in contrarium facientibus quibuscumque etc.

[c.31][XXXII] De casibus reseruatis sedi apostolice

Propositum fuit de casibus reseruatis sedi apostolice, in quibus absoluit maior penitentiarius sine speciali mandato, quod committeretur episcopis, vel quod in partibus alicui daretur potestas circa hoc.

Conclusum per maiorem partem quod stetur iuri communi; tamen aliqui dixerunt quod super occultis bonum esset prouidere. Et aliqui etiam dixerunt quod vellent magis deliberare de occultis; de notoriis autem fuerunt omnes concordes quod stetur iuri communi.

[c.32][XXXIII] De vicariis perpetuis in ecclesiis instituendis Rubrica

Item quod in singulis ecclesiis appropriatis et unitis sit unus

---

4 aut] in M; a D   5 dampnate] dampnatus M   6 quasi] in D   8–9 inueniantur] reperiantur DM   10 sancta] sacro S   11 taliter] ex pura simplicitate *add.* DM   aliter] taliter M   commode] ad sacros ordines DM   12 poterant] potens D, potentes M   13 aut] et M   14 eorum] coram DM   delicta] debita DM   19 in officiis] officio DM   20 dispensando] pensamus M   20–21 non . . . etc. *om.* DM   22 apostolice] Detur. *add. in marg.* E; Fiat, ad minus ad presens, etc. *add. in marg.* D   30 communi] De hac conclusione habes 27 Nouembris. *add. in marg.* E; *text of E end here, with colophon:* Finitum VIII Octobris anno M°<CCC>XVI° per familiarem Nicolai Elstraw, etc.   31 in] et M   instituendis] constitudendis M   33 quod *om.* D   33–p. 359 line 1 sit . . . uicarius *om.* M

vicarius, alias curatus perpetuus, qui cure insistat animarum, bene
et competenter dotatus per ordinarium auctoritate apostolica pro
hospitalitate tenenda et oneribus incumbentibus sufficienter sup-
portandis reuocatis litteris apostolicis, priuilegiis, consuetudinibus,
prescriptionibus, pactis, contrariis sententiis latis omnibus aliis in   5
contrarium facientibus quibuscumque tamquam irrationabilibus et
in preiudicium diuini cultus concessis.
[c.33][VI 2] De exemptionibus
    Item quod omnes exemptiones, etc.: Ista materia non est deliber-
ata prout apparet die veneris XXII Nouembris.   10
[c.34][XXXV 1] De examine ordinandorum Rubrica
    [EW, *in marg.*: Ista materia non est discussa plene prout habetur
XIX Octobris.]
    Fuit dictum quod examinator teneatur examinare, etiam cum
examinatio pertineat ad alium ex priuilegio vel alio iure; tunc si   15
dubitet de ydoneitate non tenetur eum admittere, nisi se offerat
examinationi.
[c.35][XXXVI] De facultatibus religiosorum
    Conclusum quod facultates concesse religiosis non mendicanti-
bus pro beneficiis extra suum ordinem reuocentur si non sint sortite   20
effectum; secus si sint sortite. Dictum tamen fuit quod oportet
considerare quia sunt aliqui canonici regulares qui tenent habitum
canonicorum regularium et tamen habent beneficium monachorum
et econtra. Item de litteris facultatum dicatur indistincte, quomodocumque habeant, tamen ista videnda sunt a capite.   25
    [EW, *in marg.*: De ista materia habes XX. Octobris et prout
apparet in fine non est conclusa.]
    Item quod reuocentur omnes littere facultatum concesse mendi-
cantibus etiam si sortite sunt effectum, et si per modum commendarum; sed concesse aliis religiosis pro beneficiis extra suum   30
ordinem, si non sunt sortite effectum, indistincte reuocentur. Secus
si effectum sortite sunt. In futurum autem indistincte non concedantur, et si concedantur non valeant.
    [EW, *in marg.*: Detur. De hac materia habes ultima Septembris
conclusiue.]   35
[c.36][XIII 4] [No rubric]

---

1 animarum] ecclesiarum D   2 pro] et D   5 sententiis] M *only*   in] D
only   5—6 prescriptionibus ... quibuscumque] *add.* DM   7 concessis *om.* S
8 exemptionibus] Non detur. *add. in marg.* EW   11 Rubrica *om.* EW
14 examinator] ordinator EW   24–25 quomodocumque] quecumque (?)
E   25 a] in E   26 ista materia] isto modo W   29 sortite] forte E

[EW, *in marg.*: XIII. Septembris conclusum quod tota ista materia referatur ad nations (!)]

[1] In collatione beneficiorum primo attendatur ad dignitatem personarum maxime circa scientiam, quod ad episcopatum nullus promoueatur vel eligatur nisi sit persona sublimis vel doctor in theologia vel in iure canonico. Attendatur tamen qualitas regionum, quia alicubi sunt ita tenues redditus episcopatuum quod forte hoc non poterit obseruari, et raritas episcoporum.

[2] Ad abbatias non videtur tantum requiri gradus scientie, quia aliquando scientia prebet materiam euagandi, quantum adminis tratio et bona solertia ad diuinum cultum et honestas in obseruantia regulari.

[EW, *in marg.*: Penultima Augustus fuit conclusum, quod in magnis abbatiis, maxime si habeunt monasteria sub se, attendatur, quod sint doctores, sicut in episcopatibus. In aliis stetur littere. Sed adhuc istius particule pendet deliberatio ex particula precedenti.]

[3] In primis etiam dignitatibus post pontificalem et curatis cathedralibus soli doctores, licentiati in theologia vel iure; in aliis dignitatibus ecclesiarum cathedralium et in principalibus ut collegiatis et curatis magnis iidem vel baccalarii in theologia formati.

[4] Item in qualibet ecclesia cathedrali sit certus numerus prebendarum ad quas perpetuo non possint nisi predicti ultimi ullomodo assumi, et supradicti gradus scientie requirantur siue per ordinarios suos, siue per expectatiuas, siue per electionem, siue prouisionem apostolicam prouideatur; alias nulla sit prouisio. Habeatur tamen ratio nobilitatis tam ad episcopatus quam ad alias dignitates secundum quod videbitur expedire. Item consideratio regionum ut supra.

[5] De gratiis expectatiuis videtur quod papa principaliter det gratias in communi forma pauperum in datis consuetis et quod paribus in datis preferantur litterati quia sunt iustitie potius quam gratie.

---

2 nations] uacatonis E   3 beneficiorum] Non detur, quia non expedita *add. in marg.* W; Expedita *add. in marg.* W²   6 canonico *om.* D   7 alicubi] alicui E   8 et . . . episcoporum *om.* DE   9 Ad abbatias] autem *add.* DE; Expedita *add. in marg.* W²   tantum] tantus S   tantum requiri] tantum sed requiritur D   10 quantum] bona *add.* DE   11 solertia] solacia S   15 episcopatibus] episcopalibus E   17 In primis] Expedita *add. in marg.* W²   18 doctores] et *add.* D   20 iidem] idem E   formati] si possunt reperiri. Alias habeatur respectus ad equiualentias. *add.* D   21 Item *om.* D; Expedita *add. in marg.* W²   cathedrali] etiam *add.* D   22 perpetuo *om.* DE   22–23 ullomodo] nullomodo (!) D   24 suos *om.* E   25 prouideatur *om.* DE   28 ut supra] Communiter placet ista particula omnibus, ita quod habeatur consideratio quod ecclesie sint sufficientes ad hoc. *add. in marg.* W   31 litterati *om.* D   quia sunt] quod sint E   gratie] Videtur quod de beneficiis infra X marcharum in captione papa non habeat se intromittere. *add.* D

[EW, *in marg.*: Varie fuerunt opiniones. Nam aliis et maiori parti
placuit textus, aliis quod limitantur, aliis quod materia pro nunc
remaneat indiscussa. Et sic finaliter fuit conclusum quod differ-
atur.]

[6] Item det rotulos ordinatos pro familiaribus suis, pro officiali-   5
bus, pro regibus, pro uniuersitatibus, pro familiaribus cardinalium,
pro ducibus et aliis consuetis, sed in certo numero et cum moderamine debito secundum ordinatum obseruatum tempore Urbani
quinti et Gregorii XI. Et ultra rotulos per totum primum annum
possit secundum exigentiam meritorum et statuum dare expecta-   10
tiuas in primis datis secundum quod moderate sibi videbitur; post
annum vero primum nullam nisi sub data currenti.

[7] Item quod non dentur expectatiue nisi ad unum beneficium
tantum et unam collationem nisi esset infra summam 40 florenorum et tunc ad duo vel distinguantur regiones ubi detur ad unum vel   15
duo vel plura secundum consuetas regulas cancellarie.

[8] Item non dentur expectatiue ad prioratus conuentuales nec ad
dignitates electiuas.

[9] Item fiat constitutio quod certus locus remaneat liber ordinariis sed quod similis scientie conferant ut supra et alias prouisio   20
sit nulla.

[10] Item quod maior in gradu scientie preferatur in pari data et
diocesanus non diocesano.

[11] In beneficiis vacantibus minoribus utatur solum reseruationibus iuris scripti et extrauagantis "Ad regimen,"[10] que ita   25
moderata est et consueta quod pro iure satis reputari potest.

[12] Item in episcopatibus et abbatiis minoribus usque ad centum florenos libera sit electio et confirmatio ordinariis; in maioribus libera sit electio sed papa confirmet.

---

10 Extrav. comm. 3.3.13

---

5 det] dat S   8 ordinatum] ordinem D   9 XI] XII E   et *om.* D
10 statuum] statum E   11 videbitur] videtur E   14 collationem] tantum
add. E   17 expectatiue *om.* E   19 remaneat] maneat D   20 alias]
alia DE   23 diocesanus] *corr.* from ideo E   24 In] Item in D; Item
E   beneficiis] non *add. and struck out* E   24–25 reseruationibus] reforma-
tionibus (!) S   26 potest] aut quia in extrauagante fit mentio de ecclesiis
cathedralibus *add.* D   27 Item *om.* E   28–29 et confirmatio ... electio
om. D

[13] Communia seruitia prelaturarum solui non possint etiam a volentibus ante annum; et fiat talis constitutio quod seruetur ex neccesitate. A fine anni a die habite possessionis soluatur medietas, et alterius anni altera medietas, et si bis in anno vacauerit non soluatur nisi semel, et ecclesie ac monasteria que sunt indebite taxata debite taxentur.

[14] Item quod papa pro tempore existens in suis prouisionibus ad prelaturas et alia beneficia ecclesiastica mentem habeat et gerat specialem ad doctores in theologia, iure canonico, et ciuili et ipsis iuxta eorum habilitates et sufficientias ad gubernandum in spiritualibus et temporalibus prouideat et eos promoueat inter alios.

[15] Item quod archiepiscopi, episcopi, abbates, priores et alii quicumque spirituales beneficiorum spiritualium collatores doctores in theologia, iure canonico vel ciuili, necnon baccalarios in theologia ad quecumque beneficia cum cura extra ecclesias cathedrales existentia, quamdiu aliqui huiusmodi doctores, magistri siue licentiati nati in diocesibus ubi huiusmodi beneficia existant non promoti fuerint, semper unum ex huiusmodi beneficiis ex nunc simul vel successiue vacaturus conferant seu ad ea presentent in forma iuris de tempore in tempus. Qui quidem doctores in theologia at alii predicti sic promouendi super eisdem suis beneficiis resideant et suis doctrinis et exemplis populum informent in lege Christi et ad hoc per suos ordinarios compellantur.

[EW, in marg.: XVIII. Nouembris conclusum, quod stetur capitulo, quantum ad id, quod ibi dicitur de residentia priuilegiis uniuersitatum studiorum. Illi tamen de natione Gallicana dixerunt, quod super hoc contulerant inter se, sed nondum erant concordes.]

[16] Item archiepiscopi et episcopi in collationibus beneficiorum in ecclesiis cathedralibus et collegiatis doctores in theologia, iure canonico sic habeant recommissos, quod in ecclesiis cathedralibus, dignitates et beneficia pro theologia siue iure canonico in eisdem ecclesiis legendis fundata vel per huiusmodi doctores in theologia et iure canonico et non per alios quouismodo occupentur iuxta naturas et fundationes eorundem beneficiorum. Qui quidem doctores theologiam et iura canonica in eisdem ecclesiis iuxta easdem naturas et fundationes personaliter et continue legant.

---

1 prelaturarum] prelatorum E   2 seruetur] seruentur (!) S   3 A (*first*)] in E   die] anni *add.* D   6 taxata] taxate D   taxentur] taxantur. Prouideatur de statu cardinalium quantum et unde. D (*See above, Table 3*)   7 Item] Non detur, quia non expedita et pendit adhuc *add. in marg.* EW; Expedita *add. in marg.* W². 10 sufficientias] insufficientias S   12 Item] Expedita *add. in marg.* W².   17 nati] ac E   19 vacaturus] vacatura E   28 Item] Expedita *add. in marg.* W².   32 per] *om.* S

[EW, *in marg.*: Conclusum, quod stetur capitulo, et addatur, quod collatio aliis facta quam theologo vel canoniste sit nulla. Item, quod predicti theologi et canoniste teneantur exequi id, quod est eis iniunctum per fundatores. Et possint ad hoc per subtractionem fructuum compelli.]   5

[17] Preterea iidem archiepiscopi, episcopi alias dignitates, canonicatus et prebendas in singulis suis ecclesiis cathedralibus et collegiatis sic conferant quod, quamdiu aliqui huiusmodi doctores, baccalarii siue licentiati in suis diocesibus nati et non promoti seu unicum beneficium tantum habentes reperiri poterunt ydonei, inter   10
quatuor huiusmodi dignitates seu prebendas per mortem siue resignationem in eisdem ecclesiis cathedralibus et collegiatis vacaturis unam conferant alicui eorundem.

[18] Et preterea alios huiusmodi doctores et licentiatos et baccalarios iuxta sua merita, scientias ac abilitates extra suas dioceses   15
natos habeant in aliis collationibus suis ad huiusmodi dignitates et prebendas in eisdem ecclesiis cathedralibus vacaturas, recommissos, iuxta suas conscientias et secundum quod pro utilitate ecclesiarum videbitur expedire; et omnes doctores et licentiati et magistri et baccalarii predicti vigore presentis ordinationis siue   20
decreti promouendi super beneficia huiusmodi iuxta naturas et fundationes eorundem resideant et morentur, nisi habeant causam iuridicam siue rationabilem absentie sue. Et ad finem quod premissa exequi valeant cancellarii vel doctores uniuersitatum pro tempore existentes de nominibus huiusmodi doctorum, licentiatorum   25
ac magistrorum et baccalariorum ordinariis locorum in quibus nati existunt certificent de tempore in tempus.

[19] Item quod in qualibet ecclesia cathedrali ad minus quarta pars prebendarum sit pro doctoribus seu licentiatis in sacra pagina, iure canonico vel ciuili aut in medicina aut baccalariis in theologia.   30

[20] Item quod in qualibet alia ecclesia collegiata ad minus quarta pars prebendarum sit pro dictis doctoribus, licentiatis aut baccalariis vel pro magistris in artibus aut baccalariis in iure canonico vel ciuili.

[21] Item quod ad minus tertia pars ecclesiarum parrochialium   35
sit pro graduatis et aliis supradictis, sic tamen quod quo ad ecclesias parrochiales existentes in locis insignibus aut alias habentes magnas plebes habeatur respectus ad theologos et canonistas.

---

3 canoniste] canonici E   6 Preterea] Et E; Expedita *add. in marg.* W²
iidem] idem E   13 unam] unant S (with correction sign, but no correction);
una ut (?) E   14 Et (*first*)] Expedita *add. in marg.* W²   19 et (*third*) *om.* E
21 super] supra E   28 Item] Expedita *add. in marg.* W²   31 Item] Expedita
add. in marg. W²   32 aut] ac E   35 Item] Ponitur (?) *add. in marg.* W²
37 aut] ut E   38 magnas] magna E

[22] Item quod episcopatibus et aliis prelaturis non prouideatur nisi graduatis aut alias scientie eminentis aut generosis si tamen illi sint sufficientis litterature.

[23] Item quod nati de diocesi in quibus sunt huiusmodi beneficia preferantur extraneis et magis graduatus minus graduato nisi rationabilis causa aliud exposcat.   5

[24] Item quod nullum habens beneficium preferatur habenti ceteris paribus. Item prouideatur quod per illam prouisionem graduatorum diuinus cultus et edificatio populi crescat et augeatur.

[c.37][IV 1] De translationibus   10
[EW, *in marg.*: Hec est in constitutione supra iam data que incipit "Quia decet"; XX Augusti fuit determinatum quod non nisi in concilio fiant et quod sic statuatur.]

Translationes inuitorum patriarcharum, archiepiscoporum, episcoporum seu abbatum, saluo iure constitutionum ordinum   15
suorum, papa non faciat usque ad proximum futurum concilium; licet, ubi immineret scandalum et periculum ecclesie spectando celebrationem futuri proximi concilii generalis licitum sit Romano pontifici cum consilio et consensu cardinalium seu maioris partis eorum absque translatione facienda de inuito scandalo huiusmodi   20
prouidere.

[c.38][XXIII 1] Quod electiones, prouisiones et postulationes decetero non fiant per preces Rubrica
[EW, *in marg.*: Conclusio facta XII Septembris.]

XI Septembris placuit quod constitutio fiat eo modo et forma   25
quod non fiat inutilis vel periculosa, et fuerunt deputati pro forma dictanda reuerendissimi cardinalis Pisanus et patriarcha Antiocenus, qui postea exhibuerunt cedulam que incipit "Statutum felicis recordationis Innocentii pape III."[11]

[c.39][XXXVII] Contra concubinarios   30
Ad arcendum concubinatus crimen et de clero penitus ad eliminandum summo studio per sacros canones prouisum est. Quia tamen quam plures ordinarii et alii ad quos pertinet, non adhi-

---

11 X 1.6.43

---

1 Item] Expedita. *add. in marg.* W²   quod] dictis *add.* E   4 Item] Ponitur *add. in marg.* W²   9 et (*second*)] ut E   10 translationibus] Expedita *add. in marg.* W²   14 inuitorum] inimicorum (!) E   15 episcoporum *om.* S   20 inuito] inimico (!) E   23 Rubrica] Ponitur (?) *add. in marg.* W²   27 dictanda] dictandi E   cardinalis] Cardinales E   29 III] etc. *add.* EW; see Common, c.9 above.   31 ad (*second*) *om.* M   32 quia] qui D

buerunt nec adhibent diligentiam quam deberent in eisdem
prouisionibus crimen prefatum in multis locis cum maximo catholi-
corum scandalo et totius clericalis contemptu ordinis frequentatur.
Cui morbo volens hec sacra sinodus occurrere decernit ut deinceps omnes in sacris ordinibus existentes vel religionem aliquam de   5
apparatis professi, qui votum continentie, ad quod se sponte obli-
gauerunt, concubinatus feditate violauerint penis infrascriptis ipso
facto subiaceant, ut videlicet si habuerint beneficia secularia
vel regularia, etiam si sint episcopatus vel superiora beneficia, et
concubinas notorie tenuerint, nisi infra mensem prorsus a se re-   10
mouerint, ipso iure intelligantur suis beneficiis per hanc constitutionem priuati, et possint ipsa beneficia libere per habentes potestatem aliis conferri et impetrari; vel aliis canonicis modis et aliis
ydoneis reformari. Si vero beneficiati non fuerint, sint ipso iure
inhabiles ad exequenda quecumque beneficia, penis aliis a sacris   15
canonibus contra tales proditis in suo robore remanentibus.
Quia vero circa euitationem talium diuerse reperiuntur opiniones, aliis asserentibus quod a presbiteris notoriis concubinariis
quamdiu tollerantur ab episcopis et aliis superioribus ita quod per
eos non est facta mentio specialis et nominatim, quod euitentur,   20
licitum est audire diuina et alia suscipere ecclesiastica sacramenta
ab eis; aliis affirmantibus ipsam notorietatem sufficere ut quilibet
possit et debeat etiam alia monitione non precedente tales euitare;
volens eadem sinodus animarum salutem consulere et sentiens ex
huiusmodi euitatione, quam priuati auctoritate propria fecerunt, in   25
nonnullis locis grauissima scandala exorta fuisse, decernit priorem
opinionem que monitionem precedentem exigit tamquam tutiorem
et non scandalosam esse preferendam.

---

1 deberent] haberent D   3 contemptu] contemptum DS   4 volens DM
only; after word synodus in D   ut] et DS   5 existentes] vel etiam in minoribus beneficiati *add.* M   6 apparatis] probatis M   6–7 obligauerent] obli-
garunt DS   9 vel regularia] aut officia, administrationes vel dignitates M
superiora beneficia] superiores dignitates M   10 mensem] duos menses M
11 beneficiis] officiis, administrationibus et dignitatibus predictis *add.* M   12
beneficia] officia, administrationes et dignitates predicte *add.* M   13 et
(*second*)] de DS   15 exequenda] assequenda M   16 proditis] prodit (!) S;
prodita D   suo] honore *add.* M   17 Quia] Etiam euitationem concubinar-
iorum *add. in marg.* D   reperiuntur] reueniuntur (?) M   17–18 opiniones]
opinionibus M   20 mentio] monitio M   quod] quia D   euitentur] omit-
tantur M   21 est] ab eis M   alia] *corr. from* talia D   22 affirmantibus]
confirmantibus (*corr. from* conformantibus) D   21–22 sacramenta ... affirman-
tibus] faciens firmantibus aliis M   24 salutem] saluti M   25 in] et D   27
monitionem] nominationem M   tutiorem *om.* M   28 preferendam] Videatur
de executione. *add. in marg.* D

[c.40][XI 1] De vestibus clericorum Rubrica

Statutum felicis recordationis Clementis pape quinti contra clericos absque rationabili causa vestes virgatas aut partitas publice deferentes editum in Concilio Viennensi[12] locum habere decernit sancta sinodus in omnibus clericis etiam si pontificali prefulgeant dignitate, qui absque causa similes vestes viridas rubeas supra talum curtas fissas stampatas aut manicas latas ultra palmam seu foderaturam usque ad oram habentes, ut alias prohibitas in concilio generali, decetero publice portare presumant; additiens et, ultra penas ibidem promulgatas, ordinarii locorum clericos sibi subditos in premissis excedentes siue exemptos apostolica auctoritate monere teneantur, ut vestem talem habentes infra certum tempus dimittant et sibi tradant pauperibus in elemosinam erogandam; quod si post trinam monitionem non fecerint beneficiis suis sint ipso facto priuati. Vel si beneficium non habuerint sint omnino inhabiles ad eandem. Ordinarii vero qui circa monitiones predictas et executiones earum reperti fuerint negligentes secundum negligentie modum per superiorem proximum etiam si sint pontifices appellatione postposita procellantur siue puniantur.

[c.41][XIII 5] De qualitate promouendorum ad beneficia; de collationibus beneficiorum

Ad episcopatum nullus eligatur vel assumatur nisi doctor in theologia, iure canonico vel ciuili vel notorie sufficiens doctor reputatus. Excipe paruos episcopatus qui non ascendunt ad IIII C. florenos, ut sunt in ciuitatibus non insignibus.

Ad abbatiam si est capud ordinis vel prior abbas, id est si alias habens vel habere debens conuentum XXV monachorum, sufficiat licentia in iure canonico vel baccalariatus formatus in theologia, in minoribus auditio triennalis, nisi esset Cisterciensis vel Premonstratensis ordinis, in quibus competens grammatica cum bona administracione sufficiat.

In dignitatibus primis post pontificalem in cathedralibus vel principalibus collegiatis et aliis iurisdictionem habentibus doctoratus vel licentia diuini vel humani iuris requiratur. In ceteris dignitatibus sufficiat baccalariatus cum lectura triennii.

---

12 Clem. 3.1.2

---

2 quinti] IIII M   4 editum] additum V   6 similes vestes *om.* M   7 talum *om.* M   8 usque ad oram] adoram S; odorem (*corr. from* odoram) D   habentes] habens M   ut] aut D; et M   9 et] ut M   13 et] teneantur ut vestem talem sibi *add. and struck out* D   sibi *om.* D   13–14 erogandam] erogandas M   15 Vel si] Si vero   16 predictas] prefatas M   17 earum] eorum DS   20–21 De . . . beneficiorum *om.* DS   23 sufficiens] et *add.* M   28 licentia] licentiatus M   32–35 In dignitatibus . . . sufficiat *om.* S (*homoiotel.*)

In qualibet ecclesia cathedrali sit una prebenda pro magistro in theologia, qui saltem bis in septimana legat et aliquando predicet; et una pro doctore iuris canonici vel ciuilis, qui in causis ecclesie patrocinari teneatur; nec aliis conferri possint. Excipe ecclesias habentes adeo prebendas exiles ut non inueniant doctorem qui se velit ad premissa obligare. De aliis vero prebendis quarta pars 5 graduatis debeatur in theologia, iure canonico vel ciuili. In collegiatis vero quarta pars predictis vel medicine vel artium magistro debeatur.

In ecclesiis parrochialibus que sunt in villis insignibus et valent C florenos vel ultra in portatis requiratur licentia iuris canonici vel 10 ciuilis aut baccalareatus formatus in theologia. Si vero fuerint extra insignes villas sufficiat gradus baccalareatus in scientiis predictis seu magisterii medicine vel artium. In ceteris parrochialibus et aliis beneficiis requiratur semper competens grammatica et alia iuxta dispositionem iuris communis. Et semper graduatus non graduato 15 vel magis graduatus minus graduato et diocesanus non diocesano preferatur in pari data. Et predicta intelligantur siue per electionem siue per collationem aut promotionem in Curia vel extra assumatur.

[c.42][XIII 9] De pessima consuetudine cathedralium et regular- 20 ium ecclesiarum quod in eis non admittuntur nisi de nobilium aut militarium genere procreati

Quia in ecclesiis quibusdam regularibus pessima seruatur et inoleuit consuetudo, vel potius corruptela, sic quod in eis non admittantur nisi de nobilium aut militarium genere procreati, qui, 25 velut ex militia geniti moribus laicalibus inbuti, studia non frequentant neque curant et sic ignari remanent et ydiote. Ex quibus tunc consequenter per electionem talem qualem ad ecclesias cathedrales huiusmodi militia dediti in prelatos promouentur interdum vix latinum fari scientes; et actus militares, tam in vestibus 30 quam in bellorum conflictibus et armorum insultibus, quia exercitati sunt in illis, magis pretendentes, quam quod actibus pontificalibus pro acquirendis, conseruandis et pascendis animabus et ouibus sibi subiectis, se ingererent, contra iura tam diuina quam

---

1 qualibet] quacumque M   2 legat] leget D   3 ecclesie] ecclesiasticis M   5 pars *om.* S   6 debeatur] debeant M   7 vero] non cathedralibus *add. in marg.* D   magistro *om.* M   10 licentia] licentiatus M   11 fuerint] sint M   13 magisterii] magisterium M   aliis *om.* M   19 assumatur *om.* S; Nota de graduatis promouendis. *add. in marg.* D   23 quibusdam] presertim cathedralibus et etiam quibusdam *add.* M   25 militarium] *corr. from* militarum D   26 velut] volunt M   27 ydiote] indocti M   28 ad] per M   29 dediti] deducti (?) M   30 fari] infari M   32 in illis, magis] magis in illis DS

humana. Et unde multa in populo ipsis subiecto scandala oriuntur. Et ecclesie ipse grauia, dampna et pericula patiuntur, et specialiter plura sollempnia monasteria de ordine sancti Benedicti desolata sunt et deserta, ita quod in quibusdam vix duo aut tres monachi inueniuntur, qui nec religiose viuere nec diuina curant ministrare seu frequentare officia. Bona etiam, res et possessiones monasteriorum male dispensantes, in esse seu statu eorum non conseruant, sed eorum aliqua ab ipsis monasteriis alienant. Idcirco petitur super hiis prouideri.

Ad idem.   1

Omnes constitutiones seu consuetudines quantumcumque seruatas, etiam si tanto tempore cuius contraria memoria non existat, etiam per sedem apostolicam confirmatas, quod ad episcopatum, dignitates seu prebendas aut monachatum, nisi nobiles vel illustres aut cuiuscumque gradus nobilitatis recipiantur, declarat   1 hec sancta sinodus non valere, sed reputandas corruptelas; nisi forte in ipsa fundatione ecclesiarum seu beneficiorum probari possit ex voluntate patroni sic fuisse statutum. Quo casu ex ecclesie tolerantia seruari possint, nisi talis nobilitatis homines de facili reperiri non possint, quo casu ad explendum numerum canonicor-   2 um seu monachorum tales ecclesie vel conuentus etiam ignobiles admittere vel recipere teneantur. Gradum etiam doctoratus vel licentie in sacra pagina, iure canonico vel ciuili pro quacumque nobilitate reputentur.

[c.43][VIII 1] De fructibus indebite perceptis per prelatos.   2

Aduersus dampnabilem abusum quo quidam ecclesiastici prelati requirunt, exigunt et recipiunt et sibi inbursant fructus integros aut duorum vel medios duorum annorum vel etiam unius in magnum detrimentum et grauamen pauperum qui multa litigando exposuerunt ac in principio introitus sui multis indigent pro regimine   3 domestico et hospitalitate seruanda. Cum tamen huiusmodi prelati alias sint sufficienter habundantes et redditus pro suis mensis habeant copiosos, petitur igitur super hiis etiam prouideri.

---

1 humana] et *add.* M.   multa] multis S   ipsis] illis M   4 deserta] desecrata D; et deserta *om.* M   5 inueniuntur] reperiuntur M   5–6 ministrare seu *om.* M   6 frequentare] frequenter D   et *om.* M   9 prouideri] *Text in M ends here.*   15 gradus] dignitatis *add. and struck out* D   19 seruari] seruati S; *corr. from* seruati D   18–21 ecclesie . . . tales *appears twice in S (homoiotel.)*   24 reputentur] Nota gradum nobilitate comparari. *add. in marg.* D   26 prelati *om.* M   27 requirunt] et *add.* M   integros] unius *add.* SM   28 etiam *om.* D   29 grauamen] gramamine M   30 ac] ut M   multis] multi D   33 igitur] etiam M

[c.44][XXIX 3] De iniquis statutis ecclesiarum et monasteriorum

Quoniam nonnulla ecclesiarum ac monasteriorum capitula et conuentus quedam nimis intolerabilia pauperibus exorbitantia statuta habere noscuntur, videlicet quod nullus de nouo admittatur nisi magna pecuniarum soluta quantitate, ita etiam quod talem 5 admittendum pluribus annis antequam integram prebende portionem accipiat oporteat expectare, quo contingit quod pauperes etiam quantumcumque alias ydonei nimium pregrauentur, idcirco talibus grauaminibus et exactionibus succurrendo petitur prouideri.

[c.45][XXXVIII] De exactionibus per principes impositis clericis 10 Rubrica

Cum prelati ecclesiastici, principes seculares et alie persone singulari exactionis genere clericos seculares et religiosos per nimias hospitalitates, vecturas, aliasque seruitutes, venatores, falconarios canes et aues, quos clericis et religiosis committunt nutriendos, ac 15 etiam porcos, boues et animalia ad impinguandum tradunt, nimis grauant; id circo petitur super hoc per opportunum remedium prouideri.

[c.46][XXXVIII] Ad idem contra libertatem ecclesiasticam Rubrica. 20

Quia per diuersa loca fiunt et hactenus facta sunt statuta contra libertatem ecclesiasticam, collecte aliaque grauamina per dominos temporales et communitates spreta et calcata omni reuerentia, quibuscumque clericis et eorum bonis pariformiter ac laicis imposite ac passim imponuntur, peroptimum videtur quod, etsi pre- 25 missa a iure satis dampnata sunt, tamen denuo per hoc sacrum concilium pro maiori firmitate adhibeatur omnis cura possibilis quod illa omnia de facto tollantur; et noua pena formidabilior taliter statuentibus et clericis aut bonis ipsorum grauamina seu collectas imponentibus statuatur. Quia pene alias a iure inflicte 30 contempnuntur et nichili penduntur.

[c.47][XXXIX] Quod reuocetur auditor camere qui est in Auinione et potestas penitentiarii minoris extra curiam et questores extraordinarii

---

6 prebende] prebendalem M   9 grauaminibus] grauibus M   exactionibus] actionibus D; exactionationibus (!) M   12–13 singulari] singulares DS   15 nutriendos] manendos M   16 impinguandum] pungnandum S; impignandum (?) D   17 grauant] tradant (!) D   15–17 ac etiam . . . grauant *om.* M   17 super] circa M; *corr. from* circa S   per *om.* M   oportunum] optimum D   18 prouideri] adhiberi M   21 fiunt] sint M   24 ac] et M   29 statuentibus] statuentur D   30 Quia] qua D   31 nichili penduntur] nichil penduntur S;   vilipenduntur D (*corr. from* nichilipenduntur)   33–34 questores extraordinarii] questore extraordinati (!) D; questiones extraordinarii M

Conclusum quod reuocetur auditor camere qui est in Auinione tamquam superfluus et per cuius officium nimium preiudicatur officio auditoris camere qui est in Curia. Reuocentur etiam omnes concessiones facte aliquibus extra Curiam per quas conceditur eis illa potestas quam habent penitentiarii minores in Curia. Reuocentur etiam omnes questores extraordinarii, ut illi qui de consuetudine non habent, vel ex priuilegio concesso locis vel hospitalibus, quod possint facere questum.

[c.48][XI 2] Contra prelatos qui non incedunt in habitu et tonsura decenti.

Fuit conclusum quod prelati, videlicet patriarche, archiepiscopi, episcopi, abbates, si omiserint incedere in habitu et tonsura clericali per annum, sint ipso iure priuati suis beneficiis, et libere possint habentes potestatem eligendi vel conferendi eligere et conferre. Et sub habitu clericali intelligatur quoad prelatos seculares, quod portent rothetum et cappam vel troccam vel mantellu, et quoad regulares, quod portent habitum sue religioni conuenientem.

[c.49][XL] Quod prelati habeant vicarios non uxoratos et bene litteratos

Et fuit conclusum quod hoc est de iure communi; tamen fiet constitutio in qua decernatur quod omnes prelati et persone ecclesiastice habentes iurisdictionem spiritualem non possint eam exercere, nisi per clericos non uxoratos et bene litteratos id est in iure peritos, et si per non clericos fuerint late sententie, sint nulle. Et quod imponantur pene sufficientes contrarium facientibus.

[c.50][XLI] De iuramentis capitulorum preiudicantibus ecclesiis Rubrica.

Propositum fuit de iuramentis que exiguntur per capitula vel conuentus ante electionem, vacante sede, que singuli de capitulo iurant, quod si eligentur, faciant talia etc. que sunt in graue preiudicium ecclesiarum seu mense episcopalis aut alterius prelature. Ad quod dictum fuit quod iuramentum non tenent; sed quia non obseruatur de facto, quod apponantur pene, puta quod electio

---

3 Curia. Reuocentur] Curia Romana, M   5–6 habent ... ut *om.* M   8 quod] que D   questum *om.* D   12–13 clericali *om.* D   16 troccam] *corr. from* troccamus S   18 et] sed MS   20 est] fuit D   fiet *om.* D   22 eam] causam (?) D   23 et] sed M   in iure] iuris M   23–24 non uxoratos ... clericos] *om.* S (*homoiotel*)   25 contrarium facientibus] contra contrafacientes D; contra facientes S   29 sede] apostolica *add.* DS   31 mense episcopalis] capitulis M   32 iuramentum non tenent] iuramenta non tenentur D; iuramenta de iure non tenent. M   33 obseruatur] obseruantur D

sit nulla et eligentes priuentur iure eligendi pro illa vice seu vacatione. Addiderunt etiam aliqui quod electus sentiatur inhabilis
perpetue ad illam dignitatem. Dixerunt et alii quod etiam quoad
eligentes adderetur maior pena.

[c.51][XLII] Quod prelatus contra prelatum non possit propria   5
auctoritate indicere bellum Rubrica.

Item omnes conuenerunt quod erat iustum quando dicitur ad
offensam, quia tunc hoc non debet fieri sine licentia superioris, nisi
in defectum iustitie; sed de pena indicenda fuit varietas. Ideo
dixerunt quod cogitaretur maxime per nationem Germanicam, ubi   10
talia plus quam alicubi eueniunt. Dictum etiam fuit quod Germanici sint cum domino cardinali Florentino et declarent premissa duo
capitula ut videbitur, et tunc iterum hic videatur etc.

---

2 sentiatur] censeantur M   4 pena] penitentia M   6 Rubrica *om*. M   7
dicitur] indicitur M   11–12 Germanici sint] Germania fuit M   13 tunc
om. D

THE VATICAN MANUSCRIPTS (V AND M)

VAT. LAT. 12572 = V

[372r] Cedule exhibite coram dominis reformatoribus super constitutionibus faciendis et determinata per ipsos sequuntur ut infra:
[c.1][VI 1] Cedula oblata per dominum pisanum die martis III Septembris
    Lettere apostolice tam de gratia quam de iustitia expediantur per cancellariam . . . [373v] . . . Ordinentur sessiones in Curia ut materia hec plenius deliberetur. Nota hic de doctoribus non fiendis in Curia quia super hoc facta est constitutio que incipit "Eo iam multos" et infra sequitur . . .
[See Common, c.6]
    Cum multe cedule fuerunt oblate et multa proposita de nullo sint deliberatum nisy quod die iouis XVIII Septembris super cedula de dispensationibus que sequitur: Deliberata.
[c.2][X I] De non dispensando cum promotis ad episcopatus et abbatias quod non teneantur ad sacros ordines promoueri
    Intentio quod papa non dispenset cum aliquo promoto ad episcopatum . . . presentis concilii. [See Common, c.10]
[c.3][X 2] De dispensatione ad incompatebilia (!) cum promotis ad maiores dignitates vel diuersarum regionum
    Intentio quod ex nunc reuocentur omnes concessiones facte episcopis . . . [374r] . . . canonicis regularibus. [See Common, c.11]
[c.4][X 3] De dispensatione ad incompatibilia cum secularibus de parrochialibus ecclesiis et dignitatibus et ceteris curatis
    Quod papa non dispenset nisi ex causa rationabili . . . in uno beneficio. [See Common, c.12]
[c.5][X 4] De preteritis dispensationibus reuocentur ille que non sunt sortite effectum . . . permutare. [See Common, c.13]
[c.6][X 6] De dispensatione de non residendo
    Quilibet summus pontifex in principio sue assumptionis proponat edictum . . . [374v] . . . referatur pape. [See Common, c.14]
[c.7][X 8] De dispensatione ad ordines

---

7 deliberetur] debberetur V

Quod prelati seruent capitulum Cum ex eo . . . ad annum tantum. [See Common, c.15]

[c.8][X 9] De dispensatione super defectu etatis
Non dispenset papa nisy in tribus annis infra etatem iuris . . .
[375r] . . . de etate. [See Common, c. 16]   5

[c.9][XXIV] Non inponat papa silentium litigantibus nec extinguat lites nisy causa cognita per sententiam nec restituat contra rem iudicatam nisy ex causa legittima et cognita. [=Common, c.17]

[c.10][XV] Cedula exhibita per dominum pisanum die Iouis XIX Septembris de doctoribus et magistris non creandis per bullam   10
apostolicam.

Eo iam multos perduxit ambitio ut qui primas capiant cathedras . . . [375v] . . . reputentur. [See Common, c.8]

[c.11][XXIII 2] Constitutio de inpressionibus et precibus exhibita per dominum Florentinum deliberata die veneris XX Septembris   15

Statutum felicis recordationis Innocentii pape III editum in concilio generali contra electiones . . . ecclesiasticas dignitates. [See Common, c.9]

[c.12][XXII 1] De decimis non imponendis per papam propositum die veneris XX Septembris de mane   20

Conclusum est quod papa non inponat decimas clero toti vel parti . . . dominos P et F. [See Common, c.18]

[c.13][XXV 2] De infidelibus conuersis ad fidem recipiendis ad baptisma propositum die martis XXIIII Septembris

Dominus Bathoniensis presidens proposuit de Iudeis et aliis   25
infidelibus . . . auferatur. [See Common, c.19]

[c.14][XXI 1] De indulgentiis et questibus et abusibus eorum tollendis Rubrica. Propositum die marcurii (!) XX die Septembris de mane.

Dominus Bathoniensis proposuit de indulgentiis et questibus   30
inordinatis et scandalosis et quod prouidendum esset aduersus scandalum quod ex abusibus eorum prouenit. Et scrutatis votis maiori parti placuit quod indulgentie que de pena et culpa, perpetue, et ad instar aliarum indulgentiarum reuocentur. Questus vero non vendantur. Sed nihilominus commissum est Cameracensi, Are-   35
tino, et priori Celestinarum ut faciant formam constitutionis que postea in congregatione recitetur.

[c.15][XXI 2] Ad succidendas ambitiones mortalium et ne

---

20 die . . . de mane] die XXV Septembris M   25 Bathoniensis] Bartholomeus M   33 que] commune (?) M   36 Celestinarum] Celsiniorum (?)
M   formam] fomam (!) V   37 recitetur] Diliberatum (!) ut supra add. in
marg.   38 succidendas] succedendas M

thesaurus ecclesie prodige effusus vilescat, ut congruit, sacrosancta
generalis synodus Constantiensis prouidendo ac statuendo reuocat,
cassat, irritat, et annullat omnes et singulas indulgentias hactenus
a tempore exorti scismatis citra quibuscumque ecclesiis, locis aut
uniuersitatibus tam ecclesiasticis quam laycalibus apostolica vel
alia quauis auctoritate ad tempus nondum finitum plenam peccatorum remissionem vel partem aut quotam aliquam; aut anni
iubilei seu proficiscentium in terre sancte subsidium vel similes
indulgentias sub quauis verborum conceptione appareant; aut pre-
dicationem verbi crucis siue inplorationem subsidiorum quorum-
libet continentes, quomodocumque et qualitercumque concessas;
nec non quasuis alias ad instar indulgentiarum sepultu Dominici,
beati Iacobi in Compostella, basilicarum quarumuis alme urbis,
sancte Marie in Portiuncula alias de angelis extra muros assisinates, sancti Marci de Venetiis, de Colle Madio, et de Aquisgrani
sanctorum martirum et similium concessis; ac etiam que predica-
tionem verbi crucis [376v] et inplorationem subsidiorum seu ques-
torum aliquas quomodolibet continerent; et facultates quascumque
de concedendis indulgentiis huiusmodi vel earum aliquam ac etiam
contenta in illis, ita quod proinde censeantur ac si concessa ac
indulta non essent; iubens et decernens [ut] locorum ordinarii sub
pena excommunicationis ac suspensionis ad annum ab officio, quas
ipso facto si neglexerint incurrant, de cetero in suis prouinciis,
ciuitatibus aut diocesibus aliquos ex talibus predicatoribus, inplor-
atoribus aut questuariis, seu deputatos ab eis, officium seu exercitium huiusmodi per se vel alios directe vel indirecte vel quouis
quesito colore gerere non permittant aut exercere. Layci autem hoc
permittentes vel dantes in predictis auxilium, consilium seu
fauorem post admonitionem prelatorum, si non destiterint, excommunicationis sententia incidant ipso facto. Indulgentiis singular-
ibus personis in mortis articulo aut semel in vita et semel in mortis
articulo et similibus in specie hactenus concessis plene remissionis
peccatorum in suo robore permansuris. Et, ne sacre predicationis
officium vilescat, prohibet, ne quis questor possit vel audeat aut
presumat per se vel alios aut predicator quiuis super premissis aut

---

2 ac] ad V   10 subsidiorum] subsidium V   12 quasuis] quauis V   sepultu *om.* V   14 Portiuncula *om.* M (*blank space of 4 cm. in text*)   14–15
assisinates *om.* V (*blank space of 4 cm. in text*)   15 Marci] Martii V   16
sanctorum martirum] sanctarum Marie V   17–18 questorum] questas (?)
V   20 ita quod] itaque V   21 essent] nisi essent facti contra hereses vel
scismates aut pro defensione fidei contra infideles *add.* M   ut *om.* MV   25 seu] vel
V   28 seu] vel M   30 incidant] incidit V   34 vel] aut M   35 quiuis]
quemuis (?) M

eorum aliquo officium aut exercitium quomodolibet exercere nisy sit bone vite, conditionis aut fame ac litteratus; et examinari et approbari debeat per loci ordinarium, et aliter admitti non possit. Presumentes aut secus vel aliter agere huiusmodi sententias ipso facto incurrant tam prelati et clerici quam laici.

Item dominus Bathoniensis proposuit infrascripta postridie capitula de tribus materiis die XXVII Septembris de mane et primo [c.16][VI 1] De exemptionibus

 Quod omnes exemptiones quibuscumque religiosis domibus aut locis . . . annullentur. [See Common, c.20]

[c.17][XXVI 1] De priuilegiis concessis inferioribus prelatis de utendo pontificalibus, mitris, sandaliis et huiusmodi ad dignitatem pontificalem pertinentibus, ab obitu fe. re. Gregorii citra indistincte reuocentur.

Item quod omnia priuilegia et indulgentie concesse inferioribus . . . reuocentur. [See Common, c.21] [377r]

[c.18][XXXV 2] Item quod omnes et singuli, cuiuscumque religionis aut conditionis extiterint, ab ordinantibus debite sicut seculares de eorum ydoneitate examinentur.

Et super premisso capitulo de ordinandis fuit exhibita constitutio tenoris qui sequitur:

[c.18a][XXXV 3] Quod examinatores examinent ordinandos

 Quod diligenter examinandi sint qui ad ordines promoueri postulant, plene in sacris canonibus est constitutum. Quos quia minus bene a nonnullis temporibus citra quidam ordinatores obseruauerunt, ventum est ad hoc, ut plurimi reperiantur promoti etiam ad sacros quibus nec assunt merita vite nec scientia nec alia que in eis de iure requiruntur. Hec itaque sacrosancta Constantiensis synodus huic morbo volens occurrere decernit, ut ordinator sub pena neminem nisi per se vel fides commissarios suos unum vel plures diligenter examinatum et habilem repertum ordinare presumat. Si vero contingat, ut predicta examinatio ad aliquem pertineat ex consuetudine, priuilegio vel statuto vel alio iure, tunc ipse ad quem pertinet premissam examinationem faciat. Quam si

---

3 possit] *corr. from* debeat 4 sententias *om.*V 6 postridie] tridie MV 8 exemptionibus] Deliberata die XXVII Septembris *add. in marg.* V 14 reuocentur] *At this point in* V, *the rubric for* c.18a *below* Quod ordinatores examinent ordinandos *has been erroneously inserted.* 19 aut *om.* V 20 eorum] eodem V examinentur] Conclusum est quod ordinator examinet ordinandos, etiam si fuerint de ordine mendicantium. *add. in marg.* V 22 sequitur] Deliberata die mercurii VIII Octobris. *add. in marg.* 24 Quod] Quoniam M 26 quedam ordinatores] quedam ordinationes V 27 plurimi] plurimum M 31 pena] *Blank space of approx. one line follows in* V, *but not* M

omiserit, ordinator autem cui predicti per alium examinati fuerint presentati, si dubitet de ipsorum ydoneitate, possit licite ipsos non admittere, nisi se offerant examinationi per ipsum ordinatorem vel eius commissarium modo premisso faciende.

[V, *in marg.*: Fuit conclusum, quod in religionibus licet possint recipi pueri tamen ad professionem non admittantur nisy puberes qui sint in XVIII annos constituti et maxime quo ad puellas. Nec etiam obligentur expressione tacita ante dictam etatem et quod nouitii non admittantur ad professionem nisy sciant conpetenter legere et cantare, nisi in religione sancti Johannis et similibus; nec admittantur ad sacros ordines, nisi sint professi et sint competenter in grammatica instructi. De promouendis ad ordines fuit dictum quod ordinator teneatur eos examinare, etsi examinatio pertineat ad alium, tamen si episcopus dubitet de idoneitate non teneatur admittere nisi se offert examinationi ordinandus.]

[c.19][XXXVI para. 2] Domino Aniciensi presidente propositum fuit die ultimo Septembris de religiosis habentibus litteras facultatis ad beneficia.

Conclusum fuit scrutatis votis quod reuocentur omnes littere facultatum ... non valeant. [See Common, c.23a]

[c.20][XXVII 2] Domino Aniciensi presidente prefato fuit repetita materia de non [377v] dispensando super ydoneitate die iouis III Octobris

Et super hoc fuit constitutio domini Gregorii XI que sequitur. [See Common, c.22]

[c.21][VII 1] Proposita fuit cedula constitutionis exhibite per dominum Florentinum super unionibus die lune VIII Octobris presidente domino: "Diuinum cultum volentes" [See M, c.44]

Scrutatis votis de futuris unionibus communiter omnibus placuit quod stetur textui, videlicet quod non fiant nisi causa rationabili et cognita et similiter quo ad ordinarios stetur textui. De preteritis varie fuerunt sententie sed tamen dictum fuit communiter quod reuocentur seu declarentur nulle facte causa rationabili [non] subsistente et super hoc eligantur quatuor videlicet unus pro qualibet natione qui auisent de causis rationabilibus. Item pro parte ali-

1 omiserit] *Blank space of approx. one-third line follows in V, but not M*   4 faciende] faciendi V   24 fuit] allegato *add.* M   que sequitur] *om.* M; Conclusum est quod innouetur et extendatur ad ordinarios. *add. in marg.*   28 domino] Feltrensi *add.* M *(Blank space of one-half line appears here in V)*   volentes] Deliberata die martis VIII Octobris *add. in marg.* V; *blank space of one and one-half lines follows*   30 videlicet ... fiant *add. above line* V   33 causa] cause MV non *om.* MV

quorum maxima facta fuit instantia quod uniones de vicariis omnino reuocarentur.

[c.22][XXIX 1] Quod tollantur iniqua statuta et praue consuetudines ecclesiarum.

Reuerendissimi patres et domini. In plerisque locis prouincie Coloniensis capitula cathedralium seu collegiatarum ecclesiarum iam diu fecerunt et facere conantur pessima et iniqua statuta, que personis in huiusmodi ecclesiis beneficiandis multum sunt contraria et rationi totaliter dissona, per que totalis honestas dictarum ecclesiarum et diuinus in eisdem cultus notorie diminuitur et deperit.

Primo videlicet antequam aliquem admittant ad possessionem alicuius prebende qualitercumque vacantis oportet ipsum admittendum soluere magnam pecunie quantitatem et vocantur denarii vini.

Secundo quod solutis huiusmodi denariis vini, que communiter ad magnam summam ascendunt, et similiter mediis fructibus camere apostolice, oportet huiusmodi soluentem et ad beneficium admissum alicubi ad tres alicubi ad quatuor alicubi ad VI alicubi ad octo vel plures annos expectare antequam de corpore huiusmodi beneficii vel prebende aliquid percipiat. Et sic quod sepissime accidit quod in huiusmodi ecclesiis personas beneficiatas mori in paupertate et debitis magnis propter prefatam pecunie solutionem id est post prebende denegationem, que valde cedunt in obprobrium clericorum et diuini cultus diminutionem, quia persone nihil recipientes non resident. Ex quo unde nunc non habent, sed potius euagantur per [378r] mundum, mala potius quam bona exercentes et adiscentes.

Dignentur igitur paternitates vestre ad huiusmodi mala aduertere et reformare predicta statuta siue constitutiones dictarum ecclesiarum sic et taliter quod de cetero huiusmodi mala non committantur vel ad minus quo ad huiusmodi pecunias et annos moderare ita quod tollerari possint ne diuinus cultus minuatur et personis beneficiatis detur occasio vagandi vel male faciendi.

[c.23][XXXI] De consiliis prouincialibus

Conclusum fuit quod consilia prouincialia fiant saltem de triennio in triennium . . . quinque diebus. [See Common, c.29]

---

12 videlicet] quod *add.* M   19 alicubi *om.* M   20 annos] alicui *add.* M
21 vel] seu M   aliquid] quecumque M   24 id est] et ex V   26 recipientes] percipientes M   28 adiscentes] adicentes M   32 annos] in nos V   33 tollerari] collocari M

VAT. LAT. 3884 = M

[fol. 1r] Cedula date nationibus pro mundatis et primo
[c.1][XII 1] (begins in middle of schedule in MS) . . . assistant,
non de una tantum mundi regione . . . non subsistat.
[c.2][XV 1] (Rubric) De reformatione curie. (Incipit) Littere apostolice tam de gratia quam de iustitia . . . [3v] . . . tantum. Sequitur
videre de auditore camere et eius notariis.
[c.3][XV 1] (Rubric) De doctoribus et magistris non creandis per
bullam apostolicam (Incipit) Eo multos produxit ambitio . . .
[4r] . . . reputentur.
[c.4][XXIII 2] (Rubric) Constitutio de impressionibus et precibus   l
exhibita per d. florentinum (Incipit) Statutum fe. re. Innocentii . . .
dignitates.
[c.5][V 1] (Rubric) De spoliis prelatorum decedentium non auferendis (Incipit) Dudum fuit prouide dispositum . . . [4v] . . .
duraturis.   l
[c.6][VII 2] (Rubric) De unionibus (Incipit) Vniones de benefitiis
cuiuscumque status . . . reuocate.
[c.7][XXXVI para.2] (Rubric) De literis facultatum concessis
mendicantibus et aliis religiosis ad bona secularia et extra suum
ordinem. (Incipit) Item quod reuocentur omnes littere faculta-   2
tum . . . ualent.
[c.8][XXVIII] (Rubric) De beneficiatis citra episcopos et abbates
non residentibus (Incipit) Quod omnes habentes bona requirentia
residentiam . . . [5r] . . . residentiam.
[c.9][IX 1] (Rubric) Contra symoniacos (Incipit) Conclusum ex-   2
pediens est quod per concilium concedatur contra . . . [5v] . . .
deputet.
[c.10][XXIX 2] (Rubric) De iniquis statutis (Incipit) De oneribus
seu solutionibus peccuniarum . . . potior. [6r]
[c.11][XXX] (Rubric) De tempore professionis fiende (Incipit)   3
Fuit conclusum quod in conclusionibus licet possint recepi . . .
constructi.
[c.12][XXXI] (Rubric) De conciliis prouincialibus et synodis episcoporum Rubrica (Incipit) Fuit conclusum quod concilia prouincialia saltem fiant . . . sequenti.   3
[c.13][VI 1] (Rubric) De exemptionibus (Incipit) Quod omnes
exemptiones quibuscumque religiosis domibus . . . [6v] . . . generalibus.
[c.14][XXXIII] (Rubric) De vicariis perpetuis et ecclesiis constituendis Rubrica (Incipit) Item quod in singulis ecclesiis appro-   4
priatis et unitis . . . concessis.

[c.15][XXXIX] (Rubric) Quod reuocetur auditor camere qui est
in auinion et potestas penitentiarii minorum extra curiam et questiones extraordinarii Rubrica (Incipit) Conclusum quod reuocetur
auditor camere qui est in Auinioni . . . questum.

[c.16][XL] (Rubric) Quod prelati habeant vicarios non uxoratos 5
sed bene litteratos (Incipit) Et fuit conclusum quod hoc est de
iure . . . facientibus.

[c.17][XLI] (Rubric) De iuramentis capitulorum preiudicantibus
ecclesiis Rubrica (Incipit) Propositum fuit de iuramentis que exigantur per capitula . . . [7r] . . . penitentia. 10

[c.18][XLII] (Rubric) Quod prelatus contra prelatum non possit
propria auctoritate indicare bellum. (Incipit) Item omnes conuenerunt quod erat iustum quando indicitur . . . uideatur.

[c.19][XXXIV] (Rubric) Quod pontifices ordines, consecrationes,
et alia pontificalia . . . (Incipit) Quia a longis temporibus humani 15
generis hoste procurante . . . [8r] . . . pensamus.

[c.20][XXXVII] (Rubric) Contra concubinarios (Incipit) Ad
arcendum concubinatus crimen . . . [8v] preferendam.

[c.21][XI 1] (Rubric) De vestibus clericorum (Incipit) Statutum
fe. re. Clementis pape IIII . . . [9r] puniantur. 20

[c.22][XI 2] (Rubric) Contra prelatos qui non incedunt habitu et
tonsura decenti (Incipit) Fuit conclusum quod prelati videlicet
patriarche . . . conueniente.

[c.23][XIII 5] (Rubric) De qualitate promouendorum ad bona de
collationibus bonorum Rubrica (Incipit) Ad episcopatum nullus 25
eligatur vel assumatur . . . [9v] . . . assumatur.

[c.24][XIII 9] (Rubric) De pessima consuetudine cathedralium et
regularium ecclesiarum quod in eis non admittantur nisi de nobilium aut militarium genere procreati (Incipit) Quia in ecclesiis
quibusdam presertim cathedralibus . . . [10r] . . . prouideri. 30

[c.25][VIII 1] (Rubric) De fructibus indebite perceptis per prelatos (Incipit) Aduersus dampnabilem abusum quo quidam ecclesiastici . . . prouideri.

[c.26][XXIX 3] (Rubric) De iniquis statutis ecclesiarum et monasteriorum (Incipit) Quoniam nonnulla ecclesiarum et monaste- 35
riorum capitula et conuentus . . . prouideri.

[c.27][XXXVIII] (Rubric) De exactionibus per principes seculares impositis clericis (Incipit) Cum prelati ecclesiastici principes
seculares et alie persone . . . adhiberi. [10v]

[c.28][XXXVIII] (Rubric) Ad idem contra liberatem ecclesiasti- 40
cam Rubrica (Incipit) Quia per diuersa loca sint et hactenus facta
sint statuta contra libertatem . . . perduntur.

[c.29][X 2] (Rubric) De dispensatione ad incompatibilia (Incipit)

Intentio quod ex nunc reuocentur omnes concessiones facte episcopis . . . religionis.

[c.30][X 3] (Rubric) De dispensatione ad incompatibilia cum secularibus de parrochialibus ecclesiis et dignitatibus etc. curatis (Incipit) Quod papa non dispenset nisi ex causa rationabili expressa   5
specifice . . . [11r] . . . in uno benefitio.

[c.31][X 4] (Rubric) De preteritis dispensationibus Rubrica (Incipit) Reuocentur ille que non sint sortite effectum in totum . . .
permutare.

[c.32][X 6] (Rubric) De dispensatione de non residendo (Incipit)   10
Quilibet summus pontifex in principio sue assumptionis pro-
ponat . . . [11v] . . . per concilium efferetur papa.

[c.33][X 8] (Rubric) De dipsensatione ad ordines (Incipit) Quod
prelati seruent capitulum Cum ex eo . . . ad annum tantum.

[c.34][X 9] (Rubric) De dispensatione super defectu etatis (In-   15
cipit) Non dispenset papa nisi in tribus annis . . . [12r] . . . de etate.

[c.35][XXIV] (No rubric)(Incipit) Non imponat papa silentium
litigantibus nec extinguat lites . . . et cognita.

[c.36][XXII 1] (Rubric) De decimis non imponendis per papam
propositum die veneris XX Septembris (Incipit) Conclusum est   20
quod papa non imponat decimas clero toti . . . et florentinum.

[c.37][XXV 2] (Rubric) De infidelibus conuersis ad fidem recipiendis ad baptisma propositum die martis XXIIII Septembris
(Incipit) Domimus Bartholomeus presidents proposuit de iudeis et
aliis infidelibus . . . auferatur. [12v]   25

[c.38][XXI 1] (Rubric) De indulgentiis et questibus aliis ac abusibus eorum tollendis Rubrica propositum die XXV Septembris
(Incipit) Dominus bartholomeus presidens proposuit de indulgentiis et questibus . . . recitetur.

[c.39][XXI 2] (No rubric) Ad succedendas ambitiones mortalium   30
et ne thesaurus ecclesie . . . [13r] quam laici.

[c.40][XXXV 2] (Rubric) Quod ordinatores examinent ordinandos (Incipit) Item quod omnes et singuli cuiuscumque religionis
aut conditionis . . . examinentur.

[c.41][XXXV 3] (Rubric) Et super primisso capitulo de ordinan-   35
dis fuit exibita constitutio thenorum que sequitur (Incipit)
Quoniam diligenter examinandi sint qui ad ordines promoueri
postulant . . . [13v] . . . faciende.

[c.42][XXXVI para. 1] (Rubric) Domino Aniciensi presidente
propositum fuit die ultima Septembris de religiosis habentibus   40
litteras facultatum ad beneficia. (Incipit) Conclusum fuit scrutatis
vocis quod reuocentur omnes littere facultatum . . . ualeant.

[c.43][XXVII 2] Domino Aniciensi presidente prefato fuit repetita materia de non dispensando super idoneitate die iouis tertia Octobris. Et super hoc fuit allegato constitutio d. Gregorii XI.

[c.44][VII 1] (Rubric) Proposita fuit constitutionis cedula exhibite per dominum Florentinum super unionibus die lune VII Octobris presidente domino Feltrensi. De unionibus et incorporationibus. 5

Diuinum cultum volentes ut est conueniens non diminui sed augeri decernimus ut si que uniones beneficiorum quorumcunque siue ecclesiarum cathedralium vel regularium [14r] per summum pontificem faciende fuerint, ad eas procedatur causa cognita et vocatis quorum interest, et confitiatur exinde scriptura publica vel 10
bulla apostolica in qua inseratur causa rationabilis ipsius unionis faciende, et hiis non obseruatis ipso iure nullum sit quicquid super hoc gestum fuerit. Et quoniam temporibus creationis precipue tempore huius pestiferi scysmatis plurime facte sunt, premissis non seruatis, in graue dampnum et detrimentum ecclesiarum vel bono- 15
rum unitorum et in grauamen et scandalum fundatorum et ordinariorum quibus suberant, easdem a tempore scysmatis supradicti omnes et singulas quecunque per eos qui in suis obedientiis habiti sunt et reputati pro summis pontificibus facte sunt, premissis non seruatis, tamquam irrationabiles et per quas cultus diuinus dimi- 20
nuatur, et maxime si nondum sortite sunt effectum, cassamus et irritamus ac reuocamus, non intendentes per hoc preiudicare unionibus que reperiuntur facte ad instantiam regum et principum pro ampliandis suis propriis capellis, vel etiam si que facte sunt ad fundandas vel erigendas cathedrales ecclesias vel aliqua collegia vel 25
clericorum vel studiorum in sacra pagina vel in iure canonico vel ciuili data rationabili compensationi his quorum intererat. Hortamur tamen eosdem reges et principes ut in ipsis ecclesiis et beneficiis unitis non permittant cultum diuinum deserui vel alia rationabilia opera ibi fieri consueta omitti. 30

[c.45][XXIX 1](Rubric) Quod tollantur iniqua statuta et praue consuetudines ecclesiarum (Incipit) Reuerendissimi patres et domini. In plerisque locis prouincie Coloniensis capitula cathedralium ... [14v] ... faciendi.

---

4 VII] VIII MV   5 incorporationibus] corporationibus MV   7 que] qui
MV   13 creationis] recentioribus (?)   15–16 bonorum] beneficiorum
(?)   18 qui] que MV   21 si nondum] sinodum MV

SECOND REFORM COMMITTEE

S = Stuttgart, Landesbibliothek, Cod. iur. Fol. 130, fol. 85r–90r
(= S², cc.1–14)
D = Vienna, Österreichische Nationalbibliothek, lat. 5113, fol.
1r–4v (= D², cc. 1–10)
W = Vienna, Österreichische Nationalbibliothek, lat. 5094, fol.
1r–11v, 46r–v, and 156r (= W², cc. 1–25)

[c.1][I 4] Auisamentum de futuris conciliis celebrandis
   Quamuis ex sacrorum generalium conciliorum celebrationibus,
statutis et ordinationibus retroactis temporibus fides catholica
plurimum roborata, multe hereses extirpate, scismata sedata et
dubia fuerunt declarata, sanctaque mater ecclesia laudabilibus   5
fuerit moribus adornata; quia tamen iam multis annis non fuit
conciliorum huiusmodi celebratio frequentata, errores, scismata et
scandala inualuisse non modica heu nostra etas miserabilis experitur. Unde postquam sancto efflante spiritu tandem hic aliquamdiu
fuimus, et sumus congregati in vinculo caritatis volentes futura   10
quantum in nobis erit tempora sub sacrorum generalium conciliorum frequentatione pro euitandis sedandisque si, quod absit,
orta fuerint scismatibus, et aliis ecclesie opportunitatibus in fide et
bonis moribus regulare; hoc decreto perpetuo sancimus, decernimus atque ordinamus, ut amodo generalia concilia celebrentur ita   15
quod primum a fine huius concilii in quinquennium immediate
sequens, secundum vero a fine illius sequentis concilii in septennium, et deinceps de decennio in decennium perpetuo celebrentur,
in locis que summus pontifex per mensem ante finem cuiuslibet
concilii approbante et consentiente concilio vel in eius defectum   20
ipsum concilium deputare et assignare teneatur, ut sic per quamdam continuationem semper aut concilium vigeat aut per termini
pendentiam expectetur. Quem terminum liceat summo pontifici de
fratrum suorum sancte Romani ecclesie Cardinalium consilio ob
emergentes forte casus abbreuiare, sed nullatenus liceat eidem   25

---

1 Auisam . . . . cele.] Ut generalium conciliorum celebratio frequentetur W; *W, in
marg.:* "Prima"   2 celebrationibus] celebratione W   9 efflante] afflante
W   12 si *struck out* S   14 hoc] Actum *add. in marg.* W (*in middle of paragraph
which begins here*)   16 quinquennium] quinquagenium (!) S   17 illius] immediate *add.* W   23–24 liceat . . . consilio] *struck out* W

summo pontifici, etiam de fratrum predictorum consilio, prorogare.

Locum autem pro futuro concilio celebrando deputatum absque euidenti necessitate non mutet. Sed si forte casus aliquis occurrerit quo necessarium videretur ipsum locum mutari puta obsidionis, guerre, pestis, aut similis, tunc liceat summo pontifici de predicto- rum fratrum aut duarum partium ipsorum consensu atque subscrip- tione alium locum prius deputato loco viciniorem et aptum, sub eadem tamen natione, surrogare, nisi idem impedimentum per totam illam nationem vigeret; tunc ad aliquem alium viciniorem alterius nationis locum aptum huiusmodi concilium poterit con- uocari. Ad quem prelati et alii qui ad concilium solent conuocare accedere teneantur ac si a principio locus ille fuisset deputatus. Quam tamen loci mutationem vel termini abbreuiationem per annum ante prefixum terminum teneatur dictus supremus pontifex legitime et sollempniter publicare et intimare, ut ad dictum con- cilium celebrandum possint predicti statuto termino conuenire.

[c.2][II] Prouisio aduersus futura scismata [W = W², c.13; W³ = W², c.15; see analysis of Vienna lat. 5094, pp. 399–400 below]

Si vero, quod absit, in futurum scisma oriri [85v] contingeret, ita quod duo [85v] vel plures pro summis pontificibus se gererent, a die quo ipsi duo vel plures insignia pontificatus publice assump- serint et ministrare ceperint intelligatur ipso iure terminus concilii tunc forte ultra annum pendens ad annum proximum abbreuiatus; ad quod omnes prelati et ceteri qui ad concilium ire tenentur sub penis iuris et aliis per concilium imponendis absque alia conuoca- tione conueniant necnon imperator ceterique reges et principes vel personaliter aut per sollempnes nuncios tamquam ad commune incendium extinguendum per viscera misericordie Iesu Christi ex

1 prorogare] *altered to* prorogetur W   4 ipsum] *in marg.* W   5 guerre] qua rarum (!) S   6 atque] *corr. from* absque W   8 idem] *struck out*; id vel similem *add. above line* W   10–11 conuocari] conuocare DS   13 quam] quia S   13–14 per . . . terminum] *appears in marg. in* W; *two different places marked for insertion, either here and after word* sollempniter.   14 supremus] summus W   15 dictum] ipsum W   16 conuenire] Placuit nationi. *add. in marg.* S   17 scismata] precauenda *add.* D   19 Si vero] Prima Octobris con- cordatum est etiam per Hispanos *add. in marg.* W³   quod . . . futurum] quod absit nouum sit umquam *in original text of* W, *but these words struck out and* quod absit in futurum *add. above line.*   oriri] orire S   20 pontificibus] ex quacumque causa *add.in text, but struck out* W; pretextu electionis facte ab hiis eidem cuius partem ius pertinet eligendum *add in marg. and struck out* W   21–22 assumpserint] assumentes W; assumpserunt D   22 et ministrare] seu administrare DWW³   23 abbreuiatus] breuiatus DWW³   25–26 conuocacione] voca- tione DWW³ (*corr. from* conuocacione WW³)   26 et *om.* S   27 aut] vel D; *corr. from* vel WW³   sollempnes] suos *add.* D   28 misericordie] domini nos- tri *add. in marg. but struck out* W³

nunc exhortati concurrant. Et quilibet ipsorum pro Romano pontifice se gerentium infra mensem a die qua scientiam habere potuit alium vel alios assumpsisse papatus insignia vel in papatu administrasse, teneatur sub interminatione maledictionis eterne et amissione iuris, si quod forte sibi quesitum esset in papatu, quam ipso facto incurrat et ultra hoc ad quaslibet dignitates actiue et passiue sit inhabilis, concilium ipsum ad terminum anni predictum loco prius deputato celebrandum indicere, publicare [et] per suas litteras competitori vel competitoribus ipsum vel ipsos prouocando ad causam et ceteris prelatis et principibus quantum in eo fuerit intimare; necnon termino prefixo sub penis prefixis ad locum concilii personaliter se transferre nec inde discedere donec per concilium causa scismatis plenarie sit finita; hoc adiuncto quod nullus ipsorum contendentium de papatu in ipso concilio ut papa presideat, quinimmo ut tanto liberius et citius ecclesia unico et indubitato pastore gaudeat, sint ipsi omnes de papatu contendentes, postquam dictum concilium inceptum fuerit, auctoritate huius sacre sinodi ipso iure ab omni administratione suspensi, nec eis aut eorum alteri, donec causa ipsa per concilium terminata fuerit, quomodolibet a quoquam sub pena fautorie scismatis obediatur.

Quod si forte pretenderetur electionem Romani pontificis per metum qui caderet in constantem seu impressionem fieri contingat, ipsam nullius decernimus et statuimus efficacie vel momenti; nec posse per consequentem consensum, etiam metu predicto cessante, ratificari vel approbari.

Non tamen liceat cardinalibus ad aliam electionem procedere quantumcumque impressio notoria existat, nisi ille sic electus forte renunciet vel decedat donec per generale concilium de electione illa fuerit iudicatum, et si procedant nulla sit electio ipso iure. Sintque sic secundo eligentes et electus si se papatu ingesserit, omni dignitate, honore et statu, etiam cardinalatus et pontificali ipso iure priuati et inhabiles decetero ad easdem et etiam ad papalem. Nec

1 exhortati] exorati WW³; *corr. from* exortati S   quilibet] quemlibet W   2 a die] *add. above line* W³   4 et *om.* D   5 si] sui D   forte] forsan D 8 indicere] *corr. from* indicetur W; et *add.* DWW³ et *om.* S   9 prouocando] et *add. in text, but struck out* W   10 et (*second*)] ac DWW³   11 prefixis] predictis DWW³   13 nullus] *In* W, *text ends here (fol. 4v)*   19 alteri] altero W³   20 obediatur] etc. *add.* D; *in* D, *the remaining text of this schedule appears as a separate schedule, with the rubric* De remedio electionis pape facte [*corr. from* facta] per metum.   21 pretenderetur] S *only*   22 impressionem] de cetero *add. in marg.* W³   23 nullius] et statuimus et *add. in marg.* W³ (statuimus *underscored*)   et statuimus *om.* DW³   24 consequentem] sequentem DW³   27 quantumcumque . . . existat *om.* DW³   30 papatu] papatui W³   32 et (*sec*) *om.* D; *corr. from* ac W³

aliquis eidem secundo electo ut pape sub pena fautorie scismatis
obediat quoquomodo, et eo casu quo omnes cardinales sic
elegerint, [86r] concilium de electione pape prouideat illa vice.

Sed liceat, immo et teneatur, totum collegium aut saltem maior
pars eorum quam cito sine periculo personarum poterunt, etiam si   5
periculum omnium bonorum immineat, se transferre ad locum
tutum et metum predictum allegare coram notariis publicis et
notabilibus personis ac multitudini populi in loco insigni.

[*Marginal glosses on* insigni, S,W³:
S: Attende hic videtur auisamentum nationis Germanice melius, et   10
si omnibus nationibus placebit textus, natio Germanica consentit.
S,W3: Ita tamen quod allegantes metum huiusmodi habeant in
ipsius metus allegatione exprimere et exponere speciem et qualitatem dicti metus et iurare sollempniter quod metus taliter allega-
tus est verus et quod credant ipsum posse probare et quod propter   15
malitiam et calumpniam huiusmodi metum non proponant.]

Nec ultra proximum futurum concilium ullo modo possint differre.

Tenentur insuper postquam se transtulerint et metum allegauerint modo predicto prouocare sic electum ad concilium. Quod
concilium, si ultra annum pendeat a die prouocationis huiusmodi,   20
intelligatur ad annum ut supra ipso iure terminus abbreuiatus. Et
nichilominus teneatur electus ipse sub penis predictis et cardinales
prouocantes sub pena amissionis cardinalatus et omnium beneficiorum suorum, quam ipso facto incurrant infra mensem a die
prouocationis, concilium ipsum ut supradicitur indicere, publicare 25
et quam citius poterunt intimare et ad locum concilii tempore
conuenienti personaliter se transferre et usque ad finem cause
expectare. Teneantur quoque prelati et ceteri ut supra ad conuocationem cardinalium tantum, si forte sic electus conuocare cessaret,
accedere. Qui sic electus in ipso concilio non presideat. Quinimmo 30

2–3 quo omnes . . . eligerint] S *only*   4 et] *add. above line* W³   totum col-
legium] *struck out in* W³ *and replaced in marg. with* electores omnes   aut] certe *added
and struck out* S   5 eorum] ipsorum DW³   6 immineat] *altered to* immineret
W³   12 metum] *corr. from* metus W³   13 et exponere *om.* W³   15 credant]
credunt W³; se *add. above line* W³   propter] per W³   16 et] vel W   propo-
nant] Hoc etiam placet Anglicis et Hyspaniis. *add.* S   17 futurum *om.* D   dif-
ferre] transferre *corr. in marg. to* differri allegatio dicti metus W³   18 Tenentur]
Teneantur D   19 prouocare . . . electum] pro vocatione sic electioni D   21
abbreuiatus] breuiatus DW³   22 Cardinales] W³: cardinales *struck out, replaced
in marg. with* cardinales electores *which is in turn struck out, then* cardinales *written in
again above line.*   23 cardinalatus] W³, *in marg.:* actum ut po. dignitates   25
ipsum *om.* D. 26 et (*second*)]*struck out* W³; ac cardinales ipsi ceterique electores *add. in
marg.*W³   29 cardinalium] electorum *add. above line* W³

sit a termino initiandi concilii ipso iure ab omni administratione papatus suspensus nec sibi a quoquam sub pena fautorie scismatis quomodolibet obediatur.

Quod si infra annum ante diem indicti concilii contingant supradicti casus, videlicet quod plures se gerant pro papa vel quod unus per metum seu impressionem eligatur, censeantur ipso iure tam gerentes se pro papa quam electus per metum seu impressionem et cardinales ad dictum concilium prouocati, teneanturque in ipso concilio comparere personaliter, causam exponere et iudicium concilii expectare.

Sed si dictis casibus occurrentibus contingat forte aliquis casus quo necessarium sit locum concilii mutare, ut obsidionis vel guerre aut pestis aut similis, teneantur nichilominus tam omnes supradicti quam omnes prelati ceterique qui ad concilium ire tenentur ad locum proximiorem ut premittitur qui sit habilis ad concilium conuenire. Possitque maior pars prelatorum qui infra mensem ad locum certum declinauerint illum sibi et aliis pro loco concilii deputare, ad quem ceteri conuenire teneantur ac si a principio fuisset deputatus.

Et si forsan generali vigente et durante concilio electio per metum seu per impressionem pretenderetur fuisse facta, teneantur huiusmodi metum aut impressionem pretendentes, dum tamen metus et impressio notorie et euidenter cessauerint, ipsum metum seu impressionem antequam ipsum concilium dissoluatur publice et canonice allegare [86v] et deducere. Et si ipsum metum seu impressionem in ipso concilio allegare non curauerint, ipsum seu ipsam finito predicto concilio allegandi sit audientia penitus interdicta. Tunc autem metus seu impressio notorie et euidenter cessasse intelligantur quando ipsa cessasse per sacrum concilium fuerit declarata. Si vero metus seu impressio huiusmodi non cessauerint teneantur ipsam pretendentes illo finito concilio prosequi ut superius continetur.

Concilium autem, ut prefertur, conuocatum et congregatum de

---

1 initiandi] nunciandi D   3 obediatur] Placet nationi *add. in marg.* S 4 indicti] in dicti S   6 censeantur] sentiantur S   11 Sed] *Rubric in marg*, D: [De] mutatione concilii, etc.   13 tam] hic *add. and struck out* S   18–19 ad quem . . . deputatus] *add. in marg.* D   21 seu] aut DW³; (*corr. from* ad D)   per *om.* DW³   21–22 teneantur . . . pretendentes *om.* W³   23 metus] *corr. from* mens W³   et (*first*)] seu W³   24 seu] aut W³   27 finito] dicto DW³ (*in D, add. above line*)   predicto] dicto DW³   29 intelligantur] intelligatur D; intelligitur W   30 declarata] declaratum DW³   31 ipsam] ipsi D   20–32 Et si forsan . . . continetur *struck out* W³   33 et] aut S

huiusmodi scismatis causa cognoscens et in contumatiam electorum seu gerentium se pro papa seu cardinalibus, si forte venire
neglexerint, litem dirimat causamque diffiniat ac culpabiles in scismate procurando seu nutriendo vel administrando aut obediendo
vel administrantibus fauendo seu contra interdictum superius   5
eligendo vel calumpniosos in allegando metum etiam ultra predictas penas, cuiuscumque gradus, status seu preeminentie existant,
ecclesiastice vel mundane sic puniat, ut vindicte rigor ceteris transeat in exemplum.

Ut autem metus seu impressionis molestia in electione pape eo   10
formidolosius euitetur, quo toti Christianitati lamentabilius eorum
incussio seu factio perpetratur ultra predicta specialiter duximus
statuendum quod si quis huiusmodi metum vel impressionem aut
violentiam electoribus ipsis vel alicui eorum in electione pape in-
tulerit seu fecerit aut fieri procurauerit vel factum ratum habuerit   15
aut in hoc consilium dederit vel fauorem facientemue scienter
receptauerit vel defensauerit aut negligentes in executione penarum
inferius memoratarum extiterit, cuiuscumque status, gradus vel
preeminentie fuerit, etiam si imperiali, regali, pontificali aut alia
quauis ecclesiastica aut seculari prefulgeret dignitate, illas penas   20
ipso facto incurrat que in constitutione felicis recordationis Bonifatii pape VIII que incipit "Felicis"[1] continentur illisque effectualiter
puniantur. Ciuitas vero, etiam si, quod absit, urbs Romana fuerit,
vel alia queuis uniuersitas que talia facienti consilium vel auxilium
dederit vel fauorem vel infra mensem saltem taliter delinquentem,   25
prout tanti facinorum enormitas exegerit et facultas ei affuerit, non
duxerit puniendum, eo ipso subiaceat ecclesiastico interdicto, et
nichilominus preter dictam urbem pontificali ut supra sit eo ipso
dignitate priuata non obstantibus priuilegiis quibuscumque.

---

1 VI 5.9.5

---

2 seu *struck out*; vel *add. above line* W³   cardinalibus] cardinalium W³   4 vel]
in add. W³   aut] *in add. and struck out* S   7 existant] etiam cardinalatus *add.
in marg. and struck out* W³   10 Ut] *Rubric in marg.* D: De pena inferunt.
11 euitetur] seuitetur S   14 vel] aut W³   16 vel *om.* S   17 aut] *corr.
from* vel W³   negligentes] negligens W³   19 aut] vel W³   20 aut] vel
DW³   23 etiam] *add. in marg.* W³   si quod] sicut S   24 vel (*first*)] et
D   vel (*second*)] aut DW³   25 saltem] talem S; *corr. from* talem W³   26
facinorum] facinoris W³   28 ut] *struck out; et add. above line* W³   eo ipso *in
marg.* W³

Volumus insuper quod in fine cuiusuis concilii generalis hoc
decretum sollempniter publicetur necnon quandocumque et ubicumque Romani pontificis electio imminebit facienda ante ingressum conclauis legatur et intimetur. [87r]

[c.3][III 3] Professio pape

Quanto Romanus pontifex eminentiori inter mortales fungitur
potestate, tanto clarioribus ipsum decet fidei vinculis et sacramentorum ecclesiasticorum obseruandis ritibus alligari. Eapropter ut in futuris Romanis pontificibus in sue creationis primordiis
singulari splendore luceat plena fides, statuimus et ordinamus quod   1
deinceps quilibet in Romanum pontificem eligendus, antequam sua
electio publicetur, coram suis electoribus publice confessionem et
professionem faciat infrascriptas.

In nomine sancte et indiuidue trinitatis, patris et filii et spiritus
sancti, Amen. Anno a natiuitate domini M° CCCC XVII° indic-   1
tione decima etc. Ego N. electus in papam omnipotenti deo cuius
ecclesiam suo presidio regendam suscipio et beato Petro beatorum
apostolorum principi corde et ore profiteor et confiteor, quamdiu in
hac fragili vita constitutus fuero, me firmiter credere et tenere fidem
catholicam secundum traditiones apostolorum, generalium con-   2
ciliorum et aliorum sanctorum patrum, maxime autem sacrorum
octo conciliorum uniuersalium, videlicet primi Niceni, secundi
Constaninopolitani, tertii Ephesini, quarti Calcedonensis, quinti
et sexti item Constantinopolitani, et septimi item Niceni, octaui
quoque Constantinopolitani, necnon Lateranensis, Lugdunensis et   2
Vienensis generalium etiam conciliorum, et illam fidem usque ad
unum apicem immutilatam seruare et usque ad animam et sanguinem confirmare, defensare et predicare, ritumque taliter
sacramentorum catholice ecclesie canonice traditum omnimode
prosequi et obseruare. Hanc autem confessionem et professionem   3
meam per notariis scriniarium sancte Romane ecclesie me iubente
scriptam propria manu subscripsi et tibi, omnipotens deus, pura
mente et deuota conscientia super altare tali etc. sinceriter offero in
presentia talium etc. testium actuum in tali loco etc.

---

1 cuiusuis] cuiuslibet DW³; *corr. from* cuiuslibet S   4 et] publicetur D; publice
add. in marg. W³   intimetur] etc. *add.* D   5 pape] Concordatum etiam per
dominos Hispanos. *add. in marg.* W   16 decima *om.* W   17 beatorum *om.*
DW   19 firmiter *om.* D; *add. in marg.* W   28 confirmare] et *add. and struck
out* W   taliter] pariter DW   29 catholice] *corr. from* canonice W   omni-
mode] *corr. from* commode W   31 meam *om.* D   notariis] notarium
DW; et *add. and struck out* W   scriniarium] scriniarum D   32 tibi] ibi S
33 altare tali] altari D; tali altari W   34 etc. *om.* W; Placet nationi *add. in marg.*
S   testium . . . etc.] actum, etc. DW

[c.4][XIX 2] Quod papa non solum de heresi sed etiam de alio
crimine scandalizanti uniuersalem ecclesiam potest deponi

Ne sancta mater ecclesia summi pontificis, si quod absit,
laberetur, detestanda cogatur vitia sub dissimulatione lamentabili
pertransire, nonullorum antique dubietatis articulum declarantes,   5
hoc decreto perpetuo diffinimus, quod summus pontifex non solum
de heresi, sed etiam de simonia notoria, tam circa sacramenta
quam circa beneficia ecclesiastica, et quolibet alio notorio crimine
graui ecclesiam dei uniuersalem notorie scandalizante, de quo
canonice monitus et incorrigibilis extiterit, per generale concilium   10
puniri valeat ac deponi etiam de papatu. [87v]

[c.5][XIII 7] De promouendis ad ecclesias cathedrales et abba-
tiales maiores

Licet diuina eloquia sanctorumque patrum canones de prelatorum superiorum et inferiorum aliorumque sacris ecclesiasticis   15
ministeriis deputatorum moribus, conuersatione, vita atque scientia multa salubria statuerint obseruanda, labentis tamen seculi
procliua fragilitas a sacris regulis plurimum deuiauit. Cernimus
enim quosdam, nedum insufficientis sed quandoque valde modice,
scientie, vel nullius, episcopales cathedras proch dolor ascendisse,   20
necnon in illis et minoribus dignitatibus, beneficiis et officiis ecclesiasticis exhortationem sane doctrine et populorum edificationem
nostris temporibus lamentabiliter defecisse, intantum ut pauci
hodie reperiantur qui ecclesiasticum ministerium perficiant in
efficacia verbi dei; ex quo nimirum clerus vilipenditur, neruus   25
ecclesiastice discipline dissoluitur, virtutum regula infringitur,
vitiorum correctio negligitur et innumera crescunt pericula animarum.

Volentes itaque detestabili huic morbo possibili occurrere cum
medela ultra priores sanctiones specialibus duximus remediis iuxta   30
dignitatum, beneficiorum et officiorum gradus expressius prouidendum, hoc sinodali statuto perpetuo decernentes quod, presupposita
morum et vite honestate, nullus deinceps ad episcopalem vel supra
aut abbatialem que caput alicuius ordinis fuerit dignitatem assu-

---

1–2 Quod . . . deponi] Quod papa accusari et deponi potest super alio crimine
quam heresi W   5 pertransire] pertransiri S   antique] *add. in marg.*
W   11 papatu] Placet nationi. *add. in marg.* S   12–13 De . . . maiores]
Quod nullus eligatur in episcopum vel abbatem nisi sit doctor sacre theologie vel
iuris canonici vel ciuilis D; Quales de cetero assumi debeant ad cathedrales et alias
dignitates W   13 maiores] Non placet nationi, sed stat cum c. Cum in cunctis
[X 1.6.7] et quod fiat dicti capituli executio. *add. in marg.* S   17 statuerint]
statuerunt D   21 et (*first*)] in *add.* DW   27–28 animarum]*See below, p. 390,*
lines 20–21.   31 dignitatum] dignitatem D   et] ac W   33 vite] vita D;
corr. from vita S   34 dignitatem] dignitatum S

matur seu promoueatur, nisi in theologia seu iure canonico aut
ciuili doctor vel licentiatus debite examinis cum rigore.

Ad maiores autem post pontificalem aliasue curatas in ecclesiis
cathedralibus dignitates soli in dictis facultatibus doctores aut
licentiati; ad alias vero in cathedralibus et principales in ecclesiis
collegiatis dignitates eiusdem gradus vel saltem baccalarii dictarum facultatum aut in medicina vel notabiles in artibus magistri
decetero admittantur.

Ubi vero dignitatibus predictis cura non imminet animarum, viri
morigerati, presertim nobiles, valeant admitti, saltem taliter litterati quod verba latina intelligere et congrue nouerint explicare.
Preterea in qualibet ecclesia cathedrali adminus sexta pars prebendarum, si prius in eadem tales persone non fuerint, doctoribus aut
licentiatis in theologia aut altero iurium assignetur. Omnia tamen
predicta intelligantur si infra mensem postquam dignitates aut
prebende premisse vacauerint vel aliqua earum, taliter, ut premittitur, graduati vel graduatus reperti seu repertus fuerit seu fuerint
qui voluerint et canonice potuerint acceptare, saluis semper statutis
rationabilibus fundationis ecclesiarum et iuribus patronatus.

[D, *in text*; W, *in marg.*: Nota quod aliqui volebant inseri postillas
infrascriptas sed maior pars residebat in textu. Postille: Quod si
forsan ecclesie notorie utilitas et sanguinis preclara generositas
suaserint, possint regum, ducum, magnorum marchionum, aut
prepotentum comitum ad episcopales aut supra aut infra, aliique
baronum filii seu militares ex utroque parente ad alias predictas
dignitates etiam sine gradibus supradictis dum tamen alias com-
petentis litterature fuerint promoueri.]

[S, *in marg.*: Lectum. Non placet textus sed stant in c. Cum in
cunctis et aliis antiquis iuribus et quod ceteris paribus doctor
preferatur. Item quod in ecclesiis cathedralibus sexta pars prebendarum stet pro doctoribus ac licentiatis et baccalaureatis formatis
et hoc si infra mensem etc.]

---

2 licentiatus] extiterit *add.* DW   debite] debiti DW   rigore] vel saltem in
scientia equipollens. Additio. *add.* D²; vel saltem in scientia equipollens *add. in
marg.* W   3 pontificalem] *altered to* pontificales W   7 medicina] magistri
add. above line and struck out W   8 admittantur] *see below lines 21–27*   14 aut]
vel D²W   15 infra mensem *underscored* S   16–17 premittitur *add. in marg.*
W; *corr. from* promittitur D²   17 seu fuerint] *om.* D; vel fuerint *add. in
marg.* W   19 fundationis] fundationibus S   et] laicorum *add.* DW
20 aliqui] domini *add.* W   inseri] addere W   20–21 Nota . . . textu] *Appears
in W as gloss on* animarum; *see above, p. 389 line 27–28*   22 forsan] forsitan
W   24 aut (*first*)] vel D   25 ex utroque parente *in marg.* W   21–27 Postille . . . promoueri] *Appears in W as a gloss on* admittantur; *see above, line 8*

[c.6][IV 2] De translationibus prelatorum

Cum ex prelatorum translationibus ecclesie de quibus trans-
feruntur plerumque grauibus in spiritualibus et temporalibus subiaceant dispendiis [88r] et iacturis, prelati quoque nonnumquam
iura et libertates ecclesiarum suarum translationis formidine non   5
adeo solerter ut alias prosequantur, ne ad importunitatem quorundam que sua et non que Iesu Christi sunt querentium, Romanus
pontifex forsan ut homo facti nescius in huiusmodi circumueniatur
aut alias leuiter inclinetur, presentibus statuimus, ordinamus et
declaramus inuitorum patriarcharum, archiepiscoporum et episco-   10
porum translationes ac etiam exemptorum abbatum, quorum
monasteria immediate sedi apostolice sunt subiecta, saluo iure
constitutionum ordinum suorum, absque magna, rationabili,
notoria et euidenti causa que vocata parte de consilio sancte
Romane ecclesie cardinalium vel maioris partis et subscriptione   15
eorundem cognita fuerit et decisa de cetero fieri non debere.

[W, in marg.: Inferiores vero, ut abbates aliique perpetue beneficiati, absque iusta et rationabili causa cognita p. Addicientes:
Et de consilio sancte Romane ecclesie cardinalium vel maioris
partis et cum subscriptione eorundem de cetero fieri non debere;   20
inferiores vero, ut abbates aliique perpetuo beneficiati, inuiti absque iusta et rationabili causa cognita mutari, ammoueri seu priuari
non debeant. Addicientes quod in mutationibus abbatum subscriptio cardinalium interueniat sicut in episcopis est premissum, saluis
constitutionibus, consuetudinibus et priuilegiis ecclesiarum,   25
monasteriorum et ordinum quorumcumque.]

[c.7][XVIII 1] Quod papa non alienet bona ecclesie Romane et
recuperet deperdita iuxta suum posse.

Ut Romanus pontifex, nedum circa spiritualia attenta consideratione versetur, sed etiam temporalia, sine quibus spiritualia diu   30
subsistere nequeant, prouida dispensatione studeat gubernare, hoc
perpetuo valituro decreto rationi fore consonum et moribus antiquis conueniens declaramus, quod quilibet Romanus pontifex ante

---

1 De . . . praelatorum] De prelatis inuitus non transferendis W; om. D   praela-
torum] II. Octobris, placuit Hyspanis add. in marg. W   4 dispendiis] stipendiis
(!) S   6 ut] aut S   7 sunt om. S   9 statuimus . . . et] om. in text DW
10 declaramus] struck out, statuimus et ordinamus add. in marg. W   10–11
patriarcharum . . . episc.] episcoporum et superiorum W (patriarcharum,
archiepiscoporum struck out, et superiorum add. above line.) In minoribus beneficiatis fiat idem. add. in marg. W   11–13 ac etiam . . . suorum] struck out
in W   13 magna] et add. above line W   14 notoria et euidenti struck
out W   15 et subscriptione om. DW; et cum subscriptione add. in
marg. W   14–16 de consilio . . . eorundem struck out W   16 de cetero . . .
debere struck out W; S, in marg.: Placet nationi.   27–28 Quod . . . posse]
Iuramentum pape super non alienando W   29 circa om. D

sui intronisationem promissionem faciat, solempni interposito
iuramento, quod regna, dominia, prouincias, ciuitates, oppida,
castra, villas, territoria, possessiones, superioritates, iurisdictiones,
nobilitates, pensiones, census, decimas, redditus et alias res cetera-
que iura et quecumque bona immobilia Romane et aliarum ecclesiarum non alienabit, nec in feudum seu emphiteosim dabit, sed ea
omnia indiminuta quantum in eo fuerit conseruabit recuperabitque
deperdita iuxta posse.

[c.8][IX 3] Contra symoniacos

Contra labem simoniace pestis, qua decor ecclesie plurimum
denigratur, multa remedia per apostolicos patres et sacra concilia
hactenus excogitata fuerunt salubriterque prouisa, que tamen temporum excrescente malitia, ut experientia docet, optatum non
attulerunt effectum. Volentes igitur quantum possumus radicem
pestis huius penitus extirpare hoc decreto perpetuo statuimus,
quod quicumque ecclesiasticus, cuiuscumque status, gradus, ordinis aut preeminentie fuerit, etiam si archiepiscopali, episcopali,
patriarchatus vel cardinalatus prefulget dignitate, qui decetero circa beneficii ecclesiastici [88v] impetrationem, collationem,
prouisionem, presentationem seu dispositionem qualemcumque
etiam ordinum aut ecclesiasticorum sacramentorum pactis precedentibus simonie crimen in Romana curia vel extra per conuentionem aut pactionem siue dando, recipiendo, promittendo aut
remittendo, paciscendo siue mediando, commiserit, ipso facto omni
dignitate, officio ecclesiastico et omnibus beneficiis suis perpetuo sit
priuatus. Possuntque beneficia sua tamquam vacantia, declaratione tamen per prius legitime facta super commissione criminis
predicti, vocatis tamen vocandis, libere impetrari et conferri. Laici
vero qui in huiusmodi culpabiles fuerint excommunicationem ipso
facto incurrant. Ceterum uniuersis et singulis ordinariis districte
precipientes mandamus, quatenus cum omni solertia circa punitionem sic delinquentium taliter intendant, quod de negligentia
minime redargui valeant; quod si negligentes extiterint per suos
superiores prout facti qualitas exposcit sic puniantur quod ceteris
cedat in exemplum.

---

1 sui] suam DW   5–6 ecclesiarum] monasteriorum et piorum locorum *add. in
marg.* W   6 feudum] nouum *add.* DW   8 posse] Placet nationi. *add. in
marg.* S   17 fuerit] fuerint D   18 prefulget] prefulgeat D   19 beneficii]
beneficia (!) S   20 seu] siue D   21–22 etiam . . . precedentibus *om.* D
precedentibus] presidentibus S   23 pactionem] taxationem (!) S   25 per-
petuo] perpetue D   28 vocatis] vocantis D   30 facto] iure D   35 exem-
plum] Placet nationi, sed detur modus probandi. *add. in marg.* S

[c.9][XVIII 3] Reuocatio alienatorum tempore schismatis

Cum post obitum felicis recordationis Gregorii pape XI scisma pestiferum Romanam omnium ecclesiarum matrem ecclesiam iam fere XL annis tenuerit laceratam, illoque durante ceca quorundam cupiditas diuersis ingeniis et conatibus sub fauoris aut assistentie vel alterius necessitatis aut utilitatis velamine, fictis quandoque titulis seu extortis aut pretensis hincinde presidentium auctoritatibus taliter qualiter adhibitis, immo nonnumquam pro temeritate Romane et aliarum ecclesiarum bona sibi attraxerit occupanda; nos indempnitati omnium ecclesiarum contra huiusmodi quantum in nobis est consulere cupientes, omnes et singulas bonorum immobilium scilicet censuum, decimarum et iurisdictionum et aliorum iurium alienationes et usurpationes preter aut contra iuris formam in Romane aut alterius cuiuscumque ecclesie seu piorum locorum siue ordinum aut monasteriorum preiudicium a tempore scismatis inchoati usque ad presentem diem factas, etiam si pretensa alicuius pro Romano pontifice tunc se gerentis auctoritate apostolica fulciantur, tenore presentium annullamus, cassamus et penitus irritamus. Bonaque huiusmodi in ius et proprietatem ecclesiarum, monasteriorum et aliorum piorum locorum a quibus alienata seu usurpata fuerant reuocamus, etiam si motu proprio de plenitudine potestatis aut cum defectuum et sollempnitatum [89r] suppletione facti extitissent, priuilegiis non obstantibus quibuscumque.

[c.10][V 2] De spoliis et procurationibus causa visitationibus non recipiendis

Cum per papam facta reseruatio et exactio et perceptio procurationum ordinariis et aliis inferiorum prelatis debitarum ratione visitationis necnon et spoliorum decedentium prelatorum aliorum-

1 tempore scismatis] et usurpatorum Romane et aliarum ecclesiarum W   3 omnium] omnem (!) S   7 titulis] Ponitur fo. 16   contra add. in marg. W   aut] ac W   7–8 auctoritatibus] auctoribus (!) S   8 pro] propria W   12 scilicet] corr. from se S; om. W   12–13 censuum … iurium] in marg. W   14–15 seu … monasteriorum] om. W; monasteriorum, piorum locorum, seu ordinis add. in marg. W   15–16 a … diem add above line W (replaces dicto durante scismate which is in text but struck out)   21–23 etiam … extitissent] om. W; moto proprio aut cum defectuum suppletione extitisset add. in marg. W   25–26 De … recipiendis] De reseruatione spoliorum amplius non faciendis nec recipiendis W   26 recipiendis] XXVᵃ Septembris concordatum. Placuit etiam Hispanis II. Octobris. add. in marg. (two separate notes) W   27 Cum … reseruatio] corr. from Cum pape reseruatio W   et (first)] ac W

que clericorum grauia ecclesiis monasteriis et aliisque beneficiis
ecclesiasticisque personis detrimenta afferant, presenti declaramus
edicto rationi fore consentaneum et reipublice accomodum tales
per papam reseruationes, ac per collectores et alios auctoritate
apostolica deputatos seu deputandos, exactiones seu perceptiones
decetero nullo modo fieri aut attemptari; quinimmo procurationes
huiusmodi ac quorumcumque prelatorum, etiam cardinalium vel
ipsius pape familiarium officialium et aliorum quorumuis clericorum, in Curia Romana et extra ubicumque et quandocumque
decedentium spolia, seu bona eorum mortis tempore reperta, plene   1
et libere pertineant illis et per illos recipiantur quibus alias prefatis
reseruationibus, mandatis et exactionibus cessantibus competerent
aut pertinere deberent. Prelatis etiam inferioribus et aliis huiusmodi spoliorum exactiones preter et contra iuris communis formam
fieri interdicimus, constitutione felicis recordationis Bonifatii pape   1
VIII que incipit "Presenti"² super hoc edita in suo robore duratura.
[c.11][XII 2] De numero cardinalium et qualitate eorum
    Statuimus ut deinceps numerus dominorum cardinalium sancte
Romane ecclesie adeo sit moderatus et non excessiuus quod nec sit   2
grauis ecclesie nec superflua in numerositate vilescat. Qui de omnibus partibus Christianitatis proportionaliter quantum fieri poterit
assumantur, ut notitia causarum et negotiarum in ecclesia emer-
gentium facilius haberi possit, et equalitas regionum in honori-

---

2   VI 1.16.9

---

1 clericorum] quam collectores iurium camere apostolice et alii auctoritate
apostolica deputati aliquando facere solent longe *add. and struck out* W   1–2
grauia . . . afferant *add. in marg.* W   1 grauia] *corr. from* grauiora W   et] ac
W   2 afferant] *appears in* W *before* detrimenta, *written above the line. The following
passage is added and struck out in* W: afferant quam ipsi camere apostolice comoda
conferunt seu emolumenta, cumque statui ecclesiastico (?) congruentius, decen-
tius, uberius, utilius, et cum minori onere subditorum possit prouideri aliunde, ea
propter hiis aliisque iustis rationabilibusque causis moti   3 et] ac W   4 ac
per collectores] collatores S   5 exactiones seu perceptiones] exactionis seu
perceptionis S   6 aut] seu W   7 ac] a S   8 officialium] *add. in marg.*
W   9 et (*first*)] vel W   11 pertineant] *add. in marg.* W   recipiantur] recip *in
text*; iantur *add. above line* S   13 aut] et W (*but struck out and replaced with* ac)   14
exactiones] exactionem W   communis] communem S   15 constitutione]
corr. from decretali W; tamen *add.* W   felicis recordationis] *in marg.* W   16
Presenti] De officio ordinarii, Liber sextus *add. in marg.* W   edita] specialiter
add. W   16–17 duratura] Placet nationi. *add. in marg.* S   18 cardinalium . . .
eorum] et qualitate dominorum cardinalium W   19 dominorum *om.*
W   21 in *om.* W

bus ecclesiasticis obseruetur, sic tamen quod numerum XXIIII
non excedant; sint autem viri in scientia moribus et rerum experientia excellentes. Qui non minores sint XXX annis doctores in
theologia saltem quatuor propter causas fidei aut in iure canonico
vel ciuili preter admodum paucos qui forte de stirpe regia vel ducali   5
aut magni principis oriundi existant, in quibus competens litteratura sufficiat; non affines seu attinentes alicuius cardinalis viuentis
usque ad quartum gradum inclusiue; nec de [89v] eadem stirpe,
familia, domo vel agnatione, nec de uno ordine mendicantium ultra
unum, non illegitime nati, non corpore vitiati vel alicuius criminis   10
aut infamie nota respersi. Nec fiat eorum electio per auricularia
vota solummodo, sed cum consilio dominorum cardinalium collegialiter et verbaliter sicut in promotione episcoporum fieri consueuit, qui modus etiam obseruetur quando aliquis ex dominis
cardinalibus vel aliquis in episcopum cardinalem assumetur.   15
[c.12][XXIII 2] Quod electiones et prouisiones decetero non fiant
per preces seu impressionem
Statutum felicis recordationis Innocentii pape III editum in
concilio generali contra electiones, eligentes et electionibus consentientes per secularis potestatis abusum locum habere decernimus in   20
prouisionibus quibuscumque factis etiam per summum pontificem
faciendis quo ad prouisiones ipsas ac prouisionibus consentientes.
Et nichilominus decernimus electionem seu prouisionem per secularis potestatis abusum factam censeri debere non solum si expressa vis aut metus fiat electoribus aut prouisori sed etiam si   25
preces litteratorie vel vocales sint tales quod si non pareatur possint
electores vel prouisor seu prouisores dampna vel incommoda in
personis suis vel suorum vel rebus vel ecclesiis suis verisimiliter
formidari. Et publicetur hec constitutio in singulis sinodis et capitulis prouincialibus episcopalibus vel regularibus et alias ubi vide-   30
bitur expedire, et specialiter cum fuerit ad electionem vel
prouisionem prouidendum. Et ubi in capitulo "Quisquis" dicitur
de suspensione dicatur ipse et procurantes preces ultra penas pre-

---

1 quod] *corr. from* qui W   1–3 sic . . . excellentes] *appears in W as two separate*
additions in right and left margins (Sic . . . excedant *and* Sint . . . excellentes). Sic . . .
excedant *replaces an earlier, cancelled note*: Hic addatur quod non excedant numerum
XXIIII^or. Numerum XXIIII conclusit natio Germanica.   4 propter . . . fidei *struck*
out W   7 affines seu attinentes] consangwinei seu attinentes W *(in marg.)*
viuentis] Arcendum ne sit consangwineus pape. add. in marg. W   10 vel] non
W   11 nota] note S   10–11 non corpore . . . respersi] *in marg.* W
12 consilio] *corr. from* consensu W   dominorum *om.* W   13 verbaliter]
verbabiliter S   14 dominis *om.* W   15 aliquis] alius W   assumetur] Placet
quod restringatur ad numerum XVIII. add. in marg. S

dictas sit excommunicatus ipso iure. Volumus autem predictam constitutionem extendi ad electiones, collationes, prouisiones, presentationes seu quasuis alias dispositiones quorumcumque beneficiorum etiam si aliqua ipsorum dignitas seu personatus seu officium etiam cum cura existat.

[c.13][X 9] De dispensatione etatis episcoporum, abbatum, curatorum et ordinum

Non dispenset papa nisi in tribus annis infra etatem iuris et in episcopo si expleuit XXVII annum, in abbatibus et curatis etc. si XXII attingerit, et similiter in ordine presbiteratus etc.; et tunc ex causa rationabili et specialiter in litteris expressa. Preterite dispensationes reuocentur que non sunt sortite effectum. Si ipsas habentes hodie sint infra dictas etates dispensationes, sint reuocate; hoc adiecto quod dispensationes ipse que dicuntur facte cum infantibus ad dignitates suprascriptas, etiam si sint sortite effectum, sint reuocate quia contra ius naturale. In prebendis ecclesiarum cathedralium stet regula cancellarie, [90r] videlicet quod non possit conferri nisi in XIIII° anno existentibus; possit tamen papa conferre existenti in XII anno facta mentione de etate.

[c.14][XIV] De causis tractandis in Curia et remittendis a penis friuole appellantium [Rubric only]

Vienna, Österreichische Nationalbibliothek, MS lat. 5094, fol. 1r–11v, 46r–v, and 156r–v = W²

[c.1][XIII 7] Quales de cetero assummi debeant ad cathedrales et alias dignitates

Licet diuina eloquia sanctorumque patrum canones de prelatorum . . . iuribus patronatus. [See S², c.5] [1v]

[c.2][XVII] Ad quem spectabit confirmatio electorum ad ecclesias cathedrales et alias dignitates

Vacantibus ecclesiis cathedralibus papa electionem expectet et si reperiatur eam canonicam confirmet vel prouideat; et idem de abbatibus et ecclesiis quorum valores quingentorum florenorum de camera excedunt.   In aliis autem et in omnibus monasteriis monialium et ceteris beneficiis electiuis superiores confirment.

[c.3][XIII 8] De collatione beneficiorum et reseruationibus

De beneficiis vacantibus conclusum est per maiorem partem [quod] papa et ordinarii conferant alternis vicibus, videlicet papa medietatem et ordinarii medietatem. Et quod stent reseruationes

---

5 existat] Placet nationi. *add. in marg.* S   19 etate] Placet nationi. *add. in marg.* S   33 camera] non *add., but struck out*

iuris scripti. Et hec omnia cum modificationibus olim per dominos
cardinales in primo reformatorio oblatis super gratiis expectatiuis,
que ponuntur infra fo. 23 ibi de gratiis expectatiuis usque ibi "In
beneficiis" exclusiue.

[c.4][XVIII 2] Die lune XVI Augusti de mane   5
Congregatis dominis reformatoribus fuit proposita materia de
reuocandis alienationibus factis de bonis tam Romane ecclesie
quam aliarum quarumcumque et monasteriorum et piorum locorum. Et conclusum fuit nemine contradicente quod alienata a
Romana ecclesia omnino reuocentur. Usurpata vero omnia tam a   10
Romana quam alibi ubicumque reuocentur. De alienatis vero
aliarum ecclesiarum a maiori parte conclusum fuit quod indebite
alienata reuocentur.

[c.5][XII 2] De numero et qualitate dominorum cardinalium
Statuimus ut deinceps numerus cardinalium sancte Romane   15
ecclesie . . . assumetur. [See S², c. 11] [2r]

[c.6][V 2] De reseruatione spoliorum amplius non faciendis nec
recipiendis
Cum per papam facta reseruatio ac exactio et perceptio procurationum . . . duratura. [See S², c. 10] [2v]   20

[c.7][XVIII 1] Iuramentum pape super non alienando
Ut Romanus pontifex nedum circa spiritualia attenta consideratione . . . iuxta posse. [See S², c. 7]

[c.8][XIX 2] Quod papa accusari et deponi postest super alio
crimine quam heresi   25
Ne sancta mater ecclesia summi pontificis siquod absit
laberetur . . . de papatu. [See S², c.4]

[c.9][IV 2] De prelatis inuitus non transferendis
Cum ex prelatorum translationibus ecclesie de quibus trans-
feruntur . . . non debere. [See S², c.6] [3r]   30

[c.10][III 3] Professio pape
Quanto Romanus pontifex eminentiori inter mortales fungitur
potestate . . . actum etc. [See S², c.3] [3v]

[c.11][I 4] Ut generalium conciliorum celebratio frequentetur
Quamuis ex sacrorum generalium conciliorum celebratione sta-   35
tutis et . . . conuenire. [See S², c.1] [4r]

[c.12][I 2] De consiliis generalibus celebrandis
Sacrosancta synodus Constantiensis ad perpetuam rei memor-
iam. Quantis iam quasi xl annorum retroactis curriculis deploran-
do orto scismate ecclesia dei multitudo fidelium onerosis sub- 40
iacuerit dispendiis, quotque et quantis fuerit plena periculis, adeo
ut columpna dei viuentis pene videretur immutare et sagena summi
piscatoris procellis intumescentibus timeretur in naufragii summa
demergi, exacti temporis consideratio edocet, et considerata

prudenter temporum preteritorum horrenda discrimina luce clarius manifestant. Hinc euidens nos vincat ratio, ut, dum hoc sacro generali Constanciensi concilio pro reformandis singulis sedula nostra iacet intentio curisque excitemur innumeris, ea que periculosiora sunt, et ceteris malis casum et incitamenta ministrant, absque prouisionis nostre remedio nullatenus relinquamus. Et si hactenus sanctorum patrum et sacrorum generalium conciliorum traditionibus et decretis aduersus futura scismata diuersa excogita fuere remedia, eo tamen procurante pacis emulo, cuius secundum scripturas proprium est unitatem scindere et genus humanum versutiis plurimis impungnare, speratum non produxerunt effectum. Cupientes igitur feruentibus votis futuris casibus et periculis, auxiliante cunctorum saluatore, occurrere et ecclesiastico statui multitudinique fidelium, ne normam scismatum, quod absit, recidiua mala suscitentur et preualeant, inposterum prout nobis est possibile prouidere. Et quia ex generalium conciliorum omissione orta et in longum tracta fuisse detestanda scismata, et in ecclesia dei scandala et errores innumeros dampnabiliter succreuisse experientia teste cognouimus, incipientes igitur ab eo quod aliorum subsecutorum errorum fomentum extitit et origo.

In nomine sancte et indiuidue trinitatis patris et filii et spiritus sancti Amen. Hoc perpetuo decreto sanctimus, decernimus, atque ordinamus ut amodo generalia concilia celebrentur ita quod a fine huius concilii in quinquennium secundum vero a fine illius sequentis concilii in septennium et deinceps de decennio in decennium perpetuo celebrentur in locis que summus pontifex ante finem cuiuslibet concilii approbante et consentiente concilio vel in eius defectum ipsum concilium deputare et assignare teneantur ut sic per quamdam continuationem semper aut Concilium vigeat aut per termini pendentiam expectetur, quem terminum liceat summo pontifici de fratrum suorum consilio ac duorum patrum (!) ipsorum ob emergentes forte casus abbreuiare sed nullatenus liceat prorogare.

---

22 decreto *add above line*   23 amodo] *corr. from* deinceps   quod] primum *add. in marg.*   24 in] *corr. from* usque ad   quinquennium] immediate sequens *add. in marg.*   25 in] *corr. from* usque ad   septennium] sempiternum (!) MS   et] sic *add. and struck out*   26 pontifex] per mensem *add. in marg.*   29 vigeat] P. *add.*   31 suorum] Sancte Romane ecclesie cardinalium *add. in marg.*   consilio] et assensu *add. and struck out*   ac . . . ipsorum *underscored*   32 abbreuiare *corr. from* breuiare   liceat] eidem summo pontifici *add. in marg.*   32–33 prorogare] *struck out*; etiam de fratrum predictorum consilio prorogare *add. in marg.* (*corr. from* etiam de consensu eorundem dominorum cardinalium prorogare)

[4v] Locum autem pro futuro concilio celebrando deputatum absque euidenti necessitate non mutet, sed si forte casus aliquis occurreret quo necessarium videretur ipsum locum mutari puta obsidionis, gwerrarum, pestis aut similis tunc liceat summo pontifici de predictorum fratrum aut duarum partium ipsorum consensu   5
atque subscriptione alium locum prius deputato loco viciniorem et aptum sub eadem tamen natione surrogare nisi idem impedimentum per totam illam nationem vigeret tunc ad aliquem alium viciniorem alterius nationis locum huiusmodi concilium poterit conuocari. Ad quem prelati et alii qui ad concilium solent   10
conuocari accedere teneantur acsi a principio pro locus ille fuisset deputatus; quam tamen loci mutationem teneatur sollempniter intimare et publicare ut ad ipsum concilium celebrandum possint predicti statuto termino convenire.

[c.13][II] Prouisio aduersus futura scismata   15

Si vero quod absit in futurum scisma oriri contingeret ita quod duo vel plures [*The text breaks off with the words* quod nullus *at the end of fol. 4v; the end of the schedule is lacking in this manuscript.*] [See S², c.2, where the variants from this text are identified as W (W³=W², c.15 below)]   20

[c. 13a][III 2]

[5r] . . . remittam. Nec terminum ad soluendum huiusmodi census ultra biennium prorogabo nisi euidens immineret scandalum et periculum ecclesie expectando in premissis celebrationem futuri proximi concilii generalis.   25

Annus etiam iubileus prout antiquitus institutus fuit de L in L annum celebrabitur sic quod venientibus et currentibus annis domini M°CCCC^{mo}L^{mo} sit primus et ex tunc sic deinceps perpetuo de quinquagesimo in quinquagesimum obseruabitur. Nec hoc umquam mutabo nisi de consensu consilii generalis excepto tamen ut   30
abiecta vetustate noxia in omnibus renouari mereamur possum pro salute animarum omnium Christifidelium de consilio et assensu presentis concilii Constantiensis si sibi videbitur instituere annum iubileum dumtaxat vice breuiori termino celebrandum.

---

4 obsidionis] *corr. from* ob synode huius ecclesie Cardinalium *add. and struck out crossed out, then added again in marg.*   5 fratrum] suorum sancte Romane   6 locum] aptum *add. above line, then crossed out, then added again in marg.*   10 conuocari] *corr. from* conuocare   12 mutationem] vel termini abbreuiationem *add. in marg.*   teneatur] omnibus *add. and struck out*; dictus summus pontifex legitime et *add. in marg.*   12 sollempniter] per annum ante prefixum terminum *add. in marg.*   14 termino] predicto *add. above line and struck out*   conuenire] Attende de pena aut iuret post professionem. *add. in marg.*   16 vero] quod absit nouum sit unquam *add. and struck out*   24 celebrationem] celebrationum

[c.14][XIX 1] Quod papa etiam pro alio crimine quam heresi si notorie scandalisat ecclesiam et monitus non desistat deponi possit.

Et quoniam decet Romanum pontificem, in quem cunctorum respiciunt oculi, quanto pluribus ecclesie ministris et rectoribus prelatus est, tanto sanctiori vita et celebriori fama fulgere . . . [*From this point on, the text agrees generally with the Common collection, c. 5 above; variants from this manuscript are given there*] . . . [5v] . . . publicare. [6r] [c.15][II] Prouisio aduersus futura scismata

Si vero quod absit in futuris scisma oriri contingeret ita quod duo . . . [7v] . . . vel facienda ante ingressum conclauis legatur et intimetur. [*Collated with S², c.2, where the variants are identified as W³*] [*Rest of fol. 7v blank*]

[8r][c.16][XX 1] (*collated with A, p. 45; see above, p. 290*) Prolocuta et aduisata per dominos deputatos sacri collegii et reformatorii continentia commendas et alia beneficia quas domini cardinales habent de presenti

1. Primo dimittent domini cardinales omnes et singulas ecclesias parrochiales et omnia alia beneficia que in inportatis non valent ultra LXX lib. Turon., et hoc infra annum a die assumptionis summi pontificis, ut interim habeant facultatem permutandi cum beneficiis alterius generis; vel papa possit eis recompensare sicut sue Sanctitati placebit.

2. Item dimittant domini cardinales ex nunc omnia hospitalia, leprosarias, zenodochia et alia pia loca, que pro hospitalitate tenenda sunt fundata, superioribus dictorum locorum. Quia tamen unus de dominis obtinet unam preceptoriam sancti Antonii que non cadit sub nomine hospitalis tunc paratus est illam dimittere, facta sibi aliquali pensione, licet non plena sed ad arbitrium boni viri.

3. Item paratus est quilibet dominorum cardinalium, in casu quo sibi fiat per summum pontificem futurum realis et actualis assignatio usque ad summam sex milium florenorum camere annuatim iuxta aduisamentum reformatorii, dimittere omnia beneficia que habent, reseruando tamen sibi unam commendam etiam metropolitanam vel cathdralem seu abbatialem, aut aliud beneficium, quod nunc habeat vel in futurum habebit, ita tamen quod valor commende seu beneficii retenti in summa VI M florenorum includatur. Presens tamen articulus non comprehendat dominos Ostiensem et de Saluciis quo ad summam predictam VI

---

14 sacri] concilii *add.* A   16 presenti] Immediate *add. in marg.* W   18 in *om.* A   27 dimittere] Petitio dominii C. de Brancaciis super hospitali detur etiam nationibus. *add. in marg.* W   29 quilibet] dimittere *add.* A   33 reseruando] sibi *add. and struck out* W

milium. Tum propter longeuitatem temporis assumptionis eorum
ad cardinalatum, tum etiam propter deperditionem beneficiorum,
que occasione scismatis perpessi sunt, ad dictam summam non
reducentur.

4. Item quilibet cardinalis habens episcopatum, abbatiam aut   5
prioratum conuentualem teneatur creato papa quilibet eorum et
singulariter singulas renunciare et illa dimittere dummodo et in
casu quo papa in ipsa renunciatione seu ante tantundem sibi
assignauerit in prouentu aut redditu perpetuo quantum valebat
importatis episcopatus, abbatia aut prioratus quem dimittet. Hoc   10
tamen non intelligatur de commenda seu beneficio quod cardinalis
sibi elegerit retinendum iuxta dispositionem capituli precedentis.
Quod autem dicitur de prioratu conuentuali intelligitur si habeat
conuentum XII monachorum.

[8v] 5. Item quod supra dictum est de episcopatu, abbatia, aut   15
prioratu dimittendis intelligatur de dignitatibus primis post pontificales in metropolitanis aut cathedralibus et principalibus in ecclesiis collegiatis.

6. Item domini cardinales abbatias seu prioratus conuentuales
habentes debeant ex nunc et interim unum religiosum eiusdem   20
ordinis ponere ad curam et regimen monachorum circa obseruantiam regularem.

7. Item etiam tenebunt debitum numerum monachorum in
abbatia et prioratu predictis secundum quod abbates aut priores
habere tenentur et dictis monacis prouidebunt de fructibus abbatie   25
aut prioratus condecenter et honeste.

8. Item si abbatia aut prioratus indiget reparatione tenebuntur
ipsam facere dicti domini cardinales ad arbitrium ordinariorum seu
superiorum dictorum locorum quis (!) ius habent eas visitandi, qui
loca illa visitabunt ut prius seu visitari facient et reparari, prout   30
fuerit rationis; ac potuerunt ordinarii seu superiores predicti con-
stringere firmarios dictorum locorum etiam per arrestum fructuum
ad reparationes predictas peragendas.

9. Item idem intelligatur de aliis beneficiis que tenent si certum
numerum ministrorum habere debent, aut etiam reparatione in-   35
digeant, quia ministris fiet decens prouisio, et locorum reparatio, ut
prefertur.

10. Item abbatia aut prioratus interim nullo modo dabuntur ad
firmam laicis, sed religiosis eiusdem ordinis. [9r]

---

1 propter *om.* A   6 creato] *om.* A   7 singulas] singulis A   8 seu ante
om. A   14 monachorum] vel supra *add.* A

[c.17][XX 2] Aduisamenta per dominos deputatos sacri collegii et reformatorii super prouisione cardinalium de nouo creandorum

1. Primo, nullus cardinalium creandorum poterit habere aut tenere aliquam ecclesiam parrochialem.

2. Item non habebunt beneficia aliqua quorum cuiuslibet valor inportatis summam LXX librorum Turonensium non excedat.

3. Item non habebunt dignitates maiores post pontificales in ecclesiis cathedralibus seu principales in ecclesiis collegiatis.

4. Item non habebunt abbatias aut prioratus conuentuales qui habeant conuentum XII monachorum vel supra.

5. Item nullas ecclesias metropolitanas dicti domini cardinales creandi.

6. Item quilibet dominorum cardinalium etiam creandorum poterit habere commendam unam unius ecclesie cathedralis vel abbatialis non tamen metropolitane ad quam se possit reducere in antiquitate aut qualitate temporis exigente.

7. Item ecclesia cathedralis que fuerit commendata cardinali, eo defuncto vel cedente, nullo modo possit cardinali alteri illa vice in commendam dari sed necessario habere habeat post cardinalem episcopum seu administratorem non cardinalem. [9v]

[c.18][VIII 3] Decet Romanum pontificem hiis uti legibus quas in aliis ipse sanxerit, quoniam illius existit vicarius qui cepit facere et docere. Digna enim vox est maiestate regnantis alligatam legibus se principem profiteri et maius est imperio summittere legibus principatum.[3] Cum itaque dudum Romani pontifices perpetuis et diuersis edictis prohibuerunt vacantibus cathedralibus regularibus et collegiatis ecclesiis, necnon dignitatibus, personatibus, prioratibus, vel ecclesiis quibuscumque bona a prelatis, rectoribus, aut ministros ipsorum et ipsarum dimissa seu post ipsorum obitum inuenta aut vacationis tempore obuenientia, a quibuscumque preterquam in certis casibus occupari, declaramus et decernimus bona huiusmodi, etiam si defuncti sancte Romane ecclesie cardinales fuerint, et ubicumque, etiam si in Romana curia bona eadem extiterint vel obuenerint, per Romanos pontifices seu eorum officiarios aut ministros non deberi occupari aut sibi vel apostolice camere applicari; per hoc autem de fructibus primi anni quos

---

3 Digna ... principatum] cf. Cod. 1.14.4

---

21 Decet] Super eo de hera.(?) liber VI. *add. in marg.*   23 maiestate] *corr. from* maiestatem   31 casibus] *corr. from* causis

vacantias seu annatas vocant, quos apostolica camera aliquando
pro suis necessitatibus percepit, nichil intendimus ordinare. [10r]
[c.19][XXII 2] Videtur sancte synodo expediens fore quod papa
non imponat decimam vel aliam quottam seu exactionem et quod
imposite reuocentur clero toti vel eius parti nisi in concilio generali,   5
et cum consensu concilii. Possit tamen postulare caritatiuum subsidium cum caritate quando res exiget. Super concedendis vero
decimis vel aliis subsidiis et collectis laicis quibuscumque super
ecclesiis ecclesiasticisque personis et eorum bonis ad instar felicis
re. domini Clementis pape quinti, qui in sua constitutione incipiente   10
"Quoniam"[4] penitus reuocauit constitutionem Bonifatii pape
octaui que incipit "Clericis laicos"[5] et declarationes eiusdem et
quidquid ex eis et ob eas secutum erat et eos haberi voluit pro
infectis, hec sancta synodus duo concilia infra designata super hoc
renouando vult et firmiter statuit illud contra quoscumque laicos   15
exigentes seu extorquentes ab ecclesiis ecclesiasticisque personis
tallias seu collectas aut exactiones quascumque et contra id facien-
dum consilium auxilium vel fauorem necnon et circa prestandas
subuentiones laicis ab ecclesiarum prelatis (?) et aliis viris ecclesiasticis inuiolabiliter obseruari quod super hiis a predecessoribus   20
suis Romanis pontificibus in lateranensi et generali conciliis, que
sub obtestatione diuini iudicii eadem synodus precipit obseruari
districti, salubriter est prouisum. [10v]
[c.20][XX 3] Primo, infra annum a die coronationis futuri summi
Romani pontificis inchoandum, domini cardinales qui beneficia   25
ecclesiastica quorum fructus, redditus et prouentus oneribus supportatis LXX librorum Turonensium valorem annuum excedunt,
de presenti possident tenebuntur dimittere omnes et singulas ecclesias parrochiales et omnia et singula officia claustralia indistincte,
cuiuscumque valoris eorum fructus etc. existerent. Necnon tene-   30
buntur etiam dimittere omnia beneficia alia ecclesiastica quorum
fructus etc., XX si in Italia usque ad XXV, si alibi sita sunt usque
ad LXX, librorum Turonensium valorem annuum, ordinariis
oneribus debite supportatis, non ascendunt. Habebunt autem
facultatem ipsi domini infra dicti anni spatium huiusmodi par-   35
rochiales ecclesias, officia claustralia, et beneficia ipsa minora cum
beneficiis alterius generis, inferius tamen non prohibitis, permu-

---

4 Clem. 3.17.un.
5 VI 3.23.3

---

tare; vel papa eisdem recompenset incommodum quod ex dimissione predicta ipsi domini cardinales incurrant; seu prouideat alias prout sibi videbitur expedire. Canonicatus tamen et prebendas quas ante assumptionem, necnon et prebendas quas cum dignitate et officio post assumptionem cardinalatus forte fuerunt assecuti, licet eorum fructus etc. ad summam LXX librorum Turonensium non ascendunt, ipsi nichilominus retinere valeant. Et insuper ex nunc omnia hospitalia, leprosarias, xenodochia, et alia pia loca que pro hospitalitate tenenda sunt fundata dimittere tenebuntur in manibus superiorum huiusmodi locorum absque recompensatione alia. Ab hoc tamen edicto dominus Ragusinus excipiatur, presertim propter sue tenuis prouisionis notoriam exiguitatem. Porro quilibet ex dominis cardinalibus iam creatis, si unum solum archiepiscopatum, episcopatum, abbatiam, prioratum conuentualem aut dignitatem aliam vel beneficium aliud quodcumque preter sui cardinalatus Romane titulum de presenti obtinet, vel in futurum secundum ordinationem concilii obtinebit, illum, illam seu illud (si vero plures seu plura ex dignitatibus beneficiis eiusdem generis vel diuersarum obtineat, illum, illam seu illud quem, quam seu quod ex illis, infra mensem a die oblationis realis infrascripte sibi facte optare maluerit) ad manus suas retinere valebat, in qua in antiquitate aut alias temporis exigente qualitate reducere [11r] se possit. Et hoc saluo quotienscumque futurus summus pontifex ipsis dominis cardinalibus iam creatis vel ipsorum alteri recompensationem valoris fructuum prouentuum etc. aurorum qui communiter supersunt oneribus supportatis huiusmodi reliquorum beneficiorum seu dignitatum realiter et cum effectu obtulerit, seu prouisionem in equiualenti valorem ipsorum fructuum in redditu seu prouentu perpetuo, presertim in patrimonio ecclesie Romane in communibus seruitiis, primis annatis, vel camere apostolice iuribus aliis eisdem dominis cardinalibus vel ipsorum alteri fecerit, decurso prefati temporis mense a die oblationis ipsius inchoate, omne ius in huiusmodi reliquis beneficiis pro quo vel quibus facta fuerit recompensatio (presertim et primo vacantibus decanatibus, preposturis conuentualibus XII religiosorum et in primis cathedralium ecclesiarum post pontificalem dignitatibus et in collegiatis principalibus) eisdem dominis cardinalibus vel ipsorum alteri quomodolibet competens censeatur fore reuocatum, etiam eis inuitis, ipso iure, vacatioque beneficiorum ipsorum et dignitatum de iure inducta, ut sic alteri conferri possint. Ita quod, pro singulis huiusmodi beneficiis fiet eisdem prouisio in equiualenti fructuum prouentuum

32 inchoate] inchoati MS   41 fructuum] redditum ac *add. and struck out*

etc. valore, beneficium ipsum equiualens relinquere teneatur, qui
illud obtinebat. Et si pro omnibus beneficiis ipsis simul vel successiue prouisionem huiusmodi fieri contingat, equiualentia beneficia
proportionaliter semper relinquere teneatur; hoc adhibito moderamine, quod si uniuersalis valor fructuum seu prouentuum etc.   5
omnium predictorum beneficiorum cuiusuis cardinalis ultra summam sex milium librorum Turonensium ascenderet, nichilominus
facta eidem prouisione vel recompensatione dumtaxat usque ad
valorem VI. milium, beneficia omnia et singula de facto relinquere
teneantur. Neque eisdem cardinalibus seu ipsorum alicui (Ostienso   10
et Saluciarum, qui propter prosecutionem unionis ecclesie quam-
plures suos redditus perdiderunt singulari priuilegio gaudere debent, dumtaxat exceptis) ultra dictam summam VI M fiat recompensatio seu prouisio, etiam si valor annuus oneribus supportatis
suorum beneficiorum plus ascenderet. Illis vero duobus fiat usque   15
ad valorem beneficiorum que de presenti obtinent, antequam
omnia vacare dicantur et quam omnia relinquere teneantur. [11v]
Ceteris vero dominis cardinalibus recompensatio seu prouisio
usque ad illam summam VI M, ut predicitur, et non ultra fieri
valeat. Etiam si valor suorum beneficiorum tantum non ascendat,   20
beneficia tamen ipsa relinquere teneantur quotienscumque facta
fuerit recompensatio in equiualente ipsorum valore. De summa
vero VI milium recompensationis predicte, vel alterius equiualentis
valoris, semper deducatur (semper in illa computetur, et in illa
comprehendatur), valor dignitatis seu beneficii per quemuis domi-   25
num cardinalem pro sua reductione ut premittitur retenti. Nomine
autem beneficii etiam maiora quecumque, etiam si archiepiscopatus existeret, intelligere volumus in premissis. Hac vero lege
reuocationis, iuris, priuationis et dimissionis comprehendere non
intendimus dominum cardinalem Remensem tantum ad archiepis-   30
copatum Pictauensem, quem tenet in titulum quacumque obla-
tione sibi inuito facienda non obstante, quam protestationem faci-
mus ex superhabundanti.
Domini cardinales quoque abbatias, prioratus, preposituras, de-
canatus regulares conuentuales vel non conuentuales habentes in-   35
terim et ex nunc teneantur et debeant unum religiosum ad hoc
ydoneum euisdem ordinis seu religionis ibi ponere ad curam et
regimen religiosorum circa obseruantiam regularem et totius admi-
nistrationis beneficiorum ipsorum; etiam si ad firmam censeantur
illa dari velle, ut scilicet non seculari sed religioso huiusmodi firma   40

---

34 Domini] vero *add. and struck out*

detur. Tenebunt ibi numerum debitum religiosorum in abbatiis et predictis beneficiis secundum quod abbates vel huiusmodi benefiorum prelati et intitulati habere teneantur. Ipsisque monacis seu religiosis de fructibus beneficiorum ipsorum prouidebunt condecenter et honeste, et secundum obseruantiam regularem quemadmodum abbates et alii beneficiati huiusmodi beneficiorum prelati facerent seu facere deberent. Tenebuntur etiam tenere hospitalitates pro religiosis et pauperibus et elimosinas tribuere secundum modum ab antiquo, scilicet antequam ad manus dominorum cardinalium peruenissent, tenebantur et teneri et fieri debebant.

[46r]
[c.21][X 10] Reuerendi patres et domini reformatores dignemini prouidere circa infrascripta

Primo, quod tollantur dispensationes concesse quibuscumque ratione dignitatum etiam episcopalium et beneficiorum ecclesiasticorum quorumcumque sacros ordines requirentium, quod ad receptionem eorundem ordinum non teneantur.

Item tollantur dispensationes facte cum patientibus defectus natalium ut ad prebendas necnon dignitates etc. ecclesiarum kathedralium etiam ad pontificales et alia beneficia promoueantur. Sed dispensationes huiusmodi fiant solum ad beneficia simplicia nisi scientia vel litteratura aut euidens neccessitas seu utilitas et persone promouende conditio aliter permittat.

Item quod de cetero non dispensetur cum constitutis in sacris ordinibus nisi in casibus premissis quod matrimonia contrahant a voto continentie recedendo, quorum aliqui, de fructibus beneficiorum et patrimonio Christi saturati, ad seculum redeunt.

Item reuocentur indulta de fructibus percipiendis in absentia nisi in casibus a iure expressis, et inhibeatur ne de cetero fiant.

Item reuocentur dispensationes ad incompatibilia ultra duo habito tamen respectu ad conditiones personarum, et prouideatur ne de cetero fiant.

Item reuocentur dispensationes ad contrahendum matrimoniam in gradibus consanguineitatis et affinitatis prohibitis nondum sortite effectum, et inhibeatur ne tales de cetero fiant, nisi ex rationabilibus causis.

[c.22][X 10]
Item reuocentur omnes indulgentie que tempore scismatis et presertim ille que reperiuntur ad instar indulgentiarum anni Iubilei, ecclesie Sancti Marcii (!) in Venetiis, in Aquisgrani, in loco heremitarum beate Marie aut alias contra stilum Curie et regulas Cancellarie concesse, et potissime ille que a dominis cardinalibus ad pia loca extra Curia Romana emanarunt quarum [46v] alique

continent in effectu ut presentes decantationi certarum anthipha-
narum (!) de qualibet nota centum dies indulgentiarum habeant
circumeuntes vero ipsa pia loca totidem dies, que magis ad decep-
tionem et derisionem populi Christiani, quam ad salutem animarum tendunt, et quod de cetero nulle indulgentie, ut premittitur   5
inconsuete extra Curia concedantur donec populus in fide deuius
ad pristinam deuotionem reducatur. Et huiusmodi abusiones et
peccuniarum extorsiones penitus extirpentur.
[c.23][X 10] [No rubric]
Item inhibeatur ne aliquis in Curia Romana super absolutionem   10
a pena et a culpa aut Confessionale seu Altare portatile, et ad
audiendum diuina in loco interdicto litteras impetrare nec impetra-
tis uti presumant (!) nisi ab ordinario suo petita licentia et obtenta,
cum per huiusmodi impetrationes neruus ecclesiasticus vilipenditur, potestas ordinariorum despicitur, deuotio impetrantium dimi-   15
nuitur, symonia nutritur, et auaritia recipit incrementum. [156r]
[c.24][XVIII 3] Reuocatio alienatorum et usurpatorum Romane
et aliarum ecclesiarum
Cum post obitum felicis recordationis Gregorii pape XI. . .
quibuscumque.   20
[c.25][VIII 2] De fructibus medii temporis vacationis non recipiendis
Vacantibus ecclesiis aut monasteriis aliisue dignitatibus officiis
seu beneficiis ecclesiasticis quibuscumque satis esse videtur incom-
odum quod suis sunt pastoribus aut presidentibus destituta, ne   25
ergo afflictis detur afflictio presentibus declaramus quod fructus,
redditus et prouentus ecclesiarum, monasteriorum, dignitatum,
officiorum et beneficiorum ecclesiasticorum vacantium quocumque
huiusmodi vacationis tempore venientes ecclesiis ac successoribus
proximis reseruentur. Nec Romanus pontifex aut aliquis alius sua   30
vel alterius cuiuscumque auctoritate illos fructus, redditus et
prouentus sibi attribuat quouismodo, priuilegiis, fundationibus,
dotationibus ac rationabilibus et prescriptis consuetudinibus inferiorum ecclesiarum in suo robore duraturis, in aliquo derogare.

21–22 recipiendis] Tradatur; XIIII Septembris conclusus *add. in marg.*   23
Vacantibus] Placuit materia sed non forma. *add. in marg.*   monasteriis] maioribus seu minoribus *add. and struck out*   24 ecclesiasticis *in marg.*   27 redditus
et prouentus *in marg.*   28 ecclesiasticorum *in marg.*   29 venientes *corr. from*
excrescentes W   31–32 redditus et prouentus *in marg.*   31 et *corr. from*
aut   32 attribuat] Hec autem per premissa tamen (premissa tamen *struck out*)
non intendit *add. in marg.*

Vienna, Österreichische Nationalbibliothek lat. 5113, fol. 1r–4v
(=D2)

[c.1][III 3] Professio pape auisata in concilio Constanciense
  Quanto Romanus pontifex eminentiori inter mortales fungitur . . . actum etc. [See S², c.3]
[c.2][XVIII 1] Quod papa non <alienat> bona ecclesie
<Romane> et recuperet d<eperdita> iuxta suum po<sse>
  Vt Romanus pontifex ne dum spiritualia attenta consideratione
versetur . . . iuxta posse. [See S², c.7]   1(
[c.3][XIX 2] Quod papa n<on solum> de heresi sed <etiam> de
alio crimine <scan>dalizante ecc<lesiam> uniuersalem et
<potest> deponi
  Ne sancta mater ecclesia summi pontificis si quod absit
laberetur . . . de papatu. [See S², c.4]   1
[1v] [Blank]
[2r] Auisata in reformatorio per XXV prelatos et doctores.
[c.4][I 3] De futuris conciliis celebrandis.
  Hoc decreto perpetuo sanximus, decernimus et ordinamus ut
amodo generalia concilia celebrentur, ita quod primum a fine huius   2(
concilii in quinquennium immediate sequens, secundum vero a fine
illius sequentis concilii in septennium et deinceps de decennio ad
decennium perpetuo celebrentur, in locis que summus pontifex per
mensem ante finem cuiuslibet concilii approbante et consentiente
concilio vel in eius defectum ipsum concilium deputare et assignare   2
teneatur; ut sic per quamdam continuationem semper aut concilium vigeat aut per termini pendentiam exspectetur. Quem terminum liceat summo pontifici de fratrum suorum sancte Romane
ecclesie cardinalium consilio ob emergentis forte casus abreuiare,
sed nullatenus liceat eidem summo pontifici etiam de fratrum   3(
consilio prorogare. Locum autem pro futuro concilio celebrando
deputatum absque euidenti necessitate non mutet. Sed si forte
casus aliquis occurreret quo necessarium videretur ipsum locum
mutare, puta obsidionis, guerrarum, pestis, aut similis; tunc liceat
summo pontifici de predictorum fratrum aut duarum partium   3
ipsorum consensu atque subscriptione alium locum prius deputato
loco viciniorem et aptum sub eadem tamen natione surrogare, nisi
idem impedimentum per totam illam nationem vigeret. Tunc ad
alium viciniorem alterius nationis locum aptum huiusmodi concilio
poterit conuocari, ad quem prelati et alii qui ad concilium solent   4(
conuocari accedere teneantur ac si a principio locus ille fuisset

---

38 ad] aliquem add. in marg.

deputatus; quam tamen loci mutationem vel termini abreuiationem teneatur dictus summus pontifex legitime et solempniter per annum ante prefixum terminum publicare et intimare, ut ad ipsum concilium celebrandum possint predicti statuto termino conuenire.

[c.5][II] Prouisio aduersus futura cismata precauenda   5

Si vero quod absit in futurum cisma oriri contingeret ita quod duo vel plures . . . obediatur. [See S², c.2] [2v]

[c.6] De remedio electionis pape facte per metum

Quod si forte electionem Romani pontificis per metum que caderet in constantem . . . [3r] . . . intimetur. [See S², c.2 (appears   10
there as part of decree "Si vero")] [3r]

[c.7][XLIII] De indebita et inordinata electione prelatorum preteritorum in Alamania et de precauenda futura. Auisamentum per M. Iop

Quia proch dolor nimius abusus in promotione episcoporum,   15
presertim in partibus Alamanie, inoleuit, nec speratur de facili posse executioni demandari quod elegantur doctores vel graduati, maxime quia imperfectum scientie quasi communiter in tota Alamania non tam supplet perfectio caritatis⁶ quam nobilitas san-   20
guinis vel potentia amicorum; et quia decretalis Cum nobis olim, De electione,⁷ circa scientiam aliqualiter laxe loquitur et doctores dicunt contra eam cum nobili potente, si alias temporalia ecclesie periclitentur, posse dispensari; idcirco visum est aliquibus dominis deputatis ad reformationem pro Germanica natione quod pro refor-   25
matione episcoporum tam presentium quam futurorum fiat una constitutio generalis in qua primo recitetur per modum exordii qualiter institutum sit nomine et figura episcopi seu pontificis ex vi vocabuli et etiam veteri testamento ac ex doctrina apostoli ad Thymoteum⁸ et ad Tytum⁹ et quomodo sacri canones ex hiis reg-   30
ulas posuerunt, prout a xxv di. usque ad quinquagesimam prosequitur Gratianus. Et specialiter tangantur ea que in c. Qui episcopus, xxiii di.¹⁰ et in c. Que ipsis et se., xxxviii di.¹¹ habentur, necnon

---

6 Cf. 1 Cor. 8,1
7 X 1.6.19
8 Cf. 1 Tim. 4,13
9 Cf. Tit. 2,1
10 D.23 c.2
11 D.38 c.5

---

4 statuto termino] *corr. from* prefixum terminum   8 facte] *corr. from* facta
10 intimetur] IIII S *add.*

in c. Cum in cunctis, De electione[12] et in c. ult., De etate et qualitate[13] et in c. Nisi para. Pro defectu, De renuntiationibus[14] cum similibus. Et post hec deploretur lamentabilis epicoporum status modernus in aliquibus partibus, quia nonnulli sunt penitus ydeote, aliqui non in sacris, alii semper in guerris et armis [3v] et plerique numquam vel raro per se exercent pontificalia aut celebrant ordines vel predicant aut visitant, ut tenentur. Sed principale sui officii committunt titularibus etiam leuibus personis et officialibus seu vicariis et id quod accessorium est et per alios facere deberent, vel potius obmittere, personaliter faciunt, die noctuque placitis et tractatibus prophanis et secularibus insudantes. Nec recorduntur etiam consecrari per professionem quam fecerunt, ex quibus tepescit fides, exulat caritas et spes salutis adimitur Christianis infinitaque scandala sunt secuta. Quare statuit et ordinat hec sacrosancta synodus quod archiepiscopi et episcopi deinceps sua officia personaliter exerceant predicando, visitando, ordines celebrando et in suis ecclesiis in festiuitatibus diuina ministrando etc., nisi iusta et rationabili causa fuerint impediti. Quodque in elegendis et promouendis episcopis examen canonicum de singulis ad hoc requisitis precedat sic quod omnino persone ad caute dignitatis fastigium ex omni parte ydonee et non alie preferantur. Nec contra hoc nisi ex magna, rationabili et notoria causa in iure expressa aliquatenus dispensetur sub grauibus penis que sacro concilio videbuntur optime. Hec autem constitutio que in effectu mandabit sacras canones seruari tam in exercitio officii episcopalis per nunc promotos quam in promouendo futuros in omnibus cathedralibus ecclesiis singulis annis bis vel ter, et presertim imminentis electionis tempore cum intellectu debito publicetur, etc.

[c.8][XIII 7] Quod nullus eligatur in episcopum vel abbatem nisi sit doctor sacre theologie vel iuris canonici vel ciuilis

Licet diuina eloquia sanctorumque patrum canones de prelatorum . . . [4r] . . . promoueri. [See S², c.5]

[c.9][IV 2] [No rubric]

Cum ex prelatorum translationibus ecclesie de quibus transferunt plerumque . . . non debere. [See S², c.6]

[c.10][IX 3] Contra symoniacos

Contra labem symoniace pestis qua decor ecclesie plurimum denigratur . . . [4v] . . . cedat in exemplum. [See S², c.8]

---

12 X 1.6.7
13 X 1.14.15
14 X 1.9.10

EXTRAVAGANTES

Additional proposal in A (Augburg, Staats- und Stadtbibliothek, 2°
Cod 226), p. 579:
[Extrav. 1] In Reformatorio:
Quod quilibet episcopus teneatur in synodo monere per edictum
omnes clericos sue diocesis ut nullus teneat concubinam publice uel 5
occulte sub penis a iure statutis et insuper sub aliis penis inferius
denotatis.
Item quod teneatur facere diligentem inquisitionem per suam
diocesim contra clericos concubinarios. Et si aliquem repererit
talem qui sit beneficiatus, si quidem ille curatus fuerit aut alias 10
sacerdos debeat omnibus de sua dyocesis mandare ut nullus ab eo
missam audiat aut ab eo recipere audeat ecclesiastica sacramenta.
Nec ante huiusmodi sententiam seu mandatum teneatur par-
rochianus suum curatum seu alium in diuinis officys ex huiusmodi
causa vitare; post vero liceat ei a quocumque maluerit curam 15
animarum habente ecclesiastica percipere sacramenta. Ceteros
vero beneficiatos ab ingressu ecclesie suspendat donec concubinas
dimiserit. Quod si uel isti uel illi superiores post mandatum seu
suspensionem infra mensem eas non dimiserint, aut in elusionem
mandati concubinas de loco ad locum transtulerint, transacto 20
mense debeat episcopus illos beneficysque suis priuare, non
habentes vero beneficia et in sacris ordinibus constitutos inhabiles
decernere ad ecclesiastica beneficia obtinenda etc.
Item quod si episcopus negligens fuerit in premissis, aut ipse qui
debet esse ceteris continentie et castitatis exemplum tenuerit con- 25
cubinam, possit tam propter crimen quam etiam propter neg-
ligentiam ecclesia sua priuari, non solum a papa, sed etiam a
concilio prouinciali, si due partes episcoporum qui fuerint in eodem
in hanc penam consenserint inferendam.
Frater Petrus fatetur esse exemplar de manu domini P. Pauli. 30

Additional paragraph in D (found in Common, c.6, para. 29 in D;
see above, Table 3, p. 306):
[Extrav. 2] Item quod officiales curie Romane non permittantur
publice nutrire concubinas, ludere ad taxillos, aut alias dissolu-
tiones facere, sed sint disciplinati moribus, verbis, et exemplis, sic 35

quod curia sit speculum sanctitatis et norma; alioquin absque
dissimulatione officiis suis priuentur si moniti non desistant.

Paris, Bibliothèque Nationale, lat. 1485B, fol. 213r [Extrav. 3]
Cedula recepta per familiarem patriarche Anthocheni die VIII.
Februarii anno XVII. de reformatione capitis ecclesie uniuersalis   5

Primo quod officium pape versetur principaliter ad orandum pro
salute animarum et pace christianitatis predicandumque et in-
struendum in fide et moribus populum christianum et ad ponen-
dum pacem inter reges et principes christianitatis exhortandique
eos ad passagium pro recuperatione terre sancte dando eis, quan-   10
tum ad eum pertinet, fauores speciales.

Item quod non sit bellicosus nec teneat seu stipendiet capitaneos
gentium armorum ad effundendum sanguinem humanum, sed
quando indigebit auxilio iustitie, utatur gladio spirituali secundum
quod sancti patres hactenus soliti sunt facere, et quando illi non   15
obedietur, inuocet brachium seculare imperatorum, regum et principum christianitatis, sicut sancti patres antiquitus faciebant.

Item non indicat aut indici faciat aut suo nomine indici permittat
taillias, gabellas seu alias exactiones populis patrimonii ecclesie
Romane, sed illos teneat in illa libertate, in qua sancti patres eius   20
predecessores illos tenere consueuerunt.

Item in ciuitatibus et aliis locis temporalitatis Romane ecclesie
non recipiat mercedem ab usurariis ut in illis fenerari possint, sed
illos repellat de dictis locis et, quod a talibus desistant, compescat.

Item in terris et locis dicte temporalitatis ecclesie Romane non   25
recipiat mercedem prostibuli nec de trechariis, sed illas exterminet,
sicut requirunt decreta sanctorum patrum.

Item pro quocumque negotio spirituali uel ecclesiastico per eum
ratione sui officii ministrando nichil recipiat, quod pertineat ad
pecuniam uel ad aliam commoditatem temporalem, sed litteras,   30
bullam et registrum et omnia alia inde necessaria gratis ministret,
sic quod symonia ab ecclesia Dei totaliter repellatur et omnia puro
corde et mundis manibus ministrentur. Et si patrimonium ecclesie
ad premissorum onera non sufficiat, per sacrum concilium cum
assistentia imperatoris, regum et principum christianitatis taliter   35
prouideatur, quod Romanus pontifex et omnes officiales Romane
curie de publico satis habeant ad premissa onera sine symonia siue
extorsione quacumque supportanda.

Item reducat numerum notariorum sedis apostolice et aliorum
officialium ad numerum antiquum, quo sancti patres contenti erant   40
antiquitus.

Item quod papa non sit litigiosus, sed litium extinctor existat

quodque de nullis causis recipiat cognitionem, nisi sint fidei uel alie
maiores, sed omnes alias si per querelam uel appellationem ad eum
deferantur ordinariis locorum uel ex causa aliis personis ydoneis in
partibus usque ad tres sententias inclusiue per sua rescripta apostolica committat, sicut antiquitus per sanctos patres predecessores   5
suos solitum est fieri.

[213v] Item non reseruet nec recipiat fructus ecclesiarum vacantium nec annatas beneficiorum nec prelationes, procurationes prelatorum ratione visitationis debitas, nec aliquas exactiones supra
clerum contra morem dictorum sanctorum patrum indicat.   10

Item non utatur gratiis expectatiuis nisi pro suppositis uniuersitatum studiorum que rectores earundem uniuersitatum vera et non
ficta et ad hoc digna sub testimonio sue consciencie reputabunt et
nominabunt nec utatur reseruationibus ecclesiarum cathedralium,
monasteriorum aut aliorum beneficiorum quorumcumque illis que 15
corpore iuris sunt clause dumtaxat exceptis nec utatur antidatis
quoquomodo nec dispensationibus ultra morem antiquum sanctorum patrum super impedimentis consanguineitatis uel affinitatis
cognationis spiritualis uel aliis quibuscumque.

Item quod dominis cardinalibus prouideat de publico competen- 20
ter secundum statum et dignitates eorundem. Et si patrimonium
Romane ecclesie ad hoc non sufficit per concilium, reges, et principes ut supradictum est eidem taliter prouideatur quod premissam
prouisionem de publico facere valeat. Et cum hoc teneantur prefati
domini cardinales dimittere ecclesias cathedrales, monasteria et 25
alia quecumque beneficia que obtinent, et sit cautus Romanus
pontifex quod de cetero talia eis non concedat.

Item in prouisionem diuturne vacationis ecclesiarum et monasteriorum vacantium, et ut cum omni puritate de pastoribus ydoneis
illis prouideat, confirmet hoc sacrum concilium electiones dictarum 30
ecclesiarum vacantium quas reperiet canonice factas, ne in spiritualibus et temporalibus amplius patiantur detrimentum.

Additional proposals in Vat. lat. 12572:
[52v] [Extrav. 4] Ex concilio Constanciensi

Inter ceteros prelatorum excessus hic maxime inoleuit, quod 35
spreta in vestibus forma ecclesiastice honestatis plurimi delectantur
esse deformes et cupiunt laicis se conformari, quodque mente
gerunt habitu profitentur. Unde, preter ea que circa vestes, tonsur-
am et habitus clericorum tam in formis quam in coloribus atque
comam seu capillos vitamque et honestatem clericorum iura sta- 40
tuunt, et que nimium collapsa sunt tam in secularibus quam regularibus, sacro approbante consilio, [53r] innouamus et precipimus

diligentius obseruari, illum specialiter abusum eodem approbante consilio decernimus penitus abolendum: quod in quibusdam partibus clerici et persone eclesiastice seculares et regulares etiam quod magis execramur prelati eclesiarum manicas ad cubitum pendentes et longas cum magna et sumptuosa superfluitate vestes etiam scis- 5 sas retro et in lateribus cum foderaturis ultra ora excedentibus in scissuris deferunt, et cum talibus in eclesiis cum superpelliciis aut aliis vestibus ad cultum et officium eclesiasticum ordinatis etiam intra eclesias ipsas in quibus beneficiati existunt non verentur diuinis officiis interesse, hanc vestium deformitatem in quibuscum- 10 que prius eclesiasticis reprobamus ac usum talium inhibemus. Contrarium autem facientes ut transgressores canonum puniantur, specialiter statuentes ut quicumque beneficiatus aut officium in eclesia gerens in habitu huiusmodi presumpserit diuinis officiis interesse pro qualibet vice, a perceptione prouentuum ecclestiasti- 15 corum per mensem nouerit se suspensum. Fructusque illi fabrice illius ecclesie applicentur.

[47r] [Extrav. 5] Ex concilio Constanciensi

Consulta Romani pontificis, que documentis publicis inscribi sacri canones instituunt, que, ne coram Romano pontifice deducta 20 necesse sit ob fidem rei geste auctoritate publica comprobari et desuper instrumenta describi, sedi apostolice notarii et eiusdem camere clerici ipsiusque Romani pontificis secretarii ut publicis funguntur officiis instituti in monumenta publica describant et desuper instrumenta conficiant, ceterisque quibuscumque tabel- 25 lionibus quauis auctoritate conprobatis aut quouis officio publico fungentibus instrumenta seu scripta huiusmodi conficiendi potestate penitus interdicta, ne, si forte sedem apostolicam et Romanum pontificem adeuntes desuper petitis, expositis, relatis et gestis inscribi tabellionibus ibidem assistentibus ignotis instrumenta secre- 30 to mandauerint, in apostolicam sedem seu Romanum pontificem inconsulte malignandi seu molestiam inferendi in alienis partibus occasio prebentur.

INDEX BY INCIPIT

(Numerals in square brackets refer to the *ACC*)

ANONYMOUS ANNATE TRACT, "AD OSTENDENDUM" EXCERPT

A = Augsburg, Staats- und Stadtbibliothek, cod. 2° 226, p. 392
P = Paris, Bibliothèque Nationale, lat. 14644, fol. 364v

Sed et nunc ostendetur quod nec actio in rem aut aliud ius reale nasci aut produci in hoc potest; quod patet a sufficienti partium casuumque enumeratione, quia hoc non potest dici ex parte illius contra quem dicitur acquisitum, nec ex parte illius cui, nec ex parte rei. De qua primum patet quia cum natura naturans, que deus est, homines et res quascumque produxerit liberas ab earum prima creatione, ut nec homo homini nec res rei alicuius seruitutis uel oneris speciem astricti fuit, res tamen inferiores creauit ad usum et seruitiam hominis ad sui similitudinem et ymaginationem procreati et super illas ei dedit dominium, Genesi i.[1] et psalmo viiii:[2] "Omnia subiecisti sub pedibus eius oues et boues etc.", Psalmo cxiii:[3] "Terram autem dedit filiis hominum"; pro quo ff. de usuris l. In pecudum:[4] Seruitutem igitur, que nature contraria est, oportet dicentem probare, quia pro libertate stat ius commune omne, videlicet diuinum, naturale et positiuum. Et cum terram deus dedisset filiis hominum et que in ea sunt secuta distinctione dominiorum ex iure gentium, ut patet in lege Ex hoc iure ff. de iustitia et iure,[5] ex quo aliqua res mea est loquendo etiam in prophanis et eius habeo dominium et omnimodam dispositionem iuxta l. In re mandata C. Mandati,[6] in re illa nullus potest ius acquirere nisi ex meo

1 Gen. 1,26
2 Ps. 8,6
3 Ps. 115,16
4 Dig. 22.1.28
5 Dig. 1.1.5
6 Cod. 4.35.21

1 et] ex A   aliud] aliquod A   3 casuumque] et casuum P   enum.] et *add.* P   5 naturans] *corr. from* naturalis P   8 fuit] sed *add.* A   9 seruitiam] seruitium P   8 ymaginationem] ymaginem P   10 ei] et P   14 commune *om.* P   16 distinctione] in distinctione P   17 in lege] *add. in marg.* A   18 etiam] tamen P   et *om.* P   19 et] sicud *add.* P

vero et expresso consensu uel saltim presumptione, quia contrarium repugnaret nature dominii et iuris totalis quod habeo in re mea. Apparet autem quod verus aut expressus hic non interuenit consensus cleri ut iste vacancie levarentur uel imponerentur seu exigerentur, quia exigere iuxta legis diffinitionem est ab inuito 5
extorquere. Saltim oportet quod de quo constaret ex facto meo et expresso verbo uel litteris uel alio modo quo consenserim exprimi ordinant iura, nec taciturnitas in ista materia haberetur pro consensu, ymo pro expresso dissensu et contradictione. Nam quando agitur de seruitute uel onere alicui rei imponendo dominus illius 10
dicitur vere et realiter contradicens et inuitus nisi expresse consenserit, l. Inuitum ff. de seruitutibus urbanorum prediorum.[7] Et licet sit regula iuris quod qui tacet nec consentit nec dissentit, tamen in ista materia istarum seruitutum et onerum est speciale quod tacens habeatur pro expresso contradicente, ut patet dicta lex. Que mul- 15
tum est notabilis in ista materia; et ratio est quia seruitus repugnat nature et libertati, et, ut dicit alibi, lex magna est ratio, quia pro libertate facit. Preterea nec consensus presumptus potest allegari quia iuris et nature presumptione, nullus presumitur velle iactare suum, ff. de probationibus. l. Cum de indebito[8] in secundo 20
responsu; et maxime in ista materia ubi preter interesse pecunia verteretur [A 393] anime detrimentum committendo symoniam, ut supra probatum est, et imponendo seruitutem ecclesie sue, cuius tenetur conseruare libertatem, et cui a iure inhibitum est, ne illi aliquam seruitutem imponat, peccatum mortale incurreret et 25
[P365r] periurum quod prestitit in provisione sibi facta; et nemo presumitur esse inmemor sue salutis eterne.

Nunc veniendo ad secundum membrum, ostenditur quod nec ex parte camere apostolice fuit consensus imponere ecclesiis istud onus etiam reale et presertim ad perpetuum uel longum tempus. 30
Hoc primo probatur ex tenore litterarum introductionis istarum

---

7 Dig. 8.2.5
8 Dig. 22.4.25.2

20–1 meo . . . expresso] mere ac uere et expresse A   1 presumptione] presumptio MSS   3 Apparet . . . quod *om.* A   4 consensus] *in marg.* A   cleri *om.* A   6 oportet] oporteret P   meo] mero P   8 haberetur] habetur P   11 et realiter *om.* A   nisi] nec A   16 repugnat] *corr. from* expugnat (?) A   17 quia] que A   20 suum] sumi A   22 de (*second*) *om.* P secundo] tertio A   21 ubi] *corr. from* nisi A   pecunia] pecuniam MSS 22 symoniam] symoniacus (?) P   25 imponat] imponit P   incurreret] incurretur A   26 periurum . . . et *om.* A

vacantiarum, ubi expresse ponit de triennio; ergo eo finito finiuit onus. Item cum princeps teneatur viuere secundum leges, uel saltim presumatur secundam illas viuere velle, et quandocumque iura concedunt posse imponi talia onera, hoc non ad perpetuum sed modicum tempus concedunt, ut infra plenius dicetur, cum respondebitur ad rationes que videntur facere pro alia parte non presumitur illas voluisse perpetuas vel ad longum tempus.

Item non debet fieri nisi ex iusta causa et hec etiam duo requirit textus in c. Ut nostrum, Ut ecclesiastica beneficia;[9] et ista causa que potest esse iusta a principio, postmodum possit cessare uel esse iniusta; et ita non debet imponi pro perpetuo, presertim quia in dicta constitutione *Cum nonnulle*[10] dicit quod pro necessitatibus Romane ecclesie; ergo non potest esse perpetua quia necessitas cessare potest prout de facto cessauit pluries ab illo tempore citra. Item dicit Johannes Andree glosans Clementinam Si beneficiorum, De decimis,[11] *Inquam*: "Papa loquitur de decima quam aliquando concedit alicui ad tempus. Dicit sic 'Ad tempus'" Johannes dicit, "quia Curia Romana onera non consueuit inponere in perpetuum sed ad tempus nec pro futuro facere intendit." Et si non esset de illa intentione informatus, non sic scripsisset, quia tempore domini Jo. XXII, qui librum illum dedit in commune anno secundo sui pontificatus, et vixit XIX annis Johannes Andree, sed contemporaneas glosas illas scripsit.

Preterea, quod est fortius, quod non fuerat mens camere nec dominorum Cardinalium istas vacantias exigentium hoc habere pro iure reali patet euidenter ex modo exigendi, quia exigebant solutionem uel obligationem, quod idem est, ut superius est probatum, ante bullarum traditionem et possessionis et receptionem et communiter ante fructuum perceptionem. Ex quo sequitur quod non intendebant illud ius esse reale quia cum nulla actio realis detur nisi contra possessorem nec dari potest obstantibus principiis iuris que habent quod in rem accionem possessio parit, C. de alienatione mutandi iudicii causa facta, l. una,[12] et prouisus ante

---

9   X 3.12.un.
10   Extrav. comm. 3.2.11
11   Clem. 3.8.2
12   Cod. 2.54.un. *Cum in rem*

---

1 vacantiarum] vacantium MSS   4 imponi] poni A   9 in *om.* P   10 potest] potuit P   iusta] iuxta P   esse (*second*)] etiam P   19 facere] tempore P   24 fuerat] fuit P   27–28 probatum] saltim post introductum scisma *add.* P   31 dari] dare A   principiis] *corr. from* principalibus A

possessionem adeptam non sit possessor; ergo actio illa realis nondum erat nata et sine actione nemo [A 394] experitur. Ergo est impossibile dicere quod ratione oneris realis illud petierint uel exigere potuerint; et cum nemo acquirat sibi ius aliud quam quod vult acquirere, et apparet quod non intendebant acquirere ius reale cum de facto ante possessionem habitam vacantiam exigerent, quod per medium iuris realis fieri non poterat; ergo ius reale non acquisierant, cum ad hoc non intenderent et de intentione ipsorum per eorum factum apparet, et plus uel saltim tantum ostenditur alicuius voluntas facto quam verbo, ff. de legibus l. De quibus[13] cum infinitis concordantibus.

Item prout nota in dicta lege ista de alienatione iudicii mutandi causa facta sicut ex parte rei in actione reali requiritur possessio, ita ex parte actoris dominium directum uel utile, et supra probatum est quod collator beneficiorum non est nec esse potest dominus; ergo nullo modo potuit in hoc [P365v] ius reale constitui. Item camera etiam a translato qui desiit esse possessor etiam si et quando vult petit istas vacantias ergo non ratione iuris uel onere realis, quod dumtaxat habet locum contra possessorem; ex quo patet quod ipsi non potuerunt nec intenderunt ius aliquod reale in istis acquirere et per consequens acquirere non potuerunt.

Sed ad tertium veniendo quod ex parte rei de qua agitur non fuerit in istis acquisitum ius reale; et primo hoc probatur ex parte materie et ipsius indispositionis, quia hoc, si esset, competerit ex causa prouisionis facte, cum alias non esset habituri, ut supra plene est deductum. Sed ita est quod sicut prohibetur a iure obligatio personalis ita realis in prouentibus uel fructibus saltim in eo qui non perciperit commodum, nisi quia dedit in dicto c. Ut nostrum;[15] et de hoc etiam est textus i q iii c. Quesitum,[16] ibi "Venalitatem omnem tam ex rebus quam ex ministris"; etiam ergo utroque modo est prohibitum et eadem causa et questione, c. Si quis prebendas in fine:[17] "Libere absque diminitione aliqua collata sibi dignitate et beneficio perfruatur"; idem tam beatus Thomas secunda secunde questione centensima articulo primo in responsione ad ultimum

---

13 Dig. 1.3.32
14 Cod. 2.54.un.
15 X 3.12.un.
16 C.1 q.3 c.4
17 C.1 q.3 c.15

---

7 fieri] facti P   12–13 de . . . facta om. A   13 sicut] in add. P   in] add. above line P   15 collator] collatio P   16 nullo om. A   26 deductum] deductio P   27 ita] et add. P   29 Quesitum] Quantum A   31 et (first) struck out A   c. struck out A   quis] quibus A

argumentum,[18] videlicet quod papa recipiens a prouiso pecuniam quoquomodo siue de redditibus ecclesie symoniam committit. Et certe eadem seu maior est ibi ratio, quia magis videretur quod prouisus posset se obligare in fauorem prouisionis sibi facte quam quod posset ad hoc ecclesia teneri uel obligari in eius favorem. Aliud nullomodo sit sed expresse in dampnum et ita per argumentum de maiori ad minus, quod tenet, destructive obligari ecclesia non potuit nec teneri. [A 395]

Et ultra hoc magis laxando materiam etiam ad materias in quibus non caderet symonia uel aliud vicium, certum est ex determinatione concilii generalis Lateranensis, de quo habetur extra de censibus c. Prohibemus,[19] quod ecclesiasticis beneficiis nulli noui census uel onera inponantur, ut de aut super fructibus eorundem aliquid percepi possit cum decreto irritante et prohibentur indistincte et generaliter per modum precepti negatiui quod obligat semper et ad semper, preterea recipiatur textus et ratio ipsius in c. Grauis, eodem titulo,[20] ubi prohibetur quod non contingente beneficiorum vacatione caueatur ne in aut ex eorum collatione aliquis inponatur census, et etiam si obligatio uel iuramentum interuenerit non ligat. Et textus mandat eos absolui, et glosa exponit, id est absolutos nunciari, saltim non potest negari et effectiue non tenet et ad hoc propositum c. Cum clerici[21] et c. Peruenit[22] eodem titulo, ubi dicitur quod oportet "quod quando et ad quid inponitus sit census presciatur." Nunc si queritur "Quando?", respondetur quod tempore Johannis XXII, sed ad terminum finitum. Iam sunt octaginta anni. Si queritur "Ad quid?" pro vero respondebitur ad grauamen ecclesiarum et cum modo symonie uel alterius peccati mortalis, ut supra est deductum, maxime in illius continuatione et perpetuatione, quam ille etiam noluit, ut patet ex litterarum suarum tenore.

Quin ymmo, quod notandum est, statutum fuit in concilio generali Toletano, de quo habetur x q iii Quia cognouimus,[23] quod superior non potest inponere censum uel aliud onus super particu-

---

18 Thomas Aquinas, *Summa theologiae* 2^a 2^{ae} 100.1 Resp. ad Obj.7.
19 X 3.39.7
20 X 3.39.15
21 X 3.39.11
22 X 3.39.5
23 C.10 q.3 c.6

---

5 eius] cuius P   6 Aliud] Id A   10 symonia] symonie A   16 ratio ipsius] primo ipsi ius (?) P   19 etiam] per *add.* P   24 Nunc *om.* A   29 noluit] sic uoluit A   31 statutum] constitutum P

lares ecclesias nisi ea que a constitutionibus sanctorum veterum
patrum fuerunt ordinata ne videantur in dei ecclesia potius ex-
actores quam pontifices et pastores, et si de facto fiat, potest de
facto propria auctoritate a subditis denegari et illos ab illa exacta
poterunt consuetudine spoliare, ut ibi habetur; nec supportari de- 5
bet superiorum auctoritas in contraueniendo cum id de se sit
illicitum, arguit ff. de conditionibus institutionum. l. Que sub
conditione[24] c. ultimo de le in l. fidei commisa (?) c. Si quis illicite;
et notat de electione, c. Venerabilem,[25] glosa super verbo "Venite".
Et si obligatio uel iuramentum interuenerit [P366r] non tenet per 10
predictum c. Grauis[26] supra allegatum, quod bene notandum in
nostro casu quod Jo. glossator decreti intelligit de quacumque
prescriptione cuiuscumque temporis cum talia clam vi uel peccato
fuerit possessam, in c. Seruitium, circa finem magne glose, xviii q.
ii[27] ad idem glosa iii c. Duo, extra de officio ordinarii,[28] pro quo c. 15
[A 396] Conquestus ix q. iii,[29] et c. 1 xviii q. ii,[30] cum multis
similibus; et licet enim qui possedit a tanto tempore de cuius
contradictio hominum memoria non existit videantur iura in tali
possessione tueri et talem possessionem haberi pro titulo seu iure
constituti, ff. de aqua cotidiana et estiua l. Hoc iure Para. Ductus 20
aque,[31] et de prescriptionibus, c. 1 in finem libro sexto:[32] Actum ubi
esset mala fides tanti temporis prescriptio nil prodesset, presertim
de iure canonico ut ibidem notat glosa penultima, Mala fides;
autem ex eo probatur, quia super re a iure diuino et humano
prohibita hoc interuenerit, et ut dicit iuris regula, "Qui contra iura 25
mercatur bonam fidem presumitur non habere,"[33] et est presumptio iuris et de iure, ut patet per exempla ibi posita in glosa inter que
ponit exemplum: Ubi in beneficio ecclesiastico uel pretextu illius
interuenit datio pecunie violenta autem debet dici ista exactio facta
a   superiore   ad   inferiorem,   ut   supponit   dictum   c.   Quia 30

---

24 Dig. 28.7.8
25 X 1.6.34
26 X 3.39.15
27 C.18 q.2 c.31
28 X 1.31.9 *Duo sunt*
29 C.9 q.3 c.8
30 C.18 q.2 c.1 *Hoc tantum*
31 Dig. 43.20.3.4
32 VI 2.13.1
33 VI 5.12 Reg. 82

---

5 ibi habetur] uidetur habere P   5–9 nec . . . "Venite." *om.* P   15 extra]
episcopi P   18 contradictio] contrario A   iura *om.* P   25 prohibita]
prohibitos P   dicit] habet A

cognouimus,[34] et presertim ubi est talis superior qui super se alium non habet, ad quem possit haberi recursus, arguit c. Licet de vitanda[35] in fine, extra de electione, et de hoc dicetur plenius infra cum respondebitur ad rationes que videntur facere pro parta contraria.

34   C.10 q.3 c.6
35   X 1.6.6

2 arguit] argumento A

ABBREVIATIONS

ACC	*Acta concilii Constanciensis.* Ed. Heinrich Finke et al. Münster, 1896–1928.
AHC	*Annuarium historiae conciliorum*
COD	*Conciliorum oecumenicorum decreta.* 3d ed. Ed. Josephus Alberigo. Bologna, 1973.
DuPin	Gerson, Jean, *Opera omnia.* Ed. L. DuPin. Antwerp, 1706.
EHR	English Historical Review
G	Gerson, Jean, *Oeuvres complètes.* Ed. Palémon Glorieux. Paris, 1960–1968.
H	Hardt, Hermann von der, *Magnum oecumenicum Constantiense concilium.* Frankfurt and Leipzig, 1692–1700.
HZ	*Historische Zeitschrift*
Hinschius	*Decretales Pseudo-Isidoriani.* Ed. P. Hinschius. Leipzig, 1863.
Mansi	Mansi, Joannes Domenicus. *Sacrorum conciliorum nova et amplissima collectio.* Florence-Venice, 1759–1798.
MIÖG	*Mitteilungen des Instituts für Österreichische Geschichtsforschung*
QFIAB	*Quellen und Forschungen aus italienischen Archiven und Bibliotheken*
RHE	*Revue d'histoire ecclésiastique*
RQ	*Römische Quartalschrift für christliche Altertumskunde und Kirchengeschichte*
Schneyer	Schneyer, Johannes. "Konstanzer Konzilspredigten." (See bibliography.)
W	Walch, Christian Wilhelm. *Monimenta medii aevi.* Göttingen, 1757–1764
ZKG	*Zeitschrift für Kirchengeschichte*
ZRG Kan.	*Zeitschrift der Savigny-Stiftung für Rechtsgeschichte. Kanonistische Abteilung*
ZRG Rom.	*Zeitschrift der Savigny-Stiftung für Rechtsgeschichte. Romanistische Abteilung*

BIBLIOGRAPHY

Primary Sources

Manuscripts

Augsburg, Staats- und Stadtbibliothek, 2° Cod 226
Bernkastel-Kues, St. Nikolaus-Hospitalbibliothek 168
Karlsruhe, Landesbibliothek, Rei 23, 48
Paris, Bibliothèque Nationale, lat. 1485-I,II, 8902, 9514, 14457, 14644
Stuttgart, Landesbibliothek, Iur. Fol. 130, Theol. et phil. Fol. 50, 137
Tübingen, Universitätsbibliothek, Mc 282
Biblioteca Apostolica Vaticana, Pal. lat. 595, Vat. lat. 3884, 12572
Vienna, Österreichische Nationalbibliothek, lat. 3896, 4292, 4300, 4948, 4958, 5069, 5094, 5113

Printed Sources

Acta concilii Constanciensis. Ed. Heinrich Finke et al. 4 vols. Münster, 1896–1928.
Caro, J. "Aus der Kanzlei Sigismunds," Archiv für österreichische Geschichte 59 (1880) 1–176.
Clamangiis, Nicolaus de (Nicolas of Clémanges). De ruina ecclesiastica, in Alfred Coville, Le traité de la ruine de l'Église. Paris, 1936.
Conciliorum oecumenicorum decreta. 3d ed. Ed. Josephus Alberigo. Bologna, 1973.
Decretales Pseudo-Isidoriani. Ed. P. Hinschius. Leipzig, 1863.
Dietrich von Nieheim. Dialog über Union und Reform der Kirche, 1410 (De modis uniendi ac reformandi ecclesiam in concilio universali). Ed. Hermann Heimpel. Leipzig, 1933.
Döllinger, Ignaz. Beiträge zur politischen, kirchlichen und Cultur-Geschichte der sechs letzten Jahrhunderte. Vol. 2: Materialen zur Geschichte des 15. und 16. Jahrhunderts. Regensburg, 1863. Pp. 299–392.
Firnhaber, F. "Petrus de Pulka, Abgesandter der Wiener Universität am Concilium zu Constanz," Archiv für die Kunde österreichischer Geschichts-Quellen 15 (1856) 1–70, repr. Graz, 1970.
Gerson, Jean. Oeuvres complètes. Ed. Palémon Glorieux, 7 vols. Paris, 1960–1968.
———. Opera omnia. Ed. L. DuPin, 5 vols. Antwerp, 1706.
Gobelinus Persona. Cosmodromius: Cosmidromius Gobelini Person und als Anhang desselben Verfassers Processus translacionis et reformacionis monasterii Budecensis. Ed. Max Jansen. Münster, 1900.
Hardt, Hermann von der. Historia litteraria reformationis. Vol. 3. Frankfort, 1717.
———. Magnum oecumenicum Constantiense concilium. 6 vols. Frankfurt and Leipzig, 1692–1700.
Heimpel, Hermann. "Regensburger Berichte vom Konstanzer Konzil," Festschrift für Karl Gottfried Hugelmann zum 80. Geburtstag. Aalen, 1959. Vol. 1, pp. 213–279.
Koeppen, H. Die Berichte der Generalprokuratoren des Deutschen Ordens an der Kurie, vol. 2: Peter von Wormditt (1403–1419). Göttingen, 1960.
Leidinger, Georg. Sämtliche Werke des Andreas von Regensburg. Munich, 1903.

Mansi, Joannes Domenicus. *Sacrorum conciliorum nova et amplissima collectio*. 31 vols. Florence-Venice, 1759–1798, repr. Graz, 1960–61).

Martène, Edmond and Ursin Durand. *Thesaurus novus anecdotorum*, Vol. 2. Paris, 1717.

Mateusza z krakowa [Matthew of Cracow] "De praxi Romanae Curiae". Ed. Wjadyslaw Senko. Wroclaw, 1969.

Raccolta di concordati su materie ecclesiastiche tra la Santa Sede e le autorità civili. Ed. Angelo Mercati. Città del Vaticano, 1954.

Regulae cancellariae apostolicae: Die päpstliche Kanzleiregeln von Johannes XXII. bis Nikolaus V. Ed. Emil von Ottenthal. Innsbruck, 1888, repr. Aalen, 1968.

Richental, Ulrich von. *Chronik des Constanzer Conzils 1414 bis 1418*, ed. Michael Buck. Stuttgart, 1882, repr. Hildesheim, 1962.

Schneyer, Johannes. "Konstanzer Konzilspredigten," *Zeitschrift für die Geschichte des Oberrheins*, 115 (n.s. 76, 1967) 117–166; 116 (n.s. 77, 1968) 127–164; 118 (n.s. 79, 1970) 99–155; 119 (n.s. 80, 1971) 175–231; 120 (n.s. 81, 1972) 125–214.

Stephanus de Geri [Bishop of Volterra]. In "Gli avanzi dell'archivio di un Pratese vescovo di Volterra," *Archivio storico Italiano*, ser. 4, 13 (1884) 339–359.

Vidal, J.M. "Un recueil manuscrit de sermons prononcés aux conciles de Constance et de Bâle," *RHE* 10 (1909) 493–520.

Vladimiri, Paulus. "De annatis I and II," ed. M. Bobrzynski in *Rerum publicarum scientiae quae in S. XV in Polonia viguit, monumenta litteraria (Staradwne prawa Polskiego pomniki* 5). Cracow, 1878.

———. *Speculum aureum de beneficiis ecclesiasticis*. In Christian Wilhelm Walch, *Monimenta medii aevi*.

Walch, Christian Wilhelm. *Monimenta medii aevi*. Göttingen, 1757–1764, repr. London, 1966. (Contains editions of Constance sermons.)

Wilkins, David, *Concilia Magnae Britanniae et Hiberniae*, vol. 3. London, 1737. In *Councils and ecclesiastical documents relating to Great Britain and Ireland*, ed. Arthur Haddan and William Stubbs. Oxford, 1964.

Zumkeller, Adolar. "Unbekannte Konstanzer Konzilspredigten des Augustiner-Theologen Gottfried Schale und Dietrich Vrie," *Analecta Augustiniana* 33 (1970) 5–74.

Secondary Sources

Alberigo, Giuseppe. *Cardinalato e collegialità*. Florence, 1969.

———. *Chiesa conciliare: Identità e significato del conciliarismo*. Brescia, 1981.

———. "Réforme en tant que critère de l'Histoire de l'Église," *RHE* 76 (1981) 72–81.

Angermeier, Heinz. *Die Reichsreform, 1410–1555: Die Staatsproblematik in Deutschland zwischen Mittelalter und Gegenwart*. Munich, 1984.

Arendt, Paul. *Die Predigten des Konstanzer Konzils*. Freiburg, 1933.

Arquillière, H. "L'origine des théories conciliaires," *Séances et travaux de l'Académie des Sciences Morales et Politiques*, 175 (1911) 573–586.

Baix, François. *La Chambre apostolique et les "Libri Annatarum" de Martin V (1417–1431)*. Brussels and Rome, 1947.

Barraclough, Geoffrey. *Papal Provisions: Aspects of Church History Constitutional, Legal and Administrative in the Later Middle Ages* (Oxford, 1935, repr. Westport, Conn., 1971).

Bartoš, František. "Das Reformprogramm des Mag. Joh. Cardinalis von Bergreichenstein, des Gesandten der Karls Universität in Prag für das Konzil zu Konstanz," in *Festschrift Heimpel zum 70. Geburtstag*. Göttingen, 1972. Vol. 2, pp. 652–85.

Batany, Jean. "États du monde (revues de)." In *Dictionnaire des Littératures de la Langue Française*. Ed. J.-P. Beaumarchais, *et al*. Paris, 1984. Pp. 774–775.

Bäumer, Remigius. "Die Erforschung des Konstanzer Konzils," in *Das Konstanzer Konzil*. Ed. Remigius Bäumer. Darmstadt, 1977.

————. "Die Erforschung des Konziliarismus," in *Die Entwicklung des Konziliarismus*. Ed. Remigius Bäumer. Darmstadt, 1976.

Baumgarten, Paul Maria von. *Untersuchungen und Urkunken über die camera collegii cardinalium für die Zeit von 1295 bis 1437.* Leipzig, 1898.

Becker, Hans-Jürgen. *Die Appellation vom Papst an ein allgemeines Konzil: Historische Entwicklung und kanonistische Diskussion im späten Mittelalter und in der frühen Neuzeit.* Cologne, 1988.

Becker, Petrus. "Benediktinische Reformbewegungen im Spätmittelalter: Ansätze, Entwicklungen, Auswirkungen," in *Untersuchungen zu Kloster und Stift*, pp. 167–187.

————. "Erstrebte und erreichte Ziele benediktinischer Reformen im Spätmittelalter," in *Reformbemühungen und Observanzbestrebungen*, pp. 23–34.

————. "Verfall und Erneuerung des Ordenswesens im Spätmittelalter: Forschungen und Forschungsaufgaben," in *Untersuchungen zu Kloster und Stift*, pp. 188–238.

Der Begriff der Repraesentatio im Mittelalter: Stellvertretung, Symbol, Zeichen, Bild. Berlin, 1971.

Belch, Stanislaus. *Paulus Vladimiri and His Doctrine Concerning International Law and Politics.* London, 1965.

Benson, Robert. "Plenitudo potestatis: Evolution of a formula from Gregory IV to Gratian," *Studia Gratiana* 14 (1967) 193–218.

Bertagna, Bruno. "Il problema della 'plenitudo ecclesiasticae potestatis' nella dottrina ecclesiologica di Giovanni Gersone (1363–1429)," *Apollinaris* 43 (1970) 555–612.

Bess, Bernhard. "Das Bündnis von Canterbury," *MIÖG*, 22 (1901) 639–658.

————. "Die Annatenverhandlungen der 'natio gallicana' des Konstanzer Konzils," *ZKG*, 22 (1901) 48–70.

Binz, Louis. *Vie religieuse et réforme ecclésiastique dans le diocèse de Genève pendant le grand schisme et la crise conciliaire (1378–1450).* Geneva, 1973.

Black, Antony. "The Conciliar Movement," in *The Cambridge History of Medieval Political Thought.* Ed. J.H. Burns. Cambridge, Engl., 1988. Pp. 573–587.

————. *Council and Commune: The Conciliar Movement and the Fifteenth-century Heritage.* London/Shepherdstown, 1979.

————. *Monarchy and Community: Political Ideas in the Later Conciliar Controversy, 1430–1450.* Cambridge, 1970.

————. "Political Languages in Later Medieval Europe." In *The Church and Sovereignty*, pp. 313–28.

————. "The Universities and the Council of Basel: Ecclesiology and Tactics," *AHC*, 6 (1974) 341–51.

————. "What Was Conciliarism? Conciliar Theory in Historical Perspective," in *Authority and Power: Studies on Medieval Law and Government Presented to Walter Ullmann on his Seventieth Birthday.* Ed. Brian Tierney and Peter Linehan. Cambridge, Engl., 1980. Pp. 213–224.

Bliemetzrieder, Franz. *Das Generalkonzil im grossen abendländischen Schisma.* Paderborn, 1904.

Boelens, Martin. "Die Klerikerehe in der kirchlichen Gesetzgebung vom II. Laterankonzil bis zum Konzil von Basel," in *Ius sacrum: Klaus Mörsdorf zum 60. Geburtstag*, ed. Audomar Scheuermann and Georg May. Paderborn, 1969. Pp. 600–614.

Bonicelli, Silvio. *I concili particolari da Graziano al concilio di Trento.* Brescia, 1971.

Boockmann, Hartmut. *Johannes Falkenberg, der Deutsche Orden und die polnische Politik: Untersuchungen zur politischen Theorie des späteren Mittelalters.* Göttingen, 1975.

————. "Zur politischen Geschichte des Konstanzer Konzils," *ZKG* 85 (1974) 45–63.

Bourgeois du Chastenet, Louis. *Nouvelle histoire du concile de Constance.* Paris, 1718.

Brandmüller, Walter. "Besitzt das Konstanzer Dekret 'Haec sancta' dogmatische Verbindlichkeit?" *AHC* 1 (1969) 96–113.

————. "Causa reformationis: Ergebnisse und Probleme der Reformen des Konstanzer Konzils," *AHC* 13 (1981) 49–66.

————. "Das Konzil, demokratisches Kontrollorgan über den Papst?" *AHC* 16 (1984) 328–347.

————. *Das Konzil von Konstanz (1414–1418).* Vol. 1: Bis zur Abreise Sigismunds nach Narbonne. Paderborn, 1991.

Breck, Allen. "The Leadership of the English Delegation at Constance," *University of Colorado Studies* ser. B, Vol. 1, No. 3 (1941) 289–299.

Broderick, John, S.J. "The Sacred College of Cardinals: Size and Geographical Composition (1099– 1986)," *Archivum historiae pontificiae* 25 (1987) 7–72.

Brosius, Dieter. "Päpstlicher Einfluss auf die Besetzung von Bistümern um die Mitte des 15. Jahrhunderts," *QFIAB*, 56 (1976) 199–228.

Brys, Joseph. *De dispensatione in iure canonico.* Bruges, 1925.

Buisson, Ludwig. *Potestas und caritas: Die päpstliche Gewalt im Spätmittelalter.* Cologne, 1958.

Burger, Christoph. *Aedificatio, fructus, utilitas: Johannes Gerson als Professor der Theologie und Kanzler der Universität Paris.* Tübingen, 1986.

Buschbell, G. "Die professiones fidei der Päpste," *RQ*, 10 (1896) 251–97, 421–50.

Cambridge History of Medieval Political Thought c. 350 – c. 1450, ed. J.H. Burns. Cambridge, 1988.

Caron, Pier Giovanni. *"Aequitas" romana, "misericordia" patristica, ed "epicheia" aristotelica nella dottrina dell' "aequitas" canonica.* Milan, 1971.

Chambers, D.S. "Studium Urbis and *gabella studii*: the University of Rome in the fifteenth century," in *Cultural Aspects of the Italian Renaissance: Essays in Honour of Paul Oskar Kristeller.* Ed. Cecil Clough. Manchester, 1976. Pp. 68–110.

Christianson, Gerald. *Cesarini, the Conciliar Cardinal: The Basel Years, 1431–1438.* Sankt Ottilien, 1979.

Chroust, Anton. "Zu den Konstanzer Concordaten," *Deutsche Zeitschrift für Geschichtswissenschaft* 4.1 (1890) 1–13.

Chroust, Th. "The Corporate Idea and the Body Politic in the Middle Ages," *Review of Politics*, 9 (1947) 423–52.

Clergeac, André. *La Curie et les bénéfices consistoriaux: Études sur les communs et menus services (1300–1600).* Paris, 1911.

The Church and Sovereignty, c. 590–1915: Essays in honour of Michael Wilks. Ed. Diana Wood. Oxford, 1991.

Le concile et les conciles: Contribution à l'histoire de la vie conciliaire de l'Église, ed. B. Botte et al. Paris, 1960.

Combes, André. "Facteurs dissolvants et principe unificateur au Concile de Constance," *Divinitas* 5 (1961) 299–310.

————. *La théologie mystique de Gerson, profil de son évolution: Leçons professées à l'Université pontificale du Latran en janvier-février 1960.* Rome, 1963–65.

Congar, Yves. "Aspects ecclésiologiques de la quérelle entre mendiants et séculiers dans la séconde moitié du XIIIe siècle et le début du XIVe," *Archives d'histoire doctrinale et littéraire du Moyen Age,* 36 (1961) 35–151.

————. *L'ecclésiologie du haut Moyen Age.* Paris, 1968.

————. "Incidence ecclésiologique d'un thème de dévotion mariale," *Mélanges des sciences religieuses,* 8 (1951) 277–92.

————. *Die Lehre von der Kirche von Augustinus bis zum Abendländischen Schisma.* Basel, 1971.

————. *Power and Poverty in the Church.* Baltimore, 1964.

————. "Status ecclesiae," *Studia gratiana,* 15 (1972) 3–31.

The Council of Constance, trans. Louise Loomis, ed. John Mundy and Kennerly Woody. New York, 1961.

Coville, Alfred. *Jean Petit: La question du tyrannicide au commencement du XVe siècle.* Paris, 1932.

————. *Recherches sur quelques écrivains du XIVe et du XVe siècle.* Paris, 1935.

Crowder, C.M.D., "Le concile de Constance et l'édition de Von der Hardt," *RHE*, 57 (1962) 409–45.

———. "Constance Acta in English Libraries," in *Das Konzil von Konstanz*, pp. 477–517.

———. "Correspondence between England and the Council of Constance, 1414–1418," *Studies in Church History* 1 (1964), ed. C.W. Dugmore and C. Duggan, pp. 184–206.

———. "Four English Cases Determined in the Roman Curia during the Council of Constance, 1414–1418," *AHC* 12 (1980) 315–411 and 13 (1981) 67–145.

———. "Henry V, Sigismund and the Council of Constance, a reexamination," *Historical Studies* 4 (1963), ed. G.A. Hayes-McCoy, pp. 93–110.

———. "Politics and the Councils of the Fifteenth Century," *The Canadian Catholic Historical Association*, 36 (1969) 41–55.

———. *Unity, Heresy, and Reform, 1378–1460: The Conciliar Response to the Great Schism*. London, 1977.

Czismadia, A. "Die Auswirkungen der 'Bulle' von Konstanz auf die Entwicklung des Oberpatronatsrechts," *Acta Iuridica Academiae Scientiarum Hungaricae* 2 (1960) 53–82.

Dax, Lorenz. *Die Universitäten und die Konzilien von Pisa und Konstanz*. Freiburg, 1910.

Decker, Wolfgang. "Die Politik der Kardinäle auf dem Basler Konzil," *AHC*, 9 (1977) 112–53, 315–400.

Delaruelle, Étienne, E.-R. Labande, and Paul Ourliac. *L'Église au temps du Grand Schisme et de la crise conciliaire, 1378–1449*. Paris, 1962–64.

Dempf, Alois. *Sacrum imperium: Geschichts- und Staatsphilosophie des Mittelalters und der politischen Renaissance*. 3d edition. Munich, 1962.

Denifle, Heinrich. "Les délégués des universités françaises au Concile du Constance: Nouvelle rectification aux ouvrages de M. Fournier," *Revue des bibliothèques*, 2 (1892) 341–48.

Diener, Hermann. "Rubrizellen zu Kanzleiregistern Johanns XXIII. und Martins V.," *QFIAB* 39 (1959).

———. "Die Vergabe von Klöstern als Kommende durch Papst und Konsistorium (1417–1523)," *QFIAB* 68 (1988) 271–283.

Dohna, Lothar. *Reformatio Sigismundi: Beiträge zum Verständnis einer Reformschrift des fünfzehnten Jahrhunderts*. Göttingen, 1960.

Duby, Georges. *Les Trois Ordres ou l'Imaginaire du féodalisme*. Paris, 1978.

Eberhard, Winfried. "'Gemeiner Nutzen' als oppositionelle Leitvorstellung im Spätmittelalter," in *Renovatio et reformatio: Wider das Bild vom "finsteren" Mittelalter: Festschrift für Ludwig Hödl*, ed. Manfred Gerwing and Godehard Ruppert. Münster, 1985.

Ebers, Godehard. *Devolutionsrecht vornehmlich nach katholischem Kirchenrecht*. Stuttgart, 1906, repr. Amsterdam, 1965.

Ehrhardt, Arnold. "Das corpus Christi und die Korporationen im spät-römischen Recht," *ZRG Rom.*, 70 (1953) 299–347.

Elm, Kaspar. "Reform- und Observanzbestrebungen im spätmittelalterlichen Ordenswesen: Ein Überblick," in *Reformbemühungen und Observanzbestrebungen*. Pp. 3–19.

Engels, Odilo. "Der Reichsgedanke auf dem Konstanzer Konzil," *Historisches Jahrbuch*, 86 (1966) 80–106.

———. "Zur Konstanzer Konzilsproblematik in der nachkonziliaren Historiographie des 15. Jahrhunderts," in *Von Konstanz nach Trient*, pp. 233–259.

Die Entwicklung des Konziliarismus (Wege der Forschung). Ed. Remigius Bäumer. Darmstadt, 1976.

Esch, Arnold. "Simonie-Geschäft in Rom 1400: 'Kein Papst wird das tun, was dieser tut," *Vierteljahrschrift für Sozial- und Wirtschaftsgeschichte* 61 (1974), 433–457.

Eschmann, I. Th. "Bonum commune melius est quam bonum unius'," *Mediaeval Studies*, 6 (1944) 62–120.

———. "A Thomistic Glossary on the Principle of a Common Good," *Mediaeval Studies*, 5 (1943) 123–165.

Fasolt, Constantin. *Council and Hierarchy: The Political Thought of William Durant the Younger*. Cambridge, Engl., 1990.

———. "Die Erforschung von Wilhelm Durants d. J. 'Tractatus de modo generalis concilii celebrandi,'" *AHC* 12 (1980) 205–268.

———. "The Manuscripts and Editions of William Durant the Younger's 'Tractatus de modo generalis concilii celebrandi,'" *AHC* 10 (1978) 290–309.

———. "A New View of William Durant the Younger's 'Tractatus de modo generalis concilii celebrandi,'" *Traditio* 37 (1981) 291–324.

———. "Die Rezeption der Traktate des Wilhelm Durant d.J. im späten Mittelalter und in der frühen Neuzeit," in *Das Publikum politischer Theorie im 14. Jahrhundert*, ed. Jürgen Miethke. Munich, 1992.

Favier, Jean, *Les finances pontificales à l'époque du Grand Schisme d'Occident*. Paris, 1966.

———. "Temporels ecclésiastiques et taxation fiscale: le poids de la fiscalité pontificale au XIVᵉ siècle", *Journal des savants* (1964), pp. 102–27.

Figgis, John. *Studies of Political Thought from Gerson to Grotius*. 2d edition. Cambridge, 1916.

Fink, Karl August. "Die konziliare Idee im späten Mittelalter," in *Die Welt zur Zeit des Konstanzer Konzils*. Constance/Stuttgart, 1965. Pp. 119–134.

———. "Papsttum und Kirchenreform nach dem Grossen Schisma," *Theologische Quartalschrift* 126 (1946) 110– 122.

———. "Das Scheitern der Kirchenreform im 15. Jahrhundert," *Mediaevalia Bohemica*, 3 (1970) 237–244.

———. "Die Wahl Martins V.", in *Das Konzil von Konstanz*, pp. 138–151, repr. in *Das Konstanzer Konzil*, pp. 306–322.

———. "Die weltgeschichtliche Bedeutung des Konstanzer Konzils," *ZRG Kan.*, 51 (1965) 1–23.

———. "Zu den Quellen für die Geschichte des Konstanzer Konzils," in *Das Konzil von Konstanz*, pp. 471–76.

———. "Zum Finanzwesen des Konstanzer Konzils," in *Festschrift Heimpel zum 70. Geburtstag*. Göttingen, 1972. Vol. 2, pp. 627–51.

———. "Zur Beurteilung des grossen abendländischen Schismas," *ZKG*, 73 (1962) 335–43.

Finke, Heinrich. *Aus den Tagen Bonifaz' VIII*. Münster, 1902.

———. "Die Nation in den spätmittelalterlichen allgemeinen Konzilien," *Historisches Jahrbuch*, 57 (1937) 323–38.

———. *Forschungen und Quellen zur Geschichte des Konstanzer Konzils*. Paderborn, 1889.

———. "Das Quellenmaterial zur Geschichte des Konstanzer Konzils," *Zeitschrift für die Geschichte des Oberrheins*, n.s., 31 (1916) 253–75.

Fransen, Gérard. "Papes, conciles, évêques du XIIe au XVe siècle," in *Problemi di storia della Chiesa: Il Medioevo dei secoli XII–XV*. Milan, 1976.

Franzen, August. "Zur Vorgeschichte des Konstanzer Konzils," in *Das Konzil von Konstanz*, pp. 3–35.

———. "Das Konzil der Einheit," in *Das Konzil von Konstanz*.

Frenz, Thomas. "Zum Problem der Reduzierung der Zahl der päpstlichen Kanzleischreiber nach dem Konzil von Konstanz." In *Grundwissenschaften und Geschichte: Festscrift für P. Ach*. Ed. W. Schlögl and P. Herde. Kallmünz, 1976. Pp. 256–73.

Fromme, Bernhard. "Der erste Prioritätstreit auf dem Konstanzer Konzil," *RQ*, 10 (1896) 509–518.

———. *Die Spanische Nation und das Konstanzer Konzil*. Münster, 1894.

Fuhrmann, Horst. *Einfluss und Verbreitung der pseudoisidorischen Fälschungen: Von ihrem Auftauchen bis in die neuere Zeit*. Stuttgart, 1972–73.

Gardi, Andrea. "La Fiscalità pontificia tra medioevo ed età moderna," *Società e storia* 33 (1986) 509–557.

Gatzemeier, Karl. *Stellung und Politik der Kardinäle auf dem Konstanzer Konzil nach der Absetzung Johanns XXIII.* Mosbach, 1937.

Gazzaniga, J.L. "L'appel 'omisso medio' au pape et l'autorité pontificale au Moyen Age," *Revue historique du droit français et étranger* 60 (1982) 395–414.

Genet, J.-P. "English Nationalism: Thomas Polton at the Council of Constance," *Nottingham Historical Studies* 28 (1984) 60–78.

Gierke, Otto. *Das deutsche Genossenschaftsrecht.* 4 vols. Berlin, 1868–1913, repr. Graz, 1954.

Girgensohn, Dieter. "Berichte über Konklave und Papstwahl auf dem Konstanzer Konzil," *AHC* 19 (1987) 351–363.

———. *Petrus von Pulkau und die Wiedereinführung des Laienkelches.* Göttingen, 1964.

Göller, Emil. *Die päpstliche Pönitentiarie von ihrem Ursprung bis zu ihrer Umgestaltung unter Pius V.* Rome, 1907–1911.

———. "Zur Geschichte der apostolischen Kanzlei auf dem Konstanzer Konzil," *RQ* 20 (1906) 205–213.

Goñi Gaztambide, J. "Los españoles en el concilio de Constanza," *Hispania sacra*, v. 15, no. 30 (1962) 253– 386; v. 18, n. 35 (1965) 103–58; vol. 18, no. 36 (1965) 265–332.

Grayzel, S. "Jews and the Ecumenical Councils," in *The Seventy-fifth Anniversary Volume of Jewish Quarterly Review*, ed. A.A. Neumann and S. Zeitlin. Philadelphia, 1976. pp. 287–311.

Grévy-Pons, N. *Célibat et nature: Une controverse médiévale.* Paris, 1975.

Grundmann, Herbert. "Freiheit als religiöses, politisches und persönliches Postulat im Mittelalter," *HZ* 183 (1956) 23–53.

Hackett, J. "State of the Church: A Concept of the Medieval Canonists," *The Jurist*, 23 (1963) 259–290.

Haller, Johannes. *Papsttum und Kirchenreform, vier Kapitel zur Geschichte des ausgehenden Mittelalters.* Berlin, 1903, repr. Berlin 1966.

Hänggi, Erwin. Review of *Das Konzil von Konstanz.* In *Zeitschrift für schweizerische Kirchengeschichte*, 60 (1966) 187–94.

Harriss, G.L. *Cardinal Beaufort: A Study of Lancastrian Ascendancy and Decline.* Oxford, 1989.

Harvey, Margaret. "The Benefice as Property: An Aspect of Anglo-Papal relations during the pontificate of Martin V (1417–1431)" in *The Church and Wealth*, ed. W.J. Sheils and Diana Wood. Oxford, 1987, pp. 161–173.

———. *England, Rome, and the papacy, 1417–1464: The Study of a Relationship.* Manchester, Engl., 1993.

Hasenohr, Wilhelm. *Patriarch Johannes Maurosii von Antiochien.* Berlin and Leipzig, 1909.

Hashagen, Justus. *Staat und Kirche vor der Reformation: Eine Untersuchung der vorreformatorischen Bedeutung der Laieneinflüsse in der Kirche.* Essen, 1931.

Heimpel, Hermann. *Dietrich von Niem.* Münster, 1932.

———. "Konrad von Soest und Job Vener, Verfasser und Bearbeiter der Heidelberger Postillen (Glossen) zu der Berufung des Konzils von Pisa: Zum Regierungsstil am Hofe König Ruprechts von der Pfalz," *Westfalen* 51 (1973) 115–24.

———. "Studien zur Kirchen- and Reichsreform des 15. Jahrhunderts. II. Zu zwei Kirchenreform-Traktaten des beginnenden 15. Jahrhunderts: Die Reformschrift 'De praxi curiae Romanae ('Squalores Romanae curiae,' 1403) des Matthäus von Krakau und ihr Bearbeiter—Das 'Speculum aureum de titulis beneficiorum (1404/5)' und sein Verfasser," *Sitzungsberichte der Universität Heidelberg, phil.-hist. Klasse*, 1974, no. 1.

———. *Die Vener von Gmünd und Strassburg, 1162–1447.* Göttingen, 1982.

Heinemann, Wolfgang. "Zur Ständedidaxe in der deutschen Literatur des 13. – 15. Jahrhunderts," *Beiträge zur Geschichte der deutschen Sprache und Literatur (Halle)* 88 (1966) 1–90; 89 (1967) 290–403; 92 (1970) 388–437.

Helmrath, Johannes. *Das Basler Konzil, 1431–1449: Forschungsstand und Probleme.* Cologne, 1987.

————. "Kommunikation auf den spätmittelalterlichen Konzilien," in *Die Bedeutung der Kommunikation für Wirtschaft und Gesellschaft*, ed. Hans Pohl. Stuttgart, 1989. Pp. 116–172.

————. "Reform als Thema der Konzilien des Spätmittelalters," in *Christian Unity*, ed. Giuseppe Alberigo. Louvain, 1991. Pp. 75–152.

Hendrix, Scott. "In Quest of the Vera Ecclesia: The Crises of Late Medieval Ecclesiology," *Viator*, 7 (1976) 347–78.

Herde, Peter. *Audientia litterarum contradictarum: Untersuchungen über die päpstliche Justizbriefe und die päpstliche Gerichtsbarkeit vom 13. bis zum Beginn des 16. Jahrhunderts.* Vol. 1. Tübingen, 1970.

Hernandez, R. "La reforma domenicana entre los concilios de Constanza y Basilea," *Archivo Domenicano* 8 (1987) 5–50.

Hirsch, K. *Die Ausbildung der konziliaren Theorie im 14. Jahrhundert.* Vienna, 1903.

Hofmann, Hasso. *Repräsentation: Studien zur Wort- und Begriffsgeschichte von der Antike bis ins 19. Jahrhundert.* Berlin, 1974.

Hofmann, Walther. *Forschungen zur Geschichte der kurialen Behörden vom Schisma bis zur Reformation.* Rome, 1914.

Hollnsteiner, Johannes. König Sigismund auf dem Konstanzer Konzil," *MIÖG*, 41 (1926) 185–200.

————. "Studien zur Geschäftsordnung am Konstanzer Konzil," in *Abhandlungen aus dem Gebiete der mittleren und neueren Geschichte und ihre Hilfswissenschaften (Festgabe Heinrich Finke).* Münster, 1925. Pp. 240–56, reprinted in *Das Konstanzer Konzil*, pp. 121–142.

Hübler, Bernhard. *Die Constanzer Reformation und die Concordate von 1418.* Leipzig, 1867, repr. Ann Arbor, 1980.

Huppert, George. *Les Bourgeois Gentilhommes: An Essay on the Development of Elites in Renaissance France.* Chicago, 1977.

Izbicki, Thomas. "*Clericis laicos* and the canonists." In *Popes, Teachers, and Canon Law in the Middle Ages*, ed. J.R. Sweeney and S. Chodorow. Ithaca, 1989. Pp. 179–190.

————. "The Council of Ferrara-Florence and Dominican Papalism." In *Christian Unity*, ed. Giuseppe Alberigo. Louvain, 1991. Pp. 429–443.

————. "Papalist Reaction to the Council of Constance: Juan de Torquemada to the Present," *Church History* 55 (1986) 7–20.

————. *Protector of the Faith: Cardinal Johannes de Turrecremata and the Defense of the Institutional Church.* Washington, D.C., 1981.

Jacob, Ernest Fraser. *Essays in the Conciliar Epoch.* 2d edition. Manchester, 1953.

————. *The Fifteenth Century, 1399–1485.* Oxford, 1961.

————. "A Note on the English Concordat of 1418." In *Medieval Studies presented to A. Gwynn.* Ed. J.H. Watt, et al. Dublin, 1961. Pp. 349–58.

————. "Petitions for Benefices from English Universities during the Great Schism," *Transactions of the Royal Historical Society*, 4th ser. 27 (1945) pp. 41–59.

————. *The Register of Henry Chichele, Archbishop of Canterbury, 1414–1443*, 4 vols. Oxford, 1937–47.

————. "Wilkin's *Concilia* and the Fifteenth Century," *Transactions of the Royal Historical Society.* 4th ser. 15 (1932) 91–131.

Jedin, Hubert. *Bischöfliches Konzil oder Kirchenparlament? Ein Beitrag zur Ekklesiologie der Konzilien von Konstanz und Basel*, 2d ed. Basel, 1965.

————. *Geschichte des Konzils von Trient.* Freiburg, 1951– 1975.

————. "Kann der Papst Simonie begehen?" in *idem, Kirche des Glaubens—Kirche der Geschichte* 2 (Freiburg, 1966) 264–284.

Kaminsky, Howard. *A History of the Hussite Revolution.* Berkeley and Los Angeles, 1967.

————. "The Politics of France's Subtraction of Obedience from Pope Benedict XIII, 27 July, 1398," *Proceedings of the American Philosophical Society* 115 (1971) 366–97.

————. *Simon de Cramaud and the Great Schism.* New Brunswick, N.J., 1983.
Kantorowicz, Ernst. *The King's Two Bodies.* Princeton, 1957.
Keussen, Hermann. "Die Stellung der Universität Köln im Grossen Schisma und zu den Reformkonzilien des 15. Jahrhunderts," *Annalen des Historischen Vereins für den Niederrhein* 115 (1929) 225–254.
Kirsch, J.-P. *Die Finanzverwaltung des Kardinalkollegiums im XIII. und XIV. Jahrhundert.* Munster, 1895.
Kneer, August. *Die Entstehung der konziliaren Theorie: Zur Geschichte des Schismas und der kirchenpolitischen Schriftsteller, Konrad von Gelnhausen und Heinrich von Langenstein.* Rome, 1893.
Koller, Gerda. *Princeps in Ecclesia: Untersuchungen zur Kirchenpolitik Herzog Albrechts V. von Österreich.* Vienna, 1964.
König, Erich. *Kardinal Giordano Orsini (+ 1438): Ein Lebensbild aus der Zeit der Grossen Konzilien und des Humanismus.* Freiburg, 1906.
Das Konstanzer Konzil (Wege der Forschung). Ed. Remigius Bäumer. Darmstadt, 1977.
Das Konzil von Konstanz: Beiträge zu seiner Geschichte und Theologie (Festschrift H. Schäufele), ed. August Franzen, et al. Freiburg, 1964.
Koselleck, Reinhart. "Staat und Souveränität," in *Geschichtliche Grundbegriffe,* 6 (Stuttgart, 1990), pp. 1–154.
Krämer, Werner. *Konsens und Rezeption: Verfassungsprinzipien der Kirche im Basler Konziliarismus.* Münster, 1980.
————. "Die ekklesiologische Auseinandersetzung um die wahre Repräsentation auf dem Basler Konzil," in *Der Begriff der repraesentatio,* pp. 202–37.
Kummer, Franz. *Die Bischofswahlen in Deutschland zur Zeit des grossen Schismas, 1378–1418.* Jena, 1892.
Küng, Hans. *Strukturen der Kirche.* Freiburg, 1962.
Kurdziałek, Marian. "Der Mensch als Abbild des Kosmos," in *Der Begriff der repraesentatio,* pp. 35–75.
Kvapil, Bohumil. "Mistr Mařik Rvačka," in *Sborník J.B. Novákovi* (Festschrift J.B. Novák). Prague, 1932. Pp. 192–99.
Ladner, Gerhart. "Aspects of Mediaeval Thought on Church and State," *Review of Politics,* 9 (1947) 403–22.
"The Concepts: Ecclesia, Christianitas, plenitudo postestatis," *Miscellanea historiae pontificiae,* 19 (1954) 49–78.
————. *The Idea of Reform.* Cambridge, Mass., 1959.
————. *Images and Ideas in the Middle Ages: Selected Studies in History and Art.* 2 vols. Rome, 1983.
————. "Die mittelalterliche Reform-Idee und ihr Verhältnis zur Idee der Renaissance," *MIÖG,* 60 (1952) 31–59.
————. "Terms and Ideas of Renewal in the Twelfth Century," in *Renaissance and Renewal in the Twelfth Century.* Ed. Robert Benson, et al. Cambridge, Mass., 1982.
————. "Two Gregorian Letters: On the Sources and Nature of Gregory's Reform Ideology," *Studi gregoriani,* 5 (1956) 221–242.
————. "Vegetation Symbolism and the Concept of Reanissance," in *De artibus opuscula XL.* Essays in Honor of Erwin Panofsky. Edited by Millard Meiss. New York, 1961. Vol. 1, pp. 303–22.
Ladner, Pascal. "Der Ablass-Traktat des Heymericus de Campo: Ein Beitrag zur Geschichte des Basler Konzils," *Zeitschrift für Schweizerische Kirchengeschichte* 71 (1977) 93–140.
Laehr, Gerhard. "Die Konstantinische Schenkung in der abendländischen Literatur des ausgehenden Mittelalters," *QFIAB* 23 (1932) 120–81.
Lagarde, Georges de. *La naissance de l'esprit laïque au déclin du moyen âge,* 5 vols. Louvain, 1956–1963.
Landi, Aldo. *Il papa deposto (Pisa 1409): L'idea conciliare nel Grande Schisma.* Turin, 1985.

Lauterbach, K.H. *Geschichtsverständnis, Zeitdidaxe, und Reformgedanke an der Wende zum sechzehnten Jahrhundert.* Freiburg, 1985.

LeGoff, Jacques. *Le bourse et la vie: Économie et religion au Moyen Age.* Paris, 1986.

———. *L'Imaginaire médiéval: Essais.* Paris, 1985.

Lehmann, Paul. "Konstanz und Basel als Büchermärkte während der grossen Kirchenversammlungen," *Zeitschrift des deutschen Vereins für Buchwesen und Schrifttum,* 4 (1921) 6–11, 17–27, repr. in Lehman, Paul. *Erforschung des Mittelalters* 4 (Stuttgart, 1961) 189–205.

Lenfant, Jacques. *Histoire du Concile de Constance.* Amsterdam, 1714.

Lenné, Albert. "Die erste literarische Kampf auf dem Konstanzer Konzil im November und Dezember 1414," *RQ,* 28 (1914) 3–40 and 61–86.

Loomis, Louise. "The Organization by Nations at Constance," *Church History,* 1 (1932) 191–210.

———. "Nationality at the Council of Constance: An Anglo–French Dispute," *American Historical Review,* 44 (1939) 508–27.

Lovejoy, Arthur and George Boas. *Primitivism and Related Ideas in Antiquity.* New York, 1965.

Lubac, Henri de. *Corpus mysticum: L'eucharistie et l'Église au Moyen âge,* 2d ed. Paris, 1949.

———. *Exégèse médiévale: Les quatres sens de l'Écriture.* Paris, 1959–1964.

Lulvès, Jean. "Die Machtbestrebungen des Kardinalkollegiums gegenüber dem Papsttum," *MIÖG,* 35 (1914) 455–83.

———. "Päpstliche Wahlkapitulationen," *QFIAB,* 12 (1909) 212–235.

Lumpe, Adolf. "Zur Bedeutungsgeschichte des Verbums 'reformare' und seiner Ableitungen," *AHC* 14 (1982) 1–12.

———. "Zu repraesentare und praesentare im Sinne von 'rechtsgültig vertreten,'" *AHC* 6 (1974) 272–90.

Lunt, William. *Financial Relations of the Papacy with England, 1327–1534.* Cambridge, Mass., 1962.

———. *Papal Revenues in the Middle Ages.* New York, 1934.

Maccarrone, Michele. *'Vicarius Christi': Storia del titolo papale.* Rome, 1952.

MacGowen, John. *Pierre d'Ailly and the Council of Constance.* Washington, D.C., 1936.

MacGrade, Arthur. *The Political Thought of William of Ockham: Personal and Institutional Principles.* Cambridge, 1974.

Madre, Alois. *Nikolaus von Dinkelsbühl, Leben und Schriften.* Münster, 1965.

Mályusz, Elemér. *Kaiser Sigismund in Ungarn, 1387–1437.* Budapest, 1990.

———. *Das Konstanzer Konzil und das königliche Patronatsrecht in Ungarn.* Budapest, 1959.

Mann, Jill. *Chaucer and Medieval Estates Satire: The Literature of Social Classes and the General Prologue to the Canterbury Tales.* Cambridge, 1973.

Manz, Luise. *Der Ordo-Gedanke: Ein Beitrag zur Frage des mittelalterliche Ständesgedankens.* Stuttgart/Berlin, 1937.

Marongiu, Antonio. "La parola stato," *Rivista internazionale di filosofia del diritto* 50 (1973) 723–753.

Martin, Victor. *Les origines du Gallicanisme.* Paris, 1939, repr. Geneva, 1978.

Matthiessen, Wilhelm. "Ulrich Richenthals Chronik des Konstanzer Konzils: Studien zur Behandlung eines universalen Grossereignisses durch die bürgerliche Chronistik," *AHC* 17 (1985) 71–192.

McDonald, Peter. "The Papacy and Monastic Observance in the Later Middle Ages: The *Benedictina* in England," *Journal of Religious History* 14 (1986) 117–132.

McFarlane, K.B. "Henry V, Bishop Beaufort, and the Red Hat, 1417–1421," *EHR* 60 (1945) 316–348.

Mersch, Émile. *Le corps mystique du Christ.* Paris, 1933.

Mertens, Dieter. "Reformkonzilien und Ordensreform im 15. Jahrhundert," in *Reformbemühungen und Observanzbestrebungen,* pp. 431–457.

——. "Riforma monastica e potere temporale nella Germania sud-occidentale prima della Riforma," in *Strutture ecclesiastiche in Italia e in Germania prima della Riforma*, ed. Paolo Prodi and Peter Johanek. Bologna, 1984. Pp. 171–205.

Merzbacher, Friedrich, "Die ekklesiologische Konzeption des Kardinals Francesco Zabarella (1360– 1417)" in *Festschrift Karl Pivec*, ed. Anton Haidachers et al. Innsbruck, 1966. Pp. 279–87.

——. "Wandlungen des Kirchenbegriffs im Spätmittelalter," *ZRG Kan.* 39 (1953) 274–361.

Meuthen, Erich. *Das Trierer Schisma von 1430 auf dem Basler Konzil: Zur Lebensgeschichte des Nikolaus von Kues.* Münster, 1964.

Meyer, Andreas. "Das Wiener Konkordat von 1448— eine erfolgreiche Reform des Spätmittelalters," *QFIAB* 66 (1986) 108–152.

——. *Zürich und Rom: Ordentliche Kollatur und päpstliche Provisionen am Frau- und Grossmünster 1316–1523.* Tübingen, 1986.

Michaud-Quantin, Pierre. *Études sur le vocabulaire philosophique du Moyen Age.* Rome, 1971.

——. *Universitas: Expressions du mouvement communautaire dans le moyen âge latin.* Paris, 1970.

Miethke, Jürgen, "Die Konzilien als Forum der öffentlichen Meinung im 15. Jahrhundert," *Deutsches Archiv* 37 (1981) 736–773.

Millet, Hélène. "Du conseil au concile: Recherches sur la nature des assemblées du clergé en France pendant le Grand Schisme d'Occident," *Journal des savants* (1985) 137–159.

Mirus, J. "On the Deposition of Popes for Heresy," *Archivum Historiae Pontificiae* 13 (1975) 131– 148.

Mohl, Ruth. *The Three Estates in Medieval and Renaissance Literature.* New York, 1933.

Mollat, Guillaume, *La collation des bénéfices ecclésiastiques sous les papes d'Avignon, 1305–1378.* Paris, 1921.

——. "Contribution à l'histoire du Sacré Collège de Clément V à Eugène IV," *RHE* 46 (1951) 22–112.

——. "Les origines du gallicanisme parlementaire au XIVe et XVe siècles," *RHE* 43 (1948) 90–147.

——. *Les papes d'Avignon.* Paris, 1964.

Moore, R. "Heresy as Disease." In *The Concept of Heresy in the Middle Ages*, 1–11. Louvain, 1976.

Moraw, Peter, "Kanzlei und Kanzleipersonal König Ruprechts," *Archiv für Diplomatik* 15 (1969) 428–531.

——. "Die kurfürstliche Politik der Pfalzgrafschaft im Spätmittelalter, vornehmlich im späten 14. u. frühen 15. Jahrhundert," *Jahrbuch für westdeutsche Landesgeschichte* 9 (1983) 75–97.

Morrall, John. *Gerson and the Great Schism.* Manchester, 1960.

Morrison, Karl. *The Mimetic Tradition of Reform in the West.* Princeton, 1982.

——. *Tradition and Authority in the Western Church, 300–1140.* Princeton, 1969.

Morrissey, Thomas, "Cardinal Franciscus Zabarella (1360–1417) as a Canonist and the Crisis of his Age: Schism and the Council of Constance," *Zeitschrift für Kirchengeschichte* 96 (1985) 196–208.

——. "Cardinal Zabarella on Papal and Episcopal Authority," in *Proceedings of the Patristic, Medieval, and Renaissance Conference*, vol. 1. Villanova, Pennsylvania, 1976, pp. 39–52.

——. "The Decree 'Haec Sancta' and Cardinal Zabarella: His Role in its Formulation and Interpretation," *AHC* 10 (1978) 145–176.

——. "The Emperor-elect Sigismund, Cardinal Zabarella, and the Council of Constance," *Catholic Historical Review* 69 (1983) 353–370.

——. "Franciscus Zabarella (1360–1417): Papacy, Community, and the Limitations on Authority," in *Reform and Authority in the Medieval and Reformation Church*, ed. Guy Lytle. Washington, D.C., 1981, pp. 37–54.

——. "Surge, Illuminare: A Lost Address by Richard Fleming at the Council of

Constance [Clm 28433]" *AHC* 22 (1990) 86–130.

Mulder, W. "Leonardus Statius auf dem Konstanzer Konzil." In *Abhandlungen aus dem Gebiete der mittleren und neueren Geschichte (Festgabe H. Finke)*, 257–269. Münster, 1925.

Müller, Heribert. "Der bewunderte Erbfeind: Johannes Haller, Frankreich und das Französische Mittelalter," *HZ* 252 (1991) 265–317.

———. *Die Franzosen, Frankreich und das Basler Konzil (1431–1449)*. 2 vols. Paderborn, 1990.

———. "Lyon et le Concile de Bâle: Etudes prosopographiques," *Cahiers d'histoire* 28, n. 4 (1983), 33–57.

Myers, A.R. *The Household of Edward IV: The Black Book and the Ordinance of 1478*. Manchester, 1959.

Nimmo, Duncan. "The Franciscan Regular Observance: The Culmination of Medieval Franciscan Reform," in *Reformbemühungen und Observanzbestrebungen*, pp. 189–205.

———. *Reform and Division in the Medieval Franciscan Order, from Saint Francis to the Foundation of the Capuchins*. Rome, 1987.

———. "Reform at the Council of Constance: The Franciscan Case." In *Renaissance and Renewal in Church History* (Studies in Church History, vol. 14, ed. Derek Baker; Oxford, 1977), pp. 159–174.

Oakley, Francis. "Figgis, Constance, and the Divines of Paris," *AHR* 75 (1969) 368–86.

———. *Omnipotence, Covenant, and Order: An Excursion in the History of Ideas from Abelard to Leibniz*. Ithaca, 1984.

———. *The Political Thought of Pierre d'Ailly: The Voluntarist Tradition*. New Haven, 1964.

———. "Pseudo-Zabarella's *Capitula agendorum*: An Old Case Reopened," *AHC* 14 (1982) 111–123.

———. *The Western Church in the Later Middle Ages*. Ithaca, 1979.

Oberman, Heiko. "'Et tibi dabo claves regni caelorum': Kirche und Konzil von Augustin bis Luther. Tendenzen und Ergebnisse II," *Nederlands Theologisch Tijdschrift* 29 (1975) 97–188.

———. *The Harvest of Medieval Theology*. Cambridge, Mass., 1963.

Olsen, Glenn. "The Idea of the Ecclesia primitiva in the Writings of the Twelfth-Century Canonists," *Traditio* 25 (1969) 61–86.

O'Malley, John. "Fulfillment of the Christian Golden Age under Pope Julius II," *Traditio* 25 (1969) 265–338.

———. *Giles of Viterbo on Church and Reform: A Study in Renaissance Thought*. Leiden, 1968.

Ouy, Gilbert. "Simon de Plumetot (1371–1443) et sa bibliothèque," in *Miscellanea codicologica F. Masai dicata*. Ghent, 1979. Pp. 353–81.

Ozment, Steven. "The University and the Church: Patterns of Reform in Jean Gerson," *Mediaevalia et Humanistica* n.s. 1 (1970) 111–126.

Pantin, William. *The English Church in the Fourteenth Century*. Cambridge, Engl., 1955; repr. Toronto, 1980.

Partner, Peter. *The Papal State under Martin V: The Administration and Government of the Temporal Power in the Early Fifteenth Century*. London, 1958.

———. "Papal Financial Policy in the Renaissance and Counter-Reformation," *Past and Present* 88 (1980), 17–62.

———. *The Pope's Men: The Papal Civil Service in the Renaissance*. Oxford, 1990.

Pascoe, Louis. *Jean Gerson: Principles of Church Reform*. Leiden, 1973.

———. "Jean Gerson: Mysticism, Conciliarism, and Reform," *AHC* 6 (1974) 379–409.

———. "Jean Gerson: The 'Ecclesia Primitiva' and Reform," *Traditio* 30 (1974) 379–409.

———. "Nobility and Ecclesiastical Office in Fifteenth-Century Lyons," *Mediaeval Studies* 38 (1976) 313–331.

————. "Religious Orders, Evangelical Liberty, and Reform in the Thought of Jean Gerson," in *Reformbemühungen und Observanzbestrebungen*, pp. 504–511.

————. "Theological Dimensions of Pierre d'Ailly's Teaching on Papal Plenitude of Power," *AHC* 11 (1979) 357–366.

Paulus, Nicolaus. *Geschichte des Ablasses im Mittelalter vom Ursprunge bis zur Mitte des 14. Jahrhunderts.* Paderborn, 1922–1923.

Pennington, Kenneth. *Pope and Bishops: The Papal Monarchy in the Twelfth and Thirteenth Centuries.* Philadelphia, 1984.

Peterson, David. "Conciliarism, Republicanism, and Corporatism: The 1415–1420 Constitution of the Florentine Clergy," *Renaissance Quarterly* 42 (1989) 183–226.

Petry, R.C. "Unitive Reform Principles of the Late Medieval Conciliarists," *Church History* 31 (1967) 164–181.

Pichler, Isfried. *Die Verbindlichkeit der Konstanzer Dekrete: Untersuchungen zur Frage der Interpretation und Verbindlichkeit der Superioritätsdekrete "Haec sancta" und "Frequens."* Vienna, 1967.

Pichler, Johannes. *Necessitas: Ein Element des mittelalterlichen und neuzeitlichen Rechts.* Berlin, 1983.

Podlech, Adalbert. "Repräsentation," in *Geschichtliche Grundbegriffe*, 5 (Stuttgart, 1984), pp. 509–549.

Post, Gaines. *Studies in Medieval Legal Thought: Public Law and the State, 1100–1322.* Princeton, 1964.

Posthumus Meyjes, G.H.M. "Exponents of Sovereignty: Canonists as Seen by Theologians in the Late Middle Ages," in *Church and Sovereignty*, pp. 299–328.

————. *Jean Gerson: Zijn kerkpolitiek en ecclesiologie.* 's-Gravenhage, 1963.

Pouchelle, Marie-Christine. *Corps et chirurgie à l'apogée du Moyen Age: Savoir et imaginaire du corps chez Henri de Mondeville, chirurgien de Philippe le Bel.* Paris, 1983.

Powers, George. *Nationalism at the Council of Constance.* Washington, D.C., 1927.

Prosperi, Adriano. "'Dominus beneficiorum': il conferimento dei benefici ecclesiastici tra prassi curiale e ragioni politiche negli stati italiani tra '400 e '500," in *Strutture ecclesiastiche in Italia e in Germania prima della Riforma*, ed. Paolo Prodi and Peter Johanek. Bologna, 1984. Pp. 51–86.

Quicke, Fr. "Les relations diplomatiques entre le Roi des Romains Sigismond et la Nation de Bourgogne," *Bulletin de la Commission royale d'histoire; Académie royale des sciences, des lettres, et des beaux-arts de Belgique* 90 (1926) 193–241.

Quillet, Jeannine. "Universitas populi et représentation au XIV⁰ siècle," in *Der Begriff der repraesentatio*, pp. 186–201.

Quirk, R.N. "Bishop Robert Hallum and the Council of Constance," in *Friends of Salisbury Cathedral: Twenty-second Annual Report* (1952) 3–15.

Rashdall, *The Universities of Europe in the Middle Ages*, ed. F.M. Powicke and A.B. Emden (Oxford, 1936).

Reformbemühungen und Observanzbestrebungen im spätmittelalterlichen Ordenswesen, ed. Kaspar Elm. Berlin, 1989.

Riedlinger, Helmut. "Hermeneutische Überlegungen zu den Konstanzer Dekreten," in *Das Konzil von Konstanz.*

Riegel, Johannes. *Die Teilnehmerlisten des Konstanzer Konzils: Ein Beitrag zur mittelalterlichen Statistik.* Freiburg, 1916.

Rössler, Augustin. *Cardinal Johannes Dominici, O.P.: Ein Reformatorenbild aus der Zeit des grossen Schisma.* Freiburg, 1893.

Ryder, Alan. *Alfonso the Magnanimous: King of Aragon, Naples, and Sicily, 1396–1458.* Oxford, 1990.

Salembier, Louis. *Le Cardinal Pierre d'Ailly, chancelier de l'Université de Paris, évêque du Puy et de Cambrai, 1350–1420.* Tourcoing, 1932.

Samaran, Charles and Guy Mollat. *La fiscalité pontificale en France au XIV siècle (période d'Avignon et grand schisme d'Occident).* Paris, 1905.

Sawicki, John and Stump, Phillip H. "New Evidence of the Reform Committee at the Council of Constance in Vat. lat. 3884," *Bulletin of Medieval Canon Law,* n.s. 8 (1978) 50–55.

Schimmelpfennig, Bernard. "Der Papst als Territorialherr im 15. Jahrhundert," in *Europa 1500,* ed. Ferdinand Seibt and Winfried Eberhard. Stuttgart, 1987. Pp. 84–95.

Schmiedel, Hans. *Nikolaus Lubich (1360–1431): Ein detuscher Kleriker im Zeitalter des grossen Schismas und der Konzilien, Bischof von Merseburg, 1411–1431.* Berlin, 1911, repr. 1965.

Schneider, Hans. *Der Konziliarismus als Problem der neueren katholischen Theologie: Die Geschichte der Auslegung der Konstanzer Dekrete von Febronius bis zur Gegenwart.* Berlin, 1976.

———. "Die Siegel des Konstanzer Konzils: Ein Beitrag zur Geschichte der spätmittelalterlichen Reformkonzile," *AHC* 10 (1978) 310–345.

Schneyer, Johannes Baptist. "Neuaufgefundene Konstanzer Konzilspredigten," *AHC* 2 (1970) 66–77.

Schreiner, Klaus. "Mönchtum im Geist der Benediktregel: Erneuerungswille und Reformstreben im Kloster Blaubeuren während des hohen und späten Mittelalters," in *Blätter für Württembergische Kirchengeschichte* 86 (1986) 105–95.

Schüssler, Hermann. *Der Primat der Heiligen Schrift als theologisches und kanonistisches Problem im Spätmittelalter.* Wiesbaden, 1977.

Schwarz, Brigide. "Die Abbreviatoren unter Eugen IV.: Päpstliches Reservationsrecht, Konkordatspolitik und kuriale Ämterorganisation," *QFIAB* 60 (1980) 33–107.

———. "Die Entstehung der Ämterkäuflichkeit an der Römischen Kurie," in *Ämterhandel im Spätmittelalter und in 16. Jahrhundert.* Berlin, 1984. Pp. 61–65.

———. *Die Organisation kurialer Schreiberkollegien von ihrer Entstehung bis zur Mitte des 15. Jahrhunderts.* Tübingen, 1972.

Seibt, Ferdinand. "Geistige Reformbewegungen zur Zeit des Konstanzer Konzils," in *Die Welt zur Zeit des Konstanzer Konzils,* pp. 31–46; repr. in *Das Konstanzer Konzil,* pp. 323–44.

Seidlmayer, Michael. *Die Anfänge des grossen abendländischen Schismas: Studien zur Kirchenpolitik insbesondere der spanischen Staaten und zu den geistigen Kämpfen der Zeit.* Münster, 1940.

Sieben, Hermann. *Traktate und Theorien zum Konzil: Vom Beginn des Grossen Schismas bis zum Vorabend der Reformation (1378–1521).* Frankfort, 1983.

Sikes, J.K. "John de Pouilli and Peter de la Palu," *EHR* 49 (1934) 219–240.

Silano, Giulio. "Episcopal Elections and the Apostolic See. The Case of Aquileia: 1251–1420," in *Diritto e potere nella storia europea: Atti in onore di Bruno Paradisi.* Florence, 1982. Pp. 163–194.

Souchon, Martin. *Die Papstwahlen in der Zeit des Grossen Schismas.* Braunschweig, 1898–1899, repr. Aalen, 1970.

Sousa Costa, António. "Due 'sermones' sui Concili Ecumenici dei teologi portoghesi del secolo XV: Fra Andrea Dias e Fra Andrea do Prado," in *Proceedings of the Seventh International Congress of Medieval Canon Law.* Città del Vaticano, 1988. Pp. 385–403.

———. *Mestré André Dias de Escobar.* Rome, 1967.

Stieber, Joachim. *Pope Eugenius IV, the Council of Basel and the Secular and Ecclesiastical Authorities in the Empire.* Leiden, 1978.

Stockmeier, Peter. "Causa Reformationis und Alte Kirche: Zum Geschichtsverständnis der Reformbewegungen," in *Von Konstanz nach Trient.* Ed. Remigius Bäumer. Munich, 1972, pp. 1–13.

Storey, Robin. "Clergy and the Common Law in the Reign of Henry IV," *Medieval Legal Records edited in Memory of C.A.F. Meekings,* ed. R.F. Hunnisett and J.B. Post. London, 1978, pp. 342–408.

———. "Recruitments of English Clergy in the Period of the Conciliar Movement," *AHC* 7 (1975) 290–313.

Strnad, Alfred. "Konstanz und der Plan eines deutschen 'Nationalkardinals.'

Neue Dokumente zur Kirchenpolitik König Siegmunds von Luxemburg," in *Das Konzil von Konstanz*, pp. 397–428.
Stump, Phillip, "The Official Acta of the Council of Constance in the Edition of Mansi," in *The Two Laws: Studies in Medieval Legal History Dedicated to Stephan Kuttner*, ed. Laurent Mayali and Stephanie Tibbetts. Washington, D.C., 1990.
———. "The Reform of Papal Taxation at the Council of Constance (1414–1418)," *Speculum* 64 (1989) 69–105.
Suarez Fernandez, Luis. *Castilla, el cisma y la crisis conciliar (1378–1440)*. Madrid, 1960.
Swanson, R.N. *Universities, Academics, and the Great Schism*. Cambridge, Engl., 1979.
Szentirmai, Alexander. "De 'iure supremi patronatus' regum Hungariae," *Monitor ecclesiasticus* 86 (1961) 281–291.
Sznuro, Joseph. "Les origines du droit d'alternative bénéficiale," *Revue des sciences religieuses* 5 (1925) 1–13, 389–415; 6 (1926) 1–25.
Tatnall, Edith. "The Condemnation of John Wyclif at the Council of Constance," in *Councils and Assemblies*. Ed. C.J. Cuming and Derek Baker. Cambridge, Engl., 1971. Pp. 209–218.
Thompson, John. *Popes and princes, 1417–1517: Politics and Polity in the Late Medieval Church*. London, 1980.
Tierney, Brian. "'Divided Sovereignty' at Constance: A Problem of Medieval and Early Modern Political Theory," *AHC* 7 (1975) 238–256.
———. *Church, Law, and Constitutional Thought in the Middle Ages*. London, 1979.
———. *The Foundations of the Conciliar Theory: The Contribution of the Canonists from Gratian to the Great Schism*. Cambridge, 1955.
———. "Hermeneutics and History," in *Essays in Medieval History Presented to Bertie Wilkinson*, ed. T.A. Sandquist and F.M. Powicke. Toronto, 1969. Pp. 354–70.
———. "Ockham, the Conciliar Theory, and the Canonists," *Journal of the History of Ideas* 15 (1954) 40–70, reprinted with bibliographic introduction by Heiko Oberman, Philadelphia, 1974.
———. *Religion, Law, and the Growth of Constitutional Thought, 1150–1650*. Cambridge, 1982.
Tillinghast, Pardon. "An Aborted Reformation: Germans and Papacy in the Mid-Fifteenth Century," *Journal of Medieval History* 2 (1976) 57–79.
Trexler, Richard. "The Bishop's Portion: Generous Pious Legacies in the Late Middle Ages in Italy," *Traditio* 28 (1972) 397–450; repr. Richard Trexler, *Church and Community, 1200–1600: Studies in the History of Florence and New Spain*. Rome, 1987. Pp. 289–353.
Tschackert, Paul. *Peter von Ailli*. Gotha, 1877.
Ullmann, Walter. *The Origins of the Great Schism: A Study in Fourteenth-century Ecclesiastical History*. London, 1948.
———. "The Legality of the Papal Electoral Pacts," *Ephemerides iuris canonici* 12 (1956) 3–25.
Untersuchungen zu Kloster und Stift. Göttingen, 1980.
Valois, Noël. *La France et le Grand Schisme d'Occident*. Paris, 1896–1902.
Vincke, Johannes. "Die Königin-Witwe Violant von Aragon im Wirkungsbereich des Konstanzer Konzils," in *Von Konstanz nach Trient*, pp. 27–46.
Von Konstanz nach Trient: Beiträge zur Geschichte der Kirche von den Reformkonzilien bis zum Tridentinum. Festgabe für August Franzen. Ed. Remigius Bäumer. Paderborn, 1972.
Vooght, Paul de. "Jean Huss et ses juges," in *Das Konzil von Konstanz*, pp. 152–173.
———. "Le concile oecuménique de Constance et le conciliarisme," *Istina* 10 (1963) 57–86.
———. "Le conciliarisme aux conciles de Constance et Bâle," in *Le concile et les conciles*, ed. O. Rousseau. Paris, 1960, pp. 143–181.
———. "Le conciliarisme aux conciles de Constance et de Bâle. Compléments et précisions," *Irenikon* 36 (1968) 61–75.

————. *Les pouvoirs du concile et l'autorité du pape au concile de Constance: Le décret Haec sancta synodus du 6 avril 1415*. Paris, 1965.

Walther, Rudolf. "Stand, Klasse," in *Geschichtliche Grundbegriffe*, 6 (Stuttgart, 1990) pp. 155–284.

Wefers, Sabine. *Das politische System Kaiser Sigmunds*. Stuttgart, 1989.

Weiss, Sabine. "Päpstliche Expectanzen in Theorie und Praxis," in *Ecclesia peregrinans: Josef Lenzenweger zum 70. Geburtstag*, ed. Karl Amon, et al. Vienna, 1986, pp. 143–152.

Die Welt zur Zeit des Konstanzer Konzils: Reichenau Vorträge im Herbst 1964. Constance, 1965.

Wenck, Karl. "Konrad von Gelnhausen und die quellen der konziliaren Theorie," *HZ* 76 (1896) 6–61.

Werminghoff, Albert. "Ständische Probleme in der Geschichte der deutschen Kirche des Mittelalters," *ZRG kan.* 1 (1911) 33–67.

Wohlhaupter, E. *Aequitas canonica*. Munich, 1931.

Wolgast, Eike. "Reform, Reformation," in *Geschichtliche Grundbegriffe*, 5 (Stuttgart, 1984) 313–360.

Wriedt, Klaus. "Der Heidelberger Hof und die Pisaner Kardinäle: Zwei Formen des Konzilsgedankens," in *Aus Reichsgeschichte und nordischer Geschichte (Festgabe für K. Jordan)*, ed. Horst Fuhrmann, et al. Kiel, 1972.

Yunck, John. "Economic Conservatism, Papal Finance and the Medieval Satires on Rome," *Mediaeval Studies* 23 (1961) 334–351.

Zacour, Norman. "Papal Regulations of Cardinals' Households in the Fourteenth Century," *Speculum* 50 (1975) 434–55.

Zeller, Joseph. "Das Provinzialkapitel im Stifte Petershausen im Jahre 1417: Ein Beitrag zur Geschichte der Reformen im Benediktinerorden zur Zeit des Konstanzer Konzils," *Studien und Mitteilungen zur Geschichte des Benediktinerordens und seiner Zweige* 41 (n.s. 10, 1921/22) 1–73.

Zimmermann, Harald. "Die Absetzung der Päpste auf dem Konstanzer Konzil," in *Das Konzil von Konstanz*, pp. 113–137 at pp. 129–135.

————. *Papstabsetzungen des Mittelalters*. Graz, 1968.

Zumkeller, Adolar. "Die Beteilung der Mendikanten an der Arbeit der Reformkonzilien von Konstanz und Basel," in *Reformbemühungen und Observanzbestrebungen*, pp. 459–467.

————. *Leben, Schrifttum und Lehrrichtung des Erfurter Universitätsprofessors Johannes Zachariae O.S.A. († 1428)*. Würzburg, 1984.

————. *Manuskripte von Werken der Autoren des Augustiner-Eremitenordens in mitteleuropäischen Bibliotheken*. Würzburg, 1966.

Zwölfer, Richard. "Die Reform der Kirchenverfassung auf dem Konzil zu Basel," *Basler Zeitschrift für Geschichte und Altertumskunde* 28 (1929) 141–247 and 29 (1930) 1–58.

INDEX OF PERSONS AND PLACES

INDEX OF MODERN SCHOLARS

INDEX OF BIBLICAL TEXTS

INDEX OF LEGAL CITATIONS

INDEX OF SUBJECTS

Studies in the History
of Christian Thought

EDITED BY HEIKO A. OBERMAN

50. HOENEN, M. J. F. M. *Marsilius of Inghen*. Divine Knowledge in Late Medieval Thought. 1993
51. O'MALLEY, J. W., IZBICKI, T. M. and CHRISTIANSON, G. (eds.) *Humanity and Divinity in Renaissance and Reformation*. Essays in Honor of Charles Trinkaus. 1993
52. REEVE, A. (ed.) and SCREECH, M. A. (introd.) *Erasmus' Annotations on the New Testament*. Galatians to the Apocalypse. 1993
53. STUMP, Ph. H. *The Reforms of the Council of Constance (1414-1418)*. 1994
54. GIAKALIS, A. *Images of the Divine*. The Theology of Icons at the Seventh Ecumenical Council. With a Foreword by Henry Chadwick. 1994

Prospectus available on request

E. J. BRILL — P.O.B. 9000 — 2300 PA LEIDEN — THE NETHERLANDS

DATE DUE

			Printed in USA